A Manual for t

the General Court

1997-1998

Edward B O'Neill,

Robert E. MacQueen

Alpha Editions

This edition published in 2020

ISBN : 9789354019180

Design and Setting By
Alpha Editions
email - alphaedis@gmail.com

MANUAL

FOR THE

GENERAL COURT

1997-1998

CALENDAR 1997

JANUARY

Su	Mo	Tu	We	Th	Fr	Sa
			1	2	3	4
5	6	7	8	9	10	11
12	13	14	15	16	17	18
19	20	21	22	23	24	25
26	27	28	29	30	31	

FEBRUARY

Su	Mo	Tu	We	Th	Fr	Sa
						1
2	3	4	5	6	7	8
9	10	11	12	13	14	15
16	17	18	19	20	21	22
23	24	25	26	27	28	

MARCH

Su	Mo	Tu	We	Th	Fr	Sa
						1
2	3	4	5	6	7	8
9	10	11	12	13	14	15
16	17	18	19	20	21	22
23/30	24/31	25	26	27	28	29

APRIL

Su	Mo	Tu	We	Th	Fr	Sa
		1	2	3	4	5
6	7	8	9	10	11	12
13	14	15	16	17	18	19
20	21	22	23	24	25	26
27	28	29	30			

MAY

Su	Mo	Tu	We	Th	Fr	Sa
				1	2	3
4	5	6	7	8	9	10
11	12	13	14	15	16	17
18	19	20	21	22	23	24
25	26	27	28	29	30	31

JUNE

Su	Mo	Tu	We	Th	Fr	Sa
1	2	3	4	5	6	7
8	9	10	11	12	13	14
15	16	17	18	19	20	21
22	23	24	25	26	27	28
29	30					

JULY

Su	Mo	Tu	We	Th	Fr	Sa
		1	2	3	4	5
6	7	8	9	10	11	12
13	14	15	16	17	18	19
20	21	22	23	24	25	26
27	28	29	30	31		

AUGUST

Su	Mo	Tu	We	Th	Fr	Sa
					1	2
3	4	5	6	7	8	9
10	11	12	13	14	15	16
17	18	19	20	21	22	23
24/31	25	26	27	28	29	30

SEPTEMBER

Su	Mo	Tu	We	Th	Fr	Sa
	1	2	3	4	5	6
7	8	9	10	11	12	13
14	15	16	17	18	19	20
21	22	23	24	25	26	27
28	29	30				

OCTOBER

Su	Mo	Tu	We	Th	Fr	Sa
			1	2	3	4
5	6	7	8	9	10	11
12	13	14	15	16	17	18
19	20	21	22	23	24	25
26	27	28	29	30	31	

NOVEMBER

Su	Mo	Tu	We	Th	Fr	Sa
						1
2	3	4	5	6	7	8
9	10	11	12	13	14	15
16	17	18	19	20	21	22
23/30	24	25	26	27	28	29

DECEMBER

Su	Mo	Tu	We	Th	Fr	Sa
	1	2	3	4	5	6
7	8	9	10	11	12	13
14	15	16	17	18	19	20
21	22	23	24	25	26	27
28	29	30	31			

CALENDAR 1998

JANUARY

Su	Mo	Tu	We	Th	Fr	Sa
				1	2	3
4	5	6	7	8	9	10
11	12	13	14	15	16	17
18	19	20	21	22	23	24
25	26	27	28	29	30	31

FEBRUARY

Su	Mo	Tu	We	Th	Fr	Sa
1	2	3	4	5	6	7
8	9	10	11	12	13	14
15	16	17	18	19	20	21
22	23	24	25	26	27	28

MARCH

Su	Mo	Tu	We	Th	Fr	Sa
1	2	3	4	5	6	7
8	9	10	11	12	13	14
15	16	17	18	19	20	21
22	23	24	25	26	27	28
29	30	31				

APRIL

Su	Mo	Tu	We	Th	Fr	Sa
			1	2	3	4
5	6	7	8	9	10	11
12	13	14	15	16	17	18
19	20	21	22	23	24	25
26	27	28	29	30		

MAY

Su	Mo	Tu	We	Th	Fr	Sa
					1	2
3	4	5	6	7	8	9
10	11	12	13	14	15	16
17	18	19	20	21	22	23
24/31	25	26	27	28	29	30

JUNE

Su	Mo	Tu	We	Th	Fr	Sa
	1	2	3	4	5	6
7	8	9	10	11	12	13
14	15	16	17	18	19	20
21	22	23	24	25	26	27
28	29	30				

JULY

Su	Mo	Tu	We	Th	Fr	Sa
			1	2	3	4
5	6	7	8	9	10	11
12	13	14	15	16	17	18
19	20	21	22	23	24	25
26	27	28	29	30	31	

AUGUST

Su	Mo	Tu	We	Th	Fr	Sa
						1
2	3	4	5	6	7	8
9	10	11	12	13	14	15
16	17	18	19	20	21	22
23/30	24/31	25	26	27	28	29

SEPTEMBER

Su	Mo	Tu	We	Th	Fr	Sa
		1	2	3	4	5
6	7	8	9	10	11	12
13	14	15	16	17	18	19
20	21	22	23	24	25	26
27	28	29	30			

OCTOBER

Su	Mo	Tu	We	Th	Fr	Sa
				1	2	3
4	5	6	7	8	9	10
11	12	13	14	15	16	17
18	19	20	21	22	23	24
25	26	27	28	29	30	31

NOVEMBER

Su	Mo	Tu	We	Th	Fr	Sa
1	2	3	4	5	6	7
8	9	10	11	12	13	14
15	16	17	18	19	20	21
22	23	24	25	26	27	28
29	30					

DECEMBER

Su	Mo	Tu	We	Th	Fr	Sa
		1	2	3	4	5
6	7	8	9	10	11	12
13	14	15	16	17	18	19
20	21	22	23	24	25	26
27	28	29	30	31		

CALENDAR 1999

JANUARY

Su	Mo	Tu	We	Th	Fr	Sa
					1	2
3	4	5	6	7	8	9
10	11	12	13	14	15	16
17	18	19	20	21	22	23
24/31	25	26	27	28	29	30

FEBRUARY

Su	Mo	Tu	We	Th	Fr	Sa
	1	2	3	4	5	6
7	8	9	10	11	12	13
14	15	16	17	18	19	20
21	22	23	24	25	26	27
28						

MARCH

Su	Mo	Tu	We	Th	Fr	Sa
	1	2	3	4	5	6
7	8	9	10	11	12	13
14	15	16	17	18	19	20
21	22	23	24	25	26	27
28	29	30	31			

APRIL

Su	Mo	Tu	We	Th	Fr	Sa
				1	2	3
4	5	6	7	8	9	10
11	12	13	14	15	16	17
18	19	20	21	22	23	24
25	26	27	28	29	30	

MAY

Su	Mo	Tu	We	Th	Fr	Sa
						1
2	3	4	5	6	7	8
9	10	11	12	13	14	15
16	17	18	19	20	21	22
23/30	24/31	25	26	27	28	29

JUNE

Su	Mo	Tu	We	Th	Fr	Sa
		1	2	3	4	5
6	7	8	9	10	11	12
13	14	15	16	17	18	19
20	21	22	23	24	25	26
27	28	29	30			

JULY

Su	Mo	Tu	We	Th	Fr	Sa
				1	2	3
4	5	6	7	8	9	10
11	12	13	14	15	16	17
18	19	20	21	22	23	24
25	26	27	28	29	30	31

AUGUST

Su	Mo	Tu	We	Th	Fr	Sa
1	2	3	4	5	6	7
8	9	10	11	12	13	14
15	16	17	18	19	20	21
22	23	24	25	26	27	28
29	30	31				

SEPTEMBER

Su	Mo	Tu	We	Th	Fr	Sa
			1	2	3	4
5	6	7	8	9	10	11
12	13	14	15	16	17	18
19	20	21	22	23	24	25
26	27	28	29	30		

OCTOBER

Su	Mo	Tu	We	Th	Fr	Sa
					1	2
3	4	5	6	7	8	9
10	11	12	13	14	15	16
17	18	19	20	21	22	23
24/31	25	26	27	28	29	30

NOVEMBER

Su	Mo	Tu	We	Th	Fr	Sa
	1	2	3	4	5	6
7	8	9	10	11	12	13
14	15	16	17	18	19	20
21	22	23	24	25	26	27
28	29	30				

DECEMBER

Su	Mo	Tu	We	Th	Fr	Sa
			1	2	3	4
5	6	7	8	9	10	11
12	13	14	15	16	17	18
19	20	21	22	23	24	25
26	27	28	29	30	31	

CALENDAR 2000

JANUARY

Su	Mo	Tu	We	Th	Fr	Sa
						1
2	3	4	5	6	7	8
9	10	11	12	13	14	15
16	17	18	19	20	21	22
23/30	24/31	25	26	27	28	29

FEBRUARY

Su	Mo	Tu	We	Th	Fr	Sa
		1	2	3	4	5
6	7	8	9	10	11	12
13	14	15	16	17	18	19
20	21	22	23	24	25	26
27	28	29				

MARCH

Su	Mo	Tu	We	Th	Fr	Sa
			1	2	3	4
5	6	7	8	9	10	11
12	13	14	15	16	17	18
19	20	21	22	23	24	25
26	27	28	29	30	31	

APRIL

Su	Mo	Tu	We	Th	Fr	Sa
						1
2	3	4	5	6	7	8
9	10	11	12	13	14	15
16	17	18	19	20	21	22
23/30	24	25	26	27	28	29

MAY

Su	Mo	Tu	We	Th	Fr	Sa
	1	2	3	4	5	6
7	8	9	10	11	12	13
14	15	16	17	18	19	20
21	22	23	24	25	26	27
28	29	30	31			

JUNE

Su	Mo	Tu	We	Th	Fr	Sa
				1	2	3
4	5	6	7	8	9	10
11	12	13	14	15	16	17
18	19	20	21	22	23	24
25	26	27	28	29	30	

JULY

Su	Mo	Tu	We	Th	Fr	Sa
						1
2	3	4	5	6	7	8
9	10	11	12	13	14	15
16	17	18	19	20	21	22
23/30	24/31	25	26	27	28	29

AUGUST

Su	Mo	Tu	We	Th	Fr	Sa
		1	2	3	4	5
6	7	8	9	10	11	12
13	14	15	16	17	18	19
20	21	22	23	24	25	26
27	28	29	30	31		

SEPTEMBER

Su	Mo	Tu	We	Th	Fr	Sa
					1	2
3	4	5	6	7	8	9
10	11	12	13	14	15	16
17	18	19	20	21	22	23
24	25	26	27	28	29	30

OCTOBER

Su	Mo	Tu	We	Th	Fr	Sa
1	2	3	4	5	6	7
8	9	10	11	12	13	14
15	16	17	18	19	20	21
22	23	24	25	26	27	28
29	30	31				

NOVEMBER

Su	Mo	Tu	We	Th	Fr	Sa
			1	2	3	4
5	6	7	8	9	10	11
12	13	14	15	16	17	18
19	20	21	22	23	24	25
26	27	28	29	30		

DECEMBER

Su	Mo	Tu	We	Th	Fr	Sa
					1	2
3	4	5	6	7	8	9
10	11	12	13	14	15	16
17	18	19	20	21	22	23
24/31	25	26	27	28	29	30

𝕿𝖍𝖊 𝕮𝖔𝖒𝖒𝖔𝖓𝖜𝖊𝖆𝖑𝖙𝖍 𝖔𝖋 𝕸𝖆𝖘𝖘𝖆𝖈𝖍𝖚𝖘𝖊𝖙𝖙𝖘

A MANUAL

FOR THE USE OF THE

GENERAL COURT

FOR

1997-1998

*Prepared under Section 11 of Chapter 5 of the General Laws,
as most recently amended by Chapter 170 of the Acts of 1962.*

BY

EDWARD B. O'NEILL
CLERK OF THE SENATE

AND

ROBERT E. MacQUEEN
CLERK OF THE HOUSE

EAGLE GRAPHICS, INC.
BOSTON, MA
1997

DECLARATION OF INDEPENDENCE

DECLARATION OF INDEPENDENCE.

A DECLARATION BY THE REPRESENTATIVES OF THE UNITED STATES OF AMERICA IN CONGRESS ASSEMBLED.

[July 4, 1776.]

When in the Course of human events, it becomes necessary for one people to dissolve the political bands which have connected them with another, and to assume among the Powers of the earth, the separate and equal station to which the Laws of Nature and of Nature's God entitle them, a decent respect to the opinions of mankind requires that they should declare the causes which impel them to the separation.

We hold these truths to be self-evident, that all men are created equal, that they are endowed by their Creator with certain unalienable Rights, that among these are Life, Liberty and the pursuit of Happiness. That to secure these rights, Governments are instituted among Men, deriving their just powers from the consent of the governed. That whenever any Form of Government becomes destructive of these ends, it is the Right of the People to alter or to abolish it, and to institute new Government, laying its foundation on such principles and organizing its powers in such form, as to them shall seem most likely to effect their Safety and Happiness. Prudence, indeed, will dictate that Governments long established should not be changed for light and transient causes; and accordingly all experience hath shewn, that mankind are more disposed to suffer, while evils are sufferable, than to right themselves by abolishing the forms to which they are accustomed. But when a long train of abuses and usurpations, pursuing invariably the same Object evinces a design to reduce them under absolute Despotism, it is their right, it is their duty, to throw off such Government, and to provide new Guards for their future security. Such has been the patient sufferance of these

Colonies: and such is now the necessity which constrains them to alter their former Systems of Government. The history of the present King of Great Britain is a history of repeated injuries and usurpations, all having in direct object the establishment of an absolute Tyranny over these States. To prove this, let Facts be submitted to a candid world.

He has refused his Assent to Laws, the most wholesome and necessary for the public good.

He has forbidden his Governors to pass Laws of immediate and pressing importance, unless suspended in their operation till his Assent should be obtained; and when so suspended; he has utterly neglected to attend to them.

He has refused to pass other Laws for the accommodation of large districts of people, unless those people would relinquish the right of Representation in the Legislature, a right inestimable to them and formidable to tyrants only.

He has called together legislative bodies at places unusual, uncomfortable, and distant from the Depository of their Public Records, for the sole purpose of fatiguing them into compliance with his measures.

He has dissolved Representative Houses repeatedly, for opposing with manly firmness his invasions on the rights of the people.

He has refused for a long time, after such dissolutions, to cause others to be elected; whereby the Legislative Powers, incapable of Annihilation, have returned to the People at large for their exercise; the State remaining in the meantime exposed to all the dangers of invasion from without, and convulsions within.

He has endeavored to prevent the Population of these States; for that purpose obstructing the Laws for Naturalization of Foreigners; refusing to pass others to encourage their migrations hither, and raising the conditions of new Appropriations of Lands.

He has obstructed the Administration of Justice, by refusing his Assent to Laws for establishing Judiciary Powers.

He has made Judges dependent on his Will alone, for the tenure of their offices, and the amount and payment of their salaries.

He has erected a multitude of New Offices, and sent hither swarms of Officers to harrass our People, and eat out their substance.

He has kept among us, in times of peace, Standing Armies without the Consent of our legislature.

He has affected to render the Military independent of and superior to the Civil Power.

He has combined with others to subject us to a jurisdiction foreign to our constitution, and unacknowledged by our laws; giving his Assent to their Acts of pretended Legislation:

For quartering large bodies of armed troops among us:

For protecting them, by a mock trial, from Punishment for any Murders which they should commit on the Inhabitants of these States:

For cutting off our Trade with all parts of the world:

For imposing Taxes on us without our Consent:

For depriving us in many cases, of the benefits of Trial by Jury:

For transporting us beyond Seas to be tried for pretended offenses:

For abolishing the free System of English Laws in a neighboring Province, establishing therein an Arbitrary government, and enlarging its Boundaries so as to render it at once an example and fit instrument for introducing the same absolute rule into these Colonies:

For taking away our Charters, abolishing our most valuable Laws, and altering fundamentally the Forms of our Governments:

For suspending our own Legislatures, and declaring themselves invested with Power to legislate for us in all cases whatsoever.

He has abdicated Government here, by declaring us out of his Protection and waging War against us.

He has plundered our seas, ravaged our Coasts, burnt our towns, and destroyed the lives of our People.

He is at this time transporting large Armies of foreign Mercenaries to compleat the works of death, desolation and tyranny, already begun with circumstances of Cruelty & perfidy scarcely paralleled in the most barbarous ages, and totally unworthy the Head of a civilized nation.

He has constrained our fellow-Citizens taken Captive on the high Seas to bear Arms against their Country, to become the executioners of their friends and Brethren, or to fall themselves by their Hands.

He has excited domestic insurrections amongst us, and has endeavored to bring on the inhabitants of our frontiers, the merciless Indian Savages, whose known rule of warfare, is an undistinguished destruction of all ages, sexes and conditions.

In every stage of these Oppressions We have Petitioned for Redress in the most humble terms: Our repeated Petitions have been answered only by repeated injury. A Prince, whose character is thus marked by every act which may define a Tyrant, is unfit to be the ruler of a free People.

Nor have We been wanting in attentions to our British brethren. We have warned them from time to time of attempts by their legislature to extend an unwarrantable jurisdiction over us. We have reminded them of the circumstances of our emigration and settlement here. We have appealed to their native justice and magnanimity, and we have conjured them by the ties of our common kindred to disavow these usurpations, which, would inevitably interrupt our connections and correspondence. They too have been deaf to the voice of justice and of consanguinity. We must, therefore, acquiesce in the necessity which denounces our Separation, and hold them, as we hold the rest of mankind, Enemies in War, in Peace Friends.

We, therefore, the REPRESENTATIVES OF THE UNITED STATES OF AMERICA, IN GENERAL CONGRESS, Assembled, appealing to the Supreme Judge of the World for the rectitude of our intentions, do, in the Name, and by Authority of the good People of these Colonies, solemnly PUBLISH AND DECLARE, That these United Colonies are, and of Right ought to be FREE AND INDEPENDENT States; that they are Absolved from all Allegiance to the British Crown, and that all political connection between them and the State of Great Britain, is and ought to be totally dissolved; and that as FREE AND INDEPENDENT STATES, they have full Power to levy War, conclude Peace, contract Alliances, establish Commerce, and to do all other Acts and Things which INDEPENDENT STATES may of right do. And for the support of this Declaration, with a firm reliance on the Protection of Divine Providence. We mutually pledge to each other our Lives, our Fortunes and our sacred Honor.

The foregoing declaration was, by order of Congress, engrossed and signed by the following members:

JOHN HANCOCK,

New Hampshire.

JOSIAH BARTLETT,
WM. WHIPPLE,

MATTHEW THORNTON.

Massachusetts Bay.

SAML. ADAMS,
JOHN ADAMS,

ROBT. TREAT PAINE,
ELBRIDGE GERRY.

Rhode Island, etc.

STEP. HOPKINS,

WILLIAM ELLERY.

Connecticut.

ROGER SHERMAN,
SAM'EL HUNTINGTON,

WM. WILLIAMS,
OLIVER WOLCOTT.

New York.

WM. FLOYD,
PHIL LIVINGSTON,

FRANS. LEWIS,
LEWIS MORRIS.

New Jersey.

RICHD. STOCKTON,
JNO. WITHERSPOON,
FRAS. HOPKINSON,

JOHN HART,
ABRA. CLARK.

Pennsylvania.

ROBT. MORRIS,
BENJAMIN RUSH,
BENJA. FRANKLIN,
JOHN MORTON,
GEO. CLYMER,

JAS. SMITH,
GEO. TAYLOR,
JAMES WILSON,
GEO. ROSS.

Delaware.

CESAR RODNEY,
GEO. READ,

THO. M'KEAN.

Maryland.

SAMUEL CHASE,   THOS. STONE,
WM. PACA,   CHARLES CARROLL OF
                            Carrollton.

Virginia.

GEORGE WYTHE,   THOS. NELSON, jr.,
RICHARD HENRY LEE,   FRANCIS LIGHTFOOT LEE,
TH. JEFFERSON,   CARTER BRAXTON.
BENJA. HARRISON,

North Carolina.

WM. HOOPER,   JOHN PENN,
JOSEPH HEWES,

South Carolina.

EDWARD RUTLEDGE,   THOMAS LYNCH, junr.,
THOS. HEYWARD, junr.,   ARTHUR MIDDLETON.

Georgia.

BUTTON GWINNETT,   GEO. WALTON.
LYMAN HALL,

Resolved. That copies of the Declaration be sent to the several assemblies, conventions, and committees or councils of safety, and to the several commanding officers of the Continental Troops: That it be PROCLAIMED in each of the UNITED STATES, and at the HEAD OF THE ARMY. — [Jour. Cong., vol. 1, p. 396.]

CONSTITUTION

OF THE

UNITED STATES OF AMERICA

CONSTITUTION OF THE UNITED STATES OF AMERICA.

PREAMBLE.

Objects of the Constitution

ARTICLE I.

ARTICLE V.

Constitution, how amended — Proviso. 25.

ARTICLE VI.

Certain debts, &c., adopted — Supremacy of Constitution, treaties, and laws of the United States — Oath to support Constitution, by whom taken — No religious test. 25, 26.

ARTICLE VII.

Ratification necessary to establish Constitution. 26.

AMENDMENTS.

I. — Religious establishment prohibited — Freedom of speech, of the press, and the right to petition. 27.
II. — Right to keep and bear arms. 27.
III. — No soldier to be quartered in any house, unless, &c. 27.
IV. — Right of search and seizure regulated. 27.
V. — Provisions concerning prosecutions, trials, and punishments — Private property not to be taken for public use, without, &c. 27.
VI. — Further provisions respecting criminal prosecutions. 27, 28.
VII. — Right of trial by jury secured. 28.
VIII. — Bail, fines, and punishments. 28.
IX. — Rule of construction. 28.
X. — Same subject. 28.
XI. — Same subject. 28.
XII. — Manner of choosing President and Vice-President. 28, 29.
XIII. — Slavery abolished. 29.
XIV. — Citizenship defined — Apportionment of representatives — Persons engaged in rebellion excluded from office — Debts of United States, and of States contracted during the rebellion. 29, 30.
XV. — Right of citizenship not to be abridged. 31.
XVI. — Congress may tax incomes without apportionment or regard to census. 31.
XVII. — Senators, number, term, qualifications of electors, filling of vacancies. 31.

We the people of the United States, in order to form a more perfect union, establish justice, insure domestic tranquility, provide for the common defence, promote the general welfare, and secure the blessings of liberty to ourselves and our posterity, do ordain and establish this CONSTITUTION for the United States of America.

ARTICLE I.

SECTION 1. All legislative powers herein granted shall be vested in a congress of the United States, which shall consist of a senate and house of representatives.

SECT. 2. The house of representatives shall be composed of members chosen every second year by the people of the several states, and the electors in each state shall have the qualifications requisite for electors of the most numerous branch of the state legislature.

No person shall be a representative who shall not have attained to the age of twenty-five years, and been seven years a citizen of the United States, and who shall not, when elected, be an inhabitant of that state in which he shall be chosen.

*Representatives and direct taxes shall be apportioned among the several states which may be included within this Union, according to their respective numbers, which shall be determined by adding to the whole number of free persons, including those bound to service for a term of years, and excluding Indians not taxed, three-fifths of all other persons. The actual enumeration shall be made within three years after the first meeting of the congress of the United States, and within every subsequent term of ten years, in such manner as they shall by law direct. The number of representatives shall not exceed one for every thirty thousand, but each state shall have at least one representative; and until such enumeration shall be made, the state of New Hampshire shall be entitled to choose three, Massachusetts eight, Rhode Island and Providence Plantations one, Connecticut five, New York six, New Jersey four, Pennsylvania eight, Delaware one, Maryland six, Virginia ten, North Carolina five, South Carolina five, and Georgia three.

When vacancies happen in the representation from any state, the executive authority thereof shall issue writs of election to fill such vacancies.

The house of representatives shall choose their speaker and other officers; and shall have the sole power of impeachment.

Sect. 3. †[The senate of the United States shall be composed of two senators from each state, chosen by the legislature thereof, for six years; and each senator shall have one vote.]

Immediately after they shall be assembled in consequence of the first election, they shall be divided as equally as may be into three classes. The seats of the senators of the first class shall be vacated at the expiration of the second year, of the second class at the expiration of the fourth year, and of the third class at the expiration of the sixth year, so that one-third may be chosen every second year; †[and if vacancies happen by resignation, or otherwise, during the recess of the legislature of any state, the executive thereof may make temporary appointments until the next meeting of the legislature, which shall then fill such vacancies].

*See Section 2 of Fourteenth Amendment.
†See Seventeenth Amendment.

No person shall be a senator who shall not have attained to the age of thirty years, and been nine years a citizen of the United States, and who shall not, when elected, be an inhabitant of that state for which he shall be chosen.

The vice-president of the United States shall be president of the senate, but shall have no vote, unless they be equally divided.

The senate shall choose their other officers, and also a president *pro tempore,* in the absence of the vice-president, or when he shall exercise the office of president of the United States.

The senate shall have the sole power to try all impeachments. When sitting for that purpose, they shall be on oath or affirmation. When the president of the United States is tried, the chief justice shall preside: and no person shall be convicted without the concurrence of two-thirds of the members present.

Judgment in cases of impeachment shall not extend further than to removal from office, and disqualification to hold and enjoy any office of honor, trust or profit under the United States: but the party convicted shall nevertheless be liable and subject to indictment, trial, judgment and punishment, according to law.

SECT. 4.   The times, places and manner of holding elections for senators and representatives, shall be prescribed in each state by the legislature thereof; but the congress may at any time by law make or alter such regulations, except as to the places of choosing senators.

*[The congress shall assemble at least once in every year, and such meeting shall be on the first Monday in December, unless they shall by law appoint a different day.]

SECT. 5.   Each house shall be the judge of the elections, returns and qualifications of its own members, and a majority of each shall constitute a quorum to do business: but a smaller number may adjourn from day to day, and may be authorized to compel the attendance of absent members, in such manner, and under such penalties as each house may provide.

Each house may determine the rules of its proceedings, punish its members for disorderly behavior, and, with the concurrence of two-thirds, expel a member.

*See Twentieth Amendment.

Each house shall keep a journal of its proceedings. and from time to time publish the same. excepting such parts as may in their judgment require secrecy: and the yeas and nays of the members of either house on any question shall. at the desire of one-fifth of those present. be entered on the journal.

Neither house. during the session of congress. shall. without the consent of the other. adjourn for more than three days. nor to any other place than that in which the two houses shall be sitting.

SECT. 6. The senators and representatives shall receive a compensation for their services. to be ascertained by law. and paid out of the treasury of the United States. They shall in all cases. except treason. felony and breach of the peace. be privileged from arrest during their attendance at the session of their respective houses. and in going to and returning from the same: and for any speech or debate in either house. they shall not be questioned in any other place.

No senator or representative shall. during the time for which he was elected. be appointed to any civil office under the authority of the United States. which shall have been created. or the emoluments whereof shall have been increased during such time; and no person holding any office under the United States. shall be a member of either house during his continuance in office.

SECT. 7. All bills for raising revenue shall originate in the house of representatives: but the senate may propose or concur with amendments as on other bills.

Every bill which shall have passed the house of representatives and the senate. shall. before it become a law. be presented to the president of the United States: if he approve he shall sign it. but if not he shall return it. with his objections. to that house in which it shall have originated. who shall enter the objections at large on their journal. and proceed to reconsider it. If after such reconsideration two-thirds of that house shall agree to pass the bill. it shall be sent. together with the objections. to the other house. by which it shall likewise be reconsidered. and if approved by two-thirds of that house. it shall become a law. But in all such cases the votes of both houses shall be determined by yeas and nays. and the names of the persons voting for and against the bill shall be entered on the journal of each house respectively. If any bill shall not be returned by the president within ten days (Sundays excepted) after it shall have been presented to him, the same shall be a law, in like manner as if he had signed it, unless the congress by their adjournment prevent its return, in which case it shall not be a law.

Every order, resolution, or vote to which the concurrence of the senate and house of representatives may be necessary (except on a question of adjournment) shall be presented to the president of the United States; and before the same shall take effect, shall be approved by him, or being disapproved by him, shall be repassed by two-thirds of the senate and house of representatives, according to the rules and limitations prescribed in the case of a bill.

SECT. 8. The congress shall have power — to lay and collect taxes, duties, imposts and excises, to pay the debts and provide for the common defence and general welfare of the United States; but all duties, imposts and excises shall be uniform throughout the United States; — to borrow money on the credit of the United States; — to regulate commerce with foreign nations, and among the several states, and with the Indian tribes; — to establish an uniform rule of naturalization, and uniform laws on the subject of bankruptcies throughout the United States; — to coin money, regulate the value thereof, and of foreign coin, and fix the standard of weights and measures; — to provide for the punishment of counterfeiting the securities and current coin of the United States; — to establish post offices and post roads; — to promote the progress of science and useful arts, by securing for limited times to authors and inventors the exclusive right to their respective writings and discoveries; — to constitute tribunals inferior to the supreme court; — to define and punish piracies and felonies committed on the high seas, and offences against the law of nations; — to declare war, grant letters of marque and reprisal, and make rules concerning captures on land and water; — to raise and support armies, but no appropriation of money to that use shall be for a longer term than two years; — to provide and maintain a navy; — to make rules for the government and regulation of the land and naval forces; — to provide for calling forth the militia to execute the laws of the Union, suppress insurrections, and repel invasions: — to provide for organizing, arming, and disciplining the militia, and for governing such part of them as may be employed in the service of the United States, reserving to the states respectively, the appointment of the officers, and the authority of training the militia according to the discipline prescribed by congress: — to exercise exclusive legislation in all cases whatsoever, over such district (not exceeding ten miles square) as may, by cession of particular states, and the acceptance of congress, become the seat of the government of the United States, and to exercise like authority over all places purchased by the consent of the legislature of the state in which the same shall be, for the erection of forts, magazines, arsenals, dock yards, and other needful buildings: — and to make all laws which shall be necessary and proper for carrying into execution the foregoing powers, and all other powers vested by this constitution in the government of the United States, or in any department or officer thereof.

Sect. 9. The migration or importation of such persons as any of the states now existing shall think proper to admit, shall not be prohibited by the congress prior to the year one thousand eight hundred and eight, but a tax or duty may be imposed on such importation, not exceeding ten dollars for each person.

The privilege of the writ of *habeas corpus* shall not be suspended, unless when in cases of rebellion or invasion the public safety may require it.

No bill of attainder or *ex post facto* law shall be passed.

No capitation, or other direct tax, shall be laid, unless in proportion to the census or enumeration hereinbefore directed to be taken.

No tax or duty shall be laid on articles exported from any state.

No preference shall be given by any regulation of commerce or revenue to the ports of one state over those of another: nor shall vessels bound to, or from, one state, be obliged to enter, clear or pay duties in another.

No money shall be drawn from the treasury, but in consequence of appropriations made by law: and a regular statement and account of the receipts and expenditures of all public money shall be published from time to time.

No title of nobility shall be granted by the United States; and no person holding any office of profit or trust under them shall, without the consent of the congress, accept of any present, emolument, office or title, of any kind whatever, from any king, prince, or foreign state.

SECT. 10. No state shall enter into any treaty, alliance, or confederation; grant letters of marque and reprisal; coin money; emit bills of credit; make any thing but gold and silver coin a tender in payment of debts; pass any bill of attainder, *ex post facto* law, or law impairing the obligation of contracts, or grant any title of nobility. No state shall, without the consent of the congress, lay any imposts or duties on imports or exports, except what may be absolutely necessary for executing its inspection laws; and the net produce of all duties and imposts, laid by any state on imports or exports, shall be for the use of the treasury of the United States; and all such laws shall be subject to the revision and control of the congress. No state shall, without the consent of congress, lay any duty of tonnage, keep troops, or ships of war in time of peace, enter into any agreement or compact with another state, or with a foreign power, or engage in war, unless actually invaded, or in such imminent danger as will not admit of delay.

ARTICLE II.

SECTION 1. The executive power shall be vested in a President of the United States of America. He shall hold his office during the term of four years, and, together with the vice-president, chosen for the same term, be elected, as follows: —

Each state shall appoint, in such manner as the legislature thereof may direct, a number of electors, equal to the whole number of senators and representatives to which the state may be entitled in the congress; but no senator or representative, or person holding an office of trust or profit under the United States, shall be appointed an elector.

*[The electors shall meet in their respective states, and vote by ballot for two persons, of whom one at least shall not be an inhabitant of the same state with themselves. And they shall make a list of all the persons voted for, and of the number of votes for each; which list they shall sign and certify, and transmit sealed to the seat of the government of the United States, directed to the president of the senate. The president of the senate shall, in the presence of the senate and house of representatives, open all the certificates, and the votes shall then be counted. The person having the greatest number of votes shall be the president, if such number be a majority of the whole number of electors appointed; and if there be more than one who have such majority, and have an equal number of votes, then the house of representatives shall immediately choose by ballot one of them for president; and if no person have a majority, then from the five highest on the list the said house shall in like manner choose the president. But in choosing the president, the votes shall be taken by states, the representation from each state having one vote; a quorum for this purpose shall consist of a member or members from two-thirds of the states, and a majority of all the states shall be necessary to a choice. In every case, after the choice of the president, the person having the greatest number of votes of the electors shall be the vice-president. But if there should remain two or more who have equal votes, the senate shall choose from them by ballot the vice-president.]

The congress may determine the time of choosing the electors, and the day on which they shall give their votes; which day shall be the same throughout the United States.

No person except a natural born citizen, or a citizen of the United States, at the time of the adoption of this constitution, shall be eligible to the office of president; neither shall any person be eligible to that office who shall not have attained to the age of thirty-five years, and been fourteen years a resident within the United States.

In case of the removal of the president from office, or of his death, resignation or inability to discharge the powers and duties of the said office, the same shall devolve on the vice-president,

---

*See Twelfth Amendment.

and the congress may by law provide for the case of removal, death, resignation, or inability, both of the president and vice-president, declaring what officer shall then act as president, and such officer shall act accordingly, until the disability be removed, or a president shall be elected.

The president shall, at stated times, receive for his services, a compensation, which shall neither be increased nor diminished during the period for which he shall have been elected, and he shall not receive within that period any other emolument from the United States, or any of them.

Before he enter on the execution of his office, he shall take the following oath or affirmation: —

"I do solemnly swear (or affirm) that I will faithfully execute the office of president of the United States, and will to the best of my ability, preserve, protect and defend the constitution of the United States."

SECT. 2.   The president shall be commander-in-chief of the army and navy of the United States, and of the militia of the several states, when called into the actual service of the United States; he may require the opinion, in writing, of the principal officer in each of the executive departments, upon any subject relating to the duties of their respective offices, and he shall have power to grant reprieves and pardons for offences against the United States, except in cases of impeachment.

He shall have power, by and with the advice and consent of the senate, to make treaties, provided two-thirds of the senators present concur; and he shall nominate, and by and with the advice and consent of the senate, shall appoint ambassadors, other public ministers and consuls, judges of the supreme court, and all other officers of the United States, whose appointments are not herein otherwise provided for, and which shall be established by law: but the congress may by law vest the appointment of such inferior officers, as they think proper, in the president alone, in the courts of law, or in the heads of departments.

The president shall have power to fill up all vacancies that may happen during the recess of the senate, by granting commissions which shall expire at the end of their next session.

SECT. 3. He shall from time to time give to the congress information of the state of the Union, and recommend to their consideration such measures as he shall judge necessary and expedient; he may, on extraordinary occasions, convene both houses, or either of them, and in case of disagreement between them, with respect to the time of adjournment, he may adjourn them to such time as he shall think proper; he shall receive ambassadors and other public ministers; he shall take care that the laws be faithfully executed, and shall commission all the officers of the United States.

SECT. 4. The president, vice-president, and all civil officers of the United States, shall be removed from office on impeachment for, and conviction of, treason, bribery, or other high crimes and misdemeanors.

ARTICLE III.

SECTION 1. The judicial power of the United States shall be vested in one supreme court, and in such inferior courts as the congress may from time to time ordain and establish. The judges, both of the supreme and inferior courts, shall hold their offices during good behavior, and shall, at stated times, receive for their services, a compensation, which shall not be diminished during their continuance in office.

SECT. 2. The judicial power shall extend to all cases, in law and equity, arising under this constitution, the laws of the United States, and treaties made, or which shall be made, under their authority; — to all cases affecting ambassadors, other public ministers, and consuls; — to all cases of admiralty and maritime jurisdiction; — to controversies to which the United States shall be a party; — to controversies between two or more states; — between a state and citizens of another state; — between citizens of different states; — between citizens of the same state claiming lands under grants of different states, and between a state, or the citizens thereof, and foreign states, citizens or subjects.

In all cases affecting ambassadors, other public ministers and consuls, and those in which a state shall be a party, the supreme court shall have original jurisdiction. In all the other cases before mentioned, the supreme court shall have appellate jurisdiction, both as to law and fact, with such exceptions, and under such regulations as the congress shall make.

The trial of all crimes, except in cases of impeachment, shall be by jury; and such trial shall be held in the state where the said crimes shall have been committed; but when not committed within any state, the trial shall be at such place or places as the congress may by law have directed.

SECT. 3. Treason against the United States, shall consist only in levying war against them, or in adhering to their enemies, giving them aid and comfort. No persons shall be convicted of treason unless on the testimony of two witnesses to the same overt act, or on confession in open court.

The congress shall have power to declare the punishment of treason, but no attainder of treason shall work corruption of blood, or forfeiture except during the life of the person attainted.

ARTICLE IV.

SECTION 1. Full faith and credit shall be given in each state to the public acts, records, and judicial proceedings of every other state. And the congress may by general laws prescribe the manner in which such acts, records and proceedings shall be proved, and the effect thereof.

SECT. 2. The citizens of each state shall be entitled to all privileges and immunities of citizens in the several states.

A person charged in any state with treason, felony, or other crime, who shall flee from justice, and be found in another state, shall, on demand of the executive authority of the state from which he fled, be delivered up to be removed to the state having jurisdiction of the crime.

No person held to service or labor in one state, under the laws thereof, escaping into another, shall, in consequence of any law or regulation therein, be discharged from such service or labor, but shall be delivered up on claim of the party to whom such service or labor may be due.

SECT. 3. New states may be admitted by the congress into this Union; but no new state shall be formed or erected within the jurisdiction of any other state; nor any state be formed by the junction of two or more states, or parts of states, without the consent of the legislatures of the states concerned as well as of the congress.

The congress shall have power to dispose of and make all needful rules and regulations respecting the territory or other property belonging to the United States; and nothing in this constitution shall be so construed as to prejudice any claims of the United States or of any particular state.

SECT. 4. The United States shall guarantee to every state in this Union a republican form of government, and shall protect each of them against invasion, and on application of the legislature, or of the executive (when the legislature cannot be convened) against domestic violence.

ARTICLE V.

The congress, whenever two-thirds of both houses shall deem it necessary, shall propose amendments to this constitution, or, on the application of the legislatures of two-thirds of the several states, shall call a convention for proposing amendments, which, in either case, shall be valid to all intents and purposes, as part of this constitution, when ratified by the legislatures of three-fourths of the several states, or by conventions in three-fourths thereof, as the one or the other mode of ratification may be proposed by congress; provided that no amendment which may be made prior to the year one thousand eight hundred and eight shall in any manner affect the first and fourth clauses in the ninth section of the first article; and that no state, without its consent, shall be deprived of its equal suffrage in the senate.

ARTICLE VI.

All debts contracted and engagements entered into before the adoption of this constitution, shall be as valid against the United States under this constitution, as under the confederation.

This constitution, and the laws of the United States which shall be made in pursuance thereof; and all treaties made, or which shall be made, under the authority of the United States, shall be the supreme law of the land; and the judges in every state shall be bound thereby, any thing in the constitution or laws of any state to the contrary notwithstanding.

The senators and representatives before mentioned, and the members of the several state legislatures, and all executive and judicial officers, both of the United States and of the several states, shall be bound by oath or affirmation, to support this constitution; but no religious test shall ever be required as a qualification to any office or public trust under the United States.

ARTICLE VII.

The ratification of the conventions of nine states, shall be sufficient for the establishment of this constitution between the states so ratifying the same.

ARTICLES
IN ADDITION TO, AND AMENDMENT OF,

The Constitution of the United States of America, proposed by congress, and ratified by the legislatures of the several states, pursuant to the fifth article of the original constitution.

ARTICLE I. Congress shall make no law respecting an establishment of religion, or prohibiting the free exercise thereof; or abridging the freedom of speech, or of the press; or the right of the people peaceably to assemble, and to petition the government for a redress of grievances.

ART. II. A well regulated militia, being necessary to the security of a free state, the right of the people to keep and bear arms shall not be infringed.

ART. III. No soldier shall, in time of peace, be quartered in any house, without the consent of the owner, nor in time of war, but in a manner to be prescribed by law.

ART. IV. The right of the people to be secure in their persons, houses, papers and effects, against unreasonable searches and seizures, shall not be violated, and no warrants shall issue, but upon probable cause, supported by oath or affirmation, and particularly describing the place to be searched, and the persons or things to be seized.

ART. V. No person shall be held to answer for a capital, or otherwise infamous crime, unless on a presentment or indictment of a grand jury, except in cases arising in the land or naval forces, or in the militia, when in actual service in time of war or public danger; nor shall any person be subject for the same offence to be twice put in jeopardy of life or limb; nor shall be compelled in any criminal case to be a witness against himself, nor be deprived of life, liberty or property, without due process of law; nor shall private property be taken for public use, without just compensation.

ART. VI. In all criminal prosecutions, the accused shall enjoy the right to a speedy and public trial, by an impartial jury of the state and district wherein the crime shall have been committed, which district shall have been previously ascertained by law, and to be informed of the nature and cause of the accusation; to be confronted with the witnesses against him; to have compulsory process for obtaining witnesses in his favor, and to have the assistance of counsel for his defence.

ART. VII. In suits at common law, where the value in controversy shall exceed twenty dollars, the right of trial by jury shall be preserved, and no fact tried by a jury shall be otherwise re-examined in any court of the United States, than according to the rules of the common law.

ART. VIII. Excessive bail shall not be required, nor excessive fines imposed, nor cruel and unusual punishments inflicted.

ART. IX. The enumeration in the constitution, of certain rights, shall not be construed to deny or disparage others retained by the people.

ART. X. The powers not delegated to the United States by the constitution, nor prohibited by it to the states, are reserved to the states respectively, or to the people.

ART. XI. The judicial power of the United States shall not be construed to extend to any suit in law or equity, commenced or prosecuted against one of the United States by citizens of another state, or by citizens or subjects of any foreign state.

ART. XII. The electors shall meet in their respective states, and vote by ballot for president and vice-president, one of whom, at least, shall not be an inhabitant of the same state with themselves; they shall name in their ballots the person voted for as president, and in distinct ballots the person voted for as vice-president, and they shall make distinct lists of all persons voted for as president, and of all persons voted for as vice-president, and of the number of votes for each, which lists they shall sign and certify, and transmit sealed to the seat of the government of the United States, directed to the president of the senate; — the president of the senate shall, in presence of the senate and house of representatives, open all the certificates and the votes shall then be counted; — the person having the greatest number of votes for president, shall be the president, if such number be a majority of the whole number of electors appointed; and if no person have such majority, then from the persons having the highest numbers not exceeding three on the list of those voted for as president, the house of representatives shall choose immediately, by ballot, the president. But in choosing the president, the votes shall be taken by states, the representation from each state having one vote; a quorum for this purpose shall consist of a member or members from two-thirds of the states, and a majority of all the states shall be necessary to a choice. And if the house of representatives shall not choose a president whenever the right of choice shall devolve upon them, before the fourth day of March next following, then the vice-president shall act as president, as in the case of the death or other constitutional disability of the president.

The person having the greatest number of votes as vice-president, shall be the vice-president, if such number be a majority of the whole number of electors, appointed, and if no person have a majority, then from the two highest numbers on the list, the senate shall choose the vice-president; a quorum for the purpose shall consist of two-thirds of the whole number of senators, and a majority of the whole number shall be necessary to a choice.

But no person constitutionally ineligible to the office of president shall be eligible to that of vice-president of the United States.

ART. XIII. SECT. 1. Neither slavery nor involuntary servitude, except as a punishment for crime whereof the party shall have been duly convicted, shall exist within the United States or any place subject to their jurisdiction.

SECT. 2. Congress shall have power to enforce this article by appropriate legislation.

ART. XIV. SECT. 1. All persons born or naturalized in the United States, and subject to the jurisdiction thereof, are citizens of the United States and of the state wherein they reside. No state shall make or enforce any law which shall abridge the privileges or immunities of citizens of the United

States; nor shall any state deprive any person of life, liberty or property, without due process of law, nor deny to any person within its jurisdiction the equal protection of the laws.

SECT. 2. Representatives shall be apportioned among the several states according to their respective numbers, counting the whole number of persons in each state, excluding Indians not taxed. But when the right to vote at any election for the choice of electors for president and vice-president of the United States, representatives in congress, the executive and judicial officers of a state, or the members of the legislature thereof, is denied to any of the male inhabitants of such state, being twenty-one years of age, and citizens of the United States, or in any way abridged, except for participation in rebellion or other crime, the basis of representation therein shall be reduced in the proportion which the number of such male citizens shall bear to the whole number of male citizens twenty-one years of age in such state.

SECT. 3. No person shall be a senator, or representative in congress, or elector of president and vice-president, or hold any office, civil or military, under the United States, or under any state, who, having previously taken an oath, as a member of congress, or as an officer of the United States, or as a member of any state legislature, or as an executive or judicial officer of any state, to support the constitution of the United States, shall have engaged in insurrection or rebellion against the same, or given aid or comfort to the enemies thereof. But congress may, by a vote of two-thirds of each house, remove such disability.

SECT. 4. The validity of the public debt of the United States, authorized by law, including debts incurred for payment of pensions and bounties for services in suppressing insurrection or rebellion, shall not be questioned. But neither the United States, nor any state, shall assume or pay any debt or obligation incurred in aid of insurrection or rebellion against the United States, or any claim for the loss or emancipation of any slave; but all such debts, obligations and claims shall be held illegal and void.

SECT. 5. The congress shall have power to enforce, by appropriate legislation, the provisions of this article.

ART. XV. Sect. 1. The right of citizens of the United States to vote shall not be denied or abridged by the United States, or by any state, on account of race, color, or previous condition of servitude.

SECT. 2. The congress shall have power to enforce this article by appropriate legislation.

ART. XVI. The congress shall have power to lay and collect taxes on incomes, from whatever source derived, without apportionment among the several states, and without regard to any census or enumeration.

ART. XVII.* The senate of the United States shall be composed of two senators from each state, elected by the people thereof, for six years; and each senator shall have one vote. The electors in each state shall have the qualifications requisite for electors of the most numerous branch of the state legislatures.

When vacancies happen in the representation of any state in the senate, the executive authority of such state shall issue writs of election to fill such vacancies: *provided,* that the legislature of any state may empower the executive thereof to make temporary appointment until the people fill the vacancies by election as the legislature may direct.

This amendment shall not be so construed as to affect the election or term of any senator chosen before it becomes valid as part of the constitution.

†[ART. XVIII. SECT. 1. After one year from the ratification of this article the manufacture, sale, or transportation of intoxicating liquors within, the importation thereof into, or the exportation thereof from the United States and all territory subject to the jurisdiction thereof for beverage purposes is hereby prohibited.

SECT. 2. The Congress and the several States shall have concurrent power to enforce this article by appropriate legislation.

---

*"In lieu of the first paragraph of section three of article 1 of the constitution of the United States, and in lieu of so much of paragraph two of the same section as relates to the filling of vacancies."

†Repealed. See Twenty-first Amendment.

SECT. 3. This article shall be inoperative unless it shall have been ratified as an amendment to the Constitution by the legislatures of the several States, as provided in the Constitution, within seven years from the date of the submission hereof to the States by the Congress.]

ART. XIX. The right of citizens of the United States to vote shall not be denied or abridged by the United States or by any State on account of sex.

Congress shall have power to enforce this article by appropriate legislation.

ART. XX. SECT. 1. The terms of the President and Vice President shall end at noon on the 20th day of January, and the terms of Senators and Representatives at noon on the 3d day of January, of the years in which such terms would have ended if this article had not been ratified; and the terms of their successors shall then begin.

SECT. 2. *The Congress shall assemble at least once in every year, and such meeting shall begin at noon on the 3d day of January, unless they shall by law appoint a different day.

SECT. 3. If, at the time fixed for the beginning of the term of the President, the President elect shall have died, the Vice President elect shall become President. If a President shall not have been chosen before the time fixed for the beginning of his term, or if the President elect shall have failed to qualify, then the Vice President elect shall act as President until a President shall have qualified; and the Congress may by law provide for the case wherein neither a President elect nor a Vice President elect shall have qualified, declaring who shall then act as President, or the manner in which one who is to act shall be selected, and such persons shall act accordingly until a President or Vice President shall have qualified.

SECT. 4. The Congress may by law provide for the case of the death of any of the persons from whom the House of Representatives may choose a President whenever the right of

---

*"In lieu of the second paragraph of section 4 of article 1 of the constitution of the United States."

choice shall have devolved upon them, and for the case of the death of any of the persons from whom the Senate may choose a Vice President whenever the right of choice shall have devolved upon them.

SECT. 5. Sections 1 and 2 shall take effect on the 15th day of October following the ratification of this article.

SECT. 6. This article shall be inoperative unless it shall have been ratified as an amendment to the Constitution by the legislatures of three-fourths of the several States within seven years from the date of its submission.

ART. XXI. SECT. 1. The eighteenth article of amendment to the Constitution of the United States is hereby repealed.

SECT. 2. The transportation or importation into any State, Territory, or possession of the United States for delivery or use therein of intoxicating liquors, in violation of the laws thereof, is hereby prohibited.

SECT. 3. This article shall be inoperative unless it shall have been ratified as an amendment to the Constitution by conventions in the several States, as provided in the Constitution, within seven years from the date of the submission hereof to the States by the Congress.

ART. XXII. SECT. 1. No person shall be elected to the office of the President more than twice, and no person who has held the office of President, or acted as President, for more than two years of a term to which some other person was elected President shall be elected to the office of the President more than once. But this Article shall not apply to any person holding the office of President when this Article was proposed by the Congress, and shall not prevent any person who may be holding the office of President, or acting as President, during the term within which this Article becomes operative from holding the office of President or acting as President during the remainder of such term.

SECT. 2. This article shall be inoperative unless it shall have been ratified as an amendment to the Constitution by the legislatures of three-fourths of the several States within seven years from the date of its submission to the States by the Congress.

ART. XXIII. SECT. 1. The District constituting the seat of Government of the United States shall appoint in such manner as the Congress may direct:

A number of electors of President and Vice President equal to the whole number of Senators and Representatives in Congress to which the District would be entitled if it were a State, but in no event more than the least populous State; they shall be in addition to those appointed by the States, but they shall be considered, for the purposes of the election of President and Vice President, to be electors appointed by a State; and they shall meet in the District and perform such duties as provided by the twelfth article of amendment.

SECT. 2. The Congress shall have power to enforce this article by appropriate legislation.

ART. XXIV. SECT. 1. The right of citizens of the United States to vote in any primary or other election for President or Vice President, for electors for President or Vice President, or for Senator or Representative in Congress, shall not be denied or abridged by the United States or any State by reason of failure to pay any poll tax or other tax.

SECT. 2. The Congress shall have power to enforce this article by appropriate legislation.

ART. XXV. SECT. I. In case of the removal of the President from office or of his death or resignation, the Vice President shall become President.

SECT. 2. Whenever there is a vacancy in the office of the Vice President, the President shall nominate a Vice President who shall take office upon confirmation by a majority vote of both Houses of Congress.

SECT. 3. Whenever the President transmits to the President pro tempore of the Senate and the Speaker of the House of

Representatives his written declaration that he is unable to discharge the powers and duties of his office, and until he transmits to them a written declaration to the contrary, such powers and duties shall be discharged by the Vice President as Acting President.

SECT. 4. Whenever the Vice President and a majority of either the principal officers of the executive departments or of such other body as Congress may by law provide, transmit to the President pro tempore of the Senate and the Speaker of the House of Representatives their written declaration that the President is unable to discharge the powers and duties of his office, the Vice President shall immediately assume the powers and duties of the office as Acting President.

Thereafter, when the President transmits to the President pro tempore of the Senate and the Speaker of the House of Representatives his written declaration that no inability exists, he shall resume the powers and duties of his office unless the Vice President and a majority of either the principal officers of the executive department or of such other body as Congress may by law provide, transmit within four days to the President pro tempore of the Senate and the Speaker of the House of Representatives their written declaration that the President is unable to discharge the powers and duties of his office. Thereupon Congress shall decide the issue, assembling within forty-eight hours for that purpose if not in session. If the Congress, within twenty-one days after receipt of the latter written declaration, or, if Congress is not in session, within twenty-one days after Congress is required to assemble, determines by two-thirds vote of both Houses that the President is unable to discharge the powers and duties of his office, the Vice President shall continue to discharge the same as Acting President; otherwise, the President shall resume the powers and duties of his office.

ART. XXVI. SECT. 1. The right of citizens of the United States, who are eighteen years of age or older, to vote shall not be denied or abridged by the United States or by any State on account of age.

SECT. 2. The Congress shall have the power to enforce this article by appropriate legislation.

ART. XXVII. No law, varying the compensation for the services of the Senators and Representatives, shall take effect, until an election of Representatives shall have intervened.

[NOTE: The constitution was adopted September 17, 1787, by the unanimous consent of the states present in the convention appointed in pursuance of the resolution of the congress of the confederation of February 21, 1787, and was ratified by the conventions of the several states, as follows: viz.: By convention of *Delaware*, December 7, 1787; *Pennsylvania*, December 12, 1787; *New Jersey*, December 18, 1787; *Georgia*, January 2, 1788; *Connecticut*, January 9, 1788; *Massachusetts*, February 6, 1788; *Maryland*, April 28, 1788; *South Carolina*, May 23, 1788; *New Hampshire*, June 21, 1788; *Virginia*, June 26, 1788; *New York*, July 26, 1788; *North Carolina*, November 21, 1789; *Rhode Island*, May 29, 1790.

The first ten amendments were proposed to the legislatures of the several states at the first session of the first congress of the United States, September 25, 1789, and were finally ratified by the constitutional number of states on December 15, 1791. Subsequently they were ratified by Massachusetts on March 2, 1939.

The eleventh amendment was proposed to the legislatures of the several states at the first session of the third congress, March 5, 1794, and was declared in a message from the President of the United States to both houses of congress, dated January 8, 1798, to have been adopted by the legislatures of three-fourths of the states.

The twelfth amendment was proposed to the legislatures of the several states at the first session of the eighth congress, December 12, 1803, and was ratified by the legislatures of three-fourths of the states in 1804, according to a public notice thereof by the secretary of state, dated September 25 of the same year.

The thirteenth amendment was proposed to the legislatures of the several states by the thirty-eighth congress on February 1, 1865, and was declared, in a proclamation of the secretary of state, dated December 18, 1865, to have been ratified by the legislatures of three-fourths of the states.

The fourteenth amendment was proposed to the legislatures of the several states by the thirty-ninth congress, on June 16, 1866.

On July 20, 1868, the secretary of state of the United States issued his certificate, setting out that it appeared by official documents on file in the department of state that said amendment had been ratified by the legislatures of the states of *Connecticut, New Hampshire, Tennessee, New Jersey, Oregon, Vermont, New York, Ohio, Illinois, West Virginia, Kansas, Maine, Nevada, Missouri, Indiana, Minnesota, Rhode Island, Wisconsin, Pennsylvania, Michigan, Massachusetts, Nebraska* and *Iowa*, and by newly established bodies avowing themselves to be and acting as the legislatures of the states of *Arkansas, Florida, North Carolina, Louisiana, South Carolina* and *Alabama*; that the legislatures of *Ohio* and *New Jersey* had since passed resolutions withdrawing the consent of those states to said amendment; that the whole number of states in the United States was thirty-seven, that the twenty-three states first above named and the six states next above named together, constituted three-fourths of the whole number of states, and certifying that if the resolutions of *Ohio* and *New Jersey*, ratifying said amendment were still in force, notwithstanding their subsequent resolutions, then said amendment had been ratified and so become valid as part of the constitution.

On July 21, 1868, congress passed a resolution reciting that the amendment had been ratified by *Connecticut, Tennessee, New Jersey, Oregon, Vermont, West Virginia, Kansas, Missouri, Indiana, Ohio, Illinois, Minnesota, New York, Wisconsin, Pennsylvania, Rhode Island, Michigan, Nevada, New Hampshire, Massachusetts, Nebraska, Maine, Iowa, Arkansas, Florida, North Carolina, Alabama, South Carolina* and *Louisiana*, being three-fourths of the several states of the Union, and declaring said fourteenth article to be a part of the constitution of the United States, and making it the duty of the secretary of state to duly promulgate it as such.

On July 28, 1868, the secretary of state issued his certificate, reciting the above resolution, and stating that official notice had been received at the department of state that action had been taken by the legislatures of the states in relation to said amendment, as follows: "It was ratified in A.D. 1866, by *Connecticut*, June 30; *New Hampshire*, July 7; *Tennessee*, July 19; *Oregon*, September 19; *Vermont*, November 9. In A.D. 1867, by *New York*, January 10; *Illinois*, January 15; *West*

Virginia. January 16; *Kansas,* January 18; *Maine,* January 19; *Nevada.* January 22; *Missouri,* January 26; *Indiana,* January 29; *Minnesota,* February 1; *Rhode Island,* February 7; *Wisconsin,* February 13; *Pennsylvania,* February 13; *Michigan,* February 15; *Massachusetts,* March 20; *Nebraska,* June 15. In A.D. 1868 by *Iowa,* April 3; *Arkansas,* April 6; *Florida,* June 9; *Louisiana,* July 9; and *Alabama,* July 13.

It was first ratified and the ratification subsequently withdrawn by *New Jersey,* ratified September 11, 1866, withdrawn April, 1868; *Ohio,* ratified January 11, 1867, and withdrawn January, 1868.

It was first rejected and then ratified by *Georgia,* rejected November 13, 1866, ratified July 21, 1868; *North Carolina,* rejected December 4, 1866, ratified July 4, 1868; *South Carolina,* rejected December 20, 1866, ratified July 9, 1868.

It was rejected by *Texas,* November 1, 1866; *Virginia,* January 9, 1867; *Kentucky,* January 10, 1867; *Delaware,* February 7, 1867; and *Maryland,* March 23, 1867.

And on said July 28, 1868, and in execution of the act proposing the amendment and of the concurrent resolution of congress above mentioned and in pursuance thereof, the secretary of state directed that said amendment to the constitution be published in the newspapers authorized to promulgate the laws of the United States, and certified that it had been adopted in the manner above specified by the states named in said resolution, and that it "has become valid to all intents and purposes as a part of the constitution of the United States."

Subsequently, it was ratified by *Virginia,* October 8, 1869, by *Georgia* again, February 2, 1870, and by *Texas,* February 18, 1870.

The fifteenth amendment was proposed to the legislatures of the several states by the fortieth congress on February 27, 1869, and was declared, in a proclamation of the secretary of state, dated March 30, 1870, to have been ratified by the legislatures of the constitutional number of states and to have "become valid to all intents and purposes as part of the constitution of the United States."

The sixteenth amendment was proposed to the legislatures of the several states by the sixty-first congress, at its first session, in 1909. On February 25, 1913, the secretary of state made proclamation to the effect that, from official documents on file in the department, it appeared that the amendment had been ratified by the legislatures of the states of *Alabama, Kentucky, South Carolina, Illinois, Mississippi, Oklahoma, Maryland, Georgia, Texas, Ohio, Idaho, Oregon, Washington, California, Montana, Indiana, Nevada, North Carolina, Nebraska, Kansas, Colorado, North Dakota, Michigan, Iowa, Missouri, Maine, Tennessee, Arkansas, Wisconsin, New York, South Dakota, Arizona, Minnesota, Louisiana, Delaware* and *Wyoming*, in all thirty-six; and further, that the states whose legislatures had so ratified the said proposed amendment constituted three-fourths of the whole number of states in the United States; and, further, that it appeared from official documents on file in the department that the legislatures of *New Jersey* and *New Mexico* had passed resolutions ratifying the said proposed amendment. He further certified that the amendment had "become valid to all intents and purposes as a part of the constitution of the United States."

The seventeenth amendment was proposed to the legislatures of the several states by the sixty-second congress, at its second session, in 1912. On May 31, 1913, the secretary of state made proclamation to the effect that, from official documents on file in the department, it appeared that the amendment had been ratified by the legislatures of the states of *Massachusetts, Arizona, Minnesota, New York, Kansas, Oregon, North Carolina, California, Michigan, Idaho, West Virginia, Nebraska, Iowa, Montana, Texas, Washington, Wyoming, Colorado, Illinois, North Dakota, Nevada, Vermont, Maine, New Hampshire, Oklahoma, Ohio, South Dakota, Indiana, Missouri, New Mexico, New Jersey, Tennessee, Arkansas, Connecticut, Pennsylvania and Wisconsin*; and, further, that the states whose legislatures had so ratified the said proposed amendment constituted three-fourths of the whole number of states in the United States. He further certified that the amendment had "become valid to all intents and purposes as a part of the constitution of the United States."

The eighteenth amendment was proposed to the legislatures of the several states by the sixty-fifth congress, at its second session, in 1917. On January 29, 1919, the acting secretary of state made proclamation to the effect that, from official documents on file in the department, it appeared that the amendment had been ratified by the legislatures of the states of *Alabama, Arizona, California, Colorado, Delaware, Florida, Georgia, Idaho, Illinois, Indiana, Kansas, Kentucky, Louisiana,*

Maine, Maryland, Massachusetts, Michigan, Minnesota, Mississippi, Montana, Nebraska, New Hampshire, North Carolina, North Dakota, Ohio, Oklahoma, Oregon, South Dakota, South Carolina, Texas, Utah, Virginia, Washington, West Virginia, Wisconsin and *Wyoming;* and, further, that the states whose legislatures had so ratified the said proposed amendment constituted three-fourths of the whole number of states in the United States. He further certified that the amendment had "become valid to all intents and purposes as a part of the constitution of the United States."

The nineteenth amendment was proposed to the legislatures of the several states by the sixty-sixth congress, at its first session, in 1919. On August 26, 1920, the secretary of state made proclamation that, from official documents on file in the department, it appeared that the amendment had been ratified by the legislatures of the states of *Arizona, Arkansas, California, Colorado, Idaho, Illinois, Indiana, Iowa, Kansas, Kentucky, Maine, Massachusetts, Michigan, Minnesota, Missouri, Montana, Nebraska, Nevada, New Hampshire, New Jersey, New Mexico, New York, North Dakota, Ohio, Oklahoma, Oregon, Pennsylvania, Rhode Island, South Dakota, Tennessee, Texas, Utah, Washington, West Virginia, Wisconsin* and *Wyoming;* and, further, that the states whose legislatures had so ratified the said proposed amendment constituted three-fourths of the whole number of states in the United States. He further certified that the amendment had "become valid to all intents and purposes as a part of the constitution of the United States."

The twentieth amendment was proposed to the legislatures of the several states by the seventy-second congress, at its first session, in 1931. On February 6, 1933, the secretary of state made proclamation that, from official documents on file in the department, it appeared that the amendment had been ratified by the legislatures of the states of *Alabama, Arizona, Arkansas, California, Colorado, Connecticut, Delaware, Georgia, Idaho, Illinois, Indiana, Kansas, Kentucky, Louisiana, Maine, Massachusetts, Michigan, Minnesota, Mississippi, Missouri, Montana, Nebraska, New Jersey, New York, North Carolina, North Dakota, Ohio, Oklahoma, Pennsylvania, Rhode Island, South Carolina, South Dakota, Texas, Utah, Virginia, Washington, West Virginia, Wisconsin* and *Wyoming;* and, further, that the states whose legislatures had so ratified the said proposed amendment constituted more than the requisite three-fourths of the whole number of states in the United States. He further certified that the amendment had "become valid to all intents and purposes as a part of the constitution of the United States."

The twenty-first amendment was proposed to conventions of the several states by the seventy-second congress, at its second session, in 1933. On December 5, 1933, the acting secretary of state made proclamation that, from official notices received at the department, it appeared that the amendment had been ratified by conventions in the states of *Alabama, Arizona, Arkansas, California, Colorado, Connecticut, Delaware, Florida, Idaho, Illinois, Indiana, Iowa, Kentucky, Maryland, Massachusetts, Michigan, Minnesota, Missouri, Nevada, New Hampshire, New Jersey, New Mexico, New York, Ohio, Oregon, Pennsylvania, Rhode Island, Tennessee, Texas, Utah, Vermont, Virginia, Washington, West Virginia, Wisconsin* and *Wyoming;* and, further, that the states wherein conventions had so ratified the said proposed amendment constituted the requisite three-fourths of the whole number of states in the United States. He further certified that the amendment had "become valid to all intents and purposes as a part of the constitution of the United States."

The twenty-second amendment was proposed to the legislatures of the several states by the eightieth congress, at its first session, in 1947. On March 1, 1951, the administrator of general services certified that from official documents on file in the general services administration it appeared that the amendment had been ratified by the legislatures of the states of *Arkansas, California, Colorado, Connecticut, Delaware, Georgia, Idaho, Illinois, Indiana, Iowa, Kansas, Louisiana, Maine, Michigan, Mississippi, Missouri, Montana, Nebraska, Nevada, New Hampshire, New Jersey, New Mexico, New York, North Carolina, North Dakota, Ohio, Oregon, Pennsylvania, South Dakota, Tennessee, Texas, Utah, Vermont, Virginia, Wisconsin* and *Wyoming;* and, further, that the states whose legislatures had so ratified the said proposed amendment constituted the requisite three-fourths of the whole number of states in the United States. He further certified that the amendment had "become valid to all intents and purposes as a part of the constitution of the United States."

The twenty-third amendment was proposed by Congress on June 16, 1960. On April 3, 1961, the administrator of general services certified that from official documents on file in the general services administration it appeared that the amendment had been ratified by the legislatures of the states of *Alaska, Arizona, California, Colorado, Connecticut, Delaware, Hawaii, Idaho, Illinois, Indiana, Iowa, Kansas, Maine, Maryland, Massachusetts, Michigan, Minnesota, Missouri, Montana, Nebraska, Nevada, New Hampshire, New Jersey, New Mexico, New York, North Dakota, Ohio, Oklahoma, Oregon, Pennsylvania, Rhode Island, South Dakota, Tennessee, Utah, Vermont, Washington, West Virginia, Wisconsin* and *Wyoming;* and further that the states whose legislatures had so ratified the said proposed amendment constituted the requisite three-fourths of the whole number of states in the United States. He further certified that the amendment had "become valid to all intents and purposes as a part of the constitution of the United States."

The twenty-fourth amendment was proposed by Congress on August 27, 1962. On February 4, 1964, the administrator of general services certified that from official documents on file in the general services administration it appeared that the amendment had been ratified by the legislatures of the states of *Alaska, California, Colorado, Connecticut, Delaware, Florida, Hawaii, Idaho, Illinois, Indiana, Iowa, Kansas, Kentucky, Maine, Maryland, Massachusetts, Michigan, Minnesota, Missouri, Montana, Nebraska, Nevada, New Hampshire, New Jersey, New Mexico, New York, North Dakota, Ohio, Oregon, Pennsylvania, Rhode Island, South Dakota, Tennessee, Utah, Vermont, Washington, West Virginia* and *Wisconsin;* and further that the states whose legislatures had so ratified the said proposed amendment constituted the requisite three-fourths of the whole number of states in the United States. He further certified that the amendment had "become valid to all intents and purposes as a part of the constitution of the United States."

The twenty-fifth amendment was proposed by Congress on January 6, 1965. On February 27, 1967, the administrator of general services certified that from official documents on file in the general services administration it appeared that the amendment had been ratified by the legislatures of the states of *Alaska, Arizona, Arkansas, California, Colorado, Delaware, Hawaii, Idaho, Indiana, Iowa, Kansas, Kentucky, Louisiana, Maine, Maryland, Massachusetts, Michigan, Minnesota, Mississippi, Missouri, Montana, Nebraska, Nevada, New*

Hampshire, New Jersey, New Mexico, New York, Oklahoma, Oregon, Pennsylvania, Rhode Island, Tennessee, Utah, Vermont, Virginia, Washington, West Virginia, Wisconsin and *Wyoming;* and further that the states whose legislatures had so ratified the said proposed amendment constituted the requisite three-fourths of the whole number of states in the United States. He further certified that the amendment had "become valid to all intents and purposes as a part of the constitution of the United States."

The twenty-sixth amendment to the Constitution of the United States was submitted to the several states by a joint resolution of Congress, at the first session, ninety-second Congress, begun January 21, 1971, and was certified by the Administrator of General Services on July 5, 1971, 36 Fed. Reg. 12725, to have been ratified by the legislatures of the required number of states.

The twenty-seventh amendment was submitted to the several states pursuant to a resolution passed by the first Congress of the United States, at its first session, on Sept. 25, 1789, and was certified by the Archivist of the United States on May 19, 1992, 57 Fed. Reg. 21187, to have been ratified by the legislatures of the states of *Alabama, Alaska, Arizona, Arkansas, Colorado, Connecticut, Delaware, Florida, Georgia, Idaho, Illinois, Indiana, Iowa, Kansas, Louisiana, Maine, Maryland, Michigan, Minnesota, Missouri, Montana, Nevada, New Hampshire, New Jersey, New Mexico, North Carolina, North Dakota, Ohio, Oklahoma, Oregon, South Carolina, South Dakota, Tennessee, Texas, Utah, Vermont, Virginia, West Virginia, Wisconsin,* and *Wyoming.*]

CONSTITUTION

OR

FORM OF GOVERNMENT

FOR THE

COMMONWEALTH OF MASSACHUSETTS

CONSTITUTION OR FORM OF GOVERNMENT FOR THE COMMONWEALTH OF MASSACHUSETTS

PREAMBLE.

Objects of government – Body politic, how formed – Its nature. Page 59.

PART THE FIRST.
Declaration of Rights.

47

PART THE SECOND.
The Frame of Government

CHAPTER I.
THE Legislative Power.
SECTION I.
The General Court.

SECTION II.
Senate.

Section III.
House of Representatives.

Chapter II.
Executive Power.
Section I.
Governor.

ART. 5. Power of governor and council to adjourn or prorogue general court and convene the same. 79.

ART. 6. Governor and council may adjourn general court in cases, etc., but not exceeding ninety days. 79.

ART. 7. Governor to be commander-in-chief – Limitation. 80. [Annulled. See Amendments. Art. 54.]

ART. 8. Pardoning power. 81. [Annulled. See Amendments, Art. 73.]

ART. 9. Judicial officers, etc., how nominated and appointed. 81.

ART. 10. Militia officers, how elected – How commissioned – Election of officers – Major-generals, how appointed and commissioned – Vacancies, how filled, in case, etc. – Officers duly commissioned, how removed – Adjutants, etc., how appointed – Organization of militia. 81. [Annulled. See Amendments, Art. 53.]

ART. 11. Money, how drawn from the treasury, except, etc. 82.

ART. 12. All public boards, etc., to make quarterly returns. 82.

ART. 13. Salary of governor – Salaries of justices of supreme judicial court – Salaries to be enlarged, if insufficient. 83.

SECTION II.
Lieutenant-Governor.

ARTICLE 1. Lieutenant-governor, his title and qualifications – How chosen. 84.

ART. 2. Governor to be president of council – Lieutenant-governor a member of, except, etc. 84.

ART. 3. Lieutenant-governor to be acting governor, in case, etc. 84.

SECTION III.
Council, and the Manner of settling Elections by the Legislature.

ARTICLE 1. Council. 84.

ART. 2. Number; from whom, and how chosen – If senators become councillors, their seats to be vacated. 85.

ART. 3. Rank of councillors. 85.

ART. 4. No district to have more than two. 85.

ART. 5. Register of council. 85.

ART. 6. Council to exercise power of governor in case, etc. 85. [Annulled. See Amendments. Art. 55.]

ART. 7. Elections may be adjourned until, etc. – Order thereof. 86.

ART. 2. Plurality of officers prohibited to governor, etc., except, etc. – Incompatible offices – Bribery, etc., disqualify. 92.

ART. 3. Value of money ascertained – Property qualifications may be increased. 93.

ART. 4. Provisions respecting commission. 94.

ART. 5. Provisions respecting writs. 94.

ART. 6. Continuation of former laws, except, etc. 94.

ART. 7. Benefit of *habeas corpus* secured, except, etc. 94.

ART. 8. The enacting style. 94.

ART. 9. Officers of former government continued until, etc. 94.

ART. 10. Provision for revising constitution. 95.

ART. 11. Provision for preserving and publishing this constitution. 95.

AMENDMENTS.

ARTICLE 1. Bill, etc., not approved within five days, not to become a law, if legislature adjourn in the meantime. 96.

ART. 2. General court empowered to charter cities and to establish limited town meeting form of government - Proviso. 96.

ART. 3. Qualifications of voters for governor, lieutenant-governor, senators and representatives. 96.

ART. 4. Notaries public, how appointed and removed – Vacancies in the offices of secretary and treasurer, how filled, in case, etc. – Commissary-general may be appointed, in case, etc. – Militia officers, how removed. 97.

ART. 5. Who may vote for captains and subalterns. 97. [Annulled. See Art. 53.]

ART. 6. Oath to be taken by all officers; or affirmation in case, etc. 97.

ART. 7. Tests abolished. 98.

ART. 8. Incompatibility of officers. 98.

ART. 9. Amendments to constitution, how made. 98. [Annulled. See Art. 48.]

ART. 10. Commencement of political year; and termination – Governor, etc., term of office -- Meetings for choice of governor, lieutenant-governor, etc., when to be held; may be adjourned. 99.

ART. 11. Religious freedom established. 100.

ART. 12. Census of ratable polls – Representatives, how apportioned. 101.

ART. 13. Census – Senatorial districts – Apportionment of representatives and councillors – Freehold as a qualification for a seat in general court or council not required. 102.

ART. 14. Election by people to be plurality. 104.

ART. 36. So much of article nineteen as is contained in the words "Commissioners of Insolvency" annulled. 112.

ART. 37. Governor, with the consent of the council, may remove justices of the peace and notaries public. 112.

ART. 38. Voting machines may be used at elections, under regulations. 112.

ART. 39. Powers of legislature relative to excess takings of land, etc., for laying out, widening or relocating highways, etc. – Proviso. 113.

ART. 40. Article three of amendments amended so as to exclude from voting persons disqualified by law because of corrupt practices in elections. 113.

ART. 41. Taxation of wild or forest lands. 113. [Annulled. See Art. 110.]

ART. 42. Authority given to general court to refer acts and resolves to the people for rejection or approval. 113. [Annulled. See Art. 48.]

ART. 43. Authority given to general court to authorize the commonwealth to take land, etc., to relieve congestion of population and provide homes for citizens. 114.

ART. 44. Authority given to general court to tax income. 114.

ART. 45. Authority given to general court to provide for absent voting. 114. [Annulled. See Art. 76.]

ART. 46. Religious freedom – Public money not to be appropriated for founding, maintaining or aiding educational, charitable or religious institutions not publicly owned, except, etc. – Care or support of public charges in private hospitals – Religious services for inmates of certain institutions. 114.

ART. 47. General court may provide for maintenance and distribution of food, etc., in time of war, public exigency, emergency or distress, by the commonwealth, cities and towns. 116.

ART. 48. The Initiative and Referendum. 116. [See Arts. 74 and 81.]

ART. 49. Conservation, etc., of natural resources of commonwealth. 127. [Annulled. See Art. 97.]

ART. 50. Regulation of advertising in public places. 127.

ART. 51. Preservation and maintenance of property of historical and antiquarian interest. 128.

ART. 52. General court may take a recess. 128. [Annulled. See Art. 102.]

ART. 53. Selection of officers of the militia. 128.

ART. 54. Powers of the governor as commander-in-chief. 128.

ART. 55. Succession in cases of vacancies in the offices of governor and lieutenant-governor. 129.

Art. 92. Census of inhabitants and special enumeration of voters – House of Representatives, number. Legislature to apportion, etc. – Senate, number – Senatorial and councillor districts – Qualifications of representatives and senators. 156. [Annulled. See Art. 101.]

Art. 93. One year residency requirement to be eligible to vote within Commonwealth annulled. 157.

Art. 94. Reduction of age qualification for eligibility to vote from twenty-one to nineteen years of age. 157.

Art. 95. Word "pauper" stricken from qualification for voting. 157.

Art. 96. Resident educational grants-in-aid may be authorized by General Court. 157.

Art. 97. Environmental bill of rights. 158.

Art. 98. Retirement of judicial officers. 158.

Art. 99. Taxation of agricultural and horticultural lands. 159.

Art. 100. Voting age qualification lowered to eighteen. 159.

Art. 101. House of Representatives cut to 160 members – decennial census qualifications, etc. 159.

Art. 102. General Court recess. 161.

Art. 103. Religious freedom – Public money not to be appropriated for founding, maintaining or aiding educational, charitable or religious institutions not publicly owned, except, etc. – Educational grant-in-aid exception. 161.

Art. 104. Revenues from use of vehicles to be used for highway and mass transportation purposes only. 162.

Art. 105. Absentee voting – religious beliefs. 162.

Art. 106. Equality under law not to be denied or abridged on the basis of sex, race, color, creed or national origin. 162.

Art. 107. State budget – Time for submission by governor who has not served in preceding term as governor. 163.

Art. 108. Voter information material – households. 163.

Art. 109. State census – residence. 164.

Art. 110. Taxation of wild or forest lands. 164.

Art. 111. Public school students – No assignment or denial of admittance due to race, color, national origin or creed. 164.

Art. 112. Real property taxation – classifications by use. 164.

Art. 113. City and town charters – Time for submission to city or town councils. 164.

Art. 114. Handicapped individuals – Prohibit discrimination. 165.

PREAMBLE.

The end of the institution, maintenance and administration of government, is to secure the existence of the body politic, to protect it, and to furnish the individuals who compose it, with the power of enjoying in safety and tranquility their natural rights, and the blessings of life: and whenever these great objects are not obtained, the people have a right to alter the government, and to take measures necessary for their safety, prosperity, and happiness.

The body politic is formed by a voluntary association of individuals: it is a social compact, by which the whole people covenants with each citizen, and each citizen with the whole people, that all shall be governed by certain laws for the common good. It is the duty of the people, therefore, in framing a constitution of government, to provide for an equitable mode of making laws, as well as for an impartial interpretation, and a faithful execution of them; that every man may, at all times, find his security in them.

We, therefore, the people of Massachusetts, acknowledging, with grateful hearts, the goodness of the great Legislator of the universe, in affording us, in the course of His providence, an opportunity, deliberately and peaceably, without fraud, violence or surprise, of entering into an original, explicit, and solemn compact with each other; and of forming a new constitution of civil government, for ourselves and posterity; and devoutly imploring His direction in so interesting a design, do agree upon, ordain and establish, the following *Declaration of Rights, and Frame of Government,* as the CONSTITUTION OF THE COMMONWEALTH OF MASSACHUSETTS.

PART THE FIRST.

A Declaration of the Rights of the Inhabitants of the Commonwealth of Massachusetts.

Article I. All men are born free and equal, and have certain natural, essential and unalienable rights; among which may be reckoned the right of enjoying and defending their lives and liberties; that of acquiring, possessing, and protecting property; in fine, that of seeking and obtaining their safety and happiness. [Annulled by Amendments, Art. CVI.]

Art. II. It is the right as well as the duty of all men in society, publicly, and at stated seasons to worship the Supreme Being, the great Creator and Preserver of the universe. And no subject shall be hurt, molested, or restrained, in his person, liberty, or estate, for worshipping God in the manner and season most agreeable to the dictates of his own conscience, or for his religious procession or sentiments; provided he doth not disturb the public peace, or obstruct others in their religious worship. [See Amendments, Arts. XLVI and XLVIII.]

Art. III. [As the happiness of a people, and the good order and preservation of civil government, essentially depend upon piety, religion, and morality; and as these cannot be generally diffused through a community, but by the institution of the public worship of God, and of public instructions in piety, religion and morality; Therefore, to promote their happiness and to secure the good order and preservation of their government, the people of this Commonwealth have a right to invest their legislature with power to authorize and require, and the legislature shall, from time to time, authorize and require, the several towns, parishes, precincts, and other bodies politic, or religious societies, to make suitable provision, at their own expense, for the institution of the public worship of God, and for the support and maintenance of public Protestant teachers of piety, religion and morality, in all cases where such provision shall not be made voluntarily.

And the people of this Commonwealth have also a right to. and do, invest their legislature with authority to enjoin upon all the subjects an attendance upon the instructions of the public teachers aforesaid, at stated times and seasons, if there be any on whose instructions they can conscientiously and con-veniently attend.

Provided notwithstanding, that the several towns, parishes, precincts, and other bodies politic, or religious societies, shall, at all times, have the exclusive right of electing their public teachers, and of contracting with them for their support and maintenance.

And all moneys, paid by the subject to the support of public worship, and of the public teachers aforesaid, shall, if he require it, be uniformly applied to the support of the public teacher or teachers of his own religious sect or denomination, provided there be any on whose instructions he attends; otherwise it may be paid towards the support of the teacher or teachers of the parish or precinct in which the said moneys are raised.

And every denomination of Christians, demeaning themselves peaceably, and as good subjects of the Commonwealth, shall be equally under the protection of the law; and no subordination of any one sect or denomination to another shall ever be established by law.] [Art. XI of Amendments substituted for this.]

Art. IV. The people of this Commonwealth have the sole and exclusive right of governing themselves, as a free, sovereign, and independent state; and do, and forever hereafter shall, exercise and enjoy every power, jurisdiction, and right, which is not, or may not hereafter, be by them expressly delegated to the United States of America in Congress assembled.

Art. V. All power residing originally in the people, and being derived from them, the several magistrates and officers of government, vested with authority, whether legislative, executive, or judicial, are their substitutes and agents, and are at all times accountable to them.

Art. VI. No man, nor corporation, or association of men, have any other title to obtain advantages, or particular and exclusive privileges, distinct from those of the community, than what arises from the consideration of services rendered to the public; and this title being in nature neither hereditary, nor transmissible to children, or descendants, or relations by blood, the idea of a man born a magistrate, lawgiver, or judge, is absurd and unnatural.

Art. VII. Government is instituted for the common good; for the protection, safety, prosperity, and happiness of the people; and not for the profit, honor, or private interest of any one man, family or class of men: Therefore the people alone have an incontestable, unalienable, and indefeasible right to institute government; and to reform, alter, or totally change the same, when their protection, safety, prosperity and happiness require it.

Art. VIII. In order to prevent those, who are vested with authority, from becoming oppressors, the people have a right, at such periods and in such manner as they shall establish by their frame of government, to cause their public officers to return to private life; and to fill up vacant places by certain and regular elections and appointments.

Art. IX. All elections ought to be free; and all the inhabitants of this Commonwealth, having such qualifications as they shall establish by their frame of government, have an equal right to elect officers, and to be elected, for public employments. [See Amendments, Arts. XLV and XLVIII, The Initiative, II. sec. 2] [For compulsory voting, see Amendments, Art. LXI.] [For use of voting machines at elections, see Amendments, Art. XXXVIII.] [For absent voting, see Amendments, Art. LXXVI.]

Art. X. Each individual of the society has a right to be protected by it in the enjoyment of his life, liberty and property, according to standing laws. He is obliged, consequently, to contribute his share to the expense of this protection; to give his personal service, or an equivalent, when necessary: but no part of the property of any individual, can, with justice, be taken from him, or applied to public uses, without his own consent, or that of the representative body of the people. In fine, the people of this Commonwealth are not controllable by any other laws than those to which their constitutional representative body have given their consent. And whenever the public exigencies require, that the property of any individual should be appropriated to public uses, he shall receive a reasonable compensation therefor. [See Amendments, Arts. XXXIX, XLIII, XLVII, XLVIII, The Initiative, II, sect. 2, LXIX, L, LI and XCVII.]

Art. XI. Every subject of the Commonwealth ought to find a certain remedy, by having recourse to the laws, for all injuries or wrongs which he may receive in his person, property, or character. He ought to obtain right and justice freely, and without being obliged to purchase it; completely, and without any denial; promptly, and without delay; conformably to the laws.

Art. XII. No subject shall be held to answer for any crimes or offence, until the same is fully and plainly, substantially and formally, described to him; or be compelled to accuse, or furnish evidence against himself. And every subject shall have a right to produce all proofs, that may be favorable to him; to meet the witnesses against him face to face, and to be fully heard in his defense by himself, or his counsel, at his election. And no subject shall be arrested, imprisoned, despoiled, or deprived of his property, immunities, or privileges, put out of the protection of the law, exiled, or deprived of his life, liberty, or estate, but by the judgment of his peers, or the law of the land.

And the legislature shall not make any law, that shall subject any person to a capital or infamous punishment, excepting for the government of the army and navy, without trial by jury. [See Amendments, Art. XLVIII, The Initiative, II, sect. 2.]

Art. XIII. In criminal prosecutions, the verification of facts in the vicinity where they happen, is one of the greatest securities of the life, liberty, and property of the citizen.

Art. XIV. Every subject has a right to be secure from all unreasonable searches, and seizures, of his person, his houses, his papers, and all his possessions. All warrants, therefore, are contrary to this right, if the cause or foundation of them be not previously supported by oath or affirmation; and if the order in the warrant to a civil officer, to make search in suspected places, or to arrest one or more suspected persons, or to seize their property, be not accompanied with a special designation of the persons or objects of search, arrest, or seizure: and no warrant ought to be issued but in cases, and with the formalities prescribed by the laws. [See Amendments, Art. XLVIII, The Initiative, II, sect. 2.]

Art. XV. In all controversies concerning property, and in all suits between two or more persons, except in cases in which it has heretofore been otherways used and practiced, the parties have a right to a trial by jury; and this method of procedure shall be held sacred, unless, in causes arising on the high seas, and such as relate to mariners' wages, the legislature shall hereafter find it necessary to alter it. [See Amendments, Art. XLVIII, The Initiative, II, sect. 2.]

Art. XVI. [The liberty of the press is essential to the security of freedom in a state: it ought not, therefore, to be restrained in this Commonwealth.] [See Amendments, Art. XLVIII, The Initiative, II, sect. 2.] [Annulled and superseded by Amend- ments, Art. LXXVII.]

Art. XVII. The people have a right to keep and to bear arms for the common defense. And as, in time of peace, armies are dangerous to liberty, they ought not to be maintained without the consent of the legislature; and the military power shall always be held in an exact subordination to the civil authority, and be governed by it.

Art. XVIII. A frequent recurrence to the fundamental principles of the constitution, and a constant adherence to those of piety, justice, moderation, temperance, industry, and frugality, are absolutely necessary to preserve the advantages of liberty, and to maintain a free government. The people ought, consequently, to have a particular attention to all those principles, in the choice of their officers and representatives: and they have a right to require of their lawgivers and magistrates an exact and constant observance of them, in the formation and execution of the laws necessary for the good administration of the Commonwealth.

Art. XIX. The people have a right, in an orderly and peaceable manner, to assemble to consult upon the common good: give instructions to their representatives, and to request of the legislative body, by the way of addresses, petitions, or remonstrances, redress of the wrongs done them, and of the grievances they suffer. [See Amendments, Art. XLVIII, The Initiative, II, sect. 2.]

Art. XX. The power of suspending the laws, or the execution of the laws, ought never to be exercised but by the legislature, or by authority derived from it, to be exercised in such particular cases only as the legislature shall expressly provide for. [See Amendments, Arts. XLVIII, I. *Definition* and LXXXIX.]

Art. XXI. The freedom of deliberation, speech and debate in either house of the legislature, is so essential to the rights of the people, that it cannot be the foundation of any accusation or prosecution, action or complaint, in any other court or place whatsoever. [See Amendments, Art. XLVIII, The Initiative, II, sect. 2.]

Art. XXII. The legislature ought frequently to assemble for the redress of grievances, for correcting, strengthening and confirming the laws, and for making new laws, as the common good may require.

Art. XXIII. No subsidy, charge, tax, impost, or duties, ought to be established, fixed, laid, or levied, under any pretext whatsoever, without the consent of the people or their representatives in the legislature.

Art. XXIV. Laws made to punish for actions done before the existence of such laws, and which have not been declared crimes by preceding laws, are unjust, oppressive, and inconsistent with the fundamental principles of a free government.

Art. XXV. No subject ought, in any case, or in any time, to be declared guilty of treason or felony by the legislature.

Art. XXVI. No magistrate or court of law, shall demand excessive bail or sureties, impose excessive fines, or inflict cruel or unusual punishments. [See Amendments, Art. XLVIII, The Initiative, II, sect. 2, and CXVI.]

Art. XXVII. In time of peace, no soldier ought to be quartered in any house without the consent of the owner; and in time of war, such quarters ought not to be made but by the civil magistrate, in a manner ordained by the legislature.

Art. XXVIII. No person can in any case be subjected to law-martial, or to any penalties or pains, by virtue of that law, except those employed in the army or navy, and except the militia in actual service, but by authority of the legislature. [See Amendments, Art. XLVIII, The Initiative, II, sect. 2.]

Art. XXIX. It is essential to the preservation of the rights of every individual, his life, liberty, property and character, that there be an impartial interpretation of the laws, and administration of justice. It is the right of every citizen to be tried by judges as free, impartial and independent as the lot of humanity will admit. It is, therefore, not only the best policy, but for the security of the rights of the people, and of every citizen, that the judges of the supreme judicial court should hold their offices as long as they behave themselves well; and that they should have honorable salaries ascertained and established by standing laws. [See Amendments, Art. XLVIII, The Initiative, II, sect. 2, and The Referendum, III, sect. 2, LXVIII and XCVIII.]

Art. XXX. In the government of this Commonwealth, the legislative department shall never exercise the executive and judicial powers, or either of them: the executive shall never exercise the legislative and judicial powers, or either of them: the judicial shall never exercise the legislative and executive powers, or either of them: to the end it may be a government of laws and not of men.

PART THE SECOND.

The Frame of Government.

The people, inhabiting the territory formerly called the Province of Massachusetts Bay, do hereby solemnly and mutually agree with each other, to form themselves into a free, sovereign, and independent body politic, or state, by the name of THE COMMONWEALTH OF MASSACHUSETTS.

CHAPTER I.

THE LEGISLATIVE POWER.

SECTION I.

The General Court.

Article I. The department of legislation shall be formed by two branches, a Senate and House of Representatives: each of which shall have a negative on the other.

The legislative body shall assemble every year [on the last Wednesday in May, and at such other times as they shall judge necessary; and shall dissolve and be dissolved on the day next preceding the said last Wednesday in May;] and shall be stiled, THE GENERAL COURT OF MASSACHUSETTS. [See Amendments, Arts. X, LXXII and LXXV.]

Art. II. No bill or resolve of the senate or house of representatives shall become a law, and have force as such, until it shall have been laid before the governor for his revisal: and if he, upon such revision, approve thereof he shall signify his approbation by signing the same. But if he have any objection to the passing of such bill or resolve, he shall return the same, together with his objections thereto, in writing, to the senate or house of representatives, in whichsoever the same shall have originated: who shall enter the objections sent down by the governor, at large, on their records, and proceed to reconsider the said bill or resolve. But if after such reconsideration, two thirds of the said senate or house of representatives, shall, notwithstanding the said objections, agree to pass the same, it shall, together with the objections, be sent to the other branch of the legislature, where it shall also be reconsidered, and if approved by two thirds of the members present, shall have the force of a law: but in all such cases, the votes of both houses shall be determined by yeas and nays; and the names of the persons voting for, or against, the said bill or resolve, shall be entered upon the public records of the Commonwealth.

[And in order to prevent unnecessary delays, if any bill or resolve shall not be returned by the governor within five days after it shall have been presented, the same shall have the force of a law.] [See Amendments, Arts. I, XLVIII, LIV, LXIII, sect. 5 and XC, sect. 1.]

Art. III. The general court shall forever have full power and authority to erect and constitute judicatories and courts of record, or other courts, to be held in the name of the Commonwealth, for the hearing, trying, and determining of all manner of crimes, offenses, pleas, processes, plaints, actions, matters, causes and things, whatsoever, arising or happening within the Commonwealth, or between or concerning persons inhabiting, or residing, or brought within the same, whether the same be criminal or civil, or whether the said crimes be capital or not capital, and whether the said pleas be real, personal, or mixed; and for the awarding and making out of execution thereupon. To which courts and judicatories are hereby given and granted full power and authority, from time to time, to administer oaths or affirmations, for the better discovery of truth in any matter in controversy or depending before them. [See Amendments, ART. XLVIII, The Initiative, II, sect. 2, and The Referendum, III, sect. 2.]

Art. IV. And further, full power and authority are hereby given and granted to the said general court, from time to time, to make, ordain, and establish, all manner of wholesome and reasonable orders, laws, statutes, and ordinances, directions and instructions, either with penalties or without; so as the same be not repugnant or contrary to this constitution, as they shall judge to be for the good and welfare of this Commonwealth, and for the government and ordering thereof, and of the subjects of the same, and for the necessary support and defense of the government thereof; and to name and settle annually, or provide by fixed laws, for the naming and settling all civil officers within the said Commonwealth; the election and constitution of whom are not hereafter in this form of government otherwise provided for; and to set forth the several duties, powers and limits, of the several civil and military officers of this Commonwealth, and the forms of such oaths or affirmations as shall be respectively administered unto them for the execution of their several offices and places, so as the same be not repugnant or contrary to this constitution; and to impose and levy proportional and reasonable assessments, rates and taxes, upon all the inhabitants of, and persons resident, and estates lying, within the said Commonwealth; and also to impose and levy, reasonable duties and excises, upon any produce, goods, wares, merchandise, and commodities, whatsoever, brought into, produced, manufactured, or being within the same; to be issued and disposed of by warrant, under the hand of the governor of this Commonwealth for the time being, with the advice and consent of the council, for the public service, in the necessary defense and support of the government of the said Commonwealth, and the protection and preservation of the subjects thereof, according to such acts as are or shall be in force within the same.

And while the public charges of government, or any part thereof, shall be assessed on polls and estates, in the manner that has hitherto been practiced, in order that such assessments may be made with equality, there shall be a valuation of estates within the Commonwealth taken anew once in every ten years at least, and as much oftener as the general court shall order. [See Amendments, Arts. XLI, XLIV, XCIX and CXII.]

[For the authority of the general court to charter cities and establish limited town meeting form of government, see Amendments, Arts. II and LXX.

For power of the general court to establish voting precincts in towns, see Amendments, Art. XXIX.

For additional taxing power given to the general court, see Amendments, Arts. XLI and XLIV.

For the authority of the general court to take land, etc., for relieving congestion of population and providing homes for citizens, see Amendments, ART. XLIII.

For the power given the general court to provide by law for absentee and compulsory voting, see Amendments, ARTS. XLV, LXI and LXXVI.

For the power given the general court to determine the manner of providing and distributing the necessaries of life, etc., during time of war, public distress, etc., by the Commonwealth and the cities and towns therein, see Amendments, ART. LXVII.

For provisions relative to taking the vote on emergency measures, see Amendments, ARTS. XLVIII, The Referendum, II, and LXVII.

For new provisions authorizing the general court to provide for the taking of lands for certain public uses, see Amendments, ART. XLIX.

For provision authorizing the general court to take a recess or recesses amounting to not more than thirty days, see Amendments, ART. LII.

For new provision authorizing the governor to return a bill with a recommendation of amendment, see Amendments, ART. LVI.

For the power of the general court to limit the use or construction of buildings, see Amendments, ART. LX.

For new provisions relative to the biennial election of senators and representatives and their terms of office, see Amendments, ART. LXIV.

For new provisions that no person elected to the general court shall be appointed to any office which was created or the emoluments of which were increased during the term for which he was elected, nor received additional salary or compensation for service upon recess committees or commissions, see Amendments, ART. LXV.

For the power given the general court to prescribe the terms and conditions upon which a pardon may be granted in the case of a felony, see Amendments, ART. LXXIII.]

CHAPTER I.

SECTION II.

Senate.

Article I. [There shall be annually elected, by the freeholders and other inhabitants of this Commonwealth, qualified as in this constitution is provided, forty persons to be councillors and senators for the year ensuing their election; to be chosen by the inhabitants of the districts into which the Commonwealth may from time to time be divided by the general court for that purpose; and the general court in assigning the numbers to be elected by the respective districts, shall govern themselves by the proportion of the public taxes paid by the said districts; and timely make known to the inhabitants of the Commonwealth the limits of each district, and the number of councillors and senators to be chosen therein; provided that the number of such districts shall never be less than thirteen; and that no district be so large as to entitle the same to choose more than six senators. [See Amendments, Arts. XIII, XVI, XXII, LXIV, LXXI, XCII, CI and CIX.]

And the several counties in this Commonwealth shall, until the general court shall determine it necessary to alter the said districts, be districts for the choice of councillors and senators. (except that the counties of Dukes County and Nantucket shall form one district for that purpose) and shall elect the following number for councillors and senators, viz.: – Suffolk, six; Essex, six; Middlesex, five; Hampshire, four; Plymouth, three; Barnstable, one; Bristol, three; York, two; Dukes County and Nantucket, one; Worcester, five; Cumberland, one; Lincoln, one; Berkshire, two.]

Art. II. The senate shall be the first branch of the legislature; and the senators shall be chosen in the following manner, viz.: there shall be a meeting on the [first Monday in April,] [annually], forever, of the inhabitants of each town in the several counties of this Commonwealth; to be called by the selectmen, and warned in due course of law, at least seven days before the [first Monday in April,] for the purpose of electing persons to be senators and councillors; [and at such meetings every male inhabitant of twenty-one years of age and upwards, having a freehold estate within the

Commonwealth, of the annual income of three pounds, or any estate of the value of sixty pounds, shall have a right to give in his vote for the senators for the district of which he is an inhabitant.] And to remove all doubts concerning the meaning of the word "inhabitant" in this constitution, every person shall be considered as an inhabitant, for the purpose of electing and being elected into any office, or place within this state, in that town, district or plantation, where he dwelleth, or hath his home. [See Amendments, Arts. II, III, X, XV, XX, XXII, XXIII, XXVI, XXVIII, XXX, XXXI, XXXII, XLV, LXIV, LXXI, LXXVI, LXXX, XCII, XCIII, XCIV, XVC, C, CI and CIX.]

The selectmen of the several towns shall preside at such meetings impartially; and shall receive the votes of all the inhabitants of such towns present and qualified to vote for senators, and shall sort and count them in open town meeting, and in presence of the town clerk, who shall make a fair record, in presence of the selectmen, and in open town meeting, of the name of every person voted for, and of the number of votes against his name: and a fair copy of this record shall be attested by the selectmen and the town clerk, and shall be sealed up, directed to the secretary of the Commonwealth for the time being, with a superscription, expressing the purport of the contents thereof, and delivered by the town clerk of such towns, to the sheriff of the county in which such town lies, thirty days at least before [the last Wednesday in May] [annually]: or it shall be delivered into the secretary's office seventeen days at least before the said [last Wednesday in May]; and the sheriff of each county shall deliver all such certificates by him received, into the secretary's office, seventeen days before the said [last Wednesday in May]. [See Amendments, Arts. II and X.]

And the inhabitants of plantations unincorporated, qualified as this constitution provides, who are or shall be empowered and required to assess taxes upon themselves toward the support of government, shall have the same privilege of voting for councillors and senators in the plantations where they reside, as town inhabitants have in their respective towns: [and the plantation meetings for that purpose shall be held annually on the same first Monday in April], at such place in the plantations respectively, as the assessors thereof shall direct; which assessors shall have like authority for notifying the electors, collecting and returning the votes, as the selectmen and town clerks have in their several towns, by this constitution. And all other persons living in places unincorporated (qualified as aforesaid) who shall be assessed to the support of government by the assessors of an adjacent town, shall have the privilege of giving in their votes for councillors and senators in the town where they shall be assessed, and be notified of the place of meeting by the selectmen of the town where they shall be assessed, for that purpose accordingly. [See Amendments, Arts. XV and LXIV.]

Art. III. And that there may be a due convention of senators on the [last Wednesday in May] [annually,] the governor with five of the council, for the time being, shall, as soon as may be, examine the return copies of such records; and fourteen days before the said day he shall issue his summons to such persons as shall appear to be chosen by [a majority of] voters, to attend on that day, and take their seats accordingly: provided nevertheless, that for the first year the said return copies shall be examined by the president and five of the council of the former constitution of government; and the said president shall, in like manner, issue his summons to the persons so elected, that they may take their seats as aforesaid. [See Amendments, Arts. X. XIV. LXIV. LXXII and LXXV.]

Art. IV. The senate shall be the final judge of the elections, returns and qualifications of their own members, as pointed out in the constitution; and shall, [on the said last Wednesday in May] [annually,] determine and declare who are elected by each district to be senators [by a majority of votes; and in case there shall not appear to be the full number of senators returned elected by a majority of votes for any district, the deficiency shall be supplied in the following manner, viz.: The members of the house of representatives, and such senators as shall be declared elected, shall take the names of such persons as shall be found to have the highest number of votes in such district, and not elected, amounting to twice the number of senators wanting, if there be so many voted for; and out of these shall elect by ballot a number of senators sufficient to fill up the vacancies in such district; and in this manner all such vacancies shall be filled up in every district of the Commonwealth; and in like manner all vacancies in the senate, arising by death, removal out of the state, or otherwise, shall be supplied as soon as may be, after such vacancies shall happen.] [See Amendments, Arts. X, XIV and XXIV.]

Art. V. Provided nevertheless, that no person shall be capable of being elected as a senator, [who is not seized in his own right of a freehold within this Commonwealth, of the value of three hundred pounds at least, or possessed of personal estate to the value of six hundred pounds at least, or of both to the amount of the same sum. and] who has not been an inhabitant of this Commonwealth for the space of five years immediately preceding his election, and at the time of his election. he shall be an inhabitant in the district for which he shall be chosen. [See Amendments, Arts. XIII, XXII, LXXI, XCII. CI and CIX.]

Art. VI. The senate shall have power to adjourn themselves, provided such adjournments do not exceed two days at a time. [See Amendments, Arts. LII and CII.]

Art. VII. The senate shall choose its own president, appoint its own officers. and determine its own rules of proceedings.

Art. VIII. The senate shall be a court with full authority to hear and determine all impeachments made by the house of representatives, against any officer or officers of the Commonwealth, for misconduct and mal-administration in their offices. But previous to the trial of every impeachment the members of the senate shall respectively be sworn, truly and impartially to try and determine the charge in question, according to evidence. Their judgment, however shall not extend further than to removal from office and disqualification to hold or enjoy any place of honor, trust, or profit, under this Commonwealth: but the party so convicted, shall be, nevertheless, liable to indictment, trial. judgment, and punishment, according to the laws of the land.

Art. IX. [Not less than sixteen members of the senate shall constitute a quorum for doing business.] [See Amendments, Arts. XXII and XXXIII.]

CHAPTER I.

SECTION III.

House of Representatives.

Article I. There shall be, in the legislature of this Commonwealth, a representation of the people, [annually] elected, and founded upon the principle of equality. [See Amendments, Art. LXIV.]

Art. II. [And in order to provide for a representation of the citizens of this Commonwealth, founded upon the principle of equality, every corporate town containing one hundred and fifty ratable polls, may elect one representative; every corporate town, containing three hundred and seventy-five ratable polls, may elect two representatives; every corporate town containing six hundred ratable polls may elect three representatives; and proceeding in that manner, making two hundred and twenty-five ratable polls, the mean increasing number for every additional representative. [See Amendments, Arts. XII, XIII, XXI, LXXI, XCII, CI and CIX.]

Provided nevertheless, that each town now incorporated, not having one hundred and fifty ratable polls, may elect one representative; but no place shall hereafter be incorporated with the privilege of electing a representative, unless there are within the same one hundred and fifty ratable polls.]

And the house of representatives shall have power from time to time to impose fines upon such towns as shall neglect to choose and return members to the same, agreeably to this constitution.

[The expenses of travelling to the general assembly, and returning home, once in every session, and no more, shall be paid by the government, out of the public treasury, to every member who shall attend as seasonably as he can, in the judgment of the house, and does not depart without leave.] [See Amendments, Art. XXXV.]

Art. III. Every member of the house of representatives shall be chosen by written vote; [and for one year at least next preceding his election, shall have been an inhabitant of, and have been seized in his own right of a freehold of the value of one hundred pounds within the town he shall be chosen to represent, or any ratable estate to the value of two hundred pounds; and he shall cease to represent the said town immediately on his ceasing to be qualified as aforesaid.] [See Amendments, Arts. XIII, XXI, LXXI, XCII, CI and CIX.]

Art. IV. [Every male person, being twenty-one years of age, and resident in any particular town in this Commonwealth for the space of one year next preceding, having a freehold estate within the same town of the annual income of three pounds, or any estate of the value of sixty pounds, shall have a right to vote in the choice of a representative, or representatives for the said town.] [See Amendments, Arts. III, XX, XXIII, XXVI, XXVIII, XXX, XXXI, XXXII, XLV, LXXVI, XCIII, XCIV, XCV and C.]

Art. V. [The members of the house of representatives shall be chosen annually in the month of May, ten days at least before the last Wednesday of that month.] [See Amendments, Arts. X, XV and LXIV.]

Art. VI. The house of representatives shall be the grand inquest of this Commonwealth; and all impeachments made by them shall be heard and tried by the senate.

Art. VII. All money bills shall originate in the house of representatives; but the senate may propose or concur with amendments, as on other bills.

Art. VIII. The house of representatives shall have power to adjourn themselves; provided such adjournment shall not exceed two days at a time. [See Amendments, Arts. LII and CII.]

Art IX. [Not less than sixty members of the house of representatives, shall constitute a quorum for doing business. [See Amendments, Arts. XXI and XXXIII.]

Art. X. The house of representatives shall be the judge of the returns, elections, and qualifications of its own members, as pointed out in the constitution; shall choose their own speaker; appoint their own officers, and settle the rules and orders of proceeding in their own house. They shall have authority to punish by imprisonment, every person, not a member, who shall be guilty of disrespect to the house, by any disorderly, or contemptuous behavior in its presence; or who, in the town where the general court is sitting, and during the time of its sitting, shall threaten harm to the body or estate of any of its members, for any thing said or done in the house; or who shall assault any of them therefor; or who shall assault, or arrest, any witness, or other person, ordered to attend the house, in his way in going or returning; or who shall rescue any person arrested by the order of the house.

And no member of the house of representatives shall be arrested, or held to bail on mesne process, during his going unto, returning from, or his attending the general assembly.

Art. XI. The senate shall have the same powers in the like cases; and the governor and council shall have the same authority to punish in like cases. Provided that no imprisonment on the warrant or order of the governor, council, senate, or house of representatives, for either of the above described offenses, be for a term exceeding thirty days.

And the senate and house of representatives may try and determine all cases where their rights and privileges are concerned, and which, by the constitution, they have authority to try and determine, by committees of their own members, or in such other way as they may respectively think best.

CHAPTER II.

EXECUTIVE POWER.

SECTION I.

Governor.

Article I. There shall be a supreme executive magistrate, who shall be styled – THE GOVERNOR OF THE COMMONWEALTH OF MASSACHUSETTS; and whose title shall be – HIS EXCELLENCY.

Art. II. The governor shall be chosen [annually]: and no person shall be eligible to this office, unless at the time of his election, he shall have been an inhabitant of this Commonwealth for seven years next preceding; [and unless he shall at the same time, be seized, in his own right, of a freehold within the Commonwealth of the value of one thousand pounds; and unless he shall declare himself to be of the Christian religion.] [See Amendments, Arts. VII. XXXIV, LXIV and LXXX.]

Art. III. Those persons who shall be qualified to vote for senators and representatives within the several towns of this Commonwealth shall, at a meeting to be called for that purpose. on the [first Monday of April annually], give in their votes for a governor, to the selectmen, who shall preside at such meetings; and the town clerk, in the presence and with the assistance of the selectmen, shall, in open town meeting, sort and count the votes, and form a list of the persons voted for, with the number of votes for each person against his name; and shall make a fair record of the same in the town books, and a public declaration thereof in the said meeting; and shall, in the presence of the inhabitants, seal up copies of the said list, attested by him and the selectmen, and transmit the same to the sheriff of the county, thirty days at least before the [last Wednesday in May]; and the sheriff shall transmit the same to the secretary's office, seventeen days at least before the said [last Wednesday in May]: or the selectmen may cause returns of the same to be made to the office of the secretary of the Commonwealth, seventeen days at least before the said day: and the secretary shall lay the same before the senate and the house of representatives, on the [last Wednesday in May], to be by them examined: and in case of an election by a [majority] of all the votes returned, the choice shall be by them declared and published. But if no person shall have a [majority] of votes, the house of representatives shall, by ballot, elect two out of four persons who had the highest number of votes, if so many shall have been voted for: but, if otherwise, out of the number voted for: and make return to the senate of the two persons so elected; on which the senate shall proceed, by ballot, to elect one, who shall be declared governor. [See Amendments, Arts. II. X. XIV, XV, XLV, LXIV, LXXVI and LXXX.]

Art IV.   The governor shall have authority from time to time, at his discretion, to assemble and call together the councillors of this Commonwealth for the time being; and the governor with the said councillors, or five of them at least, shall, and may, from time to time, hold and keep a council, for the ordering and directing the affairs of the Commonwealth, agreeably to the constitution and the laws of the land.

Art. V.   The governor, with advice of council, shall have full power and authority, during the session of the general court to adjourn or prorogue the same to any time the two houses shall desire: [and to dissolve the same on the day next preceding the last Wednesday in May:] and, in the recess of the said court, to prorogue the same from time to time, not exceeding ninety days in any one recess; and to call it together sooner than the time to which it may be adjourned or prorogued, if the welfare of the Commonwealth shall require the same: and in case of any infectious distemper prevailing in the place where the said court is next at any time to convene, or any other cause happening whereby danger may arise to the health or lives of the members from their attendance, he may direct the session to be held at some other the most convenient place within the state.

[And the governor shall dissolve the said general court on the day next preceding the last Wednesday in May.] [See Amend-ments, Arts. X. LXXII and LXXV.]

Art. VI.   In cases of disagreement between the two houses, with regard to the necessity, expediency or time of adjournment, or prorogation, the governor, with advice of the council, shall have a right to adjourn or prorogue the general court, not exceeding ninety days, as he shall determine the public good shall require.

Art. VII. [The governor of this Commonwealth for the time being, shall be the commander-in-chief of the army and navy, and of all the military forces of the state, by sea and land; and shall have full power by himself, or by any commander, or other officer or officers, from time to time, to train, instruct, exercise and govern the militia and navy; and for the special defense and safety of the Commonwealth, to assemble in martial array, and put in warlike posture, the inhabitants thereof, and to lead and conduct them, and with them, to encounter, repel, resist, expel and pursue, by force of arms, as well as by sea as by land, within or without the limits of this Commonwealth, and also to kill, slay, and destroy, if necessary, and conquer, by all fitting ways, enterprises, and means whatsoever, all and every such person and persons as shall, at any time hereafter, in a hostile manner, attempt or enterprise the destruction, invasion, detriment, or annoyance of this Commonwealth; and to use and exercise, over the army and navy, and over the militia in actual service, the law martial, in time of war or invasion, and also in time of rebellion, declared by the legislature to exist, as occasion shall necessarily require; and to take and surprise by all ways and means whatsoever, all and every such person or persons, with their ships, arms, ammunition and other goods, as shall, in a hostile manner, invade, or attempt the invading, conquering, or annoying this Commonwealth: and the governor be intrusted with all these and other powers, incident to the offices of captain-general and commander-in-chief, and admiral, to be exercised agreeably to the rules and regulations of the constitution, and the laws of the land, and not otherwise.

Provided, that the said governor shall not, at any time hereafter, by virtue of any power by this constitution granted, or hereafter to be granted to him by the legislature, transport any of the inhabitants of this Commonwealth, or oblige them to march out of the limits of the same, without their free and voluntary consent, or the consent of the general court; except so far as may be necessary to march or transport them by land or water, for the defense of such part of the state to which they cannot otherwise conveniently have access.] [Annulled and superseded by Amendments, Art. LIV.]

Art. VIII. [The power of pardoning offenses, except such as persons may be convicted of before the senate by an impeach- ment of the house, shall be in the governor, by and with the advice of council: but no charter of pardon, granted by the governor, with advice of the council before conviction, shall avail the party pleading the same, notwithstanding any general or particular expressions contained therein, descriptive of the offence or offenses intended to be pardoned.] [Annulled and superseded by Amendments, Art. LXXIII.]

Art. IX. All judicial officers, [the attorney-general,] the solicitor-general, [all sheriffs,] coroners, [and registers of probate.] shall be nominated and appointed by the governor, by and with the advice and consent of the council; and every such nomination shall be made by the governor, and made at least seven days prior to such appointment. [See Amendments, Arts. XVII, XLVIII, The Initiative, II, sect. 2, The Referendum, III, sect. 2, and LXIV.] [For provision as to election of sheriffs, registers of probate, etc., see Amendments, Art. XIX.] [For provision as to appointment of notaries public, see Amendments, Arts. IV, LVII and LXIX, sect. 2.]

Art. X. [The captains and subalterns of the militia shall be elected by the written votes of the train-band and alarm list of their respective companies, of twenty-one years of age and upwards: the field officers of regiments shall be elected by the written votes of the captains and subalterns of their respective regiments: the brigadiers shall be elected in like manner, by the field officers of their respective brigades: and such officers, so elected, shall be commissioned by the governor, who shall determine their rank. [See Amendments, Art. V.]

The legislature shall, by standing laws, direct the time and manner of convening the electors, and of collecting votes, and of certifying to the governor, the officers elected.

The major-generals shall be appointed by the senate and house of representatives, each having a negative upon the other; and be commissioned by the governor. [See Amendments, Art. IV.]

And if the electors of brigadiers, field officers, captains or subalterns, shall neglect or refuse to make such elections, after being duly notified, according to the laws for the time being, then the governor, with advice of council shall appoint suitable persons to fill such offices.

And no officer, duly commissioned to command in the militia, shall be removed from his office, but by the address of both houses to the governor, or by fair trial in court-martial pursuant to the laws of the Commonwealth for the time being. [See Amendments, Art. IV.]

The commanding officers of regiments shall appoint their adjutants and quartermasters; the brigadiers their brigade-majors; and the major-generals their aids; and the governor shall appoint the adjutant-general.

The governor, with advice of council, shall appoint all officers of the continental army, whom by the confederation of the United States it is provided that this Commonwealth shall appoint, as also all officers of forts and garrisons.

The divisions of the militia into brigades, regiments and companies, made in pursuance of the militia laws now in force, shall be considered as the proper divisions of the militia of this Commonwealth, until the same shall be altered in pursuance of some future law.] [Annulled and superseded by Amendments, Art. LIII.]

Art. XI. No moneys shall be issued out of the treasury of this Commonwealth, and disposed of (except such sums as may be appropriated for the redemption of bills of credit or treasurer's notes, or for the payment of interest arising thereon) but by warrant under the hand of the governor for the time being, with the advice and consent of the council, for the necessary defense and support of the Commonwealth; and for the protection and preservation of the inhabitants thereof, agreeably to the acts and resolves of the general court. [See Amendments, Art. XLVIII, The Initiative, II, sect. 2, and The Referendum, III, sect. 2.]

Art. XII. All public boards, [the commissary-general,] all superintending officers of public magazines and stores, belonging to this Commonwealth, and all commanding officers of forts and garrisons within the same, shall once in every three months, officially, and without requisition, and at other times. when required by the governor. deliver to him an account of all goods. stores. provisions. ammunition. cannon with their appendages. and small arms with their accoutrements. and all other public property whatever under their care respectively; distinguishing the quantity. number. quality and kind of each. as particularly as may be; together with the condition of such forts and garrisons; and the said commanding officer shall exhibit to the governor. when required by him. true and exact plans of such forts. and of the land and sea or harbor or harbors adjacent.

And the said boards. and all public officers. shall communicate to the governor. as soon as may be after receiving the same. all letters. dispatches. and intelligences of a public nature. which shall be directed to them respectively. [See Amendments. Art. LIII.]

Art. XIII. As the public good requires that the governor should not be under the undue influence of any of the members of the general court by a dependence on them for his support. that he should in all cases. act with freedom for the benefit of the public. that he should not have his attention necessarily diverted from that object to his private concerns. and that he should maintain the dignity of the Commonwealth in the character of its chief magistrate. it is necessary that he should have an honorable stated salary. of a fixed and permanent value. amply sufficient for those purposes. and established by standing laws: and it shall be among the first acts of the general court. after the commencement of this constitution. to establish such salary by law accordingly.

Permanent and honorable salaries shall also be established by law for the justices of the supreme judicial court.

And if it shall be found that any of the salaries aforesaid. so established. are insufficient. they shall. from time to time be enlarged as the general court shall judge proper. [See Amendments. Art. XLVIII. The Initiative. sect. 2. The Referendum. III. sect. 2.]

CHAPTER II.

SECTION II.

Lieutenant-Governor.

Article I. There shall be [annually] elected a lieutenant-governor of the Commonwealth of Massachusetts, whose title shall be – His HONOR; and who shall be qualified, in point of [religion, property,] and residence in the Commonwealth, in the same manner with the governor, and the day and manner of his election, and the qualifications of the electors, shall be the same as are required in the election of a governor. The return of the votes for this officer, and the declaration of his election, shall be in the same manner; and if no one person shall be found to have [a majority] of all the votes returned, the vacancy shall be filled by the senate and house of representatives, in the same manner as the governor is to be elected, in case no one person shall have [a majority] of the votes of the people to be governor. [See Amendments. Arts. VII. XIV, XXXIV, LXIV and LXXX.]

Art. II. The governor, and in his absence the lieutenant-governor, shall be president of the council, but shall have no vote in council: and the lieutenant-governor shall always be a member of the council except when the chair of the governor shall be vacant.

Art. III. Whenever the chair of the governor shall be vacant, by reason of his death, or absence from the Commonwealth, or otherwise, the lieutenant-governor, for the time being, shall, during such vacancy, perform all the duties incumbent upon the governor, and shall have and exercise all the powers and authorities, which by this constitution the governor is vested with, when personally present. [See Amendments, Art. LV.]

CHAPTER II.

SECTION III.

Council, and the Manner of settling Elections by the Legislature.

Article I. There shall be a council for advising the governor in the executive part of government, to consist of [nine] persons besides the lieutenant-governor, whom the governor, for the time being, shall have full power and authority, from time to time, at his discretion, to assemble and call together. And the governor, with the said councillors, or five of them at least, shall and may, from time to time, hold and keep a council, for the ordering and directing the affairs of the Commonwealth, according to the laws of the land. [See Amendments, Art. XVI.]

Art. II. [Nine councillors shall be annually chosen from among the persons returned for councillors and senators, on the last Wednesday in May, by the joint ballot of the senators and representatives assembled in one room; and in case there shall not be found upon the first choice, the whole number of nine persons who will accept a seat in the council, the deficiency shall be made up by the electors aforesaid from among the people at large; and the number of senators left shall constitute the senate for the year. The seats of the persons thus elected from the senate, and accepting the trust, shall be vacated in the senate.] [See Amendments, Arts. X, XIII, XXV and LXIV.] [Superseded by Amendments, Art. XVI.]

Art. III. The councillors, in the civil arrangements of the Commonwealth, shall have rank next after the lieutenant- governor.

Art. IV. [Not more than two councillors shall be chosen out of any one district of this Commonwealth.] [Superseded by Amendments, Art. XVI.]

Art. V. The resolutions and advice of the council shall be recorded in a register, and signed by the members present; and this record may be called for at any time by either house of the legislature; and any member of the council may insert his opinion, contrary to the resolution of the majority.

Art. VI. [Whenever the office of the governor and lieutenant-governor shall be vacant, by reason of death, absence, or otherwise, then the council, or the major part of them, shall, during such vacancy have full power and authority to do, and execute, all and every such acts, matters and things, as the governor or the lieutenant-governor might or could, by virtue of this constitution, do or execute, if they, or either of them, were personally present.] [Annulled and superseded by Amendments, Art. LV.]

Art. VII. [And whereas the elections appointed to be made by this constitution, on the last Wednesday in May annually, by the two houses of the legislature, may not be completed on that day, the said elections may be adjourned from day to day until the same shall be completed. And the order of elections shall be as follows: the vacancies in the senate, if any, shall first be filled up: the governor and lieutenant-governor shall then be elected, provided there should be no choice of them by the people: and afterwards the two houses shall proceed to the election of the council.] [See Amendments, Art. LXIV.] [Superseded by Amendments, Arts. XVI and XXV.]

CHAPTER II.

SECTION IV.

Secretary, Treasurer, Commissary, etc.

Article I. [The secretary, treasurer and receiver general, and the commissary-general, notaries public, and naval officers, shall be chosen annually, by joint ballot of the senators and representatives in one room. And that the citizens of this Commonwealth may be assured, from time to time, that the moneys remaining in the public treasury, upon the settlement and liquidation of the public accounts, are their property, no man shall be eligible as treasurer and receiver general more than five years successively.] [See Amendments, Arts. XVII, LXIV, LXXIX, LXXX and LXXXII.] [For provision as to appointment of notaries public and the commissary-general, see Amendments, Arts. IV, LIII and LVII; see also Amendments, Art. LXIX.]

Art. II. The records of the Commonwealth shall be kept in the office of the secretary, who may appoint his deputies, for whose conduct he shall be accountable, and he shall attend the governor and council, the senate and house of representatives, in person, or by his deputies, as they shall respectively require.

CHAPTER III.

JUDICIARY POWER.

Article I. The tenure, that all commissioned officers shall by law have in their offices, shall be expressed in their respective commissions. All judicial officers, duly appointed, commissioned and sworn, shall hold their offices during good behavior, excepting such concerning whom there is different provision made in this constitution: Provided nevertheless, the governor, with consent of the council, may remove them upon the address of both houses of the legislature. [For tenure, etc. of judges, see Amendments. Art. XLVIII, The Initiative, II, sect. 2, and The Referendum, III, sect. 2.] [For retirement of judicial officers, see Amendments, Art. LVIII.] [For removal of justices of the peace and notaries public, see Amendments, Art. XXXVII.] [Annulled by Amendments, Art. XCVIII.]

Art. II. [Each branch of the legislature, as well as the governor and council, shall have authority to require the opinions of the justices of the supreme judicial court, upon important questions of law, and upon solemn occasions.] [Amended and superseded by Art. LXXXV.]

Art. III. In order that the people may not suffer from the long continuance in place of any justice of the peace, who shall fail of discharging the important duties of his office with ability or fidelity, all commissions of justices of the peace shall expire and become void, in the term of seven years from their respective dates; and upon the expiration of any commission, the same may, if necessary, be renewed, or another person appointed, as shall most conduce to the well-being of the Commonwealth. [See Amendments, Art. XXXVII.]

Art. IV. The judges of probate of wills, and for granting letters of administration, shall hold their courts at such place or places, on fixed days, as the convenience of the people shall require. And the legislature shall from time to time, hereafter appoint such times and places; until which appointments, the said courts shall be holden at the times and places which the respective judges shall direct.

Art. V. All causes of marriage, divorce, and alimony, and all appeals from the judges of probate shall be heard and determined by the governor and council, until the legislature shall, by law, make other provision.

CHAPTER IV.

DELEGATES TO CONGRESS.

[The delegates of this Commonwealth to the congress of the United States, shall, some time in the month of June annually, be elected by the joint ballot of the senate and house of representatives, assembled together in one room; to serve in congress for one year, to commence on the first Monday in November then next ensuing. They shall have commissions under the hand of the governor, and the great seal of the Commonwealth; but may be recalled at any time within the year, and others chosen and commissioned, in the same manner, in their stead.] [Annulled by the adoption of the Constitution of the United States, July 26, 1788.]

CHAPTER V.

THE UNIVERSITY AT CAMBRIDGE, AND ENCOURAGEMENT OF LITERATURE, ETC.

SECTION I.

The University.

Article I. Whereas our wise and pious ancestors, so early as the year one thousand six hundred and thirty-six, laid the foundation of Harvard College,

Constitution of Massachusetts. 89

in which university many persons of great eminence have, by the blessing of
GOD, been initiated in those arts and sciences, which qualified them for
public employments, both in church and state: and whereas the
encouragement of arts and sciences, and all good literature, tends to the
honor of GOD, the advantage of the Christian religion, and the great benefit
of this and the other United States of America – it is declared, that the
PRESIDENT AND FELLOWS OF HARVARD COLLEGE, in their corporate capacity,
and their successors in that capacity, their officers and servants, shall have,
hold, use, exercise and enjoy, all the powers, authorities, rights, liberties,
privileges, immunities and franchises, which they now have, or are entitled
to have, hold, use, exercise and enjoy: and the same are hereby ratified and
confirmed unto them, the said president and fellows of Harvard College, and
to their successors, and to their officers and servants, respectively, forever.

Art. II. And whereas there have been at sundry times, by divers persons,
gifts, grants, devises of houses, lands, tenements, goods, chattles, legacies
and conveyances, heretofore made, either to Harvard College in Cambridge,
in New England, or to the president and fellows of Harvard College, or to
the said college, by some other description, under several charters
successively: it is declared: that all the said gifts, grants, devises, legacies
and conveyances, are hereby forever confirmed unto the president and
fellows of Harvard College, and to their successors in the capacity aforesaid,
according to the true intent and meaning of the donor or donors, grantor or
grantors, devisor or devisors.

Art. III. [And whereas, by an act of the general court of the colony of
Massachusetts Bay, passed in the year one thousand six hundred and forty-
two, the governor and deputy-governor, for the time being, and all the
magistrates of that jurisdiction, were, with the president, and a number of the
clergy in the said act described, constituted the overseers of Harvard
College: and it being necessary, in this new constitution of government to
ascertain who shall be deemed successors to the said governor, deputy-
governor and magistrates: it is declared, that the governor, lieutenant-
governor, council and senate of this Commonwealth, are, and shall be
deemed, their successors, who with the president of Harvard College, for the

time being. together with the ministers of the congregational churches in the towns of Cambridge, Watertown, Charlestown, Boston, Roxbury, and Dorchester, mentioned in the said act, shall be, and hereby are, vested with all the powers and authority belonging, or in any way appertaining to the overseers of Harvard College; provided, that] nothing herein shall be construed to prevent the legislature of this Commonwealth from making such alterations in the government of the said university, as shall be conducive to its advantage, and the interest of the republic of letters, in as full a manner as might have been done by the legislature of the late Province of the Massachusetts Bay.

CHAPTER V.

SECTION II.

The Encouragement of Literature, etc.

Wisdom and knowledge, as well as virtue, diffused generally among the body of the people, being necessary for the preservation of their rights and liberties; and as these depend on spreading the opportunities and advantages of education in the various parts of the country, and among the different orders of the people, it shall be the duty of legislatures and magistrates, in all future periods of this Commonwealth, to cherish the interests of literature and the sciences, and all seminaries of them; especially the university at Cambridge, public schools and grammar schools in the towns; to encourage private societies and public institutions, rewards and immunities, for the promotion of agriculture, arts, sciences, commerce, trades, manufacture, and a natural history of the country; to countenance and inculcate the principles of humanity and general benevolence, public and private charity, industry and frugality, honesty and punctuality in their dealings; sincerity, good humor, and all social affections, and generous sentiments among the people. [See Amendments, Arts. XVIII, XLVI, XCVI and CIII.]

CHAPTER VI.

OATHS AND SUBSCRIPTIONS: INCOMPATIBILITY OF AN EXCLUSION FROM OFFICES:
PECUNIARY QUALIFICATIONS: COMMISSIONS: WRITS: CONFIRMATION OF LAWS:
HABEAS CORPUS: THE ENACTING STYLE: CONTINUANCE OF OFFICERS:
PROVISION FOR A FUTURE REVISAL OF THE CONSTITUTION, ETC.

Article I. [Any person chosen governor, lieutenant-governor, councillor, senator, or representative, and accepting the trust, shall before he proceed to execute the duties of his place or office, make and subscribe the following declaration, viz.:

"I, A. B., do declare, that I believe the Christian religion, and have a firm persuasion of its truth; and that I am seized and possessed, in my own right, of the property required by the constitution, as one qualification for the office or place to which I am elected."

And the governor, lieutenant-governor, and councillors, shall make and subscribe the said declaration, in the presence of the two houses of assembly; and the senators and representatives, first elected under this constitution, before the president and five of the council of the former constitution, and forever afterwards before the governor and council for the time being.]

And every person chosen to either of the places or offices aforesaid, as also any person appointed or commissioned to any judicial, executive, military, or other office under the govern- ment, shall, before he enters on the discharge of the business of his place or office, take and subscribe the following declaration and oaths or affirmations, viz.:

["I, A. B., do truly and sincerely acknowledge, profess, testify, and declare, that the Commonwealth of Massachusetts is, and of right ought to be, a free, sovereign and independent state; and I do swear, that I will bear true faith and allegiance to the said Commonwealth, and that I will defend that same against traitorous conspiracies and all hostile attempts whatsoever; and that I do renounce and abjure all allegiance, subjection, and obedience to the king, queen, or government of Great Britain (as the case may be) and every other foreign power whatsoever; and that no foreign prince, person, prelate, state or potentate, hath, or ought to have, any jurisdiction, superiority, pre-eminence, authority, dispensing or other power, in any matter, civil, ecclesiastical or spiritual, within this Commonwealth, except the authority and power which is or may be vested by their constituents in the congress of the United States: and I do further testify and declare, that no man or body of men hath or can have any right to absolve or discharge me from the obligation of this oath, declaration, or affirmation and that I do make this acknowledgment, profession, testimony, declaration, denial, renunciation and abjuration, heartily and truly, according to the common meaning and acceptation of the foregoing words, without any equivocation, mental evasion, or secret reservation whatsoever. So help me GOD."]

"I, A. B., do solemnly swear and affirm, that I will faithfully and impartially discharge and perform all the duties incumbent on me as   ; according to the best of my abilities and understanding, agreeably, to the rules and regulations of the constitution and the laws of this Commonwealth. So help me GOD."

Provided always, that when any person chosen or appointed as aforesaid, shall be of the denomination of the people called Quakers, and shall decline taking the said oath[s], he shall make his affirmation in the foregoing form and subscribe the same, omitting the words ["*I do swear*," "*and abjure*," "*oath or*," "*and abjuration*," in the first oath; and in the second oath, the words] "*swear and*," and [in each of them] the words "*So help me* GOD;" subjoining instead thereof, "*This I do under the pains and penalties of perjury.*" [See Amendments, Art. VI.]

And the said oaths or affirmations shall be taken and subscribed by the governor, lieutenant-governor, and councillors, before the president of the senate, in the presence of the two houses of assembly; and by the senators and representatives first elected under this constitution, before the president and five of the council of the former constitution; and forever afterwards before the governor and council for the time being: and by the residue of the officers aforesaid, before such persons and in such manner as from time to time shall be prescribed by the legislature. [See Amendments, Arts. VI and VII.]

Art. II. No governor, lieutenant-governor, or judge of the supreme judicial court, shall hold any other office or place, under the authority of this Commonwealth, except such as by this constitution they are admitted to hold, saving that the judges of the said court may hold the offices of justices of the peace through the state; nor shall they hold any other place or office, or receive any pension or salary from any other state or government or power whatever. [See Amendments. Art. VIII.]

No person shall be capable of holding or exercising at the same time. within this state more than one of the following offices. viz.: judge of probate – sheriff – register of probate – or register of deeds: and never more than any two offices which are to be held by appointment of the governor, or the governor and council, or the senate, or the house of representatives, or by the election of the people of the state at large, or of the people of any county, military offices and the offices of justices of the peace excepted. shall be held by one person.

No person holding the office of judge of the supreme judicial court – secretary – attorney-general – solicitor-general – treasurer or receiver general – judge of probate – commissary-general – [president, professor, or instructor of Harvard College –] sheriff – clerk of the house of representatives – register of probate – register of deeds – clerk of the supreme judicial court – clerk of the inferior court of common pleas – or officer of the customs, including in this description naval officers – shall at the same time have a seat in the senate or house of representatives: but their being chosen or appointed to, and accepting the same, shall operate as a resignation of their seat in the senate or house of representatives: and the place so vacated shall be filled up. [See Amendments. Arts. VIII and XXVII.]

And the same rule shall take place in case any judge of the said supreme judicial court, or judge of probate, shall accept a seat on council; or any councillor shall accept of either of those offices or places.

And no person shall ever be admitted to hold a seat in the legislature, or any office of trust or importance under the government of this Commonwealth, who shall, in the due course of law, have been convicted of bribery or corruption in obtaining an election or appointment. [See Amendments, Art. LXV.]

Art. III. [In all cases where sums of money are mentioned in this constitution, the value thereof shall be computed in silver at six shillings and eight pence per ounce: and it shall be in the power of the legislature from time to time to increase such qualifications, as to property, of the persons to be elected to offices, as the circumstances of the Commonwealth shall require.] [See Amendments, Art. XIII and XXXIV.]

Art. IV. All commissions shall be in the name of the Commonwealth of Massachusetts, signed by the governor and attested by the secretary or his deputy, and have the great seal of the Commonwealth affixed thereto.

Art. V. All writs, issuing out of the clerk's office in any of the courts of law, shall be in the name of the Commonwealth of Massachusetts: they shall be under the seal of the court from whence they issue: they shall bear test of the first justice of the court to which they shall be returnable, who is not a party, and be signed by the clerk of such court.

Art. VI. All the laws which have heretofore been adopted, used and approved in the Province, Colony or State of Massachusetts Bay, and usually practiced on in the courts of law, shall still remain and be in full force, until altered or repealed by the legislature: such parts only excepted as are repugnant to the rights and liberties contained in this constitution.

Art VII. The privilege and benefit of the writ of *habeas corpus* shall be enjoyed in this Commonwealth in the most free, easy, cheap, expeditious and ample manner; and shall not be suspended by the legislature, except upon the most urgent and pressing occasions, and for a limited time not exceeding twelve months.

Art. VIII. The enacting style, in making and passing all acts, statutes and laws, shall be – "Be it enacted by the Senate and House of Representatives in General Court assembled, and by the authority of the same."

Art. IX. [To the end there may be no failure of justice, or danger arise to the Commonwealth from a change of the form of government, all officers, civil and military, holding commissions under the government and people of Massachusetts Bay in New England, and all other officers of the said government and people, at the time this constitution shall take effect, shall have, hold, use, exercise and enjoy, all the powers and authority to them granted or committed, until other persons shall be appointed in their stead: and all courts of law shall proceed in the execution of the business of their respective departments; and all the executive and legislative officers, bodies and powers shall continue in full force, in the enjoyment and exercise of all their trusts, employments and authority; until the general court and the supreme and executive officers under this constitution are designated and invested with their respective trusts, powers and authority.]

Art. X. [In order the more effectually to adhere to the principles of the constitution, and to correct those violations which by any means may be made therein, as well as to form such alterations as from experience shall be found necessary, the general court which shall be in the year of our Lord one thousand seven hundred and ninety-five, shall issue precepts to the selectmen of the several towns, and to the assessors of the unincorporated plantations, directing them to convene the qualified voters of their respective towns and plantations, for the purpose of collecting their sentiments on the necessity or expediency of revising the constitution, in order to amendments. [See Amendments, Art. IX.]

And if it shall appear by the returns made, that two-thirds of the qualified voters throughout the state, who shall assemble and vote in consequence of the said precepts, are in favor of such revision or amendment, the general court shall issue precepts, or direct them to be issued from the secretary's office to the several towns to elect delegates to meet in convention for the purpose aforesaid.

The said delegates to be chosen in the same manner and proportion as their representatives in the second branch of the legislature are by this constitution to be chosen.] [Annulled by Amendments, Art. XLVIII.]

Art. XI. This form of government shall be enrolled on parchment and deposited in the secretary's office, and be a part of the laws of the land – and printed copies thereof shall be prefixed to the book containing the laws of this Commonwealth, in all future editions of the said laws.

ARTICLES OF AMENDMENT

Article I. [If any bill or resolve shall be objected to, and not
approved by the governor; and if the general court shall adjourn
within five days after the same shall have been laid before the
governor for his approbation, and thereby prevent his returning it
with his objections, as provided by the constitution, such bill or
resolve shall not become a law, nor have force as such.] [See
Const. Ch. I, § 1, Art. II.] [Annulled and superseded by Amendments, Art. XC, sect. 2.]

Art. II. The general court shall have full power and authority to
erect and constitute municipal or city governments, in any corporate
town or towns in this Commonwealth, and to grant to the
inhabitants thereof such powers, privileges, and immunities, not
repugnant to the constitution, as the general court shall deem
necessary or expedient for the regulation and government thereof,
and to prescribe the manner of calling and holding public meetings
of the inhabitants, in wards or otherwise, for the election of officers
under the constitution, and the manner of returning the votes given
at such meetings. Provided, that no such government shall be
erected or constituted in any town not containing twelve thousand
inhabitants, nor unless it be with the consent, and on the application
of a majority of the inhabitants of such town, present and voting
thereon, pursuant to a vote at a meeting duly warned and holden for
that purpose. And provided, also, that all by-laws, made by such
municipal or city government, shall be subject, at all times, to be
annulled by the general court. [See Amendments, Art. LXX.]
[Annulled by Amendments, Art. LXXXIX.]

Art. III. Every [male] citizen of [twenty-one] years of age and
upwards, excepting [paupers and] persons under guardianship, who
shall have resided [within the commonwealth one year, and] within
the town or district in which he may claim a right to vote, six
calendar months next preceding any election of governor,
lieutenant-governor, senators or representatives, [and who shall
have paid, by himself or his parent, master or guardian, any state or
county tax, which shall, within two years next preceding such
election, have been assessed upon him in any town or district of this

commonwealth; and also, every citizen who shall be, by law, exempted from taxation, and who shall be, in all other respects, qualified as above mentioned,] shall have a right to vote in such election of governor, lieutenant-governor, senators and representatives; and no other person shall be entitled to vote in such elections. [See Amendments, Arts. XX, XXIII, XXVI, XXVIII, XXX, XXXI, XXXII, XL, LXVIII, LXIX, XCIII, XCIV, XCV and C.] [For absent voting, see Amendments, Arts. XLV and LXXVI.]

Art. IV. Notaries public shall be appointed by the governor in the same manner as judicial officers are appointed, and shall hold their offices during seven years, unless sooner removed by the governor, with the consent of the council, upon the address of both houses of the legislature. [See Amendments, Arts. XXXVII, LVII and LXIX, sect. 2.]

[In case the office of secretary or treasurer of the commonwealth shall become vacant from any cause, during the recess of the general court, the governor, with the advice and consent of the council, shall nominate and appoint, under such regulations as may be prescribed by law, a competent and suitable person to such vacant office, who shall hold the same until a successor shall be appointed by the general court.] [This paragraph superseded by Amendments, Art. XVII.]

[Whenever the exigencies of the commonwealth shall require the appointment of a commissary-general, he shall be nominated, appointed, and commissioned, in such manner as the legislature may, by law, prescribe.

All officers commissioned to command in the militia may be removed from office in such manner as the legislature may, by law, prescribe.] [Last two paragraphs annulled and superseded by Amendments, Art. LIII.]

Art. V. [In the elections of captains and subalterns of the militia, all the members of their respective companies, as well those under as those above the age of twenty-one years, shall have a right to vote.] [Annulled by Amendments, Art. LIII.]

Art. VI. Instead of the oath of the allegiance prescribed by the constitution, the following oath shall be taken and subscribed by every person chosen or appointed to any office, civil or military, under the government of this commonwealth, before he shall enter on the duties of his office, to wit: —

"I, A. B., do solemnly swear, that I will bear true faith and allegiance to the Commonwealth of Massachusetts, and will support the constitution thereof. So help me, God."

Provided, That when any person shall be of the denomination called Quakers, and shall decline taking said oath, he shall make his affirmation in the foregoing form, omitting the word "swear" and inserting instead thereof the word "affirm;" and omitting the words "So help me, God," and subjoining, instead thereof, the words, "This I do under the pains and penalties of perjury." [See Const., Ch. VI, Art. I.]

Art. VII. No oath, declaration, or subscription, excepting the oath prescribed in the preceding article, and the oath of office, shall be required of the governor, lieutenant-governor, councillors, senators, or representatives, to qualify them to perform the duties of their respective offices.

Art. VIII. No judge of any court of this commonwealth, (except the court of sessions,) and no person holding any office under the authority of the United States, (postmasters excepted,) shall, at the same time, hold the office of governor, lieutenant-governor, or councillor, or have a seat in the senate or house of representatives of this commonwealth; and no judge of any court in this commonwealth, (except the court of sessions,) nor the attorney-general, solicitor-general, county attorney, clerk of any court, sheriff, treasurer and receiver-general, register of probate, nor register of deeds, shall continue to hold his said office after being elected a member of the Congress of the United States, and accepting that trust; but the acceptance of such trust, by any of the officers aforesaid, shall be deemed and taken to be a resignation of his said office; and judges of the courts of common pleas shall hold no other office under the government of this commonwealth, the office of justice of the peace and militia offices excepted. [See Amendments, Art. LXV.]

Art. IX. [If, at any time hereafter, any specific and particular amendment or amendments to the constitution be proposed in the general court, and agreed to by a majority of the senators and two thirds of the members of the house of representatives present and voting thereon, such proposed amendment or amendments shall be entered on the journals of the two houses, with the yeas and nays taken thereon, and referred to the general court then next to be chosen, and shall be published; and if, in the general court next chosen as aforesaid, such proposed amendment or amendments shall be agreed to by a majority of the senators and two thirds of the members of the house of representatives present and voting thereon, then it shall be the duty of the general court to submit such proposed amendment or amendments to the people; and if they shall be approved and ratified by a majority of the qualified voters voting thereon, at meetings legally warned and holden for that purpose, they shall become part of the constitution of this commonwealth.] [Annulled by Amendments. Art. XLVIII. General Provisions, VIII.]

Art. X. The political year shall begin on the first Wednesday of January, instead of the last Wednesday of May; and the general court shall assemble every year on the said first Wednesday of January, and shall proceed, at that session, to make all the elections, and do all the other acts, which are by the constitution required to be made and done at the session which has heretofore commenced on the last Wednesday of May. And the general court shall be dissolved on the day next preceding the first Wednesday of January, without any proclamation or other act of the governor. But nothing herein contained shall prevent the general court from assembling at such other times as they shall judge necessary, or when called together by the governor. [The governor, lieutenant-governor and councillors, shall also hold their respective offices for one year next following the first Wednesday of January, and until others are chosen and qualified in their stead.] [See Amendments, Arts. LXIV, LXXII and LXXV.]

[The meeting for the choice of governor, lieutenant-governor, senators, and representatives, shall be held on the second Monday of November in every year; but meetings may be adjourned, if necessary, for the choice of representatives, to the next day, and again to the next succeeding day, but no further. But in case a second meeting shall be necessary for the choice of representatives, such meetings shall be held on the fourth Monday of the same month of

November.] [See Amendments. Art. LXIV.] [This paragraph superseded by Amendments. Art. XV.]

All the other provisions of the constitution. respecting the elections and proceedings of the members of the general court, or of any other officers or persons whatever. that have reference to the last Wednesday of May. as the commencement of the political year, shall be so far altered. as to have like reference to the first Wednesday of January.

This article shall go into operation on the first day of October, next following the day when the same shall be duly ratified and adopted as an amendment of the constitution [; and the governor, lieutenant-governor. councillors. senators. representatives, and all other state officers, who are annually chosen, and who shall be chosen for the current year. when the same shall go into operation. shall hold their respective offices until the first Wednesday of January then next following. and until others are chosen and qualified in their stead, and no longer; and the first election of the governor, lieutenant-governor, senators, and representatives. to be had in virtue of this article, shall be had conformably thereunto. in the month of November following the day on which the same shall be in force. and go into operation, pursuant to the foregoing provision].

All the provisions of the existing constitution. inconsistent with the provisions herein contained. are hereby wholly annulled. [See Amendments. Art. LXIV.]

Art. XI. Instead of the third article of the bill of rights, the following modification and amendment thereof is substituted: — "As the public worship of God and instructions in piety, religion, and morality. promote the happiness and prosperity of a people, and the security of a republican government; therefore. the several religious societies of this commonwealth. whether corporate or unincorporate. at any meeting legally warned and holden for that purpose, shall ever have the right to elect their pastors or religious teachers, to contract with them for their support. to raise money for erecting and repairinghouses for public worship for the maintenance of religious instruction. and for the payment of necessary expenses; and all persons belonging to any religious society shall be taken and held to be members, until they shall file with the clerk of such society a written notice, declaring the dissolution of their membership, and thenceforth shall not be liable for any grant or contract which may be thereafter made, or entered into by such society; and all religious sects and denominations, demeaning themselves peaceably, and as good citizens of the commonwealth, shall be equally under the protection of the law; and no subordination of any one sect or denomination to another shall ever be established by law." [See Amendments, Arts. XLVI and XLVIII. The Initiative, II. sect. 2. and The Referendum, III. sect.2.]

Art. XII. [In order to provide for a representation of the citizens of this commonwealth, founded upon the principles of equality, a census of the ratable polls, in each city, town and district of the commonwealth, on the first day of May, shall be taken and returned into the secretary's office, in such manner as the legislature shall provide, within the month of May, in the year of our Lord one thousand eight hundred and thirty-seven, and in every tenth year thereafter, in the month of May, in manner aforesaid; and each town or city having three hundred ratable polls at the last preceding decennial census of polls, may elect one representative, and for every four hundred and fifty ratable polls in addition to the first three hundred, one representative more.

Any town having less than three hundred ratable polls shall be represented thus: The whole number of ratable polls, at the last preceding decennial census of polls, shall be multiplied by ten, and the product divided by three hundred; and such town may elect one representative as many years within ten years, as three hundred is contained in the product aforesaid.

Any city or town having ratable polls enough to elect one or more representatives, with any number of polls beyond the necessary number, may be represented, as to that surplus number, by multiplying such surplus number by ten and dividing the product by four hundred and fifty; and such city or town may elect one additional representative as many years, within the ten years, as four hundred and fifty is contained in the product aforesaid.

Any two or more of the several towns and districts may, by consent of a majority of the legal voters present at a legal meeting, in each of said towns and districts, respectively, called for that purpose, and held previous to the first day of July, in the year in which the decennial census of polls shall be taken. form themselves into a representative district to continue until the next decennial census of polls, for the election of a representative, or representatives; and such district shall have all the rights, in regard to representation, which would belong to a town containing the same number of ratable polls.

The governor and council shall ascertain and determine, within the months of July and August, in the year of our Lord one thousand eight hundred and thirty-seven, according to the foregoing principles, the number of representatives. which each city, town and representative district is entitled to elect, and the number of years, within the period of ten years then next ensuing, that each city, town and representative district may elect an additional representative, and where any town has not a sufficient number of polls to elect a representative each year then how many years within the ten years, such town may elect a representative, and the same shall be done once in ten years thereafter by the governor and council, and the number of ratable polls in each decennial census of polls, shall determine the number of representatives which each city, town and representative district may elect as aforesaid; and when the number of representatives to be elected by each city, town or representative district is ascertained and determined as aforesaid, the governor shall cause the same to be published forthwith for the information of the people and that number shall remain fixed and unalterable for the period of ten years.

All the provisions of the existing constitution inconsistent with the provisions herein contained, are hereby wholly annulled.] [Superseded by Amendments, Arts. XIII, XXI, LXXI, XCII, CI and CIX.]

Art. XIII. [A census of the inhabitants of each city and town, on the first day of May, shall be taken, and returned into the secretary's office. on or before the last day of June, of the year one thousand eight hundred and forty, and of every tenth year thereafter; which census shall determine the apportionment of senators and representatives for the term of ten years. [See Amendments, Arts. XXI. XXII. LXXI. XCII. CI, CIX and CXVII.]

The several senatorial districts now existing shall be permanent. The senate shall consist of forty members; and in the year one thousand eight hundred and forty, and every tenth year thereafter the governor and council shall assign the number of senators to be chosen in each district, according to the number of inhabitants in the same. But, in all cases, at least one senator shall be assigned to each district. [See Amendments, Arts. XXII, LXXI, XCII, CI, CIX and CXVII.]

The members of the house of representatives shall be apportioned in the following manner: Every town or city containing twelve hundred inhabitants may elect one representative; and two thousand four hundred inhabitants shall be the mean increasing number, which shall entitle it to an additional representative. [See Amendments, Arts. XXI, LXXI, XCII, CI and CIX.]

Every town containing less than twelve hundred inhabitants shall be entitled to elect a representative as many times within ten years as the number one hundred and sixty is contained in the number of the inhabitants of said town. Such towns may also elect one representative for the year in which the valuation of estates within the commonwealth shall be settled.

Any two or more of the several towns may, by consent of a majority of the legal voters present at a legal meeting, in each of said towns, respectively, called for that purpose, and held before the first day of August, in the year one thousand eight hundred and forty, and every tenth year thereafter, form themselves into a representative district, to continue for the term of ten years; and such district shall have all the rights, in regard to representation, which would belong to a town containing the same number of inhabitants.

The number of inhabitants which shall entitle a town to elect one representative, and the mean increasing number which shall entitle a town or city to elect more than one, and also the number by which the population of towns not entitled to a representative every year is to be divided, shall be increased, respectively, by one-tenth of the numbers above mentioned, whenever the population of the commonwealth shall have increased to seven hundred and seventy thousand, and for every additional increase of seventy thousand inhabitants, the same addition of one-tenth shall be made, respectively, to the said numbers above mentioned.

In the year of each decennial census, the governor and council shall, before the first day of September, apportion the number of representatives which each city, town, and representative district is entitled to elect, and ascertain how many years, within ten years, any town may elect a representative, which is not entitled to elect one every year; and the governor shall cause the same to be published forthwith.

Nine councillors shall be annually chosen from among the people at large, on the first Wednesday of January, or as soon thereafter as may be, by the joint ballot of the senators and representatives, assembled in one room, who shall, as soon as may be, in like manner, fill up any vacancies that may happen in the council, by death, resignation, or otherwise. No person shall be elected a councillor, who has not been an inhabitant of this commonwealth for the term of five years immediately preceding his election; and not more than one councillor shall be chosen from any one senatorial district in the commonwealth.] [See Amendments, Arts. XVI, LXIV, LXXX, XCII, CI, CIX and CXVII.]

No possession of a freehold, or of any other estate, shall be required as a qualification for holding a seat in either branch of the general court, or in the executive council.

Art. XIV.   In all elections of civil officers by the people of this commonwealth, whose election is provided for by the constitution, the person having the highest number of votes shall be deemed and declared to be elected.

Art. XV.   The meeting for the choice of governor, lieutenant-governor, senators, and representatives, shall be held on the Tuesday next after the first Monday in November, annually; but in case of a failure to elect representatives on that day, a second meeting shall be holden, for that purpose, on the fourth Monday of the same month of November. [See Amendments, Art. LXIV and LXXX.]

Art. XVI.   Eight councillors shall be annually chosen by the inhabitants of this commonwealth, qualified to vote for governor. The election of councillors shall be determined by the same rule that is required in the election of governor. The legislature, at its first session after this amendment shall have been adopted, and at its first session after the next state census shall have been taken, and at its first session after each decennial state census thereafterwards, shall divide the commonwealth into eight districts of contiguous territory, each containing a number of inhabitants as nearly equal as practicable, without dividing any town or ward of a city, and each entitled to elect one councillor: provided, however, that if, at any time, the constitution shall provide for the division of the commonwealth into forty senatorial districts, then the legislature shall so arrange the councillor districts, that each district shall consist of five contiguous senatorial districts, as they shall be, from time to time, established by the legislature. No person shall be eligible to the office of councillor who has not been an inhabitant of the commonwealth for the term of five years immediately preceding his election. The day and manner of the election, the return of the votes, and the declaration of the said elections, shall be the same as are required in the election of governor. [Whenever there shall be a failure to elect the full number of councillors, the vacancies shall be filled in the same manner as is required for filling vacancies in the senate; and vacancies occasioned by death, removal from the state, or otherwise, shall be filled in like manner, as soon as may be, after such vacancies shall have happened.] And that there may be no delay in the organization of the government on the first Wednesday of January, the governor, with at least five councillors for the time being, shall, as soon as may be, examine the returned copies of the records for the election of governor, lieutenant-governor, and councillors; and ten days before the said first Wednesday in January he shall issue his summons to such persons as appear to be chosen, to attend on that day to be qualified accordingly; and the secretary shall lay the returns before the senate and house of representatives on the said first Wednesday in January, to be by them examined; and in case of the election of either of said officers, the choice shall be by them declared and published; but in case there shall be no election of either of said officers, the legislature shall proceed to fill such vacancies in the manner provided in the constitution for the choice of such officers. [See Amendments, Arts. XXV, LXIV and LXXX.]

Art. XVII. The secretary, treasurer and receiver-general, auditor, and attorney-general, shall be chosen [annually], on the day in November prescribed for the choice of governor; and each person then chosen as such, duly qualified in other respects, shall hold his office for the term of [one year] from the third Wednesday in January next thereafter, and until another is chosen and qualified in his stead. The qualification of the voters, the manner of the election, the return of the votes, and the declaration of the election, shall be such as are required in the election of governor. In case of a failure to elect either of said officers on the day in November aforesaid, or in case of the decease, in the meantime, of the person elected as such, such officer shall be chosen on or before the third Wednesday in January next thereafter, from the [two persons who had the highest number of votes for said offices on the day in November aforesaid], by joint ballot of the senators and representatives, in one room; and in case the office of secretary, or treasurer and receiver-general, or auditor, or attorney-general, shall become vacant, from any cause, during an annual or special session of the general court, such vacancy shall in like manner be filled by choice from the people at large; but if such vacancy shall occur at any other time, it shall be supplied by the governor by appointment, with the advice and consent of the council. The person so chosen or appointed, duly qualified in other respects, shall hold his office until his successor is chosen and duly qualified in his stead. In case any person chosen or appointed to either of the offices aforesaid, shall neglect, for the space of ten days after he could otherwise enter upon his duties, to qualify himself in all respects to enter upon the discharge of such duties, the office to which he has been elected or appointed shall be deemed vacant. No person shall be eligible to either of said offices unless he shall have been an inhabitant of this commonwealth five years next preceding his election or appointment. [See Amendments, Arts. LXIV, LXXIX and LXXX.]

Art. XVIII. [All moneys raised by taxation in the towns and cities for the support of public schools, and all moneys which may be appropriated by the state for the support of common schools, shall be applied to, and expended in, no other schools than those which are conducted according to law, under the order and superintendence of the authorities of the town or city in which the money is to be expended; and such money shall never be appropriated to any religious sect for the maintenance, exclusively, of its own school.] [Superseded by Amendments, Arts. XLVI, XCVI and CIII.]

Art. XIX. The legislature shall prescribe, by general law, for the election of sheriffs, registers of probate, [commissioners of insolvency,] and clerks of the courts, by the people of the several counties, and that district-attorneys shall be chosen by the people of the several districts, for such term of office as the legislature shall prescribe. [See Amendments, Art. XXXVI.]

Art. XX. No person shall have the right to vote, or be eligible to office under the constitution of this commonwealth, who shall not be able to read the constitution in the English language, and write his name: provided, however, that the provisions of this amendment shall not apply to any person prevented by a physical disability from complying with its requisitions, nor to any person who now has the right to vote, nor to any persons who shall be sixty years of age or upwards at the time this amendment shall take effect. [See Amendments, Arts. III, XXIII, XXVI, XXVIII, XXX, XXXI, XXXII, XL, XLV and LXXVI.]

Art. XXI. [A census of the legal voters of each city and town, on the first day of May, shall be taken and returned into the office of the secretary of the commonwealth, on or before the last day of June, in the year one thousand eight hundred and fifty-seven; and a census of the inhabitants of each city and town, in the year one thousand eight hundred and sixty-five, and of every tenth year thereafter. In the census aforesaid, a special enumeration shall be made of the legal voters; and in each city, said enumeration shall specify the number of such legal voters aforesaid, residing in each ward of such city. The enumeration aforesaid shall determine the apportionment of representatives for the periods between the taking of the census.

The house of representatives shall consist of two hundred and forty members, which shall be apportioned by the legislature, at its first session after the return of each enumeration as aforesaid, to the several counties of the commonwealth, equally, as nearly as may be, according to their relative numbers of legal voters, as ascertained by the next preceding special enumeration; and the town of Cohasset, in the county of Norfolk, shall, for this purpose, as well as in the formation of districts, as hereinafter provided, be considered a part of the county of Plymouth; and it shall be the duty of the secretary of the commonwealth, to certify, as soon as may be after it is determined by the legislature, the number of representatives to which each county shall be entitled, to the board authorized to divide each county into representative districts. The mayor and aldermen of the city of Boston, the county commissioners of other counties than Suffolk, — or in lieu of the mayor and aldermen of the city of Boston, or of the county commissioners in each county other than Suffolk, such board of special commissioners in each county, to be elected by the people of the county, or of the towns therein, as may for that purpose be provided by law, — shall, on the first Tuesday of August next after each assignment of representatives to each county, assemble at a shire town of their respective counties, and proceed, as soon as may be, to divide the same into representative districts of contiguous territory, so as to apportion the representation assigned to each county equally, as nearly as may be, according to the relative number of legal voters in the several districts of each county; and such districts shall be so formed that no town or ward of a city shall be divided therefor, nor shall any district be made which shall be entitled to elect more than three representatives. Every representative, for one year at least next preceding his election, shall have been an inhabitant of the district for which he is chosen and shall cease to represent such district when he shall cease to be an inhabitant of the commonwealth. The districts in each county shall be numbered by the board creating the same, and a description of each, with the numbers thereof and the number of legal voters therein, shall be returned by the board, to the secretary of the commonwealth, the county treasurer of each county, and to the clerk of every town in each district, to be filed and kept in their respective offices. The manner of calling and conducting the meetings for the choice of representatives, and of ascertaining their election, shall be prescribed by law.] [Not less than one hundred members of the house of representatives shall constitute a quorum for doing business; but a less number may organize temporarily, adjourn from day to day, and compel the attendance of absent members.] [Annulled and superseded by Amendments. Arts. XXXIII. LXXI. XCII, CI, CIX and CXVII.]

Art. XXII. [A census of the legal voters of each city and town, on the first day of May, shall be taken and returned into the office of the secretary of the commonwealth, on or before the last day of June, in the year one thousand eight hundred and fifty-seven; and a census of the inhabitants of each city and town, in the year one thousand eight hundred and sixty-five, and of every tenth year thereafter. In the census aforesaid, a special enumeration shall be made of the legal voters, and in each city said enumeration shall specify the number of such legal voters aforesaid, residing in each ward of such city. The enumeration aforesaid shall determine the apportionment of senators for the periods between the taking of the census. The senate shall consist of forty members. The general court shall, at its first session after each next preceding special enumeration, divide the commonwealth into forty districts of adjacent territory, each district to contain, as nearly as may be, an equal number of legal voters, according to the enumeration aforesaid: provided, however, that no town or ward of a city shall be divided therefor; and such districts shall be formed, as nearly as may be, without uniting two counties, or parts of two or more counties, into one district. Each district shall elect one senator, who shall have been an inhabitant of this commonwealth five years at least immediately preceding his election, and at the time of his election shall be an inhabitant of the district for which he is chosen; and he shall cease to represent such senatorial district when he shall cease to be an inhabitant of the commonwealth.] [Not less than sixteen senators shall constitute a quorum for doing business; but a less number may organize temporarily, adjourn from day to day, and compel the attendance of absent members.] [See Amendments. Art. XXIV.] [Annulled and superseded by Amendments. Arts. XXXIII. LXXI. XCII. CI, CIX and CXVII.]

Art. XXIII. [No person of foreign birth shall be entitled to vote, or shall be eligible to office, unless he shall have resided within the jurisdiction of the United States for two years subsequent to his naturalization, and shall be otherwise qualified, according to the constitution and laws of this commonwealth: provided, that this amendment shall not affect the rights which any person of foreign birth possessed at the time of the adoption thereof; and, provided, further, that it shall not affect the rights of any child of a citizen of the United States, born during the temporary absence of the parent therefrom.] [Annulled by Amendments, Art. XXVI.]

Art. XXIV. Any vacancy in the senate shall be filled by election by the people of the unrepresented district, upon the order of a majority of the senators elected.

Art. XXV. In case of a vacancy in the council, from a failure of election, or other cause, the senate and house of representatives shall, by concurrent vote, choose some eligible person from the people of the district wherein such vacancy occurs, to fill that office. If such vacancy shall happen when the legislature is not in session, the governor, with the advice and consent of the council, may fill the same by appointment of some eligible person.

Art. XXVI. The twenty-third article of the articles of amendment of the constitution of this commonwealth, which is as follows, to wit: "No person of foreign birth shall be entitled to vote, or shall be eligible to office, unless he shall have resided within the jurisdiction of the United States for two years subsequent to his naturalization, and shall be otherwise qualified, according to the constitution and laws of this commonwealth: provided, that this amendment shall not affect the rights which any person of foreign birth possessed at the time of the adoption thereof; and provided, further, that it shall not affect the rights of any child of a citizen of the United States, born during the temporary absence of the parent therefrom," is hereby wholly annulled.

Art. XXVII. So much of article two of chapter six of the constitution of this commonwealth as relates to persons holding the office of president, professor, or instructor of Harvard College, is hereby annulled.

Art. XXVIII. No person having served in the army or navy of the United States in time of war, and having been honorably discharged from such service, if otherwise qualified to vote, shall be disqualified therefor on account of [being a pauper:] or [if a pauper,] because of the non-payment of a poll tax. [Amended by Amendments, Art. XXXI.]

Art. XXIX. The General Court shall have full power and authority to provide for the inhabitants of the towns in this Commonwealth more than one place of public meeting within the limits of each town for the election of officers under the constitution, and to prescribe the manner of calling, holding and conducting such meetings. All the provisions of the existing constitution inconsistent with the provisions herein contained are hereby annulled. [For absent voting, see Amendments, Arts. XLV and LXXVI.]

Art. XXX. No person, otherwise qualified to vote in elections for governor, lieutenant-governor, senators, and representatives, shall, by reason of a change of residence within the Commonwealth, be disqualified from voting for said officers in the city or town from which he has removed his residence, until the expiration of six calendar months from the time of such removal. [For absent and compulsory voting, see Amendments, Arts. XLV, LXI and LXXVI.]

Art. XXXI. Article twenty-eight of the Amendments of the Constitution is hereby amended by striking out in the fourth line thereof the words "being a pauper", and inserting in place thereof the words: — receiving or having received aid from any city or town, — and also by striking out in said fourth line the words "if a pauper", so that the article as amended shall read as follows: — ARTICLE XXVIII. No person having served in the army or navy of the United States in time of war, and having been honorably discharged from such service, if otherwise qualified to vote, shall be disqualified therefor on account of receiving or having received aid from any city or town, or because of the non-payment of a poll tax.

Art. XXXII. So much of article three of the Amendments of the Constitution of the Commonwealth as is contained in the following words: "and who shall have paid, by himself, or his parent, master, or guardian, any state or county tax, which shall, within two years next preceding such election, have been assessed upon him, in any town or district of this Commonwealth; and also every citizen who shall be, by law, exempted from taxation, and who shall be, in all other respects, qualified as above mentioned", is hereby annulled.

Art. XXXIII. A majority of the members of each branch of the General Court shall constitute a quorum for the transaction of business, but a less number may adjourn from day to day, and compel the attendance of absent members. All the provisions of the existing Constitution inconsistent with the provisions herein contained are hereby annulled.

Art. XXXIV. So much of article two of section one of chapter two of part the second of the Constitution of the Commonwealth as is contained in the following words: "and unless he shall at the same time be seized, in his own right, of a freehold, within the Commonwealth, of the value of one thousand pounds"; is hereby annulled.

Art. XXXV. So much of article two of section three of chapter one of the Constitution of the Commonwealth as is contained in the following words: "The expenses of travelling to the general assembly, and returning home, once in every session, and no more, shall be paid by the government, out of the public treasury, to every member who shall attend as seasonably as he can, in the judgment of the house, and does not depart without leave", is hereby annulled.

Art. XXXVI. So much of article nineteen of the articles of Amendment to the Constitution of the Commonwealth as is contained in the following words: "commissioners of insolvency", is hereby annulled.

Art. XXXVII. The governor, with the consent of the council, may remove justices of the peace and notaries public.

Art. XXXVIII. Voting machines or other mechanical devices for voting may be used at all elections under such regulations as may be prescribed by law: provided, however, that the right of secret voting shall be preserved.

Art. XXXIX. Article ten of part one of the Constitution is hereby amended by adding to it the following words: — The legislature may by special acts for the purpose of laying out, widening or relocating highways or streets, authorize the taking in fee by the Commonwealth, or by a county, city or town, of more land and property than are needed for the actual construction of such highway or street: provided, however, that the land and property authorized to be taken are specified in the act and are no more in extent than would be sufficient for suitable building lots on both sides of such highway or street, and after so much of the land or property has been appropriated for such highway or street as is needed therefor, may authorize the sale of the remainder for value with or without suitable restrictions.

Art. XL. Article three of the Amendments to the Constitution is hereby amended by inserting after the word "guardianship", in line two, the following: — and persons temporarily or permanently disqualified by law because of corrupt practices in respect to elections.

Art. XLI. Full power and authority are hereby given and granted to the general court to prescribe for wild or forest lands such methods of taxation as will develop and conserve the forest resources of the commonwealth. [Annulled by Amendments, Art. CX.]

Art. XLII. [Full power and authority are hereby given and granted to the general court to refer to the people for their rejection or approval at the polls any act or resolve of the general court or any part or parts thereof. Such reference shall be by a majority yea and nay vote of all members of each house present and voting. Any act, resolve, or part thereof so referred shall be voted on at the regular state election next ensuing after such reference, shall become law if approved by a majority of the voters voting thereon, and shall take effect at the expiration of thirty days after the election at which it was approved or at such time after the expiration of the said thirty days as may be fixed in such act, resolve or part thereof.] [Annulled and superseded by Amendments, Art. XLVIII, General Provisions, VIII.]

Art. XLIII. The general court shall have power to authorize the commonwealth to take land and to hold, improve, subdivide, build upon and sell the same, for the purpose of relieving congestion of population and providing homes for citizens: provided, however, that this amendment shall not be deemed to authorize the sale of such land or buildings at less than the cost thereof.

Art. XLIV. Full power and authority are hereby given and granted to the general court to impose and levy a tax on income in the manner hereinafter provided. Such tax may be at different rates upon income derived from different classes of property, but shall be levied at a uniform rate throughout the commonwealth upon incomes derived from the same class of property. The general court may tax income not derived from property at a lower rate than income derived from property, and may grant reasonable exemptions and abatements. Any class of property the income from which is taxed under the provisions of this article may be exempted from the imposition and levying of proportional and reasonable assessments, rates and taxes as at present authorized by the constitution. This article shall not be construed to limit the power of the general court to impose and levy reasonable duties and excises.

Art. XLV. [The general court shall have power to provide by law for voting by qualified voters of the commonwealth who, at the time of an election, are absent from the city or town of which they are inhabitants in the choice of any officer to be elected or upon any question submitted at such election.] [Annulled and superseded by Amendments, Arts. LXXVI and CV.] [For compulsory voting, see Amendments, Art. LXI.]

Art. XLVI. (In place of article XVIII of the articles of amendment of the constitution ratified and adopted April 9, 1821, the following article of amendment, submitted by the constitutional convention, was ratified and adopted November 6, 1917.) Article XVIII. Section 1. No law shall be passed prohibiting the free exercise of religion.

Section 2. All moneys raised by taxation in the towns and cities for the support of public schools, and all moneys which may be appropriated by the commonwealth for the support of common schools shall be applied to, and expended in, no other schools than those which are conducted according to law, under the order and superintendence of the authorities of the town or city in which the money is expended; and no grant, appropriation or use of public money or property or loan of public credit shall be made or authorized by the commonwealth or any political division thereof for the purpose of founding, maintaining or aiding any school or institution of learning, whether under public control or otherwise, wherein any denominational doctrine is inculcated, or any other school, or any college, infirmary, hospital, institution, or educational, charitable or religious undertaking which is not publicly owned and under the exclusive control, order and superintendence of public officers or public agents authorized by the commonwealth or federal authority or both, except that appropriations may be made for the maintenance and support of the Soldiers' Home in Massachusetts and for free public libraries in any city or town, and to carry out legal obligations, if any, already entered into; and no such grant, appropriation or use of public money or property or loan of public credit shall be made or authorized for the purpose of founding, maintaining or aiding any church, religious denomination or society.

Section 3. Nothing herein contained shall be construed to prevent the commonwealth, or any political division thereof, from paying to privately controlled hospitals, infirmaries, or institutions for the deaf, dumb or blind not more than the ordinary and reasonable compensation for care or support actually rendered or furnished by such hospitals, infirmaries or institutions to such persons as may be in whole or in part unable to support or care for themselves.

Section 4. Nothing herein contained shall be construed to deprive any inmate of a publicly controlled reformatory, penal or charitable institution of the opportunity of religious exercises therein of his own faith; but no inmate of such institution shall be compelled to attend religious services or receive religious instruction against his will, or, if a minor, without the consent of his parent or guardian.

Section 5. This amendment shall not take effect until the October first next succeeding its ratification and adoption by the people. [See Amendments, Arts. XLVIII. The Initiative, II, sect. 2, and LXII, XCVI, sect. I and CIII.]

Art. XLVII. The maintenance and distribution at reasonable rates, during time of war, public exigency, emergency or distress, of a sufficient supply of food and other common necessaries of life and the providing of shelter, are public functions, and the commonwealth and the cities and towns therein may take and may provide the same for their inhabitants in such manner as the general court shall determine.

Art. XLVIII.

I. Definition.

Legislative power shall continue to be vested in the general court; but the people reserve to themselves the popular initiative, which is the power of a specified number of voters to submit constitutional amendments and laws to the people for approval or rejection; and the popular referendum, which is the power of a specified number of voters to submit laws, enacted by the general court, to the people for their ratification or rejection.

THE INITIATIVE.

II. Initiative Petitions.

SECTION 1. *Contents.* — An initiative petition shall set forth the full text of the constitutional amendment or law, hereinafter designated as the measure, which is proposed by the petition.

SECTION 2. *Excluded Matters.* — No measure that relates to religion, religious practices or religious institutions; or to the appointment, qualification, tenure, removal, recall or compensation of judges; or to the reversal of a judicial decision; or to the powers, creation or abolition of courts; or the operation of which is restricted to a particular town, city or other political division or to particular districts or localities of the commonwealth; or that makes a specific appropriation of money from the treasury of the commonwealth, shall be proposed by an initiative petition; but if a law approved by the people is not repealed, the general court shall raise by taxation or otherwise and shall appropriate such money as may be necessary to carry such law into effect.

Neither the eighteenth amendment of the constitution, as approved and ratified to take effect on the first day of October in the year nineteen hundred and eighteen, nor this provision for its protection, shall be the subject of an initiative amendment.

No proposition inconsistent with any one of the following rights of the individual, as at present declared in the declaration of rights, shall be the subject of an initiative or referendum petition: The right to receive compensation for private property appropriated to public use; the right of access to and protection in courts of justice; the right of trial by jury; protection from unreasonable search, unreasonable bail and the law martial; freedom of the press; freedom of speech; freedom of elections; and the right of peaceable assembly.

No part of the constitution specifically excluding any matter from the operation of the popular initiative and referendum shall be the subject of an initiative petition; nor shall this section be the subject of such a petition.

The limitations on the legislative power of the general court in the constitution shall extend to the legislative power of the people as exercised hereunder.

[SECTION 3. *Mode of Originating.* — Such petition shall first be signed by ten qualified voters of the commonwealth and shall then be submitted to the attorney-general, and if he shall certify that the measure is in proper form for submission to the people, and that it is not, either affirmatively or negatively, substantially the same as any measure which has been qualified for submission or submitted to the people within three years of the succeeding first Wednesday in December and that it contains only subjects not excluded from the popular initiative and which are related or which are mutually dependent, it may then be filed with the secretary of the commonwealth. The secretary of the commonwealth shall provide blanks for the use of subsequent signers, and shall print at the top of each blank a description of the proposed measure as such description will appear on the ballot together with the names and residences of the first ten signers. All initiative petitions, with the first ten signatures attached, shall be filed with the secretary of the commonwealth not earlier than the first Wednesday of the September before the assembling of the general court into which they are to be introduced, and the remainder of the required signatures shall be filed not later than the first Wednesday of the following December.] [Section 3 superseded by section 1 of Amendments, Art. LXXIV.]

SECTION 4. *Transmission to the General Court.* — If an initiative petition, signed by the required number of qualified voters, has been filed as aforesaid, the secretary of the commonwealth shall, upon the assembling of the general court, transmit it to the clerk of the house of representatives, and the proposed measure shall then be deemed to be introduced and pending.

III. Legislative Action. General Provisions.

SECTION 1. *Reference to Committee.* — If a measure is introduced into the general court by initiative petition, it shall be referred to a committee thereof, and the petitioners and all parties in interest shall be heard, and the measure shall be considered and reported upon to the general court with the committee's recommendations, and the reasons therefor, in writing. Majority and minority reports shall be signed by the members of said committee.

SECTION 2. *Legislative Substitutes.* — The general court may, by resolution passed by yea and nay vote, either by the two houses separately, or in the case of a constitutional amendment by a majority of those voting thereon in joint session in each of two years as hereinafter provided, submit to the people a substitute for any measure introduced by initiative petition, such substitute to be designated on the ballot as the legislative substitute for such an initiative measure and to be grouped with it as an alternative therefor.

IV. Legislative Action on Proposed
Constitutional Amendments.

SECTION 1. *Definition.* — A proposal for amendment to the constitution introduced into the general court by initiative petition shall be designated an initiative amendment. and an amendment introduced by a member of either house shall be designated a legislative substitute or a legislative amendment.

[SECTION 2. *Joint Session.* — If a proposal for a specific amendment of the constitution is introduced into the general court by initiative petition signed by not less than twenty-five thousand qualified voters, or if in case of a proposal for amendment introduced into the general court by a member of either house. consideration thereof in joint session is called for by vote of either house. such proposal shall. not later than the second Wednesday in June. be laid before a joint session of the two houses. at which the president of the senate shall preside: and if the two houses fail to agree upon a time for holding any joint session hereby required. or fail to continue the same from time to time until final action has been taken upon all amendments pending. the governor shall call such joint session or continuance thereof.] [Section 2 superseded by section 1 of Amendments. Art. LXXXI.]

SECTION 3. *Amendment of Proposed Amendments.* — A proposal for an amendment to the constitution introduced by initiative petition shall be voted upon in the form in which it was introduced. unless such amendment is amended by vote of three-fourths of the members voting thereon in joint session. which vote shall be taken by call of the yeas and nays if called for by any member.

SECTION 4. *Legislative Action.* — Final legislative action in the joint session upon any amendment shall be taken only by call of the yeas and nays. which shall be entered upon the journals of the two houses: and an unfavorable vote at any stage preceding final action shall be verified by call of the yeas and nays. to be entered in like manner. At such joint session a legislative amendment receiving the affirmative votes of a majority of all the members elected, or an initiative amendment receiving the affirmative votes of not less than one-fourth of all the members elected, shall be referred to the next general court.

SECTION 5. *Submission to the People.* — If in the next general court a legislative amendment shall again be agreed to in joint session by a majority of all the members elected, or if an initiative amendment or a legislative substitute shall again receive the affirmative votes of at least one-fourth of all the members elected, such fact shall be certified by the clerk of such joint session to the secretary of the commonwealth, who shall submit the amendment to the people at the next state election. Such amendment shall become part of the constitution if approved, in the case of a legislative amendment, by a majority of the voters voting thereon, or if approved, in the case of an initiative amendment or a legislative substitute, by voters equal in number to at least thirty per cent of the total number of ballots cast at such state election and also by a majority of the voters voting on such amendment.

V. *Legislative Action on Proposed Laws.*

[SECTION 1. *Legislative Procedure.* — If an initiative petition for a law is introduced into the general court, signed by not less than twenty thousand qualified voters, a vote shall be taken by yeas and nays in both houses before the first Wednesday of June upon the enactment of such law in the form in which it stands in such petition. If the general court fails to enact such law before the first Wednesday of June, and if such petition is completed by filing with the secretary of the commonwealth, not earlier than the first Wednesday of the following July nor later than the first Wednesday of the following August, not less than five thousand signatures of qualified voters, in addition to those signing such initiative petition, which signatures must have been obtained after the first Wednesday of June aforesaid, then the secretary of the commonwealth shall submit such proposed law to the people at the next state election. If it shall be approved by voters equal in number to at least thirty per cent of the total number of ballots cast at such state election and also by a majority of the voters voting on such law, it shall become law, and shall take effect in thirty days after such state election or at such time after such election as may be provided in such law.] [Section 1 superseded by section 2 of Amendments, Art. LXXXI.]

[SECTION 2. *Amendment by Petitioners.* — If the general court fails to pass a proposed law before the first Wednesday of June, a majority of the first ten signers of the initiative petition therefor shall have the right, subject to certification by the attorney-general filed as hereinafter provided, to amend the measure which is the subject of such petition. An amendment so made shall not invalidate any signature attached to the petition. If the measure so amended, signed by a majority of the first ten signers, is filed with the secretary of the commonwealth before the first Wednesday of the following July, together with a certificate signed by the attorney-general to the effect that the amendment made by such proposers is in his opinion perfecting in its nature and does not materially change the substance of the measure, and if such petition is completed by filing with the secretary of the commonwealth, not earlier than the first Wednesday of the following July nor later than the first Wednesday of the following August, not less than five thousand signatures of qualified voters, in addition to those signing such initiative petition, which signatures must have been obtained after the first Wednesday of June aforesaid, then the secretary of the commonwealth shall submit the measure to the people in its amended form.] [Section 2 superseded by section 3 of Amendments, Art. LXXXI.]

VI. Conflicting and Alternative Measures.

If in any judicial proceeding, provisions of constitutional amendments or of laws approved by the people at the same election are held to be in conflict, then the provisions contained in the measure that received the largest number of affirmative votes at such election shall govern.

A constitutional amendment approved at any election shall govern any law approved at the same election.

The general court, by resolution passed as hereinbefore set forth, may provide for grouping and designating upon the ballot as conflicting measures or as alternative measures, only one of which is to be adopted, any two or more proposed constitutional amendments or laws which have been or may be passed or qualified for submission to the people at any one election; provided, that a proposed constitutional amendment and a proposed law shall not be so grouped, and that the ballot shall afford an opportunity to the voter to vote for each of the measures or for only one of the measures, as may be provided in said resolution, or against each of the measures so grouped as conflicting or as alternative. In case more than one of the measures so grouped shall receive the vote required for its approval as herein provided, only that one for which the largest affirmative vote was cast shall be deemed to be approved.

THE REFERENDUM.

I. When Statutes shall take Effect.

No law passed by the general court shall take effect earlier than ninety days after it has become a law, excepting laws declared to be emergency laws and laws which may not be made the subject of a referendum petition, as herein provided.

II. Emergency Measures.

A law declared to be an emergency law shall contain a preamble setting forth the facts constituting the emergency, and shall contain the statement that such law is necessary for the immediate preservation of the public peace, health, safety or convenience. [A separate vote shall be taken on the preamble by call of the yeas and nays, which shall be recorded, and unless the preamble is adopted by two-thirds of the members of each house voting thereon, the law shall not be an emergency law; but] if the governor, at any time before the election at which it is to be submitted to the people on referendum, files with the secretary of the commonwealth a statement declaring that in his opinion the immediate preservation of the public peace, health, safety or convenience requires that such law should take effect forthwith and that it is an emergency law and setting forth the facts constituting the emergency, then such law, if not previously suspended as hereinafter provided, shall take effect without suspension, or if such law has been so suspended such suspension shall thereupon terminate and such law shall thereupon take effect; but no grant of any franchise or amendment thereof, or renewal or extension thereof for more than one year shall be declared to be an emergency law. [See Amendments, Art. LXVII.]

III. Referendum Petitions.

SECTION 1. *Contents.* — A referendum petition may ask for a referendum to the people upon any law enacted by the general court which is not herein expressly excluded.

SECTION 2. *Excluded Matters.* — No law that relates to religion, religious practices or religious institutions; or to the appointment, qualification, tenure, removal or compensation of judges; or to the powers, creation or abolition of courts; or the operation of which is restricted to a particular town, city or other political division or to particular districts or localities of the commonwealth; or that appropriates money for the current or ordinary expenses of the commonwealth or for any of its departments, boards, commissions or institutions shall be the subject of a referendum petition.

SECTION 3. *Mode of Petitioning for the Suspension of a Law and a Referendum thereon.* — A petition asking for a referendum on a law, and requesting that the operation of such law be suspended, shall first be signed by ten qualified voters and shall then be filed with the secretary of the commonwealth not later than thirty days after the law that is the subject of the petition has become law. [The secretary of the commonwealth shall provide blanks for the use of subsequent signers, and shall print at the top of each blank a description of the proposed law as such description will appear on the ballot together with the names and residences of the first ten signers. If such petition is completed by filing with the secretary of the commonwealth not later than ninety days after the law which is the subject of the petition has become law the signatures of not less than fifteen thousand qualified voters of the commonwealth, then the operation of such law shall be suspended, and the secretary of the commonwealth shall submit such law to the people at the next state election, if thirty days intervene between the date when such petition is filed with the secretary of the commonwealth and the date for holding such state election: if thirty days do not so intervene, then such law shall be submitted to the people at the next following state election, unless in the meantime it shall have been repealed; and if it shall be approved by a majority of the qualified voters voting thereon, such law shall, subject to the provisions of the constitution, take effect in thirty days after such election, or at such time after such election as may be provided in such law; if not so approved such law shall be null and void; but no such law shall be held to be disapproved if the negative vote is less than thirty per cent of the total number of ballots cast at such state election.] [Section 3 amended by section 2 of Amendments, Art. LXXIV and section 4 of Amendments, Art. LXXXI.]

SECTION 4. *Petitions for Referendum on an Emergency Law or a Law the Suspension of which is not asked for.* — A referendum petition may ask for the repeal of an emergency law or of a law which takes effect because the referendum petition does not contain a request for suspension, as aforesaid. Such petition shall first be signed by ten qualified voters of the commonwealth, and shall then be filed with the secretary of the commonwealth not later than thirty days after the law which is the subject of the petition has become law. [The secretary of the commonwealth shall provide blanks for the use of subsequent signers, and shall print at the top of each blank a description of the proposed law as such description will appear on the ballot together with the names and residences of the first ten signers. If such petition filed as aforesaid is completed by filing with the secretary of the commonwealth not later than ninety days after the law which is the subject of the petition has become law the signatures of not less than ten thousand qualified voters of the commonwealth protesting against such law and asking for a referendum thereon, then the secretary of the commonwealth shall submit such law to the people at the next state election, if thirty days intervene between the date when such petition is filed with the secretary of the commonwealth and the date for holding such state election. If thirty days do not so intervene, then it shall be submitted to the people at the next following state election, unless in the meantime it shall have been repealed; and if it shall not be approved by a majority of the qualified voters voting thereon, it shall, at the expiration of thirty days after such election, be thereby repealed; but no such law shall be held to be disapproved if the negative vote is less than thirty per cent of the total number of ballots cast at such state election.] [Section 4 superseded by section 3 of Amendments, Art. LXXIV and section 5 of Amendments, Art. LXXXI.]

GENERAL PROVISIONS.

I. Identification and Certification of Signatures.

Provision shall be made by law for the proper identification and certification of signatures to the petitions hereinbefore referred to, and for penalties for signing any such petition, or refusing to sign it, for money or other valuable consideration, and for the forgery of signatures thereto. Pending the passage of such legislation all provisions of law relating to the identification and certification of signatures to petitions for the nomination of candidates for state offices or to penalties for the forgery of such signatures shall apply to the signatures to the petitions herein referred to. The general court may provide by law that no co-partnership or corporation shall undertake for hire or reward to circulate petitions, may require individuals who circulate petitions for hire or reward to be licensed, and may make other reasonable regulations to prevent abuses arising from the circulation of petitions for hire or reward.

II. Limitation on Signatures.

Not more than one-fourth of the certified signatures on any petition shall be those of registered voters of any one county.

[III. Form of Ballot.

Each proposed amendment to the constitution, and each law submitted to the people, shall be described on the ballots by a description to be determined by the attorney-general subject to such provision as may be made by law, and the secretary of the commonwealth shall give each question a number and cause such question, except as otherwise authorized herein, to be printed on the ballot in the following form: —

In the case of an amendment to the constitution: Shall an amendment to the constitution (here insert description, and state, in distinctive type, whether approved or disapproved by the general court, and by what vote thereon) be approved?

	YES.	
	NO.	

In the case of a law: Shall a law (here insert description, and state, in distinctive type, whether approved or disapproved by the general court, and by what vote thereon) be approved?

	YES.	
	NO.	

IV. Information for Voters.

The secretary of the commonwealth shall cause to be printed and sent to each registered voter in the commonwealth the full text of every measure to be submitted to the people, together with a copy of the legislative committee's majority and minority reports, if there be such, with the names of the majority and minority members thereon, a statement of the votes of the general court on the measure, and a description of the measure as such description will appear on the ballot: and shall, in such manner as may be provided by law, cause to be prepared and sent to the voters other information and arguments for and against the measure.] [*Subheading III* superseded by section 4 of Amendments, Art. LXXIV.] [*Subheading IV* superseded by section 4, Amendments, Art. LXXIV and amended by Amendments, Art. CVIII.]

V. The Veto Power of the Governor.

The veto power of the governor shall not extend to measures approved by the people.

VI. The General Court's Power of Repeal.

Subject to the veto power of the governor and to the right of referendum by petition as herein provided, the general court may amend or repeal a law approved by the people.

VII. Amendment declared to be Self-executing.

This article of amendment to the constitution is self-executing, but legislation not inconsistent with anything herein contained may be enacted to facilitate the operation of its provisions.

VIII. Articles IX and XLII of Amendments of the Constitution annulled.

Article IX and Article XLII of the amendments of the constitution are hereby annulled.

Art. XLIX. The conservation, development and utilization of the agricultural, mineral, forest, water and other natural resources of the commonwealth are public uses, and the general court shall have power to provide for the taking, upon payment of just compensation therefor, of lands and easements or interests therein, including water and mineral rights, for the purpose of securing and promoting the proper conservation, development, utilization and control thereof and to enact legislation necessary or expedient therefor. [Superseded by Amendments, Art. XCVII.]

Art. L. Advertising on public ways, in public places and on private property within public view may be regulated and restricted by law.

Art. LI.   The preservation and maintenance of ancient landmarks and other property of historical or antiquarian interest is a public use, and the commonwealth and the cities and towns therein may, upon payment of just compensation, take such property or any interest therein under such regulations as the general court may prescribe.

Art. LII.   The general court, by concurrent vote of the two houses, may take a recess or recesses amounting to not more than thirty days; but no such recess shall extend beyond the sixtieth day from the date of their first assembling. [Annulled and superseded by Amendments, Art. CII.]

Art. LIII.   Article X of Section I of Chapter II of the constitution, the last two paragraphs of Article IV of the articles of amendment, relating to the appointment of a commissary general and the removal of militia officers, and Article V of the articles of amendment are hereby annulled, and the following is adopted in place thereof: —

Article X.   All military and naval officers shall be selected and appointed and may be removed in such manner as the general court may by law prescribe, but no such officer shall be appointed unless he shall have passed an examination prepared by a competent commission or shall have served one year in either the federal or state militia or in military service. All such officers who are entitled by law to receive commissions shall be commissioned by the governor.

Art. LIV.   Article VII of Section I of Chapter II of the constitution is hereby annulled and the following is adopted in place thereof: —

Article VII.   The general court shall provide by law for the recruitment, equipment, organization, training and discipline of the military and naval forces. The governor shall be the commander-in-chief thereof, and shall have power to assemble the whole or any part of them for training, instruction or parade, and to employ them for the suppression of rebellion, the repelling of invasion, and the enforcement of the laws. He may, as authorized by the general court, prescribe from time to time the organization of the military and naval forces and make regulations for their government.

Art. LV. Article VI of Section III of Chapter II of the constitution is hereby annulled and the following is adopted in place thereof:

Whenever the offices of governor and lieutenant-governor shall both be vacant, by reason of death, absence from the commonwealth, or otherwise, then one of the following officers, in the order of succession herein named, namely, the secretary, attorney-general, treasurer and receiver-general, and auditor, shall, during such vacancy, have full power and authority to do and execute all and every such acts, matters and things as the governor or the lieutenant-governor might or could lawfully do or execute, if they, or either of them, were personally present.

Art. LVI. The governor, within five days after any bill or resolve shall have been laid before him, shall have the right to return it to the branch of the general court in which it originated with a recommendation that any amendment or amendments specified by him be made therein. Such bill or resolve shall thereupon be before the general court and subject to amend- ments and re-enactment. If such bill or resolve is re-enacted in any form it shall again be laid before the governor for his action, but he shall have no right to return the same a second time with a recommendation to amend. [Superseded by Amendments, Art. XC, Sect. 3.]

Art. LVII. Article IV of the articles of amendment of the constitution of the commonwealth is hereby amended by adding thereto the following words: — Women shall be eligible to appointment as notaries public. — [Change of name shall render the commission void, but shall not prevent reappointment under the new name.] [See Amendments, Art. LXIX.]

Art. LVIII. Article I of Chapter III of Part the Second of the constitution is hereby amended by the addition of the following words: — and provided also that the governor, with the consent of the council, may after due notice and hearing retire them because of advanced age or mental or physical disability. Such retirement shall be subject to any provisions made by law as to pensions or allowances payable to such officers upon their voluntary retirement. [Superseded by Amendments, Art. XCVIII.]

Art. LIX. Every charter, franchise or act of incorporation shall forever remain subject to revocation and amendment.

Art. LX. The general court shall have power to limit buildings according to their use or construction to specified districts of cities and towns.

Art. LXI. The general court shall have authority to provide for compulsory voting at elections, but the right of secret voting shall be preserved.

Art. LXII. Section 1. The credit of the commonwealth shall not in any manner be given or loaned to or in aid of any individual, or of any private association, or of any corporation which is privately owned and managed. [Superseded by Art. LXXXIV.]

SECTION 2. The commonwealth may borrow money to repel invasion, suppress insurrection, defend the commonwealth, or to assist the United States in case of war, and may also borrow money in anticipation of receipts from taxes or other sources, such loan to be paid out of the revenue of the year in which it is created.

SECTION 3. In addition to the loans which may be contracted as before provided, the commonwealth may borrow money only by a vote, taken by the yeas and nays, of two-thirds of each house of the general court present and voting thereon. The governor shall recommend to the general court the term for which any loan shall be contracted.

SECTION 4. Borrowed money shall not be expended for any other purpose than that for which it was borrowed or for the reduction or discharge of the principal of the loan.

Art. LXIII. Section 1. *Collection of Revenue.* — All money received on account of the commonwealth from any source whatsoever shall be paid into the treasury thereof.

SECTION 2. *The Budget.* — Within three weeks after the convening of the general court the governor shall recommend to the general court a budget which shall contain a statement of all proposed expenditures of the commonwealth for the fiscal year. including those already authorized by law. and of all taxes, revenues, loans and other means by which such expenditures shall be defrayed. This shall be arranged in such form as the general court may by law prescribe, or. in default thereof. as the governor shall determine. For the purpose of preparing his budget. the governor shall have power to require any board, commission. officer or department to furnish him with any information which he may deem necessary. [See Amendments. Arts. LXXII and LXXV.] [Annulled and superseded by Amendments. Art. CVII.]

SECTION 3. *The General Appropriation Bill.* — All appropriations based upon the budget to be paid from taxes or revenues shall be incorporated in a single bill which shall be called the general appropriation bill. The general court may increase. decrease. add or omit items in the budget. The general court may provide for its salaries. mileage. and expenses and for necessary expenditures in anticipation of appropriations. but before final action on the general appropriation bill it shall not enact any other appropriation bill except on recommendation of the governor. The governor may at any time recommend to the general court supplementary budgets which shall be subject to the same procedure as the original budget.

Section 4. *Special Appropriation Bills.* — After final action on the general appropriation bill or on recommendation of the governor. special appropriation bills may be enacted. Such bills shall provide the specific means for defraying the appropriations therein contained.

Section 5. [*Submission to the Governor.* — The governor may disapprove or reduce items or parts of items in any bill appropriating money. So much of such bill as he approves shall upon his signing the same become law. As to each item disapproved or reduced. he shall transmit to the house in which the bill originated his reason for such disapproval or reduction. and the procedure shall then be the same as in the case of a bill disapproved as a whole. In case he shall fail so to transmit his reasons for such disapproval or reduction within five days after the bill shall have been presented to him, such items shall have the force of law unless the general court by adjournment shall prevent such transmission, in which case they shall not be law.] [See Amendments. Art. XC. sect. 4.]

Art. LXIV. [Section 1. The governor, lieutenant-governor, councillors, secretary, treasurer and receiver-general, attorney-general, auditor, senators and representatives, shall be elected biennially. The governor, lieutenant-governor and councillors shall hold their respective offices from the first Wednesday in January succeeding their election to and including the first Wednesday in January in the third year following their election and until their successors are chosen and qualified. The terms of senators and representatives shall begin with the first Wednesday in January succeeding their election and shall extend to the first Wednesday in January in the third year following their election and until their successors are chosen and qualified. The terms of the secretary, treasurer and receiver-general, attorney-general and auditor, shall begin with the third Wednesday in January succeeding their election and shall extend to the third Wednesday in January in the third year following their election and until their successors are chosen and qualified.] [Section 1 superseded by Amendments, Art. LXXX.]

SECTION 2. No person shall be eligible to election to the office of treasurer and receiver-general for more than three successive terms.

SECTION 3. The general court shall assemble every year on the first Wednesday in January. [See Amendments, Arts. LXXII and LXXV.]

SECTION 4. The first election to which this article shall apply shall be held on the Tuesday next after the first Monday in November in the year nineteen hundred and twenty, and thereafter elections for the choice of all the officers before- mentioned shall be held biennially on the Tuesday next after the first Monday in November. [Annulled and superseded by Art. LXXXII.]

Art. LXV.   No person elected to the general court shall during the
term for which he was elected be appointed to any office created or
the emoluments whereof are increased during such term, nor receive
additional salary or compensation for service upon any recess
committee or commission except a committee appointed to examine a
general revision of the statutes of the commonwealth when submitted
to the general court for adoption.

Art. LXVI.   On or before January first, nineteen hundred twenty-
one, the executive and administrative work of the commonwealth
shall be organized in not more than twenty departments, in one of
which every executive and administrative office, board and
commission, except those officers serving directly under the governor
or the council, shall be placed. Such departments shall be under such
supervision and regulation as the general court may from time to time
prescribe by law. [Annulled by Amendments, Art. LXXXVII.]

Art. LXVII.   Article XLVIII of the Amendments to the
Constitution is hereby amended by striking out, in that part entitled
"II Emergency Measures", under the heading "The Referendum", the
words "A separate vote shall be taken on the preamble by call of the
yeas and nays, which shall be recorded, and unless the preamble is
adopted by two-thirds of the members of each House voting thereon,
the law shall not be an emergency law; but" and substituting the
following: — A separate vote, which shall be recorded, shall be
taken on the preamble, and unless the preamble is adopted by two-
thirds of the members of each House voting thereon, the law shall not
be an emergency law. Upon the request of two members of the Senate
or of five members of the House of Representatives, the vote on the
preamble in such branch shall be taken by call of the yeas and nays.
But.

Art. LXVIII.   Article III of the amendments to the constitution, as
amended, is hereby further amended by striking out, in the first line,
the word "male".

Art. LXIX.   Section 1.   No person shall be deemed to be ineligible
to hold state, county or municipal office by reason of sex.

SECTION 2. Article IV of the articles of amendment of the constitution of the commonwealth, as amended by Article LVII of said amendments, is hereby further amended by striking out the words "Change of name shall render the commission void, but shall not prevent reappointment under the new name", and inserting in place thereof the following words: — Upon the change of name of any woman, she shall re-register under her new name and shall pay such fee therefor as shall be established by the general court.

Art. LXX. Article II of the articles of amendment to the constitution of the commonwealth is hereby amended by adding at the end thereof the following new paragraph: —

Nothing in this article shall prevent the General Court from establishing in any corporate town or towns in this commonwealth containing more than six thousand inhabitants a form of town government providing for a town meeting limited to such inhabitants of the town as may be elected to meet, deliberate, act and vote in the exercise of the corporate powers of the town subject to such restrictions and regulations as the General Court may prescribe; provided, that such establishment be with the consent, and on the application of a majority of the inhabitants of such town, present and voting thereon, pursuant to a vote at a meeting duly warned and holden for that purpose. [Annulled by Amendments. Art. LXXXIX.]

Art. LXXI. Article XXI of the articles of amendment is hereby annulled and the following is adopted in place thereof:

Article XXI. In the year nineteen hundred and thirty-five and every tenth year thereafter a census of the inhabitants of each city and town shall be taken and a special enumeration shall be made of the legal voters therein. Said special enumeration shall also specify the number of legal voters residing in each precinct of each town containing twelve thousand or more inhabitants according to said census and in each ward of each city. Each special enumeration shall be the basis for determining the representative districts for the ten year period beginning with the first Wednesday in the fourth January following said special enumeration; provided, that such districts as established in the year nineteen hundred and twenty-six shall continue in effect until the first Wednesday in January in the year nineteen hundred and thirty-nine.

The house of representatives shall consist of two hundred and forty members, which shall be apportioned by the general court, at its first regular session after the return of each special enumeration, to the several counties of the commonwealth equally, as nearly as may be, according to their relative numbers of legal voters, as ascertained by said special enumeration; and the town of Cohasset, in the county of Norfolk, shall, for this purpose, as well as in the formation of districts as hereinafter provided, be considered a part of the county of Plymouth; and it shall be the duty of the secretary of the commonwealth to certify, as soon as may be after it is determined by the general court, the number of representatives to which each county shall be entitled, to the board authorized to divide such county into representative districts. The county commissioners or other body acting as such or, in lieu thereof, such board of special commissioners in each county as may for that purpose be provided by law, shall, within thirty days after such certification by the secretary of the commonwealth or within such other period as the general court may by law provide, assemble at a shire town of their respective counties, and proceed, as soon as may be, to divide the same into representative districts of contiguous territory and assign representatives thereto, so that each representative in such county will represent an equal number of legal voters, as nearly as may be; and such districts shall be so formed that no town containing less than twelve thousand inhabitants according to said census, no precinct of any other town and no ward of a city shall be divided therefor, nor shall any district be made which shall be entitled to elect more than three representatives. The general court may by law limit the time within which judicial proceedings may be instituted calling in question any such apportionment, division or assignment. Every representative, for one year at least immediately preceding his election, shall have been an inhabitant of the district for which he is chosen, and shall cease to represent such district when he shall cease to be an inhabitant of the commonwealth. The districts in each county shall be numbered by the board creating the same, and a description of each, with the numbers thereof and the number of legal voters therein, shall be returned by the board, to the secretary of the commonwealth, the county treasurer of such county, and to the clerk of every city or town in such county, to be filed and kept in their respective offices. The manner of calling and conducting the elections for the choice of representatives, and of ascertaining their election, shall be prescribed by law.

Article XXII of the articles of amendment is hereby annulled and the following is adopted in place thereof:

Article XXII. Each special enumeration of legal voters required in the preceding article of amendment shall likewise be the basis for determining the senatorial districts and also the councillor districts for the ten year period beginning with the first Wednesday in the fourth January following such enumeration; provided, that such districts as established in the year nineteen hundred and twenty-six shall continue in effect until the first Wednesday in January in the year nineteen hundred and thirty-nine. The senate shall consist of forty members. The general court shall, at its first regular session after the return of each special enumeration, divide the commonwealth into forty districts of contiguous territory each district to contain, as nearly as may be, an equal number of legal voters, according to said special enumeration; provided, however, that no town or ward of a city shall be divided therefore; and such districts shall be formed, as nearly as may be, without uniting two counties, or parts of two or more counties, into one district. The general court may by law limit the time within which judicial proceedings may be instituted calling in question such division. Each district shall elect one senator, who shall have been an inhabitant of this commonwealth five years at least immediately preceding his election, and at the time of his election shall be an inhabitant of the district for which he is chosen; and he shall cease to represent such senatorial district when he shall cease to be an inhabitant of the commonwealth. [Superseded by Amendments, Arts. XCII, CI, CIX and CXVII.]

Art. LXXII. [Section 1. The general court shall assemble in regular session on the first Wednesday of January in the year following the approval of this article and biennially on said Wednesday thereafter. Nothing herein contained shall prevent the general court from assembling at such other times as they shall judge necessary or when called together by the governor.

SECTION 2. The budget required by section two of Article LXIII of the amendments to the constitution shall be for the year in which the same is adopted and for the ensuing year.

SECTION 3. All provisions of this constitution and of the amendments thereto requiring the general court to meet annually are hereby annulled.] [Annulled by Amendments. Art. LXXV.]

Art. LXXIII. Article VIII of section 1 of chapter II of Part the Second of the constitution of the commonwealth is hereby annulled and the following is adopted in place thereof: —

Article VIII. The power of pardoning offenses, except such as persons may be convicted of before the senate by an impeachment of the house, shall be in the governor, by and with the advice of council, provided, that if the offence is a felony the general court shall have the power to prescribe the terms and conditions upon which a pardon may be granted, but no charter of pardon, granted by the governor, with advice of the council before conviction, shall avail the party pleading the same, notwithstanding any general or particular expressions contained therein, descriptive of the offence or offenses intended to be pardoned.

Art. LXXIV. Section 1. Article XLVIII of the amendments to the constitution is hereby amended by striking out section three, under the heading "THE INITIATIVE. *II. Initiative Petitions.*", and inserting in place thereof the following: —
SECTION 3. *Mode of Originating.* — Such petition shall first be signed by ten qualified voters of the commonwealth and shall be submitted to the attorney-general not later than the first Wednesday of the August before the assembling of the general court into which it is to be introduced, and if he shall certify that the measure and the title thereof are in proper form for submission to the people, and that the measure is not, either affirmatively or negatively, substantially the same as any measure which has been qualified for submission or submitted to the people at either of the two preceding biennial state elections, and that it contains only subjects not excluded from the popular initiative and which are related or which are mutually

dependent, it may then be filed with the secretary of the commonwealth. The secretary of the commonwealth shall provide blanks for the use of subsequent signers. and shall print at the top of each blank a fair, concise summary, as determined by the attorney-general. of the proposed measure as such summary will appear on the ballot together with the names and residences of the first ten signers. All initiative petitions, with the first ten signatures attached, shall be filed with the secretary of the commonwealth not earlier than the first Wednesday of the September before the assembling of the general court into which they are to be introduced. and the remainder of the required signatures shall be filed not later than the first Wednesday of the following December.

SECTION 2. Section three of that part of said Article XLVIII, under the heading "THE REFERENDUM. *III. Referendum Petitions.* ", is hereby amended by striking out the words "The secretary of the commonwealth shall provide blanks for the use of subsequent signers, and shall print at the top of each blank a description of the proposed law as such description will appear on the ballot together with the names and residences of the first ten signers.", and inserting in place thereof the words "The secretary of the commonwealth shall provide blanks for the use of subsequent signers. and shall print at the top of each blank a fair, concise summary of the proposed law as such summary will appear on the ballot together with the names and residences of the first ten signers."

SECTION 3. Section four of that part of said Article XLVIII, under the heading "THE REFERENDUM. *III. Referendum Petitions.* ", is hereby amended by striking out the words "The secretary of the commonwealth shall provide blanks for the use of subsequent signers, and shall print at the top of each blank a description of the proposed law as such description will appear on the ballot together with the names and residences of the first ten signers.", and inserting in place thereof the words "The secretary of the commonwealth shall provide blanks for the use of subsequent signers, and shall print at the top of each blank a fair, concise summary of the proposed law as such summary will appear on the ballot together with the names and residences of the first ten signers."

SECTION 4. Said Article XLVIII is hereby further amended by striking out, under the heading "GENERAL PROVISIONS", all of subheading "*III. Form of Ballot.*" and all of subheading "*IV. Information for Voters.*", and inserting in place thereof the following: —

III. Form of Ballot.

A fair, concise summary, as determined by the attorney-general, subject to such provision as may be made by law, of each proposed amendment to the constitution, and each law submitted to the people, shall be printed on the ballot, and the secretary of the commonwealth shall give each question a number and cause such question, except as otherwise authorized herein, to be printed on the ballot in the following form: —

In the case of an amendment to the constitution: Do you approve of the adoption of an amendment to the constitution summarized below, (here state, in distinctive type, whether approved or disapproved by the general court, and by what vote thereon)?

YES.	
NO.	

(Set forth summary here)

In the case of a law: Do you approve of a law summarized below, (here state, in distinctive type, whether approved or disapproved by the general court, and by what vote thereon)?

YES.	
NO.	

(Set forth summary here)

[IV. Information for Voters.

The secretary of the commonwealth shall cause to be printed and sent to each registered voter in the commonwealth the full text of every measure to be submitted to the people, together with a copy of the legislative committee's majority and minority reports, if there be such, with the names of the majority and minority members thereon, a statement of the votes of the general court on the measure, and a fair, concise summary of the measure as such summary will appear on the ballot; and shall, in such manner as may be provided by law, cause to be prepared and sent to the voters other information and arguments for and against the measure. [See Amendments, Art. CVIII.]

Art. LXXV.   Article LXXII of the amendments to the constitution providing for biennial sessions of the general court and a biennial budget is hereby annulled, and all provisions of this constitution and of the amendments thereto which were annulled or affected by said Article shall have the same force and effect as though said Article had not been adopted.

Art. LXXVI.   Article XLV of the articles of amendment is hereby annulled and the following is adopted in place thereof: —

Article XLV.   The general court shall have power to provide by law for voting, in the choice of any officer to be elected or upon any question submitted at an election, by qualified voters of the commonwealth who, at the time of such an election, are absent from the city or town of which they are inhabitants or are unable by reason of physical disability to cast their votes in person at the polling places. [Superseded by Amendments, Art. CV.]

Art. LXXVII.   Article XVI of Part the First is hereby annulled and the following is adopted in place thereof: —

Article XVI.   The liberty of the press is essential to the security of freedom in a state: it ought not, therefore, to be restrained in this commonwealth. The right of free speech shall not be abridged.

Art. LXXVIII.   No revenue from fees, duties, excises or license taxes relating to registration, operation or use of vehicles on public highways, or to fuels used for propelling such vehicles, shall be expended for other than cost of administration of laws providing for such revenue, making of refunds and adjustments in relation thereto, payment of highway obligations, or cost of construction, reconstruction, maintenance and repair of public highways and bridges of the enforcement of state traffic laws; and such revenue shall be expended by the commonwealth or its counties, cities and towns for said highway purposes only and in such manner as the general court may direct; provided, that this amendment shall not apply to revenue from any excise tax imposed in lieu of local property taxes for the privilege of registering such vehicles. [Annulled and superseded by Amendments. Art. CIV.]

Art. LXXIX. Article XVII of the Amendments of the Constitution, as amended, is hereby further amended by striking out, in the third sentence, the words "two persons who had the highest number of votes for said offices on the day in November aforesaid" and inserting in place thereof the words: — people at large, — so that said sentence will read as follows: — In case of a failure to elect either of said officers on the day in November aforesaid, or in case of the decease, in the meantime, of the person elected as such, such officer shall be chosen on or before the third Wednesday in January next thereafter, from the people at large, by joint ballot of the senators and representatives, in one room; and in case the office of secretary, or treasurer and receiver-general, or auditor, or attorney-general, shall become vacant, from any cause during an annual or special session of the general court, such vacancy shall in like manner be filled by choice from the people at large; but if such vacancy shall occur at any other time, it shall be supplied by the governor by appointment, with the advice and consent of the council.

Art. LXXX. [Article LXIV of the Amendments to the Constitution is hereby amended by striking out section 1 and inserting in place thereof the following section: —

Section 1. The governor, lieutenant-governor, councillors, secretary, treasurer and receiver-general, attorney-general, auditor, senators and representatives shall be elected biennially. The terms of the governor, lieutenant-governor and councillors shall begin at noon on the Thursday next following the first Wednesday in January succeeding their election and shall end at noon on the Thursday next following the first Wednesday in January in the third year following their election. If the governor elect shall have died before the qualification of the lieutenant- governor elect, the lieutenant-governor elect upon qualification shall become governor. If both the governor elect and the lieutenant-governor elect shall have died both said offices shall be deemed to be vacant and the provisions of Article LV of the Amendments to the Constitution shall apply. The terms of senators and representatives shall begin with the first Wednesday in January succeeding their election and shall extend to the first Wednesday in January in the third year following their election and until their successors are chosen and qualified. The terms of the secretary, treasurer and receiver-general, attorney-general and auditor, shall begin with the third Wednesday in January succeeding their election and shall extend to the third Wednesday in January in the third year following their election and until their successors are chosen and qualified.] [Annulled and superseded by Art. LXXXII.]

Art. LXXXI. SECTION 1. Article XLVIII of the Amendments to the Constitution is hereby amended by striking out section 2, under the heading "THE INITIATIVE. IV. LEGISLATIVE ACTION ON PROPOSED CONSTITUTIONAL AMENDMENTS.", and inserting in place thereof the following: —

Section 2. Joint Session. — If a proposal for a specific amendment of the constitution is introduced into the general court by initiative petition signed in the aggregate by not less than such number of voters as will equal three per cent of the entire vote cast for governor at the preceding biennial state election, or if in case of a proposal for amendment introduced into the general court by a member of either house, consideration thereof in joint session is called for by vote of either house, such proposal shall, not later than the second Wednesday in May, be laid before a joint session of the two houses, at which the president of the senate shall preside; and if the two houses fail to agree upon a time for holding any joint session hereby required, or fail to continue the same from time to time until final action has been taken upon all amendments pending, the governor shall call such joint session or continuance thereof.

SECTION 2. Section 1 of that part of said Article XLVIII, under the heading "THE INITIATIVE. V. *Legislative Action on Proposed Laws.* ", is hereby amended by striking out said section and inserting in place thereof the following: —

Section 1. Legislative Procedure. — If an initiative petition for a law is introduced into the general court, signed in the aggregate by not less than such number of voters as will equal three per cent of the entire vote cast for governor at the preceding biennial state election, a vote shall be taken by yeas and nays in both houses before the first

Wednesday of May upon the enactment of such law in the form in which it stands in such petition. If the general court fails to enact such law before the first Wednesday of May, and if such petition is completed by filing with the secretary of the commonwealth, not earlier than the first Wednesday of the following June nor later than the first Wednesday of the following July, a number of signatures of qualified voters equal in number to not less than one half of one per cent of the entire vote cast for governor at the preceding biennial state election, in addition to those signing such initiative petition, which signatures must have been obtained after the first Wednesday of May aforesaid, then the secretary of the commonwealth shall submit such proposed law to the people at the next state election. If it shall be approved by voters equal in number to at least thirty per cent of the total number of ballots cast at such state election and also by a majority of the voters voting on such law, it shall become law, and shall take effect in thirty days after such state election or at such time after such election as may be provided in such law.

SECTION 3. Section 2 of that part of said Article XLVIII, under the heading "THE INITIATIVE. *V. Legislative Action on Proposed Laws.*", is hereby amended by striking out said section and inserting in place thereof the following: —

SECTION 2. *Amendment by Petitioners.* — If the general court fails to pass a proposed law before the first Wednesday of May, a majority of the first ten signers of the initiative petition therefor shall have the right, subject to certification by the attorney-general filed as hereinafter provided, to amend the measure which is the subject of such petition. An amendment so made shall not invalidate any signature attached to the petition. If the measure so amended, signed by a majority of the first ten signers, is filed with the secretary of the commonwealth before the first Wednesday of the following June, together with a certificate signed by the attorney-general to the effect that the amendment made by such proposers is in his opinion perfecting in its nature and does not materially change the substance of the measure, and if such petition is completed by filing with the secretary of the commonwealth, not earlier than the first Wednesday of the following June nor later than the first Wednesday of the following July, a number of signatures of qualified voters equal in number to not less than one half of one per cent of the entire vote cast for governor at the preceding biennial state election in addition to those signing such initiative petition, which signatures must have been obtained after the first Wednesday of May aforesaid, then the secretary of the commonwealth shall submit the measure to the people in its amended form.

SECTION 4. Section 3 of that part of said Article XLVIII, under the heading "THE REFERENDUM. *III. Referendum Petitions.*", is hereby amended by striking out the sentence "If such petition is completed by filing with the secretary of the commonwealth not later than ninety days after the law which is the subject of the petition has become law the signatures of not less than fifteen thousand qualified voters of the commonwealth, then the operation of such law shall be suspended, and the secretary of the commonwealth shall submit such law to the people at the next state election, if thirty days intervene between the date when such petition is filed with the secretary of the commonwealth and the date for holding such state election; if thirty days do not so intervene, then such law shall be submitted to the people at the next following state election, unless in the meantime it shall have been repealed; and if it shall be approved by a majority of the qualified voters voting thereon, such law shall, subject to the provisions of the constitution, take effect in thirty days after such election, or at such time after such election as may be provided in such law; if not so approved such law shall be null and void; but no such law shall be held to be disapproved if the negative vote is less than thirty per cent of the total number of ballots cast at such state election." and inserting in place thereof the following sentence: — If such petition is completed by filing with the secretary of the commonwealth not later than ninety days after the law which is the subject of the petition has become law a number of signatures of qualified voters equal in number to not less than two per cent of the entire vote cast for governor at the preceding biennial state election, then the operation of such law shall be suspended, and the secretary of the commonwealth shall submit such law to the people at the next state election, if sixty days intervene between the date when such petition is filed with the secretary of the commonwealth and the date for holding such state election: if sixty days do not so intervene, then such law shall be submitted to the people at the next following state election, unless in the meantime it shall have been repealed; and if it shall be approved by a majority of the qualified voters voting thereon, such law shall, subject to the provisions of the constitution, take effect in thirty days after such election, or at such time after such election as may be provided in such law; if not so approved such law shall be null and void: but no such law shall be held to be disapproved if the negative vote is less than thirty per cent of the total number of ballots cast at such state election.

SECTION 5. Section 4 of that part of said Article XLVIII, under the heading "THE REFERENDUM. *III. Referendum Petitions.*", is hereby amended by striking out the words "If such petition filed as aforesaid is completed by filing with the secretary of the commonwealth not later than ninety days after the law which is the subject of the petition has become law the signatures of not less than ten thousand qualified voters of the commonwealth protesting against such law and asking for a referendum thereon, then the secretary of the commonwealth shall submit such law to the people at the next state election, if thirty days intervene between the date when such petition is filed with the secretary of the commonwealth and the date for holding such state election. If thirty days do not so intervene, then it shall be submitted to the people at the next following state election, unless in the meantime it shall have been repealed; and if it shall not be approved by a majority of the qualified voters voting thereon, it shall, at the expiration of thirty days after such election, be thereby repealed: but no such law shall be held to be disapproved if the negative vote is less than thirty per cent of the total number of ballots cast at such state election." and inserting in place thereof the following: — If such petition filed as aforesaid is completed by filing with the secretary of the commonwealth not later than ninety days after the law which is the subject of the petition has become law a number of signatures of qualified voters equal in number to not less than one and one half per cent of the entire vote cast for governor at the preceding biennial state election protesting against such law and asking for a referendum thereon, then the secretary of the commonwealth shall submit such law to the people at the next state election, if sixty days intervene between the date when such petition is filed with the secretary of the commonwealth and the date for holding such state election. If sixty days do not so intervene, then it shall be submitted to the people at the next following state election, unless in the meantime it shall have been repealed; and if it shall not be approved by a majority of the qualified voters voting thereon, it shall, at the expiration of thirty days after such election, be thereby repealed; but no such law shall be held to be disapproved if the negative vote is less than thirty per cent of the total number of ballots cast at such state election.

Art. LXXXII. Article LXIV of the Amendments to the Constitution, as amended by Article LXXX of said Amendments, is hereby annulled, and the following is adopted in place thereof: —

Article LXIV. Section 1. The governor, lieutenant-governor, secretary, treasurer and receiver-general, attorney-general, and auditor shall be elected quadrennially and councillors, senators and representatives shall be elected biennially. The terms of the governor and lieutenant-governor shall begin at noon on the Thursday next following the first Wednesday in January succeeding their election and shall end at noon on the Thursday next following the first Wednesday in January in the fifth year following their election. If the governor elect shall have died before the qualification of the lieutenant-governor elect, the lieutenant-governor elect upon qualification shall become governor. If both the governor elect and the lieutenant-governor elect shall have died both said offices shall be deemed to be vacant and the provisions of Article LV of the Amendments to the Constitution shall apply. The terms of the secretary, treasurer and receiver-general, attorney-general, and auditor shall begin with the third Wednesday in January succeeding their election and shall extend to the third Wednesday in January in the fifth year following their election and until their successors are chosen and qualified. The terms of the councillors shall begin at noon on the Thursday next following the first Wednesday in January succeeding their election and shall end at noon on the Thursday next following the first Wednesday in January in the third year following their election. The terms of senators and representatives shall begin with the first Wednesday in January succeeding their election and shall extend to the first Wednesday in January in the third year following their election and until their successors are chosen and qualified.

Section 2. The general court shall assemble every year on the first Wednesday in January.

Section 3. The first election to which this article shall apply shall be held on the Tuesday next after the first Monday in November in the year nineteen hundred and sixty-six, and thereafter elections for the choice of a governor, lieutenant- governor, secretary, treasurer and receiver-general, attorney- general, and auditor shall be held quadrennially on the Tuesday next after the first Monday in November and elections for the choice of councillors, senators and representatives shall be held biennially on the Tuesday next after the first Monday in November.

Art. LXXXIII. The general court shall have full power and authority to provide for prompt and temporary succession to the powers and duties of public offices, of whatever nature and whether filled by election or appointment, the incumbents of which may become unavailable for carrying on the powers and duties of such offices in periods of emergency resulting from disaster caused by enemy attack, and to adopt such other measures as may be necessary and proper for insuring continuity of the government of the commonwealth and the governments of its political subdivisions.

Art. LXXXIV. Article LXII of the Amendments to the Constitution is hereby amended by striking out section 1 and inserting in place thereof the following section: — Section 1. The commonwealth may give, loan or pledge its credit only by a vote, taken by the yeas and nays, of two-thirds of each house of the general court present and voting thereon. The credit of the commonwealth shall not in any manner be given or loaned to or in aid of any individual, or of any private association, or of any corporation which is privately owned and managed.

Art. LXXXV. Article II of Chapter III of the Constitution of the commonwealth is hereby annulled and the following is adopted in place thereof: —

Article II. Each branch of the legislature, as well as the governor or the council, shall have authority to require the opinions of the justices of the supreme judicial court, upon important questions of law, and upon solemn occasions.

Art. LXXXVI. Names of candidates of political parties for the offices of governor and lieutenant-governor shall be grouped on the official ballot for use at state elections according to the parties they represent, and the voter may cast a single vote for any such group, which shall count as a vote for each candidate in such group, but may not cast a vote for only one of the candidates in such group.

Art. LXXXVII. *Section 1.* For the purpose of transferring, abolishing, consolidating or coordinating the whole or any part of any agency, or the functions thereof, within the executive department of the government of the commonwealth, or for the purpose of authorizing any officer of any agency within the executive department of the government of the commonwealth to delegate any of his functions, the governor may prepare one or more reorganization plans, each bearing an identifying number and may present such plan or plans to the general court, together with a message in explanation thereof.

Section 2. *(a)* Every such reorganization plan shall be referred to an appropriate committee, to be determined by the Clerks of the Senate and House of Representatives, with the approval of the President and Speaker, which committee shall not later than thirty days after the date of the Governor's presentation of said plan hold a public hearing thereon and shall not later than ten days after such hearing report that it approves or disapproves such plan and such reorganization plan shall have the force of law upon expiration of the sixty calendar days next following its presentation by the governor to the general court, unless disapproved by a majority vote of the members of either of the two branches of the general court present and voting, the general court not having been prorogued within such sixty days.

(b) After its presentation by the governor to the general court, no such reorganization plan shall be subject to amendment by the general court before expiration of such sixty days.

(c) Any such reorganization plan may provide for its taking effect on any date after expiration of such sixty days and every such reorganization plan shall comply with such conditions as the general court may from time to time prescribe by statute regarding the civil service status, seniority, retirement and other rights of any employee to be affected by such plan.

Section 3. Article LXVI of the Amendments to the Constitution is hereby annulled.

Art. LXXXVIII. The industrial development of cities and towns is a public function and the commonwealth and the cities and towns therein may provide for the same in such manner as the general court may determine.

Art. LXXXIX. Article II of the Articles of Amendment to the Constitution of the Commonwealth, as amended by Article LXX of said Articles of Amendment, is hereby annulled and the following is adopted in place thereof: —

Article II. Section 1. Right of Local Self-Government. — It is the intention of this article to reaffirm the customary and traditional liberties of the people with respect to the conduct of their local government, and to grant and confirm to the people of every city and town the right of self-government in local matters, subject to the provisions of this article and to such standards and requirements as the general court may establish by law in accordance with the provisions of this article.

Section 2. Local Power to adopt, revise or amend Charters. — Any city or town shall have the power to adopt or revise a charter or to amend its existing charter through the procedures set forth in sections three and four. The provisions of any adopted or revised charter or any charter amendments shall not be inconsistent with the constitution or any laws enacted by the general court in conformity with the powers reserved to the general court by section eight.

No town of fewer than twelve thousand inhabitants shall adopt a city form of government, and no town of fewer than six thousand inhabitants shall adopt a form of government providing for a town meeting limited to such inhabitants of the town as may be elected to meet, deliberate, act and vote in the exercise of the corporate powers of the town.

Section 3. Procedure for Adoption or Revision of a Charter by a City or Town. — Every city and town shall have the power to adopt or revise a charter in the following manner: A petition for the adoption or revision of a charter shall be signed by at least fifteen per cent of the number of legal voters residing in such city or town at the preceding state election. Whenever such a petition is filed with the board of registrars or voters of any city or town, the board shall within ten days of its receipt determine the sufficiency and validity of the signatures and certify the results to the city council of the city or board of selectmen of the town, as the case may be. As used in this section, the phrase "board of registrars of voters" shall include any local authority of different designation which performs the duties of such registrars, and the phrase "city council of the city or board of selectmen of the town" shall include local authorities of different designation performing the duties of such council or board. Objections to the sufficiency and validity of the signatures on any such petition as certified by the board of registrars of voters shall be made in the same manner as provided by law for objections to nominations for city or town offices, as the case may be.

Within thirty days of receipt of certification of the board of registrars of voters that a petition contains sufficient valid signatures, the city council of the city or board of selectmen of the town shall by order provide for submitting to the voters of the city or town the question of adopting or revising a charter, and for the nomination and election of a charter commission.

If the city or town has not previously adopted a charter pursuant to this section, the question submitted to the voters shall be: "Shall a commission be elected to frame a charter for (name of city or town)?" If the city or town has previously adopted a charter pursuant to this section, the question submitted to the voters shall be: "Shall a commission be elected to revise the charter of (name of city or town)?"

The charter commission shall consist of nine voters of the city or town, who shall be elected at large without party or political designation at the city or town election next held at least sixty days after the order of the city council of the city or board of selectmen of the town. The names of candidates for such commission shall be listed alphabetically on the ballot used at such election. Each voter may vote for nine candidates.

The vote on the question submitted and the election of the charter commission shall take place at the same time. If the vote on the question submitted is in the affirmative, the nine candidates receiving the highest number of votes shall be declared elected.

Within [ten months] after the election of the members of the charter commission, said commission shall submit the charter or revised charter to the city council of the city or the board of selectmen of the town, and such council or board shall provide for publication of the charter and for its submission to the voters of the city or town at the next city or town election held at least two months after such submission by the charter commission. If the charter or revised charter is approved by a majority of the voters of the city or town voting thereon, it shall become effective upon the date fixed in the charter. [See Amendments, Art. CXIII.]

Section 4. Procedure for Amendment of a Charter by a City or Town. — Every city and town shall have the power to amend its charter in the following manner: The legislative body of a city or town may, by a two-thirds vote, propose amendments to the charter of the city or town; provided, that (1) amendments of a city charter may be proposed only with the concurrence of the mayor in every city that has a mayor, and (2) any change in a charter relating in any way to the composition, mode of election or appointment, or terms of office of the legislative body, the mayor or city manager or the board of selectmen or town manager shall be made only by the procedure of charter revision set forth in section three.

All proposed charter amendments shall be published and submitted for approval in the same manner as provided for adoption or revision of a charter.

Section 5. Recording of Charters and Charter Amendments. — Duplicate certificates shall be prepared setting forth any charter that has been adopted or revised and any charter amendments approved, and shall be signed by the city or town clerk. One such certificate shall be deposited in the office of the secretary of the commonwealth and the other shall be recorded in the records of the city or town and deposited among its archives. All courts may take judicial notice of charters and charter amendments of cities and towns.

Section 6.   Governmental Powers of Cities and Towns. — Any city or town may, by the adoption, amendment, or repeal of local ordinances or by-laws, exercise any power or function which the general court has power to confer upon it, which is not inconsistent with the constitution or laws enacted by the general court in conformity with powers reserved to the general court by section eight, and which is not denied, either expressly or by clear implication, to the city or town by its charter. This section shall apply to every city and town, whether or not it has adopted a charter pursuant to section three.

Section 7.   Limitations on Local Powers. — Nothing in this article shall be deemed to grant to any city or town the power to (1) regulate elections other than those prescribed by sections three and four; (2) to levy, assess and collect taxes; (3) to borrow money or pledge the credit of the city or town; (4) to dispose of park land; (5) to enact private or civil law governing civil relationships except as an incident to an exercise of an independent municipal power; or (6) to define and provide for the punishment of a felony or to impose imprisonment as a punishment for any violation of law; provided, however, that the foregoing enumerated powers may be granted by the general court in conformity with the constitution and with the powers reserved to the general court by section eight; nor shall the provisions of this article be deemed to diminish the powers of the judicial department of the commonwealth.

Section 8.   Powers of the General Court. — The general court shall have the power to act in relation to cities and towns, but only by the general laws which apply alike to all cities, or to all cities and towns, or to a class of not fewer than two, and by special laws enacted (1) on petition filed or approved by the voters of a city or town, or the mayor and city council, or other legislative body, of a city, or the town meeting of a town, with respect to a law relating to that city or town; (2) by a two-thirds vote of each branch of the general court following a recommen- dation by the governor; (3) to erect and constitute metropolitan or regional entities, embracing any two or more cities or towns or cities and towns, or established with other than existing city or town boundaries, for any general or special public purpose or purposes, and to grant to these entities such powers, privileges and immunities as the general court shall deem necessary or expedient for the regulation and government thereof; or (4) solely for the incorporation or dissolution of cities or towns as corporate entities, alteration of city or town boundaries, and merger or consolidation of cities and towns, or any of these matters.

Subject to the foregoing requirements, the general court may provide optional plans of city or town organization and government under which an optional plan may be adopted or abandoned by majority vote of the voters of the city or town voting thereon at a city or town election; provided, that no town of fewer than twelve thousand inhabitants may be authorized to adopt a city form of government, and no town of fewer than six thousand inhabitants may be authorized to adopt a form of town government providing for a town meeting limited to such inhabitants of the town as may be elected to meet, deliberate, act and vote in the exercise of the corporate powers of the town.

This section shall apply to every city and town whether or not it has adopted a charter pursuant to section three.

Section 9. Existing Special Laws. — All special laws relating to individual cities or towns shall remain in effect and have the force of an existing city or town charter, but shall be subject to amendment or repeal through the adoption, revision or amendment of a charter by a city or town in accordance with the provisions of sections three and four and shall be subject to amendment or repeal by laws enacted by the general court in conformity with the powers reserved to the general court by section eight.

Art. XC. *Section 1.* Article II of section I of Chapter I of Part the Second of the Constitution is hereby amended by striking out the second paragraph and inserting in place thereof the following paragraph: —

And in order to prevent unnecessary delays, if any bill or resolve shall not be returned by the governor within ten days after it shall have been presented, the same shall have the force of a law.

Section 2. Article I of the Articles of Amendment to the Constitution is hereby annulled and the following is adopted in place thereof: —

Article I. If any bill or resolve shall be objected to, and not approved by the governor, and if the general court shall adjourn within ten days after the same shall have been laid before the governor for his approbation, and thereby prevent his returning it with his objections, as provided by the constitution, such bill or resolve shall not become a law, nor have force as such.

Section 3. Article LVI of the Articles of Amendment to the Constitution is hereby annulled and the following is adopted in place thereof: —

Article LVI. The governor, within ten days after any bill or resolve shall have been laid before him, shall have the right to return it to the branch of the general court in which it originated with a recommendation that any amendment or amendments specified by him be made therein. Such bill or resolve shall thereupon be before the general court and subject to amendment and re-enactment. If such bill or resolve is re-enacted in any form it shall again be laid before the governor for his action, but he shall have no right to return the same a second time with a recommendation to amend.

Section 4. Article LXIII of the Articles of Amendment to the Constitution is hereby amended by striking out Section 5 and inserting in place thereof the following section: —

Section 5. Submission to the Governor. — The governor may disapprove or reduce items or parts of items in any bill appropriating money. So much of such bill as he approves shall upon his signing the same become law. As to each item disapproved or reduced, he shall transmit to the house in which the bill originated his reason for such disapproval or reduction, and the procedure shall then be the same as in the case of a bill disapproved as a whole. In case he shall fail so to transmit his reasons for such disapproval or reduction within ten days after the bill shall have been presented to him, such items shall have the force of law unless the general court by adjournment shall prevent such transmission, in which case they shall not be law.

Art. XCI. Whenever the governor transmits to the president of the senate and the speaker of the house his written declaration that he is unable to discharge the powers and duties of his office, the office of governor shall be deemed to be vacant within the meaning of this Constitution.

Whenever the chief justice and a majority of the associate justices of the supreme judicial court, or such other body as the general court may by law provide, transmit to the president of the senate and the speaker of the house their written declaration that the governor is unable to discharge the powers and duties of his office, the office of governor shall be deemed to be vacant within the meaning of this Constitution.

Thereafter, in either of the above cases, whenever the governor transmits to the president of the senate and the speaker of the house his written declaration that no inability exists such vacancy shall be deemed to have terminated four days thereafter and the governor shall resume the powers and duties of his office unless the chief justice and a majority of the associate justices of the supreme judicial court, or such other body as the general court may by law provide, transmit within said four days to the president of the senate and the speaker of the house their written declaration that the governor is unable to discharge the powers and duties of his office. Thereupon the general court shall decide the issue, assembling within forty-eight hours for that purpose if not in session. If the general court within twenty-one days after receipt of the latter written declaration, or, if the general court is not in session, within twenty-one days after the general court is required to assemble, determine by a vote, taken by yeas and nays, of two-thirds of each house present and voting thereon, that the governor is unable to discharge the powers and duties of his office, the office of governor shall continue to be deemed to be vacant; otherwise such vacancy shall be deemed to have terminated and the governor shall resume the powers and duties of his office.

The above provisions shall be applicable to the lieutenant-governor when the lieutenant-governor in case of a vacancy is performing all the duties incumbent upon the governor as provided in this Constitution.

If a vacancy in the office of governor, as described in this Article, continues for six months and if such six-month period expires more than five months prior to a biennial state election other than an election for governor, there shall be an election of governor at such biennial state election for the balance of the unexpired four-year term.

Art. XCII. [*Section 1.* In the year nineteen hundred and seventy-one and every tenth year thereafter a census of the inhabitants of each city and town shall be taken. Said census shall specify the number of inhabitants residing in each precinct of each town and in each precinct and ward of each city. Said census shall be the basis for determining the representative districts for the ten year period beginning with the first Wednesday in the fourth January following the taking of said census; provided that such districts as established in the year nineteen hundred and sixty-eight shall continue until the first Wednesday in January in the year nineteen hundred and seventy-five.

The house of representatives shall consist of two hundred and forty members. The general court shall, at its first regular session after the year in which said census was taken, divide the commonwealth into two hundred and forty representative districts of contiguous territory so that each representative will represent an equal number of inhabitants, as nearly as may be; and such districts shall be formed as nearly as may be, without uniting two counties or parts of two or more counties, two towns or parts of two or more towns, two cities or parts of two or more cities, or a city and a town, or parts of cities and towns, into one district; provided, however, that the county of Dukes county and Nantucket county shall each be a representative district. Such districts shall also be so formed that no town containing less than six thousand inhabitants according to said census shall be divided. The general court may by law limit the time within which judicial proceedings may be instituted calling in question any such division. Every representative, for one year at least immediately preceding his election, shall have been an inhabitant of the district for which he is chosen, and shall cease to represent such district when he shall cease to be an inhabitant of the commonwealth.

The manner of calling and conducting the elections for the choice of representatives, and of ascertaining their election, shall be prescribed by law.

Section 2. Each census of inhabitants required in section one shall likewise be the basis for determining the senatorial districts and also the councillor districts for the ten year period beginning with the first Wednesday in the fourth January following the taking of such census; provided that such districts as established prior to the year nineteen hundred and seventy-one shall continue until the first Wednesday in January in the year nineteen hundred and seventy-five. The senate shall consist of forty members. The general court shall, at its first regular session after the year in which said census is taken, divide the commonwealth into forty districts of contiguous territory, each district to contain, as nearly as may be an equal number of inhabitants according to said census; and such districts shall be formed, as nearly as may be, without uniting two counties, or parts of two or more counties, into one district. The general court may by law limit the time within which judicial proceedings may be instituted calling in question such division. Each district shall elect one senator, who shall have been an inhabitant of this commonwealth five years at least immediately preceding his election, and at the time of his election, shall be an inhabitant of the district for which he is chosen; and he shall cease to represent such senatorial district when he shall cease to be an inhabitant of the commonwealth.

Section 3. Articles XXI and XXII of the Amendments to the Constitution, as appearing in Article LXXI of said Amendments, are hereby annulled.] [Annulled and superseded by Amendments, Art. CI.]

Art. XCIII. Article III of the Amendments to the Constitution, as amended, is hereby further amended by striking out the words "within the commonwealth one year, and".

Art. XCIV. Article III of the Amendments to the Constitution, as amended, is hereby further amended by striking out the words "twenty-one" and inserting in place thereof the word: — nineteen.

Art. XCV. Article III of the Amendments to the Constitution, as amended, is hereby further amended by striking out the words "pauper and".

Art. XCVI. The general court shall have power to authorize the commonwealth to make loans, on such terms as it may deem reasonable, to any residents of the commonwealth for tuition and board at any college, university or other institution of higher learning.

Art. XCVII. Article XLIX of the Amendments to the Constitution is hereby annulled and the following is adopted in place thereof: — The people shall have the right to clean air and water, freedom from excessive and unnecessary noise, and the natural, scenic, historic, and esthetic qualities of their environment; and the protection of the people in their right to the conservation, development and utilization of the agricultural, mineral, forest, water, air and other natural resources is hereby declared to be a public purpose.

The general court shall have the power to enact legislation necessary or expedient to protect such rights.

In the furtherance of the foregoing powers, the general court shall have the power to provide for the taking, upon payment of just compensation therefor, or for the acquisition by purchase or otherwise, of lands and easements or such other interests therein as may be deemed necessary to accomplish these purposes.

Lands and easements taken or acquired for such purposes shall not be used for other purposes or otherwise disposed of except by laws enacted by a two-thirds vote, taken by yeas and nays, of each branch of the general court.

Art. XCVIII. Article 1 of Chapter III of Part the Second of the Constitution, as amended by Article LVIII of the Amend-ments to the Constitution, is hereby annulled and the following Article is adopted in place thereof: —

Article I. The tenure, that all commissioned officers shall by law have in their offices, shall be expressed in their respective commissions. All judicial officers, duly appointed, commissioned and sworn, shall hold their offices during good behavior, excepting such concerning whom there is different provision made in this

Constitution; provided, nevertheless, the governor, with the consent of the council, may remove them upon the address of both houses of the legislature; and provided, also, that the governor, with the consent of the council, may after due notice and hearing retire them because of advanced age or mental or physical disability; and provided further, that upon attaining seventy years of age said judges shall be retired. Such retirement shall be subject to any provisions made by law as to pensions or allowances payable to such officers upon their voluntary retirement.

Art. XCIX. Full power and authority is hereby given and granted to the general court to prescribe, for the purpose of developing and conserving agricultural or horticultural lands, that such lands shall be valued, for the purpose of taxation, according to their agricultural or horticultural uses; provided, however, that no parcel of land which is less than five acres in area or which has not been actively devoted to agricultural or horticultural uses for the two years preceding the tax year shall be valued at less than fair market value under this article.

Art. C. Article III of the Amendments to the Constitution, as amended, is hereby further amended by striking out the word indicating the age at which a citizen shall have a right to vote in an election of Governor and other public officers and inserting in place thereof the following word: — eighteen.

Art. CI. In the year nineteen hundred and seventy-five and every tenth year thereafter a census of the inhabitants of each city and town shall be taken. Said census shall specify the number of inhabitants residing in each precinct of each town and in each precinct and ward of each city. Said census shall be the basis for determining the representative districts for the ten year period beginning with the first Wednesday in the fourth January following the taking of said census; provided that such districts as established based on the census in the year nineteen hundred and seventy-one shall terminate on the first Wednesday in January in the year nineteen hundred and seventy-nine. [See Amendments. Arts. CIX and CXVII.]

The House of Representatives shall consist of one hundred and sixty members. The General Court shall, at its first regular session after the year in which said census was taken, divide the

Commonwealth into one hundred and sixty representative districts of contiguous territory so that each representative will represent an equal number of inhabitants. as nearly as may be; and such district shall be formed, as nearly as may be, without uniting two counties or parts of two or more counties, two towns or parts of two or more towns, two cities or parts of two or more cities, or a city and a town, or parts of cities and towns, into one district. Such districts shall also be so formed that no town containing less than twenty-five hundred inhabitants according to said census shall be divided. The General Court may by law limit the time within which judicial proceedings may be instituted calling in question any such division. Every representative, for one year at least immediately preceding his election. shall have been an inhabitant of the district for which he is chosen and shall cease to represent such district when he shall cease to be an inhabitant of the Commonwealth. The manner of calling and conducting the elections for the choice of representatives, and of ascertaining their election. shall be prescribed by law.

SECTION 2. Each such census of inhabitants required in section one shall likewise be the basis for determining the senatorial districts and also the councillor districts for the ten year period beginning with the first Wednesday in the fourth January following the taking of such census; provided that such districts as established based on the census in the year nineteen hundred and seventy-one shall terminate on the first Wednesday in January in the year nineteen hundred and seventy-nine. The Senate shall consist of forty members. The General Court shall, at its first regular session after the year in which said census is taken, divide the Commonwealth into forty districts of contiguous territory, each district to contain, as nearly as may be, an equal number of inhabitants according to said census; and such districts shall be formed, as nearly as may be, without uniting two counties, or parts of two or more counties, into one district. The General Court may by law limit the time within which judicial proceedings may be instituted calling in question such division. Each district shall elect one senator, who shall have been an inhabitant of this Commonwealth five years at least immediately preceding his election and at the time of his election shall be an inhabitant of the district for which he is chosen; and he shall cease to represent such senatorial district when he shall cease to be an inhabitant of the Commonwealth. The manner of calling and conducting the elections for the choice of senators and councillors, and of ascertaining their election, shall be prescribed by law. [Amended by Amendments, Art. CXVII, sect. 2.]

SECTION 3. Original jurisdiction is hereby vested in the supreme judicial court upon the petition of any voter of the Commonwealth, filed with the clerk of the supreme judicial court for the Commonwealth, for judicial relief relative to the establishment of House of Representatives, councillor and senatorial districts.

SECTION 4. Article XCII of the Amendments to the Constitution is hereby annulled.

Art. CII. Article LII of the Articles of Amendment to the Constitution is hereby annulled and the following is adopted in place thereof: —

Article LII. The General Court, by concurrent vote of the two houses, may take a recess or recesses amounting to not more than thirty days.

Art. CIII. Article XLVI of the Articles of Amendment to the Constitution of the Commonwealth is hereby amended by striking out section 2 and inserting in place thereof the following section: —

Section 2. No grant, appropriation or use of public money or property or loan of credit shall be made or authorized by the Commonwealth or any political subdivision thereof for the purpose of founding, maintaining or aiding any infirmary, hospital, institution, primary or secondary school, or charitable or religious undertaking which is not publicly owned and under the exclusive control, order and supervision of public officers or public agents authorized by the Commonwealth or federal authority or both, except that appropriations may be made for the maintenance and support of the Soldiers' Home in Massachusetts and for free public libraries, in any city or town and to carry out legal obligations, if any, already entered into; and no such grant, appropriation or use of public money or property or loan of public credit shall be made or authorized for the purpose of founding, maintaining or aiding any church, religious denomination or society. Nothing herein contained shall be construed to prevent the Commonwealth from making grants-in-aid to private higher educational institutions or to students or parents or guardians of students attending such institutions.

Article CIV. Article LXXVIII of the Amendments to the Constitution is hereby annulled and the following is adopted in place thereof: —

Article LXXVIII. No revenue from fees, duties, excises or license taxes relating to registration, operation or use of vehicles on public highways, or to fuels used for propelling such vehicles, shall be expended for other than cost of administration of laws providing for such revenue, making of refunds and adjustments in relation thereto, payment of highway obligations, or cost of construction, reconstruction, maintenance and repair of public highways and bridges, and mass transportation lines and of the enforcement of state traffic laws, and for other mass transportation purposes; and such revenue shall be expended by the commonwealth or its counties, cities and towns for said highway and mass transportation purposes only and in such manner as the general court may direct; provided, that this amendment shall not apply to revenue from any excise tax imposed in lieu of local property taxes for the privilege of registering such vehicles.

Art. CV. Article XLV of the articles of amendment to the constitution, as amended by Article LXXVI of said articles of amendments, is hereby annulled and the following is adopted in place thereof: —

Article XLV. The general court shall have power to provide by law for voting, in the choice of any officer to be elected or upon any question submitted at an election, by qualified voters of the commonwealth who, at the time of such an election, are absent from the city or town of which they are inhabitants or are unable by reasons of physical disability to cast their votes in person at the polling places or who hold religious beliefs in conflict with the act of voting on the day on which such an election is to be held.

Art. CVI. Article I of Part the First of the Constitution is hereby annulled and the following is adopted: —

All people are born free and equal and have certain natural, essential and unalienable rights; among which may be reckoned the right of enjoying and defending their lives and liberties; that of acquiring, possessing and protecting property; in fine, that of seeking and obtaining their safety and happiness. Equality under the law shall not be denied or abridged because of sex, race, color, creed or national origin.

Art. CVII. Section 2 of Article LXIII of the Articles of Amendment to the Constitution of the Commonwealth is hereby annulled and the following is adopted in place thereof: —

Section 2. The Budget. — Within three weeks after the convening of the general court the governor shall recommend to the general court a budget which shall contain a statement of all proposed expenditures of the commonwealth for the fiscal year, including those already authorized by law, and of all taxes, revenues, loans and other means by which such expenditures shall be defrayed. In the first year of the term of office of a governor who has not served in the preceding year said governor shall recommend such budget within eight weeks after the convening of the general court. The budget shall be arranged in such form as the general court may by law prescribe, or, in default thereof, as the governor shall determine. For the purpose of preparing his budget, the governor shall have power to require any board, commission, officer or department to furnish him with any information which he may deem necessary.

Art. CVIII. Article XLVIII of the Amendments to the Constitution of the Commonwealth is hereby amended by striking out, under the heading "GENERAL PROVISIONS," all of subheading "*IV. Information for Voters.*", as amended by section 4 of Article LXXIV of said Amendments, and inserting in place thereof the following subheading:

IV. Information for Voters.

The secretary of the commonwealth shall cause to be printed and sent to each person eligible to vote in the commonwealth or to each residence of one or more persons eligible to vote in the commonwealth the full text of every measure to be submitted to the people, together with a copy of the legislative committee's majority and minority reports, if there be such, with the names of the majority and minority members thereon, a statement of the votes of the general court on the measure, and a fair, concise summary of the measure as such summary will appear on the ballot; and shall, in such manner as may be provided by law, cause to be prepared and sent other information and arguments for and against the measure.

Art. CIX. The first paragraph of Section 1 of Article CI of the Amendments to the Constitution of the Commonwealth is hereby amended by striking out the second sentence and inserting in place thereof the following two sentences: —

For purposes of said census every person shall be considered an inhabitant of the city or town of his usual place of residence in accordance with standards used by the United States from time to time in conducting the federal census required by Section 2 of Article 1 of the Constitution of the United States subject to such exceptions as the general court may provide by law. Such census shall specify the number of inhabitants of each precinct of each town and of each precinct and ward of each city. [Amended by Art. CXVII.]

Art. CX. Article XLI of the Amendments to the Constitution is hereby annulled and the following Article is adopted in place thereof: —

Full power and authority are hereby given and granted to the general court to prescribe for wild or forest lands and lands retained in a natural state for the preservation of wildlife and other natural resources and lands for recreational uses, such methods of taxation as will develop and conserve the forest resources, wildlife and other natural resources and the environ-mental benefits of recreational lands within the commonwealth.

Art. CXI. No student shall be assigned to or denied admittance to a public school on the basis of race, color, national origin or creed.

Art. CXII. Article IV of Chapter 1 of Part the Second of the
Constitution is hereby amended by inserting after the words "and to
impose and levy proportional and reasonable assessment, rates and
taxes, upon all the inhabitants of, and persons resident, and estates
lying, within said Commonwealth" the words: —, except that, in
addition to the powers conferred under Articles XLI and XCIX of the
Amendments, the general court may classify real property according
to its use in no more than four classes and to assess, rate and tax such
property differently in the classes so established, but proportionately
in the same class, and except that reasonable exemptions may be
granted.

Art. CXIII. The first sentence of the sixth paragraph of Section 3
of Article II of the Amendments to the Constitution of the
Commonwealth, as appearing in Article LXXXIX of said
Amendments, is hereby amended by striking out the words "ten
months" and inserting in place thereof the words: — eighteen
months.

Art. CXIV. No otherwise qualified handicapped individual shall,
solely by reason of his handicap, be excluded from the participation
in, denied the benefits of, or be subject to discrimination under any
program or activity within the commonwealth.

Art. CXV. No law imposing additional costs upon two or more
cities or towns by the regulation of the compensation, hours, status,
conditions or benefits of municipal employment shall be effective in
any city or town until such law is accepted by vote or by the
appropriation of money for such purposes, in the case of a city, by the
city council in accordance with its charter, and in the case of a town,
by a town meeting or town council, unless such law has been enacted
by a two-thirds vote of each house of the general court present and
voting thereon, or unless the general court, at the same session in
which such law is enacted, has provided for the assumption by the
commonwealth of such additional cost.

Art. CXVI. Article XXVI of part 1 of the Constitution of the
Commonwealth is hereby amended by adding the following two
sentences: — No provision of the Constitution, however, shall be
construed as prohibiting the imposition of the punishment of death.
The general court may, for the purpose of protecting the general

welfare of the citizens, authorize the imposition of the punishment of death by the courts of law having jurisdiction of crimes subject to the punishment of death.

Art. CXVII. Section 1. Section 1 of Article CI of the Articles of Amendment to the Constitution is hereby amended by striking out the first paragraph, as amended by Article CIX of said Articles of Amendment, and inserting in place thereof the following paragraph: —

The federal census shall be the basis for determining the representative districts for the ten year period beginning with the first Wednesday in the fifth January following the taking of said census.

Section 2. Section 2 of said Article CI of said Articles of Amendment is hereby amended by striking out the first sentence and inserting in place thereof the following sentence: — Said federal census shall likewise be the basis for determining the senatorial districts and also the councillor districts for the ten year period beginning with the first Wednesday in the fifth January following the taking of such census.

[Note. — Soon after the Declaration of Independence, steps were taken in Massachusetts toward framing a Constitution or Form of Government. The Council and House of Representa-tives, or the General Court of 1777-78, in accordance with a recommendation of the General Court, of the previous year, met together as a Convention, and adopted a form of Constitution "for the State of Massachusetts Bay," which was submitted to the people, and by them rejected. This attempt to form a Constitution having proved unsuccessful, the General Court on the 20th of February, 1779, passed a Resolve calling upon the qualified voters to give in their votes upon the questions — Whether they chose to have a new Constitution or Form of Government made, and, Whether they will empower their representatives to vote for calling a State Convention for that purpose. A large majority of the inhabitants having voted in the affirmative to both these questions, the General Court, on the 17th of June, 1779, passed a Resolve calling upon the inhabitants to meet and choose delegates to a Constitutional Convention, to be held at Cambridge, on the 1st of September, 1779. The Convention met at time and place appointed, and organized by choosing James

Bowdoin, President, and Samuel Barrett, Secretary. On the 11th of November the Convention adjourned, to meet at the Representatives' Chamber, in Boston, January 5th, 1780. On the 2d of March, of the same year, a form of Constitution having been agreed upon, a Resolve was passed by which the same was submitted to the people, and the Convention adjourned to meet at the Brattle Street Church, in Boston, June the 7th. At that time and place the Convention again met, and appointed a Committee to examine the returns of votes from the several towns. On the 14th of June the Committee reported, and on the 15th the Convention resolved, "That the people of the State of Massachusetts Bay have accepted the Constitution as it stands, in the printed form submitted to their revision." A Resolve providing for carrying the new Constitution into effect was passed; and the Convention then, on the 16th of June, 1780, was finally dissolved. In accordance with the Resolves referred to, elections immediately took place in the several towns; and the first General Court of the COMMONWEALTH OF MASSACHUSETTS met at the State House, in Boston, on Wednesday, October 25th, 1780.

The Constitution contained a provision providing for taking, in 1795, the sense of the people as to the expediency or necessity of revising the original instrument. But no such revision was deemed necessary at that time. On the 16th of June, 1820, an Act was passed by the General Court, calling upon the people to meet in their several towns, and give in their votes upon the question, "Is it expedient that delegates should be chosen to meet in Convention for the purpose of revising or altering the Constitution of Government of this Commonwealth?" A large majority of the people of the State having voted in favor of revision, the Governor issued a proclamation announcing the fact, and calling upon the people to vote, in accordance with the provisions of the aforesaid Act, for delegates to the proposed Convention. The delegates met at the State House, in Boston, November 15th, 1820, and organized by choosing John Adams, President, and Benjamin Pollard, Secretary. Mr. Adams, however, declined the appointment, and Isaac Parker was chosen in his stead. On the 9th of January, 1821, the Convention agreed to fourteen Articles of Amendment, and after passing a Resolve providing for submitting the same to the people, and appointing a committee to meet to count the votes upon the subject, was dissolved. The people voted on Monday, April 9th, 1821, and the Committee of the Convention met at the State House to count the votes, on Wednesday, May 24th. They made their return to the General Court; and at the request of the latter the Governor issued his proclamation on the 5th of June, 1821, announcing that nine of the fourteen Articles of Amendment had been adopted. These articles were numbered in the preceding pages from *one to nine* inclusive. The *first* Article was annulled by the *ninetieth* Article, the *second* Article by the eighty-ninth Article, the *fifth* Article by the *fifty-third* Article and the ninth Article by the *forty-eighth* Article.

The *tenth* Article of Amendment was adopted by the General Court during the sessions of the political years 1829-30, and 1830-31, and was approved and ratified by the people May 11th, 1831.

The *eleventh* Article of Amendment was adopted by the General Court during the sessions of the years 1832 and 1833, and was approved and ratified by the people November 11th, 1833.

The *twelfth* Article of Amendment was adopted by the General Court during the sessions of the years 1835 and 1836, and was approved and ratified by the people November 14th, 1836.

The *thirteenth* Article of Amendment was adopted by the General Court during the sessions of the years 1839 and 1840, and was approved and ratified by the people April 6th, 1840.

The General Court of the year 1851 passed an Act calling a third Convention to revise the Constitution. The Act was submitted to the people, and a majority voted against the proposed Convention. In 1852, on the 7th of May, another Act was passed calling upon the people to vote upon the question of calling a Constitutional Convention. A majority of the people having voted in favor of the proposed Convention, election for delegates thereto took place in March, 1853. The Convention met in the State House, in Boston, on the 4th day of May, 1853, and organized by choosing Nathaniel P. Banks, Jr., President, and William S. Robinson and James T. Robinson, Secretaries. On the 1st of August, this Convention agreed to a form of Constitution, and on the same day was dissolved, after having provided for submitting the same to the people, and appointed a committee to meet to count the votes, and to make a return thereof to the General Court. The Committee met at the time and place agreed upon, and found that the proposed Constitution had been rejected.

The *fourteenth, fifteenth, sixteenth, seventeenth, eighteenth,* and *nineteenth* Articles of Amendment were adopted by the General Court during the sessions of the years 1854 and 1855, and were approved and ratified by the people May 23d, 1855. The eighteenth Article was superseded by the *forty-sixth* Article.

The *twentieth, twenty-first* and *twenty-second* Articles of Amendment were adopted by the General Court during the sessions of the years 1856 and 1857, and were approved and ratified by the people May 1st, 1857. The *twenty-first* and *twenty-second* Articles were annulled and superseded by the *seventy-first* Article, which was subsequently annulled by the *ninety-second* Article.

The *twenty-third* Article of Amendment was adopted by the General Court during the sessions of the years 1858 and 1859, and was approved and ratified by the people May 9th, 1859, and was annulled by the *twenty-sixth* Article.

The *twenty-fourth* and *twenty-fifth* Articles of Amendment were adopted by the General Court during the sessions of the years 1859 and 1860, and were approved and ratified by the people May 7th, 1860.

The *twenty-sixth* Article of Amendment was adopted by the General Court during the sessions of the years 1862 and 1863, and was approved and ratified by the people April 6th, 1863.

The *twenty-seventh* Article of Amendment was adopted by the General Court during the sessions of the years 1876 and 1877, and was approved and ratified by the people on the 6th day of November, 1877.

The *twenty-eighth* Article of Amendment was adopted by the General Court during the sessions of the years 1880 and 1881, and was approved and ratified by the people on the 8th day of November, 1881.

The *twenty-ninth* Article of Amendment was adopted by the General Court during the sessions of the years 1884 and 1885, and was approved and ratified by the people on the 3d day of November, 1885.

The *thirtieth* and *thirty-first* Articles of Amendment were adopted by the General Court during the sessions of the years 1889 and 1890, and were approved and ratified by the people on the 4th day of November. 1890.

The *thirty-second* and *thirty-third* Articles of Amendment were adopted by the General Court during the sessions of the years 1890 and 1891. and were approved and ratified by the people on the 3d day of November. 1891.

The *thirty-fourth* Article of Amendment was adopted by the General Court during the sessions of the years 1891 and 1892, and was approved and ratified by the people on the 8th day of November, 1892.

The *thirty-fifth* Article of Amendment was adopted by the General Court during the sessions of the years 1892 and 1893, and was approved and ratified by the people on the 7th day of November, 1893.

The *thirty-sixth* Article of Amendment was adopted by the General Court during the sessions of the years 1893 and 1894, and was approved and ratified by the people on the 6th day of November, 1894.

The *thirty-seventh* Article of Amendment was adopted by the General Court during the sessions of the years 1906 and 1907, and was approved and ratified by the people on the 5th day of November, 1907.

The *thirty-eighth* Article of Amendment was adopted by the General Court during the sessions of the years 1909 and 1910, and was approved and ratified by the people on the 7th day of November, 1911.

The *thirty-ninth* Article of Amendment was adopted by the General Court during the sessions of the years 1910 and 1911, and was approved and ratified by the people on the 7th day of November, 1911.

The *fortieth* and *forty-first* Articles of Amendment were adopted by the General Court during the sessions of the years 1911 and 1912, and were approved and ratified by the people on the 5th day of November. 1912. The *forty-first* Article was annulled by the *one hundred and tenth* Article.

The *forty-second* Article of Amendment was adopted by the General Court during the sessions of the years 1912 and 1913, and was approved and ratified by the people on the 4th day of November, 1913, and was annulled by the *forty-eighth* Article.

The *forty-third* and *forty-fourth* Articles of Amendment were adopted by the General Court during the sessions of the years 1914 and 1915, and were approved and ratified by the people on the 2d day of November, 1915.

In his inaugural address to the General Court of 1916, Governor McCall recommended that the question of revising the Constitution, through a Constitutional Convention, be submitted to the people: and the General Court passed a law (chapter 98 of the General Acts of 1916) to ascertain and carry out the will of the people relative thereto, the question to be submitted being "Shall there be a convention to revise, alter or amend the constitution of the Commonwealth?" The people voted on this question at the annual election, held on November 7, casting 217,293 votes in the affirmative and 120,979 votes in the negative; and accordingly the Governor on Dec. 19, 1916, made proclamation to that effect, and, by virtue of authority contained in the act, called upon the people to elect delegates at a special election to be held on the first Tuesday in May, 1917. The election was on May 1. In accordance with the provisions of the act, the delegates met at the State House on June 6, 1917, and organized by choosing John L. Bates, president, and James W. Kimball, secretary. After considering and acting adversely on numerous measures that had been brought before it, and after providing for submitting to the people the *forty-fifth, forty-sixth,* and *forty-seventh* Articles, at the state election of 1917, and the Article relative to the establishment of the popular initiative and referendum and the legislative initiative of specific amendments of the Constitution (Article forty-eight) at the state election of 1918, the Convention adjourned on November 28 "until called by the President or Secretary to meet not later than within ten days after the prorogation of the General Court of 1918."

The *forty-fifth, forty-sixth* and *forty-seventh* Articles of Amendment, ordered by the convention to be submitted to the people, were so submitted and were approved and ratified on the 6th day of November. 1917. The *forty-fifth* Article was annulled and superseded by the *seventy-sixth* and *one hundred and fifth* Articles.

On Wednesday, June 12, 1918, the convention reassembled and resumed its work. Eighteen more articles (Articles forty-nine to sixty-six, inclusive) were approved by the convention and were ordered to be submitted to the people. On Wednesday, August 21, 1918, the convention adjourned. "to meet. subject to call by the President or Secretary, not later than within twenty days after the prorogation of the General Court of 1919. for the purpose of taking action on the report of the special committee on Rearrangement of the Constitution."

The *forty-eighth* to the *sixty-sixth* (inclusive) Articles of Amendment, ordered by the convention to be submitted to the people, were so submitted and were approved and ratified on the 5th day of November. 1918. The *forty-ninth* Article was annulled by the *ninety-seventh* Article, the *fifty-second* Article by the one hundred and second Article, the *fifty-sixth* Article by the *ninetieth* Article, the *fifty-eighth* Article by the *ninety-eighth* Article, the *sixty-fourth* Article by the *eighty-second* Article and the *sixty-sixth* Article by the *eighty-seventh* Article. Section 2 of the *sixty-third* Article was annulled by the *one hundred and eighth* Article.

On Tuesday, August 12, 1919, pursuant to a call of its President, the Convention again convened. A rearrangement of the Constitution was adopted, and was ordered to be submitted to the people for their ratification. On the following day, a subcommittee of the Special Committee on Rearrangement of the Constitution was "empowered to correct clerical and typographical errors and establish the text of the rearrangement of the Constitution to be submitted to the people, in conformity with that adopted by the Convention." On Wednesday, August 13, 1919, the Convention adjourned, *sine die.* On Tuesday, November 4, 1919, the rearrangement was approved and ratified by the people; but, as to the effect thereof, see Opinion of the Justices, 233 Mass. 603; and Loring *v.* Young, decided August 8, 1921 [see

239 Mass. 349]. [For text of the *Rearrangement,* see Manuals for the years 1920 to 1932, inclusive.]

The *sixty-seventh* Article of Amendment was adopted by the General Court during the sessions of the years 1920 and 1921, and was approved and ratified by the people on the 7th day of November, 1922.

The *sixty-eighth* and *sixty-ninth* Articles of Amendment were adopted by the General Court during the sessions of the years 1921 and 1923, and were approved and ratified by the people on the 4th day of November, 1924.

The *seventieth* Article of Amendment was adopted by the General Court during the sessions of the years 1924 and 1925, and was approved and ratified by the people on the 2d day of November, 1926.

The *seventy-first* Article of Amendment was adopted by the General Court during the sessions of the years 1928 and 1930, and was approved and ratified by the people on the 4th day of November, 1930. The *seventy-first* Article was annulled by the *ninety-second* Article.

The *seventy-second* Article of Amendment (introduced by initiative petition) was approved by the General Court during the sessions of the years 1936 and 1937, and by the people on the 8th day of November, 1938, and was annulled by the *seventy-fifth* Article.

The *seventy-third, seventy-fourth, seventy-fifth* and *seventy-sixth* Articles of Amendment were adopted by the General Court during the sessions of the years 1941 and 1943, and were approved and ratified by the people on the 7th day of November, 1944. The *seventy-sixth* Article was annulled by the *one hundred and fifth* Article.

The *seventy-seventh* Article of Amendment was adopted by the General Court during the sessions of the years 1945 and 1947, and was approved and ratified by the people on the 2d day of November, 1948.

The *seventy-eighth* Article of Amendment was adopted by the General Court during the sessions of the years 1946 and 1947, and was approved and ratified by the people on the 2d day of November,

1948. The *seventy-eighth* Article was annulled by the *one hundred and fourth* Article.

The *seventy-ninth* Article of Amendment was adopted by the General Court during the sessions of the years 1946 and 1948, and was approved and ratified by the people on the 2d day of November, 1948.

The *eightieth* Article of Amendment was adopted by the General Court during the sessions of the years 1947 and 1949, and was approved and ratified by the people on the 7th day of November, 1950.

The *eighty-first* Article of Amendment was adopted by the General Court during the sessions of the years 1948 and 1949, and was approved and ratified by the people on the 7th day of November, 1950.

The *eighty-second* Article of Amendment was adopted by the General Court during the sessions of 1961 and 1963, and was approved and ratified by the people on the 3d day of November, 1964.

The *eighty-third* Article of Amendment was adopted by the General Court during the sessions of 1962 and 1963, and was approved and ratified by the people on the 3d day of November, 1964.

The *eighty-fourth* Article of Amendment was adopted by the General Court during the sessions of 1961 and 1963, and was approved and ratified by the people on the 3d day of November, 1964.

The *eighty-fifth* Article of Amendment was adopted by the General Court during the sessions of 1962 and 1963. and was approved and ratified by the people on the 3d day of November, 1964.

The *eighty-sixth, eighty-seventh, eighty-eighth* and *eighty-ninth* Articles of Amendment were adopted by the General Court during the sessions of 1963 and 1965. and were approved and ratified by the people on the 8th day of November, 1966.

The *ninetieth* Article of Amendment was adopted by the General Court during the sessions of 1965 and 1967; the *ninety-first* Article of

Amendment was adopted by the General Court during the sessions of 1966 and 1967; and both Articles were approved and ratified by the people on the 5th day of November. 1968.

The *ninety-second* Article of Amendment was approved by the General Court during the sessions of 1968 and 1969; the *ninety-third* and *ninety-fourth* Articles of Amendment were approved by the General Court during the sessions of 1967 and 1969; and all three Articles were approved and ratified by the people on the 3d day of November. 1970. The *ninety-second* Article was annulled by the *one hundred and first* Article.

The *ninety-fifth, ninety-sixth, ninety-seventh, ninety-eighth, ninety-ninth* and *one hundredth* Articles of Amendment were adopted by the General Court during the sessions of 1969 and 1971. and all six Articles were approved and ratified by the people on the seventh day of November. 1972.

The *one hundred and first* and *one hundred and second* Articles of Amendment were adopted by the General Court during the sessions 1971 and 1973. and both Articles were approved and ratified by the people on the fifth day of November. 1974.

The *one hundred and third* Article of Amendment was adopted by the General Court during the sessions of 1972 and 1973. and was approved and ratified by the people on the fifth day of November. 1974.

The *one hundred and fourth* Article of Amendment was adopted by the General Court during the sessions of 1972 and 1974. and was approved and ratified by the people on the fifth day of November. 1974.

The *one hundred and fifth* Article of Amendment was adopted by the General Court during the sessions of 1973 and 1976. and was approved and ratified by the people on the second day of November. 1976.

The *one hundred and sixth* Article of Amendment was adopted by the General Court during the sessions of 1973 and 1975. and was approved and ratified by the people on the second day of November. 1976.

The *one hundred and seventh* Article of Amendment was adopted by the General Court during the sessions of 1975 and 1977, and was approved and ratified by the people on the seventh day of November, 1978.

The *one hundred and eighth* and *one hundred and ninth* Articles of Amendment were adopted by the General Court during the sessions of 1976 and 1977, and were approved and ratified by the people on the seventh day of November, 1978.

The *one hundred and tenth* Article of Amendment was adopted by the General Court during the sessions of 1976 and 1978, and was approved and ratified by the people on the seventh day of November, 1978.

The *one hundred and eleventh* and *one hundred and twelfth* Articles of Amendment were adopted by the General Court during the sessions of 1975 and 1977, and were approved and ratified by the people on the seventh day of November, 1978.

The *one hundred and thirteenth* Article of Amendment was adopted by the General Court during the sessions of 1976 and 1977, and was approved and ratified by the people on the seventh day of November, 1978.

The *one hundred and fourteenth* and *one hundred and fifteenth* Articles of Amendment were adopted by the General Court during the sessions of 1977 and 1980, and were approved and ratified by the people on the fourth day of November, 1980.

The *one hundred and sixteenth* Article of Amendment was adopted by the General Court during the sessions of 1980 and 1982, and was approved and ratified by the people on the second day of November, 1982.

The *one hundred and seventeenth* Article of Amendment was adopted by the General Court during the sessions of 1987 and 1990, and was approved and ratified by the people on the sixth day of November, 1990.

AMENDMENTS REJECTED BY THE PEOPLE.

[A proposed Article of Amendment prohibiting the manufacture and sale of Intoxicating Liquor as a beverage, adopted by the General Court during the sessions of the years 1888 and 1889, was rejected by the people on the twenty-second day of April, 1889.]

[Proposed Articles of Amendment, (1) Establishing biennial elections of state officers, and (2) Establishing biennial elections of members of the General Court; adopted by the General Court during the sessions of the years 1895 and 1896, were rejected by the people at the annual election held on the third day of November, 1896.]

[A proposed Article of Amendment to make Women eligible to appointment as Notaries Public, adopted by the General Court during the sessions of the years 1912 and 1913, was rejected by the people on the fourth day of November, 1913.]

[A proposed Article of Amendment enabling Women to vote, adopted by the General Court during the sessions of the years 1914 and 1915, was rejected by the people on the second day of November, 1915.]

[A proposed Article of Amendment to give the General Court the power to pass an income tax at graduated or proportioned rates, adopted by the General Court during the sessions of the years 1959 and 1961 was rejected by the people on the sixth day of November, 1962; and similar Articles of Amendment adopted by the General Court during the sessions of the years 1966 and 1967, 1973 and 1975, and 1992 and 1994 were rejected by the people on the fifth day of November, 1968, the second day of November, 1976 and the eighth day of November, 1994.]

[A proposed Article of Amendment authorizing the Legislature to classify real property according to uses, and authorizing the assessment, rating and taxation of real property at different rates in the different classes so established, but proportionately in the same classes while granting reasonable exemptions and abatements, approved by the General Court during the sessions of the years of

1968 and 1969. was rejected by the people on the third day of November. 1970.]

[A proposed Article of Amendment authorizing the General Court to impose and levy a graduated income tax and to base such tax upon the federal income tax. adopted by the General Court during the sessions of the years 1969 and 1971. was rejected by the people on the seventh day of November. 1972.]

[A proposed Article of Amendment changing the procedure by which the Legislature declares a measure to be an emergency law, adopted by the General Court during the sessions of the years 1977 and 1980. was rejected by the people on the fourth day of November, 1980.]

[A proposed Article of Amendment permitting the Commonwealth or its political subdivisions to extend aid to non-public schools students within the limits of the United States Constitution, adopted by the General Court during the sessions of the years 1980 and 1982. was rejected by the people on the second day of November. 1982; and a similar Article of Amendment adopted by the General Court during the sessions of the years 1984 and 1986. was rejected by the people on the fourth day of November. 1986.]

[A proposed Article of Amendment relative to allowing the General Court to regulate the practice and public funding of abortions consistent with the United States Constitution. adopted by the General Court during the sessions of the years 1984 and 1986, was rejected by the people on the fourth day of November, 1986.]

INDEX TO THE CONSTITUTION

A

NOTE: — Ancient spelling used in text of original Constitution and
early Amendments has been continued in this edition.

PAGE

190   *Index to the Constitution.*

F

G

198   *Index to the Constitution.*

J

L

220   *Index to the Constitution.*

THE STATE HOUSE,
SEAL OF THE COMMONWEALTH,
STATE LIBRARY, ETC.

THE STATE HOUSE.

and

GOVERNMENT CENTER.

The "Bulfinch Front" of the State House was erected in 1795-7, upon land purchased of the heirs of John Hancock, by the town of Boston, for the sum of £4,000, and conveyed by said town to the Commonwealth, May 2, 1795. The Commissioners on the part of the town to convey the "Governor's Pasture," as it was styled, to the Commonwealth, were William Tudor, Charles Jarvis, John Coffin Jones, William Eustis, William Little, Thomas Dawes, Joseph Russell, Harrison Gray Otis and Perez Morton. The agents for erecting the State House were named in the deed as follows: Thomas Dawes, Edward Hutchinson Robbins and Charles Bulfinch.

The corner stone was laid July 4, 1795, by Governor Samuel Adams, assisted by Paul Revere, Grand Master of the Grand Lodge of Masons. The stone was drawn to the spot by fifteen white horses, representing the number of States of the Union at that time. The original building is 172 feet front; the height, from base course to pinnacle, is 155 feet; and the foundation is about 106 feet above the waters of the bay. The dome is 53 feet in diameter and 35 feet high. The original cost of the building was estimated at $133,333.33.

Extensive improvements, including the "Bryant addition" extending backward upon Mount Vernon Street, were made, chiefly under the direction of a commission, in the years 1853, 1854 and 1855.

Under a resolve of 1866, a commission was appointed to inquire and report concerning the whole subject of remodeling or rebuilding the State House. They reported three propositions, without deciding in favor of any. The first was a plan of remodeling at an expense of $375,430; the second, a plan of remodeling at an expense of $759,872; and the third, a plan for a new building at an expense of $2,042,574. The report of the commission was referred to the committee on the State House of the session of 1867, who recommended a plan of alterations at the estimated expense of $150,000; and by Resolve No. 84 of that year the work was ordered to be executed under the supervision of a commission consisting of the President of the Senate and the Speaker of the

House of Representatives, who were authorized by the same resolve to expend $150,000, and, by a subsequent resolve, $20,000 in addition. The President of the Senate died on the 28th of October, and thereafter the work was continued by the surviving commissioner. The improvements consisted of an almost entire reconstruction of the interior of the building, except the "Bryant addition," before referred to as having been added from 1853 to 1855. They were executed from the plans of the architects. Washburn & Son, and cost, including furniture, $270,256.96.

The Legislature of 1868 made provision for reseating the Senate Chamber and the Hall of the House, which improvements were made under the supervision of legislative committees, in season for the accommodation of the Legislature of 1869, at a cost of about $6,500.

By Resolve No. 68 of the year 1881, the sum of $45,000 was authorized to be expended for improving the basement of the State House, in accordance with plans submitted by the joint standing committee on the State House. The work was begun soon after the regular session of 1881, and was carried on under the supervision of the commissioners on the State House, consisting of Oreb F. Mitchell, Sergeant-At-Arms, Hon. Daniel A. Gleason, Treasurer and Receiver-General, and Hon. Henry B. Peirce, Secretary of State, assisted by John W. Leighton and Asa H. Caton, both of Boston, and appointed, under the resolve referred to, by the Governor and Council. Under the plans the floor of the basement was brought down to a common level, and numerous additional office rooms and needed accommodations were obtained.

Under authority of chapter 70 of the Resolves of 1885, passenger elevators were erected in the east and west ends of the building.

In accordance with the provisions of chapter 349 of the Acts of the year 1888, the Governor and Council, "for the purpose of providing suitable and adequate accommodations for the legislative and executive departments of the State government and for the several bureaus, boards and officers of the Commonwealth, whose offices are, or may be, located in the city of Boston, and for any other necessary and convenient uses of the Commonwealth," on November 7 of the same year, took possession in the name of the Commonwealth of the parcel of land lying next north of the State House, and bounded by Derne, Temple, Mount Vernon and Hancock streets, and also of a parcel of land lying to the east of

Temple Street, between Mount Vernon and Derne streets, both lots with the buildings and improvements thereon, full power being given them to settle, by agreement or arbitration, the amount of compensation to be paid any person by reason of the taking of his property. They were also authorized to discontinue the whole of Temple Street between Mount Vernon and Derne streets, and to negotiate with the city of Boston concerning the construction of new streets or ways.

By chapter 404 of the Acts of 1892, for the purpose of securing an open space around the State House, the commissioners were authorized to take, by purchase or otherwise, the land bounded north by Derne Street, east by Bowdoin Street, south by Beacon Hill Place and west by the State House, and by chapter 129, Acts of 1893, they were authorized to sell the buildings thereon. Subsequently, the commissioners were authorized to take Beacon Hill Place (chapter 450, Acts of 1893) and also the land bounded east by Bowdoin Street, south by Beacon Street, west by Mount Vernon Street and north by the land then owned by the Commonwealth; and provision was made for the removal of buildings on said land and for the improvement thereof (chapter 532, Acts of 1894; chapter 223, Acts of 1897; chapter 382, Acts of 1900; and chapter 525, Acts of 1901). In 1901 authority was given to the Governor, with the advice and consent of the Council, to take in fee simple, in behalf of the Commonwealth, a parcel of land, with the buildings thereon, on the southerly side of Mount Vernon Street, immediately west of Hancock Avenue (chapter 525, Acts of 1901).

By chapter 92 of the Resolves of 1888, the Governor and Council were allowed a sum not exceeding $5,000 to enable them to devise and report to the next General Court a general plan for the better accommodation of the State government.

A plan was accordingly submitted to the General Court of 1889, and $2,500 was appropriated for the further perfecting of said plan. A bill to provide for the enlargement of the State House was subsequently reported in the Legislature and became a law (chapter 394 of the Acts of 1889). Under this act the Governor was authorized to appoint three persons, to be known as the State House Construction Commission, and Messrs. John D. Long, Wm. Endicott, Jr. and Benjamin D. Whitcomb were appointed the commissioners. Mr. Whitcomb died in 1894, and Mr. Charles Everett Clark was appointed to fill the vacancy. The latter died in

1899. In 1894 Mr. Long resigned and Mr. George W. Johnson was appointed a member of the commission. The architects selected were Messrs. Brigham & Spofford of Boston. Subsequently to March, 1892, Mr. Charles Brigham was the sole architect of the extension.

On the twenty-first day of December, 1889, the corner stone of the new building was laid by His Excellency Governor Ames with appropriate ceremonies. The removal of the various departments and commissions to the new building was begun in the latter part of 1894. The House of Representatives of 1895 convened in the old Representatives' Chamber on the second day of January, and on the following day met for the first time in the hall set apart for it in the State House extension. It has occupied this hall ever since. Pending changes in the State House building, the Senate sat in a room numbered 239, 240 and 241, in the extension. Its first meeting in this room was on February 18, 1895. On April 8 it resumed its sittings in the old Senate Chamber.

By chapter 124 of the Resolves of 1896, the State House Construction Commission was directed to provide temporary accommodations for the Senate of 1897 and its officers. A temporary floor was accordingly constructed across the apartment, then unfinished, that has since come to be known as Memorial Hall, on a level with the present gallery; and the room thus made was finished and furnished as a Senate Chamber, with accommodations for spectators. On January 6, 1897, the Senate met in this chamber, which it continued to occupy throughout the session of that year, and it also, for the first time, made use of the reading room and the other rooms and offices intended for its permanent occupancy.

By chapter 531 of the Acts of 1896, His Honor Roger Wolcott, Acting Governor, Hon. George P. Lawrence, President of the Senate, and Hon. George v. L. Meyer, Speaker of the House, were made a committee to decide upon a plan for preserving, restoring and rendering practically fire-proof the so-called Bulfinch State House. The committee was directed to employ an architect, who was to superintend the execution of the work in accordance with such drawings and specifications as should be approved by said committee. It was provided that the State House Construction Commission should have charge of the work. Mr. Arthur G.

Everett was the architect selected by the committee, and with him was associated Mr. Robert D. Andrews. Mr. Charles A. Cummings was made consulting architect.

By chapter 470 of the Acts of 1897, His Excellency Roger Wolcott. Hon. George P. Lawrence, President of the Senate, and Hon. John L. Bates, Speaker of the House, were made a committee to decide upon plans for furnishing the so-called Bulfinch State House, with authority to employ an architect to make drawings, specifications and designs therefor, and also to superintend the execution of the work. Mr. Everett was selected for the purpose.

On the convening of the General Court of 1898, the Senate occupied for the first time the chamber in the Bulfinch building that had formerly been the Hall of the House of Representatives. The original Senate Chamber was assigned to the Senate by the Governor and Council as one of its apartments. The Senate has continued to occupy its new chamber ever since.

For the purpose of meeting the expenses incurred between 1889 and 1913 in connection with taking of land, including land damages, the construction and furnishing of the State House Extension, the finishing of the Memorial Hall therein, and the restoring and furnishing of the Bulfinch front, etc., bonds to the amount of $7,120,000 were issued from time to time.

By chapter 150 of the Resolves of 1912, the State House Commission (the Secretary of the Commonwealth, the Treasurer and Receiver-General and the Sergeant-at-Arms) was directed, with the cooperation of the State Arts Commission, to cause to be prepared plans for alterations in, and additions to, the State House, and to report to the next General Court. Report was made to the General Court of 1913 (House Document No. 133); and, by chapter 830 of the Acts of that year the State House Building Commission, to be appointed by the Governor with the advice and consent of the Council, was created, for the purpose of constructing additions substantially in accordance with the plan recommended in the report. Messrs. Albert P. Langtry, chairman, Joseph B. Russell and Neil McNeil were appointed the members of the building commission. Messrs. Robert D. Andrews, William Chapman and R. Clipston Sturgis were the architects selected by the commission. The work was begun in August, 1914. In 1915 Mr. John A. Keliher succeeded Mr. Langtry as a member of the commission and as its chairman, and Mr. J. Edward Fuller succeeded Mr. Russell.

By chapter 256 of the General Acts of 1915, the Commission was directed to construct a forward projection of the West wing, substantially the same as that already built in connection with the new East wing, and provision was made for the purchasing or taking of certain property and for the removal of the buildings thereon, etc. To meet the expenses connected with the making of these several alterations and additions, bonds to the amount of $2,265,000 were authorized and issued, as follows: chapter 830 of the Acts of 1913, $900,000; chapter 256 of the Acts of 1915, $600,000; chapter 181 of the Acts of 1916, $65,000; and chapter 250 of the Acts of 1916, $700,000. By chapter 17 of the General Acts of 1916, taking effect March 2, the State House Building Commission was abolished and its powers were transferred to the State House Commission. The members of this latter commission were Albert P. Langtry (Secretary of the Commonwealth), Charles L. Burrill (Treasurer and Receiver-General) and Thomas F. Pedrick (Sergeant-at-Arms of the General Court), Chairman; and, under their direction, the work was completed.

By item 8157-08, section 2, Chapter 711, Acts of 1956, The State Superintendent of Buildings was directed to cause the preparation of plans for, and the construction of, an archives building on the grounds of the State House. This item appropriated $1,005,000 for the project. With Maurice A. and F. Parker Reidy of Boston, engineers in charge, and the Boston firm of Perry Shaw, Hepburn and Dean as consulting architects, construction was begun July 1, 1958. The archives museum and underground vaults for the archives and the State Library were completed and accepted by the Commonwealth on September 27, 1960.

Chapter 711 of the Acts of 1956 also provided for the air conditioning of both the House and Senate chambers.

The Government Center Commission was created by Chapter 635, Acts of 1960 to construct additional buildings near the State House to house the various expanding agencies of the state government. The land bounded by Cambridge, Somerset, Bowdoin, and Ashburton Place was taken by eminent domain in 1961. The state office building at 100 Cambridge Street was designed by Emery Roth and Sons of New York. Construction was begun in 1962 under contract with Wexler Construction Company of Newton Highlands and completed by the Perini Corporation at a cost of about $26,600,000. Occupancy began in December 1965 and formal dedication ceremonies were conducted on May 17, 1966. The building has since been named for former Governor Leverett Saltonstall.

The Division of Employment Security Building on Cambridge Street was designed by Shepley, Bulfinch, Richardson, and Abbott, a Boston architectural firm. Construction was begun in 1967 by Vappi and Company. This building, completed in March 1970 at a cost of over $11,200,000, was named as a memorial to former Governor Charles F. Hurley.

Also part of the Government Center project is the Mental Health Center. Designed by Paul Rudolph of the Boston architectural firm, Desmond and Lord, this building cost approximately $10,935,000. The state took occupancy in December 1970 and it was named for Dr. Erich Lindemann, former Chief of Psychiatric Services, at the Massachusetts General Hospital. Dr. Lindemann had been greatly instrumental in the organization and staffing of the center.

A fourth building on New Chardon Street, planned to house the state health, welfare, and education agencies, never reached the construction stage.

Chapter 685, Acts of 1968 authorized the construction of an underground garage and office building on Ashburton Place. This project was designed by Hoyle, Doran and Berry of Boston. Construction began in 1971 under contract to Vappi and Company. It was completed in 1975 at an approximate cost of $34,250,000 and was designated the John W. McCormack State Office Building.

These new buildings permitted moving many state agencies out of the State House and allowed a great expansion in the space available for offices for members and staff of the General Court.

Repairs, renovations, and upgrading of the State House were authorized under the following acts: Chapter 723 of the Acts of 1983 authorized $30,800,000; Chapter 564 of the Acts of 1987 authorized $7,000,000; and Chapter 164 of the Acts of 1988 authorized $22,000,000.

The first phase of the renovations began February 8, 1988, and was completed in the Fall of 1990. The architects for the design were Shepley, Bulfinch, Richardson and Abbott, and the construction contract was awarded to the Perini Corporation.

Completed work includes: fence replacement, front lawn landscaping, entrance to west wing, two new hearing rooms, the newly created Great Hall, an underground parking garage, restoration of Ashburton Park, all mechanical (HVAC) work in Block B, some mechanical work in other blocks, relocation of electrical vaults, roof repairs, a new telecommunications system, and some structural repairs.

SEAL OF THE COMMONWEALTH.

COUNCIL RECORDS.
WEDNESDAY. DECEMBER 13TH, 1780.

Ordered, That Nathan Cushing, Esqr., be a committee to prepare a Seal for the Commonwealth of Massachusetts, who reported a Device for a Seal for said Commonwealth as follows, viz.: SAPPHIRE, an Indian, dressed in his Shirt, Maggosins, belted proper, in his right hand a Bow, TOPAZ, in his left an Arrow, its point towards the Base: of the second, on the Dexter side of the Indian's head, a Star, PEARL, for one of the United States of America.

CREST. On a Wreath a Dexter Arm clothed and ruffled proper, grasping a Broad Sword, the Pummel and Hilt, TOPAZ, with this Motto: *Ense Petit Placidam Sub Libertate Quietem.* And around the Seal: *Sigillum Reipublicae Massachusettensis.*

Advised that the said Report be Accepted as the Arms of the Commonwealth of Massachusetts.

ARMS, GREAT SEAL AND OTHER EMBLEMS OF THE COMMONWEALTH.

[Chapter 2 of the General Laws.]
ARMS, GREAT SEAL AND OTHER EMBLEMS
OF THE COMMONWEALTH.

SECTION 1. The coat of arms of the commonwealth shall consist of a blue shield with an Indian thereon, dressed in a shirt, leggings and moccasins, holding in his right hand a bow, and in his left hand an arrow, point downward, all of gold; and, in the upper right-hand corner of the field a silver star of five points. The crest shall be, on a wreath of gold and blue, a right arm, bent at the elbow, clothed and ruffled, and grasping a broad-sword, all of gold. The motto "Ense petit placidam sub libertate quietem" shall appear in gold on a blue ribbon.

SECTION 2. The seal of the commonwealth shall be circular in form, bearing upon its face a representation of the arms of the commonwealth encircled with the inscription within a beaded border, "Sigillum Reipublicae Massachusettensis". The colors of the arms shall not be an essential part of said seal, and an impression from a seal engraved according to said design, on any commission, paper, or document shall be valid without such colors or the representation thereof by heraldic lines or marks.

SECTION 3. The flag of the commonwealth shall consist of a white rectangular field, bearing on either side a representation of the arms of the commonwealth, except that the star shall be white. The naval and maritime flag of the commonwealth shall consist of a white rectangular field bearing on either side a representation of a green pine tree.

SECTION 4. The flag of the governor shall conform to the design of the flag of the commonwealth, except that the field of the flag of the governor shall be triangular in shape.

SECTION 5. The state secretary shall be the custodian of the coat of arms, seal and flags of the commonwealth and all representations of said arms, seal and flags shall conform strictly to the specifications which shall be prepared under the direction of the state secretary in the year nineteen hundred and seventy-one and deposited in his office. The proper use and display of said arms, seal and flags of the commonwealth and their manufacture are hereby subject to such regulations relating thereto which the state secretary may from time to time issue. provided that such regulations shall be in conformity with all the relevant legislation of the United States and of the commonwealth.

SECTION 6. The flag of the United States and the flag of the commonwealth shall be displayed on the main or administration building of each public institution of the commonwealth. The flags shall be of suitable dimensions and shall be flown every day when the weather permits.

SECTION 6A. The flag of the commonwealth shall be flown at half-staff at or on the main or administration building of each public institution of the commonwealth, at or on each other state-owned or state-controlled building, and at all state military installations on the following occasions for the periods indicated:—

(a) On all occasions upon which the national flag is flown at half-staff and for the same period of time;

(b) On the death of a governor or ex-governor of the commonwealth for thirty days from the day of death;

(c) On the death of a lieutenant-governor. secretary. treasurer and receiver-general, attorney general, or auditor of the commonwealth from the day of death until sunset of the day of interment;

(d) On the death of a senator in congress from the commonwealth. from the day of death until sunset of the day of interment;

(e) On the death of a representative in congress from the commonwealth. the flag of the commonwealth shall be flown at half-staff at the aforementioned sites in the representative's congressional district from the day of death until sunset of the day of interment;

(f) In the event of the death of other elected officials or former elected officials of the commonwealth. from the day of death until sunset of the day of interment in accordance with such orders or instructions as may be issued by or at the direction of the governor; and

(g) In the event two or more of the aforementioned periods coincide in full or in part. the state flag shall be displayed at half-staff for such period as will comply with the above provisions without resulting in an additional and separate period of such display for each such death.

SECTION 7. The mayflower (*epigaea repens*) shall be the flower or floral emblem of the commonwealth.

SECTION 8. The American elm (*Ulmus americana*) shall be the tree or tree emblem of the commonwealth.

SECTION 9. The chickadee (*Penthestes atricapillus*) shall be the bird or bird emblem of the commonwealth.

SECTION 10. Cranberry juice shall be the beverage of the commonwealth.

SECTION 11. The Morgan horse shall be the horse or horse emblem of the commonwealth.

SECTION 12. The Ladybug shall be the insect or insect emblem of the commonwealth.

SECTION 13. The Cod shall be the fish or fish emblem and the historic and continuing symbol of the commonwealth.

SECTION 14. The Boston terrier shall be the dog or dog emblem of the commonwealth.

SECTION 15. Rhodonite shall be the gem or gem emblem of the commonwealth.

SECTION 16. The right whale (*Eubalaena Glacialis*) shall be the marine mammal or marine mammal emblem of the commonwealth.

SECTION 17. The dinosaur track shall be the fossil or fossil emblem of the commonwealth.

SECTION 18. Babingtonite shall be the mineral or mineral emblem of the commonwealth.

SECTION 19. The song "All Hail to Massachusetts", words and music by Arthur J. Marsh, shall be the song of the commonwealth.

SECTION 20. The song "Massachusetts", words and music by Arlo Guthrie, shall be the folk song of the commonwealth.

SECTION 21. The poem, "Blue Hills of Massachusetts", composed by Katherine E. Mullen of the town of Barre, shall be the official state poem of the commonwealth.

SECTION 22. The Roxbury Puddingstone (Roxbury Conglomerate), shall be the rock or rock emblem of the commonwealth.

SECTION 23. Plymouth Rock, located in the town of Plymouth, shall be the historical rock of the commonwealth.

SECTION 24. Dighton Rock shall be the explorer rock of the commonwealth.

SECTION 25. Granite shall be the building and monument stone of the commonwealth.

SECTION 26. Deborah Samson, who fought in the War of Independence, shall be the official heroine of the commonwealth.

SECTION 27. The song "The Road to Boston", composer unknown, shall be the official ceremonial march of the commonwealth.

SECTION 28. The corn muffin shall be the official muffin of the commonwealth.

SECTION 29. The New England neptune (*neptunea lyrata decemcostatal*) shall be the shell of the commonwealth.

SECTION 30. The Tabby Cat shall be the official cat of the commonwealth.

SECTION 31. The song "Massachusetts (Because of You Our Land Is Free)", words and music by Bernard Davidson, shall be the patriotic song of the commonwealth.

SECTION 32. Square Dancing shall be the official folk dance of the commonwealth.

SECTION 33. The Paxton Soil Series shall be the official soil of the commonwealth.

SECTION 34. The memorial to be constructed in the city of Worcester by the Commonwealth of Massachusetts Vietnam

Veterans' Memorial Trust, Incorporated shall be the official memorial of the commonwealth to honor the Vietnam War veterans of the commonwealth.

SECTION 35. Bay Staters shall be the official designation of citizens of the commonwealth.

SECTION 36. The wild turkey (*Meleagris Gallopavo*) shall be the game bird and game bird emblem of the commonwealth.

SECTION 37. The memorial to be constructed in the city of Worcester by the Desert Calm Committee, Inc. shall be the official state monument for the veterans of the Southwest Asia War.

SECTION 38. The baked navy bean shall be the official bean of the commonwealth.

SECTION 39. The cranberry (*vaccinum macrocarpon*) shall be the official berry of the commonwealth.

SECTION 40. Johnny Appleseed shall be the official folk hero of the commonwealth.

SECTION 41. The Boston cream pie shall be the official dessert or dessert emblem of the commonwealth.

OATH OR AFFIRMATION OF OFFICE.

Under the Constitution and Laws of the Commonwealth and of the United States every person chosen or appointed to any office, civil or military, under the government of this Commonwealth, before he enters on the duties of his office, is required to take and subscribe the following oath or affirmation:—

THE OATH OF OFFICE.

I, (name), do solemnly swear, that I will bear true faith and allegiance to the Commonwealth of Massachusetts, and will support the Constitution thereof. *So help me God.*

I, (name), do solemnly swear and affirm, that I will faithfully and impartially discharge and perform all the duties incumbent on me as   : according to the best of my abilities and understanding, agreeably, to the rules and regulations of the Constitution, and the laws of this Commonwealth. *So help me God.*

I, (name), do solemnly swear that I will support the Constitution of the United States.

AFFIRMATION.

I, (name), do solemnly affirm, that I will bear true faith and allegiance to the Commonwealth of Massachusetts, and will support the Constitution thereof. *This I do under the pains and penalties of perjury.*

I, (name), do solemnly affirm, that I will faithfully and impartially discharge and perform all the duties incumbent on me as   : according to the best of my abilities and understanding, agreeably, to the rules and regulations of the Constitution, and the laws of this Commonwealth. *This I do under the pains and penalties of perjury.*

I, (name), do solemnly affirm that I will support the Constitution of the United States.

STATE LIBRARY OF MASSACHUSETTS.

ROOM 341, STATE HOUSE.

The State Library is a government research library maintained to meet the current information needs and research requirements of the General Court, the Executive branch and state government employees. All library materials are available to the public for research use.

The Library's collections are strong in the areas of public law, public affairs, Massachusetts state and local history, and American history. Maps, atlases, photographs, manuscripts and media collections contribute to the Library's documentation of the state and its history.

Presently, the Library contains over 1.2 million items. The law collection emphasizes public law as contrasted to the law of private practice. All states' statutory law and judicial decisions are represented in the collection. Coverage of federal law is complete as well. This collection is the only public law library in Suffolk County. Electronic access to legal resources and other specialized databases is offered to state employees.

Designated as the official repository for Massachusetts state publications (St. 1984, c. 412), the State Library has a comprehensive collection of state publications from both the legislative and executive branches. This collection, which grows daily, is historic in scope and includes many early reports. The Library expands its collection in a variety of media; recent additions to the collection include the Senate and the House of Representatives' proceedings on videotape and selected legislative committee hearings on videotape.

The State Library has been a selective depository for federal documents for over one hundred years, resulting in important historic and current collections of federal reports. The federal documents collection is notable in its coverage of Congressional reports, Census Bureau publications, Geological Survey maps, and Department of Labor documents.

The State Library is governed by a board of trustees, four of whom are citizens appointed by the Governor. The President of the Senate, the Speaker of the House of Representatives, and the State Secretary serve on the board ex officio. The Library is managed by the State Librarian who is appointed by the Governor. The Librarian is assisted by professional and support staff. In 1960, the State Library was officially designated as the George Fingold Library in tribute to the late Attorney General.

Trustees:

— The Honorable Thomas F. Birmingham, Senate President, *ex officio*

— The Honorable Thomas M. Finneran, Speaker of the House of Representatives, *ex officio*

— William F. Galvin, Secretary of State, *ex officio*

— Representative Marie J. Parente, Milford

— Frances Burke, Roslindale

— Andrea Gordon, Milton

— Robert H. McClain, Jr., Boston

State Librarian/Director — Stephen Fulchino

Chief Administrative Clerk — Joanne Swirbalus

Chief of Reference Services — Mary Ann Neary

Chief of Special Collections — Brenda Howitson

Legislative Reference Librarian — Pamela Schofield

Head Cataloger — Patricia Hewitt

Government Documents Librarian — Bette Siegel

Public Services Librarian — Tina Dong Vegelante

Serials Librarian — Anne Meringolo

BOSTON ATHENAEUM.

10fi BEACON STREET.

By the act of the General Court incorporating the Proprietors of the Boston Athenaeum, it is provided that the Governor, Lieutenant-Governor, the members of the Council, of the Senate, and of the House of Representatives, for the time being, shall have free access to the Library of the said corporation, and may visit and consult the same at all times, under the same regulations as may be provided by the by-laws of said corporation for the proprietors thereof.

The Boston Athenaeum is near the State House; and members who may wish to avail themselves of their privilege can receive a note of introduction to the Librarian by applying to the Sergeant-at-Arms.

MASSACHUSETTS HISTORICAL SOCIETY.

1154 BOYLSTON STREET, BOSTON.

Section 6 of the Act of Feb. 19, 1794, incorporating the Massachusetts Historical Society, provides that "either branch of the Legislature shall, and may have free access to the library and museum of said Society."

THE SOCIAL LAW LIBRARY.

ROOM 1200, SUFFOLK COUNTY COURT HOUSE.

The Social Law Library was founded in 1804 as a private association library, owned by and available only to its members. The Commonwealth appropriates annually a sum to the support of this library for providing law library service to the judiciary and all attorneys in the employ of the Commonwealth. Its 175,000 volume collection makes it the largest law library in Boston for the practicing lawyer. By an act of October 21, 1814 the library is open to all members of the General Court.

LEGAL HOLIDAYS IN MASSACHUSETTS

(See General Laws, Chapter 4, Section 7,
Eighteenth paragraph, as
most recently amended by
Chapter 451 of the Acts of 1985.)

New Year's Day . . . . January the first
Martin Luther King's Birthday . . . . . . Third Monday in January
Washington's Birthday . . . . Third Monday in February
Patriots' Day . . . . Third Monday in April
Memorial Day . . . . Last Monday in May
Independence Day . . . . July the fourth
Labor Day . . . . First Monday in September
Columbus Day . . . . Second Monday in October
Veterans' Day . . . . November the eleventh
Christmas Day . . . . December the twenty-fifth

And the Day designated by the Governor as a day of
Thanksgiving, customarily the fourth Thursday in November.

In Suffolk County only . . . . March the seventeenth
(Acts of 1962, Chapter 616)
June the seventeenth
(Acts of 1962, Chapter 616)

PROCLAMATIONS REQUIRED TO BE ISSUED
ANNUALLY BY THE GOVERNOR

New Orleans Day . . . . January the eighth
(General Laws, Chapter 6, Section 12F)

Albert Schweitzer's Reverence
for Life Day . . . . January the fourteenth
(General Laws, Chapter 6, Section 12T)

Martin Luther King, Jr. Day . . . . January the fifteenth
(General Laws, Chapter 6, Section 15S)

Jaycee Week and Jaycee Day . . . . . . Third week in January and
Wednesday of that week
(General Laws, Chapter 6, Section 15Y)

Child Nutrition Week . . . . Last week in January
(General Laws, Chapter 6, Section 15X)

American History Month . . . . Month of February
(General Laws, Chapter 6, Section 15C)

Tadeusz Kosciuszko Day. . . . . First Sunday in February
(General Laws, Chapter 6, Section 12BB)

USO Appreciation Day. . . . . February the fourth
(General Laws, Chapter 6, Section 12RR)

Boy Scout Week. . . . . February fifth to eleventh
(General Laws, Chapter 6, Section 15Y)

Lincoln Day . . . . February the twelfth
(General Laws, Chapter 6, Section 13)

Spanish War Memorial Day and
Maine Memorial Day . . . . February the fifteenth
(General Laws, Chapter 6, Section 14A)

Lithuanian Independence Day . . . . February the sixteenth
(General Laws, Chapter 6, Section 12GG)

Iwo Jima Day. . . . . February the nineteenth
(General Laws, Chapter 6, Section 12AA)

Homeless Unity Day . . . . February the twentieth
(General Laws, Chapter 6, Section 12QQ)

Washington Day.. . . . . Third Monday in February
(General Laws, Chapter 6, Section 12T)

Homeless Awareness Week . . . . Last week in February
(General Laws, Chapter 6, Section 15CCC)

Kalevala Day. . . . . February the twenty-eighth
(General Laws, Chapter 6, Section 15T)

Anniversary of the Boston Massacre. . . . . March the fifth
(General Laws, Chapter 6, Section 12D)

Slovak Independence Day . . . . March the fourteenth
(General Laws, Chapter 6, Section 12II)

Peter Francisco Day . . . . March the fifteenth
(General Laws, Chapter 6, Section 12S)

Evacuation Day . . . . March the seventeenth
(General Laws, Chapter 6, Section 12K)

Employ the Older Worker Week . . . . Third week in March
(General Laws, Chapter 6, Section 15GG)

Greek Independence Day . . . . March the twenty-fifth
(General Laws, Chapter 6, Section 15RR)

Italian American War Veterans of
the United States, Inc., Day . . . . . . March the twenty-seventh
(General Laws, Chapter 6, Section 15J)

Vietnam Veterans Day . . . . March the twenty-ninth
(General Laws, Chapter 6, Section 15MM)

Practical Nursing Education Week . . . . Last full week in March
(General Laws, Chapter 6, Section 15UU)

Parliamentary Law Month . . . . Month of April
(General Laws, Chapter 6, Section 15QQ)

School Library Media Month . . . . Month of April
(General Laws, Chapter 6, Section 15AAA)

Student Government Day . . . . First Friday of April
(General Laws, Chapter 6, Section 12M)

Veterans of World War I
Hospital Day . . . . First Sunday in April
(General Laws, Chapter 6, Section 12T)

Bataan-Corregidor Day . . . . April the ninth
(General Laws, Chapter 6, Section 15Z)

Former Prisoner of War
Recognition Day . . . . April the ninth
(General Laws, Chapter 6, Section 12PP)

Earth Week . . . . One week in April
(General Laws, Chapter 6, Section 14C)

George Demeter Day . . . . Second Wednesday in April
(Acts of 1989, Chapter 208)

Aunt's and Uncle's Day . . . . Second Sunday in April
(General Laws, Chapter 6, Section 12T)

Licensed Practical Nurse Week . . Second last full week in April
(General Laws, Chapter 6, Section 15LL)

Armenian Martyrs' Day . . . . April the twenty-fourth
(General Laws, Chapter 6, Section 15II)

Patriots' Day . . . . Third Monday in April
(General Laws, Chapter 6, Section 12J)

Earth Day . . . . Fourth Monday in April
(Acts of 1971, Chapter 70)

Arbor and Bird Day . . . . Last Friday in April
(General Laws, Chapter 6, Section 15)

Workers' Memorial Day . . . . Fourth Friday in April
(General Laws, Chapter 6, Section 15KKK)

Secretaries Week . . . . Last week in April
(General Laws, Chapter 6, Section 15AA)

School Principals'
Recognition Day . . . . April the twenty-seventh
(General Laws, Chapter 6, Section 12UU)

Exercise Tiger Day . . . . April the twenty-eighth
(General Laws, Chapter 6, Section 12OO)

Senior Citizens Month . . . . Month of May
(General Laws, Chapter 6, Section 15B)

Keep Massachusetts
Beautiful Month . . . . Month of May
(General Laws, Chapter 6, Section 15O)

Law Enforcement
Memorial Month . . . . Month of May
    (General Laws, Chapter 6, Section 15TTT)

Loyalty Day . . . . May the first
    (General Laws, Chapter 6, Section 12O)

Polish Constitution Day . . . . May the third
    (General Laws, Chapter 6, Section 12R)

Horace Mann Day . . . . May the fourth
    (General Laws, Chapter 6, Section 12T)

Whale Awareness Day . . . . First Thursday in May
    (General Laws, Chapter 6, Section 15ZZ)

Mother's Day . . . . Second Sunday in May
    (General Laws, Chapter 6, Section 12T)

Emergency Responders
Memorial Day . . . . Second Sunday in May
    (General Laws, Chapter 6, Section 15RRR)

Emergency Management Week . . . . Week following the
                                   second Sunday in May
    (General Laws, Chapter 6, Section 15SSS)

Police Officers' Week . . . . Week in which
                                     May 15 occurs
    (General Laws, Chapter 6, Section 15N)

Police Memorial Day . . . . May the fifteenth
    (General Laws, Chapter 6, Section 15JJJ)

Joshua James Day . . . . Third Sunday in May
    (General Laws, Chapter 6, Section 15XX)

Lafayette Day . . . . May the twentieth
    (General Laws, Chapter 6, Section 12H)

Maritime Day . . . . May the twenty-second
    (General Laws, Chapter 6, Section 12Y)

Deborah Samson Day . . . . May the twenty-third
    (General Laws, Chapter 6, Section 12FF)

American Indian Heritage Week.......... Third week in May
    (General Laws. Chapter 6. Section 12I)

Visiting Nurse Association Week......... Third week in May
    (General Laws. Chapter 6. Section 12JJ)

National Family Week................. Third week in May
    (General Laws. Chapter 6. Section 15KK)

Maritime Day.................... May the twenty-second
    (Acts of 1964. Chapter 282)

Massachusetts Art Week................ Last week in May
    (General Laws. Chapter 6. Section 15D)

Memorial Day.................... Last Monday in May
    (General Laws. Chapter 6. Section 12Q)

Presidents' Day................... May the twenty-ninth
    (General Laws. Chapter 6. Section 15VV)

Massachusetts National
  Guard Week....................... Week preceding
                               Armed Forces Day
    (General Laws. Chapter 6. Section 15BB)

Teachers' Day..................... First Sunday in June
    (General Laws. Chapter 6. Section 12X)

Garden Week .... Week beginning the
                               First Sunday in June
    (General Laws. Chapter 6. Section 12WW)

Retired Members of
  the Armed Forces Day .... First Monday in June
    (General Laws. Chapter 6. Section 15CC)

Public Employees
  Appreciation Day .... First Wednesday in June
    (General Laws. Chapter 6. Section 15TT)

Children's Day.................... Second Sunday in June
    (General Laws. Chapter 6. Section 12U)

State Walking Sunday.............. Second Sunday in June
    (General Laws. Chapter 6. Section 15NN)

Fire Fighters Memorial Sunday....... Second Sunday in June
    (General Laws. Chapter 6. Section 15JJ)

Rabies Prevention Week . . . . Second week in June
    (General Laws, Chapter 6, Section 15EEE)

Flag Day . . . . June the fourteenth
    (General Laws, Chapter 6, Section 14)

Father's Day . . . . Third Sunday in June
    (General Laws, Chapter 6, Section 12T)

Bunker Hill Day . . . . June the seventeenth
    (General Laws, Chapter 6, Section 12C)

Destroyer Escort Day . . . . Third Saturday in June
    (General Laws, Chapter 6, Section 12TT)

Battleship Massachusetts
Memorial Day . . . . Last Saturday in June
    (General Laws, Chapter 6, Section 15M)

Winthrop Beach
Awareness Day . . . . Last Saturday in June
    (Acts of 1989, Chapter 146)

John Carver Day . . . . Fourth Sunday in June
    (General Laws, Chapter 6, Section 15HH)

Korean War Veterans Day . . . . June the twenty-fifth
    (General Laws, Chapter 6, Section 12MM)

Saint Jean de Baptiste Day . . . . Fourth Sunday in June
    (General Laws, Chapter 6, Section 15OO)

Reflex Sympathetic Dystrophy
Awareness Month . . . . Month of July
    (General Laws, Chapter 6, Section 15OOO)

Independence Day . . . . July the fourth
    (General Laws, Chapter 6, Section 15DD)

Rose Fitzgerald Kennedy Day . . . . July the twenty-second
    (General Laws, Chapter 6, Section 12SS)

Jamaican Independence Day . . . . First Monday in August
    (General Laws, Chapter 6, Section 12Z)

Youth in Government Day . . . . First Friday in August
    (General Laws, Chapter 6, Section 15WW)

Public Employees Week .... First week of August
(General Laws, Chapter 6, Section 12CC)

Purple Heart Day.................... August the seventh
(General Laws, Chapter 6, Section 12T)

Liberty Tree Day................... August the fourteenth
(General Laws, Chapter 6, Section 15I)

Social Security Day................ August the fourteenth
(General Laws, Chapter 6, Section 12LL)

Susan B. Anthony Day .... August the twenty-sixth
(General Laws, Chapter 6, Section 15E)

Caribbean Week .... Last week in August
(General Laws, Chapter 6, Section 15QQQ)

Sight-Saving Month................. Month of September
(General Laws, Chapter 6, Section 12W)

Literacy Awareness Month .... Month of September
(General Laws, Chapter 6, Section 15NNN)

Grandparents Day............... Sunday following the first
Monday of September
(General Laws, Chapter 6, Section 12EE)

Labor Week..................... First week in September
(General Laws, Chapter 6, Section 12KK)

Alzheimer's Awareness Week .... First full week in
September
(General Laws, Chapter 6, Section 15GGG)

Endangered Species Day.............. Second Saturday in
September
(General Laws, Chapter 6, Section 15EE)

Commodore John Barry Day........ September the thirteenth
(General Laws, Chapter 6, Section 12E)

Constitution Day .... September the seventeenth
(General Laws, Chapter 6, Section 15A)

Native American Day ....Third Friday in September
(General Laws, Chapter 6, Section 12VV)

POW/MIA Day................. Third Friday in September
(General Laws, Chapter 6, Section 15BBB)

Cystic Fibrosis Week.................. Third full week in
September
(General Laws, Chapter 6, Section 15K)

National Hunting and
Fishing Day .... Fourth Saturday in
September
(General Laws, Chapter 6, Section 15W)

Pro-Life Month .... Month of October
(General Laws, Chapter 6, Section 15FF)

Lupus Awareness Month............... Month of October
(General Laws, Chapter 6, Section 15LLL)

Head Injury Awareness Month .... Month of October
(General Laws, Chapter 6, Section 15VVV)

Polish American Heritage Month .... Month of October
(General Laws, Chapter 6, Section 15WWW)

Employ Handicapped
Persons Week................... First Week in October
(General Laws, Chapter 6, Section 15F)

Employee Involvement and
Ownership Week................. First week in October
(General Laws, Chapter 6, Section 15HHH)

American Education Week............. One week in either
October or November
(General Laws, Chapter 6, Section 12G)

Social Justice for Ireland Day ...... First Saturday in October
(General Laws, Chapter 6, Section 15U)

Senior Citizens' Day .... First Sunday in October
(General Laws, Chapter 6, Section 12T)

Independent Living
Center Day................... First Sunday in October
(General Laws, Chapter 6, Section 15III)

Fire Prevention Week .... Date fixed by Fire Marshal

Town Meeting Day.................... October the eighth
    (General Laws, Chapter 6, Section 15PP)

Leif Ericson Day..................... October the eighth
    (General Laws, Chapter 6, Section 15YY)

Home Composting
  Recognition Week.............. Second week in October
    (General Laws, Chapter 6, Section 15UUU)

Pulaski Day........................ October the eleventh
    (General Laws, Chapter 6, Section 12B)

Columbus Day .... Second Monday in October
    (General Laws, Chapter 6, Section 12V)

White Cane Safety Day.............. October the fifteenth
    (General Laws, Chapter 6, Section 15V)

United Nations Day .... October the twenty-fourth
    (General Laws, Chapter 6, Section 12N)

State Constitution Day............ October the twenty-fifth
    (General Laws, Chapter 6, Section 14B)

Statue of Liberty
  Awareness Day............... October the twenty-sixth
    (General Laws, Chapter 6, Section 12HH)

Youth Honor Day................. October the thirty-first
    (General Laws, Chapter 6, Section 15G)

Hospice Week .... Second week in November
    (General Laws, Chapter 6, Section 15SS)

Geographic Education
  Awareness Week............ Second week of November
    (General Laws, Chapter 6, Section 15MMM)

United States Marine
  Corps Day...................... November the tenth
    (General Laws, Chapter 6, Section 15Q)

Armistice Day.................. November the eleventh
    (General Laws, Chapter 6, Section 15R)

Veterans Day................... November the eleventh
    (General Laws, Chapter 6, Section 12A)

Silver-Haired Legislature Days........ The Third Wednesday,
Thursday and Friday
in November
(General Laws, Chapter 6, Section 15DDD)

Thanksgiving Day .... Customarily the fourth
Thursday in November
(Proclamation not required by law but customarily
issued by the Governor)

John F. Kennedy Day .... Last Sunday in November
(General Laws, Chapter 6, Section 15L)

Disabled American Veterans'
Hospital Day................. First Sunday in December
(General Laws, Chapter 6, Section 12T)

Pearl Harbor Day .... December the seventh
(General Laws, Chapter 6, Section 12DD)

Civil Rights Week................... December eighth to
fourteenth
(General Laws, Chapter 6, Section 12P)

Army and Navy Union Day............ Second Saturday in
December
(General Laws, Chapter 6, Section 12T)

Human Rights Day .... December the tenth
(General Laws, Chapter 6, Section 12NN)

Samuel Slater Day .... December the twentieth
(General Laws, Chapter 6, Section 15PPP)

Veteran Fireman's Muster Day....... Date fixed by Governor
when issued
(General Laws, Chapter 6, Section 12L)

Boy Scout Week .... Date fixed by Governor
(General Laws, Chapter 6, Section 15H)

Traffic Safety Week .... Date fixed by Governor
(General Laws, Chapter 6, Section 15P)

CHAPTER 140 of the Acts of 1934.

AN ACT PROVIDING FACILITIES FOR THE PARKING OF MOTOR VEHICLES NEAR THE STATE HOUSE BY MEMBERS AND OFFICERS OF THE GENERAL COURT.

Be it enacted by the Senate and House of Representatives in General Court assembled, and by the authority of the same, as follows:

SECTION 1. The traffic commission of the city of Boston is hereby directed to provide in its regulations prohibiting or restricting the parking and standing of motor vehicles on public ways in said city that they shall not, so far as they relate to the easterly side of Hancock street between Mount Vernon and Derne streets, the southerly side of Derne street between Hancock and Bowdoin streets, and the westerly side of Bowdoin street between Mount Vernon and Beacon streets, apply to motor vehicles owned or used by members and officers of the general court.

SECTION 2. This act shall take effect upon its passage.

CHAPTER 183 of the Acts of 1962.

AN ACT REVISING THE LAW RELATIVE TO PARKING ON THE STATE HOUSE GROUNDS.

Whereas, The deferred operation of this act would tend to defeat its purpose, which is to provide forthwith for the establishment of rules and regulations relative to the parking of motor vehicles on the state house grounds in order to relieve traffic congestion in the vicinity of the state house, therefore it is hereby declared to be an emergency law, necessary for the immediate preservation of the public convenience.

Be it enacted by the Senate and House of Representatives in General Court assembled, and by the authority of the same, as follows:

SECTION 1. The parking area on the state house grounds, including that portion of Mount Vernon street between the westerly curb of Bowdoin street and the easterly curb of Hancock street, is hereby designated for the use of members of the general court, subject to such rules and regulations as the committee on rules of the two branches acting concurrently may adopt and for the use of such other persons as said committee may by such rules and regulations prescribe. Whoever violates any such rule or regulation shall be punished by a fine of not more than ten dollars for each such violation. The capitol police shall enforce said rules and regulations and for said purpose may exercise the powers conferred on them by section twelve of chapter eight of the General Laws.

SECTION 2. Chapter two hundred and eleven of the acts of nineteen hundred and fifty-one is hereby repealed.

DISTRICTS

CONGRESSIONAL, COUNCILLOR,
SENATORIAL AND REPRESENTATIVE

CONGRESSIONAL DISTRICTS

[As established by Chapter 105 of the Acts of 1992. See General Laws, Chapter 57.]

The United States census of 1990 was the basis of the apportionment.

DISTRICT NO. 1.

CITIES AND TOWNS	Population 1990	CITIES AND TOWNS	Population 1990
Berkshire County		Tyringham	369
Adams	9,445	Washington	615
Alford	418	West Stockbridge	1,483
Becket	1,481	Williamstown	8,220
Cheshire	3,479	Windsor	770
Clarksburg	1,745		
Dalton	7,155	*Franklin County.*	
Egremont	1,229	Ashfield	1,715
Florida	742	Bernardston	2,048
Great Barrington	7,725	Buckland	1,928
Hancock	628	Charlemont	1,249
Hinsdale	1,959	Colrain	1,757
Lanesborough	3,032	Conway	1,529
Lee	5,849	Deerfield	5,018
Lenox	5,069	Erving	1,372
Monterey	805	Gill	1,583
Mount Washington . . .	135	Greenfield	18,666
New Ashford	192	Hawley	317
New Marlborough . . .	1,240	Heath	716
NORTH ADAMS	16,797	Leverett	1,785
Otis	1,073	Leyden	662
Peru	779	Monroe	115
PITTSFIELD	48,622	Montague	8,316
Richmond	1,677	New Salem	802
Sandisfield	667	Northfield	2,838
Savoy	634	Orange	7,312
Sheffield	2,910	Rowe	378
Stockbridge	2,408	Shelburne	2,012

DISTRICT NO. 1. — *Concluded.*

Cities and Towns	Population 1990	Cities and Towns	Population 1990
Shutesbury	1,561	Westhampton	1,327
Sunderland	3,399	Williamsburg	2,515
Warwick	740	Worthington	1,156
Wendell	899		
Whately	1,375	*Middlesex County.*	
		Ashby	2,717
Hampden County.		Townsend	8,496
Blandford	1,187		
Chester	1,280	*Worcester County*	
Granville	1,403	Ashburnham	5,433
HOLYOKE	43,704	Athol	11,451
Montgomery	759	Barre	4,546
Russell	1,594	FITCHBURG	41,194
Southwick	7,667	GARDNER	20,125
Tolland	289	Hardwick	2,385
WESTFIELD	38,372	Hubbardston	2,797
West Springfield	27,537	LEOMINSTER	38,145
		Lunenburg:	
Hampshire County.		Prec. 1 *(in part)*	2,893
Amherst	35,228	Precinct 2	2,907
Belchertown	10,579	Precinct 3	2,942
Chesterfield	1,048	New Braintree	881
Cummington	785	North Brookfield	4,708
Easthampton	15,537	Oakham	1,503
Goshen	830	Petersham	1,131
Granby	5,565	Phillipston	1,485
Hatfield	3,184	Royalston	1,147
Huntington	1,987	Templeton	6,438
Middlefield	392	West Brookfield	3,532
Pelham	1,373	Westminster	6,191
Plainfield	571	Winchendon	8,805
Southampton	4,478		
		Totals	601,643

[John W. Olver.]

DISTRICT NO. 2.

CITIES AND TOWNS	Population 1990	CITIES AND TOWNS	Population 1990
Hampden County.		Blackstone	8,023
Agawam	27,323	Brookfield	2,968
Brimfield	3,001	Charlton	9,576
Chicopee	56,632	Douglas	5,438
East Longmeadow	13,367	Dudley	9,540
Hampden	4,709	East Brookfield	2,033
Holland	2,185	Hopedale	5,666
Longmeadow	15,467	Leicester	10,191
Ludlow	18,820	Mendon	4,010
Monson	7,776	Milford	25,355
Palmer	12,054	Millbury	12,228
Springfield	156,983	Millville	2,236
Wales	1,566	Oxford	12,588
Wilbraham	12,635	Southbridge	17,816
		Spencer	11,645
Hampshire County.		Sturbridge	7,775
Hadley	4,231	Sutton	6,824
Northampton	29,289	Uxbridge	10,415
South Hadley	16,685	Warren	4,437
Ware	9,808	Webster	16,196
Norfolk County.		Totals	601,642
Bellingham	14,877		
		[Richard E. Neal.]	
Worcester County.			
Auburn:			
Prec. 1 *(in part)*	2,827		
Precinct 2	2,987		
Prec. 3 *(in part)*	68		
Prec. 4 *(in part)*	700		
Precinct 5	2,692		

DISTRICT NO. 3.

CITIES AND TOWNS	Population 1990	CITIES AND TOWNS	Population 1990
Bristol County.		Franklin	22.095
ATTLEBORO	38.383	Medway	9.931
Dartmouth	27.244	Plainville	6.871
FALL RIVER:		Wrentham	9.006
Ward 1	10.980		
Ward 2	9.926	*Worcester County.*	
Ward 3	10.819	Auburn:	
Ward 4. Precinct A	3.411	Prec. 1 *(in part)*	14
Ward 4. Precinct B		Prec. 3 *(in part)*	3.387
(in part)	3.437	Prec. 4 *(in part)*	2.330
Ward 4. Precinct C		Berlin	2.293
(in part)	0	Boylston	3.517
Ward 6. Precincts		Clinton	13.222
A and B	6.451	Grafton	13.035
Mansfield:		Holden	14.628
Precinct 1	4.223	Lancaster:	
Precinct 2	3.655	Prec. 1 *(in part)*	1.422
Prec. 3 *(in part)*	533	Prec. 2 *(in part)*	2.318
Prec. 4 *(in part)*	727	Northborough	11.929
North Attleborough	25.038	Northbridge	13.371
Seekonk	13.046	Paxton	4.047
Somerset	17.655	Princeton	3.189
Swansea	15.411	Rutland	4.936
Westport	13.763	Shrewsbury	24.146
		Sterling	6.481
Middlesex County.		Upton	4.677
Holliston	12.926	West Boylston	6.611
Hopkinton	9.191	Westborough	14.133
		WORCESTER	169.759
Norfolk County.			
Foxborough:		Totals	601.642
Prec. 1 *(in part)*	1.685		
Prec. 3 *(in part)*	647	[James P. McGovern.]	
Prec. 4 *(in part)*	2.193		
Precinct 5	2.861		

DISTRICT NO. 4.

Cities and Towns	Population 1990	Cities and Towns	Population 1990
Bristol County.		Foxborough:	
Acushnet	9,554	Prec. 1 *(in part)*	1,604
Berkley	4,237	Precinct 2	2,847
Dighton	5,631	Prec. 3 *(in part)*	2,308
Easton:		Prec. 4 *(in part)*	492
Prec. 1 *(in part)*	2,223	Millis	7,613
Prec. 2 *(in part)*	2,903	Norfolk	9,270
Prec. 3 *(in part)*	3,389	Sharon	15,517
Prec. 4 *(in part)*	1,621	Wellesley	26,615
Fairhaven	16,132		
Fall River:		*Plymouth County.*	
Ward 4, Precinct B		Bridgewater	21,249
(in part)	296	Carver	10,590
Ward 4, Precinct C		East Bridgewater	11,104
(in part)	3,247	Halifax	6,526
Ward 5	10,423	Hanson	9,028
Ward 6, Precinct C	2,806	Lakeville	7,785
Ward 7	10,656	Marion	4,496
Ward 8	9,555	Mattapoisett	5,850
Ward 9	10,696	Middleborough	17,867
Freetown	8,522	Pembroke	14,544
Mansfield:		Plympton	2,384
Prec. 3 *(in part)*	3,325	Rochester	3,921
Prec. 4 *(in part)*	4,105	Rockland:	
New Bedford	99,922	Prec. 2 *(in part)*	431
Norton	14,265	Precinct 3	2,147
Raynham	9,867	Precinct 4	2,676
Rehoboth	8,656	Prec. 5 *(in part)*	919
		Wareham	19,232
Middlesex County.		West Bridgewater	6,389
Newton	82,585		
Sherborn	3,989	Totals	601,642
Norfolk County.			
Brookline	54,718	[Barney Frank.]	
Dover	4,915		

DISTRICT NO. 5.

Cities and Towns	Population 1990	Cities and Towns	Population 1990
Essex County.		Pepperell	10,098
Andover	29,151	Maynard	10,325
LAWRENCE	70,207	Shirley	6,118
Methuen	39,990	Stow	5,328
		Sudbury	14,358
Middlesex County.		Tewksbury	27,266
Acton	17,872	Tyngsborough	8,642
Ashland	12,066	Wayland	11,874
Ayer	6,871	Westford	16,392
Billerica	37,609		
Boxborough	3,343	*Worcester County.*	
Carlisle	4,333	Bolton	3,314
Chelmsford	32,383	Harvard	12,329
Concord	17,076	Lancaster:	
Dracut	25,594	Prec. 1 *(in part)*	2,010
Dunstable	2,236	Prec. 2 *(in part)*	911
Groton	7,511	Lunenburg:	
Hudson	17,233	Prec. 1 *(in part)*	375
Lincoln:		Southborough	6,628
Prec. 1 *(in part)*	77		
Littleton	7,051	Totals	601,643
LOWELL	103,439		
MARLBOROUGH	31,813		

[Martin T. Meehan.]

DISTRICT NO. 6.

Cities and Towns	Population 1990	Cities and Towns	Population 1990
Essex County.		Groveland	5,214
Amesbury	14,997	Hamilton	7,280
BEVERLY	38,195	HAVERHILL	51,418
Boxford	6,266	Ipswich	11,873
Danvers	24,174	LYNN	81,245
Essex	3,260	Lynnfield	11,274
Georgetown	6,384	Manchester-by-the-Sea	5,286
GLOUCESTER	28,716	Marblehead	19,971

DISTRICT NO. 6 — *Concluded.*

Cities and Towns	Population 1990	Cities and Towns	Population 1990
Merrimac	5,166	Wenham	4,212
Middleton	4,921	West Newbury	3,421
Nahant	3,828		
Newbury	5,623	*Middlesex County.*	
NEWBURYPORT	16,317	Bedford	12,996
North Andover	22,792	Burlington	23,302
PEABODY	47,039	North Reading	12,002
Rockport	7,482	Reading:	
Rowley	4,452	Precinct 1	2,993
SALEM	38,091	Prec. 8 *(in part)*	1,967
Salisbury	6,882	Wilmington	17,651
Saugus	25,549		
Swampscott	13,650	Totals	601,643
Topsfield	5,754		

[John F. Tierney.]

DISTRICT NO. 7.

Cities and Towns	Population 1990	Cities and Towns	Population 1990
Middlesex County.		Precinct 5	2,625
Arlington	44,630	Precinct 6	2,913
EVERETT	35,701	Precinct 7	3,000
Framingham	64,989	Prec. 8 *(in part)*	889
Lexington	28,974	Stoneham	22,203
Lincoln:		Wakefield	24,825
Prec. 1 *(in part)*	4,487	WALTHAM	57,878
Precinct 2	3,102	Weston	10,200
MALDEN	53,884	Winchester	20,267
MEDFORD	57,407	WOBURN	35,943
MELROSE	28,150		
Natick	30,510	*Suffolk County.*	
Reading:		REVERE	42,786
Precinct 2	2,638	Winthrop	18,127
Precinct 3	2,738		
Precinct 4	2,776	Totals	601,642

[Edward J. Markey.]

DISTRICT NO. 8.

Cities and Towns	Population 1990	Cities and Towns	Population 1990
Middlesex County.		Ward 14	31,196
Belmont	24,720	Ward 15, Precincts	
CAMBRIDGE	95,802	1, 2, 3, 4, 5, 7, 8	
SOMERVILLE	76,210	and 9	16,989
Watertown	33,284	Ward 17, Precincts	
		1, 2, 3, 5, 6, 7, 8, 9,	
Suffolk County.		10 and 11	18,168
BOSTON:		Ward 18, Precincts	
Ward 1	32,941	1, 2, 3, 4, 5, 6, 15	
Ward 2	14,718	and 21	22,565
Ward 4	28,789	Ward 21	47,011
Ward 5, Precincts		Ward 22	29,193
1, 2, 3, 4, 6, 7, 8,		Ward x Precinct x	
9 and 10	33,675	(Boston Harbor—	
Ward 5, Precinct 5		Deer Island)	1,282
(in part)	826	CHELSEA	25,431
Ward 9	14,767		
Ward 10	22,282	Totals	601,643
Ward 11, Precincts			
1, 2, 3, 4 and 5	10,817	[Joseph P. Kennedy, II.]
Ward 12	17,698	

DISTRICT NO. 9.

Cities and Towns	Population 1990	Cities and Towns	Population 1990
Bristol County.		Canton	18,530
Easton:		Dedham	23,782
Prec. 1 *(in part)*	1,645	Medfield	10,531
Prec. 2 *(in part)*	520	Milton	25,725
Prec. 3 *(in part)*	404	Needham	27,557
Prec. 4 *(in part)*	2,893	Norwood	28,700
Precinct 5	4,209	Randolph	30,093
TAUNTON	49,832	Stoughton	26,777
		Walpole	20,212
Norfolk County.		Westwood	12,557
Braintree	33,836		

DISTRICT NO. 9 — *Concluded.*

Cities and Towns	Population 1990	Cities and Towns	Population 1990
Plymouth County.		Ward 8.	11,588
BROCKTON:		Ward 11. Precincts	
Ward 1.	11,778	6, 7, 8, 9 and 10 . .	9,360
Ward 2. Precincts		Ward 13.	18,110
B. C and D	10,690	Ward 15, Prec. 6 . . .	1,135
Ward 3.	12,114	Ward 16.	24,241
Ward 4.	14,338	Ward 17, Precincts	
Ward 5. Precinct A		4, 12, 13 and 14 . .	7,569
(in part)	217	Ward 18, Precincts	
Ward 5. Precinct C .	3,337	7, 8, 9, 10, 11, 12, 13,	
		14, 16, 17, 18, 19,	
Suffolk County.		20, 22 and 23	33,744
BOSTON:		Ward 19.	23,773
Ward 3.	25,407	Ward 20.	39,477
Ward 5, Precinct 5			
(in part)	1,501	Totals	601,643
Ward 6.	15,470		
Ward 7.	19,991	[John Joseph Moakley.]	

DISTRICT NO. 10.

Cities and Towns	Population 1990	Cities and Towns	Population 1990
Barnstable County.		Sandwich	15,489
Barnstable.	40,949	Truro.	1,573
Bourne	16,064	Wellfleet.	2,493
Brewster	8,440	Yarmouth	21,174
Chatham	6,579		
Dennis	13,864	*Dukes County.*	
Eastham	4,462	Chilmark.	650
Falmouth	27,960	Edgartown	3,062
Harwich	10,275	Gay Head	201
Mashpee	7,884	Gosnold	98
Orleans	5,838	Oak Bluffs	2,804
Provincetown	3,561	Tisbury	3,120

DISTRICT NO. 10 — *Concluded.*

Cities and Towns	Population 1990	Cities and Towns	Population 1990
West Tisbury	1,704	Duxbury	13,895
		Hanover	11,912
Nantucket County		Hingham	19,821
Nantucket	6,012	Hull	10,466
		Kingston	9,045
Norfolk County		Marshfield	21,531
Avon	4,558	Norwell	9,279
Cohasset	7,075	Plymouth	45,608
Holbrook	11,140	Rockland:	
Quincy	84,985	Precinct 1	3,309
Weymouth	54,063	Prec. 2 *(in part)*	2,191
		Prec. 5 *(in part)*	1,724
Plymouth County		Precinct 6	2,726
Abington	13,817	Scituate	16,786
Brockton:		Whitman	13,240
Ward 2, Prec. A	3,822		
Ward 5, Precinct A		Totals	601,642
(in part)	3,735		
Ward 5, Precincts			
B and D	6,606	[William D. Delahunt.]	
Ward 6	12,098		
Ward 7	14,053		

COUNCILLOR DISTRICTS.

(With Councillors for 1997-98)

[As established by Chapter 274, Section 2, of the Acts of 1993, and amended by Chapter 12 of the Acts of 1994, based on the Federal Census of 1990. See General Laws, Chapter 57.]

I. The First Plymouth and Bristol, the First Bristol, the Second Bristol, the Cape and Islands and the Plymouth and Barnstable Senatorial Districts.

Barnstable, Bourne, Brewster, Chatham, Dennis, Eastham, Falmouth, Harwich, Mashpee, Orleans, Provincetown, Sandwich, Truro, Wellfleet and Yarmouth, *in the county of Barnstable*; Acushnet, Berkley, Dartmouth, Dighton, Fairhaven, FALL RIVER, Freetown, NEW BEDFORD, Raynham, Somerset, Swansea, TAUNTON, and Westport, *in the county of Bristol*; Chilmark, Edgartown, Gay Head, Gosnold, Oak Bluffs, Tisbury and West Tisbury, *in the county of Dukes County*; Nantucket, *in the county of Nantucket*; and Bridgewater, Carver, Halifax, Hanson, Kingston, Lakeville, Marion, Mattapoisett, Middleborough, Pembroke, Plymouth, Plympton, Rochester and Wareham, *in the county of Plymouth.* [David F. Constantine, New Bedford.]

II. The Middlesex, Norfolk and Worcester, the Norfolk, Bristol and Middlesex, the Norfolk, Bristol and Plymouth, the Second Plymouth and Bristol and the Norfolk and Suffolk Senatorial Districts.

ATTLEBORO, Easton, Mansfield, North Attleborough, Norton, Rehoboth and Seekonk, *in the county of Bristol*; Ashland, Framingham, Holliston, Hopkinton, Natick and Sherborn, *in the county of Middlesex*; Canton, precincts 4, 5, and 6, Dedham, Dover, Foxborough, Franklin, Medfield, Medway, Millis, Needham, Norfolk, Norwood, Plainville, Sharon, Stoughton, Walpole, Wellesley, precincts B, F and G, Westwood and Wrentham, *in the county of Norfolk*; Abington, precincts 1 and 2, BROCKTON, East Bridgewater, Hanover, Rockland, precinct 8, West Bridgewater and Whitman, *in the county of Plymouth*; BOSTON, ward 18, precincts 10, 11, 12, 17, 18, 19, 20, 22 and 23, ward 19, precincts 10, 11 and 13 and ward 20, *in the county of Suffolk*; and Westborough, precinct 3, *in the county of Worcester.* [Kelly A. Timilty, Canton.]

III. The First Middlesex, the Fifth Middlesex, the First Middlesex and Norfolk, the Middlesex and Suffolk and the Middlesex and Worcester Senatorial Districts.

Acton. Ayer, Bedford, Belmont, Boxborough, CAMBRIDGE, ward 7, precincts 3 and 4, ward 9, precinct 2, ward 10, precincts 1, 2 and 4, and ward 11, precincts 1 and 2, Carlisle, Chelmsford, Concord, Dunstable, Groton, Hudson, Lexington, precincts 2, 3, 4, 8 and 9, Lincoln, Littleton, LOWELL, MARLBOROUGH, Maynard, NEWTON, Pepperell, Shirley, Stow, Sudbury, Tyngsborough, WALTHAM, Watertown, Wayland, Westford and Weston, *in the county of Middlesex*; Brookline and Wellesley, precincts A. C, D and E, *in the county of Norfolk*; BOSTON, ward 21, precincts 9, 10, 11, 12, 13, 14, 15 and 16 and ward 22, precincts 3, 4, 5, 6, 7, 8, 9, 10, 11, 12 and 13, *in the county of Suffolk*; and Berlin, Harvard, Northborough, Southborough and Westborough, precincts 1, 2 and 4, *in the county of Worcester*. [Cynthia Stone Creem, Newton.] \

IV. The Norfolk and Plymouth, the Plymouth and Norfolk, the First Suffolk, the Second Suffolk and the Suffolk and Norfolk Senatorial Districts.

Avon, Braintree, Canton, precincts 1, 2 and 3, Cohasset, Holbrook, Milton, QUINCY, Randolph and Weymouth, *in the county of Norfolk*; BOSTON, ward 3, precincts 7 and 8, ward 4, ward 5, ward 6, ward 7, ward 8, ward 9, ward 10, ward 11, ward 12, ward 13, ward 14, ward 15, ward 16, ward 17, ward 18, precincts 1, 2, 3, 4, 5, 6, 7, 8, 9, 13, 14, 15, 16 and 21, ward 19, precincts 1, 2, 3, 4, 5, 6, 7, 8, 9 and 12, ward 21, precincts 1, 2, 3 and 4, and Boston Harbor Island, ward x, precinct x, *in the county of Suffolk*; and Abington, precincts 3 and 4, Duxbury, Hingham, Hull, Marshfield, Norwell, Rockland, precincts 1, 2, 3, 4, 5, 6 and 7, and Scituate, *in the county of Plymouth*. [Christopher A. Iannella, Jr., Boston.]

V. The First Essex, the Second Essex, the Third Essex, the First Essex and Middlesex and the Second Essex and Middlesex Senatorial Districts.

Amesbury, Andover, BEVERLY, Boxford, Danvers, Essex, Georgetown, GLOUCESTER, Groveland, Hamilton, HAVERHILL, Ipswich, LAWRENCE, LYNN, Lynnfield, Manchester-by-the-Sea, Marblehead, Merrimac, Methuen, Middleton, Nahant, Newbury, NEWBURYPORT, North Andover, PEABODY, Rockport, Rowley, SALEM, Salisbury, Saugus, precincts 1, 3, 5, 7, 8, 9 and 10, Swampscott, Topsfield, Wenham and West Newbury, *in the county of Essex*; and Dracut, North Reading, Tewksbury and Wilmington, *in the county of Middlesex*. [Patricia A. Dowling, Lawrence.]

VI. The Second Middlesex, the Third Middlesex, the Fourth Middlesex, the Middlesex, Suffolk and Essex and the Suffolk and Middlesex Senatorial Districts.

Saugus, precincts 2, 4 and 6, *in the county of Essex*; Arlington, Billerica,
Burlington, CAMBRIDGE, ward 1, ward 2, ward 3, ward 4, ward 5, ward
6, ward 7, precincts 1 and 2, ward 8, ward 9, precincts 1, 3 and 4, ward
10, precinct 3, ward 11, precinct 3, EVERETT, Lexington, precincts 1, 5,
6 and 7, MALDEN, MEDFORD, MELROSE, Reading, SOMERVILLE,
Stoneham, Wakefield, WOBURN and Winchester, *in the county of
Middlesex*; and BOSTON, ward 1, ward 2, ward 3, precincts 1, 2, 3, 4, 5
and 6, ward 5, precincts 4 and 5, ward 21, precincts 5, 6, 7 and 8 and
ward 22, precincts 1 and 2, CHELSEA, REVERE and Winthrop, *in the
county of Suffolk.* [Dorothy A. Kelly Gay, Somerville.]

VII. The First Worcester, the Worcester, Hampden, Hampshire and
Franklin, the Second Worcester, the Worcester and Middlesex, and the
Worcester and Norfolk Senatorial Districts.

Erving, New Salem, Northfield, Orange and Warwick, *in the county of
Franklin*; Brimfield, Holland, Monson, Palmer and Wales, *in the county
of Hampden*; Belchertown and Ware, *in the county of Hampshire*;
Ashby and Townsend, *in the county of Middlesex*; Bellingham, *in the
county of Norfolk*; Ashburnham, Athol, Auburn, Barre, Blackstone,
Bolton, Boylston, Brookfield, Charlton, Clinton, Douglas, Dudley,
East Brookfield, FITCHBURG, GARDNER, Grafton, Hardwick, Holden,
Hopedale, Hubbardston, Lancaster, Leicester, LEOMINSTER,
Lunenburg, Mendon, Milford, Millbury, Millville, New Braintree,
North Brookfield, Northbridge, Oakham, Oxford, Paxton, Petersham,
Phillipston, Princeton, Royalston, Rutland, Shrewsbury, Southbridge,
Spencer, Sterling, Sturbridge, Sutton, Templeton, Upton, Uxbridge,
Warren, Webster, West Boylston, West Brookfield, Westminster,
Winchendon and WORCESTER, *in the county of Worcester.* [Jordan
Levy, Worcester.]

VIII. The Berkshire, Hampden, Hampshire and Franklin, the Hampshire
and Franklin, the First Hampden and Hampshire, the Second Hampden and
Hampshire and the Hampden Senatorial Districts.

Adams, Alford, Becket, Cheshire, Clarksburg, Dalton, Egremont, Florida,
Great Barrington, Hancock, Hinsdale, Lanesborough, Lee, Lenox,
Monterey, Mount Washington, New Ashford, New Marlborough,
NORTH ADAMS, Otis, Peru, PITTSFIELD, Richmond, Sandisfield, Savoy,
Sheffield, Stockbridge, Tyringham, Washington, West Stockbridge,
Williamstown and Windsor, *in the county of Berkshire*; Ashfield,
Bernardston, Buckland, Charlemont, Colrain, Conway, Deerfield, Gill,
Greenfield, Hawley, Heath, Leverett, Leyden, Monroe, Montague,
Rowe, Shelburne, Shutesbury, Sunderland, Wendell and Whately, *in*

the county of Franklin; Agawam, Blandford, Chester, CHICOPEE, East Longmeadow, Granville, Hampden, HOLYOKE, Longmeadow, Ludlow, Montgomery, Russell, Southwick, SPRINGFIELD, Tolland, West Springfield, WESTFIELD and Wilbraham, *in the county of Hampden*; Amherst, Chesterfield, Cummington, Easthampton, Goshen, Granby, Hadley, Hatfield, Huntington, Middlefield, NORTHAMPTON, Pelham, Plainfield, South Hadley, Southampton, Westhampton, Williamsburg and Worthington, *in the county of Hampshire*. [Edward M. O'Brien, Easthampton.]

SENATORIAL DISTRICTS

(With Senators for 1997-98)

[As established by Chapter 274. Section 3, of the Acts of 1993, based on the Federal census of 1990. See General Laws, Chapter 57.]

[Average ratio for the State. Inhabitants, 150,411.]

BERKSHIRE, HAMPDEN, HAMPSHIRE AND FRANKLIN. — Adams, Alford, Becket, Cheshire, Clarksburg, Dalton, Egremont, Florida, Great Barrington, Hancock, Hinsdale, Lanesborough, Lee, Lenox, Monterey, Mount Washington, New Ashford, New Marlborough, NORTH ADAMS, Otis, Peru, PITTSFIELD, Richmond, Sandisfield, Savoy, Sheffield, Stockbridge, Tyringham, Washington, West Stockbridge, Williamstown and Windsor, *in the county of Berkshire*; Blandford, Chester, Granville and Tolland, *in the county of Hampden*; Cummington, Middlefield, Plainfield and Worthington, *in the county of Hampshire*; and Charlemont, Hawley, Heath, Monroe and Rowe, *in the county of Franklin.* [Andrea F. Nuciforo, Jr., Pittsfield.]

FIRST BRISTOL. — FALL RIVER, Freetown, Somerset, Swansea and Westport. [Thomas C. Norton, Fall River.]

SECOND BRISTOL. — NEW BEDFORD, Acushnet, Dartmouth and Fairhaven. [Mark C. Montigny, New Bedford.]

FIRST PLYMOUTH AND BRISTOL. — Bridgewater, Carver, Halifax, Lakeville, Marion, Mattapoisett, Middleborough and Rochester, *in the county of Plymouth*; and TAUNTON, Berkley, Dighton and Raynham, *in the county of Bristol.* [Marc R. Pacheco, Taunton.]

CAPE AND ISLANDS. — Barnstable, Brewster, Chatham, Dennis, Eastham, Falmouth, precincts numbered four and seven, Harwich, Mashpee, Orleans, Provincetown, Truro, Wellfleet and Yarmouth, *in the county of Barnstable*; Chilmark, Edgartown, Gay Head, Gosnold, Oak Bluffs, Tisbury and West Tisbury, *in the county of Dukes County*; and Nantucket, *in the county of Nantucket.* [Henri S. Rauschenbach, Brewster.]

FIRST ESSEX. — LYNN, Lynnfield, Marblehead, Nahant, Saugus, precincts numbered one, three, five, seven, eight, nine and ten, and Swampscott. [Edward J. Clancy, Jr., Lynn.]

SECOND ESSEX. — BEVERLY, PEABODY, SALEM and Danvers. [Frederick E. Berry, Peabody.]

THIRD ESSEX. — HAVERHILL, NEWBURYPORT, Amesbury, Merrimac, Methuen, North Andover, precincts numbered one, two, three and four, and Salisbury. [James P. Jajuga, Methuen.]

FIRST ESSEX AND MIDDLESEX. — GLOUCESTER, Boxford, Essex, Georgetown, Groveland, Hamilton, Ipswich, Manchester-by-the-Sea, Middleton, Newbury, North Andover, precincts numbered five and six, Rockport, Rowley, Topsfield, Wenham and West Newbury, *in the county of Essex*; and North Reading and Wilmington, *in the county of Middlesex*. [Bruce E. Tarr, Gloucester.]

SECOND ESSEX AND MIDDLESEX. — LAWRENCE and Andover, *in the county of Essex*; and Dracut and Tewksbury, *in the county of Middlesex*. [John D. O'Brien, Jr., Andover.]

HAMPSHIRE AND FRANKLIN. — NORTHAMPTON, Amherst, Chesterfield, Goshen, Hadley, Hatfield, Huntington, Pelham, South Hadley, Westhampton and Williamsburg, *in the county of Hampshire*; and Ashfield, Bernardston, Buckland, Colrain, Conway, Deerfield, Gill, Greenfield, Leverett, Leyden, Montague, Shelburne, Shutesbury, Sunderland, Wendell and Whately, *in the county of Franklin*. [Stanley C. Rosenberg, Amherst.]

HAMPDEN — CHICOPEE, wards numbered two, four and five, SPRINGFIELD, wards numbered one, three and four, ward numbered five, precinct A, and ward numbered six, Agawam and West Springfield. [Linda J. Melconian, Springfield.]

FIRST HAMPDEN AND HAMPSHIRE. — SPRINGFIELD, ward numbered two, ward numbered five, precincts B, C, D, E, F, G and H, and wards numbered seven and eight, East Longmeadow, Hampden, Longmeadow, Ludlow and Wilbraham, *in the county of Hampden*; and Granby, *in the county of Hampshire*. [Brian P. Lees, East Longmeadow.]

SECOND HAMPDEN AND HAMPSHIRE. — CHICOPEE, wards numbered one, three, six, seven, eight and nine, HOLYOKE, WESTFIELD, Montgomery, Russell and Southwick, *in the county of Hampden*; and Easthampton and Southampton, *in the county of Hampshire*. [Michael R. Knapik, Westfield.]

FIRST MIDDLESEX. — LOWELL, Dunstable, Groton, Pepperell, Tyngsborough and Westford. [Steven C. Panagiotakos, Lowell.]

SECOND MIDDLESEX. — MEDFORD, SOMERVILLE, ward numbered one, precincts numbered two and three, ward numbered two, precincts numbered two and three, and wards numbered three, four, five, six and seven, WOBURN, ward numbered two, and Winchester. [Charles E. Shannon, Jr., Winchester.]

THIRD MIDDLESEX — MALDEN, MELROSE, Reading, Stoneham and Wakefield. [Richard R. Tisei, Wakefield.]

FOURTH MIDDLESEX. — CAMBRIDGE, ward numbered eleven, precinct numbered three, WOBURN, wards numbered one, three, four, five, six and seven, Arlington, Billerica, Burlington and Lexington, precincts numbered one, five, six and seven. [Robert A. Havern III, Arlington.]

FIFTH MIDDLESEX. — WALTHAM, wards numbered one and two, ward numbered three, precinct numbered one, ward numbered six, precinct numbered one, and ward numbered seven, Bedford, Carlisle, Chelmsford, Concord, Lexington, precincts numbered two, three, four, eight and nine, Lincoln, Sudbury, Wayland and Weston. [Susan C. Fargo, Lincoln.]

FIRST MIDDLESEX AND NORFOLK. — NEWTON, *in the county of Middlesex*; and Brookline and Wellesley, precincts A, C, D and E, *in the county of Norfolk.* [Lois G. Pines, Newton.]

MIDDLESEX, NORFOLK AND WORCESTER. — Ashland, Framingham, Holliston, Hopkinton and Natick, precincts numbered one, two, three, four, five and eight, *in the county of Middlesex*; Franklin, and Medway, *in the county of Norfolk*; and Westborough, precinct numbered three, *in the county of Worcester.* [David P. Magnani, Framingham.]

MIDDLESEX AND SUFFOLK. — CAMBRIDGE, ward numbered seven, precincts numbered three and four, ward numbered nine, precinct numbered two, ward numbered ten, precincts numbered one, two and four, and ward numbered eleven, precincts numbered one and two, WALTHAM, ward numbered three, precinct numbered two, wards numbered four and five, ward numbered six, precinct numbered two, and wards numbered eight and nine, Belmont and Watertown, *in the county of Middlesex*; and BOSTON, ward numbered twenty-one, precincts numbered nine, ten, eleven, twelve, thirteen, fourteen, fifteen and sixteen, and ward numbered twenty-two, precincts numbered three, four, five, six, seven, eight, nine, ten, eleven, twelve and thirteen, *in the county of Suffolk.* [Warren E. Tolman, Watertown.]

MIDDLESEX AND WORCESTER. — MARLBOROUGH, Acton, Ayer, Boxborough, Hudson, Littleton, Maynard, Shirley and Stow, *in the county of Middlesex*; and Berlin, Harvard, Northborough, Southborough and Westborough, precincts numbered one, two and four, *in the county of Worcester.* [Robert A. Durand, Marlborough.]

NORFOLK AND PLYMOUTH. — QUINCY, Braintree, precincts numbered one, two, three, four, five, eight, ten, eleven and twelve, and Holbrook, *in the county of Norfolk*; and Abington, precincts numbered three and four, Norwell and Rockland, precincts numbered one, two, three, four, five, six and seven, *in the county of Plymouth.* [Michael W. Morrissey, Quincy.]

NORFOLK, BRISTOL AND PLYMOUTH. — Foxborough, Medfield, Sharon, Stoughton and Walpole, *in the county of Norfolk*; Easton, precincts numbered three and six, Mansfield, Norton, Rehoboth and Seekonk, *in the county of Bristol*; and West Bridgewater, *in the county of Plymouth.* [William R. Keating, Sharon.]

NORFOLK, BRISTOL AND MIDDLESEX. — Millis, Needham, Norfolk, Plainville, Wellesley, precincts B, F and G, and Wrentham, *in the county of Norfolk*; ATTLEBORO and North Attleborough, *in the county of Bristol*; and Natick, precincts numbered six, seven, nine and ten, and Sherborn, *in the county of Middlesex.* [Cheryl A. Jacques, Needham.]

PLYMOUTH AND NORFOLK. — Duxbury, Hingham, Hull, Marshfield and Scituate, *in the county of Plymouth*; Braintree, precincts numbered six, seven and nine, Cohasset and Weymouth, *in the county of Norfolk.* [Robert L. Hedlund, Weymouth.]

SECOND PLYMOUTH AND BRISTOL. — BROCKTON, Abington, precincts numbered one and two, East Bridgewater, Hanover, Rockland, precinct numbered eight, and Whitman, *in the county of Plymouth*; and Easton, precincts numbered one, two A, two B, four and five, *in the county of Bristol.* [Robert S. Creedon, Jr., Brockton.]

PLYMOUTH AND BARNSTABLE. — Hanson, Kingston, Pembroke, Plymouth, Plympton and Wareham, *in the county of Plymouth*; and Bourne, Falmouth, precincts numbered one, two, three, five, six and eight, and Sandwich, *in the county of Barnstable.* [Therese Murray, Plymouth.]

FIRST SUFFOLK. — BOSTON, ward numbered three, precincts numbered seven and eight, ward numbered five, precincts numbered one, three, six, seven, eight, nine and ten, wards numbered six, seven and eight, ward numbered nine, precincts numbered one, two and three, wards numbered thirteen and fifteen, ward numbered sixteen, precincts numbered one and two, ward numbered seventeen, precincts numbered one and two, ward numbered twenty-one, precincts numbered one, two, three and four, and Boston Harbor Island, ward x precinct x. [Stephen F. Lynch, Boston.]

SECOND SUFFOLK. — BOSTON, ward numbered four, ward numbered five, precinct numbered two, ward numbered nine, precincts numbered four and five, ward numbered ten, ward numbered eleven, precincts numbered one, two, three, four and five, wards numbered twelve and fourteen, ward numbered seventeen, precincts numbered three, five, seven, eight, ten and twelve, ward numbered eighteen, precincts numbered two, three, six and twenty-one, and ward numbered nineteen, precincts numbered one and three. [Dianne Wilkerson, Boston.]

MIDDLESEX, SUFFOLK AND ESSEX. — CAMBRIDGE, ward numbered three, precincts numbered two and three, ward numbered four, precincts numbered one and two, ward numbered six, precincts numbered three and four, ward numbered seven, precincts numbered one and two, ward numbered eight, ward numbered nine, precincts numbered one, three and four, and ward numbered ten, precinct numbered three, EVERETT and SOMERVILLE, ward numbered one, precinct numbered one and ward numbered two, precinct numbered one, *in the county of Middlesex;* BOSTON, ward numbered two, ward numbered twenty-one, precincts numbered five, six, seven and eight, and ward numbered twenty-two, precincts numbered one and two, CHELSEA and REVERE, ward numbered six, *in the county of Suffolk;* and Saugus, precincts numbered two, four and six, *in the county of Essex.* [Thomas F. Birmingham, Chelsea.]

SUFFOLK AND MIDDLESEX. — BOSTON, ward numbered one, ward numbered three, precincts numbered one, two, three, four, five and six, and ward numbered five, precincts numbered four and five, REVERE, wards numbered one, two, three, four and five, and Winthrop, *in the county of Suffolk;* and CAMBRIDGE, wards numbered one and two, ward numbered three, precincts numbered one and four, ward numbered four, precincts numbered three and four, ward numbered five and ward numbered six, precincts numbered one and two, *in the county of Middlesex.* [Robert E. Travaglini, Boston.]

NORFOLK AND SUFFOLK. — Canton, precincts numbered four, five and six, Dedham, Dover, Norwood and Westwood, *in the county of Norfolk;* and BOSTON, ward numbered eighteen, precincts numbered ten, eleven, twelve, seventeen, eighteen, nineteen, twenty, twenty-two and twenty-three, ward numbered nineteen, precincts numbered ten, eleven and thirteen, and ward numbered twenty, *in the county of Suffolk.* [Marian Walsh, Boston.]

SUFFOLK AND NORFOLK. — BOSTON, ward numbered eleven, precincts numbered six, seven, eight, nine and ten, ward numbered sixteen, precincts numbered three, four, five, six, seven, eight, nine, ten, eleven and twelve, ward numbered seventeen, precincts numbered four, six, nine, eleven, thirteen and fourteen, ward numbered eighteen, precincts numbered one, four, five, seven, eight, nine, thirteen, fourteen, fifteen and sixteen, ward numbered nineteen, precincts numbered two, four, five, six, seven, eight, nine and twelve, *in the county of Suffolk;* and Avon, Canton, precincts numbered one, two and three, Milton and Randolph, *in the county of Norfolk.* [W. Paul White, Boston.]

FIRST WORCESTER. — WORCESTER, wards numbered one, two, three and four, ward numbered seven, precincts numbered one, two and three, and wards numbered nine and ten, Boylston, Clinton, Holden and West Boylston. [Robert A. Bernstein, Worcester.]

WORCESTER, HAMPDEN, HAMPSHIRE AND FRANKLIN. — Athol, Barre, Brookfield, East Brookfield, Hardwick, Hubbardston, New Braintree, North Brookfield, Oakham, Paxton, Petersham, Phillipston, Royalston, Rutland, Spencer, Sturbridge, Templeton, Warren, West Brookfield and Winchendon, *in the county of Worcester;* Brimfield, Holland, Monson, Palmer and Wales, *in the county of Hampden;* Belchertown and Ware, *in the county of Hampshire;* and Erving, New Salem, Northfield, Orange and Warwick, *in the county of Franklin.* [Stephen M. Brewer, Barre.]

SECOND WORCESTER. — WORCESTER, wards numbered five and six, ward numbered seven, precincts numbered four and five, and ward numbered eight, Auburn, Grafton, Hopedale, Leicester, Millbury, Shrewsbury, Sutton and Upton. [Matthew J. Amorello, Grafton.]

WORCESTER AND MIDDLESEX. — FITCHBURG, GARDNER, LEOMINSTER, Ashburnham, Bolton, Lancaster, Lunenburg, Princeton, Sterling and Westminster, *in the county of Worcester;* and Ashby and Townsend, *in the county of Middlesex.* [Robert A. Antonioni, Leominster.]

WORCESTER AND NORFOLK. — Blackstone, Charlton, Douglas, Dudley, Mendon, Milford, Millville, Northbridge, Oxford, Southbridge, Uxbridge and Webster, *in the county of Worcester;* and Bellingham, *in the county of Norfolk.* [Richard T. Moore, Uxbridge.]

REPRESENTATIVE DISTRICTS.*

[As established under authority of Chapter 273 of the Acts of 1993.
See General Laws, Chapter 57, Section 4.]
One To Be Elected From Each District.

Average ratio for Representative: Population 37,603.

BARNSTABLE, DUKES AND NANTUCKET COUNTIES
FIVE REPRESENTATIVES.

DISTRICT

1. —Brewster, Dennis, Precincts 1, 2, 4 and 5, and Yarmouth, precincts 1, 2, 3, 4 and 5. Thomas N. George (R), Yarmouth.
2. —Barnstable, Precincts 1, 2, 3, 4, 5, 6, 7, 8, 10 and 11, and Sandwich. Precinct 4. John C. Klimm (D), Barnstable.
3. —Bourne, Precincts 3, 4, 5 and 6. Falmouth, Precincts 3, 4, 7 and 8, Mashpee and Sandwich, Precincts 5, 6 and 7. Thomas S. Cahir (D), Bourne.
4. —Chatham, Dennis, Precinct 3, Eastham, Harwich, Orleans, Provincetown, Truro and Wellfleet. Shirley Gomes (R), Harwich.

BARNSTABLE, DUKES AND NANTUCKET. — Barnstable, Precinct 9, Yarmouth, Precinct 6, Falmouth, Precincts 1, 2, 5 and 6 *(Barnstable Co)*; Chilmark, Edgartown, Gay Head, Gosnold, Oak Bluffs, Tisbury and West Tisbury *(Dukes Co.)*; and Nantucket *(Nantucket Co.)*. Eric Turkington (D), Falmouth.

BERKSHIRE COUNTY
FOUR REPRESENTATIVES.

DISTRICT

1. —Adams, Clarksburg, Florida, Savoy, Williamstown and NORTH ADAMS. Daniel E. Bosley (D), North Adams.
2. —Becket, Cheshire, Dalton, Hancock, Hinsdale, Lanesborough, New Ashbord, Peru, Richmond, Washington, Windsor and PITTSFIELD, Ward 1, Precinct B *(Berkshire Co.)*; Ashfield, Buckland, Charlemont, Hawley, Monroe, Rowe and Shelburne *(Franklin Co.)*; Chester *(Hampden Co.)*; and Cummington, Goshen, Huntington, Middlefield and Plainfield *(Hampshire Co.)*. Shaun P. Kelly (R), Dalton.
3. —PITTSFIELD, Ward 1, Precinct A, and Wards 2, 3, 5, 6 and 7. Peter J. Larkin (D), Pittsfield.

* The Federal Census of 1990 was the basis of apportionment.

4. —Alford, Egremont, Great Barrington, Lee, Lenox, Monterey, Mount Washington, New Marlborough, Otis, Sandisfield, Sheffield, Stockbridge, Tyringham, West Stockbridge, and PITTSFIELD, Ward 4. Christopher J. Hodgkins (D), Lee.

BRISTOL COUNTY
FOURTEEN REPRESENTATIVES.

DISTRICT

1. —Foxborough *(Norfolk Co.)*; and Mansfield, Precincts 2, 3 and 4, and Norton *(Bristol Co.)*. Barbara C. Hyland (R), Foxborough.

2. —ATTLEBORO. John A. Lepper (R), Attleboro.

3. —TAUNTON, Wards 1, 2, 3, 4 and 5, Ward 7, Precinct A, and Ward 8, Precinct B. James H. Fagan (D), Taunton.

4. —Rehoboth, Seekonk, Swansea, Precincts 1 and 4, and TAUNTON, Ward 7, Precinct B, and Ward 8, Precinct A. Philip Travis (D), Rehoboth.

5. —Dighton, Somerset, Swansea, Precincts 2 and 3, and TAUNTON, Ward 6. Joan M. Menard (D), Somerset.

6. —FALL RIVER, Ward 4, Precincts A and C, Ward 7, Precincts A, C and D, and Wards 8 and 9, and Freetown, Precinct 1. David B. Sullivan (D), Fall River.

7. —FALL RIVER, Ward 1, Precincts B, C and D, Wards 2 and 3, Ward 4, Precinct B, and Ward 5, Precinct A. Robert Correia (D), Fall River.

8. —FALL RIVER, Ward 1, Precinct A, Ward 5, Precincts B and C, Ward 6, Ward 7, Precinct B, and Westport. Michael J. Rodrigues (D), Westport.

9. —Berkley, Dartmouth and Freetown, Precinct 2 *(Bristol Co.)*; and Lakeville, Precinct 1 *(Plymouth Co.)*. John F. Quinn (D), Dartmouth.

10. —Fairhaven *(Bristol Co.)*; and Marion, Mattapoisett, Rochester and Middleborough, Precincts 3 and 6 *(Plymouth Co.)*. William M. Straus (D), Mattapoisett.

11. —Acushnet, Freetown, Precinct 3, and NEW BEDFORD, Ward 1 and Ward 2, Precincts E and G *(Bristol Co.)*; and Lakeville, Precinct 2 *(Plymouth Co.)*. Robert M. Koczera (D), New Bedford.

12. —NEW BEDFORD, Ward 2, Precincts A, B, C, D and F, Ward 3, Ward 4, Precincts C, E and F, and Ward 5, Precinct G. Joseph B. McIntyre (D), New Bedford.

13. —NEW BEDFORD, Ward 4, Precincts A, B, D and G, Ward 5, Precincts A, B, C, D, E and F, and Ward 6. Antonio F. D. Cabral (D), New Bedford.

14. —Mansfield. Precincts 1, 5A and 5B, and North Attleborough *(Bristol Co.)*; and Plainville *(Norfolk Co.)*. Kevin Poirier (R), North Attleborough.

ESSEX COUNTY
SEVENTEEN REPRESENTATIVES.

DISTRICT

1. —Amesbury, Salisbury and NEWBURYPORT. Kevin L. Finnegan (R), Newburyport.
2. —Georgetown. Precinct 1, Groveland, HAVERHILL, Ward 3, Precinct 2, Ward 4, Precincts 1 and 3, and Ward 7, Precincts 2 and 3, Merrimac, Newbury, Rowley and West Newbury. Harriett L. Stanley (D), Merrimac.
3. —HAVERHILL, Wards 1, 2, 5 and 6, Ward 3, Precincts 1 and 3, Ward 4, Precinct 2, and Ward 7, Precinct 1. Brian S. Dempsey (D), Haverhill.
4. —Boxford, Hamilton, Ipswich, Manchester-by-the-Sea, Wenham, and Georgetown, Precinct 2. Forrester A. Clark, Jr., (R), Hamilton.
5. —Essex, Rockport and GLOUCESTER. Anthony J. Verga (D), Gloucester.
6. —BEVERLY. Michael P. Cahill (D), Beverly.
7. —SALEM. J. Michael Ruane (D), Salem.
8. —LYNN, Ward 3, Precinct 4, Marblehead and Swampscott. Douglas W. Petersen (D), Marblehead.
9. —LYNN, Ward 1, Precincts 1, 2 and 3, Lynnfield, Precinct 2, and Saugus. Steven Angelo (D), Saugus.
10. —LYNN, Ward 1, Precinct 4, Ward 2, Ward 3, Precincts 1, 2 and 3, Ward 4 and Ward 5, Precinct 4. Robert F. Fennell (D), Lynn.
11. —LYNN, Ward 5, Precincts 1, 2 and 3, and Wards 6 and 7, and Nahant. Thomas M. McGee (D), Lynn.
12. —PEABODY, Wards 1, 2, 3, 4 and 5. John P. Slattery (D), Peabody.
13. —Danvers, PEABODY, Ward 6, and Topsfield. Theodore C. Speliotis (D), Danvers.
14. —LAWRENCE, Ward A, Precincts 1, 3 and 4, Ward E, Precincts 2 and 3, and Ward F, Precincts 1, 2 and 4, and North Andover, Precincts 1, 2, 3 and 6. Donna F. Cuomo (R), North Andover.
15. —Methuen, Precincts 1, 3, 4, 5, 6, 7, 8, 9, 10, 11 and 12. Arthur J. Broadhurst (D), Methuen.
16. —LAWRENCE, Ward A, Precinct 2, Wards B and C, Ward D, Precincts 3 and 4, and Ward F, Precinct 3, and Methuen, Precinct 2. M. Paul Iannuccillo (D), Lawrence.

17. —Andover, Precincts 1, 2, 3, 4, 6, 7 and 8, and LAWRENCE, Ward D, Precincts 1 and 2, and Ward E, Precincts 1 and 4. Barry R. Finegold (D), Andover.

FRANKLIN COUNTY
TWO REPRESENTATIVES.

DISTRICT

1. —Athol *(Worcester Co.)*; Chesterfield, Williamsburg and Worthington *(Hampshire Co.)*; and Conway, Deerfield, Leverett, Montague, New Salem, Sunderland, Wendell and Whately *(Franklin Co.)*. Stephen Kulik (D), Worthington.

2. — Bernardston, Colrain, Erving, Gill, Greenfield, Heath, Leyden, Northfield, Orange and Warwick *(Franklin Co.)*; and Royalston *(Worcester Co.)*. John F. Merrigan (D), Greenfield.

HAMPDEN COUNTY
THIRTEEN REPRESENTATIVES.

DISTRICT

1. —Brimfield, Holland and Palmer *(Hampden Co.)*; Belchertown, Precinct B, and Ware *(Hampshire Co.)*; and East Brookfield and Sturbridge, Precinct 2, *(Worcester Co.)*. Patrick F. Landers III (D), Palmer.

2. — East Longmeadow, Precincts 2 and 3, Hampden, Longmeadow, Monson, Wales and SPRINGFIELD, Ward 6, Precinct B. Mary S. Rogeness (R), Longmeadow.

3. — Agawam, Blandford, Granville, Russell, Southwick and Tolland. Daniel F. Keenan (D), Blandford.

4. —Montgomery and WESTFIELD. Cele Hahn (R), Westfield.

5. — HOLYOKE, Wards 1, 2, 4, 6 and 7, Ward 3, Precinct B, and Ward 5, Precinct A. Evelyn G. Chesky (D), Holyoke.

6. — CHICOPEE, Ward 3, Precinct C, HOLYOKE, Ward 3, Precinct A and Ward 5, Precinct B, and West Springfield. Walter A. DeFilippi (R), West Springfield.

7. —Belchertown, Precincts A and C, and Granby *(Hampshire Co.)*; and CHICOPEE, Ward 6 and Ludlow *(Hampden Co.)*. Thomas M. Petrolati (D), Ludlow.

8. — CHICOPEE, Wards 1, 7, 8 and 9, Ward 2, Precincts C and D, Ward 3, Precincts A and B, and Ward 4, Precincts A and C. Joseph F. Wagner (D), Chicopee.

9. — CHICOPEE, Ward 2, Precincts A and B, Ward 4, Precinct B and Ward 5, and SPRINGFIELD, Ward 2 and Ward 8, Precincts A and D. Dennis M. Murphy (D), Springfield.

10. — SPRINGFIELD, Ward 1, Ward 3. Precincts B, C, D, F and H, and Ward 6, Precincts A and E. Anthony M. Scibelli (D), Springfield.
11. — SPRINGFIELD, Ward 5, Precincts C, D, E, G and H, Ward 7, Precincts C, F, G and H, and Ward 8, Precincts B, C, E, F, G and H. Paul E. Caron (D), Springfield.
12. — SPRINGFIELD, Ward 3, Precincts A, E and G, Ward 4, Ward 5, Precincts A, B and F, and Ward 7, Precinct A. Benjamin Swan (D), Springfield.
13. — East Longmeadow, Precincts 1 and 4, SPRINGFIELD, Ward 6, Precincts C, D, F, G and H, and Ward 7, Precincts B, D and E, and Wilbraham. Gale D. Candaras (D), Wilbraham.

HAMPSHIRE COUNTY
THREE REPRESENTATIVES.

DISTRICT
1. — Hatfield, Southampton, Westhampton and NORTHAMPTON. William P. Nagle, Jr. (D), Northampton.
2. — Easthampton, Hadley and South Hadley. Nancy Flavin (D), Easthampton.
3. — Amherst and Pelham *(Hampshire Co.)*; and Shutesbury *(Franklin Co.)*. Ellen Story (D), Amherst.

MIDDLESEX COUNTY
THIRTY-NINE REPRESENTATIVES.

DISTRICT
1. — Ayer, Precinct 1, Groton, Pepperell and Townsend *(Middlesex Co.)*; and Lunenburg *(Worcester Co.)*. Robert S. Hargraves (R), Groton.
2. — Harvard *(Worcester Co.)*; and Ayer, Precinct 2, Littleton and Westford *(Middlesex Co.)*. Geoffrey D. Hall (D), Westford.
3. — Bolton and Lancaster *(Worcester Co.)*; and Hudson, Shirley and Stow *(Middlesex Co.)*. Patricia A. Walrath (D), Stow.
4. — Berlin and Northborough, Precinct 3 *(Worcester Co.)*; and MARLBOROUGH *(Middlesex Co.)*. Stephen P. LeDuc (D), Marlborough.
5. — Millis, Precinct 2 *(Norfolk Co.)*; and Natick and Sherborn *(Middlesex Co.)*. Douglas W. Stoddart (R), Natick.
6. — Framingham, Precincts 1, 2, 3, 4, 5, 6, 7, 9, 10 and 13. John H. Stasik (D), Framingham.
7. — Ashland and Framingham, Precincts 8, 11, 12, 14, 15, 16 and 17. John A. Stefanini (D), Framingham.

8. —Holliston and Hopkinton *(Middlesex Co.)*; Medway *(Norfolk Co.)*; and Southborough *(Worcester Co.)*. Barbara Gardner (D), Holliston.

9. —Belmont. Precinct 4. and WALTHAM, Wards 1, 2, 3, 4 and 7. David F. Gately (U), Waltham.

10. —NEWTON, Ward 1. Precinct 4. Ward 2. Precinct 1, Ward 3, Precincts 3 and 4. and WALTHAM, Wards 5, 6, 8 and 9. Peter J. Koutoujian (D). Newton.

11. —Brookline. Precinct 15 *(Norfolk Co.)*; and NEWTON, Ward 1, Precincts 2 and 3. Ward 2. Precincts 2 and 3. Ward 6, Precinct 1. Ward 7 and Ward 8. Precincts 1, 2 and 4 *(Middlesex Co.)*. David B. Cohen (D). Newton.

12. —NEWTON, Ward 3. Precincts 1 and 2. Wards 4 and 5. Ward 6, Precincts 2, 3 and 4. and Ward 8. Precinct 3. Kay Khan (D), Newton.

13. —Maynard. Sudbury and Wayland. Susan W. Pope (R), Wayland.

14. —Acton. Boxborough and Concord. Pamela P. Resor (D), Acton.

15. —Lexington and Lincoln. Jay R. Kaufman (D), Lexington.

16. —Carlisle and Chelmsford. Carol C. Cleven (R), Chelmsford.

17. —LOWELL, Ward 1. Precinct 1, Ward 2. Precinct 3. Wards 5, 6 and 9, and Ward 10. Precinct 3. Thomas A. Golden, Jr. (D), Lowell.

18. —Andover. Precinct 5 *(Essex Co.)*; LOWELL, Ward 1. Precincts 2 and 3, Ward 4. Precincts 2 and 3. Ward 10, Precincts 1 and 2, and Ward 11. and Tewksbury. Precinct 3 *(Middlesex Co.)*. Edward A. LeLacheur (D), Lowell.

19. —LOWELL, Ward 2. Precincts 1 and 2. Ward 3. Ward 4, Precinct 1, and Wards 7 and 8. Kevin J. Murphy (D), Lowell.

20. —Tewksbury. Precincts 1, 1A, 2, 2A. 3A and 4. and Wilmington, Precincts 1, 2, 4, 5 and 6. James R. Miceli (D), Wilmington.

21. —North Andover. Precincts 4 and 5 *(Essex Co.)*; and North Reading, and Reading. Precincts 1, 2, 4, 6, 7, 8A and 8B *(Middlesex Co.)*. Bradley H. Jones, Jr. (R), North Reading.

22. —Lynnfield, Precincts 1, 3 and 4, and Middleton *(Essex Co.)*; and Wakefield *(Middlesex Co.)*. Brian M. Cresta (R), Wakefield.

23. —Bedford, Burlington and Wilmington. Precinct 3. Charles A. Murphy (D), Burlington.

24. —Billerica. William G. Greene, Jr. (D), Billerica.

25. —Arlington, Precincts 8, 9, 10, 11, 12, 13, 14, 15, 16, 17, 18, 19, 20 and 21, and MEDFORD, Ward 3, Precinct 2, and Ward 6, Precinct 1. J. James Marzilli, Jr. (D), Arlington.

26. —Arlington, Precincts 1, 2, 3, 4, 5, 6 and 7, and Belmont, Precincts 1, 2, 3, 5, 6, 7 and 8. Anne M. Paulsen (D), Belmont.

27. — CAMBRIDGE, Ward 7, Precincts 3 and 4, Wards 8, 9, 10 and 11. Alice K. Wolf (D), Cambridge.
28. — CAMBRIDGE, Ward 2, Precinct 2, Ward 3, Precincts 3 and 4, Wards 4, 5 and 6, and Ward 7, Precincts 1 and 2. Alvin E. Thompson (D), Cambridge.
29. — CAMBRIDGE, Ward 1, Ward 2, Precinct 1, Ward 3, Precincts 1 and 2, and SOMERVILLE, Ward 1, Ward 2, Precincts 1 and 2, and Ward 4, Precinct 2. Timothy J. Toomey, Jr. (D), Cambridge.
30. — SOMERVILLE, Ward 2, Precinct 3, Wards 5 and 6, and Ward 3, Precincts 1, 2 and 3. Patricia D. Jehlen (D), Somerville.
31. — EVERETT and MALDEN, Ward 1, Precinct 2. Edward G. Connolly (D), Everett.
32. — NEWTON, Ward 1, Precinct 1 and Watertown. Rachel Kaprielian (D), Watertown.
33. — WOBURN. Carol A. Donovan (D), Woburn.
34. — Reading, Precincts 3 and 5, Stoneham, Precincts 1, 2 and 3, and Winchester. Paul C. Casey (D), Winchester)
35. — MELROSE and Stoneham, Precincts 4, 5 and 6. Patrick C. Guerriero (R), Melrose.
36. — MALDEN, Ward 1, Precinct 1, Wards 2, 4, 5 and 6, Ward 3, Precinct 1, and Ward 8, Precinct 2. Christopher G. Fallon (D), Malden.
37. — MEDFORD, Ward 4, Precinct 1, Ward 5, Ward 6, Precinct 2, and Ward 7, Precinct 1, and SOMERVILLE, Ward 4, Precincts 1 and 3, and Ward 7. Vincent P. Ciampa (D), Somerville.
38. — MALDEN, Ward 3, Precinct 2, and MEDFORD, Wards 1, 2 and 8, Ward 3, Precinct 1, Ward 4, Precinct 2, and Ward 7, Precinct 2. Anthony P. Giglio (D), Medford.
39. — Dracut, Dunstable and Tyngsborough. Colleen M. Garry (D), Dracut.

NORFOLK COUNTY
FIFTEEN REPRESENTATIVES.

DISTRICT

1. — QUINCY, Ward 3, Precincts 3, 4 and 5, Ward 4, Precincts 1 and 3, Ward 5, Precincts 2 and 5, and Ward 6, and Randolph, Precinct 6. Michael G. Bellotti (D), Quincy.
2. — QUINCY, Ward 1, Ward 3, Precincts 1 and 2, Ward 4, Precincts 2, 4 and 5, and Ward 5, Precincts 1, 3 and 4. A. Stephen Tobin (D), Quincy.
3. — Holbrook, Precincts 3 and 4, QUINCY, Ward 2, and Weymouth, Precincts 5, 6, 9, 12, 16 and 17. Ronald Mariano (D), Quincy.

4. —Weymouth. Precincts 1, 2, 3, 4, 7, 8, 10, 11, 13, 14, 15 and 18. Paul R. Haley (D). Weymouth.
5. —Braintree and Holbrook. Precincts 1 and 2. Joseph C. Sullivan (D), Braintree.
6. —Avon. Canton, Randolph. Precincts 1, 2 and 4, and Stoughton, Precinct 1. William C. Galvin (D), Canton.
7. —Milton. Precincts 1, 2, 4, 5, 6, 7, 8, 9 and 10, and Randolph, Precincts 3, 5, 7 and 8. Brian A. Joyce (D), Milton.
8. —Sharon and Stoughton. Precincts 2, 3, 4, 5, 6, 7 and 8. Louis L. Kafka (D), Sharon.
9. —Millis, Precinct 1, Norfolk, Walpole, precincts 1, 2, 3, 4, 5 and 6, and Wrentham. Jo Ann Sprague (R), Walpole.
10. —Bellingham, Precincts 2, 3, 4 and 5, and Franklin *(Norfolk Co.)*; and Blackstone, Precincts 2 and 3 *(Worcester Co.)*. James E. Vallee (D), Franklin.
11. —Dedham and Westwood. Maryanne Lewis (D), Dedham.
12. —Medfield, Precincts 2 and 3, Norwood and Walpole, Precinct 7. John H. Rogers (D), Norwood.
13. —Dover, Needham, and Medfield. Precincts 1 and 4. Lida E. Harkins (D), Needham.
14. —Wellesley *(Norfolk Co.)*; and Weston *(Middlesex Co.)*. John A. Locke (R), Wellesley.
15. —Brookline, Precincts 2, 3, 4, 5, 6, 7, 8, 9, 10, 11 and 14. John A. Businger (D), Brookline.

PLYMOUTH COUNTY
TWELVE REPRESENTATIVES.
DISTRICT
1. —Plymouth, Precincts 1, 2, 3, 4, 5, 6, 7, 8, 9, 10 and 12. Joseph R. Gallitano (D), Plymouth.
2. —Bourne, Precincts 1 and 2, and Sandwich, Precincts 1, 2 and 3 *(Barnstable Co.)*; and Carver, Precincts 2 and 3, and Wareham *(Plymouth Co.)*. Ruth W. Provost (D), Sandwich.
3. —Hingham and Hull *(Plymouth Co.)*; and Cohasset *(Norfolk Co.)*. Mary Jeanette Murray (R), Cohasset.
4. —Marshfield and Scituate. Frank M. Hynes (D), Marshfield.
5. —Hanover, Norwell and Rockland. Janet W. O'Brien (D), Hanover.
6. —Duxbury, Hanson and Pembroke. Francis L. Marini (R), Hanson.
7. —Abington, East Bridgewater and Whitman. Kathleen M. Teahan (D), Whitman.
8. —Bridgewater, Precincts 1, 3, 4, 5 and 6, and Halifax, Precinct 1 *(Plymouth Co.)*; and Easton, Precincts 2B, 3 and 6, and Raynham *(Bristol Co.)*. Jacqueline Lewis (R), Bridgewater.

9. — BROCKTON. Ward 1, Precincts B and D, Ward 2, Precincts B, C and D, Ward 3 and Ward 4, Precincts A, B and D. Thomas P. Kennedy (D), Brockton.
10. — BROCKTON, Ward 4, Precinct C, Ward 5, Precincts B, C and D, and Ward 6, West Bridgewater, and Bridgewater, Precincts 2 and 7. Christine E. Canavan (D), Brockton.
11. — BROCKTON, Ward 1, Precincts A and C, Ward 2, Precinct A, Ward 5, Precinct A, and Ward 7 *(Plymouth Co.)*; and Easton, Precincts 1, 2A, 4 and 5 *(Bristol Co.)*. Geraldine Creedon (D), Brockton.
12. — Carver, Precinct 1, Halifax, Precinct 2, Kingston, Middleborough, Precincts 1, 2, 4 and 5, Plymouth, Precincts 11 and 13, and Plympton. Thomas J. O'Brien (D), Kingston.

SUFFOLK COUNTY
NINETEEN REPRESENTATIVES.

DISTRICT
1. — BOSTON, Ward 1 and harbor islands; and REVERE, Ward 1, Precinct 3. Emanuel G. Serra (D), Boston.
2. — BOSTON, Ward 2, and CHELSEA, Wards 1, 2, 4 and 5. Eugene L. O'Flaherty (D), Chelsea.
3. — BOSTON, Ward 3, Ward 4, Precinct 1, Ward 5, Precincts 1 and 5, and Ward 8, Precinct 1. Salvatore F. DiMasi (D), Boston.
4. — BOSTON, Ward 6, Ward 7, Precincts 1, 2, 3, 4, 5, 6, 7, 8 and 9, Ward 8, Precinct 6, and Ward 13, Precinct 3. John A. Hart, Jr. (D), Boston.
5. — BOSTON, Ward 7, Precinct 10, Ward 8, Precincts 5 and 7, Ward 12, Precincts 4 and 6, Ward 13, Precincts 1, 2, 4, 5 and 6, Ward 14, Precincts 4 and 6, and Ward 15, Precincts 1, 2, 3, 4, 5, 7, and 8. Charlotte Golar Richie (D), Boston.
6. — BOSTON, Ward 14, Precincts 5, 8, 10, 11, 12, 13 and 14, Ward 17, Precincts 1, 3 and 5, Ward 18, Precincts 2, 3, 7, 8 and 15, and Ward 19, Precinct 12 *(Suffolk Co.)*; and Milton, Precinct 11 *(Norfolk Co.)*. Shirley Owens-Hicks (D), Boston.
7. — BOSTON, Ward 4, Precincts 8, 9 and 10, Ward 8, Precinct 4, Ward 9, Precincts 4 and 5, Ward 11, Precinct 1, Ward 12, Precincts 1, 2, 3, 5, 8 and 9, and Ward 14, Precincts 1 and 3. Gloria L. Fox (D), Boston.
8. — BOSTON, Ward 5, Precincts 3, 4, 6, 7, 8, 9 and 10, and Ward 21, Precinct 2 *(Suffolk Co.)*; CAMBRIDGE, Ward 2, Precinct 3 *(Middlesex Co.)*; and Brookline, Precinct 1 *(Norfolk Co.)*. Paul C. Demakis (D), Boston.

9. — BOSTON, Ward 4, Precincts 2, 3, 4, 5, 6, and 7, Ward 5, Precinct 2, Ward 8, Precincts 2 and 3, Ward 9, Precincts 1, 2 and 3, and Ward 21, Precinct 1. Byron Rushing (D), Boston.

10. — BOSTON, Ward 20, Precincts 3, 5, 6, 7, 8, 9, 10, 11, 12, 13, 14, 15, 16, 17, 18, 19 and 20 *(Suffolk Co.)*; and Brookline, Precinct 16 *(Norfolk Co.)*. David T. Donnelly (D), Boston.

11. — BOSTON, Ward 11, Precincts 5, 6, 7, 8, 9 and 10, Ward 12, Precinct 7, Ward 14, Precincts 2, 7 and 9, and Ward 19, Precincts 4, 6, 7, 8, 9, 11 and 13. John E. McDonough (D), Boston.

12. — BOSTON, Ward 16, Precincts 8 and 11, Ward 17, Precincts 4, 7, 8, 10, 11, 12, 13 and 14, Ward 18, Precincts 1, 4, 5, 6 and 21 *(Suffolk Co.)*; and Milton, Precinct 3 *(Norfolk Co.)*. Thomas M. Finneran (D), Boston.

13. — BOSTON, Ward 13, Precincts 7, 8, 9 and 10, Ward 15, Precincts 6 and 9, Ward 16, Precincts 1, 2, 3, 4, 5, 6, 7, 9, 10 and 12, and Ward 17, Precincts 2, 6 and 9. James T. Brett[1] (D), Boston. Martin J. Walsh[2] (D), Boston.

14. — BOSTON, Ward 18, Precincts 9, 10, 11, 12, 13, 14, 16, 17, 18, 19, 20, 22 and 23, Ward 19, Precinct 10, and Ward 20, Precincts 1, 2 and 4. Angelo M. Scaccia (D), Boston.

15. — BOSTON, Ward 10, Ward 19, Precincts 1, 2, 3 and 5, and Ward 11, Precincts 2, 3 and 4. Kevin W. Fitzgerald (D), Boston.

16. — CHELSEA, Ward 3, Precincts 1 and 2, Revere, Ward 5, Precincts 1 and 2, Ward 3, Precinct 1, and Wards 4 and 6 *(Suffolk Co.)*; and MALDEN, Ward 7 and Ward 8, Precinct 1 *(Middlesex Co.)*. William G. Reinstein (D), Revere.

17. — BOSTON, Ward 21, Precincts 3, 5, 6, 7, 8, 9, 10, 11 and 12, and Ward 22, Precincts 2, 3, 6, 9 and 10. Kevin G. Honan (D), Boston.

18. — BOSTON, Ward 21, Precincts 4, 13, 14, 15 and 16, and Ward 22, Precincts 1, 4, 5, 7, 8, 11, 12 and 13 *(Suffolk Co.)*; and Brookline, Precincts 12 and 13 *(Norfolk Co.)*. Steven A. Tolman (D), Boston.

19. — REVERE, Ward 1, Precincts 1, 2 and 4, Ward 2, Ward 3, Precincts 2 and 3 and Ward 5, Precinct 3, and Winthrop. Robert A. DeLeo (D), Winthrop.

---

1. Declined to accept office.

2. Elected Apr. 8, 1997; qualified Apr. 16, 1997.

WORCESTER COUNTY
SEVENTEEN REPRESENTATIVES.

DISTRICT

1. —Holden, Hubbardston, Phillipston, Rutland, Templeton and Winchendon. Harold M. Lane, Jr. (D), Holden.
2. —Ashburnham, FITCHBURG, Ward 4, Precinct A. Gardner and Westminster *(Worcester Co.)*; and Ashby *(Middlesex Co.)*. Brian Knuuttila (D), Gardner.
3. —FITCHBURG, Wards 1, 2, 3, 5 and 6, and Ward 4, Precinct B. Emile J. Goguen (D), Fitchburg.
4. —LEOMINSTER. Mary Jane Simmons (D), Leominster.
5. —Barre, Brookfield, Hardwick, New Braintree, North Brookfield, Oakham, Petersham, Spencer, Warren and West Brookfield. David H. Tuttle (R), Barre.
6. —Charlton, Dudley, Precincts 3 and 4, Oxford, Precinct 2, Southbridge and Sturbridge, Precinct 1. David M. Peters (R), Charlton.
7. —Auburn, Millbury, Oxford, Precincts 1, 3 and 4, and Dudley, Precinct 1. Paul K. Frost (R), Auburn.
8. —Douglas, Millville, Uxbridge, Webster, Blackstone, Precinct 1, and Dudley, Precinct 2. Paul Kujawski (D), Webster.
9. —Grafton, Northbridge, Sutton and Upton. George N. Peterson, Jr. (R), Grafton.
10. —Hopedale, Mendon and Milford *(Worcester Co.)*; and Bellingham, Precinct 1 *(Norfolk Co.)*. Marie J. Parente (D), Milford.
11. —Shrewsbury and Westborough. Ronald W. Gauch (R), Shrewsbury.
12. —Boylston, Clinton, Northborough, Precincts 1 and 2, Princeton, Sterling and West Boylston, Precinct 2. Harold P. Naughton, Jr. (D), Clinton.
13. —Paxton and WORCESTER, Wards 1 and 9. Harriette L. Chandler (D), Worcester.
14. —WORCESTER, Wards 2 and 3, and West Boylston, Precinct 1. William J. McManus II (D), Worcester.
15. —WORCESTER, Ward 4, Ward 5, Precinct 3, and Ward 10. Vincent A. Pedone (D), Worcester.
16. —WORCESTER, Ward 5, Precincts 1, 2, 4 and 5, Ward 6 and Ward 8, Precincts 1 and 5. Guy Glodis (D), Worcester.
17. —Leicester and WORCESTER, Ward 7, and Ward 8, Precincts 2, 3 and 4. John J. Binienda (D), Worcester.

CITIES AND TOWNS ALPHABETICALLY

with

Congressional Districts (as established by Chapter 105 of the Acts of 1992), Councillor and Senatorial Districts (as established by Chapter 274 of the Acts of 1993, as amended by Chapter 12 of the Acts of 1994), and Representative Districts (as established by Chapter 273 of the Acts of 1993).

Cities and Towns	Congres- sional	Coun- cillor	Senatorial	Representative
Abington	10	{ 2 ** 4 **	2d Plymouth and Bristol, Precincts 1 and 2. Norfolk and Plymouth, Precincts 3 and 4.	7th Plymouth
Acton	5	3	Middlesex and Worcester	14th Middlesex
Acushnet	4	1	2d Bristol	11th Bristol
Adams	1	8	Berkshire, Hampden, Hampshire and Franklin	1st Berkshire
Agawam	2	8	Hampden	3d Hampden
Alford	1	8	Berkshire, Hampden, Hampshire and Franklin	4th Berkshire
Amesbury	6	5	Third Essex	1st Essex
Amherst	1	8	Hampshire and Franklin	3d Hampshire
Andover	5	5	2d Essex and Middlesex	17th Essex, Precincts 1, 2, 3, 4, 6, 7, 8. 18th Middlesex, Precinct 5
Arlington	7	6	4th Middlesex	25th Middlesex, Precincts 8, 9, 10, 11, 12, 13, 14, 15, 16, 17, 18, 19, 20 and 21. 26th Middlesex, Precincts 1, 2, 3, 4, 5, 6 and 7.
Ashburnham	1	7	Worcester and Middlesex	2d Worcester

* 2d Councillor District, Precincts 1 and 2.   ** 4th Councillor District, Precincts 3 and 4

Cities and Towns	Congressional	Councillor	Senatorial	Representative
Ashby	1	7	Worcester and Middlesex	2d Worcester
Ashfield	1	x	Hampshire and Franklin	2d Berkshire
Ashland	5	2	Middlesex, Norfolk and Worcester	7th Middlesex
Athol	1	7	Worcester, Hampden, Hampshire and Franklin	
Attleboro	3*	2	Norfolk, Bristol and Middlesex	1st Franklin / 2d Bristol
Auburn	2*	7	2d Worcester	7th Worcester
Avon	10	4	Suffolk and Norfolk	6th Norfolk
Ayer	5	3	Middlesex and Worcester	1st Middlesex, Precinct 1 / 2d Middlesex, Precinct 2 / 2d Barnstable, Precincts 1, 2, 3, 4, 5, 6, 7, 8, 10 and 11
Barnstable	10	1	Cape and Islands	Barnstable, Dukes and Nantucket, Precinct 9
Barre	1	7	Worcester, Hampden, Hampshire and Franklin	5th Worcester
Becket	1	x	Berkshire, Hampden, Hampshire and Franklin	2d Berkshire
Bedford	6	3	5th Middlesex	23d Middlesex
Belchertown	1	7	Worcester, Hampden, Hampshire and Franklin	1st Hampden, Precinct B
Bellingham	2	7	Worcester and Norfolk	7th Hampden, Precincts A and C / 10th Norfolk, Precincts 2, 3, 4 and 5 / 10th Worcester, Precinct 1
Belmont	8	3	Middlesex and Suffolk	9th Middlesex, Precinct 4 / 26th Middlesex, Precincts 1, 2, 3, 5, 6, 7 and 8
Berkley	4	1	1st Plymouth and Bristol	9th Bristol
Berlin	3	3	Middlesex and Worcester	4th Middlesex
Bernardston	1	x	Hampshire and Franklin	2d Franklin
Beverly	6	5	2d Essex	6th Essex

Billerica	5	6
Blackstone	2	7
Blandford	1	8
Bolton	5	7
Boston	{ 8 # ... 2, 3, 4 ; 9 ## ... 6 }	

* 2d Congressional District, Precinct 1 (*in part*), Precinct 2, Precinct 3 (*in part*), Precinct 4 (*in part*).

** 3d Congressional District, Precinct 1 (*in part*), Precinct 3 (*in part*), Precinct 4 (*in part*).

§ 8th Congressional District, Ward 1, Ward 2, Ward 4, Ward 5, Precincts 1, 2, 3, 4, 6, 7, 8, 9, 10 and 5 (*in part*), Ward 9, Ward 10, Ward 11, Precincts 1, 2, 3, 4 and 5, Ward 12, Ward 14, Ward 15, Precincts 1, 2, 3, 4, 5, 7, 8 and 9, Ward 17, Precincts 1, 2, 3, 5, 6, 7, 8, 9, 10 and 11, Ward 18, Precincts 1, 2, 3, 4, 5, 6, 18 and 21, Ward 21, Ward 22, Ward x, Precinct x (Ocer Island.

\## 9th Congressional District, Ward 3, Ward 5, Precinct 5 (*in part*), Ward 6, Ward 7, Ward 8, Ward 11, Precincts 6, 7, 8, 9 and 10, Ward 13, Ward 15, Precinct 6, Ward 16, Ward 17, Precincts 4, 12, 13 and 14, Ward 18, Precincts 7, 8, 9, 10, 11, 12, 13, 14, 16, 17, 18, 19, 20, 22 and 23, Ward 19, Ward 30.

‖ 2d Councillor District, Ward 18, Precincts 10, 11, 12, 17, 18, 19, 20, 22 and 23, Ward 19, Precincts 10, 11 and 13, and Ward 30.

○ 3d Councillor District, Ward 21, Precincts 9, 10, 11, 12, 13, 14, 15 and 16, Ward 22, Precincts 1, 2, 3, 4, 5, 6, 7, 8, 9, 10, 11, 12 and 13.

4th Middlesex ....

Worcester and Norfolk ....

Berkshire, Hampden, Hampshire and Franklin

Worcester and Middlesex

1st Suffolk, Ward 3, Precincts 7 and 8, Ward 5, Precincts 1, 3, 6, 7, 8, 9, 10, Wards 6, 7 and 8, Ward 9, Precincts 1, 2, 3, Wards 13 and 15, Ward 16, Precincts 1, 2, Ward 21, Precincts 1, 2, Ward 21, Precincts 1, 2, 3, 4, and Boston harbor Island, Ward x, Precinct x.

2d Suffolk, Ward 4, Ward 5, Precinct 2, Ward 9, Precincts 4, 5, Ward 10, Ward 11, Precincts 1, 2, 3, 4, 5, Wards 12 and 14, Ward 17, Precincts 3, 5, 7, 8, 10, 12, Ward 18, Precincts 2, 3, 6, 21 and Ward 19, Precincts 1 and 3, Middlesex and Suffolk, Ward 21, Precincts 9, 10, 11, 12, 13, 14, 15, 16, Ward 22, Precincts 3, 4, 5, 6, 7, 8, 9, 10, 11, 12 and 13, Middlesex, Suffolk and Essex, Ward 2, Ward 21, Precincts 5, 6, 7, 8, Ward 22, Precincts 1 and 2, Suffolk and Middlesex, Ward 1, Ward 3, Precincts 1, 2, 3, 4, 5, 6, and Ward 5, Precincts 4 and 5.

24th Middlesex
10th Norfolk, Precincts 2 and 3.
8th Worcester, Precinct 1

3d Hampden
3d Middlesex

1st Suffolk, Ward 1 and harbor island
2d Suffolk, Ward 2.
3d Suffolk, Ward 3, Ward 4, Precinct 1, Ward 5, Precincts 1 and 5, Ward 8, Precinct 1.
4th Suffolk, Ward 6, Ward 7, Precincts 1, 2, 3, 4, 5, 6, 7, 8, 9, Ward 8, Precinct 6, Ward 13, Precinct 3.
5th Suffolk, Ward 7, Precinct 10, Ward 8, Precincts 5, 7, Ward 12, Ward 13, Precincts 4, 6, Ward 14, Precincts 4, 6, Ward 15, Precincts 1, 2, 3, 4, 5, 7, 8.
6th Suffolk, Ward 14, Precincts 5, 8, 10, 11, 12, 13, 14, Ward 17, Precincts 1, 3, 5, Ward 18, Precincts 2, 3, 7, 8, 15, Ward 19, Precinct 12.
7th Suffolk, Ward 4, Precincts 8, 9, 10, Ward 8, Precinct 4, Ward 9, Precincts 4 and 5, Ward 11, Precinct 1, Ward 12, Precincts 1, 2, 3, 5, 8, 9, Ward 14, Precincts 1, 2, 3 and 3.

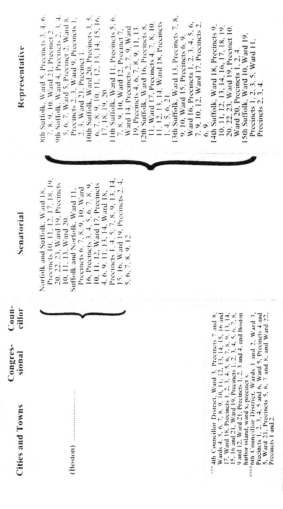

Cities and Towns	Congres-sional	Coun-cillor	Senatorial	Representative
(Boston)			Norfolk and Suffolk, Ward 18, Precincts 10, 11, 12, 17, 18, 19, 20, 22, 23, Ward 19, Precincts 10, 11, 13, Ward 20. Suffolk and Norfolk, Ward 11, Precincts 6, 7, 8, 9, 10, Ward 16, Precincts 3, 4, 5, 6, 7, 8, 9, 10, 11, 12, Ward 17, Precincts 4, 6, 9, 11, 13, 14, Ward 18, Precincts 1, 4, 5, 7, 8, 9, 13, 14, 15, 16, Ward 19, Precincts 2, 4, 5, 6, 7, 8, 9, 12.	8th Suffolk, Ward 5, Precincts 3, 4, 6, 7, 8, 9, 10, Ward 21, Precinct 2. 9th Suffolk, Ward 4, Precincts 2, 3, 4, 5, 6, 7, Ward 5, Precinct 2, Ward 8, Precincts 2, 3, Ward 9, Precincts 1, 2, 3, Ward 21, Precinct 1. 10th Suffolk, Ward 20, Precincts 3, 5, 6, 7, 8, 9, 10, 11, 12, 13, 14, 15, 16, 17, 18, 19, 20. 11th Suffolk, Ward 11, Precincts 5, 6, 7, 8, 9, 10, Ward 12, Precinct 7, Ward 14, Precincts 2, 7, 9, Ward 19, Precincts 4, 6, 7, 8, 9, 11, 13. 12th Suffolk, Ward 16, Precincts 8, 11, Ward 17, Precincts 4, 7, 8, 10, 11, 12, 13, 14, Ward 18, Precincts 1, 4, 5, 6, 21. 13th Suffolk, Ward 13, Precincts 7, 8, 9, 10, Ward 15, Precincts 6, 9, Ward 16, Precincts 1, 2, 3, 4, 5, 6, 7, 9, 10, 12, Ward 17, Precincts 2, 6, 9. 14th Suffolk, Ward 18, Precincts 9, 10, 11, 12, 13, 14, 16, 17, 18, 19, 20, 22, 23, Ward 19, Precinct 10, Ward 20, Precincts 1, 2, 4. 15th Suffolk, Ward 10, Ward 19, Precincts 1, 2, 3, 5, Ward 11, Precincts 2, 3, 4.

°°° 4th Councillor District, Ward 3, Precincts 7 and 8, Wards 4, 5, 6, 7, 8, 9, 10, 11, 12, 13, 14, 15, 16 and 17, Ward 18, Precincts 1, 2, 3, 4, 5, 6, 7, 8, 9, 13, 14, 15, 16 and 21, Ward 19, Precincts 1, 2, 3, 4, 6, 7, 8, 9 and 12, Ward 21, Precincts 1, 2, 3 and 4, and Boston harbor island, ward x, precinct x.

°°° 6th Councillor District, Wards 1 and 2, Ward 3, Precincts 1, 2, 3, 4, 5 and 6, Ward 5, Precincts 4 and 5, Ward 21, Precincts 5, 6, 7 and 8, and Ward 22, Precincts 1 and 2.

Town			Senatorial District	Representative District
(Boston)				17th Suffolk, Ward 21, Precincts 3, 5, 6, 7, 8, 9, 10, 11, 12, Ward 22. Precincts 2, 3, 6, 9, 10.
				18th Suffolk, Ward 21, Precincts 4, 13, 14, 15, 16, Ward 22, Precincts 1, 4, 5, 7, 8, 11, 12, 13.
Bourne	10	1	Plymouth and Barnstable	3d Barnstable, Precincts 3, 4, 5, 6.
				2d Plymouth, Precincts 1, 2.
Boxborough	5	3	Middlesex and Worcester	14th Middlesex
Boxford	6	5	1st Essex and Middlesex	4th Essex
Boylston	3	7	1st Worcester	12th Worcester
Braintree	9	4	Norfolk and Plymouth, Precincts 1, 2, 3, 4, 5, 8, 10, 11, 12. Plymouth and Norfolk, Precincts 6, 7, 9.	5th Norfolk
Brewster	10	1	Cape and Islands	1st Barnstable
Bridgewater	4	1	1st Plymouth and Bristol	8th Plymouth, Precincts 1, 3, 4, 5, 6.
				10th Plymouth, Precincts 2, 7.
Bramfield	2	7	Worcester, Hampden, Hampshire and Franklin	1st Hampden
Brockton	9 * 10 **	2	2d Plymouth and Bristol	9th Plymouth, Ward 1, Precincts B, D. Ward 2, Precincts B, C, D. Ward 3. Ward 4, Precincts A, B, D.
				10th Plymouth, Ward 4, Precinct C. Ward 5, Precincts B, C, D. Ward 6.
				11th Plymouth, Ward 1, Precincts A, C. Ward 2, Precinct A. Ward 5. Precinct A, Ward 7.
Brookfield	2	7	Worcester, Hampden, Hampshire and Franklin	5th Worcester

* 9th Congressional District, Ward 1, Ward 2, Precincts B, C and D, Ward 3, Ward 4, Ward 5, Precincts A (in part) and C

** 10th Congressional District, Ward 2, Precinct A, Ward 5, Precincts A (in part), B and D, Ward 6, Ward 7

Cities and Towns	Congressional	Councillor	Senatorial	Representative
Brookline	4	3	1st Middlesex and Norfolk	11th Middlesex, Precinct 15. 15th Norfolk, Precincts 2, 3, 4, 5, 6, 7, 8, 9, 10, 11, 14.
Buckland	1	8	Hampshire and Franklin	8th Suffolk, Precinct 1
Burlington	6	6	4th Middlesex. 4th Middlesex, Ward 11. Precinct 3.	10th Suffolk, Precinct 16. 18th Suffolk, Precincts 12, 13. 2d Berkshire 23d Middlesex
Cambridge	8	3 # 6 ##	Middlesex and Suffolk, Ward 7, Precincts 3, 4, Ward 9, Precinct 2, Ward 10, Precincts 1, 2, 4, Ward 11, Precincts 1, 2. Middlesex, Suffolk and Essex. Ward 3, Precincts 2, 3, Ward 4, Precincts 1, 2, Ward 6, Precincts 1, 3, 3, 4, Ward 7, Precincts 1, 2, Ward 8, Ward 9, Precincts 1, 3, 4, Ward 10, Precinct 3, Suffolk and Middlesex, Wards 1 and 2, Ward 3, Precincts 1, 4, Ward 4, Precincts 3, 4, Ward 5, Ward 6, Precincts 1, 2. Norfolk and Suffolk, Precincts 4, 5, 6.	27th Middlesex, Ward 7, Precincts 3, 4, Wards 8, 9, 10, 11. 28th Middlesex, Ward 2, Precinct 2, Ward 3, Precincts 3, 4, Wards 4, 5, 6, Ward 7, Precincts 1, 2. 29th Middlesex, Ward 1, Ward 2, Precinct 1, Ward 3, Precincts 1, 2, 8th Suffolk, Ward 2, Precinct 3
Canton	9	2 ° 4 °°	Suffolk and Norfolk, Precincts 1, 2, 3.	6th Norfolk
Carlisle	5	3	5th Middlesex	16th Middlesex 2d Plymouth, Precincts 2, 3
Carver	4	1	1st Plymouth and Bristol	12th Plymouth, Precinct 1.

Town				
Charlemont	1	x	Berkshire, Hampden, Hampshire and Franklin	2d Berkshire
Charlton	2	7	Worcester and Norfolk	6th Worcester
Chatham	10	1	Cape and Islands	4th Barnstable
Chelmsford	5	3	5th Middlesex	16th Middlesex
Chelsea	x	6	Middlesex, Suffolk and Essex	2d Suffolk, Wards 1, 2, 4, 5. 16th Suffolk, Ward 3.
Cheshire	1	x	Berkshire, Hampden, Hampshire and Franklin	2d Berkshire
Chester	1	x	Berkshire, Hampden, Hampshire and Franklin	2d Berkshire 1st Franklin
Chesterfield	1	x	Hampshire and Franklin	6th Hampden, Ward 3, Precinct C 7th Hampden, Ward 6. 8th Hampden, Wards 1, 7, 8, 9, Ward 2, Precincts C, D, Ward 3, Precincts A, B, Ward 4, Precincts A, C 9th Hampden, Ward 2, Precincts A, B, Ward 4, Precinct B, Ward 5.
Chicopee	2	x	Hampden, Wards 2, 4, 5. 2d Hampden and Hampshire, Wards 1, 3, 6, 7, 8, 9.	Barnstable, Dukes and Nantucket
Chilmark	10	1	Cape and Islands	1st Berkshire
Clarksburg	1	x	Berkshire, Hampden, Hampshire and Franklin	12th Worcester
Clinton	3	7	1st Worcester	3d Plymouth
Cohasset	10	4	Plymouth and Norfolk	2d Franklin
Colrain	1	x	Hampshire and Franklin	14th Middlesex
Concord	5	x	5th Middlesex	1st Franklin
Conway	1	x	Hampshire and Franklin	
Cummington	1	x	Berkshire, Hampden, Hampshire and Franklin	2d Berkshire
Dalton	1	x	Berkshire, Hampden, Hampshire and Franklin	2d Berkshire

1d Councillor District, Ward 7, Precincts 3 and 4, Ward 9, Precinct 2, Ward 10, Precincts 1, 2 and 4, Ward 11, Precincts 1 and 2.
and 8th Councillor District, Wards 1, 2, 3, 4, 5 and 6, Ward 7, Precincts 1 and 2, Ward 8, Ward 9, Precincts 1, 3 and 4, Ward 10, Precinct 3, Ward 11, Precinct 3
* 2d Councillor District, Precincts 4, 5 and 6.
† 4th Councillor District, Precincts 1, 2 and 3

Cities and Towns	Congressional	Councillor	Senatorial	Representative
Danvers	6	5	2d Essex	13th Essex
Dartmouth	3	1	2d Bristol	9th Bristol
Dedham	9	2	Norfolk and Suffolk	11th Norfolk
Deerfield	1	8	Hampshire and Franklin	1st Franklin
Dennis	10	1	Cape and Islands	1st Barnstable, Precincts 1, 2, 4, 5. / 4th Barnstable, Precinct 3.
Dighton	4	1	1st Plymouth and Bristol	5th Bristol
Douglas	2	7	Worcester and Norfolk	8th Worcester
Dover	4	2	Norfolk and Suffolk	13th Norfolk
Dracut	5	5	2d Essex and Middlesex	39th Middlesex
Dudley	2	7	Worcester and Norfolk	6th Worcester, Precincts 3, 4. / 7th Worcester, Precinct 1. / 8th Worcester, Precinct 2.
Dunstable	5	3	1st Middlesex	39th Middlesex
Duxbury	10	4	Plymouth and Norfolk	6th Plymouth
East Bridgewater	4	2	2d Plymouth and Bristol	7th Plymouth
East Brookfield	2	7	Worcester, Hampden, Hampshire and Franklin	1st Hampden
Eastham	10	1	Cape and Islands	4th Barnstable
Easthampton	1	8	2d Hampden and Hampshire	2d Hampshire
East Longmeadow	2	8	1st Hampden and Hampshire	2d Hampden, Precincts 2, 3 / 13th Hampden, Precincts 1, 4.
Easton	4++ / 9++	2	Norfolk, Bristol and Plymouth, Precincts 3 and 6. / 2d Plymouth and Bristol, Precincts 1, 2A, 2B, 4, 5.	8th Plymouth, Precincts 2B, 3, 6. / 11th Plymouth, Precincts 1, 2A, 4, 5.
Edgartown	10	1	Cape and Islands	Barnstable, Dukes and Nantucket
Egremont	1	8	Berkshire, Hampden, Hampshire and Franklin	4th Berkshire
Erving	1	7	Worcester, Hampden, Hampshire and Franklin	2d Franklin

Town			Senatorial District	Representative District
Essex	6	5	1st Essex and Middlesex	5th Essex
Everett	7	6	Middlesex, Suffolk and Essex	31st Middlesex
Fairhaven	4	1	2d Bristol	10th Bristol
Fall River	{ 3**, 4§§§ }	1	1st Bristol	6th Bristol, Ward 4, Precincts A, C, D, Wards 8, 9. 7th Bristol, Ward 1, Precincts B, C, D, Wards 2, 3, Ward 4, Precinct B. Ward 5, Precinct A. 8th Bristol, Ward 1, Precinct A, Ward 5, Precincts B, C, Ward 6, Ward 7, Precinct B.
Falmouth	10	1	Cape and Islands, Precincts 4 and 7. Plymouth and Barnstable, Precincts 1, 2, 3, 5, 6, 8.	3d Barnstable, Precincts 3, 4, 7, 8. Barnstable, Dukes and Nantucket, Precincts 1, 2, 5, 6,
Fitchburg	1	7	Worcester and Middlesex	2d Worcester, Ward 4, Precinct A. 3d Worcester, Wards 1, 2, 3, 5, 6, Ward 4, Precinct B
Florida	1	8	Berkshire, Hampden, Hampshire and Franklin	1st Berkshire
Foxborough	{ 3*, 4** }	2	Norfolk, Bristol and Plymouth	1st Bristol
Framingham	7	2	Middlesex, Norfolk and Worcester	6th Middlesex, Precincts 1, 2, 3, 4, 5, 6, 7, 9, 10, 13, 7th Middlesex, Precincts 8, 11, 12, 14, 15, 16, 17.
Franklin	3	2	Middlesex, Norfolk and Worcester	10th Norfolk
Freetown	4	1	1st Bristol	6th Bristol, Precinct 1, 9th Bristol, Precinct 2, 11th Bristol, Precinct 3

* 4th Congressional District, Precinct 1 (*in part*), Precinct 2 (*in part*), Precinct 3 (*in part*), Precinct 4 (*in part*), Precinct 5

§ 9th Congressional District, Precinct 1 (*in part*), Precinct 2 (*in part*), Precinct 3 (*in part*), Precinct 4 (*in part*), Precinct 5

§ 3d Congressional District, Ward 1, Ward 2, Ward 3, Ward 4, Precincts A, B (*in part*), and C (*in part*), Ward 6, Precincts A and B

§§ 4th Congressional District, Ward 4, Precincts B (*in part*), and C (*in part*), Ward 5, Ward 6, Precinct C, Ward 7, Ward 8, Ward 9

** 3d Congressional District, Precinct 1 (*in part*), Precinct 2, Precinct 3, Precinct 4 (*in part*)

** 4th Congressional District, Precinct 1 (*in part*), Precinct 2, Precinct 3 (*in part*), Precinct 4 (*in part*).

Cities and Towns	Congressional	Councillor	Senatorial	Representative
Gardner	1	7	Worcester and Middlesex	2d Worcester
Gay Head	10	1	Cape and Islands	Barnstable, Dukes and Nantucket
Georgetown	6	5	1st Essex and Middlesex	2d Essex, Precinct 1 4th Essex, Precinct 2
Gill	1	x	Hampshire and Franklin	2d Franklin
Gloucester	6	5	1st Essex and Middlesex	5th Essex
Goshen	1	x	Hampshire and Franklin	2d Berkshire
Gosnold	10	1	Cape and Islands	Barnstable, Dukes and Nantucket
Grafton	3	7	2d Worcester	9th Worcester
Granby	1	x	1st Hampden and Hampshire	7th Hampden
Granville	1	x	Berkshire, Hampden, Hampshire and Franklin	3d Hampden
Great Barrington	1	x	Berkshire, Hampden, Hampshire and Franklin	4th Berkshire
Greenfield	1	x	Hampshire and Franklin	2d Franklin
Groton	5	3	1st Middlesex	1st Middlesex
Groveland	6	5	1st Essex and Middlesex	2d Essex
Hadley	2	x	Hampshire and Franklin	2d Hampshire
Halifax	4	1	1st Plymouth and Bristol	8th Plymouth, Precinct 1, 12th Plymouth, Precinct 2.
Hamilton	6	5	1st Essex and Middlesex	4th Essex
Hampden	2	x	1st Hampden and Hampshire	2d Hampden
Hancock	1	x	Berkshire, Hampden, Hampshire and Franklin	2d Berkshire
Hanover	10	2	2d Plymouth and Bristol	5th Plymouth
Hanson	4	1	Plymouth and Barnstable	6th Plymouth
Hardwick	1	7	Worcester, Hampden, Hampshire and Franklin	5th Worcester
Harvard	5	3	Middlesex and Worcester	2d Middlesex
Harwich	10	1	Cape and Islands	4th Barnstable
Hatfield	1	x	Hampshire and Franklin	1st Hampshire

Town			District	
Haverhill	6	5	3d Essex	2d Essex, Ward 3, Precinct 2, Ward 4, Precincts 1 and 3, Ward 7, Precincts 2 and 3. 3d Essex, Wards 1, 2, 5 and 6, Ward 3, Precincts 1 and 3, Ward 4, Precinct 2 and Ward 7, Precinct 1
Hawley	1	x	Berkshire, Hampden, Hampshire and Franklin	2d Berkshire
Heath	1	x	Berkshire, Hampden, Hampshire and Franklin	2d Franklin
Hingham	10	4	Plymouth and Norfolk	3d Plymouth
Hinsdale	1	x	Berkshire, Hampden, Hampshire and Franklin	2d Berkshire
Holbrook	10	4	Norfolk and Plymouth	3d Norfolk, Precincts 3 and 4, 5th Norfolk, Precincts 1 and 2.
Holden	3	7	1st Worcester	1st Worcester
Holland	2	7	Worcester, Hampden, Hampshire and Franklin	1st Hampden
Holliston	3	2	Middlesex, Norfolk and Worcester	8th Middlesex
Holyoke	1	x	2d Hampden and Hampshire	5th Hampden, Wards 1, 2, 4, 6, 7, Ward 3, Precinct B, Ward 5, Precinct A. 6th Hampden, Ward 3, Precinct A, Ward 5, Precinct B
Hopedale	2	7	2d Worcester	10th Worcester
Hopkinton	3	2	Middlesex, Norfolk and Worcester	8th Middlesex
Hubbardston	1	7	Worcester, Hampden, Hampshire and Franklin	1st Worcester
Hudson	5	3	Middlesex and Worcester	3d Middlesex
Hull	10	4	Plymouth and Norfolk	3d Plymouth
Huntington	1	x	Hampshire and Franklin	2d Berkshire
Ipswich	6	5	1st Essex and Middlesex	4th Essex
Kingston	10	1	Plymouth and Barnstable	12th Plymouth
Lakeville	4	1	1st Plymouth and Bristol	9th Bristol, Precinct 1 11th Bristol, Precinct 2.

Cities and Towns	Congressional	Councillor	Senatorial	Representative
Lancaster	{ 3*, 5**	7	Worcester and Middlesex	3d Middlesex
Lanesborough	1	8	Berkshire, Hampden, Hampshire and Franklin	2d Berkshire
Lawrence	5	5	2d Essex and Middlesex	14 Essex, Ward A, Precincts 1, 3, 4, Ward E, Precincts 2, 3, Ward F, Precincts 1, 2, 4. 16th Essex, Ward A, Precinct 2, Wards B and C, Ward D, Precincts 3, 4, Ward F, Precinct 3. 17th Essex, Ward D, Precincts 1, 2, Ward E, Precincts 1, 4
Lee	1	8	Berkshire, Hampden, Hampshire and Franklin	4th Berkshire
Leicester	2	7	2d Worcester	17th Worcester
Lenox	1	8	Berkshire, Hampden, Hampshire and Franklin	4th Berkshire
Leominster	1	7	Worcester and Middlesex	4th Worcester
Leverett	1	8	Hampshire and Franklin	1st Franklin
Lexington	7	{ 3 +	4th Middlesex, Precincts 1, 5, 6, 7.	15th Middlesex
Leyden	1	{ 6 ++	5th Middlesex, Precincts 2, 3, 4, 8, 9. Hampshire and Franklin	2d Franklin
Lincoln	{ 5#, 7##	3	5th Middlesex	15th Middlesex
Littleton	5	3	Middlesex and Worcester	2d Middlesex
Longmeadow	2	8	1st Hampden and Hampshire	2d Hampden
Lowell	5	3	1st Middlesex	17th Middlesex, Ward 1, Precinct 1. Ward 2, Precinct 3, Wards 5, 6, 9. Ward 10, Precinct 3.

Town			Senatorial District	Representative District(s)
(Lowell)	2, 1, 5	8, 7		18th Middlesex, Ward 1, Precincts 2, 3, Ward 4, Precincts 2, 3, Ward 10, Precincts 1, 2, Ward 11. 19th Middlesex, Ward 2, Precincts 1, 2, Ward 3, Ward 4, Precinct 1, Wards 7, 8.
Ludlow			1st Hampden and Hampshire	7th Hampden
Lunenburg			Worcester and Middlesex	1st Middlesex
Lynn	6	5	1st Essex	8th Essex, Ward 3, Precinct 4. 9th Essex, Ward 1, Precincts 1, 2, 3. 10th Essex, Ward 1, Precinct 4, Ward 2, Ward 3, Precincts 1, 2, 3, Ward 4, Ward 5, Precinct 4. 11th Essex, Ward 5, Precincts 1, 2, 3, Wards 6 and 7.
Lynnfield	6	5	1st Essex	9th Essex, Precinct 2. 22d Middlesex, Precincts 1, 3 and 4. 31st Middlesex, Ward 1, Precinct 2. 36th Middlesex, Ward 1, Precinct 1, Wards 2, 4, 5, 6, Ward 3, Precinct 1, Ward 8, Precinct 2.
Malden	7	6	3d Middlesex	38th Middlesex, Ward 3, Precinct 2. 16th Suffolk, Ward 7, Ward 8, Precinct 1.
Manchester-by-the-Sea	6	5	1st Essex and Middlesex	4th Essex
Mansfield	3, 4	2	Norfolk, Bristol and Plymouth	1st Bristol, Precincts 2, 3 and 4. 14th Bristol, Precincts 1, 5A and 5B.
Marblehead	6	5	1st Essex	8th Essex
Marion	4	1	1st Plymouth and Bristol	10th Bristol

* 3d Congressional District, Precinct 1 *(in part)*, Precinct 2 *(in part)*
** 5th Congressional District, Precinct 1 *(in part)*, Precinct 2 *(in part)*
· 3d Councillor District, Precincts 2, 3, 4, 8 and 9
·· 6th Councillor District, Precincts 1, 5, 6 and 7
ⁿ 5th Congressional District, Precinct 1 *(in part)*

\#\# 7th Congressional District, Precinct 1 *(in part)*, and Precinct 2
§ 1st Congressional District, Precinct 1 *(in part)*
§§ 9th Congressional District, Precinct 1 *(in part)*, Precinct 2
3d Congressional District, Precincts 1 and 2, Precinct 3 *(in part)*, Precinct 4 *(in part)*
4th Congressional District, Precinct 3 *(in part)*, Precinct 4 *(in part)*

Cities and Towns	Congressional	Councillor	Senatorial	Representative
Marlborough	5	3	Middlesex and Worcester	4th Middlesex
Marshfield	10	4	Plymouth and Norfolk	4th Plymouth
Mashpee	10	1	Cape and Islands	3d Barnstable
Mattapoisett	4	1	1st Plymouth and Bristol	10th Bristol
Maynard	5	3	Middlesex and Worcester	13th Middlesex
Medfield	9	2	Norfolk, Bristol and Plymouth	12th Norfolk, Precincts 2 and 3; 13th Norfolk, Precincts 1 and 4; 25th Middlesex, Ward 3, Precinct 2, Ward 6, Precinct 1
Medford	7	6	2d Middlesex	37th Middlesex, Ward 4, Precinct 1, Ward 5, Ward 6, Precinct 2, Ward 7, Precinct 1; 38th Middlesex, Wards 1, 2 and 8, Ward 3, Precinct 1, Ward 4, Precinct 2, Ward 7, Precinct 2
Medway	3	2	Middlesex, Norfolk and Worcester	8th Middlesex
Melrose	7	6	3d Middlesex	35th Middlesex
Mendon	2	7	Worcester and Norfolk	10th Worcester
Merrimac	6	5	3d Essex	2d Essex
Methuen	5	5	3d Essex	15th Essex, Precincts 1, 3, 4, 5, 6, 7, 8, 9, 10, 11, 12; 16th Essex, Precinct 2
Middleborough	4	1	1st Plymouth and Bristol	10th Bristol, Precincts 3 and 6; 12th Plymouth, Precincts 1, 2, 4 and 5
Middlefield	1	8	Berkshire, Hampden, Hampshire and Franklin	2d Berkshire
Middleton	6	5	1st Essex and Middlesex	22d Middlesex
Milford	2	7	Worcester and Norfolk	10th Worcester
Millbury	2	7	2d Worcester	7th Worcester
Millis	4	2	Norfolk, Bristol and Middlesex	5th Middlesex, Precinct 2; 9th Norfolk, Precinct 1

			Representative District	Senatorial District
Millville	2	7	Worcester and Norfolk	8th Worcester
Milton	9	4	Suffolk and Norfolk	7th Norfolk, Precincts 1, 2, 4, 5, 6, 7, 8, 9, 10. 6th Suffolk, Precinct 11. 12th Suffolk, Precinct 3.
Monroe	1	x	Berkshire, Hampden, Hampshire and Franklin	2d Berkshire
Monson	2	7	Worcester, Hampden, Hampshire and Franklin	2d Hampden
Montague	1	8	Hampshire and Franklin	1st Franklin
Monterey	1	8	Berkshire, Hampden, Hampshire and Franklin	4th Berkshire
Montgomery	1	x	2d Hampden and Hampshire	4th Hampden
Mount Washington	1	x	Berkshire, Hampden, Hampshire and Franklin	4th Berkshire
Nahant	6	5	1st Essex	11th Essex
Nantucket	10	1	Cape and Islands	Barnstable, Dukes and Nantucket
Natick	7	2	Middlesex, Norfolk and Worcester, Precincts 1, 2, 3, 4, 5, 8	5th Middlesex
Needham	2	2	Norfolk, Bristol and Middlesex, Precincts 6, 7, 9 and 10.	13th Norfolk
New Ashford	1	x	Berkshire, Hampden, Hampshire and Franklin	2d Berkshire
New Bedford	4	1	2d Bristol	11th Bristol, Ward 1, Ward 2, Precincts E and G. 12th Bristol, Ward 2, Ward 3, Ward 4, Precincts C, D, E, F, Ward 5, Precinct G. 13th Bristol, Ward 4, Precincts A, B, D, G, Ward 5, Precincts A, B, C, D, E, F, Ward 6.
New Braintree	1	7	Worcester, Hampden, Hampshire and Franklin	5th Worcester
Newbury	6	5	1st Essex and Middlesex	2d Essex

Cities and Towns	Congressional	Councillor	Senatorial	Representative
Newburyport	6	5	3d Essex	1st Essex
New Marlborough	1	x	Berkshire, Hampden, Hampshire and Franklin	4th Berkshire
New Salem	1	7	Worcester, Hampden, Hampshire and Franklin	1st Franklin
Newton	4	3	1st Middlesex and Norfolk	10th Middlesex, Ward 1, Precinct 4, Ward 2, Precinct 1, Ward 3, Precincts 3, 4. 11th Middlesex, Ward 1, Precincts 2, 3, Ward 2, Precincts 2, 3, Ward 6, Precinct 1, Ward 7, Ward 8, Precincts 1, 2, 4. 12th Middlesex, Ward 3, Precincts 1, 2, Wards 4, 5, Ward 6, Precincts 2, 3, 4, Ward 8, Precinct 3. 32d Middlesex, Ward 1, Precinct 1.
Norfolk	4	2	Norfolk, Bristol and Middlesex	9th Norfolk
North Adams	1	x	Berkshire, Hampden, Hampshire and Franklin	1st Berkshire
Northampton	2	x	Hampshire and Franklin	1st Hampshire
North Andover	6	5	3d Essex, Precincts 1, 2, 3, 4. 1st Essex and Middlesex, Precincts 5 and 6.	14th Essex, Precincts 1, 2, 3, 6. 21st Middlesex, Precincts 4 and 5.
North Attleborough	3	2	Norfolk, Bristol and Middlesex	14th Bristol
Northborough	3	3	Middlesex and Worcester	4th Middlesex, Precinct 3.
Northbridge	3	7	Worcester and Norfolk	12th Worcester, Precincts 1 and 2.
North Brookfield	1	7	Worcester, Hampden, Hampshire and Franklin	9th Worcester
Northfield	1	7	Worcester, Hampden, Hampshire and Franklin	2d Franklin

Town			Senatorial District	Representative District
North Reading	6	5	1st Essex and Middlesex	21st Middlesex
Norton	4	2	Norfolk, Bristol and Plymouth	1st Bristol
Norwell	10	4	Norfolk and Plymouth	5th Plymouth
Norwood	9	2	Norfolk and Suffolk	12th Norfolk
Oak Bluffs	10	1	Cape and Islands	Barnstable, Dukes and Nantucket
Oakham	1	7	Worcester, Hampden, Hampshire and Franklin	5th Worcester
Orange	1	7	Worcester, Hampden, Hampshire and Franklin	2d Franklin
Orleans	10	1	Cape and Islands	4th Barnstable
Otis	1	8	Berkshire, Hampden, Hampshire and Franklin	4th Berkshire
Oxford	2	7	Worcester and Norfolk	6th Worcester, Precinct 2. 7th Worcester, Precincts 1, 3 and 4.
Palmer	2	7	Worcester, Hampden, Hampshire and Franklin	1st Hampden
Paxton	3	7	Worcester, Hampden, Hampshire and Franklin	13th Worcester
Peabody	6	5	2d Essex	12th Essex, Wards 1, 2, 3, 4, 5. 13th Essex, Ward 6.
Pelham	1	8	Hampshire and Franklin	3d Hampshire
Pembroke	4	1	Plymouth and Barnstable	6th Plymouth
Pepperell	5	3	1st Middlesex	1st Middlesex
Peru	1	8	Berkshire, Hampden, Hampshire and Franklin	2d Berkshire
Petersham	1	7	Worcester, Hampden, Hampshire and Franklin	5th Worcester
Phillipston	1	7	Worcester, Hampden, Hampshire and Franklin	1st Worcester
Pittsfield	1	8	Berkshire, Hampden, Hampshire and Franklin	1st Worcester 2d Berkshire, Ward 1, Precinct B 3d Berkshire, Ward 1, Precinct A. Wards 2, 3, 5, 6, 7. 4th Berkshire, Ward 4
Plainfield	1	8	Berkshire, Hampden, Hampshire and Franklin	2d Berkshire

Cities and Towns	Congressional	Councillor	Senatorial	Representative
Plainville	3	2	Norfolk, Bristol and Middlesex	14th Bristol
Plymouth	10	1	Plymouth and Barnstable	1st Plymouth, Precincts 1, 2, 3, 4, 5, 6, 7, 8, 9, 10, 12.
Plympton	4	1	Plymouth and Barnstable	12th Plymouth, Precincts 11 and 13
Princeton	3	7	Worcester and Middlesex	12th Plymouth
Provincetown	10	1	Cape and Islands	12th Worcester
				4th Barnstable
Quincy	10	4	Norfolk and Plymouth	1st Norfolk, Ward 3, Precincts 3, 4, 5, Ward 4, Precincts 1, 3, Ward 5, Precincts 2, 5, Ward 6.
				2d Norfolk, Ward 1, Ward 3, Precincts 1, 2, Ward 4, Precincts 2, 4, 5, Ward 5, Precincts 1, 3, 4.
				3d Norfolk, Ward 2.
Randolph	9	4	Suffolk and Norfolk	1st Norfolk, Precinct 6
				6th Norfolk, Precincts 1, 2, 4.
				7th Norfolk, Precincts 3, 5, 7, 8.
Raynham	4	1	1st Plymouth and Bristol	8th Plymouth
Reading	6, 7, 8	6	3d Middlesex	21st Middlesex, Precincts 1, 2, 4, 6, 7, 8A, 8B.
				34th Middlesex, Precincts 3, 5.
Rehoboth	4	2	Norfolk, Bristol and Plymouth	4th Bristol
Revere	7	6	Middlesex, Suffolk and Essex, Ward 6, Suffolk and Middlesex, Wards 1, 2, 3, 4, 5.	1st Suffolk, Ward 1, Precinct 3.
				16th Suffolk, Ward 5, Precincts 1, 2, Ward 3, Precinct 1, Wards 4 and 6.
				19th Suffolk, Ward 1, Precincts 1, 2, 4, Ward 2, Ward 3, Precincts 2, 3, Ward 5, Precinct 3
Richmond	1	8	Berkshire, Hampden, Hampshire and Franklin	2d Berkshire
Rochester	4	1	1st Plymouth and Bristol	10th Bristol

			Senatorial	Representative
Rockland	{ 4 # 10 ##	{ 2 * 4 **	2d Plymouth and Bristol, Precinct 8. Norfolk, and Plymouth, Precincts 1, 2, 3, 4, 5, 6, 7.	5th Plymouth
Rockport	6	5	1st Essex and Middlesex	5th Essex
Rowe	1	x	Berkshire, Hampden, Hampshire and Franklin	2d Berkshire
Rowley	6	5	1st Essex and Middlesex	2d Essex
Royalston	1	7	Worcester, Hampden, Hampshire and Franklin	
Russell	1	x	2d Hampden and Hampshire	2d Franklin
Rutland	3	7	Worcester, Hampden, Hampshire and Franklin	3d Hampden
Salem	6	5	2d Essex	1st Worcester
Salisbury	6	5	3d Essex	7th Essex
Sandisfield	1	x	Berkshire, Hampden, Hampshire and Franklin	1st Essex
Sandwich	10	1	Plymouth and Barnstable	4th Berkshire 2d Barnstable, Precinct 4 3d Barnstable, Precincts 5, 6, 7. 2d Plymouth, Precincts 1, 2, 3.
Saugus	6	{ 5 6	1st Essex, Precincts 1, 3, 5, 7, 8, 9, 10. Middlesex, Suffolk and Essex, Precincts, 2, 4, 6	9th Essex
Savoy	1	x	Berkshire, Hampden, Hampshire and Franklin	1st Berkshire
Scituate	10	4	Plymouth and Norfolk	4th Plymouth
Seekonk	3	2	Norfolk, Bristol and Plymouth	4th Bristol
Sharon	4	2	Norfolk, Bristol and Plymouth	8th Norfolk
Sheffield	1	x	Berkshire, Hampden, Hampshire and Franklin	4th Berkshire
Shelburne	1	x	Hampshire and Franklin	2d Berkshire
Sherborn	4	2	Norfolk, Bristol and Middlesex	5th Middlesex

§ 6th Congressional District, Precinct 1 and Precinct 8 (in part)
§§ 7th Congressional District, Precincts 2, 3, 4, 5, 6 and 7, and Precinct 8 (in part)
# 4th Congressional District, Precinct 1 (in part), Precincts 3 and 4, and Precinct 5 (in part)
10th Congressional District, Precincts 1 and 6, Precinct 2 (in part), and Precinct 5 (in part)

* 2d Councillor District, Precinct 8
** 4th Councillor District, Precincts 1, 2, 3, 4, 5, 6 and 7
*** 5th Councillor District, Precincts 1, 3, 5, 7, 8, 9 and 10
**** 6th Councillor District, Precincts 2, 4 and 6.

Cities and Towns	Congressional	Councillor	Senatorial	Representative
Shirley	5	3	Middlesex and Worcester	3d Middlesex
Shrewsbury	3	7	2d Worcester	11th Worcester
Shutesbury	1	x	Hampshire and Franklin	3d Hampshire
Somerset	3	1	1st Bristol	5th Bristol
			2d Middlesex, Ward 1, Precincts 2, 3, Ward 2, Precincts 2, 3, Wards 3, 4, 5, 6 and 7.	29th Middlesex, Ward 1, Ward 2, Precincts 1, 2, Ward 4, Precinct 2
Somerville	x	6	Middlesex, Suffolk, and Essex, Ward 1, Precinct 1, Ward 2, Precinct 1	30th Middlesex, Ward 2, Precinct 3, Wards 3, 5, 6
				37th Middlesex, Ward 4, Precincts 1, 3, Ward 7
Southampton	1	x	2d Hampden and Hampshire	1st Hampshire
Southborough	5	7	Middlesex and Worcester	8th Middlesex
Southbridge	3	x	Worcester and Norfolk	6th Worcester
South Hadley	2	x	Hampshire and Franklin	2d Hampshire
Southwick	1	x	2d Hampden and Hampshire	3d Hampden
Spencer	2	7	Worcester, Hampden, Hampshire and Franklin	5th Worcester
				2d Hampden, Ward 6, Precinct B
				9th Hampden, Ward 2, Ward 8, Precincts A and D
			Hampden, Wards 1, 3, 4, Ward 5, Precinct A, Ward 6.	10th Hampden, Ward 1, Ward 3, Precincts B, C, D, F, H, Ward 6, Precincts A, E.
Springfield	2	x	1st Hampden and Hampshire, Ward 2, Ward 5, Precincts B, C, D, E, F, G, H, Wards 7 and 8.	11th Hampden, Ward 5, Precincts C, D, E, G, H, Ward 7, Precincts C, F, G, H, Ward 8, Precincts B, C, E, F, G, H.
				12th Hampden, Ward 3, Precincts A, E, G, Ward 4, Ward 5, Precincts A, B, F, Ward 7, Precinct A.
				13th Hampden, Ward 6, Precincts C, D, F, G, H, Ward 7, Precincts B, D, E.

Town			District	
Sterling	3	7	Worcester and Middlesex	12th Worcester
Stockbridge	1	8	Berkshire, Hampden, Hampshire and Franklin	4th Berkshire
Stoneham	7	6	3d Middlesex	34th Middlesex, Precincts 1, 2, 3. 35th Middlesex, Precincts 4, 5, 6. 6th Norfolk, Precinct 1. 8th Norfolk, Precincts 2, 3, 4, 5, 6, 7 and 8.
Stoughton	9	2	Norfolk, Bristol and Plymouth	3d Middlesex
Stow	5	3	Middlesex and Worcester	1st Hampden, Precinct 2
Sturbridge	2	7	Worcester, Hampden, Hampshire and Franklin	6th Worcester, Precinct 1
Sudbury	5	3	5th Middlesex	13th Middlesex
Sunderland	1	8	Hampshire and Franklin	1st Franklin
Sutton	2	7	2d Worcester	9th Worcester
Swampscott	6	5	1st Essex	8th Essex
Swansea	3	1	1st Bristol	4th Bristol, Precincts 1, 4. 5th Bristol, Precincts 2, 3. 3d Bristol, Wards 1, 2, 3, 4, 5, Ward 7, Precinct A, Ward 8, Precinct B.
Taunton	9	1	1st Plymouth and Bristol	4th Bristol, Ward 7, Precinct B. Ward 8, Precinct A. 5th Bristol, Ward 6.
Templeton	1	7	Worcester, Hampden, Hampshire and Franklin	1st Worcester
Tewksbury	5	5	2d Essex and Middlesex	18th Middlesex, Precinct 3. 20th Middlesex, Precincts 1, 1A, 2, 2A, 3A, 4.
Tisbury	10	1	Cape and Islands	Barnstable, Dukes and Nantucket
Tolland	1	8	Berkshire, Hampden, Hampshire and Franklin	3d Hampden
Topsfield	6	5	1st Essex and Middlesex	13th Essex
Townsend	1	7	Worcester and Middlesex	1st Middlesex
Truro	10	1	Cape and Islands	4th Barnstable
Tyngsborough	5	3	1st Middlesex	39th Middlesex

Cities and Towns	Congres-sional	Coun-cillor	Senatorial	Representative
Tyringham	1	8	Berkshire, Hampden, Hampshire and Franklin	4th Berkshire
Upton	3	7	2d Worcester	9th Worcester
Uxbridge	2	7	Worcester and Norfolk	8th Worcester
Wakefield	7	6	3d Middlesex	22d Middlesex
Wales	2	7	Worcester, Hampden, Hampshire and Franklin	2d Hampden
Walpole	9	2	Norfolk, Bristol and Plymouth	9th Norfolk, Precincts 1, 2, 3, 4, 5 and 6 / 12th Norfolk, Precinct 7
Waltham	7	3	5th Middlesex, Wards 1, 2, Ward 3, Precinct 1, Ward 6, Precinct 1, Ward 7. Middlesex and Suffolk, Ward 3, Precinct 2, Wards 4, 5, Ward 6, Precinct 2, Wards 8 and 9	9th Middlesex, Wards 1, 2, 3, 4 and 7. / 10th Middlesex, Wards 5, 6, 8 and 9
Ware	2	7	Worcester, Hampden, Hampshire and Franklin	1st Hampden
Wareham	4	1	Plymouth and Barnstable	2d Plymouth
Warren	2	7	Worcester, Hampden, Hampshire and Franklin	5th Worcester
Warwick	1	7	Worcester, Hampden, Hampshire and Franklin	2d Franklin
Washington	1	8	Berkshire, Hampden, Hampshire and Franklin	2d Berkshire
Watertown	8	3	Middlesex and Suffolk	32d Middlesex
Wayland	5	3	5th Middlesex	13th Middlesex
Webster	2	7	Worcester and Norfolk	8th Worcester
Wellesley	4	2 8 / 3 8 8	Norfolk, Bristol and Middlesex, Precincts B, F, G. / 1st Middlesex and Norfolk, Precincts A, C, D, E.	14th Norfolk

Town		Senatorial District	Representative District
Wellfleet	10	Cape and Islands	4th Barnstable
Wendell	1	Hampshire and Franklin	1st Franklin
Wenham	6	1st Essex and Middlesex	4th Essex
Westborough	4	Middlesex, Norfolk and Worcester, Precinct 3. / Middlesex and Worcester, Precincts 1, 2 and 4	11th Worcester
West Boylston	3	1st Worcester	12th Worcester, Precinct 2
West Bridgewater	4	Norfolk, Bristol and Plymouth	14th Worcester, Precinct 1
West Brookfield	1	Worcester, Hampden, Hampshire and Franklin	10th Plymouth
Westfield	1	2d Hampden and Hampshire	5th Worcester
Westford	5	1st Middlesex	4th Hampden
Westhampton	1	Hampshire and Franklin	2d Middlesex
Westminster	1	Worcester and Middlesex	1st Hampshire
West Newbury	6	1st Essex and Middlesex	2d Worcester
Weston	7	5th Middlesex	2d Essex
Westport	3	1st Bristol	14th Norfolk
West Springfield	1	Hampden	8th Bristol
West Stockbridge	1	Berkshire, Hampden, Hampshire and Franklin	6th Hampden
West Tisbury	10	Cape and Islands	4th Berkshire / Barnstable, Dukes and Nantucket
Westwood	9	Norfolk and Suffolk	11th Norfolk / 3d Norfolk, Precincts 5, 6, 9, 12, 16 and 17.
Weymouth	10	Plymouth and Norfolk	4th Norfolk, Precincts 1, 2, 3, 4, 7, 8, 10, 11, 13, 14, 15 and 18.
Whately	1	Hampshire and Franklin	1st Franklin
Whitman	10	2d Plymouth and Bristol	7th Plymouth
Wilbraham	2	1st Hampden and Hampshire	13th Hampden
Williamsburg	1	Hampshire and Franklin	1st Franklin

* 2d Councillor District, Precinct 3.
** 3d Councillor District, Precincts 1, 2 and 4

§ 2d councillor District, Precincts B, F and G
§§ 3d councillor District, Precincts A, C, D and E

Cities and Towns	Congres- sional	Coun- cillor	Senatorial	Representative
Williamstown	1	8	Berkshire, Hampden, Hampshire and Franklin	1st Berkshire
Wilmington	6	5	1st Essex and Middlesex	20th Middlesex, Precincts 1, 2, 4, 5 and 6.
Winchendon	1	7	Worcester, Hampden, Hampshire and Franklin	2'd Middlesex, Precinct 3.
Winchester	7	6	2d Middlesex	1st Worcester
Windsor	1	8	Berkshire, Hampden, Hampshire and Franklin	34th Middlesex
Winthrop	7	6	Suffolk and Middlesex	2d Berkshire
				19th Suffolk
Woburn	7	6	2d Middlesex, Ward 2	33d Middlesex
			4th Middlesex, Wards 1, 3, 4, 5, 6 and 7.	
Worcester	3	7	1st Worcester, Wards 1, 2, 3, 4, Ward 7, Precincts 1, 2, 3, Wards 9 and 10.	13th Worcester, Wards 1, 9. 14th Worcester, Wards 2, 3. 15th Worcester, Ward 4, Ward 5, Precinct 3, Ward 10.
			2d Worcester, Wards 5, 6, 8, Ward 7, Precincts 4, 5.	16th Worcester, Ward 5, Precincts 1, 2, 4, 5, Ward 6, Ward 8, Precincts 1, 5. 17th Worcester, Ward 7, Ward 8, Precincts 2, 3, 4.
Worthington	1	8	Berkshire, Hampden, Hampshire and Franklin	1st Franklin
Wrentham	3	2	Norfolk, Bristol and Middlesex	9th Norfolk
Yarmouth	10	1	Cape and Islands	1st Barnstable, Precincts 1, 2, 3, 4 and 5. Barnstable, Dukes and Nantucket, Precinct 6.

VALUATION, POPULATION and VOTERS

VALUATION OF THE COMMONWEALTH.

BARNSTABLE COUNTY.

CITIES AND TOWNS	Equalized Value	Tax of $1000
Barnstable	$ 4,825,386,900	$ 12.79
Bourne	1,437,733,300	3.81
Brewster	1,129,552,100	2.99
Chatham	1,628,155,200	4.32
Dennis	2,132,188,600	5.65
Eastham	862,680,900	2.29
Falmouth	3,618,170,500	9.59
Harwich	1,626,185,400	4.31
Mashpee	1,298,760,900	3.44
Orleans	1,186,890,900	3.15
Provincetown	588,630,600	1.56
Sandwich	1,486,417,600	3.94
Truro	600,002,500	1.59
Wellfleet	703,867,400	1.87
Yarmouth	2,161,867,200	5.73
Totals	25,286,490,000	67.03

*Under the provisions of section 10C of Chapter 58 of the General Laws, the Commissioner of Revenue is required to submit final equalization and apportionment upon the several cities and towns of the amount of property and the proportion of every one thousand dollars of state or county tax which should be assessed upon each city and town. The present apportionment listed above constitutes a basis for apportionment for the year 1997 and serves for a two-year basis. The Commissioner submitted this report on January 9, 1997.

317

BERKSHIRE COUNTY.

CITIES AND TOWNS	Equalized Value	Tax of $1000
Adams	310,627,800	0.82
Alford	87,499,300	0.23
Becket	207,417,500	0.55
Cheshire	149,481,300	0.40
Clarksburg	59,068,900	0.16
Dalton	329,135,800	0.87
Egremont	182,770,200	0.48
Florida	55,857,400	0.15
Great Barrington	537,847,200	1.43
Hancock	89,283,500	0.24
Hinsdale	112,261,800	0.30
Lanesborough	235,853,100	0.62
Lee	387,403,200	1.03
Lenox	459,095,100	1.22
Monterey	164,715,400	0.44
Mount Washington	33,443,200	0.09
New Ashford	18,787,800	0.05
New Marlborough	198,830,500	0.53
NORTH ADAMS	446,712,800	1.18
Otis	274,263,800	0.73
Peru	37,080,000	0.10
PITTSFIELD	1,984,639,200	5.26
Richmond	172,806,900	0.46
Sandisfield	124,267,200	0.33
Savoy	33,713,200	0.09
Sheffield	287,818,300	0.76
Stockbridge	373,855,300	0.99
Tyringham	77,096,000	0.20
Washington	39,232,100	0.10
West Stockbridge	149,089,100	0.39
Williamstown	495,770,000	1.31
Windsor	60,074,800	0.16
Totals	8,175,797,700	21.67

BRISTOL COUNTY.

Cities and Towns	Equalized Value	Tax of $1000
Acushnet	453,683,700	1.20
ATTLEBORO	1,698,474,700	4.50
Berkley	289,696,600	0.77
Dartmouth	2,048,446,800	5.43
Dighton	313,263,400	0.83
Easton	1,229,042,000	3.26
Fairhaven	868,082,800	2.30
FALL RIVER	2,813,460,700	7.46
Freetown	478,349,400	1.27
Mansfield	1,391,011,300	3.69
NEW BEDFORD	2,950,935,400	7.82
North Attleborough	1,413,941,100	3.75
Norton	762,852,900	2.02
Raynham	706,935,600	1.87
Rehoboth	636,203,300	1.69
Seekonk	1,018,081,900	2.70
Somerset	1,402,452,300	3.72
Swansea	908,797,400	2.41
TAUNTON	2,250,229,800	5.96
Westport	1,168,931,100	3.10
Totals	24,802,872,200	65.75

DUKES COUNTY.

Cities and Towns	Equalized Value	Tax of $1000
Chilmark	830,061,200	2.20
Edgartown	1,226,925,600	3.25
Gay Head	198,164,900	0.53
Gosnold	93,475,000	0.25
Oak Bluffs	702,097,000	1.86
Tisbury	642,116,700	1.70
West Tisbury	545,653,900	1.45
Totals	4,238,494,300	11.24

ESSEX COUNTY.

Cities and Towns	Equalized Value	Tax of $1000
Amesbury	797,621,300	2.11
Andover	3,072,063,800	8.14
Beverly	2,365,546,000	6.27
Boxford	757,512,100	2.01
Danvers	2,103,970,900	5.58
Essex	319,590,500	0.85
Georgetown	469,697,100	1.25
Gloucester	2,091,570,400	5.55
Groveland	318,689,700	0.84
Hamilton	621,002,900	1.65
Haverhill	2,120,295,100	5.62
Ipswich	991,783,700	2.63
Lawrence	1,124,106,800	2.98
Lynn	2,451,325,700	6.50
Lynnfield	1,091,309,900	2.89
Manchester-by-the-Sea	854,321,900	2.27
Marblehead	2,249,236,900	5.96
Merrimac	272,194,900	0.72
Methuen	1,922,748,900	5.10
Middleton	553,789,900	1.47
Nahant	314,619,700	0.83
Newbury	501,494,200	1.33
Newburyport	1,183,744,500	3.14
North Andover	1,911,398,400	5.07
Peabody	3,330,340,100	8.83
Rockport	772,507,100	2.05
Rowley	335,021,400	0.89
Salem	2,083,065,400	5.52
Salisbury	525,853,300	1.39
Saugus	1,886,327,300	5.00
Swampscott	1,121,853,200	2.97
Topsfield	543,986,200	1.44
Wenham	363,518,900	0.96
West Newbury	334,166,900	0.89
Totals	41,756,275,000	$110.70

FRANKLIN COUNTY.

CITIES AND TOWNS	Equalized Value	Tax of $1000
Ashfield	115,968,300	0.31
Bernardston	104,335,900	0.28
Buckland	104,410,600	0.28
Charlemont	61,392,300	0.16
Colrain	94,018,600	0.25
Conway	115,030,800	0.30
Deerfield	341,103,300	0.90
Erving	143,781,100	0.38
Gill	69,805,300	0.18
Greenfield	760,475,000	2.02
Hawley	22,418,700	0.06
Heath	46,358,400	0.12
Leverett	114,412,400	0.30
Leyden	38,597,300	0.10
Monroe	17,687,700	0.05
Montague	395,147,400	1.05
New Salem	51,154,400	0.14
Northfield	164,051,700	0.43
Orange	239,221,200	0.63
Rowe	149,715,600	0.40
Shelburne	114,117,800	0.30
Shutesbury	109,450,000	0.29
Sunderland	160,751,600	0.43
Warwick	39,141,100	0.10
Wendell	43,451,100	0.12
Whately	111,349,700	0.30
Totals	3,727,347,300	9.88

HAMPDEN COUNTY.

CITIES AND TOWNS	Equalized Value	Tax of $1000
Agawam	1,394,724,700	3.70
Blandford	83,610,000	0.22
Brimfield	174,995,500	0.46
Chester	64,771,800	0.17
CHICOPEE	2,009,630,800	5.33
East Longmeadow	961,818,500	2.55
Granville	97,011,200	0.26
Hampden	283,779,600	0.75
Holland	147,859,100	0.39

HAMPDEN COUNTY — *Concluded.*

Cities and Towns	Equalized Value	Tax of $1000
Holyoke	1,121,974,300	2.98
Longmeadow	1,192,398,500	3.16
Ludlow	922,732,200	2.45
Monson	376,479,200	1.00
Montgomery	48,768,600	0.13
Palmer	546,694,100	1.45
Russell	76,402,800	0.20
Southwick	432,240,900	1.15
Springfield	4,097,775,200	10.86
Tolland	90,732,900	0.24
Wales	76,809,300	0.20
West Springfield	1,404,520,000	3.72
Westfield	1,675,556,600	4.44
Wilbraham	856,219,400	2.27
Totals	18,137,505,200	48.08

HAMPSHIRE COUNTY.

Cities and Towns	Equalized Value	Tax of $1000
Amherst	1,046,631,600	2.77
Belchertown	583,085,000	1.55
Chesterfield	62,050,000	0.16
Cummington	60,935,700	0.16
Easthampton	654,489,600	1.73
Goshen	63,117,400	0.17
Granby	292,461,000	0.78
Hadley	365,919,000	0.97
Hatfield	264,923,000	0.70
Huntington	95,752,400	0.25
Middlefield	31,068,600	0.08
Northampton	1,470,426,100	3.90
Pelham	81,502,400	0.22
Plainfield	46,114,400	0.12
South Hadley	798,598,100	2.12
Southampton	284,198,400	0.75
Ware	388,143,800	1.03
Westhampton	92,538,000	0.25
Williamsburg	142,668,500	0.38
Worthington	79,917,500	0.21
Totals	6,904,540,500	18.30

MIDDLESEX COUNTY.

Cities and Towns	Equalized Value	Tax of $1000
Acton	1,666,438,600	4.42
Arlington	2,999,301,600	7.95
Ashby	129,782,200	0.34
Ashland	903,469,400	2.39
Ayer	550,418,300	1.46
Bedford	1,293,047,700	3.43
Belmont	2,376,571,300	6.30
Billerica	2,208,107,500	5.85
Boxborough	402,723,400	1.07
Burlington	2,048,425,400	5.43
CAMBRIDGE	7,593,801,600	20.13
Carlisle	574,967,000	1.52
Chelmsford	2,129,612,700	5.65
Concord	2,269,975,300	6.02
Dracut	1,230,001,400	3.26
Dunstable	195,678,900	0.52
EVERETT	2,097,750,800	5.56
Framingham	3,955,109,800	10.48
Groton	605,556,200	1.61
Holliston	925,422,900	2.45
Hopkinton	1,036,439,600	2.75
Hudson	983,249,800	2.61
Lexington	3,689,184,800	9.78
Lincoln	837,001,800	2.22
Littleton	628,787,500	1.67
LOWELL	2,644,624,100	7.01
MALDEN	1,998,192,800	5.30
MARLBOROUGH	2,155,718,500	5.71
Maynard	594,055,900	1.57
MEDFORD	2,850,402,200	7.56
MELROSE	1,580,721,000	4.19
Natick	2,655,370,000	7.04
NEWTON	8,906,905,500	23.61
North Reading	1,043,098,800	2.77
Pepperell	533,839,800	1.41
Reading	1,675,702,200	4.44
Sherborn	607,849,500	1.61
Shirley	248,609,400	0.66
SOMERVILLE	2,805,809,000	7.44
Stoneham	1,406,201,000	3.73
Stow	470,428,500	1.25
Sudbury	1,866,486,800	4.95
Tewksbury	1,830,605,100	4.85
Townsend	411,661,700	1.09
Tyngsborough	524,052,400	1.39
Wakefield	1,712,489,800	4.54
WALTHAM	3,748,643,300	9.94

MIDDLESEX COUNTY — *Concluded.*

Cities and Towns	Equalized Value	Tax of $1000
Watertown	2,187,958,300	5.80
Wayland	1,450,192,100	3.84
Westford	1,521,187,700	4.03
Weston	2,001,436,800	5.31
Wilmington	1,689,244,100	4.48
Winchester	2,258,551,500	5.99
Woburn	2,687,725,100	7.12
Totals	99,398,588,400	263.50

NANTUCKET COUNTY.

Cities and Towns	Equalized Value	Tax of $1000
Nantucket	3,514,157,300	9.32
Totals	3,514,157,300	9.32

NORFOLK COUNTY.

Cities and Towns	Equalized Value	Tax of $1000
Avon	406,242,600	1.08
Bellingham	958,717,400	2.54
Braintree	2,449,092,000	6.49
Brookline	5,048,485,400	13.38
Canton	1,670,684,300	4.43
Cohasset	856,628,200	2.27
Dedham	1,683,887,500	4.46
Dover	933,790,700	2.48
Foxborough	1,083,159,400	2.87
Franklin	1,760,276,700	4.67
Holbrook	510,091,200	1.35
Medfield	1,039,177,400	2.76
Medway	727,465,900	1.93
Millis	474,942,900	1.26
Milton	1,811,114,100	4.80
Needham	3,131,771,600	8.30

NORFOLK COUNTY — *Concluded.*

CITIES AND TOWNS	Equalized Value	Tax of $1000
Norfolk	620,850,500	1.65
Norwood	2,162,907,600	5.73
Plainville	415,746,300	1.10
QUINCY	4,498,810,500	11.93
Randolph	1,468,588,200	3.89
Sharon	1,280,919,700	3.40
Stoughton	1,457,014,800	3.86
Walpole	1,591,345,300	4.22
Wellesley	3,914,149,200	10.38
Westwood	1,526,558,900	4.05
Weymouth	2,776,803,700	7.36
Wrentham	657,863,300	1.74
Totals	46,917,085,300	124.38

PLYMOUTH COUNTY.

CITIES AND TOWNS	Equalized Value	Tax of $1000
Abington	718,443,400	1.90
Bridgewater	997,392,300	2.64
BROCKTON	2,811,051,100	7.45
Carver	490,285,400	1.30
Duxbury	1,408,233,000	3.73
East Bridgewater	621,421,400	1.65
Halifax	333,267,900	0.88
Hanover	1,013,626,800	2.69
Hanson	490,380,200	1.30
Hingham	2,021,730,100	5.36
Hull	619,736,500	1.64
Kingston	695,879,100	1.84
Lakeville	605,001,300	1.60
Marion	602,319,400	1.60
Marshfield	1,651,966,800	4.38
Mattapoisett	620,738,100	1.65
Middleborough	918,457,000	2.43
Norwell	946,606,700	2.51
Pembroke	963,754,300	2.56
Plymouth	3,289,205,600	8.72
Plympton	161,003,800	0.43
Rochester	289,548,900	0.77
Rockland	791,190,200	2.10

PLYMOUTH COUNTY — *Concluded.*

Cities and Towns	Equalized Value	Tax of $1000
Scituate	1,498,124,400	3.97
Wareham	1,245,904,000	3.30
West Bridgewater	493,167,900	1.31
Whitman	549,559,400	1.46
Totals	26,847,995,000	71.17

SUFFOLK COUNTY.

Cities and Towns	Equalized Value	Tax of $1000
Boston	31,075,293,700	82.38
Chelsea	812,415,200	2.15
Revere	1,695,498,900	4.50
Winthrop	800,633,400	2.12
Totals	34,383,841,200	91.15

WORCESTER COUNTY.

Cities and Towns	Equalized Value	Tax of $1000
Ashburnham	254,842,400	0.68
Athol	363,713,800	0.96
Auburn	875,955,700	2.32
Barre	191,231,300	0.51
Berlin	187,963,600	0.50
Blackstone	339,983,500	0.90
Bolton	376,737,100	1.00
Boylston	265,089,100	0.70
Brookfield	121,898,800	0.32
Charlton	531,720,300	1.41
Clinton	510,779,700	1.35
Douglas	328,223,700	0.87
Dudley	389,958,100	1.03
East Brookfield	110,979,900	0.29
Fitchburg	1,178,184,300	3.12
Gardner	603,909,500	1.60

WORCESTER COUNTY— *Concluded.*

CITIES AND TOWNS	Equalized Value	Tax of $1000
Grafton	686,121,500	1.82
Hardwick	120,459,700	0.32
Harvard	524,248,300	1.39
Holden	850,242,800	2.25
Hopedale	273,138,400	0.72
Hubbardston	179,958,800	0.48
Lancaster	318,554,000	0.85
Leicester	395,974,000	1.05
LEOMINSTER	1,707,632,600	4.53
Lunenburg	496,698,400	1.32
Mendon	304,447,700	0.81
Milford	1,362,827,200	3.61
Millbury	581,586,800	1.54
Millville	113,180,900	0.30
New Braintree	45,860,800	0.12
North Brookfield	191,043,800	0.51
Northborough	964,534,800	2.56
Northbridge	538,657,200	1.43
Oakham	88,793,000	0.24
Oxford	529,357,600	1.40
Paxton	238,677,600	0.63
Petersham	79,390,700	0.21
Phillipston	75,684,800	0.20
Princeton	234,529,700	0.62
Royalston	60,049,100	0.16
Rutland	248,675,200	0.66
Shrewsbury	1,838,100,900	4.87
Southborough	836,931,400	2.22
Southbridge	524,358,400	1.39
Spencer	482,416,500	1.28
Sterling	430,076,300	1.14
Sturbridge	478,653,000	1.27
Sutton	472,689,100	1.25
Templeton	258,133,100	0.68
Upton	402,725,600	1.07
Uxbridge	547,933,000	1.45
Warren	185,870,000	0.49
Webster	703,750,400	1.87
West Boylston	405,565,700	1.08
West Brookfield	184,176,700	0.49
Westborough	1,416,340,000	3.76
Westminster	390,996,800	1.04
Winchendon	321,638,200	0.85
WORCESTER	5,409,541,600	14.34
Totals	33,131,392,900	87.83

RECAPITULATION.

COUNTIES	Equalized Value	Tax of $1000
BARNSTABLE	25.286,490,000	67.03
BERKSHIRE	8.175,797,700	21.67
BRISTOL	24.802,872,200	65.75
DUKES COUNTY	4.238,494,300	11.24
ESSEX	41.756,275,000	110.70
FRANKLIN	3.727,347,300	9.88
HAMPDEN	18.137,505,200	48.08
HAMPSHIRE	6.904,540,500	18.30
MIDDLESEX	99.398,588,400	263.50
NANTUCKET	3.514,157,300	9.32
NORFOLK	46.917,085,300	124.38
PLYMOUTH	26.847,995,000	71.17
SUFFOLK	34.383,841,200	91.15
WORCESTER	33.131,392,900	87.83
TOTALS	377,222,382,300	1000.00

POPULATION OF
CITIES IN THE COMMONWEALTH,
WITH THE DATES OF THEIR INCORPORATION.

NAME	INCORPO-RATED AS CITY	POPU-LATION, 1980 (U.S. Census)	POPU-LATION, 1985 (STATE Census)	POPU-LATION, 1990 (U.S. Census)
Boston	Feb. 23, 1822	562,994	601,094	574,283
Worcester	Feb. 29, 1848	161,799	164,651	169,759
Springfield	Apr. 12, 1852	152,319	158,763	156,983
Lowell	Apr. 1, 1836	92,148	95,339	103,439
New Bedford	Mar. 9, 1847	98,478	96,533	99,922
Cambridge	Mar. 17, 1846	95,322	86,865	95,802
Brockton	Apr. 9, 1881	95,172	97,429	92,788
Fall River	Apr. 12, 1854	92,574	89,626	92,703
Quincy	May 17, 1888	84,743	88,122	84,985
Newton	Jun. 2, 1873	83,622	82,925	82,585
Lynn	Apr. 10, 1850	78,471	78,463	81,245
Somerville	Apr. 14, 1872	77,372	71,134	76,210
Lawrence	Mar. 21, 1853	63,175	58,785	70,207
Waltham	Jun. 3, 1884	58,200	57,955	57,878
Medford	May 31, 1892	58,076	57,184	57,407
Chicopee	Apr. 18, 1890	55,112	53,325	56,632
Malden	Mar. 31, 1881	53,386	52,474	53,884
Haverhill	Mar. 10, 1869	46,865	46,172	51,418
Taunton	May 11, 1864	45,001	42,001	49,832
Pittsfield	Jun. 5, 1889	51,974	48,487	48,622
Peabody	May 8, 1916	45,976	45,766	47,039
Holyoke	Apr. 7, 1873	44,678	43,125	43,704
Revere	Jun. 19, 1914	42,423	39,512	42,786
Fitchburg	Mar. 8, 1872	39,580	39,576	41,194
Attleboro	Jun. 17, 1914	34,196	32,233	38,383
Westfield	Apr. 9, 1920	36,465	34,717	38,372
Beverly	Mar. 23, 1894	37,655	35,532	38,195
Leominster	May 13, 1915	34,508	31,113	38,145
Salem	Mar. 23, 1836	38,220	37,092	38,091
Woburn	May 18, 1888	36,626	34,793	35,943
Everett	Jun. 11, 1892	37,195	35,773	35,701
Marlborough	May 3, 1890	30,617	34,294	31,813
Northampton	Jun. 23, 1883	29,286	28,042	29,289
Gloucester	Apr. 28, 1873	27,768	24,946	28,716
Chelsea	Mar. 13, 1857	25,431	23,432	28,710
Melrose	Mar. 18, 1899	30,055	28,774	28,150
Gardner	Feb. 28, 1923	17,900	17,921	20,125
North Adams	Mar. 22, 1895	18,063	16,921	16,797
Newburyport	May 24, 1851	15,900	15,635	16,317

POPULATION AND VOTERS

COUNTIES, CITIES AND TOWNS IN THE COMMONWEALTH, WITH THE CENSUS
OF INHABITANTS IN 1990 AND 1985, AND A LIST OF VOTERS IN 1996,
THE FIGURES BEING FOR THE STATE ELECTION, REVISED AND
CORRECTED BY THE SECRETARY OF THE COMMONWEALTH.

| COUNTIES, CITIES AND TOWNS | POPULATION | | Regis-tered Voters 1996 |
	U.S. Census 1990	State Census 1985	
BARNSTABLE			
Barnstable	40,949	32,891	28,975
Bourne	16,064	15,636	10,163
Brewster	8,440	6,574	6,522
Chatham	6,579	6,332	5,772
Dennis	13,864	12,709	10,666
Eastham	4,462	3,870	3,645
Falmouth	27,960	25,974	21,440
Harwich	10,275	9,050	8,468
Mashpee	7,884	5,070	6,318
Orleans	5,838	5,979	5,140
Provincetown	3,561	3,956	3,121
Sandwich	15,489	11,589	11,733
Truro	1,573	1,431	1,431
Wellfleet	2,493	2,530	2,196
Yarmouth	21,174	18,348	17,009
Totals	186,605	161,939	142,549
BERKSHIRE			
Adams	9,445	9,611	5,667
Alford	418	353	305
Becket	1,481	1,278	994
Cheshire	3,479	3,323	2,419
Clarksburg	1,745	1,718	1,036
Dalton	7,155	6,676	4,365
Egremont	1,229	1,268	862
Florida	742	636	487
Great Barrington	7,725	6,796	4,429
Hancock	628	690	430
Hinsdale	1,959	1,727	1,163
Lanesborough	3,032	2,960	1,603
Lee	5,849	5,865	3,724

COUNTIES, CITIES AND TOWNS	POPULATION		Regis-tered Voters 1996
	U.S. Census 1990	State Census 1985	
BERKSHIRE — *Concluded*			
Lenox	5,069	5,789	3,085
Monterey	805	708	602
Mount Washington	135	105	85
New Ashford	192	171	137
New Marlborough	1,240	1,107	871
NORTH ADAMS	16,797	16,356	7,676
Otis	1,073	906	667
Peru	779	628	493
PITTSFIELD	48,622	48,876	27,355
Richmond	1,677	1,608	1,137
Sandisfield	667	771	506
Savoy	634	550	387
Sheffield	2,910	3,072	1,876
Stockbridge	2,408	2,379	1,559
Tyringham	369	322	254
Washington	615	515	378
West Stockbridge	1,483	1,237	975
Williamstown	8,220	8,135	4,884
Windsor	770	608	556
Totals	139,352	136,744	80,967
BRISTOL			
Acushnet	9,554	8,772	5,892
ATTLEBORO	38,383	32,233	19,279
Berkley	4,237	2,994	3,027
Dartmouth	27,244	24,843	15,866
Dighton	5,631	5,028	3,602
Easton	19,807	18,079	12,588
Fairhaven	16,132	15,451	9,678
FALL RIVER	92,703	89,626	44,106
Freetown	8,522	7,575	5,164
Mansfield	16,568	14,449	11,215
NEW BEDFORD	99,922	96,533	46,425
North Attleborough	25,038	22,200	14,792
Norton	14,265	12,931	8,930
Raynham	9,867	8,935	6,444
Rehoboth	8,656	7,674	5,790
Seekonk	13,046	12,271	8,141
Somerset	17,655	18,524	11,992
Swansea	15,411	14,747	9,094
TAUNTON	49,832	42,001	25,565
Westport	13,852	13,362	8,968
Totals	506,325	468,228	276,558

COUNTIES, CITIES AND TOWNS	POPULATION		Registered Voters 1996
	U.S. Census 1990	State Census 1985	
DUKES COUNTY			
Chilmark	650	520	652
Edgartown	3,062	2,617	2,608
Gay Head	201	141	276
Gosnold	98	59	126
Oak Bluffs	2,804	2,261	2,593
Tisbury	3,120	2,995	2,355
West Tisbury	1,704	1,430	1,331
Totals	11,639	10,023	9,941
ESSEX			
Amesbury	14,997	13,923	8,987
Andover	29,151	27,154	20,370
BEVERLY	38,195	35,532	24,890
Boxford	6,266	5,565	4,940
Danvers	24,174	24,224	15,598
Essex	3,260	2,971	2,404
Georgetown	6,384	5,884	4,580
GLOUCESTER	28,716	24,946	19,224
Groveland	5,214	5,089	3,565
Hamilton	7,280	7,103	4,832
HAVERHILL	51,418	46,172	26,851
Ipswich	11,873	11,368	8,568
LAWRENCE	70,207	58,785	23,804
LYNN	81,245	78,463	37,439
Lynnfield	11,274	11,135	7,726
Manchester-by-the-Sea	5,286	5,472	3,784
Marblehead	19,971	19,403	13,997
Merrimac	5,166	4,237	3,398
Methuen	39,990	36,624	22,774
Middleton	4,921	4,482	3,730
Nahant	3,828	4,070	2,549
Newbury	5,623	5,423	1,852
NEWBURYPORT	16,317	15,635	11,449
North Andover	22,792	19,711	15,756
PEABODY	47,039	45,766	30,428
Rockport	7,482	6,793	5,124
Rowley	4,452	3,803	3,026
SALEM	38,091	37,092	21,954
Salisbury	6,882	6,588	4,247
Saugus	25,549	24,628	16,337
Swampscott	13,650	13,524	9,512
Topsfield	3,754	5,480	3,809
Wenham	4,212	3,838	2,441
West Newbury	3,421	3,175	2,570
Totals	670,080	624,058	392,515

COUNTIES. CITIES AND TOWNS	POPULATION		Regis- tered Voters 1996
	U.S. Census 1990	State Census 1985	
FRANKLIN			
Ashfield	1,715	1,541	1,198
Bernardston	2,048	1,822	1,259
Buckland	1,928	1,819	1,168
Charlemont	1,249	1,159	769
Colrain	1,757	1,595	1,103
Conway	1,529	1,298	1,001
Deerfield	5,018	4,485	3,216
Erving	1,372	1,297	884
Gill	1,583	1,358	985
Greenfield	18,666	18,845	10,086
Hawley	317	298	230
Heath	716	530	445
Leverett	1,785	1,563	1,253
Leyden	662	522	434
Monroe	115	135	73
Montague	8,316	7,906	4,746
New Salem	802	770	524
Northfield	2,838	2,368	1,813
Orange	7,312	6,341	3,743
Rowe	378	335	261
Shelburne	2,012	1,924	1,244
Shutesbury	1,561	1,126	1,316
Sunderland	3,399	3,133	2,036
Warwick	740	635	504
Wendell	899	704	540
Whately	1,375	1,342	993
Totals	70,092	64,851	41,824
HAMPDEN			
Agawam	27,323	24,612	16,324
Blandford	1,187	1,039	846
Brimfield	3,001	2,386	1,905
Chester	1,280	1,107	753
CHICOPEE	56,632	53,325	29,950
East Longmeadow	13,367	12,403	8,990
Granville	1,403	1,300	938
Hampden	4,709	4,644	3,125
Holland	2,185	1,785	1,334
HOLYOKE	43,704	43,125	21,696
Longmeadow	15,467	15,971	10,619
Ludlow	18,820	16,607	10,848
Monson	7,776	7,249	4,514
Montgomery	759	667	503
Palmer	12,054	11,327	7,431
Russell	1,594	1,397	945
Southwick	7,667	7,129	4,634

COUNTIES, CITIES AND TOWNS	POPULATION		Regis-tered Voters 1996
	U.S. Census 1990	State Census 1985	

HAMPDEN — *Concluded*

SPRINGFIELD	156,983	158,763	72,776
Tolland	289	233	206
Wales	1,566	1,086	915
West Springfield	27,537	25,289	15,790
WESTFIELD	38,372	34,717	21,078
Wilbraham	12,635	11,958	8,459
Totals	456,310	438,119	244,579

HAMPSHIRE

Amherst	35,228	35,827	15,608
Belchertown	10,579	7,863	7,246
Chesterfield	1,048	963	689
Cummington	785	722	591
Easthampton	15,537	15,353	9,609
Goshen	830	729	537
Granby	5,565	5,076	3,772
Hadley	4,231	4,056	3,164
Hatfield	3,184	3,098	2,308
Huntington	1,987	1,803	1,317
Middlefield	392	374	352
NORTHAMPTON	29,289	28,042	18,061
Pelham	1,373	1,136	928
Plainfield	571	479	377
South Hadley	16,685	15,607	11,146
Southampton	4,478	4,208	3,197
Ware	9,808	8,669	5,627
Westhampton	1,327	1,213	956
Williamsburg	2,515	2,287	1,701
Worthington	1,156	1,029	813
Totals	146,568	138,534	87,999

MIDDLESEX

Acton	17,872	17,431	11,806
Arlington	44,630	46,465	27,592
Ashby	2,717	2,456	1,632
Ashland	12,066	10,531	8,495
Ayer	6,871	6,014	3,261
Bedford	12,996	11,709	7,838
Belmont	24,720	26,178	17,098
Billerica	37,609	36,687	21,099
Boxborough	3,343	3,170	2,704
Burlington	23,302	22,514	14,833

COUNTIES. CITIES AND TOWNS	POPULATION		Regis- tered Voters 1996
	U.S. Census 1990	State Census 1985	
MIDDLESEX — *Concluded*			
CAMBRIDGE	95,802	86,865	55,233
Carlisle	4,333	3,862	3,055
Chelmsford	32,383	30,684	20,233
Concord	17,076	15,636	10,811
Dracut	25,594	22,200	16,848
Dunstable	2,236	1,889	1,577
EVERETT	35,701	35,773	20,095
Framingham	64,989	61,241	36,209
Groton	7,511	6,567	5,220
Holliston	12,926	12,606	8,813
Hopkinton	9,191	7,711	7,137
Hudson	17,233	17,251	10,147
Lexington	28,974	29,224	20,435
Lincoln	7,666	6,902	3,437
Littleton	7,051	6,984	4,739
LOWELL	103,439	95,339	40,513
MALDEN	53,884	52,474	28,514
MARLBOROUGH	31,813	34,294	18,249
Maynard	10,325	9,708	6,518
MEDFORD	57,407	57,184	32,628
MELROSE	28,150	28,774	18,318
Natick	30,510	30,280	20,952
NEWTON	82,585	82,925	51,377
North Reading	12,002	11,897	8,171
Pepperell	10,098	8,661	6,072
Reading	22,539	21,993	14,748
Sherborn	3,989	4,350	3,137
Shirley	6,118	5,202	2,944
SOMERVILLE	76,210	71,134	34,935
Stoneham	22,203	21,836	14,535
Stow	5,328	5,308	3,611
Sudbury	14,358	13,736	11,413
Tewksbury	27,266	24,442	16,798
Townsend	8,496	8,140	4,999
Tyngsborough	8,642	6,194	5,375
Wakefield	24,825	24,495	16,312
WALTHAM	57,878	57,955	31,171
Watertown	33,284	32,189	21,695
Wayland	11,874	11,432	8,410
Westford	16,392	15,051	11,878
Weston	10,200	10,743	7,140
Wilmington	17,651	17,704	12,812
Winchester	20,267	20,763	13,849
WOBURN	35,943	34,793	23,379
Totals	1,398,468	1,347,546	830,800

POPULATION

COUNTIES, CITIES AND TOWNS	U.S. Census 1990	State Census 1985	Registered Voters 1996
NANTUCKET			
Nantucket	6,012	5,959	5,273
Totals	6,012	5,959	5,273
NORFOLK			
Avon	4,558	4,768	3,021
Bellingham	14,877	13,677	8,558
Braintree	33,836	35,189	20,772
Brookline	54,718	58,152	34,081
Canton	18,530	17,550	14,000
Cohasset	7,075	7,149	5,720
Dedham	23,782	23,730	14,624
Dover	4,915	4,581	3,633
Foxborough	14,637	14,522	10,025
Franklin	22,095	17,865	14,732
Holbrook	11,041	10,901	6,378
Medfield	10,531	10,330	7,462
Medway	9,931	9,037	7,035
Millis	7,613	6,689	4,858
Milton	25,725	25,589	16,915
Needham	27,557	27,870	19,755
Norfolk	9,270	8,210	5,333
Norwood	28,700	28,551	17,018
Plainville	6,871	5,683	4,163
Quincy	84,985	88,122	50,999
Randolph	30,093	28,435	16,356
Sharon	15,517	14,581	11,170
Stoughton	26,777	24,156	15,953
Walpole	20,212	18,092	14,077
Wellesley	26,615	27,052	16,791
Westwood	12,557	13,174	9,167
Weymouth	54,063	53,735	34,119
Wrentham	9,006	7,223	5,952
Totals	616,087	604,613	392,667
PLYMOUTH			
Abington	13,817	13,166	8,618
Bridgewater	21,249	18,837	11,472
BROCKTON	92,788	97,429	42,651
Carver	10,590	9,008	6,703
Duxbury	13,895	13,248	10,009
East Bridgewater	11,104	9,782	7,181
Halifax	6,526	5,925	4,295
Hanover	11,912	11,384	7,852

COUNTIES, CITIES AND TOWNS	POPULATION		Regis-tered Voters 1996
	U.S. Census 1990	State Census 1985	

PLYMOUTH — *Concluded*

Hanson	9,028	8,316	5,822
Hingham	19,821	20,648	14,314
Hull	10,466	9,791	8,315
Kingston	9,045	7,209	6,507
Lakeville	7,785	6,467	5,552
Marion	4,496	3,851	3,198
Marshfield	21,531	22,295	15,419
Mattapoisett	5,850	5,637	4,417
Middleborough	17,867	16,066	10,322
Norwell	9,279	9,031	6,431
Pembroke	14,544	13,519	9,219
Plymouth	45,608	38,836	26,734
Plympton	2,384	2,177	1,651
Rochester	3,921	3,339	2,877
Rockland	16,123	15,454	9,568
Scituate	16,786	17,287	12,734
Wareham	19,232	16,308	15,049
West Bridgewater	6,389	6,740	4,541
Whitman	13,240	13,368	7,862
Totals	435,276	415,118	269,313

SUFFOLK

BOSTON	574,283	601,094	242,373
CHELSEA	28,710	23,432	11,315
REVERE	42,786	39,512	23,891
Winthrop	18,127	18,141	11,984
Totals	663,906	682,179	289,563

WORCESTER

Ashburnham	5,433	4,322	3,298
Athol	11,451	10,321	5,930
Auburn	15,005	14,719	10,089
Barre	4,546	4,020	2,914
Berlin	2,293	2,177	1,535
Blackstone	8,023	6,522	4,639
Bolton	3,134	2,958	2,522
Boylston	3,517	3,594	2,550
Brookfield	2,968	2,542	1,942
Charlton	9,576	7,635	6,519
Clinton	13,222	12,689	7,577
Douglas	5,438	4,077	3,644
Dudley	9,540	8,592	5,236
East Brookfield	2,033	1,883	1,134

COUNTIES, CITIES AND TOWNS	POPULATION		Registered Voters 1996
	U.S. Census 1990	State Census 1985	
WORCESTER — *Concluded*			
FITCHBURG	41,194	39,576	17,142
GARDNER	20,125	17,921	9,687
Grafton	13,035	11,239	8,588
Hardwick	2,385	2,190	1,553
Harvard	12,329	12,284	3,576
Holden	14,628	13,187	9,926
Hopedale	5,666	4,233	3,305
Hubbardston	2,797	1,876	2,110
Lancaster	6,661	6,142	3,328
Leicester	10,191	9,320	6,137
LEOMINSTER	38,145	31,113	21,507
Lunenburg	9,117	8,185	5,505
Mendon	4,010	3,165	2,911
Milford	25,355	24,038	13,465
Millbury	12,228	11,486	7,372
Millville	2,236	1,783	1,529
New Braintree	881	782	528
North Brookfield	4,708	4,045	2,625
Northborough	11,929	10,887	8,243
Northbridge	13,371	12,342	7,902
Oakham	1,503	1,212	997
Oxford	12,588	11,403	7,100
Paxton	4,047	3,711	2,617
Petersham	1,131	982	833
Phillipston	1,485	1,101	713
Princeton	3,189	2,680	2,142
Royalston	1,147	964	664
Rutland	4,936	4,291	3,397
Shrewsbury	24,146	22,181	16,991
Southborough	6,628	6,334	5,120
Southbridge	17,816	16,501	8,909
Spencer	11,645	10,773	6,681
Sterling	6,481	5,956	4,285
Sturbridge	7,775	6,321	5,735
Sutton	6,824	5,895	4,898
Templeton	6,438	5,936	3,720
Upton	4,677	4,260	3,628
Uxbridge	10,415	8,730	6,610
Warren	4,437	3,717	2,570
Webster	16,196	13,985	8,542
Westborough	14,133	13,549	9,967
West Boylston	6,611	5,953	4,049
West Brookfield	3,532	2,972	2,209
Westminster	6,191	5,510	4,015
Winchendon	8,805	7,116	5,351
WORCESTER	169,759	164,651	77,132
Totals	709,705	648,529	395,343

RECAPITULATION.

COUNTIES	Number of Cities and Towns	POPULATION		Registered Voters State Election 1996
		U.S. Census 1990	State Census 1985	
BARNSTABLE	15	186,605	161,939	142,549
BERKSHIRE	32	139,352	136,744	80,967
BRISTOL	20	506,325	468,228	276,558
DUKES COUNTY	7	11,639	10,023	9,941
ESSEX	34	670,080	624,058	392,515
FRANKLIN	26	70,092	64,851	41,824
HAMPDEN	23	456,310	438,119	244,579
HAMPSHIRE	20	146,568	138,534	87,999
MIDDLESEX	54	1,398,468	1,347,546	830,800
NANTUCKET	1	6,012	5,959	5,273
NORFOLK	28	616,087	604,613	392,667
PLYMOUTH	27	435,276	415,118	269,313
SUFFOLK	4	663,906	682,179	289,563
WORCESTER	60	709,705	648,529	395,343
Totals	351	6,016,425	5,746,440	3,459,891

VOTE FOR
PRESIDENT,
MEMBERS OF CONGRESS
AND
STATE OFFICERS

VOTE FOR ELECTORS OF PRESIDENT AND VICE PRESIDENT IN 1996 (BY COUNTIES)

ELECTION, NOVEMBER 8, 1996

COUNTY OF BARNSTABLE

CITIES AND TOWNS	Browne and Jorgensen Libertarian	Clinton and Gore Democratic	Dole and Kemp Republican	Hagelin and Tompkins Natural Law	Moorehead and LaRiva Workers World	Perot and Choate Reform	All Others	Blanks	Total Votes Cast
Barnstable	153	11,543	8,317	40	9	2,108	65	232	22,467
Bourne	53	4,186	2,848	11	9	857	7	61	8,032
Brewster	46	2,873	1,930	13	7	535	12	62	5,498
Chatham	39	1,954	1,965	10	3	370	26	103	4,475
Dennis	60	4,353	3,170	10	7	767	40	86	8,493
Eastham	34	1,664	1,107	7	1	297	1	26	3,151
Falmouth	83	9,460	5,044	34	12	1,322	71	169	16,224
Harwich	42	3,355	2,621	10	2	576	42	89	6,737
Mashpee	21	2,698	1,761	5	5	413	13	46	4,962
Orleans	35	1,948	1,809	11	7	300	0	112	4,222
Provincetown	25	1,837	228	5	9	146	2	6	2,268
Sandwich	59	4,870	3,768	8	12	942	36	62	9,757
Truro	15	746	265	10	4	98	1	7	1,156
Wellfleet	14	1,132	452	4	3	127	12	24	1,768
Yarmouth	64	6,601	4,886	15	9	1,031	30	104	12,710
Totals	743	59,220	40,141	193	99	9,889	358	1,189	111,920

Adams	19	2,866	698	3	5	634	0	44	4,274
Alford	0	130	80	0	0	24	0	2	243
Becket	3	383	167	5	1	130	3	5	701
Cheshire	7	1,027	356	2	0	317	0	15	1,728
Clarksburg	2	502	157	3	0	125	1	23	813
Dalton	12	2,050	839	2	0	413	1	51	3,375
Egremont	3	417	172	1	2	100	0	16	711
Florida	0	188	80	0	0	81	0	6	355
Great Barrington	22	2,115	656	18	1	340	4	61	3,276
Hancock	4	197	89	0	0	40	8	5	343
Hinsdale	4	474	220	2	0	174	3	9	886
Lanesborough	3	840	336	1	0	241	2	6	1,429
Lee	10	1,704	623	8	4	355	7	21	2,732
Lenox	9	1,694	735	9	4	294	1	26	2,777
Monterey	3	303	102	4	1	43	0	0	472
Mount Washington	1	39	21	1	0	11	0	1	74
New Ashford	0	69	22	0	0	22	4	1	118
New Marlborough	6	331	166	7	2	97	3	5	622
NORTH ADAMS	30	3,910	989	7	6	668	18	88	5,706
Otis	3	298	190	1	2	123	0	11	628
Peru	5	164	100	5	0	75	1	4	354
PITTSFIELD	94	13,451	3,871	35	14	2,238	22	491	20,216
Richmond	1	573	245	6	1	111	5	13	955
Sandisfield	6	168	81	0	0	63	9	3	330
Savoy	0	159	77	0	0	74	1	7	318
Sheffield	11	841	477	3	0	197	24	10	1,563
Stockbridge	9	867	264	8	2	92	23	9	1,274
Tyringham	2	118	66	0	0	23	0	4	219
Washington	2	180	66	1	0	60	0	4	318
West Stockbridge	3	514	170	3	0	80	4	11	785

COUNTY OF BERKSHIRE — Concluded

Cities and Towns	Browne and Jorgensen Libertarian	Clinton and Gore Democratic	Dole and Kemp Republican	Hagelin and Tompkins Natural Law	Moorehead and LaRiva Workers World	Perot and Choate Reform	All Others	Blanks	Total Votes Cast
Williamstown	24	2,500	844	5	7	252	3	67	3,752
Windsor	6	264	96	3	0	72	2	4	448
Totals	294	39,336	13,055	143	52	7,569	149	1,023	61,795

COUNTY OF BRISTOL

Cities and Towns	Browne and Jorgensen Libertarian	Clinton and Gore Democratic	Dole and Kemp Republican	Hagelin and Tompkins Natural Law	Moorehead and LaRiva Workers World	Perot and Choate Reform	All Others	Blanks	Total Votes Cast
Acushnet	21	3,060	742	3	2	546	4	62	4,446
Attleboro	81	7,956	4,258	20	11	1,863	18	103	14,331
Berkley	23	1,223	656	5	3	378	3	24	2,321
Dartmouth	63	7,852	3,017	45	10	1,245	2	126	12,365
Dighton	14	1,444	769	6	0	403	0	46	2,682
Easton	73	5,060	3,576	9	4	868	17	78	9,697
Fairhaven	37	4,701	1,410	15	13	858	3	46	7,086
Fall River	141	22,796	4,287	43	24	2,612	2	719	30,628
Freetown	29	2,107	985	4	1	585	7	56	3,776
Mansfield	70	4,926	2,845	15	2	866	0	87	8,828
New Bedford	152	23,620	4,151	26	19	2,547	68	268	30,851
North Attleborough	75	5,733	3,715	12	7	1,339	0	119	11,000
Norton	50	3,637	2,031	11	5	746	6	52	6,546

Raynham	38	2,751	1,623	8	1	587	1	65	5,075
Rehoboth	26	2,156	1,534	6	—	584	19	31	4,357
Seekonk	27	3,452	1,943	10	3	713	20	59	6,227
Somerset	32	6,091	2,059	7	7	919	33	100	9,256
Swansea	33	4,553	1,830	12	6	870	21	74	7,399
TAUNTON	110	10,635	3,994	14	15	2,036	2	1,028	17,838
Westport	39	3,963	1,736	12	5	872	3	137	6,767
Totals	1,134	127,716	47,161	283	139	21,437	229	3,280	201,476

COUNTY OF DUKES COUNTY

Chilmark	3	373	144	2	1	38	0	4	575
Edgartown	5	1,139	500	5	2	179	3	38	1,882
Gay Head	2	156	14	1	0	11	0	2	189
Goshold	1	46	21	0	0	11	0	12	91
Oak Bluffs	14	1,297	405	2	2	157	20	44	1,941
Tisbury	12	1,215	412	7	1	168	2	14	1,851
West Tisbury	15	910	240	6	2	92	16	5	1,286
Totals	52	5,136	1,736	23	8	656	41	119	7,815

COUNTY OF ESSEX

Amesbury	59	3,774	1,774	11	3	770	33	73	6,497
Andover	134	7,906	6,604	33	12	1,084	30	93	15,938
Beverly	174	10,298	5,286	34	14	1,624	0	495	17,923
Boxford	47	1,619	2,061	5	2	329	12	42	4,117
Danvers	92	6,515	4,071	20	10	1,159	4	255	12,130
Essex	19	896	651	8	4	208	0	19	1,814
Georgetown	38	1,927	1,244	4	3	386	15	39	3,656

Vote for President in 1996.

COUNTY OF ESSEX *Concluded*

Cities and Towns	Libertarian Browne and Jorgensen	Democratic Clinton and Gore	Republican Dole and Kemp	Natural Law Hagelin and Tompkins	Workers World Moorehead and LaRiva	Reform Perot and Choate	All Others	Blanks	Total Votes Cast
GLOUCESTER	111	7,966	3,293	31	16	1,245	26	170	12,858
Groveland	30	1,502	917	5	1	312	15	24	2,806
Hamilton	39	1,820	1,860	7	2	323	12	28	4,097
HAVERHILL	174	12,314	5,751	25	9	2,104	40	213	20,675
Ipswich	75	3,757	3,359	15	2	598	36	87	6,939
LAWRENCE	84	8,615	2,804	11	15	1,096	3	352	12,986
LYNN	243	18,370	5,634	46	41	2,726	4	617	27,696
Lynnfield	55	2,975	2,832	11		508	12	76	6,470
Manchester-by-the-Sea	45	1,419	1,287	5	1	235	4	80	3,083
Marblehead	125	6,497	4,233	27	5	726	19	134	11,789
Merrimac	32	1,478	776	12	5	321	4	24	2,653
Methuen	134	9,450	5,347	18	15	1,889	0	339	17,197
Middleton	28	1,514	1,007	2	0	373	4	34	2,962
Nahant	25	1,310	628	4	0	204	10	17	2,198
Newbury	40	1,780	1,268	7	5	385	6	41	3,545
NEWBURYPORT	96	5,647	2,467	25	8	662	76	162	9,143
North Andover	102	5,916	4,718	21	14	907	20	221	11,936
PEABODY	154	14,265	5,312	20	16	2,065	57	310	22,229
Rockport	52	2,434	1,255	13	9	321	15	55	4,154
Rowley	17	1,289	876	1		304	18	19	2,525
SALEM	188	10,436	3,430	37	23	1,500	14	330	15,958

Salisbury	19	1,777	832	2	3	396	5	30	3,069
Saugus	104	7,386	3,325	23	14	1,304	8	402	12,571
Swampscott	63	4,775	1,916	8	3	458	32	116	7,369
Topsfield	30	1,477	1,466	6	3	229	0	76	3,287
Wenham	21	832	989	2	1	147	1	10	2,008
West Newbury	31	1,087	847	6	3	170	3	22	2,169
Totals	2,680	171,021	89,120	505	271	27,068	538	5,005	296,447

COUNTY OF FRANKLIN

Ashfield	11	581	224	4	5	90	46	11	972
Bernardston	9	545	315	6	1	125	2	11	1,019
Buckland	10	521	294	7	6	77	1	7	944
Charlemont	2	299	144	2	2	82	1	3	546
Colrain	8	424	245	6	1	138	22	1	845
Conway	10	626	220	4	5	100	3	7	1,011
Deerfield	15	1,659	660	11	3	294	3	7	2,693
Erving	4	401	184	1	1	101	0	7	701
Gill	10	454	152	2	0	100	10	17	745
Greenfield	48	4,694	1,884	17	12	899	97	63	7,714
Hawley	3	78	49	1	0	22	0	2	155
Heath	5	180	120	1	1	43	18	5	370
Leverett	8	741	179	5	4	57	0	5	1,066
Leyden	3	197	91	3	0	48	5	4	351
Monroe	2	31	17	0	0	6	0	2	58
Montague	19	2,410	701	20	8	422	6	30	3,664
New Salem	30	234	125	3	2	59	6	3	467
Northfield	9	826	401	6	1	166	6	16	1,448
Orange	22	1,502	859	6	3	456	24	37	2,887
Rowe	2	92	85	3	1	31	0	2	218
Shelburne	7	557	289	5	2	100	0	19	995

COUNTY OF FRANKLIN *Concluded*

CITIES AND TOWNS	Browne and Jorgensen Libertarian	Clinton and Gore Democratic	Dole and Kemp Republican	Hagelin and Tompkins Natural Law	Moorehead and LaRiva Workers World	Perot and Choate Reform	All Others	Blanks	Total Votes Cast
Shutesbury	13	682	139	5	2	69	1	4	963
Sunderland	13	1,028	305	7	8	151	24	18	1,564
Warwick	2	205	99	1	0	66	0	7	381
Wendell	6	254	59	8	2	54	4	5	429
Whately	7	505	215	0	3	92	1	6	840
Totals	278	19,726	8,055	131	72	3,848	315	306	33,046

COUNTY OF HAMPDEN

	Browne and Jorgensen Libertarian	Clinton and Gore Democratic	Dole and Kemp Republican	Hagelin and Tompkins Natural Law	Moorehead and LaRiva Workers World	Perot and Choate Reform	All Others	Blanks	Total Votes Cast
Agawam	55	7,177	3,853	10	9	1,361	2	87	12,563
Blandford	4	264	217	3	0	77	5	6	576
Brimfield	8	732	507	2	0	202	0	26	1,477
Chester	2	278	183	0	0	105	3	6	577
Chicopee	117	14,203	5,188	23	14	2,495	63	226	22,329
East Longmeadow	30	3,689	2,866	14	6	658	12	66	7,349
Granville	6	263	314	3	2	104	1	5	705
Hampden	16	1,144	1,022	5	3	285	5	11	2,491
Holland	8	469	287	3	0	171	6	8	952
Holyoke	174	9,864	3,020	21	1	1,150	11	220	14,514
Longmeadow	40	4,687	3,449	12	2	513	18	87	8,844

Ludlow	52	4,849	2,247	33	4	900	5	337	8,427
Monson	26	1,815	1,051	16	6	514	0	73	3,512
Montgomery	2	181	174	1	0	42	1	—	402
Palmer	27	3,062	1,434	13	6	681	0	82	5,305
Russell	4	320	207	2	0	113	0	3	649
Southwick	19	1,816	1,250	9	3	512	21	38	3,668
SPRINGFIELD	205	31,266	9,110	39	45	3,407	0	542	44,614
Tolland	2	75	75	1	0	31	1	2	187
Wales	7	346	186	—	2	125	0	1	671
West Springfield	60	6,589	3,824	17	13	1,202	2	72	11,782
Westfield	66	8,640	4,954	27	5	1,785	69	185	15,731
Wilbraham	30	3,320	3,092	15	2	509	26	45	7,039
Totals	960	105,049	48,510	270	133	16,942	251	2,129	174,364

COUNTY OF HAMPSHIRE

Amherst	91	7,748	1,525	55	71	530	15	117	10,467
Belchertown	33	3,112	1,487	12	9	602	16	36	5,356
Chesterfield	4	274	196	3	1	93	1	2	587
Cummington	0	271	121	3	4	57	11	2	469
Easthampton	38	4,556	1,787	16	12	973	10	99	7,546
Goshen	5	258	127	0	0	41	20	2	453
Granby	12	1,487	839	4	1	404	5	13	2,771
Hadley	12	1,569	627	8	4	304	2	78	2,649
Hatfield	12	1,184	439	2	3	177	20	16	1,853
Huntington	8	418	301	0	—	139	4	7	880
Middlefield	3	116	80	0	0	51	—	1	252
NORTHAMPTON	95	10,075	2,261	69	54	1,051	37	181	14,300
Pelham	4	547	157	3	0	57	1	9	805
Plainfield	5	163	80	3	0	47	0	—	318
South Hadley	42	4,457	2,234	14	14	805	2	457	8,052

COUNTY OF HAMPSHIRE — *Concluded*

CITIES AND TOWNS	Browne and Jorgensen, Libertarian	Clinton and Gore, Democratic	Dole and Kemp, Republican	Hagelin and Tompkins, Natural Law	Moorehead and LaRiva, Workers World	Perot and Choate, Reform	All Others	Blanks	Total Votes Cast
Southampton	14	1,347	862	8	9	364	10	19	2,633
Ware	18	2,593	927	8	4	550	1	36	4,137
Westhampton	4	399	261	4	0	117	0	5	796
Williamsburg	11	888	281	9	5	132	2	11	1,381
Worthington	2	335	191	3	0	95	0	4	649
Totals	413	41,797	14,783	226	192	6,589	158	1,096	66,354

COUNTY OF MIDDLESEX

CITIES AND TOWNS	Browne and Jorgensen, Libertarian	Clinton and Gore, Democratic	Dole and Kemp, Republican	Hagelin and Tompkins, Natural Law	Moorehead and LaRiva, Workers World	Perot and Choate, Reform	All Others	Blanks	Total Votes Cast
Acton	104	5,819	3,205	30	5	646	15	189	10,057
Arlington	312	15,312	5,687	82	57	1,385	169	789	23,793
Ashby	16	637	441	6	0	181	4	3	1,293
Ashland	50	3,848	1,728	16	4	538	0	314	6,498
Ayer	33	1,347	694	11	9	246	0	35	2,375
Bedford	75	3,639	2,174	18	9	469	9	63	6,456
Belmont	146	7,981	4,175	55	21	701	16	527	13,662
Billerica	151	9,354	4,505	21	15	1,919	20	113	16,130
Boxborough	31	1,247	712	20	2	184	3	20	2,219
Burlington	93	6,612	3,505	8	5	979	17	95	11,333

CAMBRIDGE	425	29,913	4,976	151	183	1,415	114	400	38,314
Carlisle	28	1,425	1,014	18	4	163	6	17	2,688
Chelmsford	165	9,050	5,796	29	15	1,632	47	193	16,962
Concord	97	5,441	3,123	40	13	528	36	85	9,396
Dracut	75	7,100	3,338	18	9	1,694	19	86	12,351
Dunstable	8	651	458	5	1	156	1	11	1,291
EVERETT	69	9,425	2,835	21	13	1,153	1	210	13,727
Framingham	195	16,836	6,669	39	27	1,700	110	297	25,873
Groton	67	2,260	1,503	14	7	417	4	25	4,316
Holliston	76	4,196	2,206	12	7	551	41	56	7,145
Hopkinton	52	3,199	2,098	14	4	498	17	48	5,947
Hudson	73	4,611	2,073	14	6	743	12	70	7,608
Lexington	164	10,659	4,829	45	30	793	10	204	16,761
Lincoln	39	1,973	988	12	4	131	7	27	3,209
Littleton	52	2,214	1,260	16	4	387	0	33	3,966
LOWELL	245	16,912	5,896	57	37	2,911	6	997	27,061
MALDEN	150	14,060	4,030	20	25	1,654	82	231	20,252
Marlborough	147	8,465	4,062	24	6	1,427	51	208	14,390
Maynard	44	3,204	1,345	9	11	487	7	43	5,157
MEDFORD	151	16,630	5,844	38	38	1,741	122	301	24,874
MELROSE	94	8,695	4,368	25	9	1,106	34	169	14,539
Natick	136	9,875	4,640	33	10	1,035	36	180	15,991
NEWTON	410	30,005	8,499	107	73	1,674	8	383	41,200
North Reading	51	3,632	2,386	11	5	602	14	75	6,776
Pepperell	74	2,461	1,516	6	4	649	24	25	4,759
Reading	105	6,773	4,073	22	6	933	38	111	12,061
Sherborn	32	1,161	1,162	14	11	130	16	11	2,537
Shirley	17	1,259	744	26	5	256	13	13	2,333
SOMERVILLE	272	20,206	3,983	84	120	1,455	203	369	27,030
Stoneham	71	6,506	3,169	9	9	871	37	132	10,804
Stow	49	1,648	1,045	6	5	307	23	19	3,102
Sudbury	94	4,833	3,107	17	12	475	43	64	8,648

COUNTY OF MIDDLESEX — *Concluded*

CITIES AND TOWNS	Browne and Jorgensen Libertarian	Clinton and Gore Democratic	Dole and Kemp Republican	Hagelin and Tompkins Natural Law	Moorehead and LaRiva Workers World	Perot and Choate Reform	All Others	Blanks	Total Votes Cast
Tewksbury	84	7,256	3,807	18	14	1,532	45	118	12,874
Townsend	55	1,942	1,217	10	4	490	17	32	3,767
Tyngsborough	30	2,227	1,264	2	4	540	3	33	4,103
Wakefield	115	7,661	3,869	22	12	1,127	5	173	12,992
WALTHAM	192	13,607	8,830	42	27	1,663	8	301	21,696
Watertown	139	10,234	3,646	39	27	902	30	204	15,308
Wayland	84	4,239	2,380	15	5	394	30	75	7,244
Westford	88	4,860	3,459	19	5	912	42	173	9,558
Weston	65	2,821	2,606	16	4	292	5	213	6,031
Wilmington	66	5,547	2,855	18	4	1,004	9	68	9,571
Winchester	96	6,430	4,489	33	10	734	18	120	11,969
WOBURN	146	10,107	4,614	31	11	1,593	11	169	16,682
Totals	5,898	398,014	169,897	1,488	967	48,105	1,658	8,920	636,679

COUNTY OF NANTUCKET

Nantucket	42	2,453	1,222	10	4	400	16	48	4,207
Totals	42	2,453	1,222	10	4	400	16	48	4,207

COUNTY OF NORFOLK

Avon	12	1,389	646	3	1	293	3	28	2,375
Bellingham	41	3,810	1,650	10	7	822	2	265	6,007
Braintree	117	9,721	5,401	13	13	1,479	58	192	16,994
Brookline	224	18,812	4,579	77	39	799	18	220	24,918
Canton	105	5,793	3,473	16	9	806	5	349	10,562
Cohasset	45	2,012	1,759	8	5	315	5	143	4,292
Dedham	111	6,620	3,672	21	11	914	0	411	11,760
Dover	27	1,172	1,716	3	5	177	13	66	3,188
Foxborough	54	4,588	2,673	14	5	789	6	71	8,216
Franklin	69	7,227	3,777	17	7	1,090	7	102	12,326
Holbrook	28	2,951	1,374	1	4	532	4	59	4,955
Medfield	42	3,064	2,610	11		392	20	67	6,209
Medway	59	2,946	1,722	12	3	490	0	189	5,421
Millis	44	2,207	1,287	7	8	347	9	30	3,953
Milton	95	7,888	4,764	24	12	916	3	192	13,916
Needham	111	9,558	5,595	33	14	790	36	140	16,319
Norfolk	30	2,019	1,845	11	0	392	13	43	4,353
Norwood	104	8,228	4,207	24	7	1,008	41	169	13,788
Plainville	27	1,684	1,066	0	1	382	1	31	3,196
Quincy	237	23,182	9,824	48	37	3,066	130	354	36,878
Randolph	82	8,711	2,601	11	4	921	32	117	12,479
Sharon	88	6,438	1,905	20	13	474	0	103	9,076
Stoughton	96	7,828	3,410	4	12	1,049	13	187	12,619
Walpole	90	5,995	3,961	27	12	935	0	244	11,264
Wellesley	133	7,104	5,454	32	21	578	8	370	13,720
Westwood	64	3,655	3,434	16	4	509	32	67	7,781
Weymouth	207	13,536	6,904	27	26	2,181	6	2,081	24,979
Wrentham	55	2,361	1,672	18	2	502	0	37	4,647
Totals	2,427	180,499	92,981	508	345	22,948	465	6,327	306,791

COUNTY OF PLYMOUTH

Cities and Towns	Brown and Jorgensen Libertarian	Clinton and Gore Democratic	Dole and Kemp Republican	Hagelin and Tompkins Natural Law	Moorehead and LaRiva Workers World	Perot and Choate Reform	All Others	Blanks	Total Votes Cast
Abington	45	3,657	2,069	13	11	727	2	191	6,716
Bridgewater	65	4,585	2,867	9	5	913	42	77	8,563
Brockton	247	16,361	6,972	31	28	2,738	10	1,086	27,470
Carver	22	2,585	1,453	4	1	716	16	75	4,872
Duxbury	54	3,615	3,674	12	1	592	53	60	8,071
East Bridgewater	41	2,754	1,783	5	4	668	16	45	5,317
Halifax	24	1,754	1,085	4	1	428	4	39	3,347
Hanover	47	3,255	2,416	11	8	572	5	91	6,405
Hanson	40	2,316	1,421	8	5	580	6	48	4,397
Hingham	76	5,522	4,690	14	5	714	58	194	11,273
Hull	59	3,154	1,091	13	1	468	0	280	5,070
Kingston	28	2,631	1,674	6	4	497	3	49	4,902
Lakeville	45	1,994	1,431	7	3	531	5	74	4,095
Marion	12	1,282	965	4	6	266	20	47	2,599
Marshfield	85	6,217	3,890	21	2	1,184	48	97	11,548
Mattapoisett	19	1,783	1,221	10	2	350	15	33	3,433
Middleborough	58	3,762	2,390	6	8	1,030	21	55	7,324
Norwell	53	2,523	2,226	17	6	430	7	46	5,314
Pembroke	49	4,121	2,267	15	6	836	0	75	7,370
Plymouth	148	11,331	6,521	26	15	2,425	29	131	20,666
Plympton	12	649	465	0	2	172	8	7	1,315

Rochester	20	1,028	748	3	3	297	5	19	2,123
Rockland	44	4,248	2,112	9	7	840	17	62	7,339
Scituate	94	5,142	3,694	15	3	783	27	63	9,851
Wareham	53	4,981	2,184	6	5	954	24	94	8,301
West Bridgewater	20	1,548	1,333	9	6	440	0	41	3,396
Whitman	37	3,270	1,984	7	4	687	16	68	6,077
Totals	1,497	106,068	64,626	285	155	20,808	457	3,147	197,154

COUNTY OF SUFFOLK

Boston	1,551	125,529	33,366	433	539	8,428	216	4,897	174,959
Chelsea	46	4,676	1,043	10	6	435	0	186	6,402
Revere	102	10,201	3,295	30	15	1,394	1	1,436	16,481
Winthrop	64	5,180	2,049	10	3	723	40	115	8,184
Totals	1,763	145,586	39,753	483	563	10,980	257	6,634	206,026

COUNTY OF WORCESTER

Ashburnham	15	1,331	710	3	1	329	12	27	2,428
Athol	48	2,389	1,206	5	2	735	22	38	4,446
Auburn	37	4,451	2,307	20	5	739	16	73	7,738
Barre	13	1,298	629	5	4	260	3	25	2,243
Berlin	14	642	429	5	0	154	7	9	1,260
Blackstone	23	1,876	850	5	2	522	4	44	3,326
Bolton	37	987	745	8	0	194	6	18	2,005
Boylston	12	1,063	829	6	4	205	5	18	2,142
Brookfield	5	689	407	3	4	196	0	14	1,322
Charlton	20	2,134	1,512	11	2	549	3	18	4,254
Clinton	37	3,509	1,358	10	3	526	16	107	5,566

COUNTY OF WORCESTER — *Concluded*

Cities and Towns	Brown and Jorgensen Libertarian	Clinton and Gore Democratic	Dole and Kemp Republican	Hagelin and Tompkins Natural Law	Moorehead and LaRiva Workers World	Perot and Choate Reform	All Others	Blanks	Total Votes Cast
Douglas	17	1,536	865	7	2	379	0	19	2,825
Dudley	34	2,032	1,050	7	3	494	2	258	3,880
East Brookfield	5	474	320	0	1	124	0	3	927
FITCHBURG	125	7,317	2,824	20	14	1,160	5	883	12,356
GARDNER	53	4,597	1,664	13	2	906	5	113	7,360
Grafton	42	3,642	1,986	9	—	642	13	39	6,386
Hardwick	9	698	346	14	2	158	1	9	1,242
Harvard	42	1,539	1,061	25	2	198	42	34	2,961
Holden	48	4,046	3,365	17	7	634	0	59	8,188
Hopedale	10	1,715	857	3	1	276	12	54	2,916
Hubbardston	16	821	522	—	1	254	5	7	1,634
Lancaster	25	1,324	957	60	30	245	10	18	2,671
Leicester	33	2,635	1,301	5	3	529	5	30	4,546
LEOMINSTER	113	9,348	4,192	23	8	1,621	3	263	15,574
Lunenburg	67	2,287	1,426	8	2	499	4	68	4,363
Mendon	17	1,151	820	3	6	260	7	32	2,298
Milford	73	6,756	2,641	15	8	953	6	144	10,597
Millbury	34	3,358	1,475	5	3	655	0	67	5,603
Millville	1	634	262	4	12	169	0	12	1,094
New Braintree	2	215	137	1	1	76	0	3	435
North Brookfield	17	965	743	7	6	274	7	21	2,040
Northborough	86	3,571	2,337	16	2	633	21	58	6,724

Northbridge	34	3,185	1,925	10	0	618	2	31	5,805
Oakham	5	409	311	0	0	101	0	5	833
Oxford	29	3,044	1,485	7	4	639	3	33	5,246
Paxton	13	1,006	913	2	3	172	0	28	2,137
Petersham	12	387	231	1	4	60	0	10	715
Phillipston	4	342	177	2	0	110	0	2	643
Princeton	19	827	743	1	0	139	5	15	1,764
Royalston	9	263	149	1	1	81	3	6	513
Rutland	20	1,190	914	4	3	264	0	27	2,420
Shrewsbury	90	7,705	4,905	27	2	1,153	34	128	14,045
Southborough	51	2,225	1,574	8	5	356	5	47	4,287
Southbridge	40	3,899	1,386	7	1	635	4	38	6,017
Spencer	24	2,638	1,435	7	6	607	5	37	4,759
Sterling	54	1,668	1,331	15	2	418	5	31	3,532
Sturbridge	19	2,006	1,304	6	1	388	0	23	3,748
Sutton	15	1,929	1,436	10	0	448	7	51	3,894
Templeton	21	1,653	685	2	1	408	0	42	2,811
Upton	34	1,582	994	14	3	350	20	33	3,008
Uxbridge	36	2,810	1,451	11	1	615	1	67	5,013
Warren	13	1,044	487	3	6	265	0	13	1,835
Webster	43	3,371	1,558	12	0	716	3	288	5,994
West Boylston	30	1,652	1,331	5	3	282	6	30	3,333
West Brookfield	10	803	531	8	14	199	3	10	1,570
Westborough	123	4,167	2,798	22	3	649	16	50	7,849
Westminster	20	1,733	1,022	9	3	397	3	44	3,237
Winchendon	31	1,713	840	7	58	424	15	13	3,046
Worcester	314	35,607	12,879	80		3,925	987	909	54,800
Totals	3,243	169,888	87,018	635	276	29,967	1,288	4,596	296,204

AGGREGATE

Cities and Towns	Libertarian Browne and Jorgensen	Democratic Clinton and Gore	Republican Dole and Kemp	Natural Law Hagelin and Tompkins	Workers World Moorehead and LaRiva	Reform Perot and Choate	All Others	Blanks	Total Votes Cast
BARNSTABLE	743	59,220	40,141	193	69	9,889	358	1,189	111,920
BERKSHIRE	294	39,336	13,055	143	52	7,569	149	1,023	61,795
BRISTOL	1,134	127,716	47,161	283	139	21,437	229	3,280	201,476
DUKES COUNTY	52	5,136	1,736	23	8	656	41	119	7,815
ESSEX	2,680	171,021	89,120	505	271	27,068	538	5,005	296,447
FRANKLIN	278	19,726	8,055	131	72	3,848	315	306	33,046
HAMPDEN	960	105,049	48,510	270	133	16,942	251	2,129	174,364
HAMPSHIRE	413	41,797	14,783	226	192	6,589	158	1,096	66,354
MIDDLESEX	5,898	398,014	169,897	1,488	967	48,105	1,658	8,920	636,679
NANTUCKET	42	2,453	1,222	10	4	400	16	48	4,207
NORFOLK	2,427	180,499	92,981	508	345	22,948	465	6,327	306,791
PLYMOUTH	1,497	106,068	64,626	285	155	20,808	457	3,147	197,154
SUFFOLK	1,763	145,586	39,753	483	563	10,980	257	6,634	206,026
WORCESTER	2,243	169,888	87,018	635	276	29,967	1,288	4,596	296,204
Totals	20,424	1,571,509	718,058	5,183	3,276	227,206	6,180	43,819	2,600,278

VOTE FOR SENATOR IN CONGRESS IN 1996
(BY COUNTIES)

ELECTION, NOVEMBER 5, 1996

COUNTY OF BARNSTABLE

CITIES AND TOWNS	John F. Kerry of Boston Democratic	William F. Weld of Cambridge Republican	Susan C. Gallagher of Milton Conservative	Robert C. Stowe of Cambridge Natural Law	All Others	Blanks	Total Votes Cast
Barnstable	9,789	11,926	470	65	10	207	22,467
Bourne	3,566	4,121	242	24	0	79	8,032
Brewster	2,447	2,859	103	21	2	66	5,498
Chatham	1,674	2,624	60	18	0	99	4,475
Dennis	3,710	4,458	222	28	3	72	8,493
Eastham	1,409	1,648	58	11	1	24	3,151
Falmouth	8,393	7,226	331	30	4	240	16,224
Harwich	2,856	3,547	205	29	1	99	6,737
Mashpee	2,280	2,522	103	5	2	50	4,962
Orleans	1,672	2,342	91	13	0	104	4,222
Provincetown	1,752	464	24	12	3	13	2,268
Sandwich	4,036	5,407	229	20	0	65	9,757
Truro	657	463	19	4	0	13	1,156
Wellfleet	1,025	678	38	10	0	17	1,768
Yarmouth	5,544	6,771	249	26	1	119	12,710
Totals	50,810	57,056	2,444	316	27	1,267	111,920

COUNTY OF BERKSHIRE

Adams	2,599	1,501	74	34	0	66	4,274
Alford	110	123	4	2	0	4	243
Becket	377	269	27	8	0	20	701
Cheshire	964	698	35	15	1	15	1,728
Clarksburg	445	339	10	4	0	15	813
Dalton	1,846	1,389	48	20	0	72	3,375
Egremont	401	281	10	7	0	12	711
Florida	184	150	10	1	0	10	355
Great Barrington	1,949	1,110	61	42	1	113	3,276
Hancock	154	170	9	4	0	6	343
Hinsdale	454	359	32	12	0	29	886
Lanesborough	754	596	34	14	0	31	1,429
Lee	1,515	1,071	61	23	0	62	2,732
Lenox	1,584	1,062	61	16	0	54	2,777
Monterey	307	132	19	5	0	9	472

COUNTY OF BERKSHIRE — *Concluded*

CITIES AND TOWNS	John F. Kerry of Boston Democratic	William F. Weld of Cambridge Republican	Susan C. Gallagher of Milton Conservative	Robert C. Stowe of Cambridge Natural Law	All Others	Blanks	Total Votes Cast
Mount Washington	40	33	0	0	0	1	74
New Ashford	64	49	2	2	0	1	118
New Marlborough	322	258	18	11	0	13	622
NORTH ADAMS	3,346	2,084	122	36	0	118	5,706
Otis	281	300	18	5	1	23	628
Peru	151	174	11	8	0	10	354
PITTSFIELD	12,188	6,821	461	135	0	611	20,216
Richmond	540	374	17	5	0	19	955
Sandisfield	188	114	8	4	0	16	330
Savoy	154	143	11	0	0	10	318
Sheffield	772	695	46	9	0	41	1,563
Stockbridge	820	383	34	16	0	21	1,274
Tyringham	123	79	8	0	0	9	219
Washington	181	122	9	4	0	2	318
West Stockbridge	462	277	27	2	2	15	785
Williamstown	2,245	1,354	47	11	0	95	3,752
Windsor	254	169	15	4	0	6	448
Totals	35,774	22,679	1,349	459	5	1,529	61,795

COUNTY OF BRISTOL

Acushnet	2,803	1,431	140	8	2	62	4,446
ATTLEBORO	6,539	7,069	532	67	3	121	14,331
Berkley	1,040	1,136	91	12	2	40	2,321
Dartmouth	7,216	4,584	328	44	0	193	12,365
Dighton	1,330	1,160	125	15	0	52	2,682
Easton	4,226	5,143	250	15	3	60	9,697
Fairhaven	4,397	2,343	213	25	2	106	7,086
FALL RIVER	21,162	7,100	987	101	11	1,267	30,628
Freetown	1,966	1,622	110	13	1	64	3,776
Mansfield	3,891	4,591	245	24	0	77	8,828
NEW BEDFORD	22,108	7,396	825	80	8	434	30,851
North Attleborough	4,531	5,958	373	27	0	111	11,000
Norton	3,083	3,170	220	16	1	56	6,546
Raynham	2,353	2,442	198	14	0	68	5,075
Rehoboth	1,822	2,334	128	19	3	51	4,357
Seekonk	2,900	3,014	206	24	1	82	6,227
Somerset	5,621	3,181	307	22	1	124	9,256
Swansea	4,104	2,883	289	30	1	92	7,399
TAUNTON	9,300	6,527	696	47	0	1,268	17,838
Westport	3,652	2,704	191	26	0	194	6,767
Totals	114,044	75,788	6,454	629	39	4,522	201,476

COUNTY OF DUKES COUNTY

CITIES AND TOWNS	John F. Kerry of Boston Democratic	William F. Weld of Cambridge Republican	Susan C. Gallagher of Milton Conservative	Robert C. Stowe of Cambridge Natural Law	All Others	Blanks	Total Votes Cast
Chilmark	352	210	4	1	0	6	573
Edgartown	988	815	29	2	2	46	1,882
Gay Head	149	37	1	1	0	1	189
Gosnold	45	40	4	0	0	2	91
Oak Bluffs	1.135	711	29	18	0	48	1,941
Tisbury	1,139	650	36	8	0	18	1,851
West Tisbury	855	395	13	14	0	9	1,286
Totals	4,663	2,858	116	44	2	130	7,813

COUNTY OF ESSEX

Amesbury	3,090	3,148	160	22	3	74	6,497
Andover	6,469	9,060	296	29	3	81	15,938
BEVERLY	8,444	8,480	485	40	0	473	17,922
Boxford	1,264	2,737	83	2	0	31	4,117
Danvers	5,379	6,090	376	27	0	258	12,130
Essex	766	989	42	5	0	12	1,814
Georgetown	1,545	1,987	86	9	0	29	3,656
GLOUCESTER	6,587	5,784	288	31	1	167	12,858
Groveland	1,237	1,465	82	7	0	15	2,806
Hamilton	1,488	2,392	182	1	2	32	4,097
HAVERHILL	9,768	10,068	575	61	4	199	20,675
Ipswich	3,141	3,546	176	8	3	65	6,939
LAWRENCE	7,003	5,061	421	60	0	441	12,986
LYNN	15,389	10,462	1,023	74	4	744	27,696
Lynnfield	2,370	3,891	130	13	1	65	6,470
Manchester-by-the-Sea	1,124	1,817	53	11	0	78	3,083
Marblehead	5,296	6,261	131	16	2	83	11,789
Merrimac	1,190	1,379	55	12	1	15	2,652
Methuen	7,196	9,097	564	45	1	294	17,197
Middleton	1,288	1,555	77	5	0	37	2,962
Nahant	1,160	984	38	3	0	13	2,198
Newbury	1,532	1,907	71	15	0	20	3,545
NEWBURYPORT	4,738	4,088	172	19	3	123	9,143
North Andover	4,654	6,801	285	22	1	173	11,936
PEABODY	12,121	9,172	602	34	12	288	22,229
Rockport	2,109	1,907	113	6	0	19	4,154
Rowley	1,037	1,392	63	11	1	21	2,525
SALEM	8,933	6,069	432	44	0	480	15,958
Salisbury	1,383	1,569	65	13	2	37	3,069
Saugus	6,234	5,639	311	27	0	360	12,571
Swampscott	4,033	3,108	131	9	2	86	7,369
Topsfield	1,201	1,966	56	1	0	63	3,287

COUNTY OF ESSEX — *Concluded*

CITIES AND TOWNS	John F. Kerry of Boston Democratic	William F. Weld of Cambridge Republican	Susan C. Gallagher of Milton Conservative	Robert C. Stowe of Cambridge Natural Law	All Others	Blanks	Total Votes Cast
Wenham	721	1,225	50	2	0	10	2,008
West Newbury	879	1,227	43	6	0	14	2,169
Totals	140,769	142,323	7,717	690	46	4,900	296,445

COUNTY OF FRANKLIN

Ashfield	579	368	8	7	0	10	972
Bernardston	412	571	24	2	0	10	1,019
Buckland	455	457	21	2	0	9	944
Charlemont	257	256	22	3	0	8	546
Colrain	387	422	22	4	0	10	845
Conway	610	369	23	6	0	3	1,011
Deerfield	1,478	1,145	40	10	0	20	2,693
Erving	342	330	19	2	0	8	701
Gill	389	304	36	3	0	13	745
Greenfield	3,953	3,428	209	46	4	74	7,714
Hawley	62	86	1	3	0	3	155
Heath	170	140	54	3	0	3	370
Leverett	787	246	18	5	0	10	1,066
Leyden	175	160	12	2	0	2	351
Monroe	23	30	4	0	0	1	58
Montague	2,086	1,427	104	18	0	29	3,664
New Salem	256	190	18	2	0	1	467
Northfield	713	671	38	7	0	19	1,448
Orange	1,216	1,459	171	19	0	22	2,887
Rowe	82	124	4	3	0	5	218
Shelburne	510	453	12	7	0	13	995
Shutesbury	708	232	11	7	0	5	963
Sunderland	947	554	29	7	1	26	1,564
Warwick	202	164	11	3	0	1	381
Wendell	305	109	7	6	0	2	429
Whately	434	377	21	1	0	5	838
Totals	17,538	14,072	939	178	5	312	33,044

COUNTY OF HAMPDEN

Agawam	5,174	6,951	249	49	0	140	12,563
Blandford	223	336	13	3	0	1	576
Brimfield	633	777	48	11	0	8	1,477
Chester	242	306	16	6	1	6	577

COUNTY OF HAMPDEN — *Concluded*

CITIES AND TOWNS	John F. Kerry of Boston Democratic	William F. Weld of Cambridge Republican	Susan C. Gallagher of Milton Conservative	Robert C. Stowe of Cambridge Natural Law	All Others	Blanks	Total Votes Cast
CHICOPEE	10,819	10,593	550	80	9	278	22,329
East Longmeadow	2,697	4,450	113	20	1	68	7,349
Granville	205	458	28	9	0	5	705
Hampden	838	1,567	63	8	0	15	2,491
Holland	373	526	39	5	0	9	952
HOLYOKE	7,856	5,802	316	63	5	472	14,514
Longmeadow	3,569	5,054	90	13	2	116	8,844
Ludlow	3,813	4,080	203	39	0	292	8,427
Monson	1,487	1,811	83	26	0	105	3,512
Montgomery	139	251	5	2	0	5	402
Palmer	2,611	2,452	167	18	0	57	5,305
Russell	249	374	21	1	0	4	649
Southwick	1,375	2,159	67	20	0	47	3,668
SPRINGFIELD	25,555	17,428	818	128	20	665	44,614
Tolland	72	103	6	1	1	4	187
Wales	274	354	25	11	1	6	671
West Springfield	4,888	6,426	300	34	2	132	11,782
WESTFIELD	6,510	8,583	355	49	1	233	15,731
Wilbraham	2,388	4,463	115	23	5	45	7,039
Totals	81,990	85,304	3,690	619	48	2,713	174,364

COUNTY OF HAMPSHIRE

Amherst	7,582	2,488	138	72	1	186	10,467
Belchertown	2,611	2,561	93	17	1	73	5,356
Chesterfield	255	301	17	5	0	9	587
Cummington	260	197	7	4	0	1	469
Easthampton	3,605	3,635	143	36	3	124	7,546
Goshen	229	206	15	2	0	1	453
Granby	1,115	1,553	66	10	1	26	2,771
Hadley	1,384	1,133	49	10	1	72	2,649
Hatfield	1,012	782	39	0	0	20	1,853
Huntington	383	441	36	7	0	13	880
Middlefield	121	116	9	1	0	5	252
NORTHAMPTON	9,711	4,136	237	74	8	134	14,300
Pelham	526	259	12	3	1	4	805
Plainfield	170	137	4	1	1	5	318
South Hadley	3,494	3,963	159	29	0	407	8,052
Southampton	1,026	1,514	68	8	0	17	2,633
Ware	2,201	1,773	102	20	0	41	4,137
Westhampton	343	428	18	5	0	2	796
Williamsburg	836	501	22	13	0	9	1,381
Worthington	297	320	12	4	0	16	649
Totals	37,161	26,444	1,246	321	17	1,165	66,354

COUNTY OF MIDDLESEX

Cities and Towns	John F. Kerry of Boston Democratic	William F. Weld of Cambridge Republican	Susan C. Gallagher of Milton Conservative	Robert C. Stowe of Cambridge Natural Law	All Others	Blanks	Total Votes Cast
Acton	4,923	4,898	131	24	0	81	10,057
Arlington	13,987	8,030	706	72	3	995	23,793
Ashby	493	751	37	7	0	5	1,293
Ashland	3,101	3,004	130	17	0	246	6,498
Ayer	1,099	1,189	68	5	0	14	2,375
Bedford	3,082	3,177	124	13	0	60	6,456
Belmont	7,086	5,797	293	24	1	461	13,662
Billerica	7,509	7,875	580	43	5	118	16,130
Boxborough	983	1,175	46	1	0	14	2,219
Burlington	5,466	5,373	380	17	2	94	11,332
Cambridge	28,256	9,001	485	129	26	417	38,314
Carlisle	1,200	1,448	33	3	0	4	2,688
Chelmsford	7,101	9,198	459	34	5	165	16,962
Concord	4,808	4,346	165	17	1	59	9,396
Dracut	5,347	6,444	426	35	4	95	12,351
Dunstable	466	784	35	3	0	3	1,291
Everett	8,226	4,810	409	40	0	242	13,727
Framingham	13,946	11,007	579	53	8	278	25,871
Groton	1,832	2,325	109	13	0	37	4,316
Holliston	3,363	3,548	167	16	3	48	7,145
Hopkinton	2,500	3,255	130	10	1	51	5,947
Hudson	3,279	4,058	199	13	2	57	7,608
Lexington	9,577	6,735	273	21	2	153	16,761
Lincoln	1,727	1,418	32	5	0	26	3,208
Littleton	1,774	2,082	77	15	0	18	3,966
Lowell	13,781	11,267	945	77	0	991	27,061
Malden	12,343	7,060	557	55	13	224	20,252
Marlborough	6,518	7,227	370	33	9	233	14,390
Maynard	2,582	2,356	158	11	0	50	5,157
Medford	14,715	9,087	639	64	14	355	24,874
Melrose	7,568	6,411	386	33	3	138	14,539
Natick	8,237	7,168	380	30	9	167	15,991
Newton	26,286	13,957	589	55	0	313	41,200
North Reading	2,855	3,652	192	15	0	61	6,775
Pepperell	1,915	2,625	182	16	2	19	4,759
Reading	5,673	5,976	311	20	3	77	12,060
Sherborn	928	1,544	48	4	2	11	2,537
Shirley	994	1,230	85	7	1	16	2,333
Somerville	18,941	7,016	562	109	31	371	27,030
Stoneham	5,637	4,777	265	14	2	109	10,804
Stow	1,358	1,658	58	10	9	15	3,102
Sudbury	3,986	4,469	120	7	2	64	8,648
Tewksbury	5,749	6,562	427	24	7	105	12,874
Townsend	1,451	2,139	133	15	0	29	3,767

COUNTY OF MIDDLESEX — *Concluded*

CITIES AND TOWNS	John F. Kerry of Boston Democratic	William F. Weld of Cambridge Republican	Susan C. Gallagher of Milton Conservative	Robert C. Stowe of Cambridge Natural Law	All Others	Blanks	Total Votes Cast
Tyngsborough	1,687	2,243	129	16	0	28	4,103
Wakefield	6,382	6,068	349	25	1	167	12,992
WALTHAM	11,493	9,228	645	58	4	268	21,696
Watertown	9,170	5,599	323	39	9	168	15,308
Wayland	3,578	3,503	87	12	1	63	7,244
Westford	3,748	5,426	204	18	4	158	9,558
Weston	2,254	3,529	94	4	0	150	6,031
Wilmington	4,442	4,732	311	19	0	67	9,571
Winchester	5,470	6,106	270	21	1	101	11,969
WOBURN	8,381	7,479	640	39	0	143	16,682
Totals	339,253	271,822	15,532	1,480	184	8,402	636,673

COUNTY OF NANTUCKET

Nantucket	2,201	1,866	55	16	2	67	4,207
Totals	2,201	1,866	55	16	2	67	4,207

COUNTY OF NORFOLK

Avon	1,181	1,092	73	4	0	25	2,375
Bellingham	2,929	3,157	237	20	0	264	6,607
Braintree	8,310	7,710	809	26	3	136	16,994
Brookline	16,702	7,680	240	53	8	235	24,918
Canton	4,876	4,971	333	14	0	368	10,562
Cohasset	1,700	2,332	135	8	0	117	4,292
Dedham	5,757	5,173	472	28	0	330	11,760
Dover	891	2,188	49	0	0	60	3,188
Foxborough	3,797	4,097	237	12	1	72	8,216
Franklin	5,712	6,153	319	33	0	109	12,326
Holbrook	2,453	2,243	205	11	0	43	4,955
Medfield	2,508	3,461	161	0	13	66	6,209
Medway	2,289	2,800	120	13	0	199	5,421
Millis	1,778	2,066	70	7	0	32	3,953
Milton	7,015	6,094	646	19	0	142	13,916
Needham	8,065	7,680	426	21	6	121	16,319
Norfolk	1,594	2,637	78	13	0	31	4,353
Norwood	7,086	5,979	549	30	10	134	13,788
Plainville	1,429	1,643	91	8	1	24	3,196
QUINCY	19,788	14,914	1,781	65	16	314	36,878
Randolph	7,506	4,439	381	24	2	127	12,479

COUNTY OF NORFOLK — *Concluded*

CITIES AND TOWNS	John F. Kerry of Boston Democratic	William F. Weld of Cambridge Republican	Susan C. Gallagher of Milton Conservative	Robert C. Stowe of Cambridge Natural Law	All Others	Blanks	Total Votes Cast
Sharon	5,326	3,545	121	13	0	71	9,076
Stoughton	6,594	5,515	364	12	0	134	12,619
Walpole	4,876	5,771	326	18	0	273	11,264
Wellesley	5,956	7,251	204	14	2	293	13,720
Westwood	3,167	4,286	258	8	1	61	7,781
Weymouth	12,227	10,432	1,105	46	1	1,168	24,979
Wrentham	1,940	2,465	194	12	1	35	4,647
Totals	153,452	137,774	9,984	532	65	4,984	306,791

COUNTY OF PLYMOUTH

	John F. Kerry of Boston Democratic	William F. Weld of Cambridge Republican	Susan C. Gallagher of Milton Conservative	Robert C. Stowe of Cambridge Natural Law	All Others	Blanks	Total Votes Cast
Abington	2,942	3,267	266	12	0	229	6,716
Bridgewater	3,838	4,320	293	21	10	81	8,563
BROCKTON	13,682	11,699	1,080	72	1	936	27,470
Carver	2,172	2,379	210	16	2	93	4,872
Duxbury	3,089	4,730	187	10	4	51	8,071
East Bridgewater	2,213	2,910	134	18	0	42	5,317
Halifax	1,441	1,755	100	10	1	40	3,347
Hanover	2,676	3,449	185	12	0	83	6,405
Hanson	1,932	2,263	162	4	0	36	4,397
Hingham	4,880	5,795	375	28	7	188	11,273
Hull	2,774	1,863	172	14	0	247	5,070
Kingston	2,222	2,456	172	8	1	42	4,901
Lakeville	1,716	2,108	178	7	0	86	4,095
Marion	1,121	1,354	61	7	0	56	2,599
Marshfield	5,243	5,824	358	22	4	97	11,548
Mattapoisett	1,593	1,724	74	10	1	31	3,433
Middleborough	3,206	3,749	278	20	0	71	7,324
Norwell	2,049	3,057	156	12	0	40	5,314
Pembroke	3,377	3,659	257	17	0	60	7,370
Plymouth	9,599	10,260	560	50	6	191	20,666
Plympton	545	712	48	4	0	6	1,315
Rochester	941	1,101	59	8	0	14	2,123
Rockland	3,539	3,337	369	21	5	68	7,339
Scituate	4,543	4,908	307	19	5	66	9,848
Wareham	4,404	3,494	272	24	1	106	8,301
West Bridgewater	1,291	1,905	150	11	0	39	3,396
Whitman	2,656	3,076	266	19	3	57	6,077
Totals	89,684	97,154	6,729	476	51	3,056	197,150

COUNTY OF SUFFOLK

Cities and Towns	John F. Kerry of Boston Democratic	William F. Weld of Cambridge Republican	Susan C. Gallagher of Milton Conservative	Robert C. Stowe of Cambridge Natural Law	All Others	Blanks	Total Votes Cast
Boston	114,376	50,283	4,806	403	6	5,085	174,959
Chelsea	4,116	1,912	151	27	0	196	6,402
Revere	8,811	5,776	478	47	0	1,367	16,479
Winthrop	4,500	3,370	191	16	2	105	8,184
Totals	131,803	61,341	5,626	493	8	6,753	206,024

COUNTY OF WORCESTER

Cities and Towns	John F. Kerry	William F. Weld	Susan C. Gallagher	Robert C. Stowe	All Others	Blanks	Total Votes Cast
Ashburnham	1,060	1,253	82	9	1	23	2,428
Athol	1,892	2,261	216	17	19	41	4,446
Auburn	3,426	4,037	192	24	0	59	7,738
Barre	978	1,138	80	7	0	40	2,243
Berlin	496	715	40	1	2	6	1,260
Blackstone	1,571	1,583	101	21	1	49	3,326
Bolton	808	1,135	49	4	0	9	2,005
Boylston	808	1,262	49	5	2	16	2,142
Brookfield	553	709	43	7	0	10	1,322
Charlton	1,632	2,479	107	10	1	25	4,254
Clinton	2,681	2,594	185	19	3	84	5,566
Douglas	1,136	1,578	75	6	0	30	2,825
Dudley	1,667	1,898	89	12	0	214	3,880
East Brookfield	377	509	34	3	0	4	927
Fitchburg	6,103	5,124	374	32	0	723	12,356
Gardner	3,785	3,198	233	37	0	107	7,360
Grafton	2,818	3,355	144	16	2	51	6,386
Hardwick	589	602	36	4	0	11	1,242
Harvard	1,380	1,454	90	5	1	31	2,961
Holden	2,916	4,916	162	20	0	174	8,188
Hopedale	1,330	1,493	54	3	0	36	2,916
Hubbardston	652	883	87	4	0	8	1,634
Lancaster	1,037	1,473	118	19	0	24	2,671
Leicester	2,050	2,325	130	9	4	28	4,546
Leominster	7,071	7,765	432	43	0	263	15,574
Lunenburg	1,751	2,374	142	8	0	88	4,363
Mendon	857	1,359	55	2	0	25	2,298
Milford	5,391	4,793	257	22	1	133	10,597
Millbury	2,556	2,834	137	22	1	53	5,603
Millville	530	510	42	4	0	8	1,094
New Braintree	147	284	3	0	0	1	435
North Brookfield	817	1,136	68	3	0	16	2,040

COUNTY OF WORCESTER — *Concluded*

CITIES AND TOWNS	John F. Kerry of Boston Democratic	William F. Weld of Cambridge Republican	Susan C. Gallagher of Milton Conservative	Robert C. Stowe of Cambridge Natural Law	All Others	Blanks	Total Votes Cast
Northborough	2,712	3,795	143	12	3	59	6,724
Northbridge	2,552	3,007	167	17	0	62	5,805
Oakham	334	469	22	2	0	6	833
Oxford	2,304	2,731	141	19	0	51	5,246
Paxton	782	1,283	39	8	0	25	2,137
Petersham	364	313	29	1	0	8	715
Phillipston	292	322	22	6	0	1	643
Princeton	659	1,059	25	3	3	15	1,764
Royalston	235	242	27	6	0	3	513
Rutland	909	1,406	74	10	1	20	2,420
Shrewsbury	5,936	7,658	302	33	2	114	14,045
Southborough	1,777	2,414	53	7	3	33	4,287
Southbridge	3,005	2,746	158	17	0	91	6,017
Spencer	2,084	2,434	179	16	3	43	4,759
Sterling	1,233	2,149	115	16	0	19	3,532
Sturbridge	1,490	2,136	82	25	0	15	3,748
Sutton	1,425	2,333	74	7	2	53	3,894
Templeton	1,265	1,366	128	11	0	41	2,811
Upton	1,252	1,644	76	19	0	17	3,008
Uxbridge	2,187	2,575	164	18	0	69	5,013
Warren	875	889	45	14	0	12	1,835
Webster	2,733	2,819	165	20	0	257	5,994
West Boylston	1,264	1,946	92	9	0	22	3,333
West Brookfield	615	892	41	3	1	18	1,570
Westborough	3,241	4,424	122	19	1	42	7,849
Westminster	1,366	1,721	96	10	2	42	3,237
Winchendon	1,393	1,487	114	15	3	34	3,046
WORCESTER	29,844	21,350	1,525	175	950	956	54,800
Totals	134,993	146,639	8,126	916	1,012	4,518	296,204

AGGREGATE OF VOTES FOR SENATOR

COUNTIES	John F. Kerry of Boston Democratic	William F. Weld of Cambridge Republican	Susan C. Gallagher of Milton Conservative	Robert C. Stowe of Cambridge Natural Law	All Others	Blanks	Total Votes Cast
BARNSTABLE	50,810	57,056	2,444	316	27	1,267	111,920
BERKSHIRE	35,774	22,679	1,349	459	5	1,529	61,795
BRISTOL	114,044	75,788	6,454	629	39	4,522	201,476
DUKES COUNTY	4,663	2,858	116	44	2	130	7,813
ESSEX	140,769	142,323	7,717	690	46	4,900	296,445
FRANKLIN	17,538	14,072	939	178	5	312	33,044
HAMPDEN	81,990	85,304	3,690	619	48	2,713	174,364
HAMPSHIRE	37,161	26,444	1,246	321	17	1,165	66,354
MIDDLESEX	339,253	271,822	15,532	1,480	184	8,402	636,673
NANTUCKET	2,201	1,866	55	16	2	67	4,207
NORFOLK	153,452	137,774	9,984	532	65	4,984	306,791
PLYMOUTH	89,684	97,154	6,729	476	51	3,056	197,150
SUFFOLK	131,803	61,341	5,626	493	8	6,753	206,024
WORCESTER	134,993	146,639	8,126	916	1,012	4,518	296,204
Totals	1,334,135	1,143,120	70,007	7,169	1,511	44,318	2,600,260

REPRESENTATIVES — ONE HUNDRED FIFTH CONGRESS

ELECTION, NOVEMBER 5, 1996

District

No. 1.	JOHN W. OLVER *(D)* of Amherst.
No. 2.	RICHARD E. NEAL *(D)* of Springfield.
No. 3.	JAMES P. MCGOVERN *(D)* of Worcester.
No. 4.	BARNEY FRANK *(D)* of Newton.
No. 5.	MARTIN T. MEEHAN *(D)* of Lowell.
No. 6.	JOHN F. TIERNEY *(D)* of Salem.
No. 7.	EDWARD J. MARKEY *(D)* of Malden.
No. 8.	JOSEPH P. KENNEDY, II *(D)* of Boston.
No. 9.	JOHN JOSEPH MOAKLEY *(D)* of Boston.
No. 10.	WILLIAM D. DELAHUNT *(D)* of Quincy.

VOTE FOR REPRESENTATIVES IN CONGRESS
in 1996
(BY DISTRICTS)

ELECTION, NOVEMBER 5, 1996.

CONGRESSIONAL DISTRICT NO. 1

CITIES AND TOWNS	John W. Olver of Amherst Democratic	Jane Maria Swift of North Adams Republican	All Others	Blanks	Total Votes Cast
Adams	1,872	2,345	0	57	4,274
Alford	111	129	0	3	243
Amherst	7,885	2,143	2	437	10,467
Ashburnham	1,141	1,207	0	80	2,428
Ashby	533	695	0	65	1,293
Ashfield	578	379	0	15	972
Athol	2,228	2,080	0	138	4,446
Barre	1,172	907	1	163	2,243
Becket	332	345	0	24	701
Belchertown	2,793	2,471	2	90	5,356
Bernardston	463	539	0	17	1,019
Blandford	222	345	0	9	576
Buckland	451	485	0	8	944
Charlemont	211	329	0	6	546
Cheshire	681	1,036	0	11	1,728
Chester	223	349	0	5	577
Chesterfield	244	333	0	10	587
Clarksburg	248	556	0	9	813
Colrain	370	471	0	4	845
Conway	631	371	1	8	1,011
Cummington	228	239	0	2	469
Dalton	1,592	1,715	1	67	3,375
Deerfield	1,564	1,097	1	31	2,693
Easthampton	4,020	3,363	6	157	7,546
Egremont	350	353	0	8	711
Erving	383	309	2	7	701
FITCHBURG	5,828	5,483	0	1,045	12,356
Florida	114	233	0	8	355
GARDNER	4,250	2,829	0	281	7,360
Gill	406	315	3	21	745
Goshen	217	231	0	5	453
Granby	1,290	1,399	1	81	2,771
Granville	220	468	3	14	705

CONGRESSIONAL DISTRICT NO. 1 — *Continued*

CITIES AND TOWNS	John W. Olver of Amherst Democratic	Jane Maria Swift of North Adams Republican	All Others	Blanks	Total Votes Cast
Great Barrington	1,686	1,494	3	93	3,276
Greenfield	4,216	3,365	3	130	7,714
Hancock	146	194	0	3	343
Hardwick	665	535	0	42	1,242
Hatfield	1,091	735	2	25	1,853
Hawley	57	95	1	2	155
Heath	162	182	0	26	370
Hinsdale	406	459	0	21	886
HOLYOKE	8,817	4,942	11	744	14,514
Hubbardston	756	813	4	61	1,634
Huntington	368	493	0	19	880
Lanesborough	680	728	0	21	1,429
Lee	1,270	1,399	0	63	2,732
Lenox	1,479	1,244	0	53	2,776
LEOMINSTER	7,026	7,848	3	697	15,574
Leverett	809	233	0	24	1,066
Leyden	170	176	0	5	351
Lunenburg*	1,712	2,277	0	162	4,151
Middlefield	97	153	0	2	252
Monroe	20	38	0	0	58
Montague	2,246	1,366	1	51	3,664
Monterey	276	190	0	6	472
Montgomery	147	245	0	10	402
Mount Washington	29	44	0	1	74
New Ashford	57	59	0	2	118
New Braintree	187	224	0	24	435
New Marlborough	280	331	0	11	622
New Salem	264	193	0	10	467
NORTH ADAMS	2,233	3,353	3	117	5,706
North Brookfield	977	961	0	102	2,040
Northfield	760	659	0	29	1,448
Oakham	388	404	0	41	833
Orange	1,454	1,373	0	60	2,887
Otis	235	368	0	25	628
Pelham	562	227	0	16	805
Peru	117	231	0	6	354
Petersham	383	310	0	22	715
Phillipston	331	285	1	26	643
PITTSFIELD	11,453	8,263	0	500	20,216
Plainfield	162	153	0	3	318
Richmond	478	463	0	14	955
Rowe	64	149	0	5	218
Royalston	250	235	0	28	513
Russell	271	370	0	8	649
Sandisfield	162	150	1	17	330
Savoy	104	209	0	5	318

CONGRESSIONAL DISTRICT NO. 1 — *Concluded*

CITIES AND TOWNS	John W. Olver of Amherst Democratic	Jane Maria Swift of North Adams Republican	All Others	Blanks	Total Votes Cast
Sheffield	621	904	1	37	1,563
Shelburne	470	504	3	18	995
Shutesbury	733	220	0	10	963
Southampton	1,139	1,467	0	27	2,633
Southwick	1,586	2,005	2	75	3,668
Stockbridge	753	492	0	29	1,274
Sunderland	986	532	4	42	1,564
Templeton	1,486	1,212	0	113	2,811
Tolland	65	122	0	0	187
Townsend	1,640	1,934	2	191	3,767
Tyringham	96	117	0	6	219
Warwick	214	162	0	5	381
Washington	167	149	0	2	318
Wendell	312	111	0	6	429
West Brookfield	772	700	0	98	1,570
West Springfield	5,262	6,181	0	339	11,782
West Stockbridge	420	348	2	15	785
WESTFIELD	6,972	8,350	7	402	15,731
Westhampton	338	448	0	10	796
Westminster	1,494	1,608	1	134	3,237
Whately	456	371	0	11	838
Williamsburg	883	464	0	34	1,381
Williamstown	1,943	1,701	0	108	3,752
Winchendon	1,561	1,361	0	124	3,046
Windsor	210	233	0	5	448
Worthington	299	338	0	12	649
Totals	129,232	115,801	78	8,071	253,182

*For the part of Lunenburg covered by the First Congressional District, see "Congressional Districts" (pages 257-267).

CONGRESSIONAL DISTRICT NO. 2

CITIES AND TOWNS	Richard E. Neal of Springfield Democrat	Mark Steele of Springfield Republican	Scott Andrichak of Springfield Independent	Richard Kaynor of Wilbraham Natural Law	All Others	Blanks	Total Votes Cast
Agawam	8,239	2,613	541	5,256	5	909	12,563
Auburn*	2,695	1,205	215	49	6	511	4,681
Bellingham	3,632	1,533	434	142	0	866	6,607
Blackstone	2,107	697	171	51	1	299	3,326
Brimfield	905	396	71	38	0	67	1,477
Brookfield	804	314	65	27	0	112	1,322
Charlton	2,478	1,165	202	76	2	331	4,254
Chicopee	16,314	3,915	811	370	28	891	22,329
Douglas	1,596	757	164	51	0	257	2,825
Dudley	2,384	799	155	73	0	469	3,880
East Brookfield	541	247	35	22	0	82	927
East Longmeadow	4,366	2,234	194	173	7	375	7,349
Hadley	1,826	471	78	61	4	209	2,649
Hampden	1,460	741	92	96	2	100	2,491
Holland	580	244	41	28	1	58	952
Hopedale	1,711	726	107	36	0	336	2,916
Leicester	2,737	1,048	184	77	9	491	4,546
Longmeadow	5,436	2,540	213	154	17	484	8,844
Ludlow	5,732	1,537	291	245	1	621	8,427
Mendon	1,212	690	91	23	5	277	2,298
Milford	6,685	2,133	408	107	3	1,261	10,597
Millbury	3,425	1,202	299	90	4	583	5,603
Millville	673	224	77	18	0	102	1,094
Monson	2,212	741	114	234	0	211	3,512
Northampton	10,696	1,651	522	375	62	994	14,300
Oxford	3,169	1,076	279	111	0	611	5,246
Palmer	3,660	1,021	229	149	0	246	5,305
South Hadley	5,165	1,753	286	161	4	683	8,052
Southbridge	4,233	876	178	89	1	640	6,017
Spencer	3,047	1,057	192	68	8	387	4,759
Springfield	33,202	6,789	1,301	683	41	2,598	44,614
Sturbridge	2,348	878	101	83	0	338	3,748
Sutton	2,083	1,165	172	41	8	425	3,894
Uxbridge	3,019	1,220	206	62	2	504	5,013
Wales	408	153	42	29	0	39	671
Ware	2,958	700	164	82	0	233	4,137
Warren	1,262	372	69	54	0	78	1,835
Webster	3,936	1,094	218	97	0	649	5,994
Wilbraham	4,059	1,908	169	543	5	355	7,039
Totals	162,995	49,885	9,181	5,124	226	18,682	246,093

*For the part of Auburn covered by the Second Congressional District, see "Congressional Districts" (pages 257-267).

CONGRESSIONAL DISTRICT NO. 3

Cities and Towns	Peter Blute of Shrewsbury Republican	James P. McGovern of Worcester Democratic	Dale E. Friedgen of Sterling Natural Law	All Others	Blanks	Total Votes Cast
Attleboro	6,638	7,219	199	9	266	14,331
Auburn*	1,418	1,551	21	1	66	3,057
Berlin	612	561	39	0	48	1,260
Boylston	1,176	881	25	1	59	2,142
Clinton	2,068	3,225	97	4	172	5,566
Dartmouth	4,818	6,677	190	0	680	12,365
Fall River*	3,563	10,435	184	0	695	14,877
Foxborough*	1,810	1,814	59	0	229	3,912
Franklin	5,394	6,344	158	0	430	12,326
Grafton	3,281	2,886	66	2	151	6,386
Holden	4,411	3,490	80	0	207	8,188
Holliston	3,153	3,632	88	1	271	7,145
Hopkinton	2,961	2,649	74	4	259	5,947
Lancaster*	864	763	83	1	65	1,776
Mansfield*	2,232	2,180	77	0	220	4,709
Medway	2,366	2,702	80	0	273	5,421
North Attleborough	5,668	4,818	151	0	363	11,000
Northborough	3,725	2,776	63	3	157	6,724
Northbridge	2,815	2,736	72	0	182	5,805
Paxton	1,163	889	30	0	55	2,137
Plainville	1,609	1,450	49	0	88	3,196
Princeton	943	738	31	1	51	1,764
Rutland	1,248	1,060	52	0	60	2,420
Seekonk	2,878	3,090	93	2	164	6,227
Shrewsbury	8,080	5,672	95	0	198	14,045
Somerset	3,272	5,663	87	0	234	9,256
Sterling	1,866	1,426	178	0	62	3,532
Swansea	3,095	4,002	96	3	203	7,399
Upton	1,524	1,338	49	0	97	3,008
West Boylston	1,833	1,402	54	0	44	3,333
Westborough	4,143	3,378	87	0	241	7,849
Westport	2,722	3,645	100	0	300	6,767
Worcester	19,952	31,969	475	965	1,439	54,800
Wrentham	2,393	1,983	80	0	191	4,647
Totals	115,694	135,044	3,362	997	8,220	263,317

*For the parts of the city of Fall River and the towns of Auburn, Foxborough, Lancaster and Mansfield covered by the Third Congressional District, see "Congressional Districts" pages 257-267).

CONGRESSIONAL DISTRICT NO. 4

CITIES AND TOWNS	Barney Frank of Newton Democratic	Jonathan P. Raymond of Newton Republican	All Others	Blanks	Total Votes Cast
Acushnet	3,413	865	2	166	4,446
Berkley	1,466	731	1	123	2,321
Bridgewater	5,041	3,097	9	416	8,563
Brookline	19,327	4,288	3	1,300	24,918
Carver	2,932	1,728	2	210	4,872
Dighton	1,720	838	0	124	2,682
Dover	1,407	1,637	4	140	3,188
East Bridgewater	2,958	2,059	4	296	5,317
Easton*	2,479	1,736	4	206	4,425
Fairhaven	5,237	1,522	0	327	7,086
FALL RIVER*	12,759	2,231	0	761	15,751
Foxborough*	2,767	1,337	0	200	4,304
Freetown	2,639	1,024	1	112	3,776
Halifax	1,907	1,285	2	153	3,347
Hanson	2,540	1,647	1	209	4,397
Lakeville	2,365	1,548	0	182	4,095
Mansfield*	2,590	1,359	0	170	4,119
Marion	1,495	1,008	2	94	2,599
Mattapoisett	2,167	1,185	3	78	3,433
Middleborough	4,204	2,799	3	318	7,324
Millis	2,342	1,399	5	207	3,953
NEW BEDFORD	25,283	4,334	28	1,206	30,851
NEWTON	31,273	8,256	0	1,671	41,200
Norfolk	2,332	1,828	0	193	4,353
Norton	4,131	2,186	2	227	6,546
Pembroke	4,360	2,686	0	324	7,370
Plympton	708	553	0	54	1,315
Raynham	2,910	1,931	0	234	5,075
Rehoboth	2,778	1,462	4	113	4,357
Rochester	1,245	815	1	62	2,123
Rockland*	1,747	1,012	3	135	2,897
Sharon	7,061	1,756	0	259	9,076
Sherborn	1,378	1,068	0	91	2,537
Wareham	5,551	2,475	8	267	8,301
Wellesley	7,619	5,497	0	604	13,720
West Bridgewater	1,713	1,519	0	164	3,396
Totals	183,844	72,701	92	11,396	268,033

*For the parts of the city of Fall River and the towns of Easton, Foxborough, Mansfield and Rockland covered by the Fourth Congressional District, see "Congressional Districts" (pages 257-267).

CONGRESSIONAL DISTRICT NO. 5

CITIES AND TOWNS	Martin T. Meehan of Lowell Democratic	All Others	Blanks	Total Votes Cast
Acton	7,378	74	2,605	10,057
Andover	11,090	216	4,632	15,938
Ashland	4,251	0	2,247	6,498
Ayer	1,804	0	571	2,375
Billerica	12,111	118	3,901	16,130
Bolton	1,411	0	594	2,005
Boxborough	1,605	1	613	2,219
Carlisle	1,891	7	790	2,688
Chelmsford	12,619	199	4,144	16,962
Concord	6,718	62	2,616	9,396
Dracut	9,480	169	2,702	12,351
Dunstable	967	2	322	1,291
Groton	3,110	70	1,136	4,316
Harvard	2,120	24	817	2,961
Hudson	5,699	8	1,901	7,608
Lancaster*	568	3	324	895
LAWRENCE	8,785	1	4,200	12,986
Lincoln*	100	0	32	132
Littleton	3,007	0	959	3,966
LOWELL	20,861	0	6,200	27,061
Lunenburg*	142	0	70	212
MARLBOROUGH	10,511	182	3,697	14,390
Maynard	3,868	12	1,277	5,157
Methuen	12,250	0	4,947	17,197
Pepperell	3,534	30	1,195	4,759
Shirley	1,744	11	578	2,333
Southborough	2,932	19	1,336	4,287
Stow	2,251	5	846	3,102
Sudbury	5,812	104	2,728	8,644
Tewksbury	9,747	179	2,948	12,874
Tyngsborough	3,104	4	995	4,103
Wayland	4,885	80	2,279	7,244
Westford	7,074	128	2,356	9,558
Totals:	183,429	1,708	66,558	251,695

*For the parts of the towns of Lancaster, Lincoln and Lunenburg covered by the Fifth Congressional District, see "Congressional Districts" (pages 257-267).

CONGRESSIONAL DISTRICT NO. 6

Cities and Towns	Peter G. Torkildsen of Danvers Republican	John F. Tierney of Salem Democratic	Ronald C. Fritz of Manchester-by-the-Sea Conservative	Benjamin A. Gatchell of Marblehead Independent	Martin J. McNulty of Lynn Independent	Orrin Smith of Peabody Natural Law	All Others	Blanks	Total Votes Cast
Amesbury	3,006	2,996	50	51	60	32	63	241	6,499
Bedford	3,259	2,691	40	41	49	39	0	338	6,457
BEVERLY	8,697	8,265	196	114	97	69	0	499	17,937
Boxford	2,837	1,091	23	33	27	8	1	96	4,116
Burlington	5,017	5,484	81	65	113	42	2	525	11,325
Danvers	6,991	4,644	126	69	47	52	0	201	12,130
Essex	960	760	26	18	4	6	0	40	1,814
Georgetown	1,940	1,487	31	32	35	17	0	114	3,656
GLOUCESTER	5,479	6,318	181	55	69	51	7	684	12,844
Groveland	1,420	1,192	29	25	30	15	0	95	2,806
Hamilton	2,524	1,305	105	25	24	12	0	101	4,096
HAVERHILL	8,999	10,199	189	122	174	111	6	868	20,668
Ipswich	3,571	2,951	54	35	106	22	0	201	6,940
LYNN	9,431	14,564	239	153	2,106	123	0	1,065	27,68
Lynnfield	3,827	2,268	54	30	63	24	3	204	6,47
Manchester-by-the-Sea	1,829	1,021	123	13	13	16	0	67	3,08
Marblehead	6,157	4,916	33	387	63	29	0	213	11,79
Merrimac	1,310	1,167	17	33	25	19	3	78	2,65
Middleton	1,535	1,279	28	16	19	13	1	70	2,96
Nahant	884	1,171	11	14	57	7	0	53	2,19
Newbury	1,977	1,339	25	29	27	22	0	126	3,54
NEWBURYPORT	4,115	4,438	40	47	35	51	96	326	9,14
North Andover	6,621	4,530	96	60	69	51	10	446	11,88
North Reading	3,577	2,737	40	40	62	39	2	279	6,77
PEABODY	8,823	12,299	176	88	148	195	10	475	22,21
Reading*	1,421	1,230	19	20	18	8	2	134	2,85
Rockport	2,013	1,942	70	20	14	12	0	84	4,15
Rowley	1,450	904	27	22	20	16	1	85	2,52
SALEM	5,106	10,059	128	99	88	76	0	395	15,95
Salisbury	1,320	1,466	21	28	29	21	66	125	3,07
Saugus	5,502	6,052	93	75	224	80	0	550	12,57
Swampscott	3,066	3,910	28	76	106	15	0	171	7,37
Topsfield	2,105	1,077	10	20	13	4	0	61	3,29
Wenham	1,286	618	32	11	11	5	0	46	2,00
West Newbury	1,292	773	8	8	11	4	5	69	2,17
Wilmington	3,976	4,551	99	86	127	73	0	659	9,57
Totals	133,323	133,694	2,548	2,060	4,183	1,379	278	9,784	287,24

*For the part of the town of Reading covered by the Sixth Congressional District, see "Congressional Districts" (pages 257-267).

CONGRESSIONAL DISTRICT NO. 7

CITIES AND TOWNS	Edward J. Markey of Malden Democratic	Patricia H. Long of Lexington Republican	All Others	Blanks	Total Votes Cast
Arlington	15,393	6,557	2	1,841	23,793
EVERETT	9,605	2,954	0	1,168	13,727
Framingham	16,719	7,519	16	1,615	25,869
Lexington	9,947	5,745	0	1,069	16,761
Lincoln*	1,844	1,082	0	150	3,076
MALDEN	15,100	4,054	25	1,073	20,252
MEDFORD	17,724	5,748	18	1,384	24,874
MELROSE	9,809	3,969	15	746	14,539
Natick	9,832	5,004	10	1,145	15,991
Reading*	5,650	3,130	5	423	9,208
REVERE	10,985	3,059	0	2,435	16,479
Stoneham	7,295	3,045	6	458	10,804
Wakefield	8,526	3,821	0	645	12,992
WALTHAM	12,705	6,463	2	2,526	21,696
Weston	2,706	2,878	0	447	6,031
Winchester	6,910	4,447	4	608	11,969
Winthrop	5,731	1,936	7	510	8,184
VOBURN	10,572	4,996	0	1,114	16,682
Totals	177,053	76,407	110	19,357	272,927

*For the parts of the towns of Lincoln and Reading covered by the Seventh Congressional District, see "Congressional Districts" (pages 257-267).

CONGRESSIONAL DISTRICT NO. 8

Cities and Towns	Joseph P. Kennedy, II of Boston Democratic	R. Philip Hyde of Somerville Republican	All Others	Blanks	Total Votes Cast
Belmont	9,060	3,575	0	1,027	13,662
Boston*	67,695	11,075	6	9,491	88,267
Cambridge	31,566	4,956	105	1,687	38,314
Chelsea	5,153	804	0	445	6,402
Somerville	21,907	3,985	55	1,083	27,030
Watertown	11,745	2,908	25	630	15,308
Totals	147,126	27,303	191	14,363	188,983

*For the part of the city of Boston covered by the Eighth Congressional District, see "Congressional Districts" (pages 257-267).

CONGRESSIONAL DISTRICT NO. 9

Cities and Towns	John Joseph Moakley of Boston Democratic	Paul V. Gryska of Medfield Republican	All Others	Blanks	Total Votes Cast
Boston*	63,300	11,955	7	11,430	86,692
Braintree	11,630	4,545	12	807	16,994
Brockton*	10,208	4,213	1	1,359	15,781
Canton	6,765	3,109	0	688	10,562
Dedham	7,165	3,952	0	643	11,760
Easton*	3,070	1,959	4	235	5,268
Medfield	2,346	3,675	3	185	6,209
Milton	9,497	3,686	0	733	13,916
Needham	9,745	5,878	12	684	16,319
Norwood	9,306	3,897	10	575	13,788
Randolph	8,772	3,072	11	624	12,479
Stoughton	8,389	3,651	2	577	12,619
Taunton	11,126	4,955	0	1,757	17,838
Walpole	6,419	4,276	0	569	11,264
Westwood	4,271	3,256	2	252	7,781
Totals	172,009	66,079	64	21,118	259,270

*For the parts of the cities of Boston and Brockton and the town of Easton covered by the Ninth Congressional District, see "Congressional Districts" (pages 257-267).

CONGRESSIONAL DISTRICT NO. 10

CITIES AND TOWNS	William D. Delahunt of Quincy Democratic	Edward B. Teague III of Yarmouth Republican	A. Charles Laws of West Tisbury Green	All Others	Blanks	Total Votes Cast
Abington	3,569	2,648	186	2	311	6,716
Avon	1,444	760	52	5	114	2,375
Barnstable	10,575	10,354	986	30	522	22,467
Bourne	3,665	3,675	338	4	350	8,032
Brewster	2,545	2,529	274	9	141	5,498
BROCKTON*	6,948	3,555	369	1	816	11,689
Chatham	1,859	2,273	135	5	203	4,475
Chilmark	301	173	85	0	14	573
Cohasset	2,051	1,845	130	3	263	4,292
Dennis	3,905	4,041	330	18	199	8,493
Duxbury	3,473	4,057	225	27	289	8,071
Eastham	1,527	1,387	168	6	63	3,151
Edgartown	977	598	225	1	81	1,882
Falmouth	8,407	6,522	673	43	579	16,224
Gay Head	129	20	30	1	9	189
Gosnold	42	40	5	0	4	91
Hanover	3,229	2,711	160	24	281	6,405
Harwich	3,107	3,139	259	18	214	6,737
Hingham	5,349	5,080	296	68	480	11,273
Holbrook	2,946	1,677	139	6	187	4,955
Hull	3,081	1,385	190	0	414	5,070
Kingston	2,384	2,139	150	9	219	4,901
Marshfield	6,178	4,485	332	128	425	11,548
Mashpee	2,437	2,193	190	8	134	4,962
Nantucket	2,276	1,514	177	14	226	4,207
Norwell	2,445	2,495	145	5	224	5,314
Oak Bluffs	1,035	559	267	2	78	1,941
Orleans	1,775	2,076	201	0	170	4,222
Plymouth	10,061	9,085	568	45	907	20,666
Provincetown	1,760	335	110	5	58	2,268
QUINCY	23,855	10,819	842	107	1,255	36,878
Rockland*	2,471	1,647	129	9	183	4,439
Sandwich	4,285	4,753	434	21	264	9,757
Scituate	5,012	4,172	245	83	336	9,848
Tisbury	1,012	494	289	0	56	1,851
Truro	705	358	56	2	35	1,156
Wellfleet	1,055	575	88	1	49	1,768
West Tisbury	736	300	216	0	34	1,286
Weymouth	13,208	8,324	679	11	2,757	24,979
Whitman	3,197	2,424	148	11	297	6,077
Yarmouth	5,729	6,304	392	13	272	12,710
Totals	160,745	123,520	10,913	745	13,513	309,436

*For the parts of the city of Brockton and the town of Rockland covered by the Tenth Congressional District, see "Congressional Districts" (pages 257-267).

VOTE FOR GOVERNOR AND LIEUTENANT-GOVERNOR
(BY COUNTIES)

ELECTION, NOVEMBER 8, 1994

COUNTY OF BARNSTABLE

Cities and Towns	Weld & Cellucci Republican	Roosevelt & Massie Democratic	Cook & Crawford Libertarian	Rebello & Giske LaRouche For President	All Others	Blanks	Total Votes Cast
Barnstable	14,369	4,420	81	24	4	392	19,290
Bourne	4,817	1,525	44	12	—	108	6,506
Brewster	3,431	1,073	23	4	—	69	4,600
Chatham	3,116	706	17	6	1	47	3,893
Dennis	5,460	1,672	38	14	1	117	7,302
Eastham	1,964	672	12	7	—	19	2,674
Falmouth	9,210	3,803	91	25	1	469	13,599
Harwich	4,101	1,290	41	11	—	243	5,686
Mashpee	2,942	968	22	9	—	48	3,989
Orleans	2,659	750	13	—	—	118	3,540
Provincetown	962	761	17	4	4	33	1,781
Sandwich	5,947	1,676	37	6	—	75	7,741
Truro	611	288	4	1	—	12	916
Wellfleet	943	473	13	6	—	30	1,465
Yarmouth	8,187	2,499	60	8	1	162	10,917
Totals	68,719	22,576	513	137	12	1,942	93,899

COUNTY OF BERKSHIRE

Cities and Towns	Weld & Cellucci Republican	Roosevelt & Massie Democratic	Cook & Crawford Libertarian	Rebello & Giske LaRouche For President	All Others	Blanks	Total Votes Cast
Adams	2,320	1,312	31	9	—	95	3,767
Alford	116	60	2	—	—	6	184
Becket	368	172	8	2	—	10	560
Cheshire	924	459	13	6	—	23	1,425
Clarksburg	522	170	5	—	—	16	713
Dalton	1,659	848	15	6	1	67	2,596
Egremont	358	177	6	2	—	13	556
Florida	180	91	5	1	—	7	284
Great Barrington	1,535	877	17	6	5	112	2,552
Hancock	169	89	—	—	—	2	260
Hinsdale	396	220	7	—	—	11	634
Lanesborough	685	368	13	3	1	24	1,094
Lee	1,482	736	31	5	—	92	2,346

COUNTY OF BERKSHIRE — *Concluded*

Cities and Towns	Weld & Cellucci Republican	Roosevelt & Massie Democratic	Cook & Crawford Libertarian	Rebello & Gnske LaRouche For President	All Others	Blanks	Total Votes Cast
Lenox	1,519	822	17	6	—	58	2,422
Monterey	187	156	4	1	—	10	358
Mount Washington	51	11	1	—	—	—	63
New Ashford	58	31	2	—	—	—	91
New Marlborough	310	137	9	1	—	14	471
NORTH ADAMS	3,111	1,376	34	8	5	120	4,654
Otis	199	230	10	4	—	6	449
Peru	180	72	6	—	—	5	263
PITTSFIELD	9,213	6,420	116	44	1	459	16,253
Richmond	470	284	8	—	—	10	772
Sandisfield	140	104	6	1	—	7	258
Savoy	147	77	—	—	—	6	230
Sheffield	830	345	14	3	—	31	1,223
Stockbridge	656	404	13	2	—	24	1,099
Tyringham	101	58	2	—	—	20	181
Washington	122	97	4	6	—	4	233
West Stockbridge	387	222	7	1	1	14	632
Williamstown	1,812	1,068	10	—	2	89	2,981
Windsor	223	125	4	—	—	11	363
Totals	30,430	17,618	420	117	16	1,366	49,967

COUNTY OF BRISTOL

Acushnet	2,520	1,096	26	11	—	122	3,775
ATTLEBORO	8,223	2,734	105	31	—	466	11,559
Berkley	1,059	512	16	8	—	26	1,621
Dartmouth	6,846	2,571	90	58	1	325	9,891
Dighton	1,422	724	12	3	—	54	2,215
Easton	6,341	1,768	47	7	5	124	8,292
Fairhaven	3,938	1,680	52	24	—	200	5,894
FALL RIVER	12,513	10,893	268	251	—	1,642	25,567
Freetown	2,098	881	21	12	5	57	3,074
Mansfield	5,405	1,501	45	7	—	129	7,087
NEW BEDFORD	15,648	8,653	184	152	9	972	25,618
North Attleborough	6,539	1,690	75	12	—	467	8,783
Norton	3,783	1,250	42	8	—	77	5,160
Raynham	3,111	1,112	27	7	—	112	4,369
Rehoboth	2,578	693	32	7	2	62	3,374
Seekonk	3,781	1,106	52	21	1	96	5,057
Somerset	4,608	3,082	51	48	—	172	7,961
Swansea	3,679	2,128	53	49	6	185	6,100
TAUNTON	8,334	5,842	133	44	—	721	15,074
Westport	3,325	1,786	39	29	—	216	5,395
Totals	105,751	51,702	1,370	789	29	6,225	165,866

COUNTY OF DUKES COUNTY

Cities and Towns	Weld & Cellucci Republican	Roosevelt & Massie Democratic	Cook & Crawford Libertarian	Rebello & Giske LaRouche For President	All Others	Blanks	Total Votes Cast
Chilmark	247	158	3	—	—	13	421
Edgartown	1,022	348	14	1	—	51	1,436
Gay Head	71	61	—	5	—	—	137
Gosnold	52	17	2	—	—	—	71
Oak Bluffs	918	484	11	9	1	37	1,460
Tisbury	873	515	16	1	—	52	1,457
West Tisbury	565	424	12	2	—	25	1,028
Totals	3,748	2,007	58	18	1	178	6,010

COUNTY OF ESSEX

Cities and Towns	Weld & Cellucci Republican	Roosevelt & Massie Democratic	Cook & Crawford Libertarian	Rebello & Giske LaRouche For President	All Others	Blanks	Total Votes Cast
Amesbury	3,839	1,212	48	9	—	186	5,294
Andover	11,026	2,626	73	6	1	222	13,954
BEVERLY	11,499	3,796	86	20	—	518	15,919
Boxford	2,875	465	18	1	1	47	3,407
Danvers	7,856	2,401	60	17	—	412	10,746
Essex	1,247	300	7	3	—	24	1,581
Georgetown	2,237	621	16	2	3	74	2,953
GLOUCESTER	7,941	3,008	65	12	—	268	11,294
Groveland	1,864	489	16	1	—	29	2,399
Hamilton	2,727	548	24	4	2	84	3,389
HAVERHILL	13,031	4,102	115	21	5	354	17,628
Ipswich	4,432	1,396	38	10	5	80	5,961
LAWRENCE	8,162	3,075	92	26	—	660	12,015
LYNN	16,744	7,696	195	52	—	1,092	25,779
Lynnfield	4,770	1,001	29	3	3	172	5,978
Manchester-by-the-Sea	2,064	549	21	3	—	71	2,708
Marblehead	7,895	2,258	46	7	3	241	10,450
Merrimac	1,612	454	19	5	—	28	2,118
Methuen	11,886	3,128	74	12	—	389	15,489
Middleton	1,740	516	14	5	—	67	2,342
Nahant	1,384	548	13	4	3	56	2,008
Newbury	2,342	638	30	4	—	51	3,065
NEWBURYPORT	5,472	2,116	37	7	4	219	7,855
North Andover	8,071	1,941	55	17	—	146	10,230
PEABODY	13,673	5,596	89	29	22	537	19,946
Rockport	2,632	1,027	18	5	1	57	3,740
Rowley	1,618	449	10	2	2	38	2,119
SALEM	9,374	4,521	96	21	—	440	14,452
Salisbury	1,965	567	18	1	—	52	2,603
Saugus	7,817	2,906	69	14	—	440	11,246
Swampscott	4,644	1,836	32	4	3	168	6,687
Topsfield	2,321	520	8	2	—	34	2,885
Wenham	1,432	310	3	1	—	18	1,764
West Newbury	1,426	373	13	—	—	28	1,840
Totals	189,618	62,989	1,547	330	58	7,302	261,844

COUNTY OF FRANKLIN

CITIES AND TOWNS	Weld & Cellucci Republican	Roosevelt & Massie Democratic	Cook & Crawford Libertarian	Rebello & Giske LaRouche For President	All Others	Blanks	Total Votes Cast
Ashfield	490	272	12	1	—	16	791
Bernardston	663	160	3	4	—	12	842
Buckland	572	203	4	—	—	17	796
Charlemont	307	108	3	1	—	5	424
Colrain	439	172	11	2	1	9	634
Conway	441	321	8	—	—	14	784
Deerfield	1,474	619	13	4	—	39	2,149
Erving	435	121	5	1	5	9	576
Gill	371	207	9	4	3	13	607
Greenfield	4,595	1,719	69	12	1	163	6,559
Hawley	88	21	—	—	—	4	113
Heath	161	102	4	1	—	13	281
Leverett	356	487	11	—	—	20	874
Leyden	215	90	5	—	—	6	316
Monroe	31	10	—	1	—	3	45
Montague	2,026	993	29	5	—	54	3,107
New Salem	262	105	4	—	—	9	380
Northfield	897	373	6	4	—	22	1,302
Orange	1,832	512	19	8	—	36	2,407
Rowe	119	48	1	1	—	2	171
Shelburne	560	219	13	—	—	17	809
Shutesbury	291	450	8	2	1	25	777
Sunderland	709	397	16	2	2	26	1,152
Warwick	176	107	3	2	—	10	298
Wendell	148	174	8	4	—	13	347
Whately	568	227	8	1	—	25	829
Totals	18,226	8,217	272	60	13	582	27,370

COUNTY OF HAMPDEN

Agawam	8,708	2,247	76	32	—	403	11,466
Blandford	384	110	2	1	—	8	505
Brimfield	927	317	10	2	—	14	1,270
Chester	339	129	11	2	—	4	485
Chicopee	13,914	4,976	127	49	12	395	19,473
East Longmeadow	5,179	1,045	19	2	3	137	6,385
Granville	468	80	8	—	—	12	568
Hampden	1,772	334	13	3	2	32	2,156
Holland	596	197	6	3	—	14	816
Holyoke	7,868	3,165	98	57	—	616	11,804
Longmeadow	6,254	1,316	25	7	1	106	7,709
Ludlow	4,810	1,645	70	25	3	495	7,048

COUNTY OF HAMPDEN — *Concluded*

Cities and Towns	Weld & Cellucci Republican	Roosevelt & Massie Democratic	Cook & Crawford Libertarian	Rebello & Giske LaRouche For President	All Others	Blanks	Total Votes Cast
Monson	2,057	840	35	7	—	99	3,038
Montgomery	285	66	2	1	—	2	356
Palmer	2,971	1,442	42	14	—	121	4,590
Russell	421	97	7	1	—	5	531
Southwick	2,241	596	30	3	1	70	2,941
SPRINGFIELD	26,323	10,270	317	140	—	2,190	39,240
Tolland	105	37	2	1	—	4	149
Wales	394	161	8	3	—	7	573
West Springfield	7,913	1,930	91	25	—	235	10,194
WESTFIELD	10,547	2,840	82	10	1	260	13,740
Wilbraham	5,155	1,020	24	10	—	85	6,294
Totals	109,631	34,860	1,105	398	23	5,314	151,331

COUNTY OF HAMPSHIRE

Cities and Towns	Weld & Cellucci Republican	Roosevelt & Massie Democratic	Cook & Crawford Libertarian	Rebello & Giske LaRouche For President	All Others	Blanks	Total Votes Cast
Amherst	3,540	3,849	99	8	7	275	7,778
Belchertown	2,552	1,230	55	4	—	319	4,160
Chesterfield	332	96	8	1	—	8	445
Cummington	212	154	4	1	—	5	376
Easthampton	4,508	1,604	57	12	—	120	6,301
Goshen	226	97	3	1	—	8	335
Granby	1,750	475	16	4	—	44	2,289
Hadley	1,461	726	10	2	—	54	2,253
Hatfield	1,088	503	12	—	1	31	1,635
Huntington	473	216	14	1	—	13	717
Middlefield	122	58	2	1	—	3	186
NORTHAMPTON	6,496	4,942	95	14	10	268	11,825
Pelham	351	311	5	—	2	17	686
Plainfield	159	85	4	1	—	4	253
South Hadley	5,261	1,646	45	12	—	307	7,271
Southampton	1,596	472	26	1	—	32	2,127
Ware	2,342	1,221	32	11	—	75	3,681
Westhampton	493	171	7	2	1	9	683
Williamsburg	652	429	15	—	1	23	1,120
Worthington	351	164	6	—	—	11	532
Totals	33,965	18,449	515	76	22	1,626	54,653

COUNTY OF MIDDLESEX

Cities and Towns	Weld & Cellucci Republican	Roosevelt & Massie Democratic	Cook & Crawford Libertarian	Rebello & Giske LaRouche For President	All Others	Blanks	Total Votes Cast
Acton	6,337	2,032	54	6	2	217	8,648
Arlington	12,740	7,771	157	31	12	983	21,694
Ashby	869	223	5	—	—	16	1,113
Ashland	3,876	1,205	30	7	—	226	5,344
Ayer	1,387	434	22	8	—	18	1,869
Bedford	4,089	1,362	36	7	—	94	5,588
Belmont	8,346	4,043	60	11	2	594	13,056
Billerica	10,365	3,011	96	12	5	165	13,654
Boxborough	1,373	356	15	1	—	20	1,765
Burlington	7,317	2,243	54	6	4	230	9,854
Cambridge	15,297	16,343	279	46	15	1,564	33,544
Carlisle	1,788	547	9	1	—	24	2,369
Chelmsford	11,302	2,648	83	11	7	246	14,297
Concord	5,637	2,370	38	6	3	138	8,192
Dracut	7,587	2,281	57	19	—	585	10,529
Dunstable	879	153	8	—	—	10	1,050
Everett	7,592	3,851	82	28	—	569	12,122
Framingham	16,306	6,159	132	17	4	649	23,267
Groton	2,773	762	23	2	—	44	3,604
Holliston	4,704	1,390	37	5	—	162	6,298
Hopkinton	3,653	907	32	4	4	65	4,665
Hudson	5,330	1,164	37	4	—	86	6,621
Lexington	9,994	5,049	68	14	—	348	15,473
Lincoln	1,754	840	14	2	—	143	2,753
Littleton	2,594	689	24	3	—	37	3,347
Lowell	15,897	6,454	190	51	—	1,187	23,779
Malden	10,854	5,630	130	36	1	585	17,236
Marlborough	9,088	2,393	77	9	5	358	11,930
Maynard	3,260	1,051	21	—	8	76	4,416
Medford	14,311	7,080	134	35	31	534	22,125
Melrose	9,180	3,513	75	13	11	210	13,002
Natick	9,856	3,568	115	20	—	215	13,774
Newton	22,446	13,703	161	41	—	821	37,172
North Reading	4,602	1,138	39	5	4	110	5,898
Pepperell	3,052	704	21	2	—	51	3,830
Reading	8,250	2,478	74	4	3	135	10,944
Sherborn	1,799	414	9	1	—	24	2,247
Shirley	1,458	452	19	3	—	24	1,956
Somerville	11,765	9,479	173	38	55	779	22,289
Stoneham	6,407	2,539	59	10	8	229	9,252
Stow	2,249	528	24	2	—	37	2,840
Sudbury	5,804	1,520	42	2	—	140	7,508
Tewksbury	8,232	2,480	56	14	12	135	10,929
Townsend	2,378	512	26	3	—	95	3,014
Tyngsborough	2,575	669	27	3	—	39	3,313

COUNTY OF MIDDLESEX — *Concluded*

CITIES AND TOWNS	Weld & Cellucci Republican	Roosevelt & Massie Democratic	Cook & Crawford Libertarian	Rebello & Giske LaRouche For President	All Others	Blanks	Total Votes Cast
Wakefield	8,116	3,027	65	11	1	361	11,581
WALTHAM	12,984	4,959	136	31	—	525	18,635
Watertown	8,286	4,854	87	12	15	363	13,617
Wayland	4,668	1,664	25	7	2	141	6,507
Westford	6,339	1,386	50	7	4	202	7,988
Weston	4,141	1,069	19	4	2	202	5,437
Wilmington	6,118	1,715	51	12	—	152	8,048
Winchester	7,824	2,611	43	15	—	185	10,678
WOBURN	10,672	3,766	128	55	—	282	14,903
Totals	376,500	159,189	3,528	697	220	15,430	555,564

COUNTY OF NANTUCKET

Nantucket	2,131	794	13	2	2	53	2,995
Totals	2,131	794	13	2	2	53	2,995

COUNTY OF NORFOLK

Avon	1,569	524	7	3	2	56	2,161
Bellingham	3,962	1,335	43	8	-	153	5,501
Braintree	10,878	3,950	61	16	8	424	15,337
Brookline	12,109	8,986	120	16	—	734	21,965
Canton	6,677	2,282	47	16	—	314	9,336
Cohasset	2,783	721	10	4	3	287	3,808
Dedham	7,531	2,899	63	18	—	474	10,985
Dover	2,329	396	13	—	3	43	2,784
Foxborough	4,893	1,698	50	6	5	134	6,786
Franklin	7,069	2,519	49	8	1	185	9,831
Holbrook	3,178	1,138	33	8	—	88	4,445
Medfield	4,252	1,042	16	5	—	85	5,400
Medway	3,331	948	38	12	—	130	4,459
Millis	2,593	701	25	3	—	43	3,365
Milton	8,404	3,775	54	17	1	330	12,581
Needham	10,604	3,739	53	14	15	279	14,704
Norfolk	2,993	657	19	1	1	40	3,711
Norwood	8,254	3,349	82	16	—	738	12,439
Plainville	1,925	579	22	3	—	56	2,585
QUINCY	21,497	9,582	207	72	—	1,047	32,405
Randolph	7,337	3,199	48	18	5	274	10,881
Sharon	5,456	2,257	45	6	—	137	7,901
Stoughton	7,402	2,627	53	5	—	331	10,418

COUNTY OF NORFOLK — *Concluded*

CITIES AND TOWNS	Weld & Cellucci Republican	Roosevelt & Massie Democratic	Cook & Crawford Libertarian	Rebello & Giske LaRouche For President	All Others	Blanks	Total Votes Cast
Walpole	7,409	2,091	56	8	—	226	9,790
Wellesley	9,279	2,969	72	5	2	283	12,610
Westwood	5,477	1,508	36	6	—	156	7,183
Weymouth	15,180	6,083	139	33	—	1,213	22,648
Wrentham	2,784	925	37	6	—	64	3,816
Totals	187,155	72,479	1,498	333	46	8,324	269,835

COUNTY OF PLYMOUTH

Abington	4,310	1,335	32	7	1	183	5,868
Bridgewater	5,144	1,575	51	7	11	352	7,140
BROCKTON	16,374	6,237	171	35	1	1,072	23,890
Carver	3,027	1,001	23	6	1	52	4,110
Duxbury	5,453	1,254	33	1	6	94	6,841
East Bridgewater	3,389	847	29	3	—	87	4,355
Halifax	2,035	596	21	1	3	57	2,713
Hanover	4,305	1,148	38	3	—	151	5,645
Hanson	2,822	827	27	5	—	69	3,750
Hingham	7,669	2,132	51	9	9	263	10,133
Hull	2,762	1,271	44	5	--	255	4,337
Kingston	2,886	962	24	7	—	81	3,960
Lakeville	2,616	782	36	8	—	53	3,495
Marion	1,617	451	8	3	—	29	2,108
Marshfield	7,057	2,427	52	13	—	208	9,757
Mattapoisett	2,308	597	15	3	—	52	2,975
Middleborough	4,309	1,404	45	5	7	118	5,888
Norwell	3,709	890	20	10	3	83	4,715
Pembroke	4,625	1,384	29	12	—	89	6,139
Plymouth	12,602	3,813	119	29	5	377	16,945
Plympton	874	238	3	—	1	17	1,133
Rochester	1,366	348	12	5	—	36	1,767
Rockland	4,521	1,609	51	13	1	148	6,343
Scituate	6,470	2,008	38	6	4	218	8,744
Wareham	4,854	1,880	47	6	—	108	6,895
West Bridgewater	2,434	550	16	3	2	64	3,069
Whitman	3,782	1,181	33	4	6	90	5,096
Totals	123,320	38,747	1,068	209	61	4,406	167,811

COUNTY OF SUFFOLK

CITIES AND TOWNS	Weld & Cellucci Republican	Roosevelt & Massie Democratic	Cook & Crawford Libertarian	Rebello & Griske LaRouche For President	All Others	Blanks	Total Votes Cast
BOSTON	81,160	54,705	1,055	382	8	8,129	145,439
CHELSEA	3,660	2,222	57	29	1	509	6,478
REVERE	9,719	4,678	93	31	1	800	15,322
Winthrop	5,069	2,103	49	4	5	198	7,428
Totals	99,608	63,708	1,254	446	15	9,636	174,667

COUNTY OF WORCESTER

Ashburnham	1,465	430	13	2	—	56	1,966
Athol	2,565	729	23	6	18	53	3,394
Auburn	5,052	1,446	28	6	—	85	6,617
Barre	1,416	436	12	1	1	39	1,905
Berlin	848	180	4	—	3	14	1,049
Blackstone	1,921	737	30	5	—	75	2,768
Bolton	1,322	302	13	2	—	23	1,662
Boylston	1,499	323	17	1	—	28	1,868
Brookfield	874	223	12	2	—	11	1,122
Charlton	2,753	571	21	5	2	41	3,393
Clinton	3,857	1,205	37	9	—	95	5,203
Douglas	1,646	485	19	4	—	27	2,181
Dudley	2,370	802	20	6	—	124	3,322
East Brookfield	581	154	4	2	1	17	759
FITCHBURG	7,145	2,841	79	13	—	533	10,611
GARDNER	4,392	1,898	42	14	—	205	6,551
Grafton	4,102	1,097	31	7	—	107	5,344
Hardwick	635	331	16	3	—	14	999
Harvard	1,811	630	29	1	5	41	2,517
Holden	5,928	1,172	21	2	—	94	7,217
Hopedale	1,855	535	7	1	—	48	2,446
Hubbardston	943	270	9	—	—	20	1,242
Lancaster	1,744	432	20	4	1	40	2,241
Leicester	3,071	922	24	4	1	76	4,098
LEOMINSTER	9,850	2,870	73	15	—	301	13,109
Lunenburg	2,817	679	27	3	—	87	3,613
Mendon	1,475	316	10	2	—	33	1,836
Milford	6,230	2,411	53	6	—	277	8,977
Millbury	3,546	1,091	28	4	1	114	4,784
Millville	555	260	5	2	—	21	843
New Braintree	292	73	4	1	—	8	378
North Brookfield	1,309	364	19	6	—	25	1,723
Northborough	4,469	957	38	4	3	134	5,605
Northbridge	3,556	1,089	33	9	—	70	4,757
Oakham	526	151	8	—	—	4	689

COUNTY OF WORCESTER — *Concluded*

Cities and Towns	Weld & Cellucci Republican	Roosevelt & Massie Democratic	Cook & Crawford Libertarian	Rebello & Giske LaRouche For President	All Others	Blanks	Total Votes Cast
Oxford	3,267	983	24	8	—	76	4,358
Paxton	1,671	310	6	1	—	26	2,014
Petersham	412	163	6	2	—	16	599
Phillipston	342	131	3	2	—	8	486
Princeton	1,273	237	10	—	—	11	1,531
Royalston	270	124	3	—	—	10	407
Rutland	1,564	391	14	—	—	63	2,032
Shrewsbury	9,023	2,510	46	8	3	214	11,804
Southborough	2,811	693	19	1	—	52	3,576
Southbridge	3,998	1,201	45	5	1	144	5,394
Spencer	2,983	852	33	5	—	65	3,938
Sterling	2,439	462	19	1	1	45	2,967
Sturbridge	2,630	590	20	3	—	46	3,289
Sutton	2,422	504	15	4	—	89	3,034
Templeton	1,541	625	19	5	—	33	2,223
Upton	2,000	464	15	1	—	35	2,515
Uxbridge	2,908	964	32	6	—	46	3,956
Warren	1,091	434	10	6	1	23	1,565
Webster	3,604	1,399	36	15	—	197	5,251
West Boylston	2,513	530	16	2	—	32	3,093
West Brookfield	1,027	273	7	1	1	25	1,334
Westborough	5,061	1,192	33	3	1	72	6,362
Westminster	1,982	567	12	1	—	58	2,620
Winchendon	1,655	559	13	2	—	88	2,317
WORCESTER	31,671	13,736	252	61	71	1,129	46,920
Totals	184,578	58,306	1,537	295	115	5,543	250,374

AGGREGATE OF VOTES FOR
GOVERNOR AND LT.-GOVERNOR

COUNTIES	Weld & Cellucci Republican	Roosevelt & Massie Democratic	Cook & Crawford Libertarian	Rebello & Giske LaRouche For President	All Others	Blanks	Total Votes Cast
BARNSTABLE	68,719	22,576	513	137	12	1,942	93,899
BERKSHIRE	30,430	17,618	420	117	16	1,366	49,967
BRISTOL	105,751	51,702	1,370	789	29	6,225	165,866
DUKES COUNTY	3,748	2,007	58	18	1	178	6,010
ESSEX	189,618	62,989	1,547	330	58	7,302	261,844
FRANKLIN	18,226	8,217	272	60	13	582	27,370
HAMPDEN	109,631	34,860	1,105	398	23	5,314	151,331
HAMPSHIRE	33,965	18,449	515	76	22	1,626	54,653
MIDDLESEX	376,500	159,189	3,528	697	220	15,430	555,564
NANTUCKET	2,131	794	13	2	2	53	2,995
NORFOLK	187,155	72,479	1,498	333	46	8,324	269,835
PLYMOUTH	123,320	38,747	1,068	209	61	4,406	167,811
SUFFOLK	99,608	63,708	1,254	446	15	9,636	174,667
WORCESTER	184,578	58,306	1,537	295	115	5,543	250,374
Totals	1,533,380	611,641	14,698	3,907	633	67,927	2,232,186

VOTE FOR STATE OFFICERS.

ELECTION, NOVEMBER 8, 1994

FOR ATTORNEY GENERAL.

L. Scott Harshbarger of Westwood (Democrat)	1,472,605
Janis M. Berry of Saugus (Republican)	616,506
All others	486
Blanks	142,589
Total Votes Cast	2,232,186

FOR SECRETARY.

Arthur E. Chase of Worcester (Republican)	813,062
William Francis Galvin of Boston (Democrat)	1,077,493
Peter C. Everett of Hanover (Libertarian)	77,584
All others	567
Blanks	263,480
Total Votes Cast	2,232,186

FOR TREASURER AND RECEIVER GENERAL.

Joseph Daniel Malone of Waltham (Republican)	1,319,916
Shannon Patricia O'Brien of Easthampton (Democrat)	669,567
Susan B. Poulin of Woburn (Libertarian)	44,702
Thomas P. Tierney of Framingham (Unenrolled)	60,000
All others	240
Blanks	137,761
Total Votes Cast	2,232,186

FOR AUDITOR.

A. Joseph DeNucci of Newton (Democrat)	1,432,293
Forrester A. "Tim" Clark, Jr., of Hamilton (Republican)	503,057
Geoff M. Weil of Boston (Libertarian)	52,698
All others	421
Blanks	243,717
Total Votes Cast	2,232,186

VOTE FOR EXECUTIVE COUNCILLORS.

ELECTION, NOVEMBER 5. 1996.

FIRST DISTRICT

David F. Constantine of New Bedford (Democrat)	220.107
All others	1.369
Blanks	126.256
Total Votes Cast	347,732

SECOND DISTRICT

Kelly A. Timilty of Canton (Democrat)	223.592
All others	1.123
Blanks	126.786
Total Votes Cast	351,501

THIRD DISTRICT

Cynthia Stone Creem of Newton (Democrat)	203.390
All others	822
Blanks	136.326
Total Votes Cast	340.538

FOURTH DISTRICT

Christopher A. Iannella, Jr., of Boston (Democrat)	178.362
All others	810
Blanks	107.222
Total Votes Cast	286.394

FIFTH DISTRICT

Patricia A. Dowling of Lawrence (Democrat)	175,294
Kevin J. Leach of Salem (Republican)	109,196
All others	211
Blanks	49,680
Total Votes Cast	334,381

SIXTH DISTRICT

Dorothy A. Kelly Gay of Somerville (Democrat)	194,959
All others	1,310
Blanks	121,829
Total Votes Cast	318,098

SEVENTH DISTRICT

Jordan Levy of Worcester (Democrat)	212,785
All others	1,939
Blanks	98,260
Total Votes Cast	312,984

EIGHTH DISTRICT

Edward M. O'Brien of Easthampton (Democrat)	205,685
All others	976
Blanks	101,602
Total Votes Cast	308,263

STATISTICS

STATE, POST OFFICE, COUNTY

GOVERNORS AND LIEUT.-GOVERNORS.

CHOSEN ANNUALLY BY THE PEOPLE

GOVERNORS OF PLYMOUTH COLONY.

1620 Nov. 11. John Carver	1638 June 5. Thomas Prence.	
1621 April. William Bradford	1639 June 3. William Bradford.	
1633 Jan. 1. Edward Winslow.	1644 June 5. Edward Winslow.	
1634 Mar. 27. Thomas Prence.	1645 June 4. William Bradford.	
1635 Mar. 3. William Bradford.	1657 June 3. Thomas Prence.	
1636 Mar. 1. Edward Winslow.	1673 June 3. Josiah Winslow.	
1637 Mar. 7. William Bradford.	1680 Dec. 18. Thomas Hinckley.*	

DEPUTY-GOVERNORS OF PLYMOUTH COLONY.

1680 Thomas Hinckley. †	1682 William Bradford, to 1686.
1681 James Cudworth.	1689 William Bradford, to 1692.

CHOSEN ANNUALLY UNDER THE FIRST CHARTER.

GOVERNORS OF MASSACHUSETTS BAY COLONY.

1629 Mar. 4. Matthew Cradock ‡	1646 May 6. John Winthrop.
1629 Apr. 30. John Endicott ‡	1649 May 2. John Endicott.
1629 Oct. 20. John Winthrop.‡	1650 May 22. Thomas Dudley.
1634 May 14. Thomas Dudley.	1651 May 7. John Endicott.
1635 May 6. John Haynes.	1654 May 3. Richard Bellingham.
1636 May 25. Henry Vane.	1655 May 23. John Endicott.
1637 May 17. John Winthrop.	1665 May 3. Richard Bellingham.
1640 May 3. Thomas Dudley.	1672 Dec. 12. John Leverett (act'g).
1641 June 2. Richard Bellingham.	1673 May 7. John Leverett.
1642 May 18. John Winthrop.	1679 May 28. Simon Bradstreet, to
1644 May 29. John Endicott.	May 20. 1686.
1645 May 14. Thomas Dudley	

*Mr. Hinckley was Governor till the union of the colonies in 1692, except during the administration of Andros.

†Previously there was no Deputy-Governor, a Governor *pro tem* being appointed by the Governor to serve in his absence.

‡A patent of King James I, dated Nov. 3, 1620, created the Council for New England and granted it the territory in North America from 40° to 48° N.

400   *Governors and Lieut.-Governors.*

DEPUTY-GOVERNORS OF MASSACHUSETTS BAY COLONY.

1629 Thomas Goffe, . .*to Oct. 20, 1629	1650 John Endicott . . . . to 1651
1629 Thomas Dudley 1634	1651 Thomas Dudley 1653
1634 Roger Ludlow 1635	1653 Richard Bellingham 1654
1635 Richard Bellingham 1636	1654 John Endicott 1655
1636 John Winthrop 1637	1655 Richard Bellingham 1665
1637 Thomas Dudley 1640	1665 Francis Willoughby 1671
1640 Richard Bellingham 1641	1671 John Leverett 1673
1641 John Endicott 1644	1673 Sam'l Symonds, to Oct . 1678
1644 John Winthrop 1646	1678 Oct., Simon Bradstreet . . 1679
1646 Thomas Dudley 1650	1679 Thomas Danforth 1686

latitude and from sea to sea. to be known thereafter as New England in America. By instrument of March 19, 1628. the Council for New England granted to Sir Henry Rosewell and others the territory afterwards confirmed by royal Charter to the "Governor and Company of the Massachusetts Bay in New England." This Charter, which passed the seals March 4, 1629, designated Matthew Cradock as the first Governor of the Company and Thomas Goffe as the first Deputy-Governor. Both had held similar offices from the grantee under the instrument of March 19, 1628. On May 13, 1629, the same persons were rechosen by the Company; but they never came to New England. On Oct. 20, 1629, John Winthrop was chosen Governor of the Company and John Humfrey Deputy-Governor. Humfrey having declined the service. Thomas Dudley was chosen in his stead.

John Endicott had been sent over in 1628. with a small band, as the agent of the grantees under the instrument of March 19, 1628. While Cradock was Governor of the Company, a commission, dated April 30, 1629, was sent out to Endicott at Salem appointing him "Governor of London's Plantation in the Massachusetts Bay in New England." In the exercise of this commission he was subordinate to the "Governor and Company" in London, by whom he was deputed, and who, from time to time, sent him elaborate instructions for his conduct. Cradock and Endicott were thus chief governor and local governor, respectively, from April 30, 1629, or, rather, from the time when Endicott's commission reached Salem. a few weeks later, until Oct. 20, 1629; and Winthrop and Endicott were chief and local governors, respectively, from that date until the arrival of Winthrop at Salem with the charter, June 12, 1630, when Endicott's powers merged in the general authority of Winthrop.

*Thomas Goffe, the first Deputy-Governor. never came to New England. John Humfrey was elected, but did not serve.

THE INTER-CHARTER PERIOD.

On May 25, 1686, Joseph Dudley became President of New England under a commission of King James II, and had jurisdiction over the royal dominions in New England. This office he held till December 20, the same year, when Sir Edmund Andros became Governor of New England, appointed by King James II. On April 18, 1689, Governor Andros was deposed by a revolution of the people.

AFTER THE DISSOLUTION OF THE FIRST CHARTER.

Simon Bradstreet was Governor from June 7, 1689, to May 16, 1692 and Thomas Danforth was Deputy-Governor during the same time.

APPOINTED BY THE KING UNDER SECOND CHARTER.

GOVERNORS OF THE PROVINCE OF THE MASSACHUSETTS BAY.

1692 May 16, Sir William Phips.	1730 June 11, *William Tailer.*
1694 Dec. 4, *William Stoughton.**	1730 Aug. 10, Jonathan Belcher.
1699 May 26, Richard Coote. †	1741 Aug. 14, William Shirley.
1700 July 17, *William Stoughton.*	1749 Sept. 11, *Spencer Phips.*
1701 July 7, The Council.	1753 Aug. 7, William Shirley.
1702 June 11, Joseph Dudley.	1756 Sept. 25, *Spencer Phips.*
1715 Feb. 4, The Council.	1757 April 4, The Council.
1715 Mar. 21, Joseph Dudley.	1757 Aug. 3, Thomas Pownell.
1715 Nov. 9, *William Tailer.‡*	1760 June 3, *Thomas Hutchinson.*
1716 Oct. 5, Samuel Shute.	1760 Aug. 2, Francis Bernard.
1723 Jan. 1, *William Dummer.*	1769 Aug. 2, *Thomas Hutchinson.*
1728 July 19, William Burnet.	1771 Mar. 14, Thomas Hutchinson.
1729 Sept. 7, *William Dummer.*	1774 May 17, Thomas Gage.

LIEUTENANT-GOVERNORS OF THE PROVINCE OF THE MASSACHUSETTS BAY.

1692 William Stoughton, to July, 1701	1730 William Tailer.
1702 Thomas Povey 1706	1732 Spencer Phips.
1706 Jan., vacancy to Oct 1711	1758 Thomas Hutchinson.
1711 William Tailer.	1771 Andrew Oliver.
1716 William Dummer.	1714 Thomas Oliver.

---

*Those whose names are printed in *italics* were Acting Governors.

†Richard Coote, Earl of Bellomont.

‡On Nov. 9, 1715, Elizeus Burgess was proclaimed Governor, he having been commissioned on March 17, 1715, but he never came over to perform his duties, and resigned the office in April, 1716.

UNTIL THE CONSTITUTION.

1774 Oct., a Provincial Congress   1775 July, The Council.

UNDER THE CONSTITUTION.
GOVERNORS OF THE COMMONWEALTH OF MASSACHUSETTS.

1780 John Hancock . . . . to 1785	1887 Oliver Ames 1890
1785 James Bowdoin 1787	1890 John Q. A. Brackett 1891
1787 John Hancock, Oct. 8 1793	1891 William E. Russell 1894
1794 Samuel Adams 1797	1894 Frederick T. Greenhalge† . . 1896
1797 Increase Sumner, June 7 . . . 1799	1897 Roger Wolcott 1900
1800 Caleb Strong 1807	1900 W. Murray Crane 1903
1807 Jas. Sullivan, Dec. 10 1808	1903 John L. Bates 1905
1809 Christopher Gore 1810	1905 William L. Douglas 1906
1810 Elbridge Gerry 1812	1906 Curtis Guild, Jr. 1909
1812 Caleb Strong 1816	1909 Eben S. Draper 1911
1816 John Brooks 1823	1911 Eugene N. Foss 1914
1823 Wm. Eustis, Feb. 6 1825	1914 David I. Walsh 1916
1825 Levi Lincoln 1834	1916 Samuel W. McCall 1919
1834 John Davis, March 1 1835	1919 Calvin Coolidge‡ 1921
1836 Edward Everett 1840	1921 Channing H. Cox 1925
1840 Marcus Morton 1841	1925 Alvan T. Fuller 1929
1841 John Davis 1843	1929 Frank G. Allen 1931
1843 Marcus Morton 1844	1931 Joseph B. Ely 1935
1844 George N. Briggs 1851	1935 James M. Curley 1937
1851 George S. Boutwell 1853	1937 Charles F. Hurley 1939
1853 John H. Clifford 1854	1939 Leverett Saltonstall 1945
1854 Emory Washburn 1855	1945 Maurice J. Tobin 1947
1855 Henry J. Gardner 1858	1947 Robert F. Bradford 1949
1858 Nathaniel P. Banks 1861	1949 Paul A. Dever 1953
1861 John A. Andrew 1866	1953 Christian A. Herter 1957
1866 Alexander H. Bullock 1869	1957 Foster Furcolo 1961
1869 William Claflin 1872	1961 John A. Volpe 1963
1872 William B. Washburn* 1874	1963 Endicott Peabody 1965
1875 William Gaston 1876	1965 John A. Volpe** 1969
1876 Alexander H. Rice 1879	1971 Francis W. Sargent*** . . . 1975
1879 Thomas Talbot 1880	1975 Michael S. Dukakis 1979
1880 John Davis Long . . . . . to 1883	1979 Edward J. King 1983
1883 Benjamin F. Butler 1884	1983 Michael S. Dukakis 1990
1884 George D. Robinson 1887	1991 William F. Weld . . . .

* Resigned April 29, 1874. Chosen U.S. Senator April 17, 1874.

† Died March 5, 1896.

‡ Vice President of the United States, 1921-23; President, Aug. 3, 1923, to March 4, 1929.

** Elected November 8, 1966 to a four-year term under Article LXXXII of the Amendments to the Constitution. Appointed U.S. Secretary of Transportation, Jan. 22, 1969.

*** Acting Governor from Jan. 22, 1969; elected Governor Nov. 3, 1970, qualified Jan. 7, 1971.

LIEUTENANT-GOVERNORS OF THE COMMONWEALTH OF MASSACHUSETTS.

1780	*Thos. Cushing,* to Feb. 28,*	1788
1788	Benjamin Lincoln	1789
1789	*Samuel Adams*	1794
1794	*Moses Gill,* May 20†	1800
1801	Sam'l Phillips, Feb. 10	1802
1802	Edward H. Robbins	1806
1807	*Levi Lincoln‡*	1809
1809	David Cobb	1810
1810	William Gray	1812
1812	William Phillips	1823
1823	Levi Lincoln, Feb.	1824
1824	*Marcus Morton,* July	1825
1826	Thomas L. Winthrop	1833
1833	*Samuel T. Armstrong*	1836
1836	George Hull	1843
1843	Henry H. Childs	1844
1844	John Reed	1851
1851	Henry W. Cushman	1853
1853	Elisha Huntington	1854
1854	William C. Plunkett	1855
1855	Simon Brown	1856
1856	Henry W. Benchley	1858
1858	Eliphalet Trask	1861
1861	John Z. Goodrich, Mar. 29.	1861
1862	John Nesmith, Sept.	1862
1863	Joel Hayden	1866
1866	William Claflin	1869
1869	Joseph Tucker	1873
1873	*Thomas Talbot§*	1875
1875	Horatio G. Knight	1879

1879	John Davis Long	1880
1880	Byron Weston	1883
1883	Oliver Ames	1887
1887	John Q. A. Brackett	1890
1890	William H. Haile	1893
1893	*Roger Wolcott ‖*	1897
1897	W. Murray Crane	1900
1900	John L. Bates	1903
1903	Curtis Guild, Jr.	1906
1906	Eben S. Draper	1909
1909	Louis A. Frothingham	1912
1912	Robert Luce	1913
1913	David I. Walsh	1914
1914	Edward P. Barry	1915
1915	Grafton D. Cushing	1916
1916	Calvin Coolidge	1919
1919	Channing H. Cox	1921
1921	Alvan T. Fuller	1925
1925	Frank G. Allen	1929
1929	William S. Youngman	1933
1933	Gaspar G. Bacon	1935
1935	Joseph L. Hurley	1937
1937	Francis E. Kelly	1939
1939	Horace T. Cahill	1945
1945	Robert F. Bradford	1947
1947	Arthur W. Coolidge	1949
1949	Charles F. Jeff Sullivan	1953
1953	Sumner Gage Whittier	1957
1957	Robert F. Murphy**	1960
1961	Edward F. McLaughlin, Jr.	1963

*The Lieutenant-Governors whose names are in italics were Acting Governors also during vacancies in the office of Governor.
†Mr. Gill died on the 20th of May, 1800, and the Commonwealth, for the only time under the Constitution, was without a Governor and Lieutenant-Governor. The Council, Hon. Thomas Dawes, President, officiated until the 30th of the month, when Caleb Strong was inaugurated Governor.
‡General William Heath was elected in 1806, and declined to accept the office.
§Acting Governor from April 29, 1874.
‖ Acting Governor from March 5, 1896.
**Appointed Commissioner of the Metropolitan District Commission on Oct. 6, 1960.

1963	Francis X. Bellotti 1965	1975	Thomas P. O'Neill III ...1983
1965	Elliot L. Richardson 1967	1983	John F. Kerry# 1985
1967	*Francis W. Sargent**** ...1971	1987	Evelyn F. Murphy 1990
1971	Donald R. Dwight 1975	1991	Argeo Paul Cellucci .....

*** Elected November 8, 1966 to a four-year term under Article LXXXII of the Amendments to the Constitution. Acting Governor from Jan. 22, 1969.

\# Elected November 2, 1982 to a four-year term under Article LXXXII of the Amendments to the Constitution. Resigned Jan. 2, 1985, and appointed to fill vacancy in office of United States Senator due to resignation of Paul E. Tsongas.

UNITED STATES SENATORS.

FROM MASSACHUSETTS.

Tristram Dalton 1789-91	Caleb Strong 1789-96
George Cabot 1791-96	Theodore Sedgwick 1796-99
Benjamin Goodhue 1796-1800	Samuel Dexter 1799-1800
Jonathan Mason 1800-03	Dwight Foster 1800-03
John Quincy Adams 1803-08	Timothy Pickering 1803-11
James Lloyd, Jr. 1808-13	Joseph Bradley Varnum 1811-17
Christopher Gore 1813-16	Harrison Gray Otis 1817-22
Eli Porter Ashmun 1816-18	James Lloyd 1822-26
Prentiss Mellen 1818-20	Nathaniel Silsbee 1826-35
Elijah Hunt Mills 1820-27	John Davis 1835-41
Daniel Webster 1827-41	Isaac Chapman Bates 1841-45
Rufus Choate 1841-45	John Davis 1845-53
Daniel Webster 1845-50	Edward Everett 1853-54
Robert Charles Winthrop 1850-51	Julius Rockwell 1854-55
Robert Rantoul, Jr. 1851	Henry Wilson* 1855-73
Charles Sumner † 1851-74	George S. Boutwell 1873-77
William B. Washburn 1874-75	George Frisbie Hoar‡ 1877-1904
Henry Laurens Dawes 1875-93	Winthrop Murray Crane 1904-13
Henry Cabot Lodge§ 1893-1924	John Wingate Weeks 1913-19
William Morgan Butler 1924-26	David Ignatius Walsh 1919-25
David Ignatius Walsh 1926-47	Frederick Huntington Gillett . 1925-31
Henry Cabot Lodge, Jr. 1947-53	Marcus A. Coolidge 1931-37
John Fitzgerald Kennedy** ... 1953-60	Henry Cabot Lodge, Jr ¶ ... 1937-44
Benjamin A. Smith, II †† 1960-63	Sinclair Weeks 1944
Edward M. Kennedy 1963-	Leverett Saltonstall 1945-67
	Edward W. Brooke 1967-79
	Paul E. Tsongas# 1979-85
	John F. Kerry## 1985-

* Mr. Wilson elected Vice President in 1872; George S. Boutwell chosen to fill vacancy.

† Charles Sumner died March 11, 1874; William B. Washburn chosen to fill vacancy, April 17, 1874.

‡ Mr. Hoar died September 30, 1904; Winthrop Murray Crane appointed by Governor John L. Bates October 12, 1904.

§ Mr. Lodge died November 9, 1924; William Morgan Butler temporarily appointed by Governor Channing H. Cox November 13, 1924; Mr. Walsh chosen to fill vacancy, November 2, 1926.

¶ Mr. Lodge resigned February 4, 1944; Sinclair Weeks temporarily appointed by Governor Leverett Saltonstall February 8, 1944.

** Mr. Kennedy elected President of the United States in November, 1960. Resigned from the Senate on December 22, 1960.

†† Mr. Smith temporarily appointed by Governor Foster Furcolo December 27 1960.

Mr. Tsongas' term expired January, 1985; resigned January 2, 1985.

Mr. Kerry elected to a six-year term on November 6, 1984; Mr. Kerry temporarily appointed by Governor Michael S. Dukakis on January 3, 1985.

SECRETARIES.

List of Persons who have held the Office of
SECRETARY OF THE COMMONWEALTH.

John Avery 1780-1806	Henry B. Peirce 1876-91
Jonathan L. Austin 1806-08	William M. Olin* 1891-1911
William Tudor 1808-10	Albert P. Langtry* 1911-13
Benjamin Homans 1810-12	Frank J. Donahue 1913-15
Alden Bradford 1812-24	Albert P. Langtry 1915-21
Edward D. Bangs 1824-36	Frederic W. Cook 1921-49
John P. Bigelow 1836-43	Edward J. Cronin** 1949-58
John A. Bolles 1843-44	J. Henry Goguen** 1958-59
John G. Palfrey 1844-48	Joseph D. Ward*** 1959-61
William B. Calhoun 1848-51	Kevin H. White§ 1961-67
Amasa Walker 1851-53	John F. X. Davoren† 1967-75
Ephraim M. Wright 1853-56	Paul H. Guzzi 1975-79
Francis DeWitt 1856-58	Michael Joseph Connolly . . 1979-95
Oliver Warner 1858-76	William Francis Galvin 1995-

* Secretary Olin died April 15, 1911; Mr. Langtry chosen to fill vacancy April 26, 1911.

** Secretary Cronin died Nov. 24, 1958. The vacancy was filled by the appointment of J. Henry Goguen, who qualified on Dec. 1, 1958, to fill unexpired term.

*** Office was filled by election by the Legislature of Joseph D. Ward on Jan. 20, 1959.

§ Elected November 8, 1966 to a four-year term under Article LXXXII of the Amendments to the Constitution. Resigned Dec. 20, 1967.

† Office was filled by election by the Legislature of John F. X. Davoren on Dec. 20, 1967; and on November 3, 1970. Mr. Davoren was elected to a four-year term under Article LXXXII of the Amendments to the Constitution.

TREASURERS.

List of Persons who have held the Office of
TREASURER AND RECEIVER GENERAL.

Henry Gardner	1780-83	Charles Endicott	1876-81
Thomas Ivers	1783-87	Daniel A. Gleason	1881-86
Alexander Hodgdon	1787-92	Alanson W. Beard	1886-89
Thomas Davis	1792-97	George A. Marden	1889-94
Peleg Coffin*	1797-1801	Henry M . Phillips†	1894-95
Jonathan Jackson	1802-06	Edward P. Shaw†	1895-1900
Thompson J. Skinner	1806-08	Edward S. Bradford	1900-05
Josiah Dwight	1808-10	Arthur B. Chapin‡	1905-09
Thomas Harris	1810-11	Elmer A. Stevens‡	1909-14
Jonathan L. Austin	1811-12	Frederick W. Mansfield	1914-15
John T. Apthorp	1812-17	Charles L. Burrill	1915-20
Daniel Sargent	1817-22	Fred J. Burrell§	1920
Nahum Mitchell	1822-27	James Jackson§	1920-25
Joseph Sewall	1827-32	William S. Youngman	1925-29
Hezekiah Barnard	1832-37	Karl H. Oliver‖	1929
David Wilder	1837-42	John W. Haigis‖	1929-31
Thomas Russell	1842-43	Charles F. Hurley¶	1931-37
John Mills	1843-44	Karl H. Oliver¶	1937
Thomas Russell	1844-45	William E. Hurley¶	1937-43
Joseph Barrett	1845-49	Francis X. Hurley	1943-45
Ebenezer Bradbury	1849-51	John E. Hurley	1945-47
Charles B. Hall	1851-53	Laurence Curtis	1947-49
Jacob H. Loud	1853-55	John E. Hurley**	1949-52
Thomas J. Marsh	1855-56	Foster Furcolo**	1952-55
Moses Tenney, Jr.	1856-61	John F. Kennedy	1955-61
Henry K. Oliver	1861-66	John Thomas Driscoll***	1961-64
Jacob H. Loud	1866-71	Robert Q. Crane***	1964-90
Charles Adams, Jr.	1871-76	Joseph D. Malone	1991-

* Secretary Avery had a warrant to take care of the treasury on the resignation of Mr. Coffin, May 25, 1802.

† Mr. Phillips resigned April 12, 1895; Mr. Shaw chosen to fill vacancy April 25, 1895.

‡ Mr. Chapin resigned April 1, 1909; Mr. Stevens chosen to fill vacancy April 7, 1909.

§ Mr. Burrell resigned Sept. 3, 1920; Mr. Jackson appointed to fill vacancy Sept. 8, 1920.

‖ Mr. Youngman qualified as Lieutenant-Governor Jan. 3, 1929; Mr. Oliver chosen to fill vacancy January 7; Mr. Haigis qualified January 16.

¶ Mr. Charles F. Hurley qualified as Governor, January 7, 1937; Mr. Oliver chosen to fill vacancy January 11; Mr. William E. Hurley qualified January 20.

** Mr. John E. Hurley resigned July 5, 1952; Mr. Furcolo appointed to fill vacancy July 5.

*** Mr. John Thomas Driscoll resigned May 12, 1964; Mr. Crane chosen to fill vacancy May 12; and on November 8, 1966 Mr. Crane was elected to a four-year term under Article LXXXII of the Amendments to the Constitution.

ATTORNEYS-GENERAL —
SOLICITORS-GENERAL.

[This table was prepared by Mr. A. C. Goodell, Jr., and contributed by him to the Massachusetts Historical Society's proceedings for June, 1895.]

TABLE OF ATTORNEYS-GENERAL BEFORE THE CONSTITUTION.

	CHOSEN.	APPOINTED.
Anthony Checkley	April 29, 1680.	
Under the Presidency of Joseph Dudley:		
Benjamin Bullivant		Date uncertain, but before July 1, 1686; sworn in July 26.
Under Sir Edmund Andros:		
Giles Masters		"To frame indictments, arraign and prosecute felons." April 30, 1687. He died "Kings Attorney," Feb. 29, 1688.
James Graham		Date uncertain, but as early as Aug. 25, 1687, he was "settled in Boston and made Attorney-general."
James Graham		Reappointed (2d commission) June 20, 1688.
During the inter-charter period:		
Anthony Checkley	June 14, 1689.	
Under the Province Charter:		
Anthony Checkley		Oct. 28, 1692.
Paul Dudley		July 6, 1702.
Paul Dudley	June 8, 1716.	
Paul Dudley	June 19, 1717.	
Paul Dudley*	June 25, 1718.	
John Valentine	Nov. 22, 1718.	

*Resigned Nov. 22, 1718.

CHOSEN.   APPOINTED.

John Valentine .... June 24, 1719.
Thomas Newton† .... June 19, 1720.
(*Vacancy:* John Read chosen, but negatived by Governor Shute.)
John Overing .... June 29, 1722.
John Read .... June 20, 1723.
(*Vacancy;* John Read chosen, but not consented to.)
John Read .... June 28, 1725.
John Read .... June 21, 1726.
John Read .... June 28, 1727.
Joseph Hiller .... June 19, 1728.
(Addington Davenport, Jr., chosen June 12, but declined.)
John Overing .... June 26, 1729.
(Jeremiah Gridley and others were chosen annually from 1730 to
1748, but the Governor withheld his consent. See Proceedings of
the Massachusetts Historical Society, Vol. X, Second Series, p. 254.)
Edmund Trowbridge .... June 29, 1749.
Edmund Trowbridge .... May 14, 1762.
(Made Justice of the Superior Court of Judicature, March 25, 1767.)
Jeremiah Gridley‡ .... March 25, 1767.
Jonathan Sewall .... Nov. 24, 1767.
(*Vacancy* from September, 1774, to June 12, 1777.)
Robert Treat Paine.......... June 12, 1777, ... Accepted Aug. 26.
Robert Treat Paine.......... June 19, 1778 (sworn).
Robert Treat Paine.......... Feb. 5, 1779.
Robert Treat Paine.......... Jan. 4, 1780.

SPECIAL ATTORNEY-GENERAL, ETC.

Jonathan Sewall .... March 25, 1767.

SOLICITORS-GENERAL, ETC.

Jonathan Sewall .... June 24, 1767.
(*Vacancy* from November 18, 1767, to March 14, 1771.)
Samuel Quincy§ .... March 14, 1771.

SOLICITOR-GENERAL (SINCE THE CONSTITUTION.)

Daniel Davis .... 1801-32.
(Office established in 1800, and abolished in 1832.)

†Died May 28, 1721.   ‡Died Sept. 10, 1767.
§A refugee, 1774-75.

TABLE OF ATTORNEYS-GENERAL SINCE THE CONSTITUTION.

Robert Treat Paine	1780-90	Thomas J. Boynton	1914-15
James Sullivan	1790-1807	Henry C. Attwill ⁹	1915-19
Barnabas Bidwell	1807-10	Henry A. Wyman ⁹	1919-20
Perez Morton	1810-32	J. Weston Allen	1920-23
James T. Austin	1832-43	Jay R. Benton	1923-27
John Henry Clifford	*1849-53	Arthur K. Reading ¶	1927-28
Rufus Choate+	1953-54	Joseph E. Warner ¶	1928-35
John Henry Clifford+	1854-58	Paul E. Dever	1935-41
Stephen Henry Phillips	1858-61	Robert T. Bushnell	1941-45
Dwight Foster	1861-64	Clarence A. Barnes	1945-49
Chester I. Reed‡	1864-67	Francis E. Kelly	1949-53
Charles Allen ‡	1867-72	George Fingold**	1953-58
Charles R. Train	1872-79	Edward T. Martin	Interim
George Marston	1879-83	Edward J. McCormack. Jr.**.	1958-63
Edgar J. Sherman§	1883-87	Edward W. Brooke***	1963-67
Andrew J. Waterman§	1887-91	Edward T. Martin	Interim
Albert E. Pillsbury	1891-94	Elliot L. Richardson****	1967-69
Hosea M. Knowlton	1894-1902	Robert H. Quinn****	1969-75
Herbert Parker	1902-06	Francis X. Bellotti	1975-87
Dana Malone	1906-11	James M. Shannon	1987-90
James M. Swift	1911-14	L. Scott Harshbarger	1991-

* The office of Attorney-General was abolished in 1843 and re-established in 1849.

+ Rufus Choate resigned May 12, 1854. Mr. Clifford's term began May 20, 1854.

‡ Resigned April 20, 1867. The vacancy was filled by election by the Legislature of Charles Allen, April 26, 1867.

§ Resigned October 1, 1887. The vacancy was filled by the appointment of Andrew J. Waterman.

⁹ Vacated the office August 13, 1919, by qualifying as a member of the Public Service Commission. The vacancy was filled by the appointment of Henry A. Wyman, who qualified on that day.

¶ Resigned June 6, 1928. The vacancy was filled by the choice June 13, of Joseph E. Warner.

**Attorney-General Fingold died Aug. 31, 1958. The vacancy was filled by election by the Legislature of Edward J. McCormack. Jr., on September 11, 1958.

***Resigned January 2, 1967. The vacancy was filled by the nomination by the Governor and the confirmation by the Executive Council of Edward T. Martin as interim Attorney General on January 3, 1967.

****Elected November 8, 1966 to a four-year term under Article LXXXII of the Amendments to the Constitution. Resigned January 23, 1969. Appointed Under-Secretary of State on President's Cabinet.

****Office was filled by election by the Legislature of Robert H. Quinn on January 23, 1969; and on November 3, 1970, Mr. Quinn was elected to a four-year term under Article LXXXII of the Amendments to the Constitution.

AUDITORS.

List of Persons who have held the office of
AUDITOR OF ACCOUNTS OR AUDITOR OF THE COMMONWEALTH.

[Established by Act of 1849. Name changed by Act of 1908.]

David Wilder, Jr.	1849-54	John W. Kimball	1892-1901
Joseph Mitchell	1854-55	Henry E. Turner‡	1901-11
Stephen N. Gifford	1855-56	John E. White‡	1911-14
Chandler R. Ransom	1856-58	Frank H. Pope	1914-15
Charles White	1858-61	Alonzo B. Cook	1915-31
Levi Reed*	1861-65	Francis X. Hurley	1931-35
Julius L. Clarke	1865-66	Thomas H. Buckley	1935-39
Henry S. Briggs	1866-70	Russell A. Wood	1939-41
Charles Endicott	1870-76	Thomas J. Buckley**	1941-64
Julius L. Clarke†	1876-79	Thaddeus Buczko***	1964-81
Charles R. Ladd†	1879-91	John J. Finnegan***	1981-87
William D. T. Trefry	1891-92	A. Joseph DeNucci	1987-

* Resigned December 20, 1865.

† Mr. Clarke resigned, and Mr. Ladd was appointed in his place May 5, 1879.

‡ Mr. Turner died June 29, 1911, and Mr. White was chosen to fill the vacancy July 6, 1911.

** Mr. Buckley died September 9, 1964 and Mr. Buczko was appointed to fill the vacancy September 24, 1964; and on November 8, 1966, Mr. Buczko was elected to a four-year term under Article LXXXII of the Amendments to the Constitution.

*** Mr. Buczko resigned on February 11, 1981 and Mr. Finnegan was elected, under the provisions of Article XVII, as amended by Article LXXIX of the Amendments to the Constitution, to fill the vacancy February 23, 1981.

ORGANIZATION OF THE LEGISLATURE,
Since 1780.

The first General Court, under the Constitution of The Commonwealth of Massachusetts, assembled at Boston on Wednesday, Oct. 25, 1780, and was finally prorogued (having held three sessions) May 19, 1781. From this time until 1832 the political year commenced on the last Wednesday in May, and the General Court held two, and frequently three, sessions during each year. In 1832, by an amendment of the Constitution, the commencement of the political year was changed to the first Wednesday in January.

SENATE.

PRESIDENTS.

Thomas Cushing, *resign'd* *	} 1780-81	Samuel Lathrop	1829-30
Jeremiah Powell		Samuel Lathrop, *resign'd*	} 1830-31
Jeremiah Powell, *resign'd* *	} 1781-82	James Fowler	
Samuel Adams		Leverett Saltonstall	1831
Samuel Adams	1782-85	William Thorndike	1832
Samuel Adams, *resign'd* *	} 1785-86	Benjamin T. Pickman	1833-34
Samuel Phillips, Jr.		Benjamin T. Pickman, *died*	} 1835
Samuel Phillips, Jr.	1786-87	George Bliss	
Samuel Adams	1787-88	Horace Mann	1836-37
Samuel Phillips, Jr.	1788-90	Myron Lawrence	1838-39
Samuel Phillips	1790-1801	Daniel P. King	1840-41
Samuel Phillips, *resign'd* †	} 1801-02	Josiah Quincy, Jr.	1842
David Cobb		Phineas W. Leland, *resign'd*	} 1843
David Cobb	1802-05	Frederick Robinson	
Harrison Gray Otis	1805-06	Josiah Quincy, Jr.	1844
John Bacon	1806-07	Levi Lincoln	1845
Samuel Dana	1807-08	William B. Calhoun	1846-47
Harrison Gray Otis	1808-11	Zeno Scudder	1848
Samuel Dana	1811-13	Joseph Bell	1849
John Phillips	1813-23	Marshall P. Wilder	1850
Nathaniel Silsbee	1823-26	Henry Wilson	1851-52
John Mills	1826-28	Charles H. Warren	1853
Sherman Leland	1828-29	Charles Edward Cook	1854

* Resigned to serve in Governor's Council.
† Resigned to serve as Lieutenant-Governor.

Henry W. Benchley	1855	William D. Chapple	1907-08
Elihu C. Baker	1856	Allen T. Treadway	1909-11
Charles W. Upham	1857-58	Levi H. Greenwood	1912-13
Charles A. Phelps	1859-60	Calvin Coolidge	1914-15
William Claflin	1861	Henry G. Wells	1916-18
John H. Clifford	1862	Edwin T. McKnight	1919-20
Jonathan E. Field	1863-65	Frank G. Allen†	1921-24
Joseph A. Pond	1866-67	Wellington Wells	1925-28
George O. Brastow	1868	Gaspar G. Bacon	1929-32
Robert C. Pitman, *resign'd* *	} 1869	Erland F. Fish	1933-34
George O. Brastow		James G. Moran	1935-36
Horace H. Coolidge	1870-72	Samuel H. Wragg	1937-38
George B. Loring	1873-76	Joseph R. Cotton	1939-40
John B. D. Cogswell	1877-79	Angier L. Goodwin‡	1941
Robert R. Bishop	1880-82	Jarvis Hunt§	1942-44
George Glover Crocker	1883	Arthur W. Coolidge	1945-46
George A. Bruce	1884	Donald W. Nicholson⁰	1947
Albert E. Pillsbury	1885-86	Harris S. Richardson¶	1948
Halsey J. Boardman	1887-88	Chester A. Dolan, Jr.	1949
Harris C. Hartwell	1889	Harris S. Richardson	1950
Henry H. Sprague	1890-91	Richard I. Furbush	1951-56
Alfred S. Pinkerton	1892-93	Newland H. Holmes	1957-58
William M. Butler	1894-95	John E. Powers**	1959-64
George P. Lawrence	1896-97	Maurice A. Donahue**	1964-70
George E. Smith	1898-1900	Kevin B. Harrington***	1971-78
Rufus A. Soule	1901-02	William M. Bulger***	1978-94
George R. Jones	1903-04	Thomas F. Birmingham	1995
William F. Dana	1905-06		

CLERKS.

William Baker, Jr.	1780-84	Samuel F. McCleary	1813-21
Samuel Cooper	1785-95	Samuel F. Lyman	1822
Edward McLane	1796-99	Paul Willard	1823-29
Edward Payne Hayman	1800	Charles Calhoun	1830-42
George Elliot Vaughan	1801-02	Lewis Josselyn	1843
Wendell Davis	1803-05	Charles Calhoun	1844-50
John D. Dunbar	1806-07	Chauncy L. Knapp	1851
Nathaniel Coffin	1808-10	Francis H. Underwood	1852
Marcus Morton	1811-12	Charles Calhoun	1853-54

---

* Appointed Justice of Superior Court.

† First year under biennial elections.

‡ Resigned Dec. 29, 1941 (elected to Congress).

§ Elected at Special Session, Jan. 26, 1942.

⁰ Resigned Nov. 26, 1947 (elected to Congress).

¶ Elected Jan. 7, 1948.

** Appointed Clerk of the Supreme Judicial Court, March 25, 1964; Mr. Donahue elected March 25, 1964.

*** Resigned July 31, 1978; Mr. Bulger elected July 31, 1978.

Peter L. Cox	1855-57	William H. Sanger§	1922-32
Stephen N. Gifford	1858-86	Irving N. Hayden♀	1932-62
E. Herbert Clapp	1886-88	Thomas A. Chadwick*	1962-66
Henry D. Coolidge	1889-1922	Norman L. Pidgeon**	1967-73

***SENATE CLERK AND PARLIAMENTARIAN, Norman L. Pidgeon, 1972-73.

Edward B. O'Neill**** 1974-

CHAPLAINS.

Samuel Cooper	1780	Alonzo Potter	1831
John Clark	1781	F. W. P. Greenwood	1832
Joseph Eckley	1782	George W. Blagden	1833
Samuel Cooper	1783	Chandler Robbins	1834
Joseph Eckley	1784	Hubbard Winslow	1835
Peter Thacher	1785-89	F. W. P. Greenwood	1836
Samuel Stillman	1790	Nehemiah Adams	1837
Jeremy Belknap	1791	Ralph Sanger	1838
Peter Thacher	1792-1802	William M. Rogers	1839
William Emerson	1803-06	Daniel M. Lord	1840
Thomas Baldwin	1807	Thomas M. Clark, Jr.	1841
Joseph S. Buckminster	1808-10	Joseph H. Towne	1842
Thomas Baldwin	1811-12	William M. Rogers	1843
Joshua Huntington	1813	James F. Clarke	1844
Dr. John Lathrop	1814-15	John T. Burrill	1845
Francis Parkman	1816-17	Amos Smith	1846
Henry Ware, Jr.	1818	Austin Phelps	1847
John G. Palfrey	1819-20	C. A. Bartol	1848
John Pierpont	1821	Isaac P. Langworthy	1849
James Walker	1822	James L. T. Coolidge	1850
William Jenks	1823	A. L. Stone	1851
Daniel Sharp	1824	Warren Burton	1852
Samuel Barrett	1825	J. S. D. Farnsworth	1853
Francis Wayland	1826	A. H. Burlington	1854
William Jenks	1827-28	Lyman Whiting	1855
R. W. Emerson	1829	Daniel C. Eddy	1856
Howard Malcolm	1830	John P. Cleveland	1857

§ Elected March 1, 1922, having served as assistant clerk since 1889; retired March 12, 1932.

♀ Elected March 14, 1932, having served as assistant clerk since 1922; retired Jan. 31, 1962.

* Elected Feb. 1, 1962, having served as assistant clerk since 1932; retired Dec. 31, 1966.

** Elected Jan. 4, 1967, having served as assistant clerk since 1962.

*** First person ever appointed Parliamentarian (as well as Clerk) in the history of the Commonwealth of Massachusetts.

****Elected acting Clerk of Senate, Jan. 2, 1974 to finish the term of Norman L. Pidgeon. Elected Clerk of the Senate, Jan. 1, 1975.

Arthur Fuller	1858	A. M. Ide	1874
Jacob M. Manning	1859	George F. Warren	1875
Joseph Marsh	1860	Isaac Dunham	1876-79
A. S. Patton	1861	Edmund Dowse*	1880-1904
Edward W. Clark	1862-63	Edward A. Horton♀	1904-28
A. A. Miner	1864	Charles H. Moss❡	1928-30
George E. Ellis	1865	Arthur M. Ellis	1931-40
James B. Miles	1866	Arthur W. Olsen	1941-42
Charles E. Reed	1867	W. Harold Deacon	1943-44
Henry Morgan	1868	Frederick M. Eliot	1945-48
E. N. Kirk	1869	Francis A. Burke	1949-50
J. O. Means	1870	Frederick M. Eliot**	1951-58
S. W. Foljambe	1871	John P. Robertson***	1958
Edward Abbott	1872-73	Christopher P. Griffin #	1959-79

HOUSE OF DEPUTIES

(Usually two to five sessions a year.)

SPEAKERS.

William Hawthorne†	1644-45	Thomas Clarke	1662
George Cooke	1645	John Leverett	1663-64
William Hawthorne†	1646	Thomas Clarke	1665
Robert Bridges	1646	Richard Waldron§	1666-68
Joseph Hill	1647	Thomas Clarke	1669-70
William Hawthorne†	1648	Thomas Savage	1671
Richard Russell	1648	Thomas Clarke	1672
Daniel Denison‡	1649	Richard Waldron§	1673
William Hawthorne†	1650	Joshua Hubbard	1673-74
Daniel Gookin	1651	Richard Waldron§	1674-75
Daniel Denison‡	1651-52	Peter Buckley	1675-76
Humphrey Atherton	1653	Thomas Savage	1677-78
Richard Russell	1654	Richard Waldron§	1679
Edward Johnson	1655	John Richards	1679-80
Richard Russell	1656	Daniel Fisher	1680-82
William Hawthorne†	1657	Elisha Cooke	1683
Richard Russell	1658	John Wayte	1684
Thomas Savage	1659-60	Isaac Addington	1685
William Hawthorne†	1660-61	John Saffin	1686

* Resigned January 13, 1904.

♀ Elected January 14, 1904, resigned and chosen Chaplain emeritus February 6, 1928.

❡ Elected February 7, 1928.

** Died February 17, 1958.

*** Elected to fill vacancy on February 25, 1958.

\# Beginning on January 2, 1980, the Senate has suspended so much of Senate Rule 4 as relates to the appointment of a chaplain.

† Also spelled Hauthorne, Hawthorne, Hawthorn, Hathorne.

‡ Also spelled Dennison.

§ Also spelled Waldern, Walderne.

INTER-CHARTER PERIOD.

The General Court adjourned May 21, 1686, and did not convene until May or June, 1689.

Thomas Oakes	1689	William Bond	1691-92
John Bowles	1689-90	Penn Townsend	1692
Penn Townsend	1690-91		

UNDER THE SECOND CHARTER.

William Bond	1692-93	John Clark	1721-24
Nathaniel Byfield	1693-94	William Dudley	1724-29
Nehemiah Jewett	1694-95	John Quincy	1729-41
William Bond	1695-96	William Fairfield	1741
Penn Townsend	1696-97	John Hobson	1741-42
Nathaniel Byfield	1698	Thomas Cushing	1742-46
James Converse	1699-1700	Thomas Hutchinson	1746-49
John Leverett	1700-01	Joseph Dwight	1749-50
Nehemiah Jewett	1701-02	Thomas Hubbard	1750-59
James Converse	1702-05	Samuel White	1759-60
Thomas Oakes	1705-07	James Otis	1760-62
John Burrill	1707	Timothy Ruggles	1762-64
Thomas Oliver	1708-09	Samuel White	1764-66
John Clark	1709-11	Thomas Cushing*	1766-74
John Burrill	1711-20	James Warren	1775-78
Elisha Cooke	1720	John Pickering	1778-79
Timothy Lindall	1720-21	John Hancock	1779-80

HOUSE OF REPRESENTATIVES.

SPEAKERS UNDER THE CONSTITUTION.

Caleb Davis, *resigned*	1780-82	Timothy Bigelow	1805-06
Nathaniel Gorham	1782-83	Perez Morton	1806-08
Tristram Dalton	1783-84	Timothy Bigelow	1808-10
Samuel Allyne Otis	1784-85	Perez Morton, *resigned*	1810-11
Nathaniel Gorham	1785-86	Joseph Story, *resigned*	1811-12
Artemas Ward	1786-87	Eleazer W. Ripley	1812
James Warren	1787-88	Timothy Bigelow	1812-20
Theodore Sedgwick	1788-89	Elijah H. Mills, *resigned*	1820-21
David Cobb	1789-93	Josiah Quincy, *resigned*	1821-22
Edward H. Robbins	1793-1802	Luther Lawrence	1822
John Coffin Jones	1802-03	Levi Lincoln	1822-23
Harrison Gray Otis	1803-05	William C. Jarvis	1823-25

* Son of Thomas Cushing who served in 1742-46

Timothy Fuller	1825-26	Charles J. Noyes	1887-88
William C. Jarvis	1826-28	William E. Barrett	1889-93
William B. Calhoun	1828-34	George V. L. Meyer	1894-96
Julius Rockwell	1835-37	John L. Bates	1897-99
Robert C. Winthrop	1838-40	James J. Myers	1900-03
George Ashmun	1841	Louis A. Frothingham	1904-05
Thomas Kinnicut	1842	John N. Cole	1906-08
Daniel P. King	1843	Joseph Walker	1909-11
Thomas Kinnicut, *resign d*	1844	Grafton D. Cushing	1912-14
Samuel H. Walley, Jr.	1844-46	Channing H. Cox	1915-18
Ebenezer Bradbury	1847	Joseph E. Warner	1919-20
Francis B. Crowninshield	1848-49	Benjamin Loring Young*	1921-24
Ensign H. Kellogg	1850	John C. Hull	1925-28
Nathaniel P. Banks, Jr.	1851-52	Leverett Saltonstall	1929-36
George Bliss	1853	Horace T. Cahill	1937-38
Otis P. Lord	1854	Christian A. Herter	1939-42
Daniel C. Eddy	1855	Rudolph F. King	1943-44
Charles A. Phelps	1856-57	Frederick B. Willis†	1945-48
Julius Rockwell	1858	Thomas P. O'Neill, Jr	1949-52
Charles Hale	1859	Charles Gibbons	1953-54
John A. Goodwin	1860-61	Michael F. Skerry**	1955-57
Alexander H. Bullock	1862-65	John F. Thompson***	1958-64
James M. Stone	1866-67	John F. X. Davoren‡	1965-67
Harvey Jewell	1868-71	Robert H. Quinn⚲	1967-69
John E. Sanford	1872-75	David M. Bartley•	1969-75
John D. Long	1876-78	Thomas W. McGee#	1975-85
Levi C. Wade	1879	George Keverian	1985-90
Charles J. Noyes	1880-82	Charles F. Flaherty+	1991-96
George A. Marden	1883-84	Thomas M. Finneran#‡	1996-
John Q. A. Brackett	1885-86		

CLERKS

George Henshaw	1780-81	Benjamin Pollard	1812-21
George Richards Minot	1782-91	Pelham W. Warren	1822-31
Henry Warren	1792-1802	Luther S. Cushing	1832-43
Nicholas Tillinghast	1803-05	Charles W. Storey	1844-50
Chs. Pinckney Summer	1806-07	Lewis Josselyn	1851-52
Nicholas Tillinghast	1808-09	William Schouler	1853
Chs. Pinckney Summer	1810-11	William Stowe	1854

* First year under biennial elections.
† Resigned November 9, 1948.
** Resigned as Speaker October 14, 1957.
*** Elected Speaker January 1, 1958.
‡ Elected Secretary of the Commonwealth December 20, 1967.
⚲ Elected Speaker December 20, 1967. Elected Attorney General January 23, 1969.
• Elected Speaker January 23, 1969. Resigned July 1, 1975.
\# Elected Speaker July 1, 1975.
+ Elected Speaker January 2, 1991. Resigned April 9, 1996.
#‡ Elected Speaker April 10, 1996.

Henry A. Marsh	1855	George T. Sleeper	1896
William E. P. Haskell	1856	James W. Kimball	1897-1928
William Stowe	1857-61	Frank E. Bridgman†	1928-39
William S. Robinson	1862-72	Lawrence R. Grove‡	1939-61
Charles H. Taylor	1873	William C. Maiers**	1961-68
George A. Marden	1874-82	Wallace C. Mills+	1969-83
Edward A. McLaughlin	1883-95	Robert E. MacQueen•	1983-

CHAPLAINS.

Samuel Cooper	1780	Thomas Baldwin	1818
John Clark	1781	William Jenks	1819-26
Joseph Eckley	1782	George Ripley	1827
Samuel Cooper	1783	Henry Ware, Jr.	1828
Joseph Eckley	1784	—— —— §	1829
Peter Thacher	1785-89	Joseph Tuckerman	1830
Samuel Stillman	1790	—— ——⁹	1831
Jeremy Belknap	1791	Ralph W. Emerson	1832
Peter Thacher	1792-93	Howard Malcolm	1832-33
Samuel Stillman	1794-95	Edward T. Taylor	1834
Peter Thacher	1796-99	George W. Blagden	1835
Thomas Baldwin	1800-01	Ezra S. Gannett	1835
John T. Kirkland	1802	Samuel K. Lothrop	1836
Thomas Baldwin	1803	William M. Rogers	1836
John T. Kirkland	1804	Baron Stow	1837
Thomas Baldwin	1805-07	Thomas S. King	1837
Charles Lowell	1808	Ephraim Peabody	1838
John Lathrop	1809	George W. Blagden	1839
Thomas Baldwin	1810	Otis A. Skinner	1839
Elijah R. Sabin	1811	Joy H. Fairchild	1840
Horace Holly	1812	Benjamin Whittemore	1840
Joshua Huntington	1813	Joseph H. Towne	1841
Samuel Cary	1814	Robert C. Waterston	1842
Samuel C. Thacher	1815	Edwin H. Chapin	1842
Asa Eaton	1816	Edward N. Kirk	1843
Daniel Sharp	1817	Frederic D. Huntington	1843

† Elected April 10, 1928, having served as assistant clerk since 1897; retired March 28, 1939.

‡ Elected March 28, 1939, having served as assistant clerk since 1928; retired May 26, 1961.

** Elected May 26, 1961, having served as assistant clerk since 1946.

⁻ Elected January 1, 1969, having served as assistant clerk since 1961.

• Elected Clerk January 5, 1983, having served as assistant clerk since 1969.

§ There was no choice, and it was ordered, after balloting, that all the settled clergymen of Boston be invited by the Speaker to officiate alternately as Chaplain.

⁹ There was no choice, and it was ordered, after balloting, that the three clergymen having the highest votes should act as joint Chaplains. These were Lyman Beecher, Sebastian Streeter and Ezra S. Gannett.

Austin Phelps	1844	Noah M. Gaylord	1866
Chandler Robbins	1845	Pliny Wood	1867
William Hague	1845	William R. Alger	1868
William Jenks	1846	Orin T. Walker	1869
Samuel D. Robbins	1846	John A. M. Chapman	1870
George Richards	1847	Charles C. Sewall	1871
Silas Aiken	1848	Warren H. Cudworth	1872
S. Hale Higgins	1848	Robert G. Seymour	1873-78
Rollin H. Neale	1849	Daniel W. Waldron	1879-1918
Henry V. Degen	1850	William F. Dusseault	1919-22
George M. Randall	1851	Donald B. Aldrich	1923-24
Rufus W. Clark	1852	Harry W. Kimball	1925-28
Stephen Lovell	1853	Gardiner M. Day	1929
Arthur B. Fuller	1854	Abbot Peterson	1930-32
John H. Twombly	1855	Dan Huntington Fenn	1933-36
Abraham D. Merrill	1856	J. Caleb Justice	1937-38
Daniel Foster	1857	Cornelius P. Trowbridge	1939-42
Warren Burton	1858	Howard P. Horn	1943
Thomas Dodge	1859	Howard P. Bozarth	1943-44
Warren Burton	1860	Elmore Brown	1945-48
Andrew L. Stone	1861	Richard J. Quinlan	1949-52
Phineas Stowe	1862	Arthur Joseph Snow	1953-54
George S. Ball	1863	Christopher P. Griffin	1955-58
David Brenner	1864	George V. Kerr•	1959-83
Samuel F. Upham	1865	Robert F. Quinn#	1983-

SERGEANT-AT-ARMS.†

Benjamin Stevens	1835-59	James Beatty	1920
John Morrissey	1859-74	Charles O. Holt¶	1921-49
Oreb F. Mitchell	1875-85	Arthur R. Driscoll*	1949-62
John G. B. Adams	1886-1900	Leopold Lepore**	1962-63
Charles G. Davis	1901-03	John J. Cavanaugh	1963-75
David T. Remington	1904-09	Charles M. McGowan***	1976-90
Thomas F. Pedrick	1910-20	Michael J. Rea, Jr.§§	1990-

SERGEANT-AT-ARMS FOR THE HOUSE.

Octave O. Desmarais♀   1949-52

---

† The office of Sergeant-at-Arms was established by law in 1835. Previous to that time Jacob Kuhn was Messenger to the General Court from 1786. William Baker preceded him from the first session under the Constitution in 1780-81, he having also served in a similar position for many years previously thereto.

¶ Resigned March 21, 1949. Mr. Driscoll was elected to fill the vacancy August 31, 1949.

* Retired March 8, 1962. Mr. Lepore was elected to fill vacancy April 25, 1962.

** Died May 24, 1963. Mr. Cavanaugh was elected to fill the vacancy November 13, 1963.

♀ The office of Sergeant-at-Arms for the House was established by Chapter 806 of the Acts of 1949.

*** Elected January 26, 1976; Retired eff. May 1, 1990.

• Died January 23, 1983.

Appointed to fill vacancy in the office of Chaplain, February 7, 1983.

§§ Elected November 30, 1990.

Table showing the Length of the Session of the Legislature in
Each Year since 1832

YEAR	Convened	Prorogued		Total Days	No. of Reps.
1832	January 4	March	24	80	528
1833	2		28	86	574
1834	1	April	2	92	570
1835*	7		8	92	615
1836	6		16	102	619
1837	4		20	107	635
1838	3		25	113	480
1839	2		10	99	521
1840	1	March	24	84	521
1841	6		18	72	397
1842*	5		3	58	336
1843	4		24	80	352
1844	3		16	74	321
1845	1		26	85	271
1846	7	April	16	100	264
1847	6		16	111	255
1848*	5	May	10	127	272
1849	3		2	120	263
1850	2		3	122	297
1851	2		24	146	396
1852	7		22	137	402
1853	5		25	142	288
1854	4	April	29	116	310
1855	3	May	21	138	380
1856	1	June	6	158	329
1857*	7	May	30	144	357

* There was an extra session of sixty-two days in 1835, to revise the statutes;
one of nine days in 1842, to divide the Commonwealth into Congressional Districts;
one of three days in 1848, to choose electors of President and Vice-President; one
of eighteen days in 1857, to establish districts for the choice of Councillors,
Representatives and Senators, one of one hundred and thirteen days in 1859, to revise
the general statutes; one of fourteen days in 1860, to consider the subject of the disease
among the cattle of the Commonwealth; one of ten days in 1861, to consider the duty
of the Commonwealth in relation to public affairs, consequent on the Rebellion;
one of eight days in 1863, to provide for raising the quota under the call of the
President of the United States of the 17th of October, 1863, for 300,000 men; one
of thirty days in 1872, to consider what legislation was necessary by reason of the
great fire in Boston, November 9 and 10; one of ten days in 1881 and one of seven
days in 1901, to act upon the report of a joint special committee to revise the statutes;
one of three days in 1916, to legislate for Massachusetts soldiers called to the Mexican
border and to provide for the reapportionment of Suffolk County into Representative
districts; one of thirty-six days in 1919, to consider the street railway situation, the
compensation of the State Guard for special duty in Boston, the appropriations of
cities and towns for compensating school teachers and for other municipal purposes.

YEAR	Convened		Prorogued		Total Days	No. of Reps.
1858†	January	6	March	27	81	240†
1859*		5	April	6	92	—
1860*		4		4	92	—
1861*		2		11	100	—
1862		1		30	120	—
1863*		7		29	113	—
1864		6	May	14	130	—
1865		4		17	137	—
1866		3		30	147	—
1867		2	June	1	150	—
1868		1		12	164	—
1869		6		24	170	—
1870		5		23	170	—
1871		4	May	31	148	—
1872*		3		7	126	—
1873		1	June	12	163	—
1874		7		30	175	—
1875		6	May	19	134	—
1876		5	April	28	115	—
1877		3	May	17	135	—
1878		2		17	136	—
1879		1	April	30	120	—
1880		7		24	109	—
1881*		5	May	13	129	—
1882		4		27	144	—
1883		5	July	27	206	—
1884		2	June	4	155	—
1885		7		19	164	—
1886		6		30	176	—
1887		5		16	163	—
1888		4	May	29	147	—
1889		2	June	7	157	—
1890		1	July	2	183	—
1891		7	June	11	156	—

the recognition of Provincetown in the Pilgrim Tercentenary celebration, etc.; one of sixteen days in 1920, to act upon the report of a joint special committee to revise the General Laws; one of three hours on October 20, 1930, to commemorate the tercentenary of the first General Court held in Massachusetts; one of forty-six days in 1931, to consider changing the law relative to rates for compulsory motor vehicle liability insurance; one of twenty-seven days in 1933, to consider regulation and control of the liquor traffic; one of three days in 1938, to provide funds for the devastation caused by hurricane and floods; one of six days in 1942, to provide for the safety of the Commonwealth during the existence of the war emergency; one of fifteen days in 1944, to facilitate voting by citizens in the armed forces, and to issuance of licenses based upon safety of places of public assembly; one of six days in 1952

† The number of Representatives remained at 240 from 1858 through 1978; the number of Representatives beginning in 1979 has been 160.

YEAR	Convened	Prorogued		Total Days	DAYS OF SITTING	
					Senate	House
1892	January 6	June	17	163	112	112
1893	4		9	157	107	107
1894	3	July	2	181	121	126
1895	2	June	5	155	102	107
1896	1		10	162	112	112
1897	6		12	158	108	110
1898	5		23	170	115	120
1899	4		3	151	104	104
1900	3	July	17	196	131	133
1901*	2	June	19	169	114	117
1902	1		28	179	123	124
1903	7		26	171	119	121
1904	6		9	156	109	110
1905	4	May	26	143	101	101
1906	3	June	29	178	123	123
1907	2		28	178	125	125
1908	1		13	165	117	119
1909	6		19	165	116	116
1910	5		15	162	114	114
1911	4	July	28	206	140	141
1912	3	June	13	163	113	112
1913	1		20	171	120	120
1914	7	July	7	182	127	126
1915	6	June	4	150	104	104
1916*	5		2	150	105	105
1917	3	May	26	144	101	101
1918	2	June	3	153	107	107
1919*	1	July	25	206	144	144
1920*	7	June	5	151	108	105
1921	5	May	28	144	100	100
1922	4	June	13	161	110	111
1923	3	May	26	144	99	99
1924	2	June	5	156	108	110
1925	7	May	2	116	79	81
1926	6		29	144	86	102
1927	5	April	28	114	69	78
1928	4	July	25	204	105	124

to repeal provisions of law providing pensions or retirement allowances for members of the General Court and other elected state officials and to revise the laws providing travel and other expenses for members and employees of the legislative branch; one of one day in 1954 to provide funds for the alleviation of the destruction caused by the hurricane and to revise the law relative to the retirement of certain veterans of World War I; and one of three days in 1960 to consider the purchase of part of the former Old Colony Railroad right-of-way, the establishment of a state medical school, the continuity of terms of chairmen of the commissions on transportation and public

YEAR	Convened	Prorogued		Total Days	Days of Sitting	
					Senate	House
1929	January 2	June	8	158	92	109
1930*	1	May	29	149	89	107
1931*	7	June	10	155	100	107
1932	6		7	154	92	106
1933*	4	July	22	200	123	139
1934	3	June	30	179	114	122
1935	2	Aug.	15	226	124	126
1936	1	July	2	184	106	103
1937	6	May	29	144	75	84
1938*	5	Aug.	24	232	115	135
1939†	4		12	221	107	145
1941*	1	Nov.	1	305	166	170
1943*	6	June	12	158	89	90
1945‡	3	July	25	204	119	119
1946	2	June	15	165	98	98
1947	1	July	1	182	111	109
1948	7	June	19	165	97	96
1949	5	Aug.	31	239	140	152
1950	4		19	228	135	136
1951	3	Nov.	17	319	179	189
1952*	2	July	5	186	89	103
1953	7		4	179	92	102
1954*	6	June	11	157	91	99
1955	5	Sept.	16	255	141	158
1956	4	Oct.	6	277	145	151
1957	2	Sept.	21	262	142	137
1958	1	Oct.	17	290	162	159
1959	7	Sept.	17	254	143	145
1960*	6	Nov.	24	324	173	172
1961	4	May	27	144	82	94
1962	3	July	27	206	138	127
1963	2	Nov.	16	319	181	182
1964	1	July	4	186	126	110
1965**	6	Jan. 4, '66		364	204	222
1966*	5	Sept.	7	246	136	136
1967**	4	Jan. 2, '68		364	197	200
1968	3	July	20	200	107	103
1969	1	Aug.	25	237	135	131
1970	7	Aug.	25	237	135	127

utilities, the establishment of the salaries of the clerks of the Newton District Court
and the Second Plymouth District Court and the appropriation of money for the
urban renewal division; one of one day in 1962 relative to cessation of service by
the Metropolitan Transit Authority; one of twenty-four days in 1966 relative to
mental health and mental retardation services, the extension of a runway at Logan
Airport and establishing home rule procedures for cities and towns; one of six days

YEAR	Convened	Prorogued		Total Days	Days of Sitting	
					Senate	House
1971	January 6	Nov.	10	309	171	167
1972	5	July	9	187	105	103
1973	3	Nov.	30	331	180	179
1974	2	Aug.	2	213	112	116
1975**	1	Jan. 6, '76		371	158	191
1976	7	Oct.	14	282	106	128
1977**	5	Jan. 3, '78		364	167	173
1978*	4	July	12	190	96	83
1979§	3	Nov.	4	306	134	149
1980*	2	July	5	186	72	88
1981**	7	Jan. 5, '82		364	124	134
1982**	6	Jan. 2, '83		364	156	139
1983**	5	Jan. 3, '84		363	134	159
1984**	4	Jan. 1, '85		362	119	117
1985**	2	Dec. 31, '85		364	136	142
1986**	1	Jan. 6, '87		371	136	147
1987	7	Jan. 5, '88		364	144	153
1988	6	Nov. 23, '88		322	103	123
1989**	4	Jan. 2, '90		364	128	148
1990**	3	Jan. 1, '91		364	127	135
1991**	2	Dec. 31, '91		364	124	147
1992	1	Jan. 5, '93		371	155	144
1993	6	Jan. 4, '94		364	153	150
1994	5	Jan. 3, '95		364	129	120
1995	4	Jan. 2, '96		364	115	119
1996	3	Dec. 31, '96		364	130	122
1997	1	—		—	—	—

in 1973 relative to the energy crisis; and one of two days in 1978 to consider the removal from office of Robert M. Bonin, Chief Justice of the Superior Court; one of five days in 1980 for the purpose of continuing the unfinished Constitutional Convention; one of three days in 1980 to consider legislation to permit the continuation of the Massachusetts Bay Transportation Authority; and one of six days in 1980 to consider legislation to permit the continuation of the Massachusetts Bay Transportation Authority.

* See note on extra sessions on pages 422-426.
† First year of biennial session.
‡ First year of return to annual sessions.
** Dissolved under Article X of the Amendments to the Constitution.
§ First year of 160-member House of Representatives.

POST OFFICES IN MASSACHUSETTS,

WITH THE CITIES OR TOWNS AND COUNTIES IN WHICH
THEY ARE SITUATED

The spelling of the names of post offices is that established
by the United States Postal Service.]

[Post offices marked † are in the Boston Postal Area.]

POST OFFICES	CITIES AND TOWNS	COUNTIES
Abington 02351	Abington	Plymouth
Accord 02018	Hingham	Plymouth
Acton 01720	Acton	Middlesex
Acushnet 02743	Acushnet	Bristol
Adams 01220	Adams	Berkshire
Agawam 01001	Agawam	Hampden
Airport 02109†	Boston	Suffolk
Allerton 02045	Hull	Plymouth
Allston 02134†	Boston	Suffolk
Amesbury 01913	Amesbury	Essex
Amherst 01002	Amherst	Hampshire
Andover 01810	Andover	Essex
Aquinnah 02535	Chilmark	Dukes
Arlington 02174†	Arlington	Middlesex
Arlington Heights 02175†	Arlington	Middlesex
Ashburnham 01430	Ashburnham	Worcester
Ashby 01431	Ashby	Middlesex
Ashfield 01330	Ashfield	Franklin
Ashland 01721	Ashland	Middlesex
Ashley Falls 01222	Sheffield	Berkshire
Assinippi 02339	Hanover	Plymouth
Assonet 02702	Freetown	Bristol
Assumption College 01609	Worcester	Worcester
Astor 02123†	Boston	Suffolk
Athol 01331	Athol	Worcester
Attleboro 02703	Attleboro	Bristol

426 *Post Offices in Massachusetts.*

POST OFFICES	CITIES AND TOWNS	COUNTIES
Attleboro Falls 02763	North Attleborough...	Bristol
Auburn 01501	Auburn	Worcester
Auburndale 02166†	Newton	Middlesex
Avon 02322	Avon	Norfolk
Ayer 01432	Ayer	Middlesex
Babson Park 02157†	Wellesley	Norfolk
Back Bay Annex 02117†	Boston	Suffolk
Baldwinville 01436	Templeton	Worcester
Ballardvale 01810	Andover	Essex
Barnstable 02630	Barnstable	Barnstable
Barre 01005	Barre	Worcester
Bass River 02664	Dennis	Barnstable
Becket 01223	Becket	Berkshire
Bedford 01730	Bedford	Middlesex
Belchertown 01007	Belchertown	Hampshire
Bellingham 02019	Bellingham	Norfolk
Belmont 02178†	Belmont	Middlesex
Berkley 02779	Berkley	Bristol
Berkshire 01224	Lanesborough	Berkshire
Berlin 01503	Berlin	Worcester
Bernardston 01337	Bernardston	Franklin
Beverly 01915	Beverly	Essex
Beverly Farms 01915	Beverly	Essex
Billerica 01821	Billerica	Middlesex
Blackstone 01504	Blackstone	Worcester
Blandford 01008	Blandford	Hampden
Bolton 01740	Bolton	Worcester
Bondsville 01009	Palmer	Hampden
Boston (Postmaster) 02205†	Boston	Suffolk
Boston College 02167†	Newton	Middlesex
Boston University 02215†	Boston	Suffolk
Bourne 02532	Bourne	Barnstable
Boxboro 01719	Boxborough	Middlesex
Boxford 01921	Boxford	Essex
Boylston 01505	Boylston	Worcester
Bradford 01835	Haverhill	Essex
Braintree 02184†	Braintree	Norfolk
Brant Rock 02020	Marshfield	Plymouth
Brewster 02631	Brewster	Barnstable
Bridgewater 02324	Bridgewater	Plymouth
Brighton 02135†	Boston	Suffolk
Brightwood 01107	Springfield	Hampden

POST OFFICES	CITIES AND TOWNS	COUNTIES
Brimfield 01010	Brimfield	Hampden
Brockton 02403	Brockton	Plymouth
Brookfield 01506	Brookfield	Worcester
Brookline 02146†	Brookline	Norfolk
Brookline Village 02147†	Brookline	Norfolk
Bryantville 02327	Pembroke	Plymouth
Buckland 01338	Buckland	Franklin
Burlington 01803	Burlington	Middlesex
Buzzards Bay 02532	Bourne	Barnstable
Byfield 01922	Newbury	Essex
Cambridge 02138†	Cambridge	Middlesex
Cambridge A (Campt.) 02139†	Cambridge	Middlesex
Cambridge B (N. Cam.) 02140†	Cambridge	Middlesex
Cambridge C (E. Cam.) 02141†	Cambridge	Middlesex
Canton 02021	Canton	Norfolk
Carlisle 01741	Carlisle	Middlesex
Carver 02330	Carver	Plymouth
Cataumet 02534	Bourne	Barnstable
Cathedral 02118†	Boston	Suffolk
Center 02361	Plymouth	Plymouth
Centerville 02632	Barnstable	Barnstable
Central Village 02790	Westport	Bristol
Charlemont 01339	Charlemont	Franklin
Charles Street 02114†	Boston	Suffolk
Charlestown 02129†	Boston	Suffolk
Charlton 01507	Charlton	Worcester
Charlton City 01508	Charlton	Worcester
Charlton Depot 01509	Charlton	Worcester
Chartley 02712	Norton	Bristol
Chatham 02633	Chatham	Barnstable
Chelmsford 01824	Chelmsford	Middlesex
Chelsea 02150†	Chelsea	Suffolk
Cherry Valley 01611	Leicester	Worcester
Cheshire 01225	Cheshire	Berkshire
Chester 01011	Chester	Hampden
Chesterfield 01012	Chesterfield	Hampshire
Chestnut Hill 02167†	Newton	Middlesex
Chicopee 01021	Chicopee	Hampden

POST OFFICES	CITIES AND TOWNS	COUNTIES
Chicopee Center 01013	Chicopee	Hampden
Chilmark 02535	Chilmark	Dukes
Clarksburg 01247	North Adams	Berkshire
Clinton 01510	Clinton	Worcester
Cochituate 01778	Wayland	Middlesex
Cohasset 02025	Cohasset	Norfolk
Colrain 01340	Colrain	Franklin
Concord 01742	Concord	Middlesex
Conway 01341	Conway	Franklin
Cotuit 02635	Barnstable	Barnstable
Craigville 02636	Barnstable	Barnstable
Cummaquid 02637	Barnstable	Barnstable
Cummington 01026	Cummington	Hampshire
Cushman 01002	Amherst	Hampshire
Cuttyhunk 02713	Gosnold	Dukes
Dalton 01226	Dalton	Berkshire
Danvers 01923	Danvers	Essex
Dartmouth 02714	Dartmouth	Bristol
Dedham 02026	Dedham	Norfolk
Deerfield 01342	Deerfield	Franklin
Dennis 02638	Dennis	Barnstable
Dennis Port 02639	Dennis	Barnstable
Dighton 02715	Dighton	Bristol
Division Street 02744	New Bedford	Bristol
Dorchester 02122†	Boston	Suffolk
Dorchester Center 02124†	Boston	Suffolk
Dover 02030	Dover	Norfolk
Dracut 01826	Dracut	Middlesex
Drury 01343	Florida	Berkshire
Dudley 01571	Dudley	Worcester
Dudley Hill 01570	Webster	Worcester
Dunstable 01827	Dunstable	Middlesex
Duxbury 02332	Duxbury	Plymouth
East Arlington 02174†	Arlington	Middlesex
East Boston 02128†	Boston	Suffolk
East Bridgewater 02333	East Bridgewater	Plymouth
East Brookfield 01515	East Brookfield	Worcester
East Dedham 02026	Dedham	Norfolk
East Dennis 02641	Dennis	Barnstable
East Douglas 01516	Douglas	Worcester
East Falmouth 02536	Falmouth	Barnstable
East Freetown 02717	Freetown	Bristol

POST OFFICES	CITIES AND TOWNS	COUNTIES
Eastham 02642	Eastham	Barnstable
Easthampton 01027	Easthampton	Hampshire
East Longmeadow 01028	East Longmeadow	Hampden
East Lynn 01904	Lynn	Essex
East Mansfield 02031	Mansfield	Bristol
Easton 02334	Easton	Bristol
East Orleans 02643	Orleans	Barnstable
East Otis 01029	Otis	Berkshire
East Princeton 01517	Princeton	Worcester
East Sandwich 02537	Sandwich	Barnstable
East Taunton 02718	Taunton	Bristol
East Templeton 01438	Templeton	Worcester
East Walpole 02032	Walpole	Norfolk
East Wareham 02538	Wareham	Plymouth
East Watertown 02172†	Watertown	Middlesex
East Weymouth 02189†	Weymouth	Norfolk
Edgartown 02539	Edgartown	Dukes
Elms College 01013	Chicopee	Hampden
Elmwood 02337	East Bridgewater	Plymouth
Erving 01344	Erving	Franklin
Essex 01929	Essex	Essex
Essex 02112†	Boston	Suffolk
Everett 02149†	Everett	Middlesex
Fairhaven 02719	Fairhaven	Bristol
Fall River 02722	Fall River	Bristol
Falmouth 02540	Falmouth	Barnstable
Fayville 01745	Southborough	Worcester
Federal 01601	Worcester	Worcester
Feeding Hills 01030	Agawam	Hampden
Fiskdale 01518	Sturbridge	Worcester
Fitchburg 01420	Fitchburg	Worcester
Flint 02723	Fall River	Bristol
Florence 01060	Northampton	Hampshire
Florida 01247	Florida	Berkshire
Forestdale 02644	Sandwich	Barnstable
Forest Park 01108	Springfield	Hampden
Forge Village 01886	Westford	Middlesex
Fort Devens 01433	Ayer	Middlesex
Foxboro 02035	Foxborough	Norfolk
Framingham 01701	Framingham	Middlesex
Framingham Center 01701	Framingham	Middlesex
Franklin 02038	Franklin	Norfolk

430   *Post Offices in Massachusetts.*

POST OFFICES	CITIES AND TOWNS	COUNTIES
Highlands 01851	Lowell	Middlesex
Hingham 02043	Hingham	Plymouth
Hinsdale 01235	Hinsdale	Berkshire
Holbrook 02343	Holbrook	Norfolk
Holden 01520	Holden	Worcester
Holland 01521	Holland	Hampden
Holliston 01746	Holliston	Middlesex
Holyoke 01040	Holyoke	Hampden
Hopedale 01747	Hopedale	Worcester
Hopkinton 01748	Hopkinton	Middlesex
Housatonic 01236	Great Barrington	Berkshire
Hubbardston 01452	Hubbardston	Worcester
Hudson 01749	Hudson	Middlesex
Hull 02045	Hull	Plymouth
Humarock 02047	Scituate	Plymouth
Huntington 01050	Huntington	Hampshire
Hyannis 02601	Barnstable	Barnstable
Hyannis Port 02647	Barnstable	Barnstable
Hyde Park 02136†	Boston	Suffolk
Incoming Mail Center, North 02150	Chelsea	Suffolk
Indian Orchard 01151	Springfield	Hampden
Inman Square 02139†	Cambridge	Middlesex
Internal Revenue Service Center 05501	Andover	Essex
Ipswich 01938	Ipswich	Essex
Islington 02090	Westwood	Norfolk
Jamaica Plain 02130†	Boston	Suffolk
Jefferson 01522	Holden	Worcester
John Fitzgerald Kennedy 02114†	Boston	Suffolk
John Fitzgerald Kennedy Library 02125†	Boston	Suffolk
John W. McCormack Building 02108†	Boston	Suffolk
Kendall Square 02142†	Cambridge	Middlesex
Kenmore 02215†	Boston	Suffolk
Kingston 02364	Kingston	Plymouth
Lake Pleasant 01347	Montague	Franklin
Lakeville 02347	Lakeville	Plymouth

POST OFFICES	CITIES AND TOWNS	COUNTIES
Lancaster 01523	Lancaster	Worcester
Lanesboro 01237	Lanesborough	Berkshire
Lanesville 01930	Gloucester	Essex
Lawrence 01842	Lawrence	Essex
Lee 01238	Lee	Berkshire
Leeds 01053	Northampton	Hampshire
Leicester 01524	Leicester	Worcester
Lenox 01240	Lenox	Berkshire
Lenox Dale 01242	Lenox	Berkshire
Leominster 01453	Leominster	Worcester
Leverett 01054	Leverett	Franklin
Leverett Saltonstall State Office Building 02202†	Boston	Suffolk
Lexington 02173†	Lexington	Middlesex
Leyden 01301	Greenfield	Franklin
Lincoln 01773	Lincoln	Middlesex
Lincoln Center 01773	Lincoln	Middlesex
Linwood 01525	Uxbridge	Worcester
Littleton 01460	Littleton	Middlesex
Longmeadow 01106	Longmeadow	Hampden
Lowell 01853	Lowell	Middlesex
Ludlow 01056	Ludlow	Hampden
Lunenburg 01462	Lunenburg	Worcester
Lynn 01901	Lynn	Essex
Lynnfield 01940	Lynnfield	Essex
Magnolia 01930	Gloucester	Essex
Main Street 02532	Bourne	Barnstable
Main Street 01601	Worcester	Worcester
Malden 02148†	Malden	Middlesex
Manchaug 01526	Sutton	Worcester
Manchester 01944	Manchester-by-the-Sea	Essex
Manomet 02345	Plymouth	Plymouth
Mansfield 02048	Mansfield	Bristol
Marblehead 01945	Marblehead	Essex
Marion 02738	Marion	Plymouth
Marlborough 01752	Marlborough	Middlesex
Marshfield 02050	Marshfield	Plymouth
Marshfield Hills 02051	Marshfield	Plymouth
Marstons Mills 02648	Barnstable	Barnstable
Mashpee 02649	Mashpee	Barnstable
Mattapan 02126†	Boston	Suffolk

POST OFFICES	CITIES AND TOWNS	COUNTIES
Mattapoisett 02739	Mattapoisett	Plymouth
Maynard 01754	Maynard	Middlesex
Medfield 02052	Medfield	Norfolk
Medford 02155†	Medford	Middlesex
Medway 02053	Medway	Norfolk
Medway Village 02053	Medway	Norfolk
Melrose 02176†	Melrose	Middlesex
Mendon 01756	Mendon	Worcester
Menemsha 02552	Chilmark	Dukes
Merrimac 01860	Merrimac	Essex
Merrimack College 01845	North Andover	Essex
Methuen 01844	Methuen	Essex
Middleboro 02346	Middleborough	Plymouth
Middlefield 01243	Middlefield	Hampshire
Middleton 01949	Middleton	Essex
Milford 01757	Milford	Worcester
Millbury 01527	Millbury	Worcester
Millers Falls 01349	Montague	Franklin
Millis 02054	Millis	Norfolk
Mill River 01244	New Marlborough	Berkshire
Millville 01529	Millville	Worcester
Milton 02186†	Milton	Norfolk
Milton Village 02187†	Milton	Norfolk
Minot 02055	Scituate	Plymouth
M.I.T. 02139†	Cambridge	Middlesex
Monponsett 02350	Hanson	Plymouth
Monroe 01350	Monroe	Franklin
Monroe Bridge 01350	Monroe	Franklin
Monson 01057	Monson	Hampden
Montague 01351	Montague	Franklin
Monterey 01245	Monterey	Berkshire
Montgomery 01085	Montgomery	Hampden
Monument Beach 02553	Bourne	Barnstable
Mount Herman 01354	Northfield	Franklin
Mount Pleasant 02745	New Bedford	Bristol
Mount Saint James 01610	Worcester	Worcester
Mount Tom 01027	Easthampton	Hampshire
Nabnasset 01886	Westford	Middlesex
Nahant 01908	Nahant	Essex
Nantucket 02554	Nantucket	Nantucket
Natick 01760	Natick	Middlesex
Needham 02192†	Needham	Norfolk

POST OFFICES	CITIES AND TOWNS	COUNTIES
Needham Heights 02194†	Needham	Norfolk
New Ashford 01237	New Ashford	Berkshire
New Bedford 02740	New Bedford	Bristol
New Braintree 01531	New Braintree	Worcester
Newbury 01951	Newbury	Essex
Newburyport 01950	Newburyport	Essex
New Salem 01355	New Salem	Franklin
New Seabury 02649	Mashpee	Barnstable
Newton 02158†	Newton	Middlesex
Newton Center 02159†	Newton	Middlesex
Newton Highlands 02161†	Newton	Middlesex
Newton Lower Falls 02162†	Newton	Middlesex
Newton Upper Falls 02164†	Newton	Middlesex
Newtonville 02160†	Newton	Middlesex
New Town 02258†	Newton	Middlesex
Nonantum 02195†	Newton	Middlesex
Noquochoke 02790	Westport	Bristol
Norfolk 02056	Norfolk	Norfolk
North 02746	New Bedford	Bristol
North Abington 02351	Abington	Plymouth
North Adams 01247	North Adams	Berkshire
North Amherst 01059	Amherst	Hampshire
Northampton 01060	Northampton	Hampshire
North Andover 01845	North Andover	Essex
North Attleboro 02760	North Attleborough	Bristol
North Billerica 01862	Billerica	Middlesex
Northborough 01532	Northborough	Worcester
Northbridge 01534	Northbridge	Worcester
North Brookfield 01535	North Brookfield	Worcester
North Carver 02355	Carver	Plymouth
North Chatham 02650	Chatham	Barnstable
North Chelmsford 01863	Chelmsford	Middlesex
North Dartmouth 02747	Dartmouth	Bristol
North Dighton 02764	Dighton	Bristol
North Eastham 02651	Eastham	Barnstable
Northeastern University 02115†	Boston	Suffolk
North Easton 02356	Easton	Bristol
North Egremont 01252	Egremont	Berkshire
North Falmouth 02556	Falmouth	Barnstable
Northfield 01360	Northfield	Franklin
North Grafton 01536	Grafton	Worcester
North Hatfield 01066	Hatfield	Hampshire

POST OFFICES	CITIES AND TOWNS	COUNTIES
North Marshfield 02059	Marshfield	Plymouth
North Oxford 01537	Oxford	Worcester
North Pembroke 02358	Pembroke	Plymouth
North Quincy 02171†	Quincy	Norfolk
North Reading 01864	North Reading	Middlesex
North Scituate 02060	Scituate	Plymouth
North Truro 02652	Truro	Barnstable
North Uxbridge 01538	Uxbridge	Worcester
North Waltham 02154†	Waltham	Middlesex
North Weymouth 02191†	Weymouth	Norfolk
Norton 02766	Norton	Bristol
Norwell 02061	Norwell	Plymouth
Norwood 02062	Norwood	Norfolk
Nutting Lake 01865	Billerica	Middlesex
Oak Bluffs 02557	Oak Bluffs	Dukes
Oakdale 01539	West Boylston	Worcester
Oakham 01068	Oakham	Worcester
Ocean Bluff 02065	Marshfield	Plymouth
Onset 02558	Wareham	Plymouth
Orange 01364	Orange	Franklin
Orchard Street 02744	New Bedford	Bristol
Orleans 02653	Orleans	Barnstable
Osterville 02655	Barnstable	Barnstable
Otis 01253	Otis	Berkshire
Otis Air Force Base 02542	Bourne	Barnstable
Oxford 01540	Oxford	Worcester
Padanaram Village 02748	Dartmouth	Bristol
Palmer 01069	Palmer	Hampden
Paxton 01612	Paxton	Worcester
Peabody 01960	Peabody	Essex
Pelham 01002	Pelham	Hampshire
Pembroke 02359	Pembroke	Plymouth
Pepperell 01463	Pepperell	Middlesex
Peru 01235	Peru	Berkshire
Petersham 01366	Petersham	Worcester
Phillipston 01331	Phillipston	Worcester
Pigeon Cove 01966	Rockport	Essex
Pinehurst 01866	Billerica	Middlesex
Pittsfield 01201	Pittsfield	Berkshire
Plainfield 01070	Plainfield	Hampshire
Plainville 02762	Plainville	Norfolk

POST OFFICES	CITIES AND TOWNS	COUNTIES
Plymouth 02360	Plymouth	Plymouth
Plympton 02367	Plympton	Plymouth
Pocasset 02559	Bourne	Barnstable
Porter Square 02140†	Cambridge	Middlesex
Prides Crossing 01965	Beverly	Essex
Princeton 01541	Princeton	Worcester
Provincetown 02657	Provincetown	Barnstable
Prudential Center 02199†	Boston	Suffolk
Quincy 02269†	Quincy	Norfolk
Quinsigamond Village 01607	Worcester	Worcester
Randolph 02368	Randolph	Norfolk
Raynham 02767	Raynham	Bristol
Raynham Center 02768	Raynham	Bristol
Reading 01867	Reading	Middlesex
Readville 02137†	Boston	Suffolk
Rehoboth 02769	Rehoboth	Bristol
Revere 02151†	Revere	Suffolk
Richmond 01254	Richmond	Berkshire
Riverdale 01930	Gloucester	Essex
Rochdale 01542	Leicester	Worcester
Rochester 02770	Rochester	Plymouth
Rockland 02370	Rockland	Plymouth
Rockport 01966	Rockport	Essex
Roslindale 02131†	Boston	Suffolk
Rowe 01367	Rowe	Franklin
Rowley 01969	Rowley	Essex
Roxbury 02119†	Boston	Suffolk
Roxbury Crossing 02120†	Boston	Suffolk
Royalston 01368	Royalston	Worcester
Russell 01071	Russell	Hampden
Rutland 01543	Rutland	Worcester
Sagamore 02561	Bourne	Barnstable
Sagamore Beach 02562	Bourne	Barnstable
Salem 01970	Salem	Essex
Salem State College 01970	Salem	Essex
Salisbury 01952	Salisbury	Essex
Salisbury Beach 01952	Salisbury	Essex
Sandisfield 01255	Sandisfield	Berkshire
Sandwich 02563	Sandwich	Barnstable
Saugus 01906	Saugus	Essex
Savoy 01256	Savoy	Berkshire

POST OFFICES	CITIES AND TOWNS	COUNTIES
Saxonville 01701	Framingham	Middlesex
Scituate 02066	Scituate	Plymouth
Seekonk 02771	Seekonk	Bristol
Sharon 02067	Sharon	Norfolk
Shattuckville 01369	Colrain	Franklin
Shawsheen Village 01810	Andover	Essex
Sheffield 01257	Sheffield	Berkshire
Shelburne Falls 01370	Shelburne	Franklin
Sheldonville 02070	Wrentham	Norfolk
Sherborn 01770	Sherborn	Middlesex
Shirley 01464	Shirley	Middlesex
Shirley Center 01464	Shirley	Middlesex
Shrewsbury 01545	Shrewsbury	Worcester
Shutesbury 01072	Shutesbury	Franklin
Siasconset 02564	Nantucket	Nantucket
Silver Beach 02565	Falmouth	Barnstable
Snug Harbor 02332	Duxbury	Plymouth
Soldiers Field 02163†	Boston	Suffolk
Somerset 02726	Somerset	Bristol
Somerville 02143†	Somerville	Middlesex
South 02724	Fall River	Bristol
Southampton 01073	Southampton	Hampshire
South Attleboro 02703	Attleboro	Bristol
South Barre 01074	Barre	Worcester
Southborough 01772	Southborough	Worcester
South Boston 02127†	Boston	Suffolk
Southbridge 01550	Southbridge	Worcester
South Carver 02366	Carver	Plymouth
South Chatham 02659	Chatham	Barnstable
South Chelmsford 01824	Chelmsford	Middlesex
South Dartmouth 02748	Dartmouth	Bristol
South Deerfield 01373	Deerfield	Franklin
South Dennis 02660	Dennis	Barnstable
South Easton 02375	Easton	Bristol
South Egremont 01258	Egremont	Berkshire
Southfield 01259	New Marlborough	Berkshire
South Framingham 01701	Framingham	Middlesex
South Grafton 01560	Grafton	Worcester
South Hadley 01075	South Hadley	Hampshire
South Hamilton 01982	Hamilton	Essex
South Harwich 02661	Harwich	Barnstable
South Lancaster 01561	Lancaster	Worcester

POST OFFICES	CITIES AND TOWNS	COUNTIES
South Lee 01260	Lee	Berkshire
South Lynnfield 01940	Lynnfield	Essex
South Orleans 02662	Orleans	Barnstable
South Postal Annex 02205†	Boston	Suffolk
South Royalston 01331	Royalston	Worcester
South Walpole 02071	Walpole	Norfolk
South Waltham 02154†	Waltham	Middlesex
South Wellfleet 02663	Wellfleet	Barnstable
South Weymouth 02190†	Weymouth	Norfolk
Southwick 01077	Southwick	Hampden
South Yarmouth 02664	Yarmouth	Barnstable
Spencer 01562	Spencer	Worcester
Springfield 01101	Springfield	Hampden
State House 02133†	Boston	Suffolk
Sterling 01564	Sterling	Worcester
Still River 01467	Harvard	Worcester
Stockbridge 01262	Stockbridge	Berkshire
Stoneham 02180†	Stoneham	Middlesex
Stoughton 02072	Stoughton	Norfolk
Stow 01775	Stow	Middlesex
Sturbridge 01566	Sturbridge	Worcester
Sudbury 01776	Sudbury	Middlesex
Sunderland 01375	Sunderland	Franklin
Sutton 01590	Sutton	Worcester
Swampscott 01907	Swampscott	Essex
Swansea 02777	Swansea	Bristol
Taunton 02780	Taunton	Bristol
Teaticket 02536	Falmouth	Barnstable
Templeton 01468	Templeton	Worcester
Tewksbury 01876	Tewksbury	Middlesex
Thomas P. O'Neill, Jr., Federal Office Building 02222†	Boston	Suffolk
Thorndike 01079	Palmer	Hampden
Three Rivers 01080	Palmer	Hampden
Tolland 01034	Tolland	Hampden
Topsfield 01983	Topsfield	Essex
Townsend 01469	Townsend	Middlesex
Tremont 02116†	Boston	Suffolk
Truro 02666	Truro	Barnstable
Tufts University 02153 †	Medford	Middlesex
Turners Falls 01376	Montague	Franklin
Turnpike 01545	Shrewsbury	Worcester

POST OFFICES	CITIES AND TOWNS	COUNTIES
Tyngsboro 01879	Tyngsborough	Middlesex
Tyringham 01264	Tyringham	Berkshire
Univ. of Massachusetts 01003	Amherst	Hampshire
Univ. of Massachusetts 02125†	Boston	Suffolk
Uphams Corner 02125†	Boston	Suffolk
Upton 01568	Upton	Worcester
Uxbridge 01569	Uxbridge	Worcester
Village of Nagog Woods 01718	Acton	Middlesex
Vineyard Haven 02568	Tisbury	Dukes
Waban 02168†	Newton	Middlesex
Wakefield 01880	Wakefield	Middlesex
Wales 01081	Wales	Hampden
Wallis Street 01960	Peabody	Essex
Walpole 02081	Walpole	Norfolk
Waltham 02154†	Waltham	Middlesex
Waquoit 02536	Falmouth	Barnstable
Ward Hill 01835	Haverhill	Essex
Ware 01082	Ware	Hampshire
Wareham 02571	Wareham	Plymouth
Warren 01083	Warren	Worcester
Warwick 01378	Warwick	Franklin
Watertown 02172†	Watertown	Middlesex
Waverly 02179†	Belmont	Middlesex
Wayland 01778	Wayland	Middlesex
Webster 01570	Webster	Worcester
Webster Square 01603	Worcester	Worcester
Wellesley 02181†	Wellesley	Norfolk
Wellesley Hills 02181†	Wellesley	Norfolk
Wellfleet 02667	Wellfleet	Barnstable
Wendell 01379	Wendell	Franklin
Wendell Depot 01380	Wendell	Franklin
Wenham 01984	Wenham	Essex
West Acton 01720	Acton	Middlesex
West Barnstable 02668	Barnstable	Barnstable
Westborough 01581	Westborough	Worcester
West Boxford 01885	Boxford	Essex
West Boylston 01583	West Boylston	Worcester
West Bridgewater 02379	West Bridgewater	Plymouth
West Brookfield 01585	West Brookfield	Worcester
West Chatham 02669	Chatham	Barnstable
West Chesterfield 01084	Chesterfield	Hampshire

POST OFFICES	CITIES AND TOWNS	COUNTIES
West Chop 02573	Vineyard Haven	Dukes
West Concord 01742	Concord	Middlesex
West Dennis 02670	Dennis	Barnstable
West Falmouth 02574	Falmouth	Barnstable
Westfield 01085	Westfield	Hampden
Westford 01886	Westford	Middlesex
West Groton 01472	Groton	Middlesex
Westhampton 01027	Westhampton	Hampshire
West Hanover 02339	Hanover	Plymouth
West Harwich 02671	Harwich	Barnstable
West Hatfield 01088	Hatfield	Hampshire
West Hyannisport 02672	Barnstable	Barnstable
West Lynn 01905	Lynn	Essex
West Medford 02156†	Medford	Middlesex
Westminster 01473	Westminster	Worcester
West Newbury 01985	West Newbury	Essex
West Newton 02165†	Newton	Middlesex
Weston 02193†	Weston	Middlesex
West Otis 01245	Otis	Berkshire
Westover AFB 01022	Chicopee	Hampden
West Peabody 01960	Peabody	Essex
Westport 02790	Westport	Bristol
Westport Point 02791	Westport	Bristol
West Roxbury 02132†	Boston	Suffolk
West Side 01602	Worcester	Worcester
West Somerville 02144†	Somerville	Middlesex
West Springfield 01089	West Springfield	Hampden
West Stockbridge 01266	West Stockbridge	Berkshire
West Tisbury 02575	West Tisbury	Dukes
West Townsend 01474	Townsend	Middlesex
West Wareham 02576	Wareham	Plymouth
West Warren 01092	Warren	Worcester
Westwood 02090	Westwood	Norfolk
West Yarmouth 02673	Yarmouth	Barnstable
Weymouth 02188†	Weymouth	Norfolk
Whately 01093	Whately	Franklin
Wheelwright 01094	Hardwick	Worcester
White Horse Beach 02381	Plymouth	Plymouth
Whitinsville 01588	Northbridge	Worcester
Whitman 02382	Whitman	Plymouth
Wilbraham 01095	Wilbraham	Hampden
Wilkinsonville 01590	Sutton	Worcester

POST OFFICES	CITIES AND TOWNS	COUNTIES
Williamsburg 01096	Williamsburg	Hampshire
Williamstown 01267	Williamstown	Berkshire
Wilmington 01887	Wilmington	Middlesex
Winchendon 01475	Winchendon	Worcester
Winchendon Springs 01477	Winchendon	Worcester
Winchester 01890	Winchester	Middlesex
Windsor 01270	Windsor	Berkshire
Winter Hill 02145†	Somerville	Middlesex
Winthrop 02152†	Winthrop	Suffolk
Woburn 01801	Woburn	Middlesex
Wollaston 02170†	Quincy	Norfolk
Woods Hole 02543	Falmouth	Barnstable
Woodville 01784	Hopkinton	Middlesex
Worcester 01613	Worcester	Worcester
Woronoco 01097	Russell	Hampden
Worthington 01098	Worthington	Hampshire
Wrentham 02093	Wrentham	Norfolk
Yarmouth Port 02675	Yarmouth	Barnstable

COUNTY OFFICERS.

By the provisions of the designated sections of chapter 54 of the General Laws (see also chapter 221), county officers are chosen at biennial State elections by the voters of each of the several counties or districts, as follows: —

Section 155, *a Clerk of the Supreme Judicial Court for the County of Suffolk and two Clerks of the Superior Court* of said county, one for civil and one for criminal business, and *Clerk of the Courts* in each of the other counties who shall act as clerk of the Supreme Judicial Court, of the Superior Court and of the County Commissioners, — 1922 and every sixth year thereafter. Section 156, *A Register of Probate and Family Court,* — 1924 and every sixth year thereafter. Section 157, *a Register of Deeds* (district or county), — 1922 and every sixth year thereafter. Section 158 (as amended by chapter 31 of the Acts of 1939), *two County Commissioners* (except in Hampshire, Suffolk and Nantucket counties, which see), — 1940 and every fourth year thereafter; and *one County Commissioner,* — 1942 and every fourth year thereafter. Section 159, *a Sheriff,* — 1926 and every sixth year thereafter. Section 160, *a County Treasurer* (except in Suffolk, Nantucket and Franklin counties, which see), — 1924 and every sixth year thereafter.

All of the foregoing officers hold office beginning with the first Wednesday of January following their election, and until their successors are chosen and qualified. Vacancies are filled in accordance with the provisions of section 142, 143 or 144 of chapter 54 of the General Laws.

BARNSTABLE COUNTY — INCORPORATED 1685.
Shire Town, Barnstable.

Register of Probate and Family Court — Frederic P. Claussen, Cotuit.
   First Assistant — Robert D. Farrell, Barnstable.
   Second Assistant — Priscilla Young, Bourne.

Sheriff — John F. DeMello, Barnstable.

Clerk of Courts — Phyllis A. Day, Falmouth.
   First Assistant Clerk — Linda C. Morin, Marstons Mills.
   Second Assistant Clerk — Kathleen C. Serpa, Barnstable.

County Treasurer — E. Mark Zielinski, Attleboro.

Register of Deeds — John F. Meade, Centerville.
   Assistant Register — Peter C. Bennett, Sandwich.

County Commissioners —
   Robert A. O'Leary, Barnstable . . . . Term expires January, 1999.
   Mary J. LeClair, Mashpee . . . . Term expires January, 2001.
   Christine B. Dolen, Falmouth . . . . Term expires January, 2001.

BERKSHIRE COUNTY — INCORPORATED 1761.
Shire Town, Pittsfield.

Register of Probate and Family Court —
   Francis B. Marinaro, Pittsfield.
   First Assistant Register — Gary W. Roy, Pittsfield.
   Assistant Register — James P. Mazzeo, Pittsfield.

Sheriff — Carmen C. Massimiano, Jr., Pittsfield.

Clerk of Courts — Deborah S. Capeless, Pittsfield.
   Assistant Clerk — Elizabeth A. Gingras, Pittsfield.

County Treasurer — Peter G. Arlos, Pittsfield.

Register of Deeds —
   Central District, Mary K. O'Brien, Pittsfield.
   Northern District, Christopher J. Solari, Adams.
   Southern District, Irene Skorput, Great Barrington.

Assistant Registers —
   Central District, Elaine Costanzo, Pittsfield.

County Commissioners —
   William "Smitty" Pignatelli, Lenox . . . Term expires January, 1999.
   Robert H. Melle, Becket . . . . Term expires January, 2001.
   Ronald E. Kitterman, Pittsfield . . . . Term expires January, 2001.

BRISTOL COUNTY — INCORPORATED 1685.
Shire Towns, Taunton and New Bedford.

Register of Probate and Family Court — Robert E. Peck, Dartmouth.
Assistant Registers --
Stephen J. Hanna, Taunton.
Margaret Atwood, New Bedford.
Clare Gamberoni, Newton.
Susan M. Paris, Fairhaven.
Sheriff — Thomas Hodgson, New Bedford (Acting).
Clerk of Courts — Marc J. Santos, Fairhaven.
First Assistant Clerk -- Robert J. Martin, Taunton.
Assistant Clerks --
Marcel W. Gautreau, Dartmouth.
Peter R. Andrade, Taunton.
Philip F. Leddy, Taunton.
Valerie A. Brodeur, Westport.
Erin J. Tierney, New Bedford.
Mark A. Ferriera, Seekonk.
Joseph T. Vincent, Taunton.

County Treasurer — Patrick H. Harrington, Somerset.

Register of Deeds —
Northern District, Joseph L. Amaral, Taunton.
Southern District, James L. Henry, New Bedford.
Fall River District, Bernard J. McDonald III, Fall River.
Assistant Registers --
Northern District, Francis J. McGuirk, Raynham.
Fall River District, John P. Collias, Fall River
County Commissioners —
Maria F. Lopes, Taunton . . . . Term expires January, 1999.
Christopher J. Saunders, New Bedford . . Term expires January, 2001.
Arthur R. Machado, Fall River . . . . Term expires January, 2001.

DUKES COUNTY — INCORPORATED 1695.
Shire Town, Edgartown.

Register of Probate and Family Court — Elizabeth J. Herrmann,
Edgartown.
Sheriff — Christopher S. Look, Jr., Edgartown.

Clerk of Courts — Joseph E. Sollitto, Jr., Chilmark.

County Treasurer — Noreen Mavro Flanders, Tisbury.

Register of Deeds — Diane E. Powers, West Tisbury.
Assistant Register — Debra Levesque, Tisbury.

Executive Board —

John S. Alley, West Tisbury	Term expires January, 1999.
Daniel Flynn, Oak Bluffs	Term expires January, 1999.
Elizabeth S. Talbot, Oak Bluffs	Term expires January, 1999.
Randall F. Vega, Edgartown	Term expires January, 1999.
Leonard Jason, Jr., Chilmark	Term expires January, 2001.
Linda B. Sibley, West Tisbury	Term expires January, 2001.
Timothy Carroll, Chilmark	Term expires January, 2001.

ESSEX COUNTY — INCORPORATED 1643.
Shire Towns, Salem, Lawrence and Newburyport.

Register of Probate and Family Court — Pamela Casey O'Brien, Saugus.
First Assistant Register — Mary T. Defrancisco, Andover.
Assistant Registers —
Ralph E. Fink, Jr., North Andover.
Julie Stiles Matuschak, Marblehead.
Kim J. Wright, Lawrence.

Sheriff — Frank G. Cousins, Jr., Newburyport.

Clerk of Courts — James Dennis Leary, Peabody.
First Assistant Clerk — Robert P. Murphy, Peabody.
Assistant Clerks —
Arthur V. Kelleher, Jr., Peabody.
JoDee Sylvester Doyle, Newburyport.
Judith Brennan, Georgetown.
Elaine J. Nally, Peabody.
John M. Raftery, Lynn.
Kevin Jones, Danvers.
James E. Clancy, Lynn.
John P. Greenler, Groveland.
Edward D. Sullivan, Haverhill.

County Treasurer -- Timothy A. Bassett, Marblehead.

Register of Deeds —
Northern District, Thomas J. Burke, Methuen.
Southern District, John L. O'Brien, Jr., Lynn.

Assistant Registers —
Northern District, David J. Burke, Methuen
.Southern District:
   First Assistant, Michael T. Miles, Lynn.
   Second Assistant, Robin A. Harvey, Salem.

County Commissioners —
Christopher T. Casey, Lynn .... Term expires January, 1999.
John V. O'Brien, Beverly .... Term expires January, 2001.
Marguerite P. Kane, Lawrence .... Term expires January, 2001.

FRANKLIN COUNTY — INCORPORATED 1811.
Shire Town, Greenfield.

Register of Probate and Family Court — John A. Barrett, Greenfield.
   Assistant Register — Stephen A. Rainaud, South Hadley.

Sheriff — Frederick B. Macdonald, Deerfield.

Clerk of Courts — Doris G. Doyle, Greenfield.
   Assistant Clerk — Eve M. Blakeslee, Charlemont.

*County Treasurer** — Carolyn Olsen, Erving.

Register of Deeds — H. Peter Wood, Greenfield.
   Assistant Register — Susanne Wolfram, Greenfield.

County Commissioners —
Mary L. Forbes, Greenfield .... Term expires January, 1999.
Daniel Hammock, Erving .... Term expires January, 2001.
John Stobierski, South Deerfield ...... Term expires January, 2001.

*Under the provisions of Chapter 12 of the Acts of 1995, the Treasurer of the county of Franklin is an appointive position.

HAMPDEN COUNTY — INCORPORATED 1812.
Shire Town, Springfield.

Register of Probate and Family Court — Thomas P. Moriarty, Jr., Wilbraham.
   Assistant Registers —
   Charles T. Eliopoulos, Springfield.
   Arlene Meregian, Wilbraham.
   Lawrence R. Sisitsky, Longmeadow.
   Geraldine A. Twining, Springfield.

Sheriff — Michael J. Ashe, Jr., Springfield.

Clerk of Courts — Marie G. Mazza, Springfield.
Assistant Clerks —
  Kathleen M. McGreal, Springfield.
  Elizabeth R. Jangrow, East Longmeadow.
  William L. Eason, Springfield.
  Terrence Ginley, Holyoke.
  John Fitzgerald, Springfield.
  Shirley Hiter, Springfield.
  Laura Gentile, Springfield.

County Treasurer — Rose Marie Coughlin, Springfield.

Register of Deeds — Donald E. Ashe, Springfield.
Assistant Registers.
  Kelly Kelly, Westfield.
  Maureen Moriarty, Springfield.

County Commissioners —
  Leonard J. Collamore, Springfield . . . . . . Term expires January, 1999.
  Abraham Kasparian, Agawam . . . . Term expires January, 2001.
  Richard S. Thomas, West Springfield . . . Term expires January, 2001.

HAMPSHIRE COUNTY — INCORPORATED 1662.
Shire Town, Northampton.

Register of Probate and Family Court — Robert F. Czelusniak,
  Northampton.
First Assistant Register — Mary Lynn Carroll, Hatfield.
Second Assistant Register — Kathleen T. Dean, Easthampton.

Sheriff — Robert J. Garvey, Amherst.

Clerk of Courts — Harry J. Jekanowski, Jr., Hadley.
Assistant Clerk — Nancy A. Foley, Northampton.

County Treasurer — Harold T. Chadwick, Hadley.

Register of Deeds — Marianne L. Donohue, Florence.
Assistant Register --- Patricia Plaza, Florence.

Executive Board —
  Bernard R. Kubiak, Belchertown . . . . Term expires May, 1997.
  Marilyn M. Bigelow, Pelham . . . . Term expires May, 1997.
  Sean M. Barry, Hatfield . . . . Term expires May, 1997.
  Vincent J. O'Connor, Amherst . . . . Term expires May, 1997.
  Joseph A. Wilhelm III, Northampton . Term expires December, 1997.

MIDDLESEX COUNTY — INCORPORATED 1643.
Shire Towns, Cambridge (East) and Lowell.

Register of Probate and Family Court — Robert A. Antonelli. Woburn.
First Assistant — Marie A. Gardin, Arlington.
Assistants —
Veronica Crowley, Dedham.
Edward F. Donnelly, Jr., Maynard.
Arthur W. Havey, Boxford.
James J. Hurley. Melrose.
Irene M. Thomas, Arlington.

Sheriff — James V. DiPaola, Malden.

Clerk/Magistrate of Courts — Edward J. Sullivan. Cambridge.
First Assistant Clerk Magistrate — Whitney J. Brown, Esq., Reading.
Second Assistant Clerk/Magistrate — James J. Lynch III, Medford.
Assistants —
John A. Drohan. Belmont.
Austin Parsons, West Roxbury.
Jane M. Haviland. Stoneham.
Michael H. Powers, Holliston, Magistrate.
Wayne Emerson, Cambridge.
George M. Loiacono, Revere.
Constance A. Carney, Cambridge.
Robert McDade, Watertown.
John E. Dunn, Jr., Watertown.
Leona Kusmirek, Watertown.
Arthur DeGuglielmo, Peabody.
David J. Quinn, Medford.
Michael M. Brennan, Arlington. Magistrate.
David N. Barry, Cambridge.
Daniel H. Doherty. Melrose.
Brian F. Burke, Medford.
Lucille M. Pasquale, Medford, Magistrate,
Terence O'Reilly, Watertown.
David Arsenault, Somerville (Temporary).

County Treasurer — James E. Fahey, Jr., Watertown.

Register of Deeds —
Northern District, Richard P. Howe, Jr., Lowell.
Southern District, Eugene C. Brune, Somerville.

Assistant Registers —
Southern District, Michael J. Ring, Andover.
John Allen MacRae, Littleton.

Northern District, Anthony Accardi, Jr., Tewksbury.

County Commissioners —
Francis X. Flaherty, Arlington .... Term expires January, 1999.
Thomas J. Larkin, Bedford .... Term expires January, 2001.
Edward J. Sullivan. Cambridge .... Term expires January, 2001.

NANTUCKET COUNTY — INCORPORATED 1671.
Shire Town, Nantucket.

Register of Probate and Family Court — Sylvia D. Howard, Nantucket.

Sheriff — Harry E. Clute, Nantucket.

Clerk of Courts — Patricia R. Church, Nantucket.

County Treasurer — Jeffrey Cannon, Nantucket.

Register of Deeds — Sandra M. Chadwick, Nantucket.
Assistant Register — Joanne L. Kelly, Nantucket.

Executive Board —
Charles J. Gardner, Nantucket .... Term expires April, 1997.
Arthur L. Desrocher, Nantucket .... Term expires April, 1998.
Pamela Killen, Nantucket .... Term expires April, 1998.
Vincent M. Vacca. Nantucket .... Term expires April, 1999.
Timothy Soverino, Nantucket .... Term expires April, 1999.

NORFOLK COUNTY — INCORPORATED 1793.
Shire Town. Dedham.

Register of Probate and Family Court — Thomas Patrick Hughes,
Quincy.
Assistant Registers —
Michael C. Stevens, Dedham.
John H. Cross, Needham.
John B. Jenney, Wayland.
Judith A. Murray, Dedham.
Helene C. Pike, Walpole.
Richard P. Schmidt, Weymouth.

Sheriff — John V. Flood, Canton.

Clerk of Courts — Nicholas Barbadoro, Braintree.
First Assistant, Mary K. Hickey, Norwood.

Assistant Clerks —
Nancy J. Delaney, Norwell
Michael T. Hulak, Hanson..
James M. McDermott, Blackstone.
Edward W. Sheehan, Avon.
Walter F. Timilty, Milton
Janice C. Uguccioni, Dedham.

County Treasurer — Timothy Cahill, Quincy.

Register of Deeds –– Barry T. Hannon, Braintree.
 First Assistant Register — Richard F. Kennedy, Jr., Wrentham.
 Second Assistant Register — Chester E. Svenson, Jr., Foxborough.
 Technical Advisor — John R. Curran, Quincy.

County Commissioners —
 Peter Collins, Quincy . . . . Term expires January, 1999.
 William P. O'Donnell, Norwood . . . . . . Term expires January, 2001.
 John M. Gillis, Quincy . . . . Term expires January, 2001.

PLYMOUTH COUNTY — INCORPORATED 1685.
Shire Town, Plymouth.

Register of Probate and Family Court — John J. Daley, Bridgewater.

Sheriff — Peter Forman, Plymouth.

Clerk of Courts — Francis R. Powers, Scituate.
 First Assistant Clerk — Clare P. Sheehan, Scituate.
 Assistant Clerks —
 Joseph M. Walsh, Boston.
 John B. Deady, Dedham.
 David M. Biggs, Mansfield.
 Leo P. Foley, Franklin.
 Brendan P. Sullivan, Quincy.
 John C. Barr, Plymouth.

County Treasurer — John F. McLellan, Abington.

Register of Deeds — John D. Riordan, Abington.

County Commissioners —
 Robert J. Stone, Whitman . . . . Term expires January, 1999.
 Peter B. Asiaf, Jr., Brockton . . . . Term expires January, 2001.
 Joseph F. McDonough, Scituate . . . . Term expires January, 2001.

SUFFOLK COUNTY — Incorporated 1643.
Shire Town, Boston.

Register of Probate and Family Court — Richard P. Ianella, Boston.
  First Assistant -- John C. Harney, Canton.
  Assistant Registers —
    James E. Collins, Braintree.
    Dorothy M. Gibson, Boston.
    John J. Scully, Jr., Boston.
    Kathleen G. Kavey, Waltham.
    Angela M. Syrbick, Boston.
  Deputy Assistant Registers—
    Edward F. Conley, Winthrop.
    Roseanne Lagoria, Stoneham.
    Robert A. Reveliotis, West Bridgewater.
    James J. Twomey, Malden.

Sheriff — Robert C. Rufo, Boston.

*Clerk of Supreme Judicial Court*** — Maura S. Doyle, Boston.
  *First Assistant Clerk of Supreme Judicial Court*** — Lillian
    Andruszkiewicz, Melrose.
  Second Assistant Clerk — George E. Slyva, Milton.
  Third Assistant Clerk — Francis V. Kenneally, Boston.

*Clerk of Court Magistrate for the Superior Court Department
  of the Trial Court for Civil Business* —
    Michael Joseph Donovan, Boston.
  First Assistant Clerk Magistrate — (vacant).
  First Assistant Clerk Magistrate for Equitable Remedies —
    John J. Lynch, Boston.
  Second Assistant Clerk — (vacant).

Assistant Clerk Magistrate for Caseflow Management — John Peter
  Connolly, Milton.

Assistant Clerks —
  Helen M. Foley-Bousquet, Southborough.
  Daniel L. Dailey, Braintree.
  Stephen W. Donovan, Medford.
  Francis T. Foley, Braintree.
  James P. Kelly, Canton..
  James J. O'Reilly, Wellesley.
  Jane M. Mahon, Milton.

** For the County.

Anna K. Flaherty, South Boston..
John F. Reveliotis, Charlestown.
Elizabeth A. Moore, Milton.
Martin J. Conley, Stoneham.
Michael W. Neighbors, Roxbury.
Catherine G. DeSimone, West Roxbury.
Three vacancies.

Clerk of Court/Magistrate for the Superior Court Department of the Trial Court for Criminal Business — John A. Nucci, East Boston.
Assistant Clerks —
Frank R. Barbour, Stoughton.
Marybeth Brady, Braintree.
James T. Flanagan, Sharon.
Thomas M. Ford, Buzzards Bay.
Benjamin F. Forde, Jr., Scituate.
Richard A. Hannaway, Stoughton.
Donna M. Harvey, Dorchester.
Irwin R. Macey, Lexington.
William D. Manning, Jr.
Paul D. Nagle, Braintree.
James M. Pardi, Revere.
Richard T. Parsons, Duxbury.
John R. Powers, Weymouth.
Diana M. Prift, Jamaica Plain.
Paula A. Sordillo, Medford.
Robin E. Vaughan, Boston.
Gary D. Wilson, Norwood.
William K. Walsh, Norwood.

County Treasurer§ — John C. Simmons, Boston.

Register of Deeds — Paul R. Tierney, Esq., Hyde Park.
Assistant Registers —
James C. Doyle, Jr., Esq., Arlington.
Joseph Ciardi, Esq., Hyde Park.
Ronald Itri, Esq., Roslindale.
Michael T. O'Brien, Esq., South Boston.

§ Treasurer for the city of Boston.
NOTE: — The Mayor and the City Council of Boston, the Board of Aldermen of Chelsea and the City Council of Revere, in their respective cities and the Selectmen of Winthrop, in said town, have most of the powers and duties of County Commissioners.

WORCESTER COUNTY — Incorporated 1731.
Shire Towns, Worcester and Fitchburg.

Register of Probate and Family Court — Leonard P. Flynn,
Shrewsbury.
First Assistant — Robert E. Hanlon, Auburn.
Assistant Registers —
Maureen A. Metterville, Worcester.
Theresa Butkiewicz, Worcester.
Ronald W. King, Worcester.
Robert T. Hackenson, Dudley.

Sheriff — John M. Flynn, West Boylston.

Clerk of Courts — Loring P. Lamoureux, Worcester.
First Assistant — Leonard F. Tomaiolo, Holden.
Assistants —
John F. O'Connor, Worcester.
Thomas F. Gallen, Worcester.
Philip T. Breen, Sutton.
Kevin M. Golden, Worcester.
Alexander Rodriguez, III, Southbridge.
Kathleen F. Stukowski, Rutland.
Karen A. Zona, Shrewsbury.
Eugene G. Sullivan, Holden.
Corinne L. McDermott, Leominster.
Denise D. Foley, Worcester.
Mary F. Stratford, Worcester.

County Treasurer — Michael J. Donoghue, Worcester.

Register of Deeds —
Northern District, John B. McLaughlin, Leominster.
Worcester District, Anthony J. Vigliotti, Worcester.

Assistant Register — Northern District, Ruth Piermarini, Leominster.
First Assistant Register — Worcester District, John J. Mitchell,
Clinton.

County Commissioners —
John C. Burke, Fitchburg . . . . Term expires January, 1999.
John J. Finnegan, Worcester . . . . Term expires January, 2001.
Peter A. Amorello, Sutton . . . . Term expires January, 2001.

MEDICAL EXAMINERS
[See Chapter 38 of the General Laws.]

Office of the Chief Medical Examiner
Headquarters
720 Albany Street
Boston, MA 02118
(617) 267-6767
(800) 962-7877 (within Massachusetts)

Richard J. Evans, M.D., Chief Medical Examiner
Stanton C. Kessler, M.D., Associate Chief Medical Examiner for
     Headquarters
Gerald Feigin, M.D., Associate Chief Medical Examiner
Leonard Atkins, M.D., Forensic Pathologist Medical Examiner
George Kury, M.D., Medical Examiner
Antonio Boschetti, M.D., Medical Examiner

Catchment areas: Suffolk County, Norfolk County, Essex County,
     Middlesex County, parts of Worcester County including the
     city of Worcester and towns east.
District Medical Examiners may be contacted via Headquarters.

Office of the Chief Medical Examiner
Southeast Region
870 County Road
Pocasset, MA 02559
(508) 564-6371
(800) 222-5999 (within Massachusetts)

James Weiner, M.D., Associate Chief Medical Examiner
William Zane, M.D., Forensic Pathologist Medical Examiner

Catchment areas: Barnstable County, Plymouth County, Dukes County,
     Nantucket County.
District Medical Examiners may be contacted via the Southeast Regional
     Office.

Office of the Chief Medical Examiner
Western Region
1400 State Street
Springfield, MA 01109
(413) 739-0525
(800) 445-5889 (within Massachusetts)

Joann Richmond. M.D., Deputy Chief Medical Examiner
Loren J. Mednick. M.D., Forensic Pathologist/Medical Examiner

Catchment areas: Hampden County, Hampshire County, Berkshire County, Franklin County, and parts of Worcester County west of the city of Worcester.
District Medical Examiners may be contacted through their regional offices.

THE JUDICIARY
AND
DISTRICT ATTORNEYS

JUDICIARY.

*Judges of the Superior Court of Judicature of the Province of
Massachusetts Bay, from 1692 to 1775.**

CHIEF JUSTICES.

APPOINTED.		LEFT THE BENCH		DIED.
1692.	William Stoughton,	1701.	Resigned.	1701.
1701.	Wait Winthrop,	1701.	Resigned.	1717.
1702.	Isaac Addington,	1703.	Resigned.	1715.
1708.	Wait Winthrop,	1717.		1717.
1718.	Samuel Sewall,	1728.	Resigned.	1730.
1729.	Benjamin Lynde,	1745.		1745.
1745.	Paul Dudley,	1751.		1751.
1752.	Stephen Sewall,	1760.		1760.
1761.	Thomas Hutchinson,	1769.	Resigned.	1780.
1769.	Benjamin Lynde,	1771.	Resigned.	1781.
1772.	Peter Oliver,	1775.	Removed at Revolution.	1791.

JUSTICES.

1692.	Thomas Danforth,	1699.		1699.
1692.	Wait Winthrop,	1701.	Resigned.	1717.
1692.	John Richard,	1694.		1694.
1692.	Samuel Sewall,	1728.	(Appointed C. J., 1718.)	1730.
1695.	Elisha Cooke,	1702.	Removed.	1715.
1700.	John Walley,	1712.		1712.
1701.	John Saffin,	1702.	Removed.	1710.
1702.	John Hathorne,	1712.	Resigned.	1717.
1702.	John Leverett,	1708.	Resigned.	1724.
1708.	Jonathan Curwin,	1715.	Resigned.	1718.
1712.	Benjamin Lynde,	1745.	(Appointed C. J., 1729.)	1745.
1712.	Nathaniel Thomas,	1718.	Resigned.	1718.
1715.	Addington Davenport,	1736.		1736.
1718.	Paul Dudley,	1751.	(Appointed C. J., 1745.)	1751.
1718.	Edmund Quincy,	1737.		1737.
1728.	John Cushing,	1733.	Removed.	1737.
1733.	Jonathan Remington,	1745.		1745.
1736.	Richard Saltonstall,	1756.		1756.
1737.	Thomas Greaves,	1738.	Resigned.	1747.

* The judges died in office, except where otherwise stated. See "Sketches of the
Judicial History of Massachusetts," by Emory Washburn, 1840, p. 241.

APPOINTED		LEFT THE BENCH.		DIED
1739.	Stephen Sewall,	1760.	(Appointed C. J., 1752.)	1760
1745.	Nathaniel Hubbard,	1746.	Resigned.	1748
1745.	Benjamin Lynde,	1771.	(Appointed C. J., 1769.)	1781
1747.	John Cushing,	1771.	Resigned.	1778
1752.	Chambers Russell,	1766.		1766.
1756.	Peter Oliver,	1775.	(Appointed C. J., 1772.)	1791
1767.	Edmund Trowbridge,	1775.	Resigned.	1793
1771.	Foster Hutchinson,	1775.	Removed at Revolution.	1799
1772.	Nathaniel Ropes,	1774.		1774
1772.	William Cushing,	1775.	Removed at Revolution.	1810
1774.	William Browne,	1775.	Removed at Revolution.	1802

*Justices of the Superior Court of Judicature and the
Supreme Judicial Court of Massachusetts since the Revolution.
The latter was established July 3, 1782.*

CHIEF JUSTICES.

APPOINTED		LEFT THE BENCH		DIED
1775.	John Adams,	1776.	Resigned.*	1826
1777.	William Cushing,	1789.	Resigned.†	1810
1790.	Nathaniel Peaslee Sargent,	1791.		1791
1791.	Francis Dana,	1806.	Resigned.	1811
1806.	Theophilus Parsons,	1813.		1813
1814.	Samuel Sewall,	1814.		1814
1814.	Isaac Parker,	1830.		1830
1830.	Lemuel Shaw,	1860.	Resigned.	1861
1860.	George Tyler Bigelow,	1868.	Resigned.	1878
1868.	Reuben Atwater Chapman,	1873.		1873
1873.	Horace Gray,‡	1882.		1902
1882.	Marcus Morton,	1890.	Resigned.	1891
1890.	Walbridge Abner Field,	1899.		1899
1899.	Oliver Wendell Holmes,§	1902.		1935
1902.	Marcus Perrin Knowlton,	1911.	Resigned.	1918
1911.	Arthur Prentice Rugg,	1938.		1938

* Mr. Adams never took his seat on the bench.
† Chief Justice Cushing resigned on being appointed one of the Justices of the Supreme Court of the United States.
‡ Chief Justice Gray vacated his office by accepting an appointment as one of the Justices of the Supreme Court of the United States.
§ Chief Justice Holmes vacated his office by accepting an appointment as one of the Justices of the Supreme Court of the United States.

Judiciary. 461

938.	Fred Tarbell Field,	1947.	Resigned.	1950.
947.	Stanley Elroy Qua,	1956.	Resigned.	1965.
956.	Raymond Sanger Wilkins, ..	1970.	Resigned.	1971.
970.	G. Joseph Tauro,	1976.	Retired.	1994.
976.	Edward F. Hennessey,	1989.	Retired.	
989.	Paul J. Liacos,	1996.	Retired.	
996.	Herbert P. Wilkins.			

JUSTICES.

775.	William Cushing,	1789.	(Appointed C. J., 1777.)	1810.
775.	Nathaniel Peaslee Sargent, ..	1791.	(Appointed C. J., 1790.)	1791.
775.	William Reed,	1776.	Superseded.	1780.
776.	Jedediah Foster,	1779.		1779.
776.	James Sullivan,	1782.	Resigned.	1808.
777.	David Sewall,	1789.	Resigned.*	1825.
782.	Increase Sumner,	1797.	Res. to become Gov'r.	1799.
785.	Francis Dana,	1806.	(Appointed C. J., 1791.)	1811.
790.	Robert Treat Paine,	1804.	Resigned.	1814.
790.	Nathan Cushing,	1800.	Resigned.	1812.
792.	Thomas Dawes,	1802.	Resigned.	1825.
797.	Theophilus Bradbury,	1803.	Removed.†	1803.
800.	Samuel Sewall,	1814.	(Appointed C. J., 1814.)	1814.
801.	Simeon Strong,	1805.		1805.
801.	George Thacher,	1824.	Resigned.	1824.
802.	Theodore Sedgwick,	1813.		1813.
806.	Isaac Parker,	1830.	(Appointed C. J., 1814.)	1830.
813.	Charles Jackson,	1823.	Resigned.	1855.
814.	Daniel Dewey,	1815.		1815.
814.	Samuel Putnam,	1842.	Resigned.	1853.
815.	Samuel Sumner Wilde,	1850.	Resigned.	1855.
824.	Levi Lincoln,	1825.	Res. to become Gov'r.	1868.
825.	Marcus Morton,	1840.	Res. to become Gov'r.	1864.
837.	Charles Augustus Dewey, ..	1866.		1866.
842.	Samuel Hubbard,	1847.		1847.
848.	Charles Edward Forbes, ...	1848.	Resigned.	1881.
848.	Theron Metcalf,	1865.	Resigned.	1875.
848.	Richard Fletcher,	1853.	Resigned.	1869.
850.	George Tyler Bigelow,	1868.	(Appointed C. J., 1860.)	1878.
852.	Caleb Cushing,	1853.	Resigned.‡	1879.

* Mr. Justice Sewall resigned on being appointed Judge of the United States District ourt for the District of Maine.
† Mr. Justice Bradbury was removed on account of physical disability.
‡ Mr. Justice Cushing resigned on being appointed to the office of Attorney-General of e United States.

APPOINTED		LEFT THE BENCH		DIED.
1853.	Benj. Franklin Thomas, ...	1859.	Resigned.	1878.
1853.	Pliny Merrick, ...	1864.	Resigned.	1867.
1859.	Ebenezer Rockwood Hoar, .	1869.	Resigned.*	1895.
1860.	Reuben Atwater Chapman, .	1873.	(Appointed C. J., 1868.)	1873.
1864.	Horace Gray, Jr., ...	1882.	(Appointed C. J., 1873.)	1902.
1865.	James Denison Colt, ...	1866.	Resigned.	1881.
1866.	Dwight Foster, ...	1869.	Resigned.	1884.
1866.	John Wells, ...	1875.		1875.
1868.	James Denison Colt, ...	1881.		1881.
1869.	Seth Ames, ...	1881.	Resigned.	1881.
1869.	Marcus Morton, ...	1890.	(Appointed C. J., 1882.)	1891.
1873.	Wm. Crowninshield Endicott,	1882.	Resigned.	1900.
1873.	Charles Devens, Jr., ...	1877.	Resigned.†	1891.
1875.	Otis Phillips Lord, ...	1882.	Resigned.	1884.
1877.	Augustus Lord Soule, ...	1881.	Resigned.	1887.
1881.	Walbridge Abner Field, ...	1890.	(Appointed C. J., 1890.)	1899.
1881.	Charles Devens,†	1891.		1891.
1881.	William Allen, ...	1891.		1891.
1882.	Charles Allen, ...	1898.	Resigned.	1913.
1882.	Waldo Colburn, ...	1885.		1885.
1882.	Oliver Wendell Holmes, ...	1902.	(Appointed C. J., 1899.)	1935.
1885.	William Sewall Gardner, ...	1887.	Resigned.	1888.
1887.	Marcus Perrin Knowlton, ...	1911.	(Appointed C. J., 1902.)	1918.
1890.	James Madison Morton, ...	1913.	Resigned.	1923.
1891.	John Lathrop, ...	1906.	Resigned.	1910.
1891.	James Madison Barker, ...	1905.		1905.
1898.	John Wilkes Hammond, ...	1914.	Resigned.	1922.
1899.	William Caleb Loring, ...	1919.	Resigned.	1930.
1902.	Henry King Braley, ...	1929.		1929.
1905.	Henry Newton Sheldon, ...	1915.	Resigned.	1925.
1906.	Arthur Prentice Rugg, ...	1938.	(Appointed C. J., 1911.)	1938.
1911.	Charles Ambrose DeCourcy,	1924.		1924.
1913.	John Crawford Crosby, ...	1937.		1943.
1914.	Edward Peter Pierce, ...	1937.		1938.
1915.	James Bernard Carroll, ...	1932.		1932.
1919.	Charles Francis Jenney, ...	1923.		1923.
1923.	William Cushing Wait, ...	1934.		1935.
1924.	George Augustus Sanderson,	1932.		1932.

* Mr. Justice Hoar resigned on being appointed to the office of Attorney-General of the United States.

† Mr. Justice Devens resigned on being appointed to the office of Attorney-General of the United States, and was reappointed to the Supreme Bench in 1881.

APPOINTED.		LEFT THE BENCH.		DIED.
1929.	Fred Tarbell Field, ...	1947.	(Appointed C. J., 1938.)	1950.
1932.	Charles Henry Donahue, . . .	1944.	Resigned.	1952.
1932.	Henry Tilton Lummus, ...	1955.	Resigned.	1960.
1934.	Stanley Elroy Qua, ...	1956.	(Appointed C. J., 1947.)	1965.
1937.	Arthur Walter Dolan, ...	1949.	Resigned.	1949.
1937.	Louis Sherburne Cox, ...	1944.	Retired.	1961.
1938.	James Joseph Ronan, ...	1959.	Retired.	1960.
1944.	Raymond Sanger Wilkins, . .	1970.	(Appointed C. J., 1956.)	1971.
1944.	John Varnum Spalding, ...	1971.	Retired.	1981.
1947.	Harold Putnam Williams, . . .	1962.	Resigned.	1965.
1949.	Edward A. Counihan, Jr., . . .	1960.	Retired.	1961.
1955.	Arthur E. Whittemore, ...	1969.		1969.
1956.	R. Ammi Cutter, ...	1972.	Retired.	1993.
1960.	Paul G. Kirk, ...	1971.	Retired.	1981.
1961.	Jacob J. Spiegel, ...	1972.		
1962.	Paul Cashman Reardon, ...	1977.	Retired.	1988.
1969.	Francis J. Quirico, ...	1981.	Retired.	
1970.	G. Joseph Tauro, ...	1976.	(Appointed C. J., 1970.)	1994.
1971.	Robert Braucher, ...	1981.		1981.
1971.	Edward F. Hennessey, ...	1989.	(Appointed C. J., 1976.)	
1972.	Benjamin Kaplan, ...	1981.	Retired.	
1972.	Herbert P. Wilkins, ...		(Appointed C. J., 1996.)	
1976.	Paul J. Liacos, ...	1996.	(Appointed C. J., 1989.)	
1977.	Ruth I. Abrams.			
1981.	Joseph R. Nolan, ...	1995.	Retired.	
1981.	Neil L. Lynch.			
1981.	Francis P. O'Connor.			
1989.	John M. Greaney.			
1995.	Charles Fried.			
1996.	Margaret H. Marshall.			

Justices of the Appeals Court since its Establishment in 1972.

CHIEF JUSTICES.

APPOINTED.		LEFT THE BENCH.		DIED.
1972.	Allan M. Hale, ...	1984.	Retired.	
1984.	John M. Greaney, ...	1989.	(App'd to Sup. Jud. Ct., 1989.)	
1989.	Joseph P. Warner.			

ASSOCIATE JUSTICES.

APPOINTED		LEFT THE BENCH		DIED
1972.	David A. Rose.	1976.	Retired.	1995
1972.	Edmund V. Keville.	1979.	Retired.	
1972.	Reuben Goodman.	1982.		1982
1972.	Donald R. Grant.	1988.	Retired.	
1972.	Christopher J. Armstrong.			
1976.	Frederick L. Brown.			
1978.	John M. Greaney.	1989.	(App'd to Sup. Jud. Ct., 1989.)	
1978.	Charlotte Anne Peretta.			
1979.	Raya S. Dreben.			
1979.	Rudolph Kass.			
1980.	Joseph R. Nolan.	1981.	(App'd to Sup. Jud. Ct., 1981.)	
1981.	Kent B. Smith.			
1982.	Joseph P. Warner.		(Appointed C. J., 1989.)	
1984	Edith W. Fine.	1995.	Retired.	1995
1989.	George Jacobs.			
1990.	Gerald Gillerman.	1994.	Retired.	
1990.	Elizabeth A. Porada.			
1990.	Roderick L. Ireland.			
1990.	Mel L. Greenberg.			
1990.	Kenneth Laurence.			
1995.	J. Harold Flannery.			
1995.	Barbara A. Lenk.			

Justices of the Court of Common Pleas, from its Establishment in 1820 until its Abolition in 1859.

CHIEF JUSTICES.

APPOINTED		LEFT THE BENCH		DIED
1820.	Artemas Ward.	1839.	Resigned.	1847
1839.	John Mason Williams.	1844.	Resigned.	1868
1844.	Daniel Wells.	1854.		1854
1854.	Edward Mellen.	1859.		1875

JUSTICES.

1820.	Solomon Strong.	1842.	Resigned.	1850
1820.	John Mason Williams.	1844.	(Appointed C. J., 1839.)	1868
1820.	Samuel Howe.	1828.		1828
1828.	David Cummins.	1844.	Resigned.	1855
1839.	Charles Henry Warren.	1844.	Resigned.	1874

APPOINTED.		LEFT THE BENCH.		DIED.
1842.	Charles Allen, ...	1844.	Resigned.	1869.
1843.	Pliny Merrick, ...	1848.	Resigned.	1867.
1844.	Joshua Holyoke Ward, ...	1848.		1848.
1844.	Emory Washburn, ...	1847.	Resigned.	1877.
1844.	Luther Stearns Cushing, ...	1848.	Resigned.	1856.
1845.	Harrison Gray Otis Colby, . . .	1847.	Resigned.	1853.
1847.	Charles Edward Forbes, ...	1848.	App'd to Sup. Jud. Ct.	1881.
1847.	Edward Mellen, ...	1859.	(Appointed C. J., 1854.)	1875.
1848.	George Tyler Bigelow, ...	1850.	App'd to Sup. Jud. Ct.	1878.
1848.	Jonathan Cogswell Perkins, . .	1859.		1877.
1848.	Horatio Byington, ...	1856.		1856.
1848.	Thomas Hopkinson, ...	1849.	Resigned.	1856.
1849.	Ebenezer Rockwood Hoar, .	1855.	Resigned.	1895.
1850.	Pliny Merrick, ...	1853.	App'd to Sup. Jud. Ct.	1867.
1851.	Henry Walker Bishop, ...	1859.		1871.
1853.	George Nixon Briggs, ...	1859.		1861.
1854.	George Partridge Sanger, . . .	1859.		1890.
1855.	Henry Morris, ...	1859.		1888.
1856.	David Aiken, ...	1859.		1895.

Justices of the Superior Court for the County of Suffolk from its Establishment in 1855 until its Abolition in 1859.

CHIEF JUSTICES.

APPOINTED.		LEFT THE BENCH.	DIED.
1855.	Albert Hobart Nelson, ...	1857.	1858.
1858.	Charles Allen,*	1859.	1869.

JUSTICES.

1855.	Josiah Gardner Abbot, ...	1858.	1891.
1855.	Charles Phelps Huntington, . .	1859.	1868.
1855.	Stephen Gordon Nash, ...	1859.	1894.
1858.	Marcus Morton,†	1859.	1891.

* In 1859 Charles Allen became the first Chief Justice of the Superior Court of the Commonwealth.

† In 1859 Marcus Morton became one of the Associate Justices of the Superior Court of the Commonwealth.

Justices of the Superior Court since its Establishment in 1859.

CHIEF JUSTICES.

APPOINTED		LEFT THE BENCH		DIED
1859.	Charles Allen,	1867.	Resigned.	1869.
1867.	Seth Ames,	1869.	App'd to Sup. Jud. Ct.	1881.
1869.	Lincoln Flagg Brigham,	1890.	Resigned.	1895.
1890.	Albert Mason,	1905.		1905.
1905.	John Adams Aiken,	1922.	Resigned.	1927.
1922.	Walter Perley Hall,	1937.	Resigned.	1942.
1937.	John Patrick Higgins,	1955.		1955.
1955.	Paul Cashman Reardon,	1962.	App'd to Sup. Jud. Ct.	1988.
1962.	G. Joseph Tauro,	1970.	App'd C. J., Sup. Jud. Ct.	1994.
1970.	Walter H. McLaughlin,*	1977.	Retired.	
1977.	Robert M. Bonin,	1978.	Resigned.	
1978.	James P. Lynch, Jr.,**	1983.		
1983.	Thomas R. Morse, Jr.,	1988.	Retired.	
1988.	Robert L. Steadman,	1993.	Retired.	
1993.	John J. Irwin, Jr.,	1994.	App'd. C. A. J. Trial Court.	
1994.	Robert A. Mulligan.			

JUSTICES.

APPOINTED		LEFT THE BENCH		DIED
1859.	Julius Rockwell,	1886.	Resigned.	1888.
1859.	Otis Phillips Lord,	1875.	App'd to Sup. Jud. Ct.	1884.
1859.	Marcus Morton,	1869.	App'd to Sup. Jud. Ct.	1891.
1859.	Seth Ames,	1869.	(Appointed C. J., 1867.)	1881.
1859.	Ezra Wilkinson,	1882.		1882.
1859.	Henry Vose,	1869.		1869.
1859.	Thomas Russell,	1867.	Resigned.	1887.
1859.	John Phelps Putnam,	1882.		1882.
1859.	Lincoln Flagg Brigham,	1890.	(Appointed C. J., 1869.)	1895.
1867.	Chester Isham Reed,	1871.	Resigned.	1873.
1867.	Charles Devens, Jr.,	1873.	App'd to Sup. Jud. Ct.	1891.
1869.	Henry Austin Scudder,	1872.	Resigned.	1895.
1869.	Francis Henshaw Dewey,	1881.	Resigned.	1887.
1869.	Robert Carter Pitman,	1891.		1891.
1871.	John William Bacon,	1888.		1888.

* In 1977 Chief Justice Walter H. McLaughlin was compelled to retire once he reached the mandatory retirement age of 70.

** Under the provisions of Chapter 478 of the Acts of 1978 (Judicial Reform Act) the term of the office for the Chief Justice of the Superior Court is five years. After a term has been completed, the former chief justice reverts to being an associate justice of the Superior Court.

APPOINTED.		LEFT THE BENCH.		DIED.
1871.	William Allen, ...	1881.	App'd to Sup. Jud. Ct.	1891.
1873.	Peleg Emory Aldrich, ...	1895.		1895.
1875.	Waldo Colburn, ...	1882.	App'd to Sup. Jud. Ct.	1885.
1875.	William Sewall Gardner, ...	1885.	App'd to Sup. Jud. Ct.	1888.
1881.	Hamilton Barclay Staples, . . .	1891.		1891.
1881.	Marcus Perrin Knowlton, . . .	1887.	App'd to Sup. Jud. Ct.	1918.
1882.	Caleb Blodgett, ...	1900.	Resigned.	1901.
1882.	Albert Mason, ...	1905.	(Appointed C. J., 1890.)	1905.
1882.	James Madison Barker, ...	1891.	App'd to Sup. Jud. Ct.	1905.
1885.	Charles Perkins Thompson, . .	1894.		1894.
1886.	John Wilkes Hammond, ...	1898.	App'd to Sup. Jud. Ct.	1922.
1886.	Justin Dewey, ...	1900.		1900.
1887.	Edgar Jay Sherman, ...	1911.	Retired.	1914.
1888.	John Lathrop, ...	1891.	App'd to Sup. Jud. Ct.	1910.
1888.	James Robert Dunbar, ...	1898.	Resigned.	1915.
1888.	Robert Roberts Bishop, ...	1909.		1909.
1890.	Daniel Webster Bond, ...	1911.		1911.
1891.	Henry King Braley, ...	1902.	App'd to Sup. Jud. Ct.	1929.
1891.	John Hopkins, ...	1902.		1902.
1891.	Elisha Burr Maynard, ...	1906.		1906.
1891.	Franklin Goodridge Fessenden,	1922.	Resigned.	1931.
1892.	John William Corcoran, ...	1893.	Resigned.	1904.
1892.	James Bailey Richardson, . .	1911.		1911.
1893.	Charles Sumner Lilley, ...	1900.	Resigned.	1931.
1894.	Henry Newton Sheldon, ...	1905.	App'd to Sup. Jud. Ct.	1925.
1895.	Francis Almon Gaskill, ...	1909.		1909.
1896.	John Henry Hardy, ...	1917.		1917.
1896.	Henry Wardwell, ...	1898.	Resigned.	1922.
1898.	William Burnham Stevens, .	1917.	Resigned.	1931.
1898.	Charles Upham Bell, ...	1917.	Resigned.	1922.
1898.	John Adams Aiken, ...	1922.	(Appointed C. J., 1905.)	1927.
1900.	Frederick Lawton, ...	1926.	Resigned.	1941.
1900.	Edward Peter Pierce, ...	1914.	App'd to Sup. Jud. Ct.	1938.
1900.	Jabez Fox, ...	1921.	Retired.	1923.
1902.	Charles Ambrose DeCourcy,	1911.	App'd to Sup. Jud. Ct.	1924.
1902.	Robert Orr Harris, ...	1911.	Resigned.	1926.
1902.	Lemuel LeBaron Holmes, . .	1907.		1907.
1902.	William Cushing Wait, ...	1923.	App'd to Sup. Jud. Ct.	1935.
1902.	William Schofield, ...	1911.	Resigned.	1912.
1903.	Lloyd Everett White, ...	1921.	Resigned.	1921.
1903.	Loranus Eaton Hitchcock, . .	1920.		1920.
1905.	John Crawford Crosby, ...	1913.	App'd to Sup. Jud. Ct.	1943.

468   *Judiciary.*

APPOINTED.	LEFT THE BENCH.		DIED.
1925.	Franklin Freeman, ...	1926.	1926.
1925.	Wilford Drury Gray, ...	1939.	1939.
1926.	David Francis Dillon, ...	1948.	1948.
1926.	Harold Putnam Williams. ...	1947.	App'd to Sup. Jud. Ct.	1965.
1928.	Walter Leo Collins.	1959.	Resigned.	1975.
1928.	Daniel Theodore O'Connell.	1958.	Resigned.	1958.
1929.	Thomas Jasper Hammond, ..	1946.	1946.
1929.	John Mellen Gibbs, ...	1937.	1937.
1929.	Raoul Henri Beaudreau, ...	1956.	Resigned.	1956.
1929.	Edward Francis Hanify, ...	1954.	1954.
1930.	Abraham Edward Pinanski, .	1949.	1949.
1931.	James Corcoran Donnelly, ..	1952.	1952.
1931.	John Joseph Burns, ...	1934.	Resigned.	1957.
1932.	Frank Joseph Donahue, ...	1973.	Retired.	1979.
1932.	Lewis Goldberg, ...	1973.	Retired.	1974.
1933.	John Edward Swift, ...	1967.	1967.
1934.	Vincent Brogna, ...	1960.	1960.
1934.	George Francis Leary, ...	1954.	1954.
1935.	Joseph Alphonsus Sheehan, .	1942.	1942.
1935.	Thomas Henry Dowd, ...	1958.	Resigned.	1958.
1935.	Joshua Arthur Baker, ...	1951.	1951.
1937.	Joseph Leo Hurley, ...	1956.	1956.
1937.	Francis Joseph Good, ...	1958.	1958.
1937.	Jesse Whitman Morton, ...	1962.	1962.
1937.	William Clement Giles, ...	1956.	Retired.	1959.
1937.	Paul Grattan Kirk, ...	1960.	App'd to Sup. Jud. Ct.	1981.
1939.	Allan Gordon Buttrick, ...	1951.	Retired.	1954.
1939.	Felix Forte, ...	1973.	Retired.	1975.
1940.	Joseph Everett Warner, ...	1958.	1958.
1942.	John Varnum Spalding, ...	1944.	App'd to Sup. Jud. Ct.	1981.
1943.	Charles Codman Cabot, ...	1947.	Resigned.	1976.
1944.	John Vincent Sullivan.	1962.	1962.
1945.	Richard M. Walsh, ...	1946.	Retired.	1952.
1946.	Eugene A. Hudson, ...	1972.	1972.
1946.	Edward J. Voke, ...	1965.	1965.
1946.	Frank J. Murray, ...	1967.	App'd U.S. Dist. Ct.	1995.
1946.	Daniel D. O'Brien, ...	1963.	1963.
1947.	Horace Tracy Cahill, ...	1973.	Retired.	1976.
1947.	Frank Edward Smith, ...	1973.	Retired.	1978.
1948.	Charles Fairhurst, ...	1973.	Retired.	1975.
1949.	Charles A. Rome, ...	1959.	1959.
1949.	David G. Nagle, ...	1960.	1960.

APPOINTED		LEFT THE BENCH		DIED
1951.	John Henry Meagher.	1978.	Retired.	
1952.	Wilfred J. Paquet.	1973.	Retired.	1987.
1952.	Edward A. Pecce.	1970.	Retired.	1973.
1954.	Edmund R. Dewing.	1965.	Retired.	1981.
1954.	Reuben L. Lurie.	1973.	Retired.	1985.
1956.	Donald M. Macaulay.	1971.	Retired.	1980.
1956.	George E. Thompson.	1973.		1973.
1956.	Francis J. Quirico,	1969.	App'd to Sup. Jud. Ct.	
1956.	Charles S. Bolster,	1966.	Retired.	
1958.	John M. Noonan,	1971.	Retired.	1975
1958.	Frank W. Tomasello.	1973.	Retired.	1986
1958.	Edward O. Gourdin.	1966.		1966
1958.	August C. Taveira,	1983.	Retired.	
1958.	John W. Coddaire, Jr.,	1975.	Retired.	1989
1958.	Stanley W. Wisnioski.	1961.		1961
1958.	James L. Vallely,	1983.	Retired.	
1958.	Edward J. DeSaulnier. Jr.,	1972.	Resigned.	1990
1958.	Robert Sullivan.	1976.		1976
1959.	Jennie Loitman Barron.	1969.		1969
1959.	Francis John Good.	1982.	Retired.	1994
1960.	Daniel J. O'Connell. Jr.	1962.	Resigned.	1977
1960.	David A. Rose.	1972.	App'd Appeals Court.	1995
1960.	Thomas J. Spring.	1974.	Retired.	1980
1960.	Vincent R. Brogna.	1982.	Retired.	
1961.	G. Joseph Tauro,	1970.	(Appointed C. J., 1962.)	1994
1962.	Francis L. Lappin,	1985.	Retired.	1993
1962.	Joseph Ford.	1984.	Retired.	
1962.	Thomas J. O'Malley.	1969.		1969
1962.	Harry Kalus,	1974.	Retired.	1980
1962.	Amedeo V. Sgarzi,	1973.	Retired.	
1962.	Robert H. Beaudreau,	1980.		1980
1962.	Henry H. Chmielinski, Jr.,	1982.	Retired.	1983
1963.	Cornelius J. Moynihan.	1975.	Retired.	1986
1963.	George P. Ponte,	1975.	Retired.	1991
1965.	Frederick S. Pillsbury,	1966.	Resigned.	
1965.	Joseph K. Collins,	1973.	Retired.	1988
1966.	Joseph S. Mitchell, Jr.,	1992.	Retired.	
1967.	Edward F. Hennessey,	1971.	App'd to Sup. Jud. Ct.	
1967.	Allan M. Hale,	1972.	App'd C. J. Appeals Court.	
1967.	Walter H. McLaughlin,	1977.	(Appointed C. J., 1970.)	
1967.	Samuel T. Tisdale,	1979.	Retired.	
1968.	James Charles Roy,	1977.	Retired.	1990
1968.	Andrew R. Linscott.	1984.	Retired.	1989

APPOINTED.		LEFT THE BENCH		DIED.
1968.	Edward H. Bennett, Jr., ...	1983.	Retired.	
1968.	Henry M. Leen, ...	1977.	Retired.	
1969.	Alan J. Dimond, ...	1986.	Retired.	
1969.	Levin H. Campbell, ...	1972.	App'd Fed. Court.	
1969.	Paul V. Rutledge, ...	1986.	Retired.	
1970.	Paul K. Connolly, ...	1976.	Retired.	
1970.	Thomas E. Dwyer.	1986.	Retired.	
1971.	John Francis Moriarty.			
1971.	Herbert F. Travers, Jr.			
1972.	Paul A. Tamburello, ...	1976.	Retired.	
1972.	John J. McNaught, ...	1979.	App'd U.S. District Ct.	
1972.	Ruth I. Abrams, ...	1977.	App'd to Sup. Jud. Ct.	
1972.	George J. Hayer, ...	1985.	Retired.	
1972.	James P. Lynch, Jr..		(Chief Justice 1978-1983.)	
1972.	Kent Benedict Smith.	1981.	App'd Appeals Ct.	
1973.	Raymond R. Cross.	1991.	Retired.	
1973.	Roger Joseph Donohue.	1994.	Retired.	
1973.	Eileen P. Griffin, ...	1986.	Retired.	
1973.	Arthur M. Mason, ...	1978.	App'd Ch. Adm. Judge-Trial Ct.	
1973.	David S. Nelson.	1979.	App'd U.S. Dist. Ct.	
1973.	Harry Zarrow, ...	1976.	Retired.	1990.
1973.	Robert J. Hallisey.	1990.	Retired.	
1973.	James P. McGuire.	1979.	Retired.	
1973.	Samuel Adams, ...	1982.	Resigned.	
1973.	John P. Sullivan.	1992.	Retired.	
1973.	Thomas R. Morse. Jr., ...	1988.	Retired. (C. J. 1983-1988.)	
1973.	John Tracy Ronan, ...	1992.	Retired.	
1974.	Francis W. Keating.	1987.		1987.
1974.	Robert S. Prince, ...	1988.	Retired.	
1976.	A. David Mazzone, ...	1978.	App'd U.S. Dist. Ct.	
1976.	John M. Greaney.	1978.	App'd App. Ct. & S.J.C.	
1976.	Francis P. O'Connor.	1981.	App'd to Sup. Jud. Ct.	
1976.	Charles R. Alberti, ...	1992.	Retired.	
1976.	John J. Irwin, Jr., ...	1994.	App'd Ch. Adm. Judge-Trial Ct.	
1976.	Paul G. Garrity, ...	1984.	Resigned.	
1976.	Gordon L. Doerfer, ...	1981.	Resigned.	
1977.	Edith W. Fine, ...	1984.	App'd Appeals Court.	1995.
1978.	William W. Simons, ...	1993.	Retired.	
1978.	William G. Young, ...	1985.	App'd U.S. Dist. Ct.	
1978.	Joseph R. Nolan, ...	1980.	App'd App. Ct. & S.J.C.	
1979.	Robert A. Barton.			
1979.	Robert V. Mulkern, ...	1972.	Retired.	
1979.	Rudolph F. Pierce, ...	1985.	Resigned.	

472 *Judiciary.*

1979.	John F. Murphy, Jr.			
1979.	James P. Donohue.			
1979.	Augustus F. Wagner, Jr., . . .	1986.	Resigned.	
1979.	Chris Byron, ...	1992.	Retired.	
1979.	Herbert Abrams, ...	1993.	Retired.	
1979.	Andrew G. Meyer, ...	1993.	Retired.	
1979.	Robert L. Steadman, ...	1996.	Retired. (C. J. 1988-1993.)	
1979.	William C. O'Neil. Jr., ...	1991.		1991.
1979.	Hiller B. Zobel.			
1979.	Elizabeth Dolan.			
1979.	Peter F. Brady.			
1979.	Richard S. Kelley	1996.	Retired.	
1979.	William K. Mone, ...	1982.		1982.
1980.	George N. Hurd. Jr., ...	1989.	Retired.	
1980.	Lawrence B. Urbano, ...	1991.	Retired.	
1980.	Walter E. Steele, ...	1996.	Retired.	
1981.	William H. Carey, ...	1996.	Retired.	
1981.	George Jacobs, ...	1989.	App'd Appeals Court.	
1982.	Elizabeth Porada, ...	1990.	App'd Appeals Court.	
1982.	Sandra L. Hamlin.			
1982.	Gerald F. O'Neill, Jr.			
1982.	James D. McDaniel, Jr.			
1982.	John D. Sheehan, ...	1992.	Retired.	
1982.	George C. Keady, Jr., ...	1994.	Retired.	
1982.	Vieri Volterra.			
1982.	James J. Nixon, Jr., ...	1992.	Retired.	
1982.	Elbert Tuttle, ...	1992.	Retired.	
1982.	Robert A. Mulligan.		(Appointed C. J., 1994)	
1982.	John L. Murphy, Jr., ...	1994.	Retired.	
1983.	Mel L. Greenberg, ...	1990.	App'd Appeals Court.	
1983.	Harry J. Elam, ...	1988.	Retired.	
1983.	Katherine Liacos Izzo, ...	1996.	Retired.	
1984.	J. Harold Flannery, ...	1995.	App'd Appeals Court.	
1985.	Paul A. Chernoff.			
1985.	Barbara J. Rouse.			
1985.	James F. McHugh.			
1985.	Cortland A. Mathers, ...	1994.	Retired.	
1985.	Charles M. Grabau.			
1985.	Suzanne DelVecchio.			
1985.	Robert W. Banks.			
1986.	R. Malcolm Graham.			
1986.	William H. Welch.			
1986.	Constance M. Sweeney.			

APPOINTED.		LEFT THE BENCH		DIED.
1987.	Catherine A. White.			
1987.	John C. Cratsley.			
1988.	John M. Xifaras.			
1988.	J. Owen Todd, ...	1992.	Resigned.	
1989.	Barbara A. Dortch.			
1989.	Wendie I. Gershengorn.			
1989.	Patrick J. King.			
1989.	Daniel A. Ford.			
1989.	Robert H. Bohn, Jr.			
1989.	David M. Roseman.			
1989.	Elizabeth A. Donovan.			
1989.	Margot Botsford.			
1989.	Peter M. Lauriat.			
989.	Patrick F. Brady.			
989.	Patti B. Saris, ...	1994.	App'd U.S. Dist. Ct.	
990.	Gordon L. Doerfer.			
990.	Julian T. Houston.			
990.	Charles F. Barrett.			
990.	Thomas E. Connolly.			
990.	John A. Tierney.			
990.	Richard G. Stearns, ...	1994.	App'd U.S. Dist. Ct.	
990.	Elizabeth Butler.			
990.	John J. O'Brien.			
990.	Richard F. Connon.			
990.	George A. O'Toole, ...	1995.	App'd U.S. Dist. Ct.	
990.	Charles J. Hely.			
991.	Judith A. Cowin.			
992.	Charles T. Spurlock.			
992.	Stephen E. Neel.			
992.	Regina L. Quinlan.			
992.	Isaac Borenstein.			
992.	Mary-Lou Rup.			
993.	Daniel F. Toomey.			
993.	Francis X. Spina.			
993.	Martha B. Sosman.			
993.	Maria I. Lopez.			
993.	E. Susan Garsh.			
993.	Margaret R. Hinkle.			
993.	Howard J. Whitehead.			
993.	Judd J. Carhart.			
993.	James P. Dohoney.			
993.	Thayer Fremont-Smith.			

APPOINTED		LEFT THE BENCH		DIED.
1993.	Richard J. Chin.			
1993.	Joseph A. Grasso, Jr.			
1993.	Barbara A. Lenk,	1995.	App'd Appeals Ct.	
1994.	Christine M. McEvoy.			
1994.	Richard E. Welch, III.			
1994.	Bertha D. Josephson.			
1995.	Herman J. Smith, Jr.			
1995.	Raymond J. Brassard.			
1995.	Diane M. Kottmyer.			
1996.	Francis R. Fecteau.			
1996.	Carol S. Ball.			
1996.	Philip Rivard-Rapoza.			
1996.	Lawrence B. Wernick.			
1996.	Judith Fabricant.			
1996.	Mitchell J. Sikora, Jr.			
1996.	Nonnie S. Burnes.			
1996.	Allan van Gestel.			
1996.	Nancy Merrick.			

*Judges of the Land Court since its Establishment in 1898 as the
Court of Registration.*

JUDGES.

APPOINTED.		LEFT THE BENCH.		DIED
1898.	Leonard A. Jones,	1909.	Resigned.	1909
1909.	Charles Thornton Davis,	1936.		1936
1936.	Michael A. Sullivan,	1937.		1937
1937.	John E. Fenton,	1966.	Retired.	1974
1966.	Elwood H. Hettrick,	1971.	Retired.	1972
1971.	William I. Randall,	1985.	Retired.	

ADMINISTRATIVE JUSTICES.
(NOW CHIEF JUSTICES).

APPOINTED.		LEFT THE BENCH.	DIED
1985.	Marilyn M. Sullivan, ...	1993.	
1990.	John E. Fenton, Jr., ...	1994.	(App'd C.A.J. of T.C.,'92)
1992.	Robert V. Cauchon, ...	1996.	Retired.
1996.	Peter W. Kilborn.		

ASSOCIATE JUDGES.
(NOW JUSTICES).

APPOINTED.		LEFT THE BENCH.		DIED
1898.	Charles Thornton Davis, .	1936.	(App'd Judge, 1909).	1936.
1909.	Louis M. Clark, ...	1914.		1914.
1914.	Joseph J. Corbett, ...	1937.	Retired.	1949.
1924.	Clarence C. Smith, ...	1943.		1943.
1937.	Patrick J. Courtney.	1952.	Retired.	1966.
1943.	Joseph R. Cotton, ...	1965.	Retired.	1983.
1952.	Edward McPartlin, ...	1973.	Retired.	1973.
1965.	Joseph P. Silverio.	1974.	Retired.	
1973.	Marilyn M. Sullivan.	1993.	(A. J., 1985-1990.)	
1974.	John E. Fenton, Jr., ...	1994.	(A. J., 1990-1992.)	
1986.	Robert V. Cauchon, ...	1996.	(A. J., 1992-1996.)	
1990.	Peter W. Kilborn.		(App'd C. J., 1996.)	
1994.	Karyn Faith Sheier.			
1995.	Leon J. Lombardi.			

PRESENT ORGANIZATION OF THE COURTS.

[All judges in the Commonwealth are appointed by the Governor with the advice and consent of the Council and hold office during good behavior until age seventy.]

SUPREME JUDICIAL COURT.
[General Laws, Chapter 211.]
Herbert P. Wilkins of Concord, *Chief Justice.*

Justices.

Ruth I. Abrams of Cambridge.
Neil L. Lynch of Scituate.
Francis P. O'Connor of
Shrewsbury.
John M. Greaney of Westfield.

Charles Fried of
Cambridge .
Margaret H. Marshall of
Cambridge.

Jean M. Kennett of Boston. *Clerk of the Commonwealth,* Room 1412, Suffolk County Court House.

Susan Mellen of Boston, *Assistant Clerk for the Commonwealth,* Room 1412. Court House.

Maura Sweeney Doyle of Boston, 2000, *Clerk for the County of Suffolk,* Room 1404, Court House.

Lillian Andruszkiewicz of Melrose, *First Assistant Clerk for the County of Suffolk.* Room 1404, Court House.

George E. Slyva of Milton, *Second Assistant Clerk for the County of Suffolk,* Room 1404, Court House.

Francis V. Kenneally of Boston, *Third Assistant Clerk for the County of Suffolk,* Room 1404, Court House.

C. Clifford Allen III of Beverly, *Reporter of Decisions,* Room 1407, Court House.

Catherine C. MacInnes, *Administrative Assistant to the Chief Justice,* Room 1300. Suffolk County Court House.

Maria Z. Mossaides, *Administrative Assistant to the Justices of the Supreme Judicial Court,* Room 1300, Suffolk County Court House.

Maureen McGee, *Legal Counsel to the Chief Justice,* Room 1300, Suffolk County Court House.

Henry Clay, *Chief Staff Counsel for the Appellate Bureau,* Room 1350, Suffolk County Courthouse.

APPEALS COURT.
[General Laws, Chapter 211A.]
Joseph P. Warner of Dedham, *Chief Justice.*

Justices.

Christopher J. Armstrong of Newbury.
Frederick L. Brown of Belmont.
Charlotte Anne Perretta of Boston.
Raya S. Dreben of Belmont.
Rudolph Kass of Arlington.
Kent B. Smith of Longmeadow.

George Jacobs of Dartmouth.
Elizabeth A. Porada of Hatfield.
Roderick L. Ireland of Milton.
Mel L. Greenberg of Worcester.
Kenneth Laurence of Lexington.
J. Harold Flannery of Weston.
Barbara A. Lenk of Carlisle.

Nancy Turck Foley of Boston, *Clerk,* Room 1500, Court House.
Ashley Brown Ahearn of Boston, *First Assistant Clerk.* Room 1500, Court House.
Warren L. Shields of Westwood, *Assistant Clerk,* Room 1500, Court House.
Gilbert P. Lima, Jr., of Attleboro, *Assistant Clerk,* Room 1500, Court House.
Lena M. Wong of Brookline, *Assistant Clerk,* Room 1500, Court House.
C. Clifford Allen III of Beverly, *Reporter of Decisions,* Room 1407, Court House.
Alexander M. McNeil of Newton, *Administrative Assistant to the Chief Justice,* Room 1500, Court House.

TRIAL COURT.
[General Laws, Chapter 211B.]

John J. Irwin, Jr., of Medford, *Chief Justice for Administration and Management.*
Lynne G. Reed of Belmont, *Executive Director.*

SUPERIOR COURT DEPARTMENT OF THE TRIAL COURT.
[General Laws, Chapter 212.]
Robert A. Mulligan of Boston, *Chief Justice.*

Justices.
John F. Moriarty of Holyoke.
Herbert F. Travers, Jr., of Holden.

Robert A. Barton of Bedford.
John F. Murphy, Jr., of
Northampton.
James P. Donohue of Clinton.
Hiller B. Zobel of Cohasset.
Elizabeth Dolan of Arlington.
Peter F. Brady of Lynnfield.
Sandra L. Hamlin of Brookline.
Gerald F. O'Neill, Jr.. of West
Harwich.
James D. McDaniel. Jr., of Malden.
Vieri Volterra of Brookline.
Robert A. Mulligan of Boston.
Paul A. Chernoff of Newton.
Barbara J. Rouse of Charlestown.
James F. McHugh of Lincoln.
Charles M. Grabau of Newton.
Suzanne DelVecchio of Hingham.
Robert W. Banks of Belmont.
R. Malcolm Graham of Newton.
William H. Welch of
Northampton.
Constance M. Sweeney of
Springfield.
Catherine A. White of Boston.
John C. Cratsley of Concord.
John M. Xifaras of Marion.
Barbara A. Dortch of Milton.
Wendie I. Gershengorn of
Weston.
Patrick J. King of Brookline.
Daniel A. Ford of Pittsfield.
Robert A. Bohn, Jr., of
Auburndale.
David M. Roseman of Lexington.
Elizabeth A. Donovan of
Jamaica Plain.
Margot Botsford of Brookline.
Peter M. Lauriat of Watertown.
Patrick F. Brady of Needham.
Gordon L. Doerfer of Boston.

Julian T. Houston of Brookline.
Charles F. Barrett of Milton.
Thomas E. Connolly of West
Roxbury.
John A. Tierney of New Bedford.
Elizabeth Butler of Wayland.
John J. O'Brien of Milton.
Richard F. Connon of South
Hadley.
Charles J. Hely of Needham.
Judith A. Cowin of West Newton.
Charles T. Spurlock of Cambridge.
Stephen E. Neel of Watertown.
Regina L. Quinlan of
Charlestown.
Isaac Borenstein of Andover.
Mary-Lou Rup of Whately.
Daniel F. Toomey of Holden.
Francis X. Spina of Pittsfield.
Martha B. Sosman of Boston.
Maria I. Lopez of Newton.
E. Susan Garsh of Belmont.
Margaret R. Hinkle of Newton.
Howard J. Whitehead of Lynnfield.
Judd J. Carhart of Conway.
James P. Dohoney of Great
Barrington.
Thayer Fremont-Smith of Melrose.
Richard J. Chin of Brockton.
Joseph A. Grasso, Jr., of Andover.
Christine M. McEvoy of Concord.
Richard E. Welch, III of
Newburyport.
Bertha D. Josephson of Holyoke.
Herman J. Smith, Jr., of Medford.
Raymond J. Brassard of Needham.
Diane M. Kottmyer of Winchester.
Francis R. Fecteau of Worcester.
Carol S. Ball of Boston.
Philip Rivard-Raposa of Dartmouth.
Lawrence B. Wernick of
Longmeadow.

Judith Fabricant of Brookline.
Mitchell J. Sikora, Jr., of West Roxbury.
Nonnie S. Burnes of Boston.

Allan van Gestel of Boston.
Nancy Merrick of Nahant.

APPELLATE DIVISION.
Herbert F. Travers, Jr., of Holden.
Elizabeth Dolan of Arlington.
James D. McDaniel, Jr., of Malden.

Michael Joseph Donovan of Boston, 2000, *Clerk for Civil Business for the County of Suffolk*, Room 117, Suffolk County Courthouse.
John A. Nucci of Boston, 2000, *Clerk for Criminal Business for the County of Suffolk*, Room 712, Courthouse, Boston.
James H. Klein, Esq., *Court Administrator*, Room 1112, Courthouse, Boston.
James F. Donovan of Belmont, *Messenger for the Court*, Room 1103, Courthouse, Boston.

LAND COURT

DEPARTMENT OF THE TRIAL COURT.
[General Laws, Chapter 185.]

Chief Justice, Peter W. Kilborn, Newton. *Justices*, Karyn Faith Scheier, Weston; Leon J. Lombardi, Easton; (vacancy). *Recorder*, Charles W. Trombly, Jr., North Andover. *Acting Executive Secretary*, Ellen B. Bransfield, Brookline, Room 408, Suffolk County Courthouse.

PROBATE AND FAMILY COURT
DEPARTMENT OF THE TRIAL COURT.
[General Laws, Chapter 215.]
Mary C. Fitzpatrick, *Chief Justice*.
John E. McNichols, *Court Administrator*.

Justices.

Rudolph A. Sacco, *Hampshire Division (Special Circuit).*
Sheila E. McGovern, *Middlesex Division.*

Edward M. Ginsburg, *Middlesex Division.*
Sean M. Dunphy, *Hampshire Division.*

James M. Sweeney, *Middlesex Division.*

David H. Kopelman, *Norfolk Division.*

Eliot K. Cohen, *Nantucket Division.*

Edward J. Rockett, *Essex Division.*

William Highgas, Jr., *Middlesex Division.*

John J. Moynihan, *Worcester Division.*

Mary M. Manzi, *Essex Division.*

David G. Sacks, *Hampden Division.*

Elizabeth O. LaStaiti, *Bristol Division.*

Arline S. Rotman, *Worcester Division.*

Malcolm M. Jones, *Bristol Division.*

Elaine M. Moriarty, *Suffolk Division.*

Christina L. Harms, *Norfolk Division.*

Robert E. Terry, *Barnstable Division.*

Joseph Lian, Jr., *Worcester Division.*

Eileen M. Shaevel, *Norfolk Division.*

Marie E. Lyons, *Hampden Division.*

John M. Smoot, *Suffolk Division.*

Catherine P. Sabaitis, *Plymouth Division.*

Nancy M. Gould, *Circuit Justice.*

Fernande R. V. Duffly, *Middlesex Division.*

Beverly W. Boorstein, *Middlesex Division.*

John P. Cronin, *Dukes Division.*

Anna H. Doherty, *Plymouth Division.*

David M. Fuller, *Hampden Division.*

Susan D. Ricci, *Circuit Justice.*

Prudence M. McGregor, *Bristol Division.*

Judith N. Dilday, *Circuit Justice.*

Robert A. Scandurra, *Barnstable Division.*

Jeremy A. Stahlin, *Circuit Justice.*

Anthony R. Nesi, *Circuit Justice.*

Edward J. LaPointe, *Berkshire Division.*

James V. Menno, *Plymouth Division.*

Robert W. Langlois, *Norfolk Division.*

Stephen C. Steinberg, *Plymouth Division.*

John C. Stevens, III, *Essex Division.*

HOUSING COURT OF THE TRIAL COURT.
[General Laws, Chapter 185C.]
Administrative Justice, E. George Daher.
Court Administrator, Harvey J. Chopp, Esq.

CITY OF BOSTON DIVISION.
Chief Justice, E. George Daher. *Associate Justice,* (vacant). *Clerk-Magistrate,* Robert L. Lewis. *First Assistant Clerk-Magistrate,* Laurence B. Pierce. *Assistant Clerk-Magistrates,* Joe Ann Smith Crayton, Camilla Duffy.

HAMPDEN COUNTY DIVISION.
First Justice, William H. Abrashkin. *Clerk-Magistrate,* Curtis L. Shaird. *Assistant Clerk-Magistrate,* Karen Ann Huntoon.

WORCESTER DIVISION.
First Justice, John G. Martin. *Clerk-Magistrate,* James A. Bisceglia. *First Assistant Clerk-Magistrate,* (vacant).

NORTHEASTERN DIVISION.
First Justice, David D. Kerman. *Clerk-Magistrate,* Paul J. Burke. *First Assistant Clerk-Magistrate,* Susan Trippi.

SOUTHEASTERN DIVISION.
First Justice, Manuel Kyriakakis. *Clerk-Magistrate,* Carlton M. Viveiros. *First Assistant Clerk-Magistrate,* Stephen G. Carreiro.

DISTRICT COURT DEPARTMENT OF THE TRIAL COURT.
[General Laws, Chapter 218.]
Samuel E. Zoll, *Administrative Justice.*
Jerome S. Berg, *Court Administrator.*

COURT IDENTIFICATION.
Consistent with the provisions of St. 1980, c. 83, as amended, the divisions of the District Court Department except the Northern Berkshire and Southern Berkshire divisions, shall be referred to by the name of the city or town which is the principal place of sitting of the division.

482 *Judiciary.*

The judicial districts of the several district and municipal courts are as follows:

Barnstable Division: Barnstable, Yarmouth and Sandwich. — *Justices,* Don L. Carpenter, Joseph J. Reardon, Joan E. Lynch. *Clerk-Magistrate,* Omer R. Chartrand.

Orleans Division: Provincetown, Truro, Wellfleet, Eastham, Orleans, Brewster, Chatham, Harwich and Dennis. — *Justices,* Robert A. Welsh, Jr., John B. Leonard. *Clerk-Magistrate,* Stephen I. Ross.

Falmouth Division: Bourne, Falmouth and Mashpee. — *Justices,* Kevan J. Cunningham, (vacancy). *Clerk-Magistrate,* Charles N. Decas.

BERKSHIRE.

The district courts at Adams, North Adams and Williamstown were consolidated into the Northern Berkshire District as a result of section 166 of Chapter 478 of the Acts of 1978 (Court Reorganization).

Northern Berkshire Division, held at Adams and North Adams: Adams, North Adams, Williamstown, Clarksburg, Florida, New Ashford, Cheshire, Savoy, Hancock, and Windsor; the Pittsfield Division exercising concurrent jurisdiction in Windsor and Hancock. — *Justices,* Anthony J. Ruberto, Jr., Michael J. Ripps. *Clerk-Magistrate,* Mark D. Trottier.

Pittsfield Division: Pittsfield, Hancock, Lanesborough, Peru, Hinsdale, Dalton, Washington, Richmond, Lenox, Becket and Windsor; the district court of southern Berkshire exercising concurrent jurisdiction in Lenox and Becket and the district court of northern Berkshire exercising concurrent jurisdiction in Windsor and Hancock. — *Justices,* Alfred A. Barbalunga, Rita Scales Koenigs. *Clerk-Magistrate,* Leo F. Evans.

The District Courts at Lee and Great Barrington were consolidated into the Southern Berkshire District as a result of section 166 of Chapter 478 of the Acts of 1978 (Court Reorganization).

Southern Berkshire Division, held at Great Barrington; Sheffield, Great Barrington, Egremont, Alford, Mount Washington, Monterey, New Marlborough, Stockbridge, West Stockbridge, Sandisfield, Lee, Tyringham, Otis, Lenox and Becket; the Pittsfield Division exercising concurrent jurisdiction in Lenox and Becket. — *Justices,* Fredric D. Rutberg, James B. McElroy. *Clerk-Magistrate,* Louis A. Airoldi.

BRISTOL.

Taunton Division; Taunton, Rehoboth, Berkley, Dighton, Seekonk, Easton and Raynham. — *Justices,* Andrew J. Dooley, Paul E. Ryan. *Clerk-Magistrate,* Raymond S. Peck.

Fall River Division; Fall River, Somerset, Swansea, Freetown and Westport; the New Bedford Division exercising concurrent jurisdiction in Freetown and Westport. — *Justices,* Bernadette L. Sabra, David T. Turcotte, John H. O'Neil. *Clerk-Magistrate,* Thomas E. Kitchen.

New Bedford Division; New Bedford, Fairhaven, Acushnet, Dartmouth, Freetown and Westport; the Fall River Division exercising concurrent jurisdiction in Freetown and Westport. — *Justices,* John A. Markey, James M. Quinn, Aileen H. Belford. *Clerk-Magistrate,* John M. Stellato.

Attleboro Division; Attleboro, North Attleborough, Mansfield and Norton. — *Justices,* John J. Dolan, Antone S. Aguiar, Jr. *Clerk-Magistrate,* Daniel J. Sullivan.

DUKES COUNTY.

Edgartown Division; Edgartown, Oak Bluffs and Tisbury; Dukes County. *Justices,* Robert J. Kane, Brian Rowe. *Clerk-Magistrate,* Thomas A. Teller.

ESSEX.

Salem Division; Salem, Beverly, Danvers, Middleton and Manchester-by-the-Sea. — *Justices,* Samuel E. Zoll, David T. Doyle. *Clerk-Magistrate,* Robert F. Arena.

Ipswich Division; Ipswich, Hamilton, Topsfield and Wenham. — *Justices,* Robert A. Cornetta, Joseph A. Furnari. *Clerk-Magistrate,* Kathryn Morris Early.

Haverhill Division; Haverhill, Groveland, Georgetown, Boxford and West Newbury; the Newburyport Division exercising concurrent jurisdiction in West Newbury. — *Justices,* (vacancy), (vacancy). *Clerk-Magistrate,* Frank Caruso.

Gloucester Division; Gloucester, Rockport and Essex. — *Justices,* David E. Harrison, Ellen Flatley. *Clerk-Magistrate,* Kevin P. Burke.

Lynn Division; Lynn, Swampscott, Saugus, Marblehead and Nahant. — *Justices,* Joseph I. Dever. Robert E. Hayes. *Clerk-Magistrate,* Charles E. Flynn.

Lawrence Division: Lawrence, Andover, North Andover and Methuen. — *Justices,* Kevin M. Herlihy, Michael T. Stella, Jr. *Clerk-Magistrate,* Keith McDonough.

Newburyport Division, held at Newburyport; Amesbury, Merrimac, Newbury. Newburyport, Rowley, Salisbury and West Newbury; the Central District Court of Northern Essex (Haverhill Division) exercising concurrent jurisdiction in West Newbury. — *Justices,* James J. O'Leary, Ronald D. D'Avolio, William E. Melahn, (vacancy). *Clerk-Magistrate,* J. Nicholas Sullivan.

Peabody Division; Peabody and Lynnfield. — *Justices,* Santo J. Ruma, J. Dennis Healey. *Clerk-Magistrate,* Russell H. Craig.

FRANKLIN.

Greenfield Division. held at Greenfield and at Turners Falls in Montague; Franklin County, except Orange, Erving, Warwick, Wendell and New Salem. Sessions may also be held at Shelburne Falls in Shelburne and Buckland at such times and places as the justice of said court may determine. — *Justices,* Herbert H. Hodos, (vacancy). *Clerk-Magistrate,* John R. Johnson.

Orange Division; Orange, Erving, Warwick, Wendell and New Salem, *in the county of Franklin;* and Athol, *in the county of Worcester.* — *Justices,* M. John Schubert, Jr., Thomas T. Merrigan. *Clerk-Magistrate,* Laurie N. Dornig.

HAMPDEN.

Palmer Division; Palmer, Brimfield, Hampden, Ludlow, Monson, Holland, Wales and Wilbraham. — *Justices,* Kenneth J. Cote, Jr., Robert L. Howarth. *Clerk-Magistrate,* E. Donald Riddle.

Westfield Division; Westfield, Chester, Granville, Southwick, Russell, Blandford, Tolland and Montgomery. — *Justices,* Philip A. Contant, Peter J. Rutherford. *Clerk-Magistrate,* Carol J. Casartello.

Chicopee Division; Chicopee. — *Justices,* Alphonse C. Turcotte, Mary E. Hurley-Marks. *Clerk-Magistrate,* Paul M. Kozikowski.

Holyoke Division; Holyoke. — *Justices,* William B. McDonough, Robert F. Kumor, Jr. *Clerk-Magistrate,* Manuel A. Moutinho. III.

Springfield Division; Springfield, West Springfield, Agawam. Longmeadow and East Longmeadow. — *Justices,* Jacques C. Leroy, Nancy Dusek-Gomez, William W. Teahan, Jr., George A. Sheehy. *Clerk-Magistrate,* Robert E. Fein.

HAMPSHIRE.

Northampton Division, held at Northampton; Amherst, Cummington, South Hadley, Huntington and Easthampton; Hampshire County, except Belchertown, Granby and Ware. — *Justices,* Alvertus J. Morse, W. Michael Ryan. *Clerk-Magistrate,* Genevieve L. Keller.

Ware Division, held at Ware; Belchertown, Granby and Ware and any violation of law committed on land of the metropolitan district commission comprising the Quabbin reservation or used for the supply or protection of the Quabbin reservoir. — *Justices,* (vacancy), (vacancy). *Clerk-Magistrate,* James H. Bloom.

MIDDLESEX.

Concord Division: Concord, Acton, Bedford, Carlisle, Lincoln, Maynard, Stow and Lexington. — *Justices,* James H. Wexler, Patricia G. Curtin. *Clerk-Magistrate,* Ann M. Colicchio.

Ayer Division; Ayer, Dunstable, Groton, Pepperell, Townsend, Ashby, Shirley, Westford, Littleton and Boxborough. — *Justices,* Peter J. Kilmartin, James M. Geary, Jr. *Clerk-Magistrate,* Wendy A. Wilton.

Malden Division; Malden, Wakefield, Melrose and Everett. — *Justices,* Paul F. Mahoney, Paul J. Cavanaugh, Maurice R. Flynn III, Richard A. Mori. *Clerk-Magistrate,* Joseph Croken.

Waltham Division; Waltham, Watertown and Weston. — *Justices,* Gregory C. Flynn, Janet L. Sanders. *Clerk-Magistrate,* Charles F. Graceffa.

Cambridge Division; Cambridge, Arlington and Belmont. — *Justices,* Jonathan Brant, Arthur Sherman, George R. Sprague, Marie O. Jackson, Severlin B. Singleton, Bonnie MacLeod. *Clerk-Magistrate,* Robert L. Moscow.

Woburn Division; Woburn, Winchester, Burlington, Wilmington, Stoneham, Reading and North Reading. — *Justices,* Marie T. Buckley, Tobin N. Harvey. *Clerk-Magistrate,* Kathleen McKeon.

Framingham Division; Framingham, Ashland, Holliston, Sudbury, Wayland and Hopkinton. — *Justices,* Robert C. Campion, Robert V. Greco, Paul F. Healy, Jr. *Clerk-Magistrate,* Anthony M. Colonna.

Lowell Division; Lowell, Tewksbury, Billerica, Dracut, Chelmsford and Tyngsborough. — *Justices,* Barbara S. Pearson, Neil J. Walker. *Clerk-Magistrate,* William A. Lisano.

Marlborough Division; Marlborough and Hudson. — *Justices,* (vacancy), Robert A. Belmonte. *Clerk-Magistrate,* Paul Malloy.

Natick Division; Natick and Sherborn. — *Justices,* James H. McGuinness, Jr., Edward M. Viola. *Clerk-Magistrate,* Joseph M. Hogan.

Newton Division; Newton. — *Justices,* Conrad J. Bletzer, Dyanne J. Klein. *Clerk-Magistrate,* Henry H. Shultz.

Somerville Division; Somerville and Medford. — *Justices,* Paul P. Heffernan, Mark S. Coven. *Clerk-Magistrate,* Robert A. Tomasone.

NANTUCKET.

Nantucket Division; Nantucket County. — *Justices,* W. James O'Neill, Deborah A. Dunn. *Clerk-Magistrate,* Roxana E. Viera.

NORFOLK.

Dedham Division; Dedham, Dover, Norwood, Westwood, Medfield, Needham and Wellesley. — *Justices,* Maurice H. Richardson, Gerald Alch. *Clerk-Magistrate,* Salvatore Paterna.

Quincy Division; Quincy, Randolph, Braintree, Cohasset, Weymouth, Holbrook and Milton; and, in criminal cases, concurrently with the Hingham Division, that part of Scituate described in chapter three hundred and ninety-four of the acts of nineteen hundred and twelve. Arrests and service of process in such cases may be made by an officer qualified to serve criminal process in Cohasset. — *Justices,* Gregory R. Baler, Warren A. Powers. *Clerk-Magistrate,* Arthur H. Tobin.

Stoughton Division; Stoughton, Canton, Avon and Sharon. — *Justices,* Robert B. Sheiber, Francis T. Crimmins, Jr. *Clerk-Magistrate,* Donald M. Stapleton.

Wrentham Division; Franklin, Walpole, Foxborough, Medway, Millis, Norfolk, Wrentham and Plainville. — *Justices,* John F. St. Cyr, Daniel B. Winslow. *Clerk-Magistrate,* William H. Barker, Jr.

Brookline Division; Brookline. — *Justices,* Herbert N. Goodwin, Paul K. Leary. *Clerk-Magistrate,* John J. Connors.

Hingham Division; Hingham, Rockland, Hull, Hanover, Scituate and Norwell. — *Justices,* Patrick J. Hurley, Geraldine Lombardo. *Clerk-Magistrate,* Joseph A. Ligotti.

Plymouth Division; Plymouth, Kingston, Plympton, Pembroke, Duxbury, Hanson, Halifax and Marshfield. — *Justices,* Thomas F. Brownell, Rosemary B. Minehan. *Clerk-Magistrate,* Roger W. O'Neil, Jr., John A. Sullivan *(pro tempore).*

Wareham Division, held at Middleborough and Wareham; Middleborough, Wareham, Lakeville, Marion, Mattapoisett, Rochester and Carver. — *Justices,* Richard D. Savignano, John C. Wheatley. *Clerk-Magistrate,* Paul F. Walsh.

Brockton Division; Brockton, Bridgewater, East Bridgewater, Whitman, Abington and West Bridgewater. Said court may adjourn to the Massachusetts correctional institution at Bridgewater, whenever the public convenience seems to the presiding justice to render such adjournment expedient. — *Justices,* Charles E. Black, Paul F. X. Moriarty, David E. Stevens, David G. Nagle, Jr. *Clerk-Magistrate,* Kevin P. Creedon.

Brighton Division; ward twenty-five of Boston as it existed on February first, eighteen hundred and eighty-two. — *Justices,* Albert H. Burns, R. Peter Anderson. *Clerk-Magistrate,* James B. Roche III.

Charlestown Division; wards three, four and five of Boston as they existed on February first, eighteen hundred and eighty-two, provided that in criminal matters said court shall have exclusive jurisdiction in that part of said wards which is under the care, custody and control of the lower basin division of the Metropolitan District Commission and in so much of the Charles river basin, as defined in section two of chapter five hundred and twenty-four of the acts of nineteen hundred and nine as affected by chapter two hundred and forty-five of the General Acts of nineteen hundred and sixteen as is within the district of said court. — *Justices,* Peter W. Agnes, Jr., Allen Jarasitis. *Clerk-Magistrate,* S. John Hamano.

Chelsea Division; Chelsea and Revere. — *Justices,* Eugene G. Panarese, Kathleen E. Coffey. *Clerk-Magistrate,* Kevin G. Murphy.

Dorchester Division; ward twenty-four of Boston as it existed on February first, eighteen hundred and eighty-two and the territory comprised within the limits of precinct twelve of ward thirteen of Boston as it existed on November second, nineteen hundred and forty-eight. — *Justices,* James W. Dolan, Rosalind H. Miller, Joseph M. Walker III, Sydney Hanlon. *Clerk-Magistrate,* Richard J. Dwyer.

East Boston Division; Winthrop and wards one and two of Boston as they existed on March first, eighteen hundred and eighty-six; provided that said court shall have territorial jurisdiction in matters that arise in the Sumner tunnel, so-called, and Lieutenant William F. Callahan, Jr., tunnel including any property, toll plazas and approach roads thereto under the ownership, care, custody and control of the Massachusetts Turnpike Authority as provided by chapter five hundred and ninety-eight of the acts of nineteen hundred and fifty-eight. — *Justices,* Domenic J.F. Russo, Thomas J. May. *Clerk-Magistrate,* Joseph R. Faretra.

Roxbury Division; wards nineteen, twenty, twenty-one and twenty-two of Boston as they existed on February first, eighteen hundred and eighty-two, excepting ward ten, save as hereinafter provided, as it existed on February first, nineteen hundred and seventy-six; and excepting further, cases of juvenile offenders under seventeen and cases of delinqent children when such cases arise in wards four, five, and precincts one and two of ward twenty-one of Boston as they existed on February first, nineteen hundred and seventy-six; provided however that, notwithstanding any other provision of law, said court shall have jurisdiction over matters arising in precincts one, six and seven of ward ten. — *Justices,* Gordon A. Martin, Jr., Paul L. McGill, Gregory L. Phillips, Edward R. Redd, Milton L. Wright, Jr., (vacancy). *Clerk-Magistrate,* Keesler H. Montgomery.

South Boston Division; wards thirteen, fourteen and fifteen of Boston as they existed on February first, eighteen hundred and eighty-two. — *Justices,* John P. Concannon, Mary Ann Driscoll. *Clerk-Magistrate,* John E. Flaherty.

West Roxbury Division; ward twenty-three of Boston as it existed on February first, eighteen hundred and eighty-two, and the territory comprised within the limits of the former town of Hyde Park which was annexed to Boston by chapters four hundred and sixty-nine and five hundred and eighty-three of the acts of nineteen hundred and eleven, and ward ten, except precincts one, six and seven of said ward ten, as existing on February first, nineteen hundred and seventy-six; and excepting further, cases of juvenile offenders under seventeen and cases of delinquent children when such cases arise in said ward ten. — *Justices,* (vacancy), Robert P. Ziemian. *Clerk-Magistrate,* Michael J. McCusker.

WORCESTER.

Worcester Division; Worcester, Millbury, Auburn, Paxton, West Boylston, Holden, Rutland, Barre and Oakham. — *Justices,* Richard P. Kelleher, Neil G. Snider, Dennis J. Brennan, Thomas F. Sullivan, Jr., William J. Luby, (vacancy). *Clerk-Magistrate,* Thomas J. Noonan.

Gardner Division; Gardner, Petersham, Phillipston, Royalston, Templeton, Hubbardston and Westminster. — *Justices,* Austin T. Philbin, Timothy S. Hillman. *Clerk-Magistrate,* William T. Clark.

Westborough Division; Westborough, Grafton, Shrewsbury, Southborough and Northborough. — *Justices,* Paul S. Waickowski, John S. McCann. *Clerk-Magistrate,* Thomas X. Cotter.

Clinton Division; Clinton, Berlin, Bolton, Boylston, Harvard, Lancaster and Sterling. — *Justices,* Thomas F. Fallon, Martha A. Brennan. *Clerk-Magistrate,* Raymond Salmon.

Dudley Division; Southbridge, Webster, Sturbridge, Charlton, Dudley and Oxford. — *Justices,* John C. Geenty, (vacancy). *Clerk-Magistrate,* Kenneth F. Candito.

Uxbridge Division; Blackstone, Uxbridge, Douglas, Northbridge, Millville and Sutton. — *Justices,* Sarkis Teshoian, (vacancy). *Clerk-Magistrate,* Peter D. Rigero.

Milford Division; Milford, Mendon, Upton, Hopedale, *in the county of Worcester;* and Bellingham, *in the county of Norfolk.* — *Justices,* (vacancy), (vacancy). *Clerk-Magistrate,* (vacancy).

East Brookfield Division; East Brookfield, Brookfield, Leicester, Spencer, North Brookfield, West Brookfield, Warren, Hardwick and New Braintree. Said court may adjourn to any town within its district other than East Brookfield whenever the public convenience seems to the presiding justice to render such adjournment expedient. — *Justices,* Paul F. LoConto, Patrick A. Fox. *Clerk-Magistrate,* Paul A. Losapio.

Fitchburg Division; Fitchburg, Ashburnham and Lunenburg. — *Justices,* Andre A. Gelinas, Elliott L. Zide. *Clerk-Magistrate,* Duncan E. McLeod.

Leominster Division: Leominster and Princeton. — *Justices,* John J. Curran, Edward J. Reynolds. *Clerk-Magistrate,* Philip B. O'Toole.

Winchendon Division; Winchendon. — *Justices,* Vito A. Virzi, (vacancy). *Clerk-Magistrate,* Lillian E. Bateman.

CIRCUIT JUSTICES.

Philip A. Beattie; Brian R. Merrick; Sarah B. Singer; Milton H. Raphaelson; Daniel Klubock; Anthony P. Sullivan; George H. Lebherz, Jr.; Margaret A. Zaleski; Leah W. Sprague; Timothy H. Gailey; James F. X. Dineen; Roanne Sragow; Joseph R. Welch; Thomas A. Connors; Robert C. Rufo; Michael C. Creedon.

APPELLATE DIVISIONS OF THE DISTRICT COURT DEPARTMENT.
[General Laws, Chapter 231. s. 108, as most recently amended by Acts of 1975, Chapter 377, ss. 106-107B]

Five justices assigned to each of the three Districts by the Chief Justice of the District Courts, subject to the approval of the Chief Justice of the Supreme Judicial Court:

Northern District — *Presiding Justice:* Hon. Arthur Sherman, *Cambridge Division. Associate Justices:* Hon. Robert V. Greco, *Framingham Division;* Hon. Mark S. Coven, *Somerville Division;* Hon. Brian Merrick, *Circuit Justice;* Hon. Patricia G. Curtin, *Concord Division.*

Southern District — *Presiding Justice:* Hon. Antone S. Aguiar, Jr., *Attleboro Division. Associate Justices:* Hon. Aileen H. Belford, *New Bedford Division;* Hon. Francis T. Crimmins, Jr., *Stoughton Division;* Hon. Rosemary B. Minehan, *Plymouth Division;* Hon. Robert A. Welsh, Jr., *Orleans Division.*

Western District — *Presiding Justice:* Hon. Paul F. LoConto, *East Brookfield Division. Associate Justices:* Hon. Martha A. Brennan, *Clinton Division;* Hon. Andre A. Gelinas, *Fitchburg Division;* Hon. Thomas T. Merrigan, *Orange Division;* Hon. William W. Teahan, Jr., *Springfield Division.*

BOSTON MUNICIPAL COURT
DEPARTMENT OF THE TRIAL COURT.
[General Laws, Chapter 218.]

The municipal court of the city of Boston, held at Boston; wards six, seven, eight, nine, ten, eleven, twelve, sixteen, seventeen and eighteen of

Boston as they existed on February first, eighteen hundred and eighty-two; and in criminal cases, concurrently with the municipal courts of the Roxbury and Brighton districts, the second and third district courts of eastern Middlesex, and the district court of Newton, respectively, so much of the Charles river basin, as defined in section two of chapter five hundred and twenty-four of the acts of nineteen hundred and nine, as affected by chapter two hundred and forty-five of the General Acts of nineteen hundred and sixteen, as is within the districts of said courts. — *Chief Justice,* William J. Tierney. *Associate Justices,* J. Peter Donovan, Charles Ray Johnson, Sally A. Kelly, Herbert H. Hershfang, Dermot Meagher, Raymond G. Dougan, Jr., Linda E. Giles, Mark H. Summerville, Patricia E. Bernstein, (vacancy). *Court Administrator,* Helen Quigley, Esq.

Clerk-Magistrate for Civil Business, Michael J. Coleman. *First Assistant Clerk-Magistrate,* Neil P. Murphy. *Assistant Clerk-Magistrates,* Kevin F. Callahan, Rosemarie L. Carroll, John R. Cavanaugh, Joseph V. Cronin, Jr., James P. Gianelis, Elizabeth J. Gillis, Glen Hannington, Donald F. MacKinnon, Timothy Mazobere, George L. Shea, Jr., Sean F. Durant.

Clerk-Magistrate for Criminal Business, Francis N. Shiels. *First Assistant Clerk-Magistrate,* Robert E. Block. *First Assistant Clerk-Magistrate in Charge of Jury Session,* Rosemary T. Carr. *Assistant Clerk-Magistrates,* Ruth M. Hunter, Francis X. Cunningham, John Bartlett, Mark J. Concannon, Christopher L. Ferguson, William J. Lavery, Linda M. Scanlon, M. Stella Scarinci, Daniel J. Hogan, Robert J. Kelley. Suffolk County Courthouse.

APPELLATE DIVISION.

(All Justices sit on Appellate Division.)

JUVENILE COURT DEPARTMENT OF THE TRIAL COURT.
[General Laws, Chapter 211B, §1.]

Chief Justice, Francis G. Poitrast. *Court Administrator,* Jane Strickland.

BOSTON DIVISION, JUVENILE COURT.
[General Laws, Chapter 218, §§57-60.]

Presiding Justice (Acting), Paul D. Lewis. *Associate Justices,* John J. Craven, Jr., Leslie E. Harris, Mark E. Lawton, Stephen M. Limon, June C. Miles. *Clerk-Magistrate,* John P. Bulger. Rooms 160-175, Suffolk County Courthouse.

HAMPDEN COUNTY DIVISION, JUVENILE COURT.

Presiding Justice, Joseph A. Pellegrino. *Associate Justices,* Rebekah J. Crampton, Daniel J. Swords. *Clerk-Magistrate,* Marc S. Katsoulis.

WORCESTER DIVISION, JUVENILE COURT.

Presiding Justice, Luis Perez. *Associate Justices,* Martha P. Grace, George F. Leary, Jan L. Najemy. *Clerk-Magistrate,* Craig Smith.

BRISTOL COUNTY DIVISION, JUVENILE COURT.

Presiding Justice, Ronald D. Harper. *Associate Justices,* Kenneth P. Nasif, James M. Cronin, *Clerk-Magistrate,* Ronald C. Arruda.

MIDDLESEX COUNTY DIVISION, JUVENILE COURT.

Associate Justices, Margaret Feary, Jay Blitzman, Gwen Tyre, Gail Garinger. *Clerk-Magistrate,* Paul J. Hartnett.

NORFOLK COUNTY DIVISION, JUVENILE COURT.

Associate Justices, R. Marc Kantrowicz, Mary McCallum. *Clerk-Magistrate,* James F. Poirier.

PLYMOUTH COUNTY DIVISION, JUVENILE COURT.

Associate Justices, John P. Corbett, Robert F. Murray, Carol Smith. *Clerk-Magistrate,* Thomas LeBach.

BARNSTABLE COUNTY/PLYMOUTH DIVISION, JUVENILE COURT.

Associate Justice, Louis D. Coffin. *Clerk-Magistrate,* Charles P. Andrade, Jr.

ESSEX COUNTY DIVISION, JUVENILE COURT.

Associate Justices, Jose Sanchez, Sally F. Padden, Michael F. Edgerton. *Clerk-Magistrate,* Judith M. Brennan.

BERKSHIRE COUNTY DIVISION, JUVENILE COURT.

Associate Justice, Paul Perachi. *Clerk-Magistrate,* Laura Rueli-Rilla.

———————

FRANKLIN/HAMPSHIRE COUNTY DIVISION, JUVENILE COURT.

Associate Justice, Lillian Miranda. *Clerk-Magistrate,* Christopher Reavey.

———————

494 *Judiciary.*

DISTRICT ATTORNEYS.

NORTHERN DISTRICT (Middlesex County) — Thomas F. Reilly, Watertown. *First Assistant,* John McEvoy, Jr., Belmont. *Deputy First Assistant,* Gerard T. Leone, Jr., Hopkinton. *Assistants:* Kerry A. Ahern, Lowell; Heather V. Baer, Derry, N.H.; Michael Banks, Belmont; Stephen B. Barton, Woburn; Andrew Bassock, Boston; Edward R. Bedrosian, Jr., Belmont; Yvonne R. Bellefontaine, Malden; Marini Torres-Benson, Framingham; John Benzan, Wellesley; Barbara Berenson, Newton; William F. Bloomer, Lexington; Kimberley P. Bourgeois, Belmont; Thomas A. Brant, Winthrop; Gerard A. Butler, Woburn; Judith A. Carroll, Milton; Michelle Charness, Brighton; Michael A. Chinman, Roslindale; Kenneth E. Citron, Boston; Agnes Colon, Randolph; Karen Colucci-Pelletier, Milton; Elaine L. Contant, South Boston; Anne Cosco, Winchester; David W. Cunis, Holliston; Kevin J. Curtin, Cummaquid; Julie Dale, Hingham; Robert F. Daut, Somerville; Kimberly Diaz, Danvers; Erin Duggan, Merrimac; Beth Dunigan, Lowell; Anne Edwards, Winchester; Marc A. Eichler, Boston; Michael Fabbri, Ashland; Kathleen Farmer, Norwood; Sean W. Farrell, Framingham; Daniel S. Field, Newton; Katharine Folger, Cambridge; Michael Friedland, Dorchester; Anthony H. Gemma, Milton; Dana M. Gershengorn, Weston; Marguerite T. Grant, Cambridge; Eliot J. Green, Brookline; Geraldine Griffin, Cambridge; Richard Grundy, Salem; Robert Healy, Lowell; Lee Hettinger, Marlborough; Stephen C. Hoctor, Woburn; Lincoln S. Jalelian, Arlington; Martin F. Kane, II, Brighton; Gary Katz, Cambridge; Mary Pat Kelly, Boston; Michael Koffman, Charlestown; Brian W. Leahey, Tewksbury; Linda M. Leggett, Somerville; David P. Linsky, Natick; David Losier, Acton; Adrienne Lynch, Newton; Steven Masse, Somerville; Paul Mastrocola, Medford; Allen McCarthy, Winchester; David McCauley, Revere; Ann T. McGonigle, Wakefield; Lisa S. McLean, Cambridge; David C. Megan, Cambridge; Rose Mellor, Charlestown; Beth Merachnik, Cambridge; Susan Meyer, Boston; Alexandra S. Moffatt, Dedham; Maura B. Murphy, Franklin; Joseph D. Neylon, Stoneham; Sonia Norman-Johnson, Easton; Thomas O'Reilly, South Boston; Michael A. Ortiz, Lowell; Emily R. Paradise, Brookline; Lori Parris, Dorchester; Carlene Pennell, Arlington; Barbara Piselli, Malden; Jennifer Queally, Dedham; AnneMarie Relyea-Chew, Winchester; Joan F. Renehan, Brighton; James Rice, Arlington; James R. Richards, Milton; Kimberly A. Rizzotti, Somerville; Lynn C. Rooney, Bedford; Marian Ryan, Belmont; Kevin L. Ryle, Wilmington; James Sahakian, Winchester; Pamela A. Scarlatelli, Brookline; Kurt Schwartz, Wayland; Sabita Singh, Somerville; Heather Smith, Marion; Judith B. Stephenson, Westwood; Julie Stevens,

Needham; Megan Storing, Newton; Catherine E. Sullivan, Lexington; Alison M. Takacs, Maynard; James Tamagini, Jr., Wakefield; Daniel O. Tracy, Milton; Jill Wasserman, Randolph; Melissa Weisgold, Boston; Karen Wells, Newton; David R. Yannetti, Boston; Tanis Yannetti, Boston; Nathaniel Yeager, Brighton; David Zirlen, Natick.

EASTERN DISTRICT (Essex County) — Kevin M. Burke, Beverly. *First Assistant,* Robert N. Weiner, Marblehead. *Chief, Administration and Finance,* Charles F. Grimes, Beverly. *Chief, Special Investigations Division,* Frederick B. McAlary, Andover. *Chief, District Court Operations,* William E. Fallon, Melrose. *Executive Director, Victim/ Witness Programs,* Michaelene O'Neill McCann, Lowell. *Indictment Clerk, Essex County,* George O'Connor, Lynn. *Administrative Assistant Trial List, Felonies,* Shirley Cahill, Lynn. *Assistants:* Robert Brennan, Bedford; Milton Cranney, Jr., Andover; Jean Curran, Reading; Mary Alice Doyle, Stoneham; David Duncan, Beverly; D. Dunbar Livingston, Nahant; William Melkonian, Stoneham; Kevin M. Mitchell, Boston; Antonia Nedder, Westwood; Brian O'Keefe, Salem; Gerald Shea, Newburyport; David Swartz, Haverhill; Kathe Tuttman, Andover; Eileen Whooley, Ipswich. *Chief, Appeals Division,* S. Jane Haggerty, Lexington. *Assistants:* Robert J. Bender, Merrimac; Cathleen Campbell, Allston; Elin Graydon, Chestnut Hill; Nicole Procida, South Boston; Marcia Slingerland, Beverly.

NORFOLK DISTRICT (Norfolk County) — Jeffrey A. Locke, Wellesley. *Deputy District Attorney,* Matthew T. Connolly, Needham. *First Assistant District Attorney,* John P. Kivlan, Dover. *Executive Assistant District Attorney:* Michael C. Bolden, Milton. *Assistants:* Michele M. Armour, Walpole; Jon S. Barooshian, Newton; Andrew R. Berman, Braintree; John G. Birtwell, Walpole; Thomas M. Brennan, Bedford; Christopher J. Bulger, Quincy; Courtney Cahill, Scituate; James M. Cantwell, Marshfield; Catherine A. Cappelli, Jamaica Plain; Jeanmarie Carroll, Jamaica Plain; Peter S. Casey, Milford; Susan Corcoran, Milton; Robert C. Cosgrove, Braintree; John R. Costello, South Dennis; Glenn A. Cunha, Dorchester; Robert M. Delahunt, Jr., South Weymouth; Suzanne DiPiero, Braintree; Eric T. Donovan, Dorchester; Daniel P. Flaherty, Cambridge; Timothy R. Flaherty, Cambridge; Timothy E. Gage, Weymouth; Kim S. Gainsboro, Brookline; Stephanie M. Glennon, Greenland, N.H.; Robert S. Goldstein, Concord; Brett J. Harpster, Dedham; Joseph P. Harrington, Jr., Brighton; Julio R. Hernando, Weymouth; Marianne C. Hinkle, Brookline; Sean R. Holland, Milford; Heather M. Kelley, Milton; Tanya Kaye Konjolka, Waban; Varsha Kukafka, Brookline; Julie S. Lavin, Charlestown; Grace H. Lee, Boston; Edward E. Madden, Jr., Brookline; Dennis C. Mahoney, Quincy; Charles McIntyre, Quincy; Michael Mone, Boston; Brian

O'Neill, Boston; Phillip J. Privitera, Arlington; Gerald C. Pudolsky, Canton; Elaina M. Quinn, Dorchester; Christopher M.Tauro, Marblehead; Michael H. Xifaras, Brighton; Anne S. Yas, Sharon. *Special Assistants:* Danielle E. deBenedictis, Boston; Mary E. Tufo, Quincy.

CAPE AND ISLANDS DISTRICT (Barnstable, Dukes and Nantucket Counties) — Philip A. Rollins, Mashpee. *First Assistant:* Michael D. O'Keefe, Barnstable. *Chief District Court Prosecutor, Barnstable Division:* Sharon Thibeault, Marshfield. *Chief District Court Prosecutor, Falmouth Division:* Richard J. Piazza, North Falmouth. *Chief District Court Prosecutor, Orleans Division:* Peter Lloyd, Centerville. *Assistants:* Lisa Edmonds, West Yarmouth; Brian S. Glenny, Yarmouthport; James N. Greenberg, Dennis; Michael Joyce, Yarmouthport; Monica Kraft, Truro; Edward F. X. Lynch, West Barnstable; Robert E. Manning Jr., Centerville; Nicole Manoog, Hyannis; David G. Nagle, Duxbury; Gary M. Saladino, Plymouth; Michael A. Trudeau, Harwichport; Linda Wagner, Buzzards Bay; Robert A. Welsh III, West Barnstable. *Chief Appellate Attorney:* Julia K. Holler, Sandwich. *Chief Juvenile Court Prosecutor:* Roger A. Jackson, Cotuit. *Chief Domestic Violence Prosecutor:* J. Thomas Kirkman, North Falmouth. *Chief of Operations:* Sarah C. Dale, Barnstable. *Victim/Witness Assistance Program Director:* Virginia L. Bein, Barnstable.

BRISTOL DISTRICT (Bristol County) — Paul F. Walsh, Jr., New Bedford. *First Assistant,* Gilbert J. Nadeau, Jr.. Somerset. *Chief Prosecutor, District Courts,* Lewis A. Armistead, Jr., East Providence, R.I. *Assistants:* Cynthia M. Brackett, Fall River; Matthew F. Burke, Fall River; Stephen G. Butts, Fairhaven; Kevin E. Connelly, New Bedford; David L. Crowley, Jr., Mattapoisett; Elspeth B. Cypher, New Bedford; Renee P. Dupuis, Mattapoisett; William J. Flynn III, North Easton; Pamela S. Gauvin, Fall River; Sylvia Gomes, New Bedford; Robert L. Goodale, Dedham; David L. Keighley, Fairhaven; George D. Kelly, Swansea; Lesly A. Leahy, Adamsville, R.I.; Catherine B. Ledwidge, Fall River; Cynthia A. Letourneau, Lakeville; John P. Letourneau, New Bedford; Christopher J. Markey, Dorchester; John V. Mahoney II, New Bedford; Cheryl L. Mazurek, Fall River; Timothy R. McGuire, Fall River; Stephen L. Melo, South Dartmouth; Rebecca S. Miller, Medway; Toby S. Mooney, Taunton; John D. Moses, Taunton; Ronald F. Moynahan, Scituate; Raymond G. Mullen, Jr., Fall River; Bernard J. Murphy, Mansfield; Sandra G. Saunders, Fairhaven; Walter J. Shea, Lawrence; John P. Stapleton, Bridgewater; C. Samuel Sutter, Fall River; James M. Tierney, Milton; Kenneth D. vanColen, South Dartmouth;

Cynthia A. Vincent, New Bedford; Nancy K. Wasserman, Stoughton. *Special Assistants:* John N. Flanagan, Boston; David K. Ferguson, Worcester; David Mark, Boston; Shaun S. McLean, Northampton; John C. O'Neil, Fall River; Brian J. Sullivan, Westport.

MIDDLE DISTRICT (Worcester County) — John J. Conte, Worcester. *Assistants:* James J. Reagon, Worcester; John P. Haran, Worcester; Joseph LoStracco, Worcester; Leon R. Zitowitz, Worcester; Lawrence J. Murphy, Southborough; Kathleen K. Dellostritto, Worcester; Mary E. Sawicki, Rutland; Stephen J. Prunier, Worcester. *Victim/Witness Director:* Anthony J. Pellegrini.

HAMPDEN DISTRICT (Hampden County) — William M. Bennett, Springfield. *First Assistant,* James C. Orenstein, Longmeadow. *Superior Court Assistants:* Laurel Brandt, Longmeadow; Ellen Berger, Chicopee; Patricia Campagnari, East Longmeadow; Dianne Dillon, Springfield; Elizabeth G. Dineen, East Longmeadow; Charles E. Dolan, Ludlow; Donna S. Donato, Springfield; Francis M. Dunn, Holyoke; Elizabeth Dunphy Farris, Longmeadow; David M. Jenkins, Springfield; Richard Morse, Amherst; Tina S. Page, Springfield; Carmen W. Picknally, Longmeadow; Linda Pisano, Northampton; Maria Rodriguez, West Springfield; Howard I. Safford, Feeding Hills; Matt Shea, Springfield. *Appellate Division Assistant District Attorneys:* Deborah Ahlstrom, Springfield; Jennifer Brand, Northampton; Marcia Julian, Springfield; Jane Montori, Longmeadow; Lori Odierna, Longmeadow; Jim Wodarski, Lenox. *District Court Assistant District Attorneys:* Lisa Baker, Springfield; Daniel Bergin, Longmeadow; Kimberly Brooks, Springfield; Barbara Burton, Springfield; Tina Cafaro, East Longmeadow; John DaCruz, Ludlow; Christopher Donovan, Amherst; Jeffrey Fialky, Longmeadow; John Flahive, Springfield; Theresa Flanagan, Holyoke; Christopher Gahm, East Longmeadow; James Goodhines, Longmeadow; Anthony Guardione, Longmeadow; Catherine Higgins, South Hadley; Daniel Kelly, Springfield; Jacquelyn Lee, Springfield; Joan Lynch, Holyoke; Christine Maza, Springfield; John McKenna, Springfield; Karen McCarthy, West Springfield; Christene Mertes, Springfield; Peter Murphy, Springfield; Jill O'Connor, East Longmeadow; Mary Beth Ogulewicz, Holyoke; Timothy Rogers, Wilbraham; Patrick Sabbs, South Hadley; Bethzaida Sanabria-Vega, Springfield; Grace Taylor, Springfield; Nina Vivenzio, Springfield; Jill Ziter, Springfield.

NORTHWESTERN DISTRICT (Hampshire and Franklin Counties; Town of Athol in Worcester County) — Elizabeth D. Scheibel, South Hadley. *First Assistants:* David A. Angier, Conway; W. Michael Goggins, Northampton. *Assistants:* James P. Clark, Springfield; Susan J. Loehn,

Florence; Jane E. Mulqueen, Chicopee; Judith E. Pietras, Wilbraham; Mary Lou Szulborski, Baldwinville; Joseph A. Quinlan, Colrain; Renee L. Steese, Florence; Barry Auskern, Bernardston; Deirdre Burke, Ashfield; Daniel F. Graves, Greenfield; Elizabeth Katz, Northampton; Robert S. LaMountain, Holyoke; Laurie MacLeod, Greenfield; Thomas M. O'Connor, South Hadley; Jayme A. Parent, Northampton; Cynthia M. Pepyne, South Deerfield; Ian Polumbaum, Northampton; Cora-Jean Robinson, Northampton; Matthew E. Ryan, South Hadley; Melinda A. Soffer, Eastampton; John P. Talbot, Jr., Florence; Maureen E. Walsh, North Hatfield.

BERKSHIRE DISTRICT (Berkshire County) — Gerard D. Downing, Pittsfield. *First Assistant,* David F. Capeless, West Stockbridge. *Second Assistant,* Anne M. Kendall, Dalton. *Assistants:* Stephen J. Buoniconti, Pittsfield; Paul J. Caccaviello, Pittsfield; Carolyn K. Ince, Housatonic; Robert W. Kinzer III, Pittsfield; Richard M. Locke, Pittsfield; Susan O. Mancini, Pittsfield; Joan M. McMenemy, Pittsfield; Kelly M. Mulcahy, North Adams;Alexander Z. Nappan, Housatonic; Joseph A. Pieropan, Pittsfield; Jennifer Tyne, Cheshire; Christopher J. Walsh, Pittsfield.

PLYMOUTH DISTRICT (Plymouth County) — Michael J. Sullivan, Abington. *First Assistant,* Joseph P. Gaughan, Duxbury. *Second Assistants,* Geline W. Williams; Paul C. Dawley. *Third Assistant,* Frank M. Gaziano. *Assistants:* Kathleen A. Adams; Mary L. Amrhein; William F. Asci; Jeffrey S. Beckerman; Nicholas H. Bokavich; Patrick O. Bomberg; Garrett J. Bradley; John E. Bradley; Daniel P. Bulger; Sheila M. Calkins; Colleen C. Carroll; Diane B. Cashman; William H. Connolly; Christina Crowley; Michael F. Darche; Bruce Denneen; Maria DoCouto; Kelly Anne Doherty; Sharon E. Donatelle; Daniel J. Dwyer; Patrick C. Gannon; Brian D. Griffin; Jeanne L. Holmes; Barbara J. Isola; Lisa J. Jacobs; Ruth C. Kechejian; Daniel P. Kennedy; Christine M. Kiggen; Martha J. Kovner; Patrick C. Lee; William M. McCauley; Joseph McDonald; Frank J. Middleton, Jr.; Mary E. Mullaney; Kathleen Murphy; Gregory G. Nazarian; Bridget V. Norton; Scott B. Nussbum; Michael H. O'Connell; Saundra R. Saunders; Edward H. Sharkansky; Gordon W. Spencer; James M. Sullivan; Jennifer Sullivan; Suzanne M. Sullivan; Robert C. Thompson; David G. Tobin; Carolyn C. Vantine.

SUFFOLK DISTRICT (Suffolk County) — Ralph C. Martin II, Boston. *First Assistant:* Robert P. Gittens. *Chief of Staff,* Rachel Kimmich. *Executive Secretary,* Linda Tobin. *Chief Trial Counsel,* Elizabeth Keeley. *External Affairs Coordinator,* James Borghesani. *Director, Community Relations,* Deborah McDonagh; *Chief of District Court Prosecutions,*

Marcy Cass. *District Court Administrative Assistant,* Lisa Ortiz; *Chief of Homicide,* David Meier. *Chief, Appellate Division,* Katherine McMahon; *Chief, Victim Witness Services,* Janet E. Fine. *Press Secretary,* Carmen E. Fields. *Director, Domestic Violence Unit,* Andrea Cabral. *Director, Child Abuse Unit,* Joshua Wall. *Director of Training,* Linda Bucci. *Personnel Administrator,* Constance Valenti. *Assistant District Attorneys:* Janet Abrams; Claire Ahern; Margaret F. Albertson; Gwen Allen; Kenneth Anderson; Charles Bartoloni; Robert E. Baylor; Cherise Beineke; Lynn Beland; Daniel Bennet; Patricia Blackburn; Jeff Blackshear; Timothy Bradl; Lynn Brennan; Phyllis Broker; Linda Bucci; Margaret M. Buckley; John Burke; Andrea Cabral; Thomas P. Campbell; Robert Canty; Karen S. Caplan; Nancy Carlos; Brian J. Carney; Karen M. Carrabes; Lisa Casella; Lawrence Christopher; David J. Coffey; James Coffey; Dennis Collins; Georgia Critsley; Paul Curran; Gennaro D'Ambrosio; David Deakin; Bruce Dean; Kenneth Desmond; Richard DiMeo; Carlos Dominguez; Ellen M. Donahue; Sean Donahue; Kelly Downes; Kristin Dunn; Sean Early; Francine Falbo; Michael Flaherty; Peter G. Flaherty; Stacey J. Fortes; Sharon Fray-Witzer; William Freeman; Stephen Fuller; Jill Furman; T. Jane Gabriel; Michael F. Gaffney, Jr.; Mark Grady; Gretchen Graef; Jodi Greenburg; Robert M. Griffin; Patrick Haggan; Mark Hallal; George Hardiman; Nancy Hathaway; Kevin Hayden; Elizabeth Hayes; Margaret Hegarty; Maureen Hogan; Michele Hogan; Mary Hogan-Sullivan; Daniel J. Hourihan; Mathew Iler; Marcy Jackson; Ann Johnston; Leora Joseph; John M. Julian; Jeffrey Karp; Ursula Knight; William Korman; James J. Larkin; Heather Lewis; Paul B. Linn; Ellen (Fulham) Lopez; David Lowy; Padraic Lydon; Tracy-Lee Lyons; Matthew Machera; Joseph Makalusky; Timothy Malec; Debra Markham; Kathleen M. McCarthy; Deborah A. McDonagh; Alicia McDonnell; Jane L. McDonough; Robert J. McKenna, Jr.; Katherine McMahon; David Meier; Kevin Mullen; Eileen Murphy; Michael Murphy; Amy Nechtem; Mathew Nestor; Eric Neyman; Leslie O'Brien; Catherine Oatway; Mary Orfanello; Joseph Pagliarulo; Robert Palumbo; John Pappas; Paul Poth; Linda Poulos; John E. Powers, Jr.; Robert Powers; John Paul Puleo; Shelley Richmond; Susan Rist-Sbracia; Isabel Rivera; Karen Rolley; Brian Roman; Maria F. Romero; Jennifer Rowe; Blake Rubin; Frank Sacco; Lisa Scalcione; Gary W. Schubert; Julia Schwartz; Paul Smyth; James Stanton; Gerald Stewart; Jane Sullivan; Carla Tacelli; Kristine Tammaro; Viktor Theiss; Naomi Thompson; Robert Tochka; Paul Treseler; Michael Uhlarik; Soledad Valenciano; Constance Valenti; Mai Vu; Joshua I. Wall; Pamela Wechsler; Philip L. Weiner; Joan White; Jane Woodbury; Raffi Yassayan; Onyen Yong; Barbara Young; Edmond Zabin; John Zanini; Mark Zanini.

LIST OF THE

Executive and Legislative Departments

OF THE

GOVERNMENT

OF

The Commonwealth of Massachusetts

AND OFFICERS IMMEDIATELY CONNECTED THEREWITH WITH PLACES OF RESIDENCE

1997–1998

EXECUTIVE DEPARTMENT
GOVERNOR.
HIS EXCELLENCY, WILLIAM F. WELD *(R)*
of Cambridge.
LIEUTENANT-GOVERNOR.
HIS HONOR, ARGEO PAUL CELLUCCI *(R)*
of Hudson.

District   Council.
   I. — DAVID F. CONSTANTINE *(D)* of New Bedford.
  II. — KELLY A. TIMILTY *(D)* of Canton.
 III. — CYNTHIA STONE CREEM *(D)* of Newton.
 IV. — CHRISTOPHER A. IANNELLA, JR. *(D)* of Boston.
  V. — PATRICIA A. DOWLING *(D)* of Lawrence.
 VI. — DOROTHY A. KELLY GAY *(D)* of Somerville.
VII. — JORDAN LEVY *(D)* of Worcester.
VIII. — EDWARD M. O'BRIEN *(D)* of Easthampton.

Legislative Director to Governor.
STEPHEN C. DODGE.

Chief Legal Counsel to Governor.
PAUL W. JOHNSON.

Military Establishment

His Excellency, WILLIAM F. WELD, Commander-in-Chief.

Major General RAYMOND A. VEZINA,
The Adjutant General, Shrewsbury.

Military Division
State Staff

MG Raymond A. Vezina. *The Adjutant General* Shrewsbury
BG John J. Hannon. *Executive Officer* .... Quincy
COL David W. Gavigan, *Assistant Adjutant
General* .... Kingston
COL Paul R. DesForges, *Assistant
Adjutant General, Air* .... Shrewsbury
COL Louis Volpe, *State Quartermaster* ...... Whitinsville
LTC Abraham P. Zimelman, *State Surgeon* ... Newton

U.S. Property & Fiscal Officer

COL Anthony C. Spadorcia .... Danvers

Massachusetts Regional Training Institute

COL John J. Goff, Jr., *Commandant* .... Hanover

Commanders, Massachusetts National Guard
ARMY NATIONAL GUARD

Headquarters, State Area Command, Mass. ARNG:
    MG Raymond A. Vezina .... Shrewsbury
Recruiting & Retention Command:
    LTC Thomas J. Sellars .... Randolph
79th Troop Command:
    COL Robert E. D'Alto .... Braintree
26th Infantry Brigade:
    COL Norman A. Welch .... Plymouth
1/104th Infantry Battalion:
    LTC Ronald Senez .... Springfield
1/181st Infantry Battalion:
    LTC Richard E. Hens .... Leominster
51st Troop Command:
    COL William J. Rabbe .... Duxbury

182nd Infantry Battalion (Mech):
 LTC Edward G. McNamara . . . . Sterling
181st Engineers Battalion:
 LTC Joseph G. Materia . . . . Newton
101st Engineer Battalion:
 LTC Kenneth R. Simmons . . . . Manchester, NH
726th Finance Support Command:
 LTC Roy L. Weeks . . . . Fayetteville, NC
101 Quartermaster Battalion:
 MAJ Raymond M. Murphy . . . . Burlington
Service Support Battalion:
 MAJ Brian J. Catalano . . . . Whitinsville
Maintenance Battalion Command:
 LTC Henry J. Barber . . . . Milford
211th Military Police Battalion:
 LTC Richard H. Spicer . . . . Franklin
Camp Edwards Training Site:
 COL Gregory J. Dadak . . . . Cataumet
1/101st Field Artillery Battalion:
 LTC Gaetano V. Sammartano . . . . Brighton
1/102nd Field Artillery Battalion:
 LTC Gary A. Pappas . . . . Boston
42nd Division Artillery:
 COL Edward H. Russell . . . . Windham, NH

Commanders, AIR NATIONAL GUARD

Military Division State Staff:
 COL Paul R. Desforges, *Assistant
 Adjutant General, Air* . . . . Shrewsbury
HQ Mass. Air National Guard:
 BG Richard A. Platt . . . . Westfield
102d Fighter Wing:
 LTC Samuel M. Shiver . . . . Falmouth
104th Fighter Wing:
 COL David W. Cherry . . . . Westfield
253rd Combat Communications Group:
 COL Alan L. Cowles . . . . Mashpee
267th Combat Communications Squadron:
 MAJ Donald F. Mofford . . . . Randolph

101st Air Control Squadron:
    LTC Robert A. Johnson . . . . Uxbridge
212th Engineering Installation Squadron:
    LTC Joseph B. Bellino . . . . Shrewsbury

Secretary of the Commonwealth.
WILLIAM FRANCIS GALVIN *(D)* of Boston

John K. McCarthy, Esq., Norwood, *Chief of Staff,*
    Room 337, State House, Boston.
Laurie Flynn, Malden, *Chief Legal Counsel,*
    17th Floor, McCormack Building, Boston.
Philip L. Shea, Lowell, *Director of Administrative
    Services,* 17th Floor, McCormack Building, Boston.
Roberta Baker, Worcester, *Director, Personnel,*
    16th Floor, McCormack Building, Boston.
Josephine Fatta, Everett, *Director of Graphic Communications,*
    16th Floor, McCormack Building, Boston.
Kevin Harvey, Salem, *Legislative Secretary,*
    Room 337, State House, Boston.
Michael Maresco, Marshfield, *Legislative Secretary,*
    Room 337, State House, Boston.
Laurie Flynn, Malden, *Director of Corporations,*
    17th Floor, McCormack Building, Boston.
John Cloonan, Roslindale, *Director of Elections,*
    17th Floor, McCormack Building, Boston.
John Warner, Norwood, *Archives Director,*
    State Archives, Columbia Point, Boston.
Richard Sundstrom, Westborough, *Director of Archives
    Building Facility,* State Archives, Columbia Point, Boston.
Anthony DeSantis, Worcester, *Director of State Records Center,*
    State Archives, Columbia Point, Boston.
Judy McDonough, Boston, *Director of Massachusetts Historical
    Commission,* State Archives, Columbia Point, Boston.
Carolyn Kelly MacWilliam, Everett, *Director of Public Records,*
    17th Floor, McCormack Building, Boston.
Susan Scalfani, Watertown, *Supervisor of Commissions,*
    17th Floor, McCormack Building, Boston.
Steve Kfoury, Lawrence, *Director of State
    Publications and Regulations,*
    Room 2A, State House, Boston.
Janice Coughlin, Quincy, *Director of State Bookstore,*
    Room 116, State House, Boston.

Mary Rinehart-Stankeiwicz, Andover, *Director of State House Tours,* Room 194, State House, Boston.
Josephine Albanese, Woburn, *Director of Citizens Information Service,* 16th Floor, McCormack Building, Boston.
Barry Guthery, Cambridge, *Director of Securities,* 17th Floor, McCormack Building, Boston.

Treasurer and Receiver General
JOSEPH D. MALONE *(R)* of Waltham.

Thomas H. Trimarco, *First Deputy Treasurer* . . Charlestown
Beth E. Myers, *Deputy Treasurer* . . . . Watertown
Robert Foley, *Deputy Treasurer* . . . . Framingham
Kenneth Olshansky, *Deputy Treasurer* . . . . . . Lincoln
Marie Lawlor, *Deputy Treasurer* . . . . Brighton
Eric Fehrnstrom, *Asst. Treasurer* . . . . Brookline
William Squillace, *Asst. Treasurer* . . . . Gloucester
Lina Wilson, *Asst. Treasurer* . . . . Winchester
Paul Mandeville, *Asst. Treasurer* . . . . Marshfield
Tonia Duchano, *Asst. Treasurer* . . . . Charlestown
Laureen Vaughn, *Director,*
   State Board of Retirement . . . . Brighton
Sam DePhillippo, *Dir. State Lottery* . . . . Needham

Auditor of the Commonwealth
A. JOSEPH DENUCCI *(D)* of Newton.

Robert A. Powilatis . . . . *First Deputy Auditor for Audit Operations.*
Kenneth A. Marchurs . . . . *Deputy Auditor for Administration/ Local Mandates.*
John W. Beveridge . . . . *Deputy Auditor for MIS/EDP.*
Francis W. Shannon . . . . *Deputy Auditor for Policy and Executive Affairs.*
Richard D. Sewall . . . . *Chief of Staff, Executive Division.*
Charles R. Melchin . . . . *Administrator, Audit Operations.*
Thomas F. Collins . . . . . *Director, Division of Local Mandates.*

Attorney General
L. SCOTT HARSHBARGER *(D)*, of Westwood.

First Assistant
THOMAS H. GREEN.

Senior Advisor
DONALD L. DAVENPORT.

I. Executive Bureau
Thomas E. Samoluk. Chief of Staff

   a. Director of Communication
Edward Cafasso.
   b. Community Liaison
Robert Colt.
   c. Director of Personnel
Doris S. Donovan.
   d. Executive Assistant Attorney General
William P. Lee.
   e. Director of Budget
Jeanette Maillet.
   f. Director of Support Services
Vickie Manning.
   g. Director of Management Informational Systems
Maryclare Querzoli.
   h. Director of Operations and Investigative Services
Carmen Russo.
   i. Deputy Chief of Staff, Director of Public Affairs
Carrie Smotrich.
   j. Legal Counsel to the Attorney General
Jane E. Tewksbury.
   k. Law Librarian
Karin Thurman.

II. Business and Labor Protection Bureau
Stuart Rossman, Bureau Chief.

   a. Unemployment Fraud Division
Marie St. Fleur. Assistant Attorney General.
   b. Fair Labor and Business Practices Division
Helen Moreschi, Assistant Attorney General.
   c. Insurance Fraud Division
John Ciardi, Assistant Attorney General.

    d. Medicaid Fraud Control Unit
        Nicholas Messuri, Assistant Attorney General.
        Steven McCarthy, Deputy Division Chief.

III. Criminal Bureau
    Frances A. McIntyre, Bureau Chief.
    Susan Spurlock, Deputy Bureau Chief.
    Mark Smith, Deputy Bureau Chief of Litigation.

    a. Criminal Appellate Division
        Pamela Hunt, Assistant Attorney General.
    b. Criminal Investigation Division
        Captain John Kelly, Massachusetts State Police.
    c. Economic Crimes Division
        Carol Starkey, Assistant Attorney General.
    d. Environmental Crimes Strike Force
        Martin Levin, Assistant Attorney General.
    e. Financial Investigation Division
        Paul Stewart, Assistant Attorney General.
    f. Narcotics & Organized Crime Division &
        Special Investigations Unit
        Robert Sikellis, Assistant Attorney General.
    g. Public Integrity Division
        Jeremy Silverfine, Assistant Attorney General.

IV. Family and Community Crimes Bureau
    Diane Juliar, Bureau Chief.

    a. Victim Compensation and Assistance Division
        Judith Beals, Assistant Attorney General.

V. Government Bureau
    Douglas Wilkins, Bureau Chief.
    Peter Sacks, Deputy Bureau Chief.

    Coordinator of Affirmative Litigation
        William Porter, Assistant Attorney General.
    Appeals/Bureau Training Coordinator
        John Bowman, Assistant Attorney General.

    a. Administrative Law Division
        Judith Yogman, Assistant Attorney General.
    b. Trial Division
        John Bigelow, Assistant Attorney General.
    c. Environmental Protection Division
        James Milkey, Assistant Attorney General.

VI. Public Protection Bureau
Barbara B. Anthony, Bureau Chief.
Freda Fishman, Deputy Bureau Chief.
   a. Civil Rights Investigation Division
      Karen Ortolino, Assistant Attorney General.
   b. Civil Rights Civil Liberties Division
      Richard Cole, Assistant Attorney General.
   c. Consumer Protection/Antitrust Division
      George Weber, Assistant Attorney General.
   d. Public Charities Division
      Richard Allen, Assistant Attorney General.
   e. Regulated Industries Division
      George Dean, Assistant Attorney General.

VII. Western Massachusetts Regional Office
Edward Berlin, Division Chief.
Judy Z. Kalman, Chief of Litigation.

Office of the Inspector General.
[Chapter 579 of the Acts of 1980, as amended]

ROBERT A. CERASOLI, *Inspector General*, Quincy

Fran Brown, *First Assistant Inspector
General for Legislative and Public Policy* . . West Roxbury
Janet Werkman, *First Assistant Inspector
General for Legal Affairs* . . . . Cambridge
F. Daniel Ahern, Jr., *First Assistant Inspector
General for Management* . . . . Hanover
Gregory Sullivan, *First Assistant Inspector
General for Financial Investigations* . . . . . . Norwood
Richard Finocchio, *First Assistant Inspector
General for Criminal Investigations* . . . . Marblehead
Barbara Hansberry, *General Counsel* . . . . Cambridge
Mary Beth Farrelly, *Director of
Administration and Finance* . . . . Wrentham

GOVERNOR'S CABINET

Governor's Cabinet.

[Chapter 704 of the Acts of 1969, as amended.]

[This listing includes the Secretariats, as reorganized under Chapter 57 of the Acts of 1996, and subsequently amended by sections 10 and 527 of Chapter 151 of the Acts of 1996. Executive Departments that report directly to the Governor, and boards that are appointed by the Governor.]

SECRETARIATS.

EXECUTIVE OFFICE FOR ADMINISTRATION AND FINANCE.

Executive Secretary, Charles D. Baker.
Chief of Staff, Leslie A. Kirwan.
Assistant Secretary, Joseph A. Trainor.
Assistant Secretary, Steven N. Kadish.
Assistant Secretary, Lowell L. Richards, III.
General Counsel, Susan S. Beck.
Executive Director of Minority Business Enterprise, Pablo Calderon.
Director of Information Technology, Louis Gutierrez.
Director of Communications, Joe Landolfi.

MAJOR AGENCY HEADS:
Division of Administrative Law Appeals (DALA), Christopher Connolly,
    Chief Administrative Magistrate.
Office of Affirmative Action (SOAA), Mark Bolling, Director.
Appellate Tax Board (ATB), Ken Gurge, Chairman.
Budget Bureau (FAD), Tom Graf, Director.
Bureau of State Office Buildings (BSOB), Dennis Smith, Superintendent.
Central Business Office (CBO), MaryAnn Myers, Director.
Capital Planning and Operations (DCPO), Lark Palermo,
    Commissioner.
Civil Service Commission (CSC), Chris Morris, Chairperson.
Office of the Comptroller (OSC), William T. Kilmartin, Comptroller.
Administering Agency on Developmental Disabilities (ADDA), Daniel
    Shannon, Director.
Massachusetts Office on Disability (MOD), Lorraine Grieff, Acting
    Director.
Massachusetts Commission Against Discrimination (MCD), Charles
    Walker, Acting Chairman.
Massachusetts Office of Dispute Resolution (MODR), Fredie Kay,
    Director.
Office of Employee Relations (OER), Kevin Preston, Acting Director.
Group Insurance Commission (GIC), Dolores Mitchell, Executive
    Director.

514   *Governor's Cabinet.*

Board of Library Commissioners (BLC), Keith Fiels, Director.
Division of Information Technology (ITD), Louis Gutierrez, Director.
Massachusetts Teachers' Retirement Board (MTRB), Thomas R. Lussier,
     Executive Director.
Division of Human Resources (HRD), Joseph Trainor, Administrator.
Operational Services Division (OSD), Philmore Anderson, Purchasing
     Agent.
Public Employee Retirement Administration (PERA), John J. McGlynn,
     Commissioner.
Department of Revenue (DOR), Mitchell Adams, Commissioner.
Department of Local Services (DLS), Harry Grossman, Acting Director.
State Library (George Fingold) (OSD), Stephen Fulcino, State
     Librarian Director.
Office of Veterans' Services (VET), Thomas Hudner, Commissioner.
Workers' Compensation Litigation Unit (WCL), Gillian Steinhauer,
     Director.

AGENCIES INCLUDE: —
     Division of Administrative Law Appeals (DALA).
     Office of Affirmative Action (SOAA).
     Appellate Tax Board (ATB).
     Budget Bureau (FAD).
     Bureau of State Office Buildings (BSOB).
     Central Business Office (CBO).
     Capital Planning and Operations (DCPO).
     Civil Service Commission (CSC).
     Office of the Comptroller (OSC).
     Administering Agency on Developmental Disabilities (ADDA).
     Massachusetts Office On Disability (MOD) .
     Massachusetts Commission Against Discrimination (MCD).
     Massachusetts Office of Dispute Resolution (MODR).
     Office of Employee Relations (OER).
     Group Insurance Commission (GIC).
     Board of Library Commissioners (BLC).
     Division of Information Technology (ITD).
     Massachusetts Teachers' Retirement Board (MTRB).
     Division of Human Resources (HRD).
     Operational Services Division (OSD).
     Public Employee Retirement Administration (PERA).
     Department of Revenue (DOR).
     Department of Local Services (DLS).
     State Library (George Fingold) (OSD).
     Office of Veterans' Services (VET).
     Workers' Compensation Litigation Unit (WCL).

EXECUTIVE OFFICE OF ELDER AFFAIRS.
[Chapter 1168 of the Acts of 1973.]

Executive Secretary, Franklin P. Ollivierre, Newton.

MAJOR AGENCY HEADS: —
Assistant Secretary for Policy and Program Development, Marlene Lio-MacDougall, Cambridge.
Assistant Secretary, Finance and Administration, Timothy Regan, Boston.
Assistant Secretary, Program Management, Lillian Glickman, Ph.D., Newton.
General Counsel, Pamela Dashiell, Boston.
Special Assistant, Derrek Shulman, Newton.

EXECUTIVE OFFICE OF ENVIRONMENTAL AFFAIRS.

Executive Secretary, Trudy Coxe.
Undersecretary/Policy and Programs, Jan Reitsma.
Undersecretary/Administration and Finance, George Crombie.
General Counsel, Carol Lee Rawn.
Chief of Staff, Melanie Murray-Brown.

MAJOR AGENCY HEADS: —
Office of Technical Assistance, Barbara Kelley, Director.
Coastal Zone Management, Margaret Brady, Director.
Environmental Impact Review Act (MEPA). (vacant).
Division of Conservation Services, Joel A. Lerner, Director.
Water Resources Commission, Mark Smith, Director.
DEPARTMENT OF ENVIRONMENTAL MANAGEMENT, Peter C. Webber, Commissioner.
Division of Administration, Susan Frechette, Director.
Division of Forests & Parks, Todd Frederick, Director.
Division of Resource Conservation, Martin Suuberg, Director.
DEPARTMENT OF FISHERIES, WILDLIFE & RECREATIONAL VEHICLES, John Phillips, Commissioner.
Division of Fisheries and Wildlife, Wayne F. MacCallum, Director.
Division of Marine Fisheries, Philip G. Coates, Director.
Division of Law Enforcement, Richard Murray, Director.
Public Access Board, John P. Sheppard, Director.
METROPOLITAN DISTRICT COMMISSION, David Balfour, Commissioner.
Administration and Finance, Andrew Iovanna, Director.
Operations, Brian Kerins, Director.
Policy, Samantha Overton, Director.

Engineering and Construction, Francis D. Faucher, Director.
DEPARTMENT OF FOOD AND AGRICULTURE. Jonathan Healy,
Commissioner.
Assistant Commissioner, Richard Hubbard.
Director of Administration, Virginia Richard.
Division of Agricultural Development, Mary Jordan, Director.
Pesticide Board, Brad Mitchell, Director.
Division of Fairs, Stephen Quinn, Director.
DEPARTMENT OF ENVIRONMENTAL PROTECTION, David Struhs,
Commissioner.
Environmental Results Strategic Priorities, Allan Bedwell.
Operations and Programs, Ed Kounce.
Administration Human Resources, Daniel McGillicuddy.
Strategic Policy Technology, Madeline Snow.
Strategic Programs, James Colman.
Bureau of Resource Protection, Arlene O'Donnell, Director.
Bureau of Waste Prevention, Carl Dierker, Director.
Division of Waste Site Cleanup, James Colman, Director.
MASSACHUSETTS WATER RESOURCES AUTHORITY, Trudy Coxe,
Chairman.
Executive Director, Douglas MacDonald.

BOARDS AND COMMISSIONS INCLUDE: —
Department of Environmental Management Board.
Committee for Conservation of Soil, Water and Related Resources.
Department of Fisheries, Wildlife and Recreational Vehicles
Advisory Board.
Fisheries and Wildlife Board.
Marine and Recreational Vehicles Advisory Board.
Marine Fisheries Advisory Commission.
Milk Control Board.
State Board of Food and Agriculture.
Pesticide Board.

EXECUTIVE OFFICE OF HEALTH AND HUMAN SERVICES.

Executive Secretary, Joseph Gallant.
Undersecretary for Health and Human Services, John Ford.

MAJOR AGENCY HEADS: —
Commission for the Blind, Charles Crawford, Commissioner.
Commission for the Deaf and Hard of Hearing, Barbara Jean Wood,
Commissioner.
Department of Social Services, Linda Carlisle, Commissioner.

Department of Mental Health, Marylou Sudders, Commissioner.
Department of Public Health, David Mulligan, Commissioner.
Department of Transitional Assistance, Claire McIntire, Commissioner.
Department of Youth Services, William O'Leary, Commissioner.
Office for Children, Ardith Wieworka, Director.
Soldiers' Home in Chelsea, William Thompson, Commandant.
Soldiers' Home in Holyoke, Rudy Chmura, Superintendent.
Division of Health Care Finance and Policy, Barbara Weinstein,
     Commissioner.
Massachusetts Rehabilitation Commission, Elmer C. Bartels,
     Commissioner.
Department of Mental Retardation, (vacant).

AGENCIES INCLUDE: —
     Department of Mental Health.
     Department of Social Services.
     Office for Children.
     Department of Transitional Assistance.
     Department of Public Health.
     Division of Health Care Finance and Policy.
     Massachusetts Rehabilitation Commission.
     Commission for the Blind.
     Commission for the Deaf and Hard of Hearing.
     Soldiers' Home in Chelsea.
     Soldiers' Home in Holyoke.
     Department of Youth Services.
     Department of Mental Retardation.
     Office of Refugees and Immigration.

ADVISORY BOARDS: —
     Board of Trustees of all State Hospitals and State Schools.
     Refugee Advisory Council.
     Mental Health Advisory Council.
     Commission for Licensing Radiologist Technologists.
     Health Facilities Appeal Board.
     Governor's Commission on Physical Fitness.
     State Advisory Council for the Office for Children.
     Public Health Council.
     Advisory Board for Lead Paint Poisoning Program.
     Nutrition Board.
     Organ Transplant Fund Advisory Board.
     Drug Formulatory Commission.
     Advisory Council on Radiation Protection.
     Advisory Council on Alcoholism.

Advisory Council to the Massachusetts Rehabilitation Commission.
Drug Addiction Rehabilitation Board.
Advisory Board to the Massachusetts Commission for the Blind.
Advisory Board to the Massachusetts Commission for the Deaf.
Board of Trustees of the Soldiers' Home in Chelsea.
Board of Trustees of the Soldiers' Home in Holyoke.
Advisory Committee to the Department of Youth Services.
Board of Trustees Massachusetts Hospital School.
Board of Trustees Tewksbury Hospital.
DMR Advisory Council.
Statewide Independent Living Council.
Children's Trust Fund.
Advisory Committee on Chaplains in State Institutions.
Adolescent Health Council.

EXECUTIVE OFFICE OF PUBLIC SAFETY.

Executive Secretary, Kathleen O'Toole.
Chief of Staff, Richard St. Louis.
Undersecretary, A. David Rodham.
Undersecretary, Robert C. Krekorian.

MAJOR AGENCY HEADS: --
Department of State Police, Colonel Reed Hillman.
Department of Correction, Larry E. DuBois, Commissioner.
Department of Public Safety, Winthrop Farwell, Commissioner.
Parole Board, Natalie Hardy, Executive Director.
Massachusetts Emergency Management Agency, Peter Laporte,
    Executive Director.
Committee on Criminal Justice, Richard St. Louis, Acting Executive
    Director.
Governor's Highway Safety Bureau, Nancy J. Luther, Executive
    Director.
Massachusetts Criminal Justice Training Council, Howard Lebowitz,
    Executive Director.
Military Division, Major General Raymond A. Vezina, Adjutant General.
Registry of Motor Vehicles, Jerold A. Gnazzo, Registrar.
Criminal History Systems Board, Craig Burlingame, Executive Director.
Office of Chief Medical Examiner, Richard Evans, Chief Medical
    Examiner.
Department of Fire Services, Stephen Coan, State Fire Marshal.
Architectural Access Board, Deborah Ryan, Executive Director.
Governor's Alliance Against Drugs, Brad Bailey, Executive Director.
Statewide Emergency Telecommunications Board, Robert Watkinson,
    Executive Director.

AGENCIES INCLUDE: —
    Department of Public Safety
    Board of Boiler Rules.
    Board of Elevator Appeals.
    Board of Elevator Examiners.
    Board of Elevator Regulations.
    Board of Fire Prevention Regulations.
    Bureau of Pipefitters and Refrigeration Technicians.
    Division of Inspections.
    Licensing Section.
    State Fire Marshal's Office.
    Recreational Tramway Board.
    State Boxing Commission.
    State Office of Investigations.
Massachusetts Committee on Criminal Justice Proposal Review Board.
Massachusetts Firefighting Academy.
Massachusetts Fire Training Council.
Office of Chief Medical Examiner.
Medicolegal Investigation Committee.
Registry of Motor Vehicles.
Medical Advisory Board.
Architectural Access Board.
Board of Architectural Access.
Governor's Highway Safety Bureau.
Governor's Highway Safety Committee.
Statewide Emergency Telephone Board.
Firearms Division.

EXECUTIVE OFFICE OF TRANSPORTATION AND CONSTRUCTION.

Secretary of Transportation, MassPike and MBTA Chairman, James J.
    Kerasiotes.
Undersecrerary, John J. Kriston.
General Counsel, James F. McGrail.
Deputy Secretaries:
    Surface Transportation Programs, Dr. Toye L. Brown.
    Civil Rights Program Development, Mary A. Fernandez.

MAJOR AGENCY HEADS: —
Massachusetts Aeronautics Commission, Sherman W. Saltmarsh.
    Chairman; Steven Muench, Executive Director.

Massachusetts Highway Department, Kevin J. Sullivan, Commissioner;
    Charles Kostro, Deputy Commissioner.
MassPort, Peter W. Blute, Executive Director; Mark Robinson,
    Chairman, Board of Directors.
Massachusetts Turnpike Authority, Secretary of EOTC, James J.
    Kerasiotes, Chairman.
Massachusetts Bay Transportation Authority, Secretary of EOTC,
    James J. Kerasiotes, Chairman; Patrick J. Moynihan,
    General Manager.

AGENCIES INCLUDE: —
    Massachusetts Aeronautics Commission.
    Massachusetts Highway Department.
    Massachusetts Port Authority.
    Massachusetts Turnpike Authority.
    Massachusetts Bay Transportation Authority.
    Regional transportation authorities.

DEPARTMENTS AND OFFICES REPORTING
DIRECTLY TO GOVERNOR.

OFFICE OF CONSUMER AFFAIRS AND
BUSINESS REGULATION.

Director, Michael T. Duffy, Boston.
Deputy Director, Jonathan Spampinato, Cambridge.
General Counsel, James Connelly, Hingham.
Chief Financial Officer, Gray Holmes, Wayland.
Director of Consumer Education and Information, Lynn Leonard,
    Peabody.

MAJOR AGENCY HEADS: —
Alcoholic Beverages Control Commission, Walter J. Sullivan, Jr.,
    Hingham, Chairman; Frederick W. Riley, Saugus, Suzanne Iannella,
    Boston, Commissioners.
Board of Registration in Medicine, Alexander F. Fleming, Boston,
    Executive Director; Penelope Wells, Jamaica Plain, General
    Counsel.
Division of Banks, Thomas J. Curry, Boston, Commissioner; Joseph S.
    McWhirter, Milton, Senior Deputy Commissioner; Joseph A.
    Leonard, Hyde Park, Deputy Commissioner and General Counsel;
    Edward J. Geary, Needham, First Deputy Commissioner.
Cable Television Commission, John Patrone, Boston, Commissioner;
    Martha Leavitt, Lawrence, Executive Director.

Division of Insurance, Linda Ruthardt, Ashland, Commissioner;
Ralph Ianacco, Boston, Deputy Commissioner and Chief of Staff;
Richard Mastrangelo, Watertown, First Deputy Commissioner and
General Counsel.

Department of Public Utilities, John B. Howe, Belmont, Chairman; Janet
Gail Besser, Newton, Commissioner; Timothy Shevlin, Milton,
Executive Director.

State Racing Commission, Robert M. Hutchinson, Jr., Lexington,
Chairman; Christ Decas, Wareham, Arthur M. Khoury, Lawrence,
Associate Commissioners.

Division of Registration, William Wood, Marstons Mills, Director; Anne
Collins, Cambridge, Craig Chamberlain, East Sandwich,
Commissioners.

Division of Standards, Donald Falvey, Milton, Director; Charles Carroll,
Stoneham, Assistant Director.

AGENCIES INCLUDE: —
Division of Banks.
Division of Insurance.
Department of Public Utilities.
Division of Standards.
Alcoholic Beverages Control Commission.
Cable Television Commission.
State Racing Commission.
Board of Registration in Medicine.

Division of Registration:
Board of Registration of Allied Health Professionals.
Board of Registration of Allied Mental Health.
Board of Registration of Architects.
Board of Registration of Barbers.
Board of Registration of Chiropractors.
Board of Registration of Cosmetology.
Board of Registration in Dentistry.
Board of Registration of Dispensing Opticians.
Board of Certification of Operators of Drinking Water Supply
Facilities.
Board of State Examiners of Electricians.
Board of Registration of Electrologists.
Board of Registration in Embalming and Funeral Directing.
Board of Registration of Professional Engineers and Land Surveyors.
Board of Certification of Health Officers.
Board of Registration of Landscape Architects.
Board of Registration in Nursing.
Board of Registration of Nursing Home Administrators.
Board of Registration in Optometry.

Board of Registration in Pharmacy.
Board of Registration of Physician Assistants.
Board of State Examiners of Plumbers and Gas Fitters.
Board of Registration in Podiatry.
Board of Registration of Psychologists.
Board of Public Accountancy.
Board of Registration of Radio and Television Technicians.
Board of Registration of Real Estate Appraisers.
Board of Registration of Real Estate Brokers and Salesmen.
Board of Respiratory Care.
Board of Registration of Sanitarians.
Board of Registration of Social Workers.
Board of Registration for Speech-Language Pathology and
    Audiology.
Board of Registration in Veterinary Medicine.

DEPARTMENT OF ECONOMIC DEVELOPMENT.

Director, David A. Tibbetts, Newburyport.
Deputy Director, John R. Regan, Holliston.
Chief of Staff, Daniel Grabauskas, Arlington.
General Counsel, J. Todd Fernandez, Boston.
Chief Financial Officer, Diana P. Salemy, Boston.
Director of Marketing and Communications, Donna A. Freni, Beverly.

MAJOR AGENCY HEADS: —
Division of Energy Resources, David O'Connor, Commissioner.
Massachusetts Office of Travel and Tourism, Mary Jane McKenna,
    Executive Director.
Office of Film and Video Development, Robin Dawson, Director.
Office of International Trade and Investment, Nicholas Rostow,
    Executive Director.
State Office of Minority and Women's Business Assistance, France
    Lopez, Executive Director.

QUASI-PUBLIC AGENCIES INCLUDE: —
Community Development Finance Corporation.
Corporation for Business, Work and Learning.
Massachusetts Development Finance Agency.
Massachusetts Technology Park Corporation.
Massachusetts Technology Development Corporation.

DEPARTMENT OF LABOR AND WORKFORCE DEVELOPMENT.

Director, Angelo R. Buonopane.
Chief of Staff, Kenneth J. Paradis.
General Counsel, Spencer C. Demetros.
Chief Financial Officer, Joan Cunningham.
Accounting Manager, Loreena LaMarca.
Programing Coordinator, Jennifer Roccos.
Administrative Assistants, Maria C. Hernandez, Lois Celona.

MAJOR AGENCY HEADS: —
Division of Employment and Training, Nils L. Nordberg, Deputy
    Director.
Division of Occupational Safety, Robert Prezioso, Deputy Director.
Division of Apprenticeship Training, Gayann Wilkinson, Deputy
    Director.
Labor Relations Commission, Robert C. Dumont, Chairman; William J.
    Dalton, Claudia T. Centomini, Commissioners; Mike Wallace,
    Executive Secretary.
Joint Labor-Management Committee, John T. Dunlop, Chairman, Morris
    A. Horowitz, Vice Chairman.
Board of Conciliation and Arbitration, Elizabeth Laing, Chairman;
    James F. Kelley, Jr., Vice Chairman.
Division of Industrial Accidents, James Campbell, Commissioner;
    Thomas Griffin, Deputy Commissioner.
MassJobs Council, Peter T. Koch, Executive Director.
One-Stop Career Center Office, John Buonomo, Director, Karin
    McCarthy, Deputy Director.
Corporation for Business, Work, and Learning, Suzanne Teegarden,
    President.

AGENCIES INCLUDE: —

    Board of Conciliation and Arbitration.
    Department of Industrial Accidents.
    Joint Labor-Management Committee.
    Labor Relations Commission.
    Division of Employment and Training.
    Division of Occupational Safety.
    Division of Apprenticeship Training.
    MassJobs Council.
    One-Stop Career Center Office.
    Corporation for Business, Work and Learning.

DEPARTMENT OF HOUSING AND COMMUNITY DEVELOPMENT.

Director, Jane Wallis Gumble.
Assistant Director for Policy, Marc A. Slotnick.
Assistant Director for Administration and Finance, Tom Simard.
Chief of Staff, Elizabeth S. Morse.
Director of Communications, Tara G. Frier.
Division of Community Services, Mary M. Greendale, Associate Director.
Division of Public Housing, Paul Galante, Associate Director.
Division of Private Housing, Kate Racer, Associate Director.
Division of Neighborhood Services, Roger P. Provost, Associate Director.

QUASI-PUBLIC AFFILIATIONS INCLUDE: —
Massachusetts Housing Finance Agency.
Massachusetts Housing Partnership.
Community Development Finance Corporation.
Community Economic Development Assistance Corporation.

KEY COMMISSIONS:
Manufactured Homes Commission.
Commission on Indian Affairs.
Housing Appeals Committee.

BOARDS APPOINTED BY THE GOVERNOR.

EDUCATION.

Department of Education, Robert V. Antonucci, Falmouth, Commissioner.
Board of Education, John Silber, Brookline, Chairman.
Board of Higher Education, Stanley Koplik, Boston, Chancellor; James Carlin, Wellesley, Chairman.

AGENCIES INCLUDE: —
Department of Education.
Higher Education Coordinating Council.

LEGISLATIVE DEPARTMENT.

SENATE, ALPHABETICALLY.

Amorello, Matthew J. .... *Second Worcester District.*
Antonioni, Robert A. .... *Worcester and Middlesex
District.*
Bernstein, Robert A. .... *First Worcester District.*
Berry, Frederick E. .... *Second Essex District.*
Birmingham, Thomas F.
[President] .... *Middlesex, Suffolk and Essex
District.*
Brewer, Stephen M. .... *Worcester, Hampden, Hampshire
and Franklin District.*
Clancy, Edward J., Jr. .... *First Essex District.*
Creedon, Robert S., Jr. .... *Second Plymouth and Bristol
District.*
Durand, Robert A. .... *Middlesex and Worcester
District.*
Fargo, Susan C. .... *Fifth Middlesex District.*
Havern, Robert A. .... *Fourth Middlesex District.*
Hedlund, Robert L. .... *Plymouth and Norfolk District.*
Jacques, Cheryl A. .... *Norfolk, Bristol and Middlesex
District.*
Jajuga, James P. .... *Third Essex District.*
Keating, William R. .... *Norfolk, Bristol and Plymouth
District.*
Knapik, Michael R. .... *Second Hampden and Hampshire
District.*
Lees, Brian P. .... *First Hampden and Hampshire
District.*
Lynch, Stephen F. .... *First Suffolk District.*
Magnani, David P. .... *Middlesex, Norfolk and Worcester
District.*
Melconian, Linda J. .... *Hampden District.*
Montigny, Mark C. .... *Second Bristol District.*
Moore, Richard T. .... *Worcester and Norfolk District.*
Morrissey, Michael W. .... *Norfolk and Plymouth District.*
Murray, Therese .... *Plymouth and Barnstable District.*
Norton, Thomas C. .... *First Bristol District.*

SENATE BY DISTRICTS

SENATE . . . BY DISTRICT.

Hon. Thomas F. Birmingham, President.

District.	Name.	Residence.	Address during the Session.
Berkshire, Hampden, Hampshire and Franklin	Andrea F. Nuciforo, Jr. (D)	Pittsfield, 953 West Street	At home.
First Bristol	Thomas C. Norton (D)	Fall River, 422 Reading Street	At home.
Second Bristol	Mark C. Montigny (D)	New Bedford, 94 Hawthorn St.	At home.
Cape and Islands	Henri S. Rauschenbach (R)	Brewster, 20 Depot Street	At home.
First Essex	Edward J. Clancy, Jr. (D)	Lynn, 20 Harmon Street	At home.
Second Essex	Frederick E. Berry (D)	Peabody, 210 Washington Street	At home.
Third Essex	James P. Jajuga (D)	Methuen, 146 Forest Street	At home.

First Essex and Middlesex	Bruce E. Tarr *(R)*	Gloucester, 80 Essex Avenue	At home.
Second Essex and Middlesex	John D. O'Brien, Jr. *(D)*	Andover, 237 Highland Road	At home.
Hampden	Linda J. Melconian *(D)*	Springfield, 257 Fort Pleasant Avenue	At home.
First Hampden and Hampshire	Brian P. Lees *(R)*	East Longmeadow, 5 Millbrook Circle	At home.
Second Hampden and Hampshire	Michael R. Knapik *(R)*	Westfield, 45 East Silver Street	At home.
Hampshire and Franklin	Stanley C. Rosenberg *(D)*	Amherst, 38 Webster Court	At home.
First Middlesex	Steven C. Panagiotakos *(D)*	Lowell, 191 Sanders Avenue	At home.
Second Middlesex	Charles E. Shannon *(R)*	Winchester, 17 Robinson Park	At home.
Third Middlesex	Richard R. Tisei *(R)*	Wakefield, 703 Main Street	At home.
Fourth Middlesex	Robert A. Havern III *(D)*	Arlington, 35 Bartlett Avenue	At home.

District	Name	Residence	Address during the session.
Fifth Middlesex	Susan C. Fargo (D)	Lincoln, 7 Mine Brook Road	At home.
First Middlesex and Norfolk	Lois G. Pines (D)	Newton, 40 Helene Road	At home.
Middlesex, Norfolk and Worcester	David P. Magnani (D)	Framingham, 70 Fay Road	At home.
Middlesex and Suffolk	Warren E. Tolman (D)	Watertown, 30 Stoneleigh Circle	At home.
Middlesex, Suffolk and Essex	Thomas F. Birmingham (D)	Chelsea, 9 Nichols Street	At home.
Middlesex and Worcester	Robert A. Durand (D)	Marlborough, 39 Red Spring Road	At home.
Norfolk, Bristol and Middlesex	Cheryl A. Jacques (D)	Needham, 41 Hancock Road	At home.
Norfolk, Bristol and Plymouth	William R. Keating (D)	Sharon, 111 Bay Road	At home.

District	Senator	Address	
Norfolk and Plymouth	Michael W. Morrissey (D)	Quincy, 111 Lansdowne Street	At home.
Norfolk and Suffolk	Marian Walsh (D)	Boston, 651 West Roxbury Parkway	At home.
Plymouth and Barnstable	Therese Murray (D)	Plymouth, 1 Winding Lane	At home.
First Plymouth and Bristol	Marc R. Pacheco (D)	Taunton, 7 Dartmouth Street	At home.
Second Plymouth and Bristol	Robert S. Creedon, Jr. (D)	Brockton, 393 West Elm Street	At home.
Plymouth and Norfolk	Robert L. Hedlund (R)	Weymouth, 54 Longwood Road	At home.
First Suffolk	Stephen F. Lynch (D)	Boston, 55 G Street	At home.
Second Suffolk	Dianne Wilkerson (D)	Boston, 3 Douglass Park, Suite 107	At home.

DISTRICT.	NAME.	RESIDENCE.	ADDRESS DURING THE SESSION.
Suffolk and Middlesex	Robert E. Travaglini *(D)*	Boston, 51 St. Andrew Road	At home.
Suffolk and Norfolk	W. Paul White *(D)*	Boston, 43 Boutwell Street	At home.
First Worcester	Robert A. Bernstein *(D)*	Worcester, 7 Aylesbury Road	At home.
Second Worcester	Matthew J. Amorello *(R)*	Grafton, 2 Bruce Street	At home.
Worcester, Hampden, Hampshire and Franklin	Stephen M. Brewer *(D)*	Barre, 193 Pleasant Street	At home.
Worcester and Middlesex	Robert A. Antonioni *(D)*	Leominster, 85D Winter Street	At home.
Worcester and Norfolk	Richard T. Moore *(D)*	Uxbridge, 235 Williams Street	At home.

SEATING ARRANGEMENT
OF THE SENATE
Hon. THOMAS F. BIRMINGHAM, President.

On the President's Left.

1. Hon. Thomas C. Norton
2. Hon. Linda J. Melconian
3. Hon. Robert A. Durand
4. Hon. Robert A. Havern
5. Hon. Stanley C. Rosenberg
6. Hon. Stephen F. Lynch
7. Hon. David P. Magnani
8. Hon. W. Paul White
9. Hon. Michael W. Morrissey
10. Hon. Richard T. Moore
11. Hon. Charles E. Shannon
12. Hon. Robert A. Antonioni
13. Hon. Marian Walsh
14. Hon. Michael R. Knapik
15. Hon. Bruce E. Tarr
16. Hon. Dianne Wilkerson
17. Hon. John D. O'Brien
18. Hon. Therese Murray
19. Hon. Robert E. Travaglini
20. Hon. Cheryl A. Jacques

On the President's Right.

1. Hon. Edward J. Clancy, Jr.
2. Hon. Frederick E. Berry
3. Hon. Henri S. Rauschenbach
4. Hon. Brian P. Lees
5. Hon. Richard R. Tisei
6. Hon. Matthew J. Amorello
7. Hon. Robert L. Hedlund
8. Hon. William R. Keating
9. Hon. Mark C. Montigny
10. Hon. Susan C. Fargo
11. Hon. Andrea F. Nuciforo, Jr.
12. Hon. Warren E. Tolman
13. Hon. Robert S. Creedon, Jr.
14. Hon. Stephen M. Brewer
15. Hon. Lois G. Pines
16. Hon. Marc R. Pacheco
17. Hon. Steven C. Panagiotakos
18. Hon. James P. Jajuga
19. Hon. Robert A. Bernstein
20. Vacant.

OFFICERS AND EMPLOYEES
OF THE SENATE

President of the Senate.
Hon. THOMAS F. BIRMINGHAM, CHELSEA.
Room 332, State House.

Counsel to the President.
NOAH BERGER.

Chief of Staff, Senate President's Office.
TED CONSTAN.

Fiscal Director, Senate President's Office.
JOHN McGINN

Senate Clerk.
(General Laws, Chapter 3, Sections 12-13)
EDWARD B. O'NEILL, SOUTH BOSTON.
Room 335, State House

Assistant Clerk.
PATRICK F. SCANLAN, SALEM.

*Second Assistant Clerk and
Counsel to the Clerk of the Senate.*
DAVID H. McDERMOTT, BOSTON.

Office Manager.
FRED E. DAY, JR., LOWELL.

Senate Calendar Clerk.
WILLIAM F. WELCH, MILFORD.

Supervisor of Data Processing.
JAMES M. PROCTOR, METHUEN.

Assistant Manager.
MICHAEL D. HURLEY, SOUTH BOSTON.

Administrative Assistant.
JOHN G. CRONIN, MILTON.

Clerical Assistants.
RUTHANN BROOKS, QUINCY.
PAUL J. COUGHLIN, DANVERS.
ROBERT J. YEAGER, AVON.
STACEY N. OSTIGUY, QUINCY.

Sergeant-at-Arms.
MICHAEL J. REA, JR., BILLERICA
Room 71B, State House.

Counsel to the Senate.
(General Laws, Chapter 3, Sections 51-55)
DAVID E. SULLIVAN, CAMBRIDGE.

Assistant Counsels to the Senate.
ROBERT D. BOWES, SR., LYNN.
GERARD F. BURKE, MILTON.
IRENE R. COMEAU, BOSTON.
MARTIN J. DUNN, HOLYOKE.
EILEEN S. FITZGERALD, MILTON.

**Clerk of the Committees on Rules of the two branches,
acting concurrently, on the part of the Senate.**
LEONARD C. ALKINS, BROCKTON.

**Joint Senate-House
Legislative Engrossing Division.**
ANNE D. SWEETNAM, *Chief Clerk.*
CAROLYN M. GALLAGHER, *Clerk.*
VALERIE A. SMITH, *Clerk.*
JUDITH M. O'BRIEN, *Clerk.*
COLLEEN A. CARROLL, *Clerk.*
ROBERTA MANN, *Clerk.*

HOUSE OF REPRESENTATIVES
ALPHABETICALLY

HOUSE OF REPRESENTATIVES, ALPHABETICALLY.

WITH DISTRICTS REPRESENTED, POST-OFFICE ADDRESSES AND RESIDENCES
DURING THE SESSION.

Hon. THOMAS M. FINNERAN, *Speaker.*

NAME.	District.	Post-office Address.	Residence during the session.	No. of Seat.
Angelo, Steven	9, Essex	14 Prospect Street, Saugus	At home	4
Bellotti, Michael G.	1, Norfolk	159 Standish Road, Quincy	At home	114
Binienda, John J.	17, Worcester	41 Circuit Avenue East, Worcester	At home	20
Bosley, Daniel E.	1, Berkshire	3 Elmwood Avenue, North Adams	At home	66
Brett, James T.[1]	13, Suffolk	7 Wedmore Street, Boston	At home	—

Broadhurst, Arthur J.	15. Essex	11 Westwind Drive, Methuen	At home	139
Businger, John A.	15. Norfolk	33 St. Paul St., Brookline	At home	79
Cabral, Antonio F. D.	13. Bristol	212 Maple Street, New Bedford	At home	39
Cahill, Michael P.	6. Essex	7 Robin Road, Beverly	At home	112
Cahir, Thomas S.	3. Barnstable	3 River Road, Bourne	At home	147
Canavan, Christine E.	10. Plymouth	29 Mystic Street, Brockton	At home	83
Candaras, Gale D.	13. Hampden	643 Tinkham Road, Wilbraham	At home	109
Caron, Paul E.	11. Hampden	8 Rhinebeck Avenue, Springfield	At home	36
Casey, Paul C.	34. Middlesex	6 Ardley Place, Winchester	At home	136
Chandler, Harriette L.	13. Worcester	7 Brook Hill Drive, Worcester	At home	94

1. Declined to accept office

NAME.	District.	Post-office Address.	Residence during the session.	No. of Seat.
Chesky, Evelyn G.	5, Hampden	3 Brenan Street, Holyoke	At home	97
Ciampa, Vincent P.	37, Middlesex	64 Ossipee Road, Somerville	At home	17
Clark, Forrester A., Jr.	4, Essex	308 Sagamore Road, Hamilton	At home	49
Cleven, Carol C.	16, Middlesex	4 Arbutus Avenue, Chelmsford	At home	93
Cohen, David B.	11, Middlesex	66 Vine Street, Newton	At home	121
Connolly, Edward G.	31, Middlesex	784 Broadway, Everett	At home	135
Correia, Robert	7, Bristol	1290 Plymouth Avenue, Fall River	At home	21
Creedon, Geraldine	11, Plymouth	393 West Elm Street, Brockton	At home	60

Cresta, Brian M.	22, Middlesex	183 Nahant Street, Wakefield	At home	101
Cuomo, Donna F.	14, Essex	45 Castlemere Place, North Andover	At home	55
DeFilippi, Walter A.	6, Hampden	35 Pease Avenue, West Springfield	At home	25
DeLeo, Robert A.	19, Suffolk	171 Cottage Park Road, Winthrop	At home	160 BTR
Demakis, Paul C.	8, Suffolk	46 Commonwealth Avenue, Boston	At home	80
Dempsey, Brian S.	3, Essex	15 Oxford Street, Haverhill	At home	115
DiMasi, Salvatore F.	3, Suffolk	102 Commercial Street, Boston	At home	5
Donnelly, David T.	10, Suffolk	75 Manthorne Road, Boston	At home	134
Donovan, Carol A.	33, Middlesex	455 Place Lane, Woburn	At home	43

NAME.	District.	Post-office Address.	Residence during the session.	No. of Seat.
Fagan, James H.	3, Bristol	406 Davis Street, Taunton	At home	155
Fallon, Christopher G.	36, Middlesex	49 Dexter Street, Malden	At home	102
Fennell, Robert F.	10, Essex	9 Virginia Terrace, Lynn	At home	90
Finegold, Barry R.	17, Essex	11 Lavender Hill Lane, Andover	At home	64
Finnegan, Kevin L.	1, Essex	48 Woodland Street, Newburyport, ...	At home	132
Finneran, Thomas M.	12, Suffolk	7 Countryside Drive, Boston	At home	2 SPK
Fitzgerald, Kevin W.	15, Suffolk	71 Mossdale Road, Boston	At home	116
Flavin, Nancy	2, Hampshire	5 Dragon Circle, Easthampton	At home	70

Fox, Gloria L.	7, Suffolk	7 Harold Park, Boston	At home	133
Frost, Paul K	7, Worcester	60 Berlin Street, Auburn	At home	87
Galliano, Joseph R	1, Plymouth	1 Carver Street, Plymouth	At home	35
Galvin, William C.	6, Norfolk	125 Westchester Drive, Canton	At home	91
Gardner, Barbara	8, Middlesex	114 Jennings Road, Holliston	At home	6
Garry, Colleen M.	39, Middlesex	55 Chapman Street, Dracut	At home	98
Gately, David F.	9, Middlesex	222 Totten Pond Road, Waltham	At home	125
Gauch, Ronald W	11, Worcester	396 Lake Street, Shrewsbury	At home	48
George, Thomas N.	1, Barnstable	17 Thacher Shore Road, Yarmouth	At home	72
Giglio, Anthony P.	38, Middlesex	146 Traincroft, N.W. Medford	At home	23
Glodis, Guy	16, Worcester	47 Sandra Drive, Worcester	At home	19

NAME.	District.	Post-office Address.	Residence during the session.	No. of Seat.
Goguen, Emile J.	3, Worcester	424 Shea Street, Fitchburg	At home	18
Golden, Thomas A., Jr.	17, Middlesex	60 Leeds Street, Lowell	At home	148
Gomes, Shirley	4, Barnstable	15 Ridgevale Road, Harwich	At home	75
Greene, William G., Jr.	24, Middlesex	27 Naushon Road, Billerica	At home	34
Guerriero, Patrick C.	35, Middlesex	44 Orris Street., Melrose	At home	28
Hahn, Cele	4, Hampden	P.O. Box 1248, Westfield, 01086	28 Pineridge Dr. Westfield	100
Haley, Paul R.	4, Norfolk	55 Cassandra Road, Weymouth	At home	42
Hall, Geoffrey D.	2, Middlesex	1 Pershing Street, Westford	At home	140

Name	District	Address		
Hargraves, Robert S.	1, Middlesex	21 Temple Drive, Groton	At home	26
Harkins, Lida E.	13, Norfolk	14 Hancock Road, Needham	At home	122
Hart, John A., Jr.	4, Suffolk	62 G Street, Boston	At home	110
Hodgkins, Christopher J	4, Berkshire	100 Franklin Street, Lee	At home	63
Honan, Kevin G.	17, Suffolk	192 Faneuil Street, Boston	At home	159
Hyland, Barbara C	1, Bristol	38 Bicknell Street, Foxborough	At home	27
Hynes, Frank M.	4, Plymouth	78 Meetinghouse Lane, Marshfield	At home	50
Iannuccillo, M. Paul	16, Essex	162 Jackson Street, Lawrence	At home	45
Jehlen, Patricia D.	30, Middlesex	67 Dane Street, Somerville	At home	157
Jones, Bradley H., Jr.	21, Middlesex	249 Park Street, North Reading	At home	130

NAME.	District.	Post-office Address.	Residence during the session.	No. of Seat.
Joyce, Brian A.	7, Norfolk	38 Ridge Road, Milton	At home	67
Kafka, Louis L.	8, Norfolk	2 Hart Road, Sharon	At home	89
Kaprielian, Rachel	32, Middlesex	158 Spring Street, Watertown	At home	12
Kaufman, Jay R.	15, Middlesex	1 Childs Road, Lexington	At home	11
Keenan, Daniel F.	3, Hampden	25 North Street, Blandford	At home	81
Kelly, Shaun P.	2, Berkshire	488 East Housatonic Street, Dalton	At home	54
Kennedy, Thomas P.	9, Plymouth	92 Winthrop Street, Brockton	At home	154
Khan, Kay	12, Middlesex	18 St. Mary's Street, Newton	At home	57
Klimm, John C.	2, Barnstable	20 Elmwood Circle, Cotuit	At home	144

Name	District	Address		
Knuuttila, Brian	2, Worcester	63 Holly Drive, Gardner	At home	77
Koczera, Robert M.	11, Bristol	119 Jarry Street, New Bedford	At home	16
Koutoujian, Peter J.	10, Middlesex	154 Waltham Street, Newton	At home	146
Kujawski, Paul	8, Worcester	71 Klebart Avenue, Webster	At home	88
Kulik, Stephen	1, Franklin	P.O. Box 36, Worthington, 01098	50 Thayer Hill Rd. Worthington	53
Landers, Patrick F., III	1, Hampden	33 Knox Street, Palmer	At home	30
Lane, Harold M., Jr.	1, Worcester	12 Dix Street, Holden	At home	138
Larkin, Peter J.	3, Berkshire	156 Blythewood Drive, Pittsfield	At home	71
LeDuc, Stephen P.	4, Middlesex	135 Mechanic Street Marlborough	At home	15
LeLacheur, Edward A.	18, Middlesex	63 Fruit Street, Lowell	At home	85
Lepper, John A.	2, Bristol	311 Newport Avenue, Attleboro	At home	74

NAME.	District.	Post-office Address.	Residence during the session.	No. of Seat.
Lewis, Jacqueline	8, Plymouth	1000 High Street, Bridgewater	At home	9
Lewis, Maryanne	11, Norfolk	70 Abbott Road, Dedham	At home	84
Locke, John A.	14, Norfolk	866R Washington Street, Wellesley	At home	152
Mariano, Ronald	3, Norfolk	200 Falls Boulevard, Unit F-301, Quincy	At home	40
Marini, Francis L.	6, Plymouth	580 Main Street, Hanson	At home	10
Marzilli, J. James, Jr.	25, Middlesex	15 Stevens Terrace, Arlington	At home	78
McDonough, John E.	11, Suffolk	59 Patten Street, Boston	At home	127
McGee, Thomas M.	11, Essex	9 Pine Road, Lynn	At home	117

McIntyre, Joseph B.	12, Bristol	367 Brownell Avenue, New Bedford	At home	103
McManus, William J., II	14, Worcester	100 Blue Bell Road, Worcester	At home	56
Menard, Joan M.	5, Bristol	4059 Riverside Avenue, Somerset	At home	38
Merrigan, John F.	2, Franklin	54 Congress Street, Greenfield	At home	99
Miceli, James R.	20, Middlesex	11 Webber Street, Wilmington	At home	14
Murphy, Charles A.	23, Middlesex	19 Sears Street, Burlington	At home	104
Murphy, Dennis M.	9, Hampden	221 Atwater Road, Springfield	At home	31
Murphy, Kevin J.	19, Middlesex	63 Newbury Street, Lowell	At home	145
Murray, Mary Jeanette	3, Plymouth	28 Margin Street, Cohasset	At home	106
Nagle, William P., Jr.	1, Hampshire	152 South Main Street, Northampton	At home	7

NAME.	District.	Post-office Address.	Residence during the session.	No. of Seat.
Naughton, Harold P., Jr.	12, Worcester	56 Prescott Street, Clinton	At home	95
O'Brien, Janet W.	5, Plymouth	128 Washington Street, Hanover	At home	124
O'Brien, Thomas J.	12, Plymouth	27 Longwood Circle, Kingston	At home	46
O'Flaherty, Eugene L.	2, Suffolk	318 Revere Beach Parkway, Chelsea	At home	131
Owens-Hicks, Shirley	6, Suffolk	15 Outlook Road, Boston	At home	61
Parente, Marie J.	10, Worcester	13 Reagan Road, Milford	At home	13
Paulsen, Anne M.	26, Middlesex	90 School Street, Belmont	At home	156
Pedone, Vincent A.	15, Worcester	3 Verdi Road, Worcester	At home	3
Peters, David M.	6, Worcester	105A Old Worcester Road, Charlton	At home	8

Name		District	Address		Page
Petersen, Douglas W		8, Essex	29 Rose Avenue, Marblehead	At home	68
Peterson, George N., Jr		9, Worcester	8 North Street, Grafton	At home	113
Petrolati, Thomas M		7, Hampden	106 Stevens Street, Ludlow	At home	105
Poirier, Kevin		14, Bristol	117 Grove Street, No. Attleborough	At home	47
Pope, Susan W		13, Middlesex	28 Moore Road, Wayland	At home	126
Provost, Ruth W		2, Plymouth	16 Grove Street, Sandwich	At home	65
Quinn, John F		9, Bristol	5 East River Drive, Dartmouth	At home	153
Reinstein, William G		16, Suffolk	61 Sweeney Avenue, Revere	At home	22
Resor, Pamela P		14, Middlesex	5 Proctor Street, Acton	At home	123
Richie, Charlotte Golar		5, Suffolk	29 Percival Street, Boston	At home	107
Rodrigues, Michael J		8, Bristol	428 Sanford Road, Westport	At home	29
Rogeness, Mary S		2, Hampden	22 Warren Terrace, Longmeadow	At home	128

NAME.	District.	Post-office Address.	Residence during the session.	No. of Seat.
Rogers, John H.	12, Norfolk	253 Railroad Avenue, Norwood	At home	149
Ruane, J. Michael	7, Essex	19 Nursery Street, Salem	At home	1
Rushing, Byron	9, Suffolk	25 Concord Square, Boston	At home	158
Scaccia, Angelo M.	14, Suffolk	59 Readville Street, Boston	At home	120
Scibelli, Anthony M.	10, Hampden	200 Maple Street, Springfield	At home	118
Serra, Emanuel G.	1, Suffolk	230 Orient Avenue, Boston	At home	59
Simmons, Mary Jane	4, Worcester	126 Burrage Avenue, Leominster	At home	142
Slattery, John P.	12, Essex	20 Orchard Street, Peabody	At home	96
Speliotis, Theodore C.	13, Essex	4 Ardmore Drive, Danvers	At home	51

Name	District	Address		No.
Sprague, Jo Ann	9, Norfolk	305 Elm Street, Walpole	At home	129
Stanley, Harriett L.	2, Essex	37 Hadley Road. Merrimac	At home	32
Stasik, John H.	6, Middlesex	15 Chouteau Avenue. Framingham	At home	108
Stefanini, John A.	7, Middlesex	66 Wilson Avenue. Framingham	At home	143
Stoddart, Douglas W.	5, Middlesex	15 Pauline Drive, Natick	At home	151
Story, Ellen	3, Hampshire	185 Pelham Road. Amherst	At home	62
Straus, William M.	10, Bristol	8 Nashawena Road. Mattapoisett	At home	86
Sullivan, David B.	6, Bristol	1015 Madison Street. Fall River	At home	37
Sullivan, Joseph C.	5, Norfolk	51 West Street. Braintree	At home	150
Swan, Benjamin	12, Hampden	837 State Street. Springfield	At home	24

NAME.	District.	Post-office Address.	Residence during the session.	No. of Seat.
Teahan, Kathleen M	7, Plymouth	78 Harvard Street, Whitman	At home	82
Thompson, Alvin E.	28, Middlesex	521 Green Street, Cambridge	At home	137
Tobin, A. Stephen	2, Norfolk	33 Virginia Road, Quincy	At home	44
Tolman, Steven A.	18, Suffolk	17 Madeline Street, Boston	At home	52
Toomey, Timothy J., Jr.	29, Middlesex	88 Sixth Street, Cambridge	At home	92
Travis, Philip	4, Bristol	28 County Street, Rehoboth	At home	33
Turkington, Eric	Barnstable, Dukes and Nantucket	P.O. Box 546, Falmouth 02541	4 Sheeps Crossing Lane, Falmouth	111
Tuttle, David H.	5, Worcester	16 Church Street, Barre	At home	76
Vallee, James E.	10, Norfolk	480 Maple Street, Franklin	At home	41

Verga, Anthony J.	5, Essex	66 Perkins Street, Gloucester	At home	69
Wagner, Joseph F.	8, Hampden	81 Sherman Avenue, Chicopee	At home	141
Walrath, Patricia A.	3, Middlesex	20 Middlemost Way, Stow	At home	58
Walsh, Martin J.[1]	13, Suffolk	33 Taft Street, Boston	At home	119
Wolf, Alice K.	27, Middlesex	48 Huron Avenue, Cambridge	At home	73

1. Elected Apr. 8, 1997, qualified Apr. 16, 1997.

OFFICERS AND EMPLOYEES OF THE
HOUSE OF REPRESENTATIVES

HON. THOMAS M. FINNERAN, BOSTON, *Speaker.*
Room 355, State House.
ROBERT E. MacQUEEN, WEYMOUTH, *Clerk.* Room 145,
State House.
STEVEN T. JAMES, NORTH ANDOVER, *Assistant Clerk.*
Room 145, State House.
SCOTT J. MITCHELL, BURLINGTON, *Second Assistant Clerk.*
Room 145, State House.
MICHAEL J. REA, JR., BILLERICA, *Sergeant-at-Arms.*
Room 46, State House.
REVEREND ROBERT F. QUINN, BOSTON, *Chaplain.*

Clerical Assistants to House Clerk.

JAMES J. TWOMEY, JR,	Boston
PAUL T. SULLIVAN	Boston
MICHAEL A. SMITH	Everett
ROBERT J. DeCARLO	Winthrop
CATHERINE M. SCLAFANI	Quincy
WILLIAM H. TIERNEY	Woburn
KATHLEEN M. LOGUE	Everett

COUNSEL to the HOUSE.

(General Laws, Chapter 3, Sections 51-55).
LOUIS A. RIZOLI, WESTWOOD, Room 139, State House.

Assistants to the House Counsel.

ELAINE M. FARRELL, NORTH ANDOVER, Room 139,
State House.
DAVID E. NAMET, SWAMPSCOTT, Room 139, State House.
RICHARD L. WALSH, BOSTON (Jamaica Plain), Room 139,
State House.

Assistants to the House Counsel — Concluded.

JOHN J. SLATER, CHELSEA. Room 139, State House.
CHARLES T. MARTEL, MELROSE, *Clerk of the House Committee on Bills in the Third Reading,* Room 139, State House.

ASSISTANT TO THE SPEAKER.

Chief of Staff/Chief Legal Counsel to the Speaker of the House, WILLIAM KENNEDY, BOSTON, Room 356, State House.

MONITORS OF THE HOUSE

First Division:	Rep. CONNOLLY of Everett.
	Rep. MURRAY of Cohasset.
Second Division:	Rep. HYNES of Marshfield.
	Rep. CLARK of Hamilton.
Third Division:	Rep. GIGLIO of Medford.
	Rep. CLEVEN of Chelmsford.
Fourth Division:	Rep. RUANE of Salem.
	Rep. PETERSON of Grafton.

SERGEANT-AT-ARMS AND APPOINTEES

Michael J. Rea, Jr., Billerica   Sergeant-at-Arms
                    Room 46, State House.

Appointees

Assistant Sergeant-at-Arms — James DiPerri.
Assistant Sergeant-at-Arms — A. John Clifford.
Chief Administrative Voucher Examiner — Francis B. Donnelly.
Assistant Sergeant-at-Arms — Cheryl Dennis.
Clerk — James G. Walsh.
Clerk — Carmello S. Zangla.

Document Room

Director of Documents — Robert W. Murray.
Assistant Document Room Clerks — James T. Corcoran,
    Daniel S. Elio, Thomas Hegarty, Stephen Iannessa,
    Shawn P. Linehan.

Assigned to Senate

Chief Court Officer — Paul Dooley, Joseph M. Foley, Paul L. Lynch.
Assistant Chief Court Officers — Conrad Bailey, Gerald F. Roche,
    Francis Saccardo, Paul F. Shea, John F. Tierney.
General Court Officers — James Allen, John H. Burke, Joseph Carr,
    Dennis Coffey, Daniel T. Driscoll, James Gallery, Paul Hogan,
    Benjamin Hubbart, Thomas McDonough, Joseph O'Donnell,
    Karl J. Ryan, Kenneth Schmitz, Michael Tierney
Senate Maintenance Superintendent — Edward K. Phillips.
Assistant Legislative Postmaster — Charles Dame.
Assistant Legislative Postmaster — Edward Finn.

Assigned to the House of Representatives

Chief Court Officer — Raymond J. Amaru.
Assistant Chief Court Officers — Timothy M. Leonard,
    William P. Petrigno.
General Court Officers — Katherine Adams, Joseph M. Corso,
    Eugene F. DiPersio, Lewis E. Hinkley, Leonard Liotta,
    Arthur L. LoConte, Robert F. Macaulay, Kevin O'Brien,
    Joseph A. Quinn, Odell W. Ruffin, Peter M. Wells.
Legislative Postmaster — Michael A. Luongo.
Porter — Richard Buividas.

Legislative Bulletin and Daily Lists

Daniel J. Ranieri, *Editor.*
K. Patricia Mulleague, *Assistant Editor.*
Janice Hamilton, *Assistant Editor.*
Robyn C. Plouffe, *Administrative Assistant.*

MASSACHUSETTS STATE HOUSE PRESS ASSOCIATION — 1997 MEMBERSHIP

Donald Aucoin, *Boston Globe.*
Daniel Boylan, *State House News Service.*
Pat Collins, *Ottaway News Service.*
Martin Finucane, *Associated Press.*
Michael Grunwald, *Boston Globe.*
Ed Hayward, *Boston Herald.*
*John Hoey, *Brockton Enterprise.*
Glen Johnson, *Associated Press.*
Jason Kauppi, *Lowell Sun.*
Steve LeBlanc, *Community Newspapers.*
Mark Leccese, *Community Newspapers.*
Lauren Markoe, *Quincy Patriot-Ledger.*
Edward McHugh, *Worcester Telegram & Gazette.*
*Brian McNiff, *Worcester Telegram & Gazette.*
*Leslie Miller, *Community Newspapers.*
John O'Connell, *Springfield Union-News.*
Frank Phillips, *Boston Globe.*
Dan Ring, *Ottaway News Service.*
Carolyn Ryan, *Boston Herald.*
Craig Sandler, *State House News Service.*
*Jon Tapper, *State House News Service.*
Meg Vaillancourt, *Boston Globe.*
Doris Sue Wong, *Boston Globe.*
Helen Woodman, *State House News Service.*
Wendell Woodman, *State House News Service.*

(Officers, executive committee members).

Broadcasters.

STATE HOUSE BROADCASTERS
ASSOCIATION —1997 MEMBERSHIP

Henning, John, *WBZ-TV, Channel 4,* Boston.
Hiller, Andy, *WHDH-TV, Channel 7,* Boston.
Keller, Jon, *WLVI-TV, Channel 56,* Boston.
McNicholas, Kevin, *New England Radio News Network.*
Schachter, Aaron, *WBUR, WFCR,* Boston and *NPR.*
Stevens, Carl, *WBZ Radio,* Boston.
Wu, Janet, *WCVB-TV, Channel 5,* Boston.

New England Cable News, Boston.
WFXT-TV, Channel 25, Boston

RULES OF THE SENATE

RULES OF THE SENATE.

[As adopted by the Senate on January 16, 1997.]

[The dates under each rule indicate when the rule and its amendments were adopted. The date 1817 denotes the time when the several rules against which it is placed were first preserved. Previously to that year these rules are not to be found, although from the Senate Journal it appears that they were printed.]

THE PRESIDENT.

1. The President shall take the chair at the hour to which the Senate stands adjourned, shall call the members to order, and, on the appearance of a quorum, shall proceed to business.

[1831; 1888.]

1A. Every formal session of the Senate shall open with a prayer and a recitation of the "Pledge of Allegiance to the Flag".

[1989.]

2. The President shall preserve order and decorum, may speak to points of order in preference to other members, and shall decide all questions of order subject to an appeal to the Senate. He shall rise to put a question, or to address the Senate, but may read sitting.

[1817; between 1821 and 1826; 1831; 1888.]

3. The President may vote on all questions.

[1826.]

4. The President may appoint a member to perform the duties of the chair for a period not exceeding three days at any one time. Unless the Senate shall otherwise direct, the President, at the beginning of each legislative year, shall appoint a Chaplain and in case of vacancy in said office, he shall promptly fill said vacancy.

[1831; 1862; 1865; 1888; 1971.]

4A. The Senate President shall be elected by roll call on the Senate floor.

[1993.]

5. In case of a vacancy in the office of President, or in case the President, or the member appointed by him to perform the duties of the chair, is absent at the hour to which the Senate stands adjourned, the eldest senior member present shall call the Senate to order, and shall preside until a President, or a President *pro tempore*, is elected by ballot or by roll call vote as the Senate shall by majority vote determine, and such election shall be the first business in order.

[1831; 1885; 1888; 1971; 1985.]

5A. In case of extreme emergency, the President of the Senate, may for a period not exceeding two days, in conformity with Article 6, Section II, Chapter 1 of the Constitution, cause a session of the Senate to be cancelled. Each member of the Senate insofar as is practicable shall be notified of such action. The President may also declare a session informal in nature, with prior notice given. Notice of such action shall be printed in the Journal of the Senate by the Clerk thereof and the printing of a calendar shall be suspended with reference to an informal session under this rule.

In the case of an informal session, only reports of committees and matters not giving rise to formal motion or debate shall be considered. No motion or order of business shall lose its precedence but shall be carried over until the next formal session.

[1971; 1973.]

CLERK.

6. The Clerk shall keep a journal of the proceedings of the Senate, and shall cause the same to be printed daily. He shall, in the journal, make note of all questions of order, and enter at length the decisions thereon. He shall insert in an appendix to the journal the rules of the Senate and the joint rules of the two branches.

[1882; 1888.]

7. The Clerk, with the approval and direction of the President and the Committee on Steering and Policy, shall prepare and cause to be printed each day a calendar of matters in order for consideration. The calendar for a session shall be available to the members and the public at least 24 hours prior to the start of that session, except when formal sessions are held on consecutive days. The calendar for any formal session on a day following a formal session shall be available to the members and to the public at least two hours prior to the start of that session. The printing of a calendar may only be suspended by a 2/3 vote of all members present and voting as determined by a call of the yeas and nays. The calendar shall consist of at least four separate sections. One section shall contain those matters for third reading and engrossment. No matters shall be considered for third reading that do not appear on this section of the calendar without unanimous consent. One section shall contain those matters held by the Senate committee on Bills in the Third Reading. One section shall contain those matters appearing on the Senate Calendar for the first time. No matters shall be considered for second reading that do not appear on this section of the calendar without unanimous consent. One section shall contain those matters which shall be on the Senate Calendar for the first time at the following formal session. No matters shall be considered for a second reading at a formal session that were not on the Calendar for the previous formal session. It shall be mandatory, however, that a bill or resolve ordered to third reading on one calendar day must appear on the calendar at the following formal session.

The Clerk, with the approval and direction of the President
and the Committee on Steering and Policy, may prepare
the calendar, with such memoranda as he may deem necessary, in a form designed to provide complete information
and to properly facilitate the business of the Senate. When
the printing of the calendar required under this rule is suspended under the provisions of Rule 5A, a session shall be
considered informal and no matter shall be considered if a
member prior to said session requested that the matter be
held for consideration or if a member at said session
objects thereto.

[1882; 1888; 1945; 1971; 1974; 1985; 1991; 1993.]

7A. To better facilitate the business of the Senate,
whenever possible, and notwithstanding the provisions of
any rules to the contrary, during consideration of the new
matters on the calendar each day, the chair will first
declare a recess so that members may examine the items.
The chair will then ask for passes on the second reading
matters. Second reading matters with amendments pending
will automatically be considered separately. The chair will
direct the Clerk to dispense with the reading of each
title, but the journal for that day will show that the bills
have been read a second time. The question will then
come on ordering those second reading matters which
have not been passed for debate to a third reading.
Matters passed for debate will be considered on the second call.

The same procedure will be followed with relation to
adverse reports appearing in groups on the calendar.
Adverse reports passed for debate will be considered on
the second call. The question will be put by the chair on
the acceptance of all remaining adverse reports not
passed for debate.

[1975.]

7B. The Clerk of the Senate shall be the official parliamentarian of the Senate.

[1973.]

8. [Omitted in 1969.]

9. When a bill or resolve coming from the other branch does not appear in print in the form in which it was passed in that branch, the Clerk shall either indicate the amendments on the Orders of the Day, or shall have the bill or resolve reprinted, at his discretion.

[1882.]

COUNSEL TO THE SENATE.

9A. The Counsel to the Senate and members of the staff of said Counsel shall not engage in the private practice of law during ordinary business hours while the Senate is in session. The Counsel to the Senate and the staff of said Counsel shall be available at all times for consultation with the President and members of the Senate in relation to matters pending before the Senate.

[1976.]

MEMBERS OF THE SENATE.

10. No member, officer, or employee shall use or attempt to use improper means to influence an agency, board, authority, or commission of the Commonwealth or any political subdivision thereof. No member, officer, or employee of the Senate shall receive compensation or permit compensation to accrue to his or her beneficial interest by virtue of influence improperly exerted from his or her position in the Senate. Every reasonable effort shall be made to avoid situations where it might appear that he or she is making such use of his or her official position. Members, officers, and employees should avoid accepting or retaining an economic interest or opportunity which represents a threat to their independence of judgement.

No member, officer, or employee shall use confidential information gained in the course of or by reason of his or her official position or activities to further his or her own financial interest or those of any other person.
[1977.]

10A. No member, officer, or employee shall employ anyone from state funds who does not perform tasks which contribute to the work of the Senate and which are commensurate with the compensation received; and no officer or full time employee of the Senate shall engage in any outside business activity during regular business hours, whether the Senate is in session or not. All employees of the Senate are assumed to be full time unless their personnel record indicates otherwise.
[1977.]

11. No member shall absent himself from the Senate without leave, unless there is a quorum without his presence.
[1817.]

11A. Each member of the Senate shall be assigned an office in the State House. Each member shall have full authority to employ and dismiss personal and committee staff within written guidelines developed by the Senate Committee on Administration.
[1983; 1985; 1993.]

11B. No member of the Senate shall hold, for more than eight consecutive years, any one of the following positions:

President of the Senate, Majority Leader, Assistant Majority Leader, Second Assistant Majority Leader, Minority Leader, Assistant Minority Leader, Second

Assistant Minority Leader, and Third Assistant Minority Leader.

For purposes of this rule the counting of consecutive years will commence on January 4, 1995.
[1993.]

COMMITTEES.

12. The following standing committees shall be appointed at the beginning of the first year of the two year General Court and the appointments shall be for the life of the General Court, to wit:

A Committee on Rules;

To consist of the President, the Majority Leader, the Minority Leader, two members elected by the Majority Party in caucus and one member elected by the Minority Party in caucus.

A Committee on Ways and Means;

To consist of seventeen members.

A Committee on Bills in the Third Reading;

To consist of five members.

A Committee on Post Audit and Oversight;

To consist of seven members.

A Committee on Science and Technology;

To consist of seven members.

[1831; 1836; 1840; 1844; 1847; 1863; 1864; 1870; 1876; 1882; 1885; 1886; 1888; 1891; 1896; 1897; 1920; 1937; 1939; 1941; 1945; 1946; 1957; 1960; 1963; 1965; 1969; 1971; 1972; 1982; 1989; 1991; 1993; 1995; 1997.]

12A. There shall be a standing Committee on Ethics consisting of six members to be appointed in accordance with Senate Rule 13 at the beginning of the first year of the biennial session of the General Court. All violations of rules and all questions of conduct of members, officers

and employees of the Senate shall be referred by order of
the Senate to said committee. Such orders shall be as specific as circumstances allow. The committee is also
empowered to receive sworn written complaints or evidence regarding violations of Rules 10 and 10A. Until a
hearing, if any, is held, the contents of such complaints or
evidence shall be considered confidential information,
unless they are already a matter of public record. If no
hearing is held, such contents may be made public by the
committee in a final report. Breach of confidentiality may
itself be grounds for disciplinary action.

Upon receipt of an order, a sworn written complaint
filed under penalties of perjury, or upon receipt of evidence, the committee is empowered to investigate and take
written or oral testimony on any matters specified in the
order or covered by Rules 10 and 10A. A majority of committee members must be present to receive sworn testimony unless a majority designates a lesser number to do so.
In any case, at least one member of the committee must be
present to receive such testimony. Upon majority vote of
the full Senate, the committee may require by summons
the attendance and testimony of witnesses and the produc-
tion of books and papers and such other records as said
committee may deem relevant.

Said committee shall consider and have authority to
report to the Senate any recommendations regarding any
infringement of the rules and all questions of conduct of
members, officers and employees referred to it. If after
investigation the committee determines that there has been
a violation of the rules, or other misconduct, the committee
shall file a report with the Clerk of the Senate, including a
recommendation for disciplinary action, including but not
limited to: in the case of a member, reprimand, censure,
removal from committee chairmanship or other position

of authority, or expulsion; in the case of an officer or employee, reprimand, suspension or removal. Said report shall not prevent the Senate from taking any other action as it shall deem advisable and appropriate.

Nothing in this rule shall be construed to require the disclosure of any allegation that the committee deems frivolous or without merit.

If the committee receives a sworn written complaint, evidence, order of the Senate, or request for an opinion involving a member of the committee, such member shall remove himself from the committee's deliberations on that matter.

The committee may, upon written request from a member, officer, or employee of the Senate, issue written advisory opinions on matters concerning Rules 10 and 10A. Such advisory opinions may be published, provided that the name of the person requesting the opinion, and any other identifying information shall not be included in the publication. The Senate may not penalize a member, officer or employee of the Senate for conduct satisfying the guidelines of an advisory opinion based on factually indistinguishable conduct.

At least three members shall sign all recommendations and reports of the committee.

The committee shall annually, on or before the first Wednesday in December, file a report with the Clerk summarizing its activities for the year. In addition, the committee may at any time recommend changes in the rules of conduct for the Senate or legislation relating thereto, and a majority vote of the Senate shall be required to approve any such recommended changes.

[1977; 1978; 1983; 1991.]

12B. There shall be a standing Committee on Steering and Policy consisting of the President, the chairman of the Senate Committee on Ways and Means, the leader of the majority party in the Senate, the leader of the minority party in the Senate, and seven other members to be appointed by the President, one of whom shall be a member of the minority party, at the beginning of the first year of the biennial session of the General Court. The first member appointed by the President shall be designated the chairman. The committee shall meet from time to time at the call of the chair for the purpose of assisting the President and the Senate in identifying the major matters which require consideration by the General Court during the pending session and to advise the President and the Senate on the relative priority of such matters, the relative urgency for consideration by the General Court of such matters, and alternative methods of responding to such matters by the General Court, and on scheduling legislative matters for their even distribution throughout the legislative year.

The Committee on Steering and Policy shall report on a legislative matter not later than thirty days following the day on which the matter was referred to it; provided that it shall report on all such matters prior to the last formal sitting of the legislative session. The committee shall not report that any matter referred to it ought to pass or ought not to pass, nor shall it recommend any amendment to such matter, but shall only report on what date prior to adjournment of the last formal session and within the forty-five day period referred to in the preceding sentence, the matter will be considered by the Senate.

[1983; 1985; 1986; 1991; 1993.]

12C. [Omitted in 1995.]

12D. There shall be a standing Senate Committee on Administration consisting of the President of the Senate, the Majority leader, the Minority leader and two members elected by the members of the Senate. The committee shall review applications for each member's staff and committee operating requirements and determine the allocation of resources for each member. Such allocations shall be distributed pursuant to written guidelines established by the Committee. The Committee shall also allocate office space.

[1993.]

13. (a) Unless the Senate shall otherwise specially order, the President shall nominate a candidate for chair of each standing committee, joint standing committee or special committee and the vice-chair of the Senate Committee on Ways and Means. The President may also nominate not more than three persons to majority party floor leadership positions. The minority party floor leader may nominate not more than three persons to minority party floor leadership positions. Such nominations must be ratified by a majority vote by the respective party caucus. The vote shall be by voice vote, roll call or secret ballot, as the majority vote of the caucus shall determine. In the event a nomination is rejected by such caucus another nomination may be made by the person designated in this rule to make the initial nomination which shall be subject to ratification in the same manner. In the case of the election by the Senate of a committee by ballot, the member having the highest number of votes shall act as chairman. The second named member shall be vice-chairman.

(b) Except as provided above or unless the Senate shall otherwise specially order, committees shall be appointed by the President, with the exception of the chair whose nomination and ratification shall be governed by the provisions of paragraph (a). The President shall in making such appointments give consideration to representation of both the majority and minority parties relative to their respective representation in the Senate and in any event shall reserve at least two positions on the Senate Committee on Ways and Means and at least one position upon each standing or special committee for a Senate member of the minority party and appointments to such positions shall be made by the Senate minority party leader. For the purposes of this rule the term "minority party" shall mean the political party of those members of the Senate who, in the aggregate, constitute the second largest group of members of the Senate affiliated with a political party.

(c) A vacancy in any position which is regulated by the provisions of this rule shall be filled in the same manner as provided in this rule for the original appointment. Any person in a position which is regulated by the provisions of this rule shall be subject to removal only by a majority vote of the respective party caucus by voice vote, roll call or secret ballot as the majority vote of the caucus shall determine.

[1817; between 1821 and 1826; 1831; 1888; 1973; 1983; 1985; 1991.]

13A. All motions or orders authorizing committees of the Senate to travel or to employ stenographers, all propositions involving special investigations by committees of the Senate and all motions or orders providing that information be transmitted to the Senate shall be referred without debate to the Committee on Rules, who shall report thereon, recommending what action should be taken. All other motions that create main questions, except those that relate to privilege, to procedure and

kindred matters, or to the subjects referred to in Joint Rules 29 and 30, shall also be referred without debate to the Committee on Rules and be treated in like manner.
[1904; 1913; 1921; 1953.]

13B. The President of the Senate may call a caucus at any time at which either he or a designated member of the majority leadership shall preside unless otherwise voted by a majority of the caucus. The President shall honor the request of the Minority Leader at any time while the Senate is in session, to call a minority caucus at which the Minority Leader shall preside or a designated member of the minority leadership, unless otherwise voted by a majority of the caucus.

A caucus shall also be called if twenty-five percent or more of a party's membership requests the calling of a caucus. Such request shall be made to the Senate President or Minority Leader. In the instance of such a caucus being called, said caucus may consider any subject matter, including but not limited to resolutions, motions or other means of ascertaining the sense of party members on any subject. When the Senate recesses to allow a caucus, the Senate President or presiding officer shall inform the members from the rostrum of a time certain for reconvention.
[1985; 1993.]

13C. The Senate Committee on Rules shall provide for periodic audits of Senate financial accounts to be conducted by a certified public accountant experienced in auditing governmental entities. A copy of any such audit shall be filed with the Senate Clerk and copies shall be made available upon request by any member of the Senate or the general public.
[1985.]

14. No committee shall be allowed to occupy the Senate Chamber without a vote of the Senate. [1836; 1863; 1888.]

15. No legislation affecting the rights of individuals or the rights of a private or municipal corporation, otherwise than as it affects generally the people of the whole Commonwealth or the people of the city or town to which it specifically applies, shall be proposed or introduced except by a petition, nor shall any bill or resolve embodying such legislation be reported by a committee, except upon a petition duly referred, nor shall such a bill or resolve be reported by a committee, whether on an original reference or on a recommittal with instructions to hear the parties, until it is made to appear to the satisfaction of the committee that proper notice of the proposed legislation has been given by public advertisement or otherwise to all parties interested, without expense to the Commonwealth, or until evidence satisfactory to the committee is produced that all parties interested have in writing waived notice. A committee reporting adversely for want of proper notice or of a waiver thereof shall set forth this fact in its report, and no bill or resolve shall be in order as a substitute for, or amendment of, such report. Objection to the violation of this rule may be taken at any stage prior to that of third reading. [1870; 1871; 1885; 1890; 1921; 1939; 1945; 1971.]

16. When the object of an application, by petition can be secured under existing laws, or, without detriment to the public interests, by a general law, the committee to whom the matter is referred shall report, ought not to pass, or a general law, as the case may be. The committee may report a special law on matters referred to it upon (1) a petition filed or approved by the voters of a city or town, or the mayor and city council, or other leg-

islative body, of a city, or the town meeting of a town, with respect to a law relating to that city or town; (2) a recommendation by the governor; and (3) matters relating to erecting and constituting metropolitan or regional entities, embracing any two or more cities and towns, or establishing with other than existing city or town boundaries, for any general or special public purpose or purposes.
[1882; 1885; 1888; 1891; 1893; 1967; 1971; 1973.]

Forms of Bills and Resolves.

17. Bills, resolves, resolutions and orders shall be prepared under supervision of the "Bill Drafting Division." Bills, resolves, resolutions and orders founded upon petition shall be presented in original typewritten form and double spaced without substantial erasures or interlineations, on not less than one sheet of paper, with suitable margins and spaces between the several sections or resolves. Any petition which presents a bill, resolve, resolution or order that was before the General Court in the legislative session preceding that for which it is presented shall be designated as a "refiled petition" by the presenting member, together with reference to the number assigned such matter in the preceding legislative session. Bills amending existing laws shall not provide for striking words from, or inserting words in, such laws, unless such course is the best calculated to show clearly the subject and nature of the amendment. No repealed law and no law which has expired by limitation, and no part of any such law, shall be re-enacted by reference merely.
[1844; 1857; 1880; 1882; 1885; 1888; 1889; 1947; 1972; 1985.]

INTRODUCTION OF BUSINESS.

18. Every petition (excepting as otherwise provided
for in the Constitution. or laws of the Commonwealth),
shall be presented by a member. who shall endorse his
name thereon, and a brief statement of the nature and
object of the instrument; and the reading of this instrument shall be dispensed with. unless specially ordered.
[1831; 1888; 1972; 1973.]

18A. In the event that identical legislation is filed
based upon petition, by members of the Senate, the
Clerk of the Senate may make every effort to consolidate
said petitions as one.

The Clerk shall include the name of each petitioner;
such names shall be placed on the consolidated petition
in the order in which the original petitions were filed
with the Clerk.
[1984.]

19. All motions contemplating legislation shall be
founded upon petition. Committees to whom messages
from the governor, reports of state officers, boards, commissions, and others authorized to report to the legislature shall be referred, may report by bill or otherwise
such legislation as may be germane to the subject-matter
referred to them.
[1858; 1888; 1891; 1893; 1973.]

20. All petitions for legislation accompanied by bills
or resolves embodying the subject-matter prayed for.
which are intended for presentation or introduction to
the Senate. reports of state officials, departments, commissions and boards, and reports of special committees
and commissions shall be filed with the Clerk, who shall
unless they be subject to other provisions of these rules
or of the rules of the two branches. refer them, with the

approval and direction of the President and the Committee on Steering and Policy, to the appropriate committees, subject to such change of reference as the Senate may make.

Provided, that petitions and other papers so filed, or papers received from the House, which are subject to the provisions of Joint Rules 7A, 7B or 9, shall be referred by the Clerk to the Committee on Rules. Petitions and other papers so filed which are subject to the provisions of the second paragraph of Joint Rule 12, shall be referred by the Clerk to the Committees on Rules of the two branches, acting concurrently. The reading of all such documents may be dispensed with, but they shall be entered in the journal of the same or the next legislative day after such reference, except as provided in Joint Rule 13.

All orders and resolutions intended for adoption shall be deposited with the Clerk. If they relate to questions of privilege or to procedure and kindred matters, they shall be laid before the Senate by the President as soon as may be. If they relate to other subjects, except as provided in rule 13A or in Joint Rules 29 and 30, they shall be inspected by the Committee on Rules and laid before the Senate not later than the fourth legislative day succeeding the day of their deposit with the committee.

Special reports of state officials, departments, commissions and boards, reports of special committees and commissions, bills and resolves accompanying petitions and reports, and resolutions, shall be printed on order of the President, and under the direction of the Clerk. They shall retain, during all subsequent stages, their original numbers and shall also bear such new numbers as may be necessary.

Matters which have been placed on file may be taken from the files by the Clerk upon request of any Senator or Senator-elect; and matters so taken from the files shall be referred or otherwise disposed of as provided for above.

The Senate may at any time by order make any other disposition of petitions in the hands of the Clerk.

[1891; 1893; 1894; 1916; 1921; 1925; 1927; 1933; 1939; 1945; 1953; 1963; 1967; 1971; 1973; 1985.]

21. [Omitted in 1943.]

22. [Omitted in 1949.]

23. No bill or resolve shall be proposed or introduced unless received from the House of Representatives, reported by a committee, or moved as an amendment to the report of a committee.

[1881; 1882; 1888.]

24. The consideration of any order proposed for adoption, or of any motion to suspend Senate Rule 15, or Joint Rules 8, 9 or 12, shall be postponed without question to the day after that on which the order is proposed or request made, if any member asks such postponement. The consideration of any motion to lay a matter on the table or to take a matter from the table shall be postponed without question to the day after that on which the motion is made (except during the last week of formal business under Joint Rule 12A).

[1885; 1891; 1971; 1973; 1983; 1997.]

25. [Omitted in 1929, the provisions thereof being covered by Joint Rule 9.]

COURSE OF PROCEEDINGS.

26. Bills and resolves from the House, after they are read a first time, shall be referred to a committee of the

Senate, unless they have been reported by a joint committee or substituted for the report of a joint committee. Bills and resolves reported in the Senate, and bills and resolves from the House reported by joint committees or substituted for the reports of joint committees shall, after they have been read once, be referred to the Committee on Steering and Policy, except as otherwise provided by Rule 27. Any matter reported in the Senate or received from the House concerning or restricted to a particular city or town which has received the approval of the voters of the city or town or of the town meeting shall appear on the calendar for the next session for a second reading notwithstanding any other provisions of this rule. Bills introduced by initiative petition, when reported in the Senate or received from the House, shall be referred to the Committee on Steering and Policy. Resolutions received from the House, or introduced or reported in the Senate, shall be referred to the Committee on Steering and Policy. Bills and resolves under Rule 27, when reported, shall be referred to the Committee on Steering and Policy. All reports of the Committee on Steering and Policy shall be placed in the Orders of the Day for the next session unless such matter is assigned for special consideration by said committee as provided for under the provision of Senate Rule 12B.

[1825; 1885; 1888; 1890; 1891; 1897; 1945; 1985; 1993.]

26A. Bills and resolves received in the Senate involving the physical sciences and advancements in their technological fields, shall, after their first reading, be referred to the Senate Committee on Science and Technology. The Clerk, after consulting the President, may also refer Senate petitions involving said subjects to said Committee in the first instance.

Bills and resolves reported by the Senate Committee on Science and Technology shall, if they be subject to the provisions of Senate Rule 27, be referred to the Senate Committee on Ways and Means.
[1995; 1997.]

27. Bills and resolves involving public money, or a grant of public property, unless the subject-matter has been acted upon by the joint Committee on Ways and Means, shall, after the first reading, be referred in course to the Senate Committee on Ways and Means, whose duty it shall be to report on their relation to the finances of the Commonwealth. [See Rule 36.]

Orders reported in the Senate or received from the House involving the expenditure of public money for special committees shall, before the question is taken on the adoption thereof, be referred to the Senate Committee on Ways and Means, whose duty it shall be to report on their relation to the finances of the Commonwealth.

Every such bill involving a capital expenditure for new projects, or an appropriation for repairs, or any legislation, the cost of which, in the opinion of the committee, exceeds the sum of one hundred thousand dollars, when reported into the Senate by the Committee on Ways and Means, shall be accompanied by a fiscal note indicating the amount of public money which will be required to be expended to carry out the provisions of the proposed legislation, together with an estimate of the cost of operation and maintenance for the first year if a new project is involved.
[1871; 1882; 1887; 1888; 1889; 1896; 1921; 1941; 1946; 1947; 1953; 1963; 1967; 1968; 1971; 1995.]

27A. All appropriation bills reported by the Senate Committee on Ways and Means shall be printed in such a manner so as to show: — (a) a prior year's appropriation,

(b) the sum requested by the officer having charge of the department, agency, institution or undertaking, (c) the recommendation, if any, of the secretary of the executive office within which such department, agency, institution or undertaking shall be. (d) the recommendation, if any, of the governor, and (e) the recommendation of the House and the Senate Committees on Ways and Means. The committee shall include with every appropriation bill on which it files a report an explanation of the reasons for any increase or decrease of five percent or more which results in an increase of one million dollars or more for any one appropriation item of, for the deletion of any item from, and for the addition of any new item to, an appropriation bill passed to be engrossed by the House of Representatives.

The committee on Ways and Means shall provide the membership with a copy of its proposed text of the general appropriations bill, and an executive summary which shall include a list of outside sections organized by topic, and a short summary of each outside section not later than the fifth business day prior to full Senate consideration of such bill. When the Senate considers the general appropriation bill, the Ways and Means proposed text shall be adopted and the bill shall be ordered to a third reading without other amendments. The bill shall be immediately read a third time and then be open to other amendments. Each member shall file any proposed amendments, including those relating to outside sections, with the Clerk not later than 5:00 p.m. of the third business day before Senate consideration of the bill. Each amendment shall contain a one sentence descriptive title. The Clerk shall make a list of amendments available to the membership at least twenty-four hours prior to consideration of such bill. Such list shall identify the member sponsoring the amendment and include the one-sentence descriptive title. The sponsoring member shall make available at his or her office a copy and a detailed summary of the amendment.

The committee on Ways and Means shall provide the membership with a copy of its proposed text of any other appropriations bill, and an executive summary which shall include a list of outside sections organized by topic, and a short summary of each outside section not later than the fourth business days prior to full Senate consideration of such bill. When the Senate considers such an appropriation bill, the Ways and Means proposed text shall be adopted and the bill shall be ordered to a third reading without other amendments. The bill shall be immediately read a third time and then be open to other amendments. Each member shall file any proposed amendments, including those relating to outside sections, with the Clerk not later than 5:00 p.m. of the third business day before Senate consideration of the bill. Each amendment shall contain a one sentence descriptive title. The Clerk shall make a list of amendments available to the membership at least twenty-four hours prior to consideration of such bill. Such list shall identify the member sponsoring the amendment and include the one-sentence descriptive title. The sponsoring member shall make available at his or her office a copy and a detailed summary of the amendment.

A member may withdraw an amendment to an appropriation bill after filing it, or may replace a seasonably filed amendment with a redrafted amendment which shall be clearly designated as such. Amendments in the second degree shall be in order pursuant to general parliamentary law; if necessary, the presiding officer will declare a recess and allow members to examine such second-degree amendments before their consideration.

This rule shall not be rescinded, amended or suspended, unless four-fifths of the members present consent thereto.

[1974: 1993: 1997.]

27B. All bills providing for capital outlay programs and projects reported by the Senate Committee on Ways and Means shall be itemized and classified to indicate those requests which are most urgent, those which are essential but may be delayed and those which represent future, long-range development plans; shall state: (a) the request of the agency desiring such program or project, (b) the recommendation, if any, of the secretary of the executive office within which such agency shall be, (c) the recommendation, if any, of the governor, and (d) the recommendation of the House committee and the Senate Committee on Ways and Means; and shall include a statement of the estimated annual operating and maintenance cost of the facilities to be constructed, shall indicate whether the project is to repair, enlarge or improve an existing, properly identified structure or to replace such a structure or to provide additional or hitherto unprovided facilities. Such report shall include therewith a statement showing the total indebtedness proposed to be incurred under each capital outlay program or project and the fund to be charged therefor, and a statement relative to the condition of the state debt. This rule shall not be rescinded, amended or suspended, unless four-fifths of the members present consent thereto.
[1974.]

27C. With the exception of appropriation bills and capital outlay bills, the Committee on Ways and Means and the Committee on Rules may be discharged from the further consideration of matters referred to them pursuant to the following procedure. The consideration of a motion to discharge such committees from further consideration of a certain matter shall be postponed without question to the day after that on which the motion is made. Such motion shall require a majority vote of the members present and voting for adoption, if made after the expiration of forty-five calendar days after referral to said committees, but shall require a vote of two-thirds of the members present and voting, if made prior to the expiration of said forty-five calendar days after referral to said committees. On the motion to discharge such committees, not more than fifteen minutes shall be allowed for debate, and no member shall speak more than three minutes.

In addition to the above procedure, the Committee on Ways and Means shall be discharged from further consideration of a certain matter upon the written petition of a majority of the members of such committee presented to the chairman after forty-five calendar days following referral of the matter to said committee. When directed to discharge a certain matter pursuant to this rule said committees shall either report or be discharged of said matter within five legislative days of the vote or petition calling for such discharge. A petition discharged under the provisions of this rule shall be considered as favorably reported and the matter accompanying said petition shall be designated as "discharged", and shall be placed in the Orders of the Day for the next day for a second reading or question on adoption, as the case may be, unless subject to the provisions of Senate Rule 27.

[1983; 1985.]

---

28. No bill or resolve shall pass to be engrossed without three readings on three several days.

[1817; 1836; 1841; 1859; 1878; 1881; 1882; 1885.]

29. Bills and resolves, in their several readings, and resolutions, shall be read by their titles, unless objection is made.

[1817; 1836; 1841; 1859; 1878; 1881; 1882; 1885; 1890.]

30. If a committee to whom a bill or resolve is referred reports that the same ought not to pass, the question shall be "Shall this bill (or resolve) be rejected?". If the rejection is negatived, the bill or resolve, if it has been read but once, shall go to its second reading without a question; and if it has been read more than once it shall be placed in the Orders of the Day for the next day, pending the question on ordering to a third reading, or engrossment, as the case may be.

[1817; 1836; 1841; 1859; 1878; 1881; 1882; 1885; 1897; 1921; 1939; 1945; 1971.]

31. If an amendment is offered by any member at the second or third reading of a bill or resolve, substantially changing the greater part thereof, the question shall not be put forthwith on adopting the amendment to the bill or resolve if formally requested by two members, but the bill or resolve shall be laid over and placed in the Orders of the next day after that on which the amendment is offered, with the amendment pending. The proposed amendment shall be printed in the calendar and in the journal. If an amendment is made at the second or third reading of a bill or resolve substantially changing the greater part thereof, the question shall not be put forthwith on ordering the bill or resolve to a third reading or to be engrossed, as the case may be, but the bill or resolve, as amended, shall be placed in the Orders of the next day after that on which the amendment is made, and shall then be open to further amendment before such question is put. In like manner, when an amendment is made in any proposition of such a nature as to change its character, as from a bill to an order, or the like, the proposition as amended shall be placed in the Orders of the next day after that on which the amendment was made.

[1882; 1888; 1971.]

31A. Upon recommendation of the Committee on Rules, the Senate may by order require that all amendments to a designated bill be filed with the Clerk not later than one day before consideration of the bill by the Senate. Such amendments shall be printed in the calendar and shall not be subject to the provisions of Senate Rule 31.
[1997.]

32. Bills or resolves ordered to a third reading shall be placed in the Orders for the next day for such reading.
[1817; 1836; 1841; 1859; 1878; 1881; 1882; 1885.]

32A. (1) The Senate Committee on Bills in the Third Reading may be discharged from the further consideration of matters referred to it pursuant to the following procedure:

(a) The consideration of a motion to discharge said committee from further consideration of a certain matter shall be postponed without question to the day after that on which the motion is made.

(b) The adoption of such motion shall require a simple majority vote of the members present and voting thereon.

(2) The Senate Committee on Steering and Policy may be discharged from the further consideration of matters referred to it pursuant to the following procedure:

(a) The consideration of a motion to discharge said committee from further consideration of a certain matter shall be postponed without question to the day after that on which the motion is made.

(b) Such motion shall require a majority vote of the members present and voting for adoption if made after the expiration of thirty calendar days after referral to said committee, but shall require a vote of two-thirds of the members present and voting if made prior to the expiration of said thirty calendar days after referral to said committee.

(3) When either committee is directed to discharge a certain matter pursuant to this rule, such committee shall either report or be discharged of said matter within five legislative days of the vote calling for such discharge. A matter discharged under the provisions of this rule shall be designated as "discharged" and the matter shall be placed in the Orders of the Day for the next sitting. On the motion to discharge such committee, not more than fifteen minutes shall be allowed for debate and no member shall speak more than three minutes.

[1985; 1987; 1989; 1993; 1995.]

32B. [Omitted in 1995.]

33. Bills and resolves when ordered to a third reading, and bills and resolves amended subsequently to their third reading unless the amendment was reported by the Committee on Bills in the Third Reading, shall be referred forthwith to that committee, which shall examine and correct them, for the purpose of avoiding repetitions and unconstitutional provisions, and insuring accuracy in the text and references, and consistency with the language of existing statutes, and of giving effect to the provisions of section fifty-two of chapter three of the General Laws; but any change in the sense of legal effect, or any material change in construction shall be reported to the Senate as an amendment. The committee may consolidate into one bill any two or more related bills referred to it, whenever legislation may be simplified thereby. Resolutions received from and adopted by the House or introduced or reported into the Senate, after they are read and before they are adopted, and amendments of bills, resolves and resolutions

adopted by the House and sent to the Senate for concurrence, shall also be referred, in like manner, to the Committee on Bills in the Third Reading. When a bill, resolve or resolution has been so referred, no further action shall be taken until report thereon has been made by the committee. If a bill or resolve referred to the Committee on Bills in the Third Reading contains an emergency preamble, or if it changes the compensation paid to the members of the General Court, or if it provides for the borrowing of money by the Commonwealth and comes within the provisions of Section 3 of Article LXII of the Amendments to the Constitution, or provides for the giving, loaning or pledging of the credit of the Commonwealth and comes within the provisions of Section 1 of Article LXII (as amended by Article LXXXIV) of the Amendments to the Constitution, or provides, upon recommendation of the governor, for a special law relating to an individual city or town and comes within the provisions of clause (2) of Section 8 of Article LXXXIX of the Amendments to the Constitution, the committee shall plainly indicate the fact on the outside of the bill or resolve, or on a wrapper or label attached thereto.
[1817; 1836; 1882; 1888; 1890; 1891; 1914; 1919; 1925; 1927; 1929; 1945; 1965; 1967; 1983.]

33A. All legislative matters receiving a Senate number shall be in print and available to all the members of the Senate and to the public at least twenty-four hours in advance of consideration by the Senate.

All other amendments recommended by any committee, other than the Committee on Bills in the Third Reading, shall be subject to the provisions of this rule.

This rule shall be suspended only upon a vote of two-thirds of the members present and voting thereon.
[1985.]

34. Bills and resolves prepared for final passage shall be certified by the Senate Clerk and Parliamentarian, after comparison, to be the same as the bills or resolves passed to be engrossed; and if found to be properly prepared, the Clerk shall so endorse on the envelope thereof; and the question on enactment or final passage or adopting an emergency preamble shall be taken thereon, without further reading, unless specifically ordered. When a bill or resolve prepared for final passage contains an emergency preamble or when it changes the compensation paid to members of the General Court or when it provides for the borrowing of money by the Commonwealth and comes within the provisions of Section 3 of Article LXII of the Amendments to the Constitution, or provides for the giving, loaning or pledging of the credit of the Commonwealth and comes within the provisions of Section 1 of Article LXII (as amended by Article LXXXIV) of the Amendments to the Constitution, or provides, upon recommendation of the governor. for a special law relating to an individual city or town and comes within the provisions of clause (2) of Section 8 of Article LXXXIX of the Amendments to the Constitution, the Clerk shall plainly indicate the fact on the envelope thereof.

[1817; 1831; 1882; 1888; 1914; 1919; 1965; 1967; 1971; 1983.]

ORDERS OF THE DAY.

35. The unfinished business in which the Senate was engaged at the time of the last adjournment shall have preference in the Orders of the Day next after motions to reconsider.

[1830; 1870.]

36. Reports of committees not by bill or resolve shall be referred to the Committee on Steering and Policy; except that the report of a committee asking to be discharged from the further consideration of a subject and recommending that it be referred to another committee, or a report of a committee recommending that a matter be placed on file, shall be immediately considered. All reports of the Committee on Steering and Policy shall be placed in the Orders of the Day for the next session unless such matter is assigned for special consideration by said Committee on some future date. Amendments to a measure which have been made by the House and sent back to the Senate for concurrence shall be placed in the Orders of the next day after that on which they are received; provided that amendments involving state money shall be referred to the Committee on Ways and Means.

Reports of committees on proposals for amendment of the Constitution shall be dealt with in accordance with the provisions of Joint Rule 23.

[1845; 1853; 1888; 1891; 1919; 1947; 1953; 1965; 1968; 1971; 1985; 1995.]

37. After entering upon the consideration of the Orders of the Day, the Senate shall proceed with them in regular course, as follows: Matters not giving rise to a motion or debate shall first be disposed of in the order in which they stand in the calendar; then the matters that were passed over shall be considered and disposed of in like order.

[1817; 1836; 1841; 1859; 1878; 1882; 1885.]

38. No matter which has been duly placed in the Orders of the Day shall be discharged therefrom or considered out of its regular course.

[1885.]

38A. The Senate shall not continue in session beyond the hour of eight o'clock post meridiem. This rule shall not be suspended unless a majority of the members present and voting consent thereto on a recorded yea and nay vote.

[1983.]

38B. Debate and consideration on the general appropriation bill shall begin at ten o'clock in the morning and shall be the only matter placed on the calendar for the day.
[1985.]

RULES OF DEBATE.

39. Every member, when he speaks, shall stand in his place and address the President. When recognized, the member shall confine himself to the measure and question under debate and shall at all times avoid personalities.
[1817; 1831; 1871; 1973.]

40. When two or more members rise to speak at the same time, the President shall designate the member who is entitled to the floor.
[1831; 1888.]

41. No member shall speak more than once to the prevention of any other member who has not spoken and desires to speak on the same question.
[1817; 1886.]

42. No member shall interrupt another while speaking, except by rising to call to order or to rise to a question of personal privilege or parliamentary inquiry.
[1817; 1831; 1971.]

43. After a question is put to vote no member shall speak to it.
[1817.]

43A. No appeal from a decision of the President shall be entertained unless it is seconded; and the question on the appeal shall be disposed of forthwith.
[1973.]

MOTIONS.

44. Any motion shall be reduced to writing if the President so directs. A motion need not be seconded and may be withdrawn by the mover if no objection is made.
[1817; 1844; 1871; 1888.]

44A. A motion to amend may be made by up to three members whenever it is clearly indicated thereon.
[1991.]

45. A question containing two or more propositions, capable of division, shall be divided whenever desired by any member. When a motion to strike out and insert is thus divided, the failure of the motion to strike out shall not preclude amendment; or, if the motion to strike out prevails, the matter proposed to be inserted shall be open to amendment before the question is taken on inserting it.
[1817; 1841; 1888.]

46. When a question is under debate the President shall receive no motion that does not relate to the same, except a motion to adjourn or some other motion which has precedence by express rule of the Senate, or because it is privileged in its nature; and he shall receive no motion relating to the same except:

(1) To *lay on the table* (or take from the table);
(2) To *close debate at a specified time*;
(3) To *postpone to a day certain*;
(4) To *commit* (or recommit);
(5) To *amend*;
(6) To *postpone indefinitely.*

These motions shall have preference in the order in which they stand.
[Between 1821 and 1826; 1831; 1844; 1870; 1882; 1885; 1888; 1921; 1939; 1945; 1971.]

47. Debate may be closed at any time not less than one hour from the adoption of a motion to that effect. On this motion not more than ten minutes shall be allowed for debate, and no member shall speak more than three minutes.

[1882.]

48. When motions are made to refer a subject to different committees, the committees proposed shall be considered in the following order:

(1) A standing committee of the Senate;

(2) A special committee of the Senate;

(3) A joint standing committee of the two branches;

(4) A joint special committee of the two branches.

[1844; 1888.]

49. No engrossed bill or resolve shall be amended; but this rule shall not apply to a bill or resolve returned by the Governor with a recommendation of amendment in accordance with the provisions of Article LVI of the Amendments of the Constitution; nor shall it apply to amendments of engrossed bills proposed by the House and sent to the Senate for concurrence.

[1837; 1919; 1931.]

50. No motion or proposition of a subject different from that under consideration and no measure which has been finally rejected or disposed of by the Senate shall be admitted under the color of an amendment.

[1882; 1971.]

51. In filling blanks the largest sum and the longest time shall be put first.

[1882.]

52. The motion to adjourn and the call for yeas and nays shall be decided without debate. On the motions to lay on the table and take from the table, to postpone to a time certain. to commit or recommit (except with instructions), not exceeding ten minutes shall be allowed for debate. and no member shall speak more than three minutes.

On a motion to reconsider not exceeding thirty minutes shall be allowed for debate. and no member shall speak more than five minutes: but on a motion to reconsider a vote upon any subsidiary. incidental or dependent question debate shall be limited to ten minutes. and no member shall speak more than three minutes.

On a motion to suspend any of the joint rules or Senate rules debate shall be limited to fifteen minutes, and no member shall speak more than three minutes.

[1817: 1859: 1870: 1874; 1882: 1885: 1937; 1941.]

52A. The Senate President or presiding officer of the Senate may not declare that the Senate is in recess for more than thirty minutes. without informing the members from the rostrum of a time certain for reconvention.

[1993.]

***

RECONSIDERATION.

53. No motion to reconsider a vote shall be entertained unless it is made on the same day on which the vote has passed. or on the next day thereafter on which a quorum is present and before the Orders of the Day for that day have been taken up. If reconsideration is moved on the same day, the motion shall (except during the last week of the session) be placed first in the Orders of the Day for the succeeding day; but if it is moved on the succeeding day, the motion shall be considered forthwith; *provided, however,* that this rule shall not prevent the reconsideration of a vote on a subsidiary. incidental or dependent question at any time when the main question to which it relates is under consideration; and *provided, further,* that a motion to reconsider a vote on any incidental, subsidiary or dependent question shall not remove the main subject under consideration from before the Senate, but shall be considered at the time when it is made.

There shall be no reconsideration of the vote on the question on adjourning, for the yeas and nays, on laying on the table or on taking from the table; and when a motion for reconsideration has been decided, that decision shall not be reconsidered.

[1817; between 1821 and 1826; 1858; 1885; 1888; 1891; 1902; 1946.]

REJECTED MEASURES.

54. When any measure has been finally rejected or finally disposed of by the Senate, no measure substantially the same shall be introduced by any committee or member during the session, or moved as an amendment to another measure.

[1817; dispensed with in 1831; and revived in 1838; amended in 1841; 1844; 1877; 1882; 1971.]

VOTING.

55. The President shall declare all votes; but if a member doubts a vote, the President shall order a return of the number voting in the affirmative, and in the negative, without further debate.

[1831; 1888.]

56. The sense of the Senate shall be taken by yeas and nays whenever required by one-fifth of the members present, or by a number of members equal to the total number of members of the minority party. The President may wait a period not exceeding ten minutes before ordering the Clerk to start the yeas and nays, during which time the members shall be summoned to the Senate Chamber as the President may direct. Other business of the Senate may be taken up during the ten minute period. At the end of the ten minute interval, the President shall state the question to be roll called and then direct the Clerk to begin the call. If, before the vote is taken, a member states to the Senate that he has paired with another member and how each would vote on the pending question, the fact shall be entered on the journal immediately after the record of the yeas and nays, and such member shall be excused from voting. If, after the yeas and nays have been ordered, an advanced notice of at least sixty minutes is given by the President, he may set a time certain for the vote to be taken and the ten minute waiting period above prescribed may be waived.

[1817; 1852; 1888; 1971; 1972; 1997.]

57. Whenever a question is taken by yeas and nays, the Clerk shall call the names of all members, except the President, in alphabetical order, and every member present shall answer to his name, unless excused before the vote is taken; and no member shall be permitted to vote after the decision is announced from the chair.

[1837; 1844.]

57A. The vote on enactment or final passage of any legislation which changes the compensation paid to members of the General Court shall be taken by a call of the yeas and nays.

[1983.]

ELECTIONS BY BALLOT.

58. In all elections by ballot a time shall be assigned for such election, at least one day previous thereto, except in case of an election of President or President *pro tempore*, under the provisions of Rule 5.

[1831; 1891.]

REPORTERS' GALLERY.

59. Subject to the approval and direction of the Committee on Rules during the session and of the President after prorogation, the use of the reporters' gallery of the Senate Chamber shall be under the control of the organization of legislative reporters known as the Massachusetts State House Press Association or the State House Broadcasters Association (provided that no radio, television or other electronic recording equipment shall be allowed in the Senate Chamber or Senate Reading Room under this rule). Except in the employ of the newspaper or publication which he represents as a legislative reporter, no person who is entitled to the privileges of the reporters' gallery shall seek to influence the action of the Senate or any member thereof, nor shall such person approach a member to seek to influence him in any place from which legislative agents are excluded by Rule 61. Every legislative reporter desiring admission to the reporters' gallery of the Senate Chamber shall state in writing that he is not the agent or representative of any person or corporation interested in legislation before the General Court and will not act as representative of any such person or corporation while he retains his place in the gallery; but nothing herein contained shall prevent such legislative reporter from engaging in other employment, provided such other employment is specifically approved by the Committee on Rules and reported to the Senate.

[1847; 1911; 1914; 1925; 1989.]

59A. Formal sessions of the Senate shall be made accessible to electronic media, including television and radio. The manner, conditions and extent of such access shall be established by the Committee on Rules.

This rule shall not be suspended unless by majority vote of the members present and voting thereon.

[1989.]

59B. The Clerk of the Senate shall deliver a videotape of each televised Senate session to the Majority Floor Leader and the Minority Floor Leader no later than twenty-four hours after such session has ended.

The Clerk of the Senate shall also keep a videotaped copy of every televised Senate session for reference purposes. These tapes will be made available to the public upon request.

[1993.]

THE SENATE CHAMBER AND ADJOINING ROOMS.

60. No person not a member shall be allowed to sit at the Senate table while the Senate is in session.

[1853; 1888.]

61. No person, except members of the legislative and executive departments of the state government, persons in the exercise of an official duty directly connected with the business of the Senate, and legislative reporters who are entitled to the privileges of the reporters' gallery, shall, unless invited by the President, be admitted to the floor of the Senate Chamber or to the reception room or to the corridor between the reception room and the Senate Chamber during the sessions of the Senate, or during the half hour preceding or succeeding said sessions, nor to the Senate reading room, cloak room corridor, cloak room or anterooms on any day when a session of the Senate is held, except upon written invitation bearing the name of the person it is desired to invite and the name of the Senator extending the invitation, which invitation shall be surrendered when the said person enters the apartment.

Publications desiring the privileges of the reporters' gallery of the Senate Chamber for legislative reporters, not members of the State House Press Association or the State House Broadcasters Association (provided that no radio, television or other electronic recording equipment shall be allowed in the Senate Chamber or Senate Reading Room under this rule), shall make written application to the President stating the purposes for which the privileges are required, and such privileges shall be granted only upon written approval by the President.

No legislative counsel or agent shall be admitted to the floor of the Senate Chamber, nor, on any day when a session of the Senate is held, to the reading room, the cloak room, the reception room or the Senate corridors or anterooms. No person, except members of the legislative and executive departments of the state government, persons in the exercise of an official duty directly connected with the business of the Senate and legislative reporters who are entitled to the privileges of the reporters' gallery, shall be permitted to loiter in the reading room, the cloak room, the reception room or the Senate corridors or anterooms at any time. Smoking shall not be permitted in the reception room.
[1870; 1875; 1886; 1891; 1895; 1896; 1897; 1898; 1907; 1909; 1914; 1916; 1925; 1989.]

61A. No person shall be allowed to smoke on the floor of the Senate.
[1985.]

PARLIAMENTARY PRACTICE.

62. The rules of parliamentary practice shall govern the Senate in all cases to which they are applicable, and in which they are not inconsistent with these rules or the joint rules of the two branches.
[1847; 1858; 1882; 1895; 1963.]

ALTERATIONS, SUSPENSION OR REPEAL OF RULES.

63. This rule and rules 24, 31, 33, 34 and 53 shall not be suspended if objection is made; and no other rule shall be altered, suspended or repealed, except by vote of two-thirds of the members present and voting thereon. The Committee on Rules may consider and suggest measures that shall, in its judgement, tend to facilitate the business of the Senate, and a majority vote of the Senate shall be required to approve such recommendations.

[1817; 1841; 1848; 1882; 1888; 1891; 1893; 1899; 1953; 1973.]

64. Twenty-one members shall constitute a quorum for the organization of the Senate and the transaction of business. [See Amendments to the Constitution, Art. XXXIII.]

[1973.]

65. The Senate shall meet no later than the third Friday following the convening of the first annual session of a General Court for the purpose of adopting permanent rules of the Senate.

[1991.]

66. [Omitted in 1997.]

INDEX TO SENATE RULES.

RESOLUTIONS:
    drafting division to prepare, 17.
    to be deposited with Clerk, etc., 20.
    to be printed, 20.
    to be read by title, unless objection, 29.
    to be referred to the committee on Bills in the Third Reading
        before adoption, 33.
    to be referred to the committee on Steering and Policy, 26.
Resolves. See *Bills and Resolves.*

RULES:
    alteration, suspension or repeal of, 52, 63.
    Clerk to insert in appendix to journal, 6.
    motions to suspend certain, may be postponed, on request
        of a member, 24.
    of parliamentary practice, 62.
    permanent, deadline for adoption, 65.
    violations of, 12A.
Rules, committee on, 12, 13A, 13C, 20, 27C, 59, 59A, 63.
    (See also Joint Rules 1, 14, 21, 29, 30, 32.)
    may make recommendations to facilitate business of
        the session, 63.
    may make recommendation to print amendments on
        calendar, 31A.

Science and Technology, committee on, 12, 26A.
Senate Chamber and adjoining rooms, 59, 60, 61, 61A.

SESSIONS:
    cancellation of, 5A.
    informal, 5A, 7.
    last week of, 24, 53.
    television, radio coverage for formal, 59A.
    to end at 8 o'clock P.M., 38A.
Special bills, 16.
Special reports, filed with Clerk and printed, 20.
Steering and Policy, committee on, 7, 12B, 20, 26, 32A, 36.
Stenographers, employment of, by committees, 13A. (See also
    Joint Rule 29.)
Suspension of certain rules, laid over, 24.

SUSPENSION OF RULES:
    limit of debate on, 52.
    vote required, 63.

RULES
OF THE
HOUSE OF REPRESENTATIVES

[as finally adopted on
January 14, 1997.]

RULES
OF THE
HOUSE OF REPRESENTATIVES
[As adopted on January 14, 1997
with subsequent amendments as indicated.]

**[Rule numbers have been changed. Numbers enclosed
in brackets following each rule indicate
the rule number prior to 1979.
Numbers enclosed in parentheses following each rule
indicate the corresponding Senate Rule.]**

SPEAKER.

1. The Speaker shall take the Chair at the hour to which the House stands adjourned. call the members to order, and, on the appearance of a quorum, proceed to business. [1.] (Senate Rule 1.)

1A. The House shall not be called to order before the hour of ten o'clock A.M. nor meet beyond the hour of ten o'clock P.M. At the hour of ten o'clock P.M., if the House is in session, the Speaker shall interrupt the business then pending and shall, without debate, place before the House the question of suspension of this rule which shall be decided by a majority of members present and voting by a recorded yea and nay vote. If the vote is in the affirmative, the House shall return to the pending business; and if no matter was pending, to the next order of business. However, if the vote is in the negative, the Speaker shall forthwith, and without further debate. adjourn or recess the House to a time not earlier than ten o'clock A.M. on the next succeeding calendar day.

[Adopted Jan. 12, 1983; Amended Jan. 11, 1985; Jan. 12, 1987; Jan. 14, 1997.]

2. The Speaker shall preserve decorum, including proper and appropriate attire for all members, and order; may speak to points of order in preference to other members; and shall decide all questions of order, subject to an appeal to the House. [2] (2.) [With regard to appeals, see Rule 77.]
[Amended Jan. 11, 1985.]

3. The Speaker shall declare all votes, subject to verification as hereinafter provided. [3.] (55.) [See Rules 49 to 53, inclusive.]
[Amended Jan. 11, 1985.]

4. In all cases the Speaker may vote. [4.] (3.)
[Amended Jan. 11, 1985.]

5. The Speaker may appoint a member to perform the duties of the Chair. In the event the Speaker fails to appoint a member to perform the duties of the Chair, the Majority Leader shall be the Acting Speaker until the Speaker otherwise provides or until a vacancy in the office of Speaker occurs. In the event that the Majority Leader is absent or is unable to perform the duties of Acting Speaker, the Assistant Majority Leader or the Second Assistant Majority Leader or other designee shall be the Acting Speaker. [7.] (4.)
[Amended April 18, 1979; Jan. 11, 1985; Jan. 14, 1997.]

6. In case of a vacancy in the office of Speaker, or in case the Speaker or the member named by said Speaker in accordance with the preceding rule is absent at the hour to which the House stands adjourned, the senior member present shall call the House to order, and shall preside until a Speaker *pro tempore* or a Speaker is elected, which shall be the first business in order. [8.] (5.)
[Amended Jan. 11, 1985.]

7. At the beginning of the first year of the two year General Court the Speaker shall, unless the House otherwise directs, appoint a Chaplain; and the Speaker shall promptly fill any vacancy in the office of Chaplain. [7A.] (4.)
[Amended Jan. 11, 1985.]

SCHEDULING.

7A. There shall be appointed a standing committee on Steering, Policy and Scheduling consisting of eleven members. The committee shall not be subject to the provisions of Rule 17A, but shall be authorized to meet from time to time at the call of the Chair for the purpose of assisting the Speaker and the members of the House of Representatives in identifying the major matters pending before the General Court, the relative urgency and priority for consideration of such matters, and alternative methods of responding to such matters by the General Court. Said committee shall schedule legislative matters in a manner that will provide for an even distribution and orderly consideration of reports of legislative committees on the daily Calendar.

The committee on Steering, Policy and Scheduling shall not be authorized to recommend changes or amendments to legislation or recommend that a matter ought to pass or ought not to pass, but shall only report what date a matter shall be scheduled for consideration by the House and placed in the Orders of the Day.

All matters received from the Senate or reported from standing committees of the House and joint standing committees of the General Court shall, unless subject to provisions of any other House or joint rules, be referred to the committee on Steering, Policy and Scheduling. All matters reported by said committee on Steering, Policy and Scheduling shall be placed in the Orders of the Day for the next sitting. Said committee shall report on a legislative matter not later than thirty days following the day the matter was referred.
[Adopted Jan. 14, 1997.]

7B. The committee on Rules shall be authorized to originate and report special orders for the scheduling and consideration of legislation on the floor of the House. Said committee shall not be subject to the notification provisions contained in Rule 17A but may hold public hearings and shall accept testimony only from the members of the House. A majority of the members appointed to the committee shall constitute

a quorum. When reported, such orders may be amended and shall be subject to approval by a majority of the members of the House present and voting. Debate on the question on adoption of such orders shall be limited to thirty minutes. No orders adopted pursuant to this paragraph shall limit the powers of the Speaker as provided in Rules 1 to 6, inclusive. Such orders shall not be subject to reconsideration.
[Adopted Jan. 14, 1997.]

7C. The committee on Rules may consider and make recommendations designed to improve and expedite the business and procedures of the House and its committees, and to recommend to the House any amendments to the Rules deemed necessary: provided that a majority of the members of the House present and voting shall be required to approve such recommendations.
The committee shall be privileged to report at any time.
[Adopted Jan. 14, 1997.]

7D. The Speaker shall, in consultation with the committee on Rules and the committee on Steering, Policy and Scheduling, establish a committee scheduling system that would minimize to the greatest extent possible scheduling conflicts for members of committees.
The Speaker shall determine a schedule for the House for each week relative to formal and informal sessions and shall make such schedule available to the members by Thursday of the preceding week; provided, however, that the Speaker may make, notwithstanding the provisions of Rule 7A, changes in the schedules to necessitate action on certain matters in an efficient and timely fashion.
[Adopted Jan. 14, 1997.]

MONITORS.

8. Two monitors shall be appointed by the Speaker for each division of the House, whose duty it shall be to see to the due observance of the rules, and, on request of the Speaker, to return the number of votes and members in their respective divisions. [9.]

9. If a member transgress any of the rules after being notified thereof by a monitor, it shall be the duty of such monitor to report the case to the House.

It shall be the duty of a monitor to report his or her knowledge of the occurrence of a member voting for another member, in his or her division of the House, to the Speaker of the House and the Minority Leader. [10.] [See Rules 16 and 16A.]

[Amended Jan. 9, 1991; May 5, 1993.]

9A. There shall be established a Floor Division Committee for each of the four divisions of the House. The Speaker shall appoint a Floor Division chairperson for each of the four divisions. Said committee shall consist of the members assigned to the respective divisions.

In order to create a continuous flow of debate, each chairperson shall be responsible for reviewing the daily Calendar and providing advance notice to committee members in the respective divisions of all matters scheduled for consideration in the Orders of the Day. Said committee chairpersons shall provide information to members of their committees on pending legislation and other matters of business before the House.

In addition to the legislative duties, chairpersons shall oversee the physical appearance of the Chamber and the various areas under the jurisdiction of the House of Representatives. Said chairpersons shall be authorized to act as a committee and may meet at any time at the request of at least two chairpersons. Said chairpersons, as a committee, shall be authorized to meet with the appropriate agencies and historical commissions of the Commonwealth for the purpose of requesting expeditious appraisals and necessary repairs and renovations to the interior and exterior of the State House. The committee of chairpersons shall report directly to the Speaker the results of all consultations.

[Adopted Jan. 14, 1997.]

CLERK.

10. The Clerk shall keep the Journal of the House. The Clerk shall enter therein a record of each day's proceedings, and submit it to the Speaker and the Minority Leader before the hour fixed for the next sitting, and shall cause the same to be printed daily; and provided further that a copy of said Journal shall also be made available to each member of the House. Any objection to the Journal shall be made before the House proceeds to the consideration of the Orders of the Day. [11.] (6.)
[Amended Jan. 12, 1981; Jan 11, 1985; Jan. 17, 1995.]

10A. The Clerk shall be the official parliamentarian of the House of Representatives.
[Adopted Jan. 9, 1991.]

11. Every question of order with the decision thereof shall be entered at large in the Journal, and shall be noted in an appendix, which shall also contain the rules of the House and of the two branches. [12.] (6.)

12. The Clerk shall prepare and cause to be printed each day a Calendar of matters in order for consideration and such other memoranda as the House or the Speaker may direct. The Clerk shall prepare a Calendar on which shall appear any question on passage of a bill or resolve notwithstanding the objections of His Excellency the Governor.

When, in the determination of the Clerk, a volume of matters exists for the next legislative day, the Clerk shall prepare and cause to be printed an advance calendar of the matters in order of consideration for the next legislative day and such other memoranda as the House or Speaker may direct. The Clerk may indicate on the advance calendar that the matters contained therein are subject to change.

The Clerk shall be authorized to dispense with the printing of a Calendar for designated formal sessions of the House only after two-thirds of the members present and voting consent thereto on a recorded yea and nay vote. Debate on this

question shall be limited to fifteen minutes, no member shall speak more than three minutes. and such question shall not be subject to reconsideration. [13.] (7.)
[Amended Jan. 12, 1983; Jan. 11, 1985; Jan. 12, 1987; May 5, 1993; Jan. 17, 1995.]

13. Any objection to the Calendar shall be made and disposed of before the House proceeds to the consideration of the Orders of the Day. [14.]

MEMBERS.

14. No member shall stand up. to the inconvenience of others, while a member is speaking; or be involved in disturbing conversation while another member is speaking in debate; or pass unnecessarily between the Speaker of the House and the member speaking; or stand in the passages, or in the area in front of the Chair; or stand at the Clerk's desk while a roll call is in progress; or smoke upon the floor of the House; and neither shall any person be allowed to smoke upon the floor of the House or within the confines of the House Chamber, including the galleries. [16.]
[Amended Jan. 12, 1987; Jan. 9, 1989.]

15. When it appears to the presiding officer that the presence of a quorum is endangered, the Chair shall order the doors closed. If a quorum is doubted the Chair shall order the doors closed and thereafter no member shall enter or leave the House until an initial determination has been made as to the presence of a quorum or lack thereof; and thereafter, provided that no quorum is present, no member shall leave the House unless by permission of the presiding officer, but members shall be admitted, at any time.
Upon the doubting of a quorum and after ascertaining that a quorum is not present, the Speaker may order a recorded attendance roll call to be taken on the electronic roll call machine.
Said roll call, if ordered, shall be taken at a time determined by the Speaker.

Members answering a quorum call shall vote "YES" on the roll call machine. [17.] (11.)
[Amended Jan. 12, 1981; Feb. 22, 1982; Jan. 12, 1983; Jan. 12, 1987; Jan. 9, 1991.]

ETHICS.

16. There shall be appointed a committee on Ethics as authorized by Rule 17 but shall not be subject to the provisions of Rule 17A when the committee is meeting pursuant to an alleged violation of House Rule 16A. The committee shall consist of eleven members, seven of whom shall be appointed by the Speaker, four of whom shall be appointed by the Minority Leader.

Any member appointed to this committee shall, upon declaration of candidacy for any other state or federal elective office, remove himself/herself from said committee.

The House committee on Ethics is empowered to investigate and evaluate, at the direction of the Speaker, by a sworn written complaint filed and delivered by a member, officer or employee to the chairman of the Ethics committee, or by a majority vote of the members appointed to the Ethics committee, any matters relative to alleged violations of the Code of Ethics (Rule 16A) by a member, officer or employee.

Upon the receipt of said sworn written complaint, at the direction of the Speaker or by a majority vote of the members appointed to the Ethics committee, the committee shall notify any person named of the nature of the alleged violation and a list of prospective witnesses, and also shall notify said person of the final disposition and the recommendations, if any, of the committee.

Any member, officer, or employee of the House named relative to an alleged violation shall be afforded the opportunity to appear before the committee on Ethics with counsel.

All proceedings including the filing of the initial complaint shall be considered confidential information.

If the alleged violation received in the manner described above is deemed to have merit by a majority vote of the members appointed to the committee, the committee shall file a report with the Clerk of the House. Said report shall be a public document. The committee shall not disclose any allegation deemed to be frivolous or without merit.

If a majority appointed finds that any member of the House, officer, or employee has violated any provision of the Code of Ethics, a majority appointed may, in the case of a member, recommend a reprimand, censure, removal from a chairmanship or other position of authority, or expulsion; and in the case of an officer or employee, a majority appointed may recommend a reprimand, suspension, or removal from employment.

Should such an alleged violation be filed with the committee regarding a member or members of the House Ethics committee, said member or members shall not participate in the committee deliberations on said alleged violation.

Any member of the House, officer, or employee may request in writing from the House committee on Ethics an advisory opinion concerning any contemplated personal action or potential personal conflict. The committee on Ethics shall issue written advisory opinions and clarification in response to said written request. The committee shall respond within sixty days of receipt of such a request, unless the General Court has prorogued. In that event, the committee shall respond within thirty days following the opening of the new session.

No member, officer, or employee of the House shall be penalized in any manner for having acted within the guidelines of an advisory opinion, provided that all pertinent facts are stated in the original request for an advisory opinion.

The chairman of the Ethics committee may convene the committee at any time.

The chairman shall also convene the committee at the written request of at least five members of the committee.

Upon convening of the first annual session of the General Court and after the adoption of rules, all members, officers and employees of the House shall be provided with a current copy of the Code of Ethics contained in Rule 16A. [19.] (12A.)

[Amended Jan. 12, 1987; May 5, 1993; Jan. 17, 1995; Mar. 6, 1995; Jan. 14, 1997.]

CODE OF ETHICS.

16A. (1.) While members, officers, and employees should not be denied those opportunities available to all other citizens to acquire and retain private, economic and other interests, members, officers, and employees should exercise prudence in any and all such endeavors and make every reasonable effort to avoid transactions, activities, or obligations, which are in substantial conflict with or will substantially impair their independence of judgement.

(2.) No member, officer, or employee shall solicit or accept any compensation or political contribution other than that provided for by law for the performance of official legislative duties.

(3.) No member, officer, or employee shall serve as a legislative agent as defined in Chapter 3 of the General Laws regarding any legislation before the General Court.

(4.) No member, officer, or employee shall receive any compensation or permit any compensation to accrue to his or her beneficial interest by virtue of influence improperly exerted from his or her official position in the House.

(5.) No member, officer, or employee shall accept employment or engage in any business or professional activity, which will require the disclosure of confidential information gained in the course of, and by reason of, his or her official position.

(6.) No member, officer, or employee shall willfully and knowingly disclose or use confidential information gained in the course of his or her official position to further his or her own economic interest or that of any other person.

(7.) Except as provided in Rule 49, no member shall cast a vote for any other member.

(8.) No member shall use profane, insulting, or abusive language in the course of public debate in the House Chamber or in testimony before any committee of the General Court.

(9.) No member, officer, or employee shall employ anyone from public funds who does not perform tasks which contribute substantially to the work of the House and which are commensurate with the compensation received; and no officer or full time employee of the House shall engage in any outside business activity during regular business hours, whether the House is in session or not. All employees of the House are assumed to be full time unless their personnel record indicates otherwise.

(10.) No member, officer, or employee shall accept or solicit compensation for non-legislative services which is in excess of the usual and customary value of such services.

(11.) No member, officer, or employee shall accept or solicit an honorarium for a speech, writing for publication, or other activity from any person, organization, or enterprise having a direct interest in legislation or matters before any agency, authority, board, or commission of the Commonwealth which is in excess of the usual and customary value of such services.

(12.) No member of the House, officer, or employee shall knowingly accept any gifts with an aggregate value of $100.00 or more in a calendar year from any legislative agent.

No member of the House, officer, or employee shall accept any gift of cash from any person or entity having a direct interest in legislation before the General Court (For the purpose of paragraph 12, the definitions of "gift" and "person" are defined in Chapter 268B, Section 1(g) and 1(m).).

(13.) No member shall convert campaign funds to personal use in excess of reimbursements for legitimate and verifiable campaign expenditures. Members shall consider all proceeds from testimonial dinners and other fund raising activities as campaign funds.

(14.) No member shall serve on any committee or vote on any question in which his/her private right is immediately concerned, distinct from the public interest. [19.]

(15.) No member, officer or employee shall violate the confidentiality of any proceeding before the Ethics committee. [19A.]

[Amended Jan. 12, 1981; May 5, 1993.]

COMMITTEES.

17. At the beginning of the first year of the two year General Court, standing committees shall be appointed as follows:
A committee on Rules;
(to consist of fifteen members).
A committee on Ways and Means;
(to consist of thirty-two members).
A committee on Bills in the Third Reading;
(to consist of three members).
A committee on Long-Term Debt and Capital Expenditures;
(to consist of eleven members).
A committee of each Floor Division;
(to consist of the members of each division).
A committee on Ethics;
(to consist of eleven members).
A committee on Personnel and Administration;
(to consist of thirteen members).
A committee on Post Audit and Oversight;
(to consist of eleven members).
A committee on Science and Technology;
(to consist of eleven members).
A committee on Steering. Policy and Scheduling;
(to consist of eleven members).
Committee meetings, insofar as practicable, shall not be scheduled in conflict with formal sessions of the House of Representatives. [20.] (12. 12A. 12B.)
[Amended March 6, 1979; Sept. 16, 1981; Jan. 11, 1985; Jan. 12, 1987; May 5, 1993; Oct. 6, 1993; May 23, 1996; Jan. 14, 1997.]

17A. The following terms shall have the following meanings:
"Deliberation", a verbal exchange between a quorum of members of a committee attempting to arrive at a decision on any public business within its jurisdiction.
"Emergency", a sudden, generally unexpected occurrence or set of circumstances demanding immediate action.

"Executive session", any meeting or part of a meeting of a committee which is closed to certain persons for deliberation on certain matters.

"Meeting", any corporal convening and deliberation of a committee for which a quorum is required in order to make a decision at which any public policy matter over which the committee has supervision, control, jurisdiction or advisory power is discussed or considered: but shall not include any on site inspection of any project or program.

"Quorum", a simple majority of a committee unless otherwise defined by constitution, rule or law applicable to such committee. A quorum shall be presumed to be present unless otherwise doubted.

All meetings, including hearings and executive sessions, of House standing committees, and special committees of the House of Representatives, shall be open to the public and any person shall be permitted to attend any meeting except as otherwise provided by this rule. Areas for the media and the public may be specifically designated by the presiding officer.

No quorum of a committee shall meet in private for the purpose of deciding on deliberating toward a decision on any matter except as provided by this rule.

No executive session shall be held until the committee has first convened in an open session for which notice has been given, the presiding officer having stated the authorized purpose of the executive session, a majority of the members of the committee present have voted to go into executive session and the vote of each member recorded on a roll call vote and entered into the minutes, the presiding officer has stated before the executive session if the committee will reconvene after the executive session.

Nothing except the limitations contained in this rule shall be construed to prevent the committee from holding an executive session after an open meeting has been convened and after a recorded vote has been taken to hold an executive session. Executive sessions may be held only for the following purposes:

(1) To discuss the reputation, character, physical condition or mental health rather than the professional competence of an

individual, provided that the individual to be discussed in such executive session has been notified in writing by the committee, at least forty-eight hours prior to the proposed executive session. Notification may be waived upon agreement of the parties.

A committee shall hold an open meeting if the individual involved requests that the meeting be open. If an executive session is held, such individual shall have the following rights:

(a) to be present at such executive session during discussions or considerations which involve that individual.

(b) to have counsel or a representative of his/her own choosing present and attending for the purpose of advising said individual and not for the purpose of active participation in said executive session.

(c) to speak in his her own behalf.

(2) To consider the discipline or dismissal of, or to hear complaints or charges brought against, a public officer, employee, staff member, or individual, provided that the individual involved in such executive session has been notified in writing by the committee at least forty-eight hours prior to the proposed executive session. Notification may be waived upon agreement of the parties. A committee shall hold an open meeting if the individual involved requests that the meeting be open. If an executive session is held, such individual shall have the following rights:

(a) to be present at such executive session during discussions or considerations which involve that individual.

(b) to have counsel or a representative of his/her own choosing present and attending for the purpose of advising said individual and not for the purpose of active participation in said executive session.

(c) to speak in his/her own behalf.

(3) To discuss strategy with respect to litigation if an open meeting may have a detrimental effect on the position of the committee.

(4) To consider the purchase, exchange, lease or value of real property, if such discussions may have a detrimental effect on the negotiating position of the Commonwealth and a person, firm or corporation.

This rule shall not apply to any chance meeting or social meeting at which matters relating to official business are discussed so long as no final agreement is reached. No chance meeting or social meeting shall be used in circumvention of the spirit or requirements of this section to discuss or act upon a matter over which the committee has supervision. control, jurisdiction, or advisory power.

Except in an emergency, a notice and agenda of every meeting of a committee subject to this rule shall be filed with the Clerk of the House and publicly posted on the bulletin board outside the Clerk's Office and in such other places as are designated in advance for such purpose by said Clerk. at least forty-eight hours. including Saturdays but not Sundays and legal holidays, prior to the time of such meeting and a list of the bills. petitions. and resolutions to be considered for a vote or other action by the committee. The notice shall include the date. time and place of such meeting. Such filing and posting shall be the responsibility of the officer calling such meetings. The Clerk shall furnish copies of such notices, upon request, to members and the public.

A committee shall maintain accurate records of its meetings and hearings setting forth the date. time and place thereof. and recording any action taken at each meeting. hearing or executive session. The record of each meeting shall become a public record and be available to the public: provided. however. that the records of any executive session may remain secret as long as publication may defeat the lawful purposes of the executive session. but no longer. All votes requested to be taken in executive sessions shall be recorded roll call votes and shall become a part of the record of said executive sessions.

A meeting of a committee may be recorded by a person in attendance by means of a tape recorder or any other means of sonic reproduction except when a meeting is held in executive session; provided. that during such recording there is no active interference with the conduct of the meeting.

[Adopted Nov. 17, 1983; Amended Jan. 12. 1987: Jan. 9. 1991; May 5, 1993; Jan. 17, 1995; Jan. 14. 1997.]

17B. Whenever any member of a House committee present at the committee meeting so requests, the vote to give any legislation a favorable or adverse report shall be a recorded vote of the full committee. Such votes shall be recorded on appropriate forms that show all votes for and against the particular committee action. The record of all such roll calls shall be kept in the offices of the committee and shall be available for public inspection.

No report of a House committee on any legislation shall be final until those members of the committee present and voting with the majority have been given the opportunity to sign such appropriate forms before the report is made to the House. No signature shall be valid unless the forms to which the signatures are affixed include the substantially complete text of the legislation being reported.

[Adopted Nov. 17, 1983; Amended Jan. 12, 1987.]

17C. There shall be a committee on Personnel and Administration on the part of the House consisting of thirteen members. Said committee shall be responsible for the allocation of office space as equitably as possible among the various members and joint and standing committees on the part of the House and their respective House staffs.

The committee shall allocate space among the various committees on the part of the House taking into account the work load, duties and responsibilities and size of staff of each.

The Speaker may make temporary office assignments in accordance with the foregoing principles.

The committee on Personnel and Administration may from time to time make changes in the assignment of office space for committees and the various staffs in accordance with the established standards.

Said committee shall establish the staffing levels and positions for each joint and standing committee of the House together with a classification plan for all employees of the House of Representatives.

For each person who is employed or is to be employed by a joint or standing committee on the part of the House, each committee chairman shall nominate each such person and the House members of the committee by a majority vote shall vote on whether to approve each said nominee. The House members of the committee shall approve such persons whose character and qualifications are acceptable to the majority of the House members of the committee and are in accordance with the qualifications established by the Personnel and Administration committee.

The chairman of each standing committee shall have the authority to discharge an employee.

The House staff members of each committee shall be appointed solely on the basis of fitness to perform the duties of their respective positions and consistent with section four of chapter one hundred fifty-one B of the General Laws. The said committee staff shall:

(1) not engage in any work other than committee business during business hours.

(2) not be assigned any duties other than those pertaining to committee business.

The committee shall meet on request of the chairman or any three members of the committee. Any such meeting requested shall be convened on or within the fifth business day following such request. All such requests shall be in writing and forwarded to the chairman and each member of the committee.

Funds shall be allocated from the budget to carry out the determination of the committee.

[Adopted Jan. 11, 1985; Amended Jan. 16, 1985; Jan. 12, 1987; Jan. 9, 1991.]

17D. There shall be appointed a standing committee on Long-Term Debt and Capital Expenditures consisting of eleven members. Said committee shall review all legislation providing for the giving, loaning or pledging of the credit of the Commonwealth (see Article LXII of the Amendments to the Constitution, as amended by Article LXXXIV). Said committee shall be responsible for evaluating such legislation and determining the appropriateness of enacting new legislation containing increased bond authorizations for the Commonwealth.

The committee on Long-Term Debt and Capital Expenditures shall periodically review and hold open public hearings, accepting oral and written testimony on the status of the bonds and notes of the Commonwealth: (1) general obligation debt; (2) dedicated income tax debt; and (3) special obligation debt. Said committee shall also, in its continuing study of the state's bonding practices, review the Commonwealth's liabilities relative to (a) state-supported debt; (b) state-guaranteed debt; and (c) indirect obligations.

Said committee shall consult with the various agencies of the Executive branch and the office of the Treasurer and Receiver-General relative to project expenditures, availability of funds, the sale of new bonds and the resultant debt obligations, federal reimbursements and other related funding and bonding issues.

Said committee on Long-Term Debt and Capital Expenditures shall be authorized to conduct hearings relative to the statutory authority of the Executive branch and the Treasurer and Receiver-General in the issuance and sale of bonds and notes and the expenditure of capital funds by the various agencies and authorities of the Commonwealth. Said committee shall determine whether such laws, administrative regulations and programs are being implemented in accordance with the intent of the General Court; and provided further that said committee shall be authorized to make recommendations for statutory changes and changes in the Constitution which would grant discretion to the Legislature over the allotment and expenditure of funds authorized by capital appropriations.

The committee on Long-Term Debt and Capital Expenditures shall be authorized to report to the General Court from time to time on the results of its hearings, but shall file an annual report detailing its activities during the preceding fiscal year, together with drafts of legislation and proposals for amendments to the Constitution necessary to carry its recommendations into effect, by filing the same with the Clerk of the House of Representatives on or before the first Wednesday in August following said fiscal year.

[Adopted Jan. 14, 1997.]

18. The Speaker shall appoint, and may recommend the removal of, the Majority Floor Leader, Assistant Majority Floor Leader, and Second Assistant Majority Floor Leader. The Minority Leader shall appoint, and may recommend the removal of, the Assistant Minority Floor Leader, Second Assistant Minority Floor Leader, and Third Assistant Minority Floor Leader. The Minority Leader shall be that member of the minority party who is selected for that position by the members of his/her party.

Each of the foregoing appointments and/or removals shall be ratified by a majority vote of the respective party caucus. In the event that an appointment is rejected by such caucus another appointment shall be made by the person designated to make the initial appointment, which shall also be subject to ratification in the same manner.

The Speaker shall appoint, and may recommend the removal of, the chair of each standing committee. The Speaker shall appoint, and may recommend the removal of, the vice chair and assistant vice chair of the Ways and Means committee and the vice chair of the Post Audit and Oversight committee.

The majority party shall then vote to accept or reject each such appointment and/or recommendation for removal by a majority vote.

In the event that any such appointment is rejected by the caucus, the procedure of this rule shall be repeated until an appointment for the said position has been approved by the caucus. A vacancy in any position to which the provisions of this section apply shall be filled in the same manner as provided in this section for original appointment.

[Amended Jan. 16, 1979; Nov. 17, 1983; Jan. 11, 1985; Jan. 9, 1991; Jan. 14, 1997.]

18A. There shall be one member of the minority party on all committees of conference and one on the committee on Bills in the Third Reading. On all other standing and joint committees, the percent of minority party membership shall be at least equal to the percent of minority party membership in the House of Representatives as of the first day of the session, provided however that the minority party shall under no circumstances have less than four members on the committee on Ethics, four on the committee on Personnel and Administration, three on the committee on Rules and six on the committee on Ways and Means. Where such percentage results in a fraction of a number, the fraction shall be rounded off to the nearest whole. In no case shall minority party representation be less than two members on all other standing and joint committees.

The Speaker and the Minority Leader shall appoint the members of their respective party caucuses to be assigned to each standing committee. The Speaker shall appoint the vice chair of each standing committee. The appointments, except those to which Rule 18 applies, shall be voted upon together and shall be subject to ratification by majority vote of the appropriate party caucus.

No member shall be removed from a standing committee except upon the recommendation of the Speaker or Minority Leader, as the case may be, subject to the ratification by their respective caucuses; provided, however if any vacancy occurs in a position to which Rule 18 does not apply, subsequent to the initial ratification, the Speaker or Minority Leader shall fill such vacancy.

The Speaker shall announce committee appointments of majority party members, and the member first named shall be chairman, and the second named member shall be vice-chairman. The Minority Leader shall announce committee appointments of minority party members. (13.)

[Adopted Jan. 11, 1985; Amended Jan. 12, 1987; Jan. 9, 1991; Jan. 14, 1997.]

18B. All votes on ratification by the caucus required by these rules shall be by written ballot and shall require a majority of those present and voting.

[Adopted Jan. 11, 1985.]

18C. No person shall serve more than eight years as Speaker.

[Adopted Jan. 11, 1985.]

19. A majority and minority party caucus may be called by the Speaker or Minority Leader, respectively, or upon petition of twenty-five percent of the members of the respective party caucus. A caucus may entertain resolutions, motions, or other means of ascertaining the sense of the respective party members on any subject. (13B.)
[Adopted Nov. 17, 1983; Amended Jan. 11, 1985.]

19A. The majority party and minority party shall establish caucus rules that shall dictate the procedures of each caucus.
[Adopted Nov. 17, 1983; Amended Jan. 14, 1997.]

20. The committee on Ways and Means shall report in appropriation bills the total amount appropriated. The General Appropriation Bill shall be in printed form at least seven calendar days prior to consideration thereof by the House. [25.] (27A.)
[Amended Jan. 11, 1985; Mar. 24, 1986; Jan. 14, 1997.]

21. Whenever the committee on Ways and Means reports an appropriation bill or capital outlay bill, it shall make available to the members a report which includes an explanation of any increase or decrease of five percent or more which results in an increase or decrease of one million dollars or more for any item for which the Governor has made a recommendation, and an explanation for the deletion of an item recommended by the Governor, and for the addition of an item for which the Governor has made no recommendation. [25A.] (27A.)

22. Bills and resolves when ordered to a third reading shall be referred forthwith to the committee on Bills in the Third Reading, which shall examine and correct them, for the purpose of avoiding repetitions and unconstitutional provisions, and insuring accuracy in the text and references, and consistency with the language of existing statutes; but any change in the sense or legal effect, or any material change in construction, shall be reported to the House as an amendment.

The committee may consolidate into one bill any two or more related bills referred to it. whenever legislation may be simplified thereby.

Resolutions received from and adopted by the Senate or introduced or reported into the House. after they are read and before they are adopted. shall be referred to the committee on Bills in the Third Reading.

Amendments of bills. resolves and resolutions adopted by the Senate and sent to the House for concurrence, shall, subsequently to the procedure required by rule thirty-five in respect to amendments. also be referred. in like manner, to the committee on Bills in the Third Reading.

When a bill. resolve or resolution has been so referred, no further action shall be taken until report thereon has been made by the committee. Accompanying said report shall be a written explanation prepared by the committee defining any changes made in a bill. resolve or resolution so as to facilitate the proceedings of the House.

If a bill or resolve referred to the committee on Bills in the Third Reading requires a two-thirds vote because it contains an emergency preamble. or if it provides for the borrowing of money by the Commonwealth and comes within the provisions of Section 3 of Article LXII of the Amendments to the Constitution. or provides for the giving. loaning or pledging of the credit of the Commonwealth and comes within the provisions of Section 1 of Article LXII (as amended by Article LXXXIV) of the Amendments to the Constitution, or provides. upon recommendation of the Governor, for a special law relating to an individual city or town and comes within the provisions of clause (2) of Section 8 of Article LXXXIX of the Amendments to the Constitution or provides for environmental protection within the provisions of Article XLIX as amended by Article XCVII. the committee shall plainly indicate the fact on the outside of the bill or resolve, or on a wrapper or label attached thereto. [26.] (33.)

[Amended Jan. 12. 1983: Jan. 11. 1985: May 5, 1993.]

23. Bills and resolves prepared for final passage shall be certified by the Clerk of the House. after comparison, to be the same as the bills or resolves passed to be engrossed; and if found to be properly prepared, the Clerk shall so endorse on the envelope thereof; and the question on enactment or final passage or adopting an emergency preamble shall be taken thereon, without further reading, unless specifically ordered.

When a bill or resolve prepared for final passage contains an emergency preamble or when it provides for the borrowing of money by the Commonwealth and comes within the provisions of Section 3 of Article LXII of the Amendments to the Constitution, or provides for the giving, loaning or pledging of the credit of the Commonwealth and comes within the provisions of Section 1 of Article LXII (as amended by Article LXXXIV) of the Amendments to the Constitution, or provides, upon recommendation of the Governor, for a special law relating to an individual city or town and comes within the provisions of clause (2) of Section 8 of Article LXXXIX of the Amendments to the Constitution, or provides for environmental protection within the provisions of Article XLIX as amended by Article XCVII, the Clerk shall plainly indicate the fact on the envelope thereof. [27.] (34.) [See Rule 40.]
[Amended Jan. 12, 1983.]

23A. No bill, resolve, or order affecting the compensation or allowances of the members of the General Court shall be finally acted upon by the House of Representatives except by a call of the yeas and nays; nor shall any such bill, resolve, or order be considered for final passage after a date thirty days preceding the last date set by law for filing nomination papers with the local election authority for election to the General Court at the next biennial state election. (57A.)
[Adopted Nov. 17, 1983; Amended Jan. 12, 1987.]

23B. No member of the House, except the Speaker, Majority Leader, Assistant Majority Leader, Second Assistant Majority Leader, Minority Leader, Assistant Minority Leader, Second Assistant Minority Leader, Third Assistant Minority Leader and committee chairmen with respect to committee business, shall receive privileges or compensation greater than any other member for postage.
[Adopted Jan. 11, 1985.]

24. (1) Petitions. recommendations and reports of state officials, departments, commissions and boards, and reports of special committees and commissions, shall be filed with the Clerk, who shall, unless they be subject to other provisions of these rules or the rules of the two branches, refer them, with the approval of the Speaker, to the appropriate committees, subject to such change of reference as the House may make. The reading of all such documents may be dispensed with, but they shall be entered in the Journal of the same or the next legislative day after such reference except as provided in joint rule thirteen.

(2) All orders, including motions or orders proposed for joint adoption, resolutions and other papers intended for presentation, except those hereinbefore mentioned, shall be filed with the Clerk who shall, prior to the procedure required by other provisions of these rules or of the rules of the two branches, refer them to the committee on Rules.

(3) Petitions and other papers so filed which are subject to the provisions of joint rule seven A, seven B, or nine, shall be referred by the Clerk to the committee on Rules. Petitions and other papers so filed, which are subject to the provisions of the second paragraph of Joint Rule 12, shall, prior to the procedure required by said rule, be referred by the Clerk to the committee on Rules. The reading of all such papers may be dispensed with, but they shall be entered in the Journal of the same or the next legislative day after such reference.

(4) Matters which have been placed on file during the preceding year may be taken from the files by the Clerk upon request of any member or member-elect; and matters so taken from the files shall be referred or otherwise disposed of as provided above.

(5) Recommendations and special reports of state officials, departments, commissions and boards, reports of special committees and commissions, bills and resolves accompanying petitions, recommendations and reports, and resolutions shall be printed under the direction of the Clerk, who may cause to be printed, with the approval of the Speaker, any other documents filed as herein provided.

(6) Debate upon the suspension of this rule shall be limited to ten minutes, three minutes for each member, and the Speaker shall recognize the member presenting the order, resolution or petition first; provided, however, that suspension of this rule shall require unanimous consent of the members present. Any order, except such order that would amend the Rules of the House, resolution or petition referred to the committee on Rules after the question of suspension of this rule has been negatived, or any order, resolution or petition filed after the beginning of the session and referred to the committee on Rules, shall not be discharged from said committee except by unanimous consent of the House. Motions to discharge the committee on Rules shall be subject to the provisions of paragraph 2 of Rule 28. [28.] (20.) [See Rules 36 and 85.]

[Amended April 27, 1981; Jan. 9, 1989; Jan. 9, 1991.]

25. Every petition for legislation shall be accompanied by a bill or resolve embodying the legislation prayed for. [29.] [See Joint Rule 12.]

26. When the object of an application can be secured without a special act under existing laws, or, without detriment to the public interests, by a general law, the committee to which the matter is referred shall report such general law or ought not to pass, as the case may be. The committee may report a special law on matters referred to it upon (1) a petition filed or approved by the voters of a city or town, or the mayor and city council, or other legislative body, of a city, or the town meeting of a town, with respect to a law relating to that city or town; (2) a recommendation by the Governor; and (3) matters relating to erecting and constituting metropolitan or regional entities, embracing any two or more cities and towns, or established with other than existing city or town boundaries, for any general or special public purpose or purposes. [30.] (16.) [See Joint Rule 7.]

27. With the exception of matters referred to the committee on Rules under the provisions of paragraph (3) of rule twenty-four, committees shall report on all matters referred to them. The committee on Ways and Means shall report the General Appropriation Bill not later than the second Wednesday of May; and provided further that said committee shall make available to the members all data compiled for justification of budgetary recommendations in all appropriation bills. [33.]

[Amended April 18, 1979; Jan. 14, 1997.]

27A. A committee reporting a matter which contemplates legislation, may insert a clear and explicit statement in such report which states the legislative intent and purpose of the legislation.

[Adopted Jan. 11, 1985.]

28. (1) With the exception of appropriation bills and capital outlay bills, motions directing the committee on Ways and Means or the committee on Counties on the part of the House to report certain matters to the House, or motions discharging said committees from further consideration of certain matters, shall not be considered until the expiration of seven calendar days and shall require a majority vote of the members present and voting for adoption. Committees so directed to report shall file a report with the Clerk within four legislative days.

(2) The committee on Rules, except as provided in Rule 24, and the committee on Bills in the Third Reading shall not be discharged from consideration of any measure or be directed to report on any measure within ten calendar days of its reference without the unanimous consent of the House, or after such ten day period except by a vote of a majority of the members present and voting thereon.

(3) Matters discharged under the provisions of this rule shall be placed in the Orders of the Day for the next sitting. Petitions discharged under the provisions of this rule shall be considered as favorably reported and the bill, resolve, resolution or order accompanying such petitions shall be placed in the Orders of the Day for the next sitting.

(4) During the last week of the session the provisions of paragraphs (1) and (3) of this rule shall be inoperative.

(5) A second motion to discharge a matter from a committee or a second motion to direct a committee to report a matter shall not be entertained until the first such motion has been disposed of.

(6) As an alternative procedure to that provided under the provisions of this rule, the members of the House may, by filing a petition signed by a majority of the members elected to the House, discharge the committee on Counties on the part of the House, the House committee on Ways and Means, the House committee on Bills in the Third Reading, and the House committee on Rules from further consideration of a legislative matter. Seven days following the filing of the petition with the House Clerk, the committee shall be discharged from further consideration of the legislative matter specified in the petition and the House Clerk shall place the matter in the Orders of the Day for the next calendar day that the House is meeting.

For the purpose of this rule, matters not appearing on the Calendar which are not before any committee shall be deemed to be before the Rules committee. Notwithstanding the previous sentence, a bill which has been engrossed by the House and Senate, shall be placed before the House for enactment. Any member may request that a matter, engrossed in the House and Senate, be placed before the House for enactment. The Speaker shall, in response to such a request of a member, put the matter before the House at the conclusion of the matter then pending.

(7) This rule shall not be suspended unless by unanimous consent of the members present. (27C, 32A.)

[Amended Jan. 12, 1981; April 27, 1981; Jan. 12, 1983; Nov. 17, 1983; Jan. 11, 1985; Jan. 9, 1989; Jan. 9, 1991.]

28A. The committee on Bills in the Third Reading shall report on a legislative matter not later than forty-five days following the day the matter was referred to it.

[Adopted Jan. 11, 1985.]

REGULAR COURSE OF PROCEEDINGS.

Petitions.

29. The member presenting a petition shall endorse his/her name thereon; and the reading thereof shall be dispensed with, unless specially ordered. [37.] (18.)
[Amended Jan. 11, 1985.]

Motions Contemplating Legislation, etc.

30. All motions contemplating legislation shall be founded upon petition, except as follows:

The committee on Ways and Means may originate and report appropriation bills as provided in rule twenty. Messages from the Governor shall, unless otherwise ordered, be referred to the appropriate committee, which may report by bill or otherwise thereon. A similar disposition shall, unless otherwise ordered, be made of reports by state officers and committees authorized to report to the Legislature, and similar action may be had thereon. [40.] (19.)

Bills and Resolves.

31. Bills shall be printed or written in a legible hand, without material erasure or interlineation, on not less than one sheet of paper, with suitable margins and spaces between the several sections. Bills amending existing laws shall not provide for striking words from, or inserting words in, such laws, unless such course is best calculated to show clearly the subject and nature of the amendment. No repealed law, and no part of any repealed law, shall be re-enacted by reference merely. [42.] (17.)

32. If a committee to which a bill is referred reports that the same ought not to pass, the question shall be *"Shall this bill be rejected?"*. If the question on rejection is negatived, the bill, if it has been read but once, shall go to a second reading without question; otherwise it shall be placed in the Orders of the Day for the next day, pending the question on ordering to a third reading, or to engrossment, as the case may be. [43.] (30.)

32A. Any bill providing for borrowing for new projects, and requiring the Commonwealth to issue bonds for such purpose, shall, prior to its reference to the committee on Ways and Means, be referred to the committee on Long-Term Debt and Capital Expenditures for report on its relationship to the finances of the Commonwealth.

New provisions shall not be added to such bills by the committee on Long-Term Debt and Capital Expenditures unless directly connected with the financial features thereof.

[Adopted Jan. 14, 1997.]

33. Bills involving an expenditure of public money or grant of public property, or otherwise affecting the state finances, unless the subject matter has been acted upon by the joint committee on Ways and Means, shall, after their first reading, be referred to the committee on Ways and Means, for report on their relation to the finances of the Commonwealth.

New provisions shall not be added to such bills by the committee on Ways and Means, unless directly connected with the financial features thereof.

Orders reported in the House or received from the Senate involving the expenditure of public money for special committees, shall, before the question is taken on the adoption thereof, be referred to the committee on Ways and Means, whose duty it shall be to report on their relation to the finances of the Commonwealth.

Every such bill involving a capital expenditure for new projects, or an appropriation for repairs, or any legislation, the cost of which, in the opinion of the committee, exceeds the sum of one hundred thousand dollars when reported into the House by the committee on Ways and Means, shall be accompanied by a fiscal note indicating the amount of public money which will be required to be expended to carry out the provisions of the proposed legislation, together with an estimate of the cost of operation and maintenance for the first year if a new project is involved.

Bills involving an expenditure of county money shall, after their first reading, be referred to the committee on Counties on the part of the House, for report on their relation to the finances of the county affected, unless the subject matter thereof has been previously acted upon by the joint committee on Counties; and no new provisions shall be added to such bills by the committee on Counties on the part of the House, unless directly connected with the financial features thereof.

Every such bill involving a capital expenditure for new projects, or an appropriation for repairs, or any legislation, the cost of which, in the opinion of the committee, exceeds the sum of one hundred thousand dollars, when reported into the House by the committee on Counties on the part of the House, shall be accompanied by a fiscal note indicating the amount of county money which will be required to be expended to carry out the provisions of the proposed legislation, together with an estimate of the cost of operation and maintenance for the first year if a new project is involved. [44.] (27.)

[Amended April 18, 1979; Jan. 12, 1981.]

33A. Copies of all bills shall be available to all members of the House and the public at least twenty-four hours in advance of consideration by the House.

All amendments offered by members to any legislative matter in the House shall be considered chronologically as submitted, in duplicate form, to the Clerk of the House, except for an amendment in the second degree; provided that all of said amendments shall be clearly and legibly written, and double spaced and drafted in proper form; and provided further that there shall be available to the members, at the side of the Clerk's desk, a duplicate copy of each amendment. (33A.)

[Adopted Nov. 17, 1983; Amended Nov. 28, 1984; Jan. 12, 1987; Jan. 9, 1991; Jan. 17, 1995.]

33B. Bills involving issues relating to science and technology, including, but not limited to: research and development; computers; data transmission, access and storage; communications; bio-technology; pollution control; medical technology; and classroom applications, shall, after the first reading, be referred to the committee on Science and Technology.

New provisions shall not be added to such bills by said committee unless directly connected with the science and technology features thereof.

Bills involving science and technology and an expenditure of public funds, or otherwise affecting the finances of the Commonwealth, shall, after their first reading, be referred to the committee on Science and Technology, and when reported by said committee, shall be referred to the committee on Ways and Means.

[Adopted Mar. 24, 1994.]

34. Bills from the Senate, after their first reading, shall be referred to a committee of the House, unless they were reported to the Senate by a joint committee. [45.] (26.)

35. Amendments proposed by the Senate, and sent back to the House for concurrence, shall be referred to the committee which reported the measure proposed to be amended, unless such committee is composed of members of both branches, in which case such amendments shall be placed in the Orders of the Day for the next day; provided, that amendments affecting state finances shall be referred to the committee on Ways and Means on the part of the House, and amendments involving expenditure of county money shall be referred to the committee on Counties on the part of the House, as the case may be. [46.] (36.)

[Amended April 18, 1979; Jan. 12, 1981.]

36. No bill shall be proposed or introduced unless received from the Senate, reported by a committee, or moved as an amendment to the report of a committee. [47.] (36.)

37. Bills, resolves and other papers that have been, or, under the rules or usage of the House, are to be, printed shall be read by their titles only, unless the full reading is requested by vote of a majority of those members present and voting. [48.] (29.)

38. When a bill, resolve, order, petition or memorial has been finally rejected or disposed of by the House, no measure substantially the same shall be introduced by any committee or member during the same session. This rule shall not be suspended unless by unanimous consent of the members present. [49.] (54.)

39. No bill shall be passed to be engrossed without having been read on three separate legislative days. [51.] (28.)
[Amended Jan. 11, 1985.]

40. No engrossed bill shall be amended, except by striking out the enacting clause. A motion to strike out the enacting clause of a bill shall be received when the bill is before the House for enactment. This rule shall not apply to a bill or resolve returned by the Governor with a recommendation of amendment in accordance with the provisions of Article LVI of the Amendments to the Constitution; nor shall it apply to amendments of engrossed bills proposed by the Senate and sent to the House for concurrence, which amendments shall be subject to the provisions of rule thirty-five. [53.] (49.)

41. Bills received from the Senate and bills reported favorably by committees, when not referred to another standing committee of the House, shall, after their first reading, be referred to the committee on Steering, Policy and Scheduling. Resolutions received from and adopted by the Senate, or reported in the House by committees, shall, if proposed for joint adoption, be referred to said committee on Steering, Policy and Scheduling. [56.] (26.)
[Amended Jan. 14, 1997.]

42. Reports of committees, not by bill or resolve, including orders if proposed for joint adoption, after they are received from the Senate, or made in the House, as the case may be, shall, unless subject to the provisions of any other House or joint rules, be referred to the committee on Steering, Policy and Scheduling; provided that the report of a committee asking to be discharged from further consideration of a subject, and recommending that it be referred or recommitted to another committee, or a report of a committee recommending that a matter be placed on file, shall be immediately considered. Reports of committees on proposals for amendments to the Constitution shall be dealt with in accordance with the provisions of joint rule twenty-three. [57.] (36.)

[Amended Jan. 14, 1997.]

43. Bills ordered to a third reading shall be placed in the Orders of the Day for the next day for such reading. [58.] (32.)

44. The Speaker may designate when an informal session of the House shall be held provided said Speaker gives notice of such informal session at a prior session of the House. The Speaker may, in cases of emergency, cancel a session or declare any session of the House to be an informal session. At such session the House shall only consider reports of committees, papers from the Senate, bills for enactment or resolves for final passage, bills containing emergency preambles and the matters in the Orders of the Day. Motions to reconsider moved at such informal session shall be placed in the Orders of the Day for the succeeding day, and no new business shall be entertained, except by unanimous consent.

Upon the receipt of a petition signed by at least forty percent of the House, so requesting, the Speaker shall, when the House is in session, designate a formal session, to be held within seven days of said receipt, for the purpose of considering the question of passage of a bill, notwithstanding the objections of the Governor, returned pursuant to Article 2, Section 1, Clause 1, Part 2 of the Massachusetts Constitution. This rule shall not be suspended unless by unanimous consent of the members present. [59.] (5A.)

[Amended Jan. 11, 1985; Jan. 12, 1987; Jan. 17, 1995; Jan. 14, 1997.]

45. After entering upon the consideration of the Orders of the Day, the House shall proceed with them in regular course as follows: Matters not giving rise to a motion or debate shall first be disposed of in the order in which they stand in the Calendar; after which the matters that were passed over shall be considered in like order and disposed of. The provisions of this paragraph shall not be suspended unless by unanimous consent of the members present.

Notwithstanding the provisions of this rule, during consideration of the Orders of the Day, the committee on Ways and Means and the committee on Bills in the Third Reading may present matters for consideration of the House after approval of two-thirds of the members present and voting, without debate. [59.] (37.) [See Rule 47.]

[Amended Jan. 12, 1981; Jan. 12, 1983.]

46. When the House does not finish the consideration of the Orders of the Day, those which had not been acted upon shall be the Orders of the Day for the next and each succeeding day until disposed of, and shall be entered in the Calendar, without change in their order, to precede matters added under rules forty-one and forty-two; provided, however, that all other matters shall be listed in numerical order by Calendar item.

The unfinished business in which the House was engaged at the time of adjournment shall have the preference in the Orders of the Day for the next day. [60.] (35.)

[Amended Jan. 12, 1987.]

Special Rule Affecting the Course of Proceedings.

47. No matter which has been duly placed in the Orders of the Day shall be discharged therefrom, or considered out of the regular course. [61.] (38.) [See Rule 45.]

Voting.

48. Members desiring to be excused from voting shall make application to that effect before the division of the

House or the taking of the yeas and nays is begun. Such application may be accompanied by a brief statement of reasons by the member making it, but shall be decided without debate, and shall not be subject to the provisions of rule fifty-two. [64.] (57.)

49. If the presence of a quorum is doubted, a count of the House shall be made. When a yea and nay vote is taken, the members, with the exception of the Speaker, shall vote only from their seats. A member who has been appointed by the Speaker to perform the duties of the Chair, or a person who has been elected Speaker *pro tempore*, may designate some member or a court officer to cast a vote for him/her on any vote taken on the electronic voting machine while such member is presiding. The Speaker shall state the pending question before opening the machine for voting.

Except in the case of a vote to ascertain the presence of a quorum, if a member is prevented from voting personally on the voting machine at his/her assigned seat because of physical disability, said member shall, if present in the State House, be excused from so voting and the Speaker shall assign a court officer to cast said member's vote so long as said physical disability continues; provided that the Speaker shall announce the action of the Chair to the membership prior to assigning a court officer to cast the member's vote and provided further that the Speaker shall announce the action to the membership the first time a vote is cast for that member on each successive day. [65.]
[Amended April 18, 1979; Jan. 12, 1987; Jan. 9, 1991.]

50. When a question is put, the sense of the House shall be taken by the voices of the members, and the Speaker shall first announce the vote as it appears to said Speaker by the sound. If the Speaker is unable to decide by the sound of the voices, or if the announcement made thereupon is doubted by a member rising in his/her place for that purpose, the Speaker shall order a division of the number voting in the affirmative and in the negative, without further debate upon the question. [66.] (55.)
[Amended Jan. 11, 1985.]

51. When a return by division of the members voting in the affirmative and in the negative is ordered, the members for or against the question, when called on by the Speaker, shall rise in their places, and stand until they are counted. If, upon the taking of such a vote, the presence of a quorum is doubted, a count of the House shall be had, and if a quorum is present the vote shall stand. [67.]

52. The sense of the House shall be taken by yeas and nays whenever required by twenty of the members present. The Speaker shall, after waiting up to an interval of twelve minutes, state the pending question and, after opening the electronic voting machine, instruct the members to vote for or against the question. After the voting machine has remained open for not less than two minutes and kept open for no more than twenty-two minutes, the Speaker shall close said machine and cause the totals to be displayed and a record made of how each member present voted.

Any member desiring to be recorded as being "present" when a yea and nay vote is taken on the roll call machine shall so notify the Clerk in person after said vote is ordered and before the vote is announced.

If an advance notice of at least sixty minutes is given by the Speaker a yea and nay vote may be taken at any prescribed time.

In the event the voting machine is not in operating order, the roll of the House shall be called in alphabetical order but however said vote may be taken no member shall be allowed to vote or to answer "present" who was not on the floor before the vote is declared; provided, however, that a member, who was in the State House on a previous roll call, may be recorded by reporting to the Clerk within five minutes after such vote is closed, unless objection is made thereto and it is seconded; and provided further that the presiding officer shall not, for said purpose, interrupt the member who is speaking on the floor. The Speaker *shall not* entertain any requests beyond said five minute period. Once the voting has begun it shall not be interrupted except for the purpose of questioning the validity of a member's vote before the result is announced.

Except as heretofore provided, any member who shall vote or attempt to vote for another member or any person not a member who votes or attempts to vote for a member, or any member or other person who willfully tampers with or attempts to impair or destroy in any manner whatsoever the voting equipment used by the House, or change the records thereon shall be punished in such manner as the House determines. [68.] (56, 57.)
[Amended Jan. 12, 1983; Jan. 11, 1985; Jan. 12, 1987; Jan. 9, 1991.]

53. The call for yeas and nays shall be decided without debate. If the yeas and nays have been ordered before the question is put, the proceedings under rules fifty and fifty-one relative to verification of the vote by the voices of the members or by a return of divisions shall be omitted; if not, they may be called for in lieu of a return by sections when the Speaker's announcement is doubted by a member rising in his/her place, and, if then ordered, the proceedings under rules fifty and fifty-one shall be omitted. [69.] (52.)

Reconsideration.

54. No motion to reconsider a vote shall be entertained unless it is made on the same day on which the vote was taken, or before the Orders of the Day have been taken up on the next day thereafter on which a quorum is present. If reconsideration is moved on the same day, the motion shall (if made prior to July first) be placed first in the Orders of the Day for the succeeding day; but, if it is moved on the succeeding day, the motion shall be considered forthwith except that if said motion is moved on a day on which an informal session has been designated, it shall be placed in the Orders of the Day for the succeeding day. If reconsideration is moved on July first, and thereafter, on any main question, it shall be considered forthwith. This rule shall not prevent the reconsideration of a vote on a subsidiary, incidental or dependent question at any time when the main question to which it relates is under consideration; and provided, further, that a

motion to reconsider a vote on any subsidiary, incidental or dependent question shall not remove the main subject under consideration from before the House, but shall be considered at the time when it is made. This rule shall not be suspended unless by unanimous consent of the members present. [70.] (53.)
[Amended Jan. 12, 1981.]

55. When a motion for reconsideration is decided, that decision shall not be reconsidered, and no question shall be twice reconsidered; nor shall any vote be reconsidered upon any of the following motions:
to recess,
to adjourn,
on sustaining a ruling of the Chair,
to close debate at a specified time,
to postpone if voted in the negative,
to discharge or direct a committee to report,
to commit or recommit,
for second or subsequent legislative days,
for the previous question, or
for suspension of rules.
This rule shall not be suspended unless by unanimous consent of the members present. [71.] (53.)
[Amended Jan. 12, 1981; Jan. 12, 1983; Jan. 9, 1991.]

56. Debate on motions to reconsider shall be limited to fifteen minutes, and no member shall occupy more than three minutes, but on a motion to reconsider a vote upon any subsidiary or incidental question, debate shall be limited to ten minutes, and no member shall occupy more than three minutes.
If the House has voted to close debate on any question, a motion to reconsider said question shall be decided without debate. [72.] (52.)
[Amended Jan. 12, 1981; Jan. 12, 1987.]

RULES OF DEBATE.

57. Every member, when about to speak, shall rise and respectfully address the Speaker and shall confine himself/herself to the question under debate. [73.] (39.) [Amended Jan. 11, 1985.]

58. Every member while speaking shall avoid personalities; and shall sit down when finished. No member shall speak out of his/her place without leave of the Speaker. [73.] (39.) When two or more members rise at the same time, the Speaker shall name the member entitled to the floor, preferring one who rises in his/her place to one who does not. [74.] (40.) [Amended Jan. 11, 1985.]

59. If a member repeatedly violates any of the rules of the House, or disrupts the orderly procedure of the House, the Speaker, after warning the member of such violations, shall call the member to order, and order that said member take his/her seat. A member so called to order shall lose the right to speak on the pending subject-matter but shall not be debarred from voting. A member so called to order shall remain seated until the House begins consideration of another subject-matter or unless the Speaker earlier returns to the member his/her rights to the floor.

If a member so called to order refuses to immediately take his/her seat, the Speaker shall immediately name that member, who shall be escorted from the Chamber under escort of the Sergeant-at-Arms. The matter shall thereupon, on motion, be referred to a special committee of three to be appointed by the Speaker. Said special committee shall make a report to the House of its recommendations, which report shall be read and accepted.

Having been named, a member shall not be allowed to resume his/her seat until said member has complied with the recommendations of the committee as accepted by the House.

If, after a member is seated or named, the action of the Speaker is appealed, the House shall decide the case by a

majority vote of the members present and voting, but if there
is no immediate appeal, the decision of the Speaker shall be
conclusive.
[Amended Jan. 12. 1981; Jan. 11, 1985.]

60. No member shall interrupt another while speaking
except by rising to a point of order, to a question of personal
privilege, to doubt the presence of a quorum, or to ask the
person speaking to yield.

Members may rise to explain matters personal to themselves by leave of the presiding officer, but shall not discuss
pending questions in such explanations.

Questions of personal privilege shall be limited to questions
affecting the rights, reputation, and conduct of the member in
his/her representative capacities.

Members may rise to ask questions of parliamentary inquiry concerning the pending matter by leave of the
presiding officer, but shall not debate the pending questions.
[75.] (42.)
[Amended Jan. 12. 1981.]

61. No member shall speak more than once to the prevention of those who have not spoken and desire to speak on the
same question.

This prohibition shall not apply to those members designated by the committee or committees reporting the bill.

No member shall occupy more than thirty minutes at a time
while speaking on any question where debate is unlimited.

Unless the operation of another rule provides to the contrary (such as previous question, limitation of debate, etc.), no
member shall be prohibited from speaking more than once on
any question when no other member who has not spoken is
seeking recognition by the Chair. [76.] (41.)

Motions.

62. Every motion shall be reduced to writing, if the
Speaker so directs. [77.] (44.)

63. A motion need not be seconded. except an appeal from the decision of the Chair. and may be withdrawn by the mover if no objection is made. [78.] (44.)
[Amended Jan. 12. 1981.]

Limit of Debate.

64. A motion to recess or adjourn shall always be first in order, and shall be decided without debate; and on the motions to close debate at a specified time, to postpone to a time certain, to commit or recommit, not exceeding ten minutes shall be allowed for debate, and no member shall speak more than three minutes. On the motion to discharge any committee, or on a motion directing any committee to report matters before it, not exceeding fifteen minutes shall be allowed for debate, and no member shall speak more than three minutes.

If the main motion is undebatable, any subsidiary or incidental motion made relating to it shall also be decided without debate. [79.] (52.) [See Rules 56 and 83.]
[Amended Jan. 12, 1981.]

64A. Debate on the question on adoption of orders for second and subsequent legislative days shall be limited to ten minutes, and no member shall speak more than three minutes. After entering into a second or subsequent legislative day, the House shall immediately proceed to consideration of engrossed bills, reports of committees, papers from the Senate or the Orders of the Day. This rule shall not be suspended unless by unanimous consent of the members present.
[Adopted Jan. 12, 1983.]

65. When a question is before the House, until it is disposed of, the Speaker shall receive no motion that does not relate to the same, except the motion to recess or adjourn or some other motion that has precedence either by express rule of the House, or because it is privileged in its nature; and the Speaker shall receive no motion relating to the same, except,—

for the previous question, ... See Rules 66, 67 and 68
to close debate at a specified time. See Rules 64, 69 and 70
to postpone to a time certain, ... See Rules 64 and 70
to commit (or recommit), ... See Rules 64 and 71
to amend. . . . . See Rules 72, 73, 74 and 75
— which several motions shall have precedence in the order
in which they are arranged in this rule. [80.] (46.)
[Amended Jan. 11. 1985.]

Previous Question.

66. Any member may call for the previous question on the
main question.

The previous question shall be put in the following form:
"Shall the main question be now put?" and all debate on the
main question shall be suspended until the previous question
is decided.

The adoption of the previous question shall require the
affirmative vote of two-thirds of the members present and
voting and shall put an end to all debate, and bring the House
to direct vote upon pending amendments, if any, in their
regular order. and then upon the main question.

A motion to reconsider the vote on any of the pending
amendments shall be decided without debate. [81.]
[Amended Jan. 12. 1981.]

67. Any member may call for the previous question on any
pending amendment.

The previous question shall be put in the following form:
*"Shall the question on adoption of the amendment be now
put?"* and all debate shall be suspended until the previous
question is decided.

The adoption of the previous question on a pending
amendment shall require the affirmative vote of two-thirds
of the members present and voting and shall put an end to
all debate and bring the House to a direct vote upon the
pending amendment.

A motion to reconsider the vote on the pending amendment
shall be decided without debate.
[Amended Jan. 12. 1981.]

68. The previous question shall be decided without debate.

Motion to Close Debate at a Specified Time.

69. Debate may be closed at any time not less than thirty minutes from the adoption of a motion to that effect. This rule shall not be suspended unless by unanimous consent of the members present. [85.] (47.)

Motion to Postpone to a Time Certain.

70. When a motion is made to postpone to a time certain, and different times are proposed, the question shall first be taken on the most remote time: and the time shall be determined before the question is put on postponement, which may then be rejected if the House sees fit. [87.] (51.)

Motion to Commit.

71. When a motion is made to commit, and different committees are proposed, the question shall be taken in the following order:

a standing committee of the House,

a select committee of the House,

a joint standing committee,

a joint selected committee;

and a subject may be recommitted to the same committee or to another committee at the pleasure of the House. [88.] (48.)

Motion to Amend.

72. A motion to amend an amendment may be received: but no amendment in the third degree shall be allowed. This rule shall not be suspended unless by unanimous consent of the members present. [89.]

[Amended Jan. 12. 1983.]

73. No motion or proposition on a subject different from that under consideration shall be admitted under color of amendment. This rule shall not be suspended unless by unanimous consent of the members present. [90.] (50.)
[Amended Jan. 12. 1987.]

73A. No motion to amend a release from Ways and Means or from Third Reading, when such an amendment contains an expenditure of public money or an increase or decrease in taxes. shall be considered unless a brief explanation of the amendment is stated.
[Adopted Jan. 17. 1995.]

74. A question containing two or more propositions capable of division shall be divided whenever desired by any member, if the question includes points so distinct and separate that, one of them being taken away, the other will stand as a complete proposition. The motion to strike out and insert shall be considered as one proposition and therefore indivisible. The question on ordering a bill or resolve to a third reading, or to be engrossed, or to be enacted, or similar main motions shall be considered as indivisible under this rule. This rule shall not be suspended unless by unanimous consent of the members present. [91.] (45.)
[Amended Jan. 12, 1983.]

75. In filling blanks, the largest sum and longest time shall be put first. [92.] (51.) [See Rule 70.]

Motion to Recess.

76. The Speaker may declare a recess of fifteen minutes duration, or less.
[Amended Jan. 9, 1991.]

APPEAL.

77. No appeal from the decision of the Speaker shall be entertained unless it is seconded; and no other business shall be in order until the question on the appeal has been disposed of. Debate shall be limited to fifteen minutes on the question of sustaining a ruling by the Chair, and no member shall occupy more than three minutes. [94.] (43A.) [See Rule 2.] [Amended Jan. 9, 1989.]

RESOLVES.

78. Such of these rules as are applicable to bills, whether of the House or of the Senate, shall apply likewise to such resolves as require the concurrence of the Senate and approval by the Governor in order to become law and have force as such. [95.]

SEATS.

79. (1) The desk on the right of the Speaker shall be assigned to the use of the Clerk and such persons as he/she may employ to assist said Clerk, and that on the left to the use of the chairman and vice-chairman of the committee on Bills in the Third Reading.

(2) The Speaker shall assign members to vacant seats. The seat assigned to any member, other than seats assigned under paragraph (1) of this rule, shall be his/her seat for the year and for such additional years as said member may elect so long as service in the House remains continuous. An exchange of seats may be made with the approval of the Speaker. [98.] [Amended Jan. 11, 1985; May 5, 1993.]

PRIVILEGE OF THE FLOOR.

80. The following persons shall be entitled to admission to the House of Representatives, during the session thereof, to stand in an area designated by the Speaker in the rear of the Chamber, unless otherwise invited by said Speaker to occupy seats not numbered:

(1) The Governor and the Lieutenant-Governor, members of the Executive Council, Secretary of the Commonwealth,

Treasurer and Receiver-General, Auditor of the Commonwealth, Attorney-General, Librarian and Assistant Librarian.

(2) The members of the Senate.

(3) Persons in the exercise of an official duty directly connected with the business of the House.

(4) The legislative reporters entitled to the privileges of
the reporters' galleries.

Contestants for seats in the House, whose papers are in the
hands of a special committee of the House, may be admitted,
while their cases are pending, to seats to be assigned by the
Speaker.

No other person shall be admitted to the floor during the
session, except upon the permission of the Speaker. This rule
shall not be suspended unless by unanimous consent of the
members present. [99.] (60, 61.)

[Amended Jan. 9, 1991.]

REPRESENTATIVES' CHAMBER AND ADJOINING ROOMS.

81. Use of the Representatives' Chamber shall be subject
to the approval of the committee on Rules.

No person shall be admitted to the members' corridor and
adjoining rooms, except persons entitled to the privilege of the
floor of the House, unless upon written invitation, bearing
the name of the person it is desired to invite and the name
of the member extending the invitation, which invitation shall
be surrendered upon the person entering the corridor. No
legislative agent or counsel shall be admitted to said corridor
and adjoining rooms.

No person shall be admitted to the north gallery of the
House except upon a card of the Speaker.

Subject to the approval and direction of the committee on
Rules during the session and of the Speaker after prorogation,
the use of the reporters' galleries of the House Chamber shall
be under the control of the organization of legislative reporters
known as the Massachusetts State House Press Association
and the State House Broadcasters Association.

Every legislative reporter desiring admission to the reporters' galleries shall state in writing that he/she is not the agent or representative of any person or corporation interested in legislation before the General Court, and will not act as representative of any such person or corporation while retaining a place in the galleries; but nothing herein contained shall prevent such legislative reporter from engaging in other employment, provided such other employment is specifically approved by the committee on Rules and reported to the House.

In hearing rooms under the jurisdiction of the committee on Rules, smoking shall be prohibited while a hearing is in progress.

All formal sessions of the House of Representatives shall be open to both commercial and public radio and television, except designated times during such sessions, as determined by the House, reserved for the consideration of non-controversial business which does not give rise to debate. The manner and conditions of such broadcasts shall be established by the Speaker. Television or radio broadcasts may be prohibited on any given day by the Speaker with the approval of the House. This rule shall not be suspended unless by unanimous consent of the members present. [100.] (59.)

[Amended April 18, 1979; Jan. 12, 1983; Jan. 12, 1987; Jan. 9, 1991.]

QUORUM.

82. Eighty-one members shall constitute a quorum for the organization of the House and the transaction of business. [See amendments to the Constitution, Art. XXXIII.]

In the event that a quorum is not present, the presiding officer shall compel the attendance of a quorum. During the absence of a quorum, no other business may be transacted or motions entertained except a declaration of adjournment or a recess by the Speaker. [105.]

[Amended Jan. 12, 1981; Jan. 14, 1997.]

DEBATE ON MOTIONS FOR SUSPENSION OF RULES.

83. The question of suspension of House rules 45, 47, 56, 61, 64, 66, 67, 68, 69, 77 and 83 shall be decided without debate. Debate upon the motion for the suspension of any other House rule, unless otherwise indicated, or any joint rule shall be limited to fifteen minutes and no member shall occupy more than three minutes. This rule shall not be suspended unless by unanimous consent of the members present. [102.] (52.)

[Amended Jan. 12, 1981; Jan. 9, 1989.]

84. Unless otherwise indicated, nothing in the House rules or joint rules shall be suspended, altered or repealed unless two-thirds of the members present and voting consent thereto. This rule shall not be suspended unless by unanimous consent of the members present. [103.] (63.)

[Amended Jan. 12, 1981.]

REFERENCE TO COMMITTEE ON RULES.

85. All motions or orders authorizing committees of the House to travel or to employ stenographers, all propositions involving special investigations by committees of the House, all resolutions presented for adoption by the House only, and all motions and orders except those which relate to the procedure of the House or are privileged in their nature or are authorized by rule sixty-five, shall be referred without debate to the committee on Rules, which shall report thereon, recommending what action should be taken. The committee shall not recommend suspension of joint rule nine, unless evidence satisfactory to the committee is produced that the petitioners have previously given notice, by public advertisement or otherwise, equivalent to that required by Chapter 3 of the General Laws. [104.] (13A.)

85A. The House committee on Rules shall provide that outside, independent audits of House financial accounts be conducted at the end of each fiscal year. A copy of such audit shall be filed with the Clerk of the House and copies shall be made available to the members and the general public. (13C.) [Adopted Jan. 11, 1985.]

PARLIAMENTARY PRACTICE.

86. The rules of parliamentary practice shall govern the House in all cases to which they are applicable, and in which they are not inconsistent with these rules or the joint rules of the two branches. (62.)

INDEX TO THE HOUSE RULES.

668

time for reporting. 28A.
floor amendments, 73A.

BLANKS, filling of, 75.

Calendar, 12, 13, 45, 46, 47.
Calendar, dispense with printing of, 12.
Capital outlay bills, 20, 21.
Caucus, 17C, 18, 18A, 18B, 19, 19A.
Chairpersons, etc., nomination and caucus approval, 18.
Chaplain, to be appointed by Speaker, 7.
Clerk, 10, 10A, 11, 12, 14, 17A, 17C, 20, 23, 24, 28, 79(1), 85A.
     certifying bills for final passage, 23.
     printing of bills, etc., by the, 24(5).
     amendments, submission to, 33A.
Code of Ethics, 16A.
Commit, motion to, 64, 65, 71.

COMMITTEES:
     on Steering, Policy and Scheduling, 7A, 7D, 17, 41, 42.
     on Rules, 7B, 7C, 7D, 17, 85.
     on each Floor Division, 9A, 17.
     no member to serve where his private right, etc., 16A(14).
     standing, to be appointed, 17.
     hearings and House sessions, scheduling, 17, 18.
     on Long-Term Debt and Capital Expenditures, 17, 17D, 32A.
     on Science and Technology, 17, 33B.
     on Ethics, 16, 16A.
     on Bills in the Third Reading, 17, 18A, 22, 28, 45, 79(1).
     open meetings, 17A.
     reports, 17B.
     voting, 17B.
     office space, 17C.
     staffing, 17C.
     to be appointed by Speaker and Minority Leader, 18.
     chairpersons of, ratification, 18.
     conference, minority member, 18A.
     members of, ratification, 18A.
     duty of committee on Ways and Means, 20, 21, 27, 28, 30, 33, 35.
     to report adversely in certain cases, 26, 85.
     time for reporting appropriation bill, 27.
     to make report on all matters, except, 27.
     statements of intent, 27A.
     to discharge or direct to report, 28, 55, 64.
     on Counties on the part of the House, 33, 35.

desiring to be excused from voting, etc., 48.
voting, recording within five minutes, 52.
about to speak, to rise and address the Speaker, etc., 57.
Speaker, recognition of members, 58.
naming or seating, 59.
not to interrupt another, etc., 60.
not to speak more than once, etc., 61.
seats, 79.
privilege of the floor, 80. See **Voting.**
Messages from the Governor to be referred, etc., 30.

MINORITY LEADER:
to nominate Assistant Minority Floor Leader, etc., 18.
to nominate committee members, 18A.
to call a caucus, 19.
Minority party, caucus rules, 19A.
Minority party, percentage of committee membership, 18A.
Monitors, 8, 9.
Motions, 62 to 75, 83, 85.
to be reduced to writing, 62.

Naming of members, 59.
Notice to parties, 85.

Office space, 17C.
Open meetings, 17A.
Order. See **Questions of Order.**

ORDERS:
filing of, 24.
involving expenditures for special committees, 33.
once rejected or disposed of, not to be renewed, 38.
reported by committees, 42.
providing that information be transmitted to the House, 85.
Orders of the Day, 12, 13, 28, 41 to 47.

Parliamentarian, 10A.
Parliamentary inquiry, 60.
Personal privilege, 60.
Personnel and Administration, committee on, 17, 17C.

PETITIONS, 24, 25, 29, 30.
Final disposition precludes renewal, 38.
Petition for formal session to consider veto, 44.

JOINT RULES

OF THE TWO BRANCHES

JOINT RULES OF THE SENATE AND
HOUSE OF REPRESENTATIVES

[As finally adopted by the Senate and by the House of Representatives on June 12, 1995.]

Committees.

1. Joint standing committees shall be appointed at the beginning of the political year as follows:-

A committee on Banks and Banking;
A committee on Commerce and Labor;
A committee on Counties;
A committee on Criminal Justice;
A committee on Education, Arts and Humanities;
A committee on Election Laws;
A committee on Energy;
A committee on Federal Financial Assistance;
A committee on Government Regulations;
A committee on Health Care;
A committee on Housing and Urban Development;
A committee on Human Services and Elderly Affairs;
A committee on Insurance;
A committee on the Judiciary;
A committee on Local Affairs;
A committee on Natural Resources and Agriculture;
A committee on Public Safety;
A committee on Public Service;
A committee on State Administration;
A committee on Taxation;
A committee on Transportation;

Each to consist of six members of the Senate, and eleven on the part of the House except the committee on Transportation which shall consist of seven members of the Senate and thirteen on the part of the House.

Within three calendar days of the opening of each annual session of the General Court the committees on Rules of the Senate and the House of Representatives shall meet concurrently to establish at least one designated day of each week and designated hours during that day which shall be set aside for the holding of formal sessions of the respective branches and during which the joint standing committees shall not hold public hearings or executive sessions of their members from the opening of the first annual session through the fourth Wednesday in April in that session.

Within four weeks of the appointment of joint standing committees in the first annual session of the General Court, each joint standing committee shall adopt rules of procedure regarding the conduct of said committee. Said rules of procedure shall be filed with the Clerk of the Senate and the Clerk of the House and shall be available to the public and members of the General Court.

Matters referred by either the Senate or the House to its committee on Ways and Means shall be considered by the respective committees of the two branches, acting as a joint committee, when, in the judgment of the chairmen of the respective committees of the two branches, the interests of legislation or the expedition of business will be better served by such joint consideration. Matters may also be referred to the committees on Ways and Means, of the two branches, as a joint committee.

The committees on Rules, together with the presiding officers of the two branches, acting concurrently, may consider and suggest such measures·as shall, in their judgment, tend to facilitate the business of the session and a majority vote of the two branches shall be required to approve such recommendations.

In order to assist the House and the Senate in their
(1) consideration and enactment of new legislation and
of modifications of existing laws, when either are
deemed to be appropriate; (2) evaluation of the effectiveness and administration of laws and programs
already enacted in the Commonwealth; and (3) appraisal
of conditions and circumstances which may indicate the
desirability of enacting new legislation, the various joint
committees shall have oversight responsibilities as provided in the following paragraphs:

(i) Each joint committee shall review and study, on a
continuing basis, the implementation, administration,
execution and effectiveness of those laws, or parts of
law, the subject matter of which is within the jurisdiction
of that committee, the administrative regulations adopted
to implement those laws, and those state agencies or
entities having responsibilities for the administration and
execution of such laws.

(ii) In carrying out these review and study activities,
each committee shall determine whether such laws,
administrative regulations and programs thereunder are
being implemented in accordance with the intent of the
General Court and whether such laws, administrative
regulations and programs should be continued, curtailed
or eliminated.

(iii) Each committee shall also review and study any
conditions and circumstances which may indicate the
necessity or desirability of enacting new legislation
within the jurisdiction of that committee (whether or not
any matter has been introduced with respect thereto),
and shall on a continuing basis undertake research on
matters within the jurisdiction of that committee.

Committees shall coordinate oversight activities, under the direction of the presiding officers of both branches, for the purpose of achieving the maximum objectives of clauses (i), (ii) and (iii).

Each committee shall, upon completion of its oversight hearings, be authorized to report to the General Court the results of its findings and recommendations, with accompanying corrective legislation, if any, by filing the same with the Clerk of the House of Representatives or the Clerk of the Senate. Copies of such reports shall be printed and be made available for the members and the public. The disposition of said reports shall be determined by the Clerks with the approval of the Speaker and the President.

[Amended Jan. 6, 1882; Jan. 5, 1883; Jan. 7, 1884; Jan. 8 and 26, 1885; Jan. 8, 1886; Jan. 12, 1887; Jan. 9, 1888; Jan. 28, 1889; Jan. 8, 1890; Feb. 2, 1891; Jan. 11 and Feb. 10, 1892; Feb. 7, 1893; Jan. 8, 1894; Jan. 7, 1895; Jan. 7, 1896; Jan. 11, 1897; Jan. 10, 1898; Jan. 9, 1899; Jan. 22 and 29, 1901; Jan. 6, 1902; Jan. 9, 1903; Jan. 8, 1904; Jan. 6, 1905; Jan. 4, 1907; Jan. 5, 1910; Jan. 4, 1911; Jan. 1, 1913; Jan. 12, 1914; Jan. 2, 1918; Jan. 1 and 8 and Feb. 21, 1919; Jan. 7, 1920; Jan. 5, 1921; April 17 and 30, 1925; Jan. 5, 1927; Jan. 7, 1931; Jan. 6, 1937; Jan. 4, 1939; Jan. 1, 1941; Jan. 3, 1945; Jan. 2, 1946; Jan. 6, 1947; Feb. 1, 1949; Jan. 7, 1953; Jan. 7, 1959; Jan. 30, 1961; Jan. 7, 1963; Jan. 12 and Feb. 24, 1965; Mar. 10, 1966; Jan. 30, 1967; Jan. 7, 1971; July 23, 1974; Sept. 30 and Oct. 12, 1976; Nov. 3 and Dec. 21, 1981; Mar. 15, 1982; Oct. 3, 1983; June 3, 1985; Mar. 14, 1988; Mar. 27 and June 12, 1995.]

1A. Private or executive meetings of joint committees acting concurrently. Senate and House standing committees, special committees of the Senate and House of Representatives, and joint special committees and committees of conference on the disagreeing votes of the two branches shall be open to the public, unless a majority shall vote otherwise.

[Adopted July 17, 1973. Amended July 18, 1974.]

1B. A joint standing committee must hold a public hearing on each matter referred to it in each legislative session. A joint standing committee may adopt in its rules a provision stating that during the second year of the General Court the committee will accept only written testimony on matters that were heard by that committee during the first year.

[Adopted June 3, 1985.]

1C. All joint standing committees shall schedule committee hearings and executive sessions so as not to conflict, to the extent feasible, with the schedules of other committees and so as not to conflict with the day of the week and hours of the day which have been designated under Joint Rule 1 as the day of the week and times during that day set aside for formal sessions of the respective branches from the first Wednesday in January through the fourth Wednesday of April in the first annual session.

[Adopted June 3, 1985. Amended June 12, 1995.]

1D. All meetings of joint standing committees, and special joint committees of the Senate and House of Representatives, shall be open to the public, and any person shall be permitted to attend any such meeting unless such committee convenes in private session, as provided herein. All joint standing committees will determine a schedule for committee hearings to be held from the beginning of the first annual session through the fourth Wednesday in June in said session. These committee schedules shall be submitted to the Sergeant at Arms who shall cause them to be published. Establishment of such schedules shall not preclude joint standing committees from scheduling additional hearings or meetings as needed. No private session shall be held except upon extraordinary circumstances and only after the committee has first convened in an open session for which notice has been given, the presiding officer has stated the purpose of the private session, a majority of the committee members present has voted to go into private session, the vote of each member has been recorded on a roll call vote, and the presiding officer has stated before the private session if the committee will reconvene after the private session. The records of all such roll calls shall be kept in the offices of the committee for the duration of the General Court during which said vote was recorded, and shall be available for public inspection upon reasonable notice and during regular office hours.

All joint standing committees, and special joint committees of the Senate and House of Representatives, shall give notice of the time, place and agenda of all public hearings and executive sessions no less than forty-eight hours prior to the time of such meetings.

Nothing contained in this rule shall prohibit any joint standing committee or special joint committee of the Senate and the House of Representatives from taking appropriate action, including but not limited to the exclusion of a person from a committee meeting, in order to prevent the disruption of or interference with committee proceedings.

The forty-eight hour requirement shall be suspended in an emergency only after all reasonable efforts have been made to contact all committee members and upon a recorded vote of at least a majority of the members of each branch appointed to the committee, but no less than two-thirds of the members of each branch voting.

[Adopted June 3, 1985. Amended June 12, 1995.]

2. No member of either branch shall act as counsel for any party before any committee of the Legislature.

2A. No member of either branch shall purchase, directly or indirectly, the stock or other securities of any corporation or association knowing that there is pending before the General Court any measure specially granting to such corporation or association any immunity, exemption, privilege or benefit or any measure providing for the creation of, or directly affecting any, contractual relations between such corporation or association and the Commonwealth. This rule shall not apply to the purchase of securities issued by the Commonwealth or any political subdivision thereof.

[Adopted Jan. 16, 1922.]

3. (a) When the General Court is in session authorization for any committee of the Senate or House of Representatives to travel during the session of the General Court shall be approved by a vote of two-thirds of the members of its branch present and voting. (b) When the General Court is in session, authorization for any committee of the Senate or House of Representatives to sit and travel during the recess of the General Court shall be approved by a vote of two-thirds of the members of each branch present and voting. (c) During the recess of the General Court, the President of the Senate and the Speaker of the House of Representatives may, by written consent, allow standing committees of their respective branches or appoint special committees to sit, travel and incur expenses not exceeding sums authorized in writing by said presiding officers and appropriated for such purposes. (d) When the General Court is in session, authorization for any joint committee to travel during the session. or to sit or travel during the recess, of the General Court shall be approved by a vote of two-thirds of the members of each branch present and voting. (e) During the recess of the General Court, the President of the Senate and the Speaker of the House of Representatives, acting jointly, may, by written consent, allow joint committees or appoint joint special committees to sit, travel and incur expenses not exceeding sums authorized in writing by said presiding officers and appropriated for such purposes. The Clerks of the Senate and House of Representatives shall be notified of any appointments made and authorizations granted during the recess for said committees to sit, travel and incur expenses during the recess and the Clerks shall enter such information in the journals for the next year, as soon as may be practicable. Committees authorized by the presiding officers to sit during the recess in the odd numbered year shall report not later than the fourth Wednesday of January during the following year and committees authorized by the presiding officers to sit during the recess in the even numbered year shall report not later than the fourth Wednesday of December during the same year.

No committee shall travel except at the expense of the Commonwealth. In any case when a committee is authorized to travel, the Sergeant-at-Arms shall provide transportation only for members of the committee and the officer accompanying them, and the reasonable travelling expenses of such members and officers only shall be charged to or paid by the Commonwealth. Neither the Sergeant-at-Arms nor the officer detailed by him shall permit any person to accompany such committee while in the discharge of its official duties unless invited by vote of the committee.

All bills for the travelling expenses of committees shall be submitted by the Sergeant-at-Arms to the committee by whom they have been incurred and shall be approved by a majority of said committee before being presented to the Comptroller for payment.

[Adopted Feb. 7, 1890. Amended Feb. 2, 1891; Jan. 20, 1904; April 17, 1925; March 2, 1943; July 27, 1950; Oct. 18, 1971; March 28, 1972; Jan. 15, 1973.]

3A. A joint standing committee may, upon the written and signed report of two-thirds of the members of the Senate and two-thirds of the members of the House appointed to said committee, report a bill or other form of legislation without said legislation being founded upon petition; provided, however, that matters so reported shall be germane to the subject matters regularly referred to the committee. The committee shall hold a public hearing on such bill or other form of legislation before it is reported. A bill or other form of legislation so reported shall be placed in the Orders of the Day by the Clerk of the respective branch wherein it is reported or referred to a standing committee of said branch under the rules. All reports of committees not founded upon petition shall bear the designation "committee bill, resolve, order or resolution", as the case may be, in the Orders of the Day. Committees to which messages from the Governor, reports of state officers, boards, committees, commissions and others authorized to report to the General Court, may report by bill or otherwise such legislation as may be germane to the subject-matter referred to them.

[Adopted June 3, 1985.]

4. Favorable reports, and adverse reports on subjects of legislation other than petitions, by joint committees may be made to either branch, at the discretion of the committee, having reference to an equal distribution of business between the two branches, except that reports on money bills shall be made to the House; and if adverse reports on matters other than petitions which are accompanied by "money bills" are accepted by the House, this shall constitute final rejection. Adverse reports by joint committees on petitions shall be made to the branch in which the petition was originally introduced, excepting that such adverse reports on petitions accompanied by proposed "money bills" shall be made to the House; and, if accepted by the branch in which they are made, shall be considered as a final rejection. When a report is made from any committee to either branch, and the subject-matter thereof is subsequently referred therein to a joint committee, such committee shall report its action to the branch in which the reference originated. [See also Joint Rule 5.]

A vote of a joint standing committee to give legislation a favorable or adverse report shall be conducted by a roll call upon request of two committee members present at the committee meeting. Such votes shall be recorded on appropriate forms that show all votes for and against the particular committee action. The records of all such roll calls shall be kept in the offices of the committee for the duration of the General Court during which said vote was recorded, and shall be available for public inspection upon reasonable notice and during regular office hours.

A report of a joint standing committee will not be final and shall not be filed until all committee members have been given the opportunity to sign an appropriate form to accompany said report signifying approval of, dissent or abstention from, said report. No signature shall be valid unless the report to which the signature is affixed includes the substantially complete text of the legislation being reported.

[Amended Jan. 3, 1952; April 8, 1959; June 7, 1965; Jan. 7, 1971; March 11, 1974; June 3, 1985.]

4A. In compliance with the provisions of section 38A of chapter 3 of the General Laws, all joint committees of the General Court when reporting on bills referred to them shall include therewith a fiscal note prepared in accordance with the provisions of section 3A of chapter 29 of the General Laws, showing the estimated cost or the fiscal effect of the proposed legislation, if, in the opinion of said committee, such cost exceeds the sum of one hundred thousand dollars.

[Adopted Jan. 15, 1973.]

5. Matters reported adversely by joint committees and the committees on Rules of the two branches, acting concurrently, may be recommitted to the same committees at the pleasure of the branch acting thereon, and bills or resolves may be recommitted in either branch. If a bill or resolve is laid aside in either branch for the reason that it is declared to be broader in its scope than the subject-matter upon which it is based, the subject-matter shall be recommitted to the committee. A concurrent vote shall, however, be necessary for recommittal, with instructions. After recommitment, report shall, in all cases, be made to the branch originating the recommitment.

[Amended Feb. 2, 1891; April 11, 1935; Jan. 6, 1947; May 7, 1953; March 26, 1963; Jan. 30, 1967; Jan. 7, 1971; March 11, 1974.]

6. Bills and resolves reported by joint committees shall be printed or fairly written in a legible hand, without material erasure or interlineation, and on not less than one sheet of paper, with suitable margins, and with spaces between the several sections.

[Amended Jan. 28, 1889; Jan. 9, 1941; Feb. 8, 1949.]

Joint Petitions.

6A. A member of the Senate and a member of the House of Representatives may file a joint petition in either branch and shall endorse their name thereon and a brief statement of the nature and object of the instrument; and the reading of the instrument shall be dispensed with, unless specially ordered. The petition shall be filed in the office of the Clerk of either the Senate or House of Representatives, depending on whether it is a "Joint Senate-House Petition" or a "Joint House-Senate Petition" but the Journal records in the Senate and House of Representatives shall carry both members names as presentors of the petition.

[Adopted Jan. 15, 1973.]

7. Whenever, upon any application for an act of incorporation or other legislation, the purpose for which such legislation is sought can be secured without detriment to the public interests by a general law or under existing laws, the committee to which the matter is referred shall report such general law, or "ought not to pass".

[Amended Feb. 2, 1891; Feb. 7, 1893; Jan. 7, 1971.]

7A. A petition for legislation to authorize a county to reinstate in its service a person formerly employed by it, or to retire or pension or grant an annuity to any person, or to increase any retirement allowance, pension or annuity, or to pay any sum of money in the nature of a pension or retirement allowance, or to pay any salary which would have accrued to a deceased official or employee but for his death, or to pay any claim for damages or otherwise, or to alter the benefits or change the restrictions of any county retirement or pension law, shall, subsequently to the procedure required by Senate Rule No. 20 and House Rule No. 24, be reported adversely, unless, when filed it be the petition of, or be approved by, a majority of the county commissioners.

[Adopted April 29, 1915. Amended Jan. 13, Feb. 19 and Dec. 22, 1920; May 24, 1926; April 11, 1935; April 22, 1937; Jan. 12, 1939; Jan. 15, 1945; Feb. 20, 1951; Jan. 30, 1967; Jan. 7, 1971; Jan. 15, 1973.]

7B. A petition, the operation of which is restricted to a particular city or town (and which does not affect the powers, duties, etc., of state departments, boards, commissions, etc., or which does not affect generally the laws of the Commonwealth) and which is not filed in conformity with Section 8 of Article LXXXIX of the Amendments to the Constitution shall, subsequent to the procedure required by Senate Rule 20 and House Rule 24, be reported adversely, unless when filed, be on petition filed or approved by the voters of a city or town, or the mayor and city council, or other legislative body, of a city, or the town meeting of a town. A joint committee to which is inadvertently referred a petition or other subject of legislation the operation of which is restricted to a particular city or town and which is not in conformity with Section 8 of Article LXXXIX of the Amendments to the Constitution — shall report a general law which applies alike to all cities, or to all towns, or to all cities and towns, or to a class of not fewer than two; or shall report "ought not to pass", with the further endorsement that it "would be unconstitutional to enact such special law".

[Adopted Jan. 13, 1920. Amended Feb. 19 and Dec. 22, 1920; May 24, 1926; April 11, 1935; April 22, 1937; Jan. 12, 1939; Jan. 9, 1941; Jan. 15, 1945; Feb. 20, 1951; Jan. 30, 1967; Jan. 7 and Mar. 22, 1971; Jan. 15, 1973.]

Notice to Parties Interested.

8. No legislation affecting the rights of individuals or the rights of a private or municipal corporation, otherwise than as it affects generally the people of the whole

Commonwealth or the people of the city or town to which it specifically applies, shall be proposed or introduced except by a petition, nor shall any bill or resolve embodying such legislation be reported by a committee except upon a petition duly referred, nor shall such a bill or resolve be reported by a committee, whether on an original reference or on a recommittal with instructions to hear the parties, until it is made to appear to the satisfaction of the committee that proper notice of the proposed legislation has been given by public advertisement or otherwise to all parties interested, without expense to the Commonwealth, or until evidence satisfactory to the committee is produced that all parties interested have in writing waived notice. A committee reporting adversely for want of proper notice or of a waiver thereof shall set forth this fact in its report and no bill or resolve shall be in order as a substitute for, or amendment of, such report. Objection to the violation of this rule may be taken at any stage prior to that of the third reading.

[Adopted Feb. 7, 1890. Amended Dec. 22, 1920; Jan. 12, 1939; Jan. 15, 1945; Jan. 7, 1971.]

9. A petition for the incorporation of a city or town, for the annexation of one municipality to another, for the consolidation of two or more municipalities or for the division of an existing municipality, or for the incorporation or revival of a railroad, street railway, elevated railroad, canal, telephone, telegraph, water, gas, electric light, power or other public service corporation, for the amendment, alteration or extension of the charter or corporate powers or privileges, or for the change of name, of any such company, whether specially incorporated or organized under general laws, or for authority to take water for a water supply, or relative to building structures in or over navigable or tide waters, shall be placed on file, and not referred to a committee, unless the petitioner has given the notice and followed the procedure required by section 5 of chapter 3 of the General Laws, as appearing in the Official Edition. But if, no objection being raised, any such petition is referred to a committee without such required notice or procedure, the committee shall forthwith report adversely, setting forth as the reason for such report failure to comply with the provisions of law, unless evidence satisfactory to the committee is produced that all parties interested have in writing waived notice. In case a bill or resolve is reported upon such a petition, after proof of such waiver of notice, this fact shall be set forth in the report of the committee. When an adverse report is made by a committee, on account of failure to give the required notice, no bill or resolve shall be substituted for such report, nor shall such report be recommitted or referred to another committee.

A petition for the establishment or revival, or for the amendment, alteration or extension of the charter or corporate powers or privileges, or for the change of name, of any corporation, except a petition subject to the provisions of the preceding paragraph, shall be transmitted by the Clerk of the branch in which it is filed to the office of the State Secretary. If such a petition is returned by said Secretary with a statement that the petitioner has failed to comply with the requirements of section 7 of chapter 3 of the General Laws, as appearing in the Official Edition, said petition shall be placed on file, and shall not be referred to a committee.

Any petition placed on file for want of proper notice or procedure under this rule shall not affect action upon any other measure involving the same subject matter.

[Adopted Feb. 7, 1890. Amended Feb. 2, 1891; Feb. 3, 1898; Jan. 16, 1903; Feb. 19 and Dec. 22, 1920; May 24, 1926; Feb. 27, 1929; April 11,

1935; Jan. 6, 1938; Jan. 12, 1939; Jan. 9, 1941; Jan. 15, 1945; April 8, 1959; Jan. 7, 1963; Jan. 7, 1971; Jan. 15, 1973; June 12, 1995.]

Limit of Time Allowed for Reports of Committees.

10. In the first annual session of the General Court, joint committees and the committees on Rules of the two branches, acting concurrently, shall make final report not later than the fourth Wednesday of June on all matters referred to them previously to the fifteenth day of June, and within ten days on all matters referred to them on and after said fifteenth day of June. When the time within which said committees are required to report has expired, all matters upon which no report has then been made shall forthwith be reported by the chairman of the committee on the part of the branch in which they were respectively introduced, with an adverse recommendation under this rule. If the chairman fails to make such report by the end of the legislative day next following the expiration date, all matters remaining unreported shall be placed in the Orders of the Day by the Clerk of the branch in which the matter was originally filed with an adverse report under this rule. Matters which have been referred under the provisions of Joint Rule 29, upon which the chairmen of the committees on Rules fail to make a report, shall be placed by the respective Clerks in the Orders of the Day of the branch in which the subject matter was referred to said committees. Committees to whom are referred subjects of legislation may combine petitions of similar subject matter, or other forms of legislation of similar subject matter, into one adverse report, and the report thereon shall be that said petitions or other forms of legislation "ought NOT to pass," and if the report is accepted, all the matters contained therein shall be disposed of. However, petitions upon which an adverse report is accepted in only one branch, may not be combined with other subjects of legislation upon which adverse reports must be accepted, in concurrence. The provisions of this rule shall not apply to petitions referred to the committees on Rules of the two branches, acting concurrently, under the provisions of the second paragraph of Joint Rule 12. This rule shall not be rescinded, amended or suspended, except by a concurrent vote of four-fifths of the members of each branch present and voting thereon. Notwithstanding the provisions of Joint Rule 30, this rule shall not be rescinded, amended or suspended more than three times except by unanimous consent.

[Amended Feb. 2. 1891; Jan. 25, 1894; Jan. 16, 1903; Jan. 20, 1904; Dec. 22, 1920; April 17. 1925; Jan. 12. 1939; Jan. 15. 1945; Jan. 6. 1947; May 7. 1953; Jan. 27, 1955; Jan. 30. 1967; Jan. 7. 1971; Feb. 4. 1974; June 12, 1995.]

10A. The form for all subjects of legislation receiving a favorable report shall be "ought to pass." The form for all subjects of legislation receiving an adverse report shall be "ought NOT to pass." A committee to whom is referred any other matter may report recommending that the same be placed on file.

[Adopted Jan. 7, 1971.]

Committees of Conference.

11. Committees of conference shall consist of three members on the part of each branch, representing its vote; and their report, if agreed to by a majority of each committee, shall be made to the branch asking the conference, and may be either accepted or rejected, but no other action shall be had, except through a new committee of conference.

Committees of conference to whom are referred matters of difference in respect to bills or resolves, shall, before filing their reports, have the same approved by the committee on Bills in the Third Reading of the branch to which the report is to be made.

[Amended April 22, 1937.]

11A. Committees of conference to whom are referred matters of difference in respect to appropriation bills, including capital outlay programs, shall, before filing their reports, have the same approved by the committees on Bills in the Third Reading of the two branches, acting concurrently.

Upon the appointment of a committee of conference to whom matters of difference in respect to any appropriation bill or in respect to any bill providing for capital outlay programs and projects are referred, the clerk of the branch requesting said committee of conference shall cause to be printed and made available to members of the General Court a list of the matters in disagreement identified by item number and item purpose and showing the amount appropriated therefor by each branch of the General Court, and any other matters in disagreement and the position of each of the said branches with respect thereto.

The report of said committee of conference shall consist of the matters of difference so referred and so identified, showing the amounts appropriated therefor by each of the said branches and other matters in disagreement and the position of each branch with respect thereto, and shall state said committee's recommendations with respect to the matters so referred. Matters on which there exists no disagreement between the branches shall not be disturbed by the committee of conference.

The committees on ways and means of each branch of
the General Court shall assist such committee of conference in any and all matters necessary to the preparation
and completion of its report.

[Adopted July 30. 1974. Amended Oct. 3. 1983.]

11B. No report from a committee of conference shall
be considered or acted upon by either branch until the
calendar day following during which said report shall
have been in print and available to the public and to the
members of the General Court and provided further that
in no case shall less than twelve hours expire between
such availability and consideration. except that a report
from such committee of conference that it is unable to
agree may be considered and acted upon at the time that
such report is filed.

[Adopted Oct. 3. 1983.]

Limit of Time Allowed for New Business.

12. Resolutions intended for adoption by both
branches of the General Court. petitions. and all other
subjects of legislation. shall be deposited with the Clerk
of either branch prior to five o'clock in the afternoon on
the first Wednesday in December preceding the first
annual session of the General Court.

All such matters (except messages from the Governor.
reports required or authorized to be made to the
Legislature and petitions filed or approved by the voters
of a city or town, or the mayor and city council. or other
legislative body of a city. or the town meeting of a town,
for the enactment of a special law in compliance with
the requirements of Section 8 of Article LXXXIX of the
Amendments to the Constitution and which do not affect
the powers. duties. etc.. of state departments. boards.

commissions, etc.. or which do not affect generally the laws of the Commonwealth) deposited with the respective Clerks subsequent to five o'clock on the first Wednesday of December preceding the first annual session of the General Court shall be referred by the Clerks to the committees on the Rules of the two branches, acting concurrently. No such matter shall be admitted for consideration except on report of the committees on Rules of the two branches, acting concurrently, and then upon approval of four-fifths of the members of each branch voting thereon. Matters upon which suspension of Joint Rule 12 has been negatived shall be placed on file.

At any special session called under Rule 26A, however. matters relating to the facts constituting the necessity for convening such session shall, if otherwise admissible. be admitted as though filed seasonably in accordance with the first sentence of this rule. Any recommendations from the Governor shall be similarly considered. This rule shall not be rescinded, amended or suspended, except by a concurrent vote of four-fifths of the members of each branch present and voting thereon.

[Amended Feb. 7, 1890; Feb. 2, 1891; Feb. 7, 1893; Jan. 10, 1898; Jan. 9, 1899; Feb. 15, 1901; May 4. 1904; Jan. 31, 1910; Feb. 2, 1917: Dec. 22, 1920; March 30, 1921; Jan. 30, 1923; Feb. 15, 1933; Jan. 12 and Aug. 7, 1939; Jan. 15. 1945; Jan. 6. 1947; May 27, 1948; Jan. 30, 1967; March 26, 1969; Jan. 7, 1971; Jan. 15 and Oct. 2, 1973; Oct 3, 1983 June 12, 1995.]

12A. All formal business of the first annual session of the General Court shall be concluded no later than the third Wednesday in November of that calendar year and all formal business of the second annual session shall be concluded no later than the last day of July of that calendar year.

In order to assist the Senate and House in its analysis and appraisal of laws enacted by the General Court, each joint standing committee, upon conclusion of the formal business of the annual sessions, shall, as authorized by Joint Rule 1, initiate oversight hearings for the purpose of evaluating the effectiveness, application and administration of the subject matter of laws within the jurisdiction of that committee.

[Adopted, June 12, 1995.]

Unfinished Business of the Session.

12B. Any matter pending before the General Court at the end of the first annual session and any special session held in the same year shall carry over into the second annual session of the same General Court in the same legislative status as it was at the conclusion of the first annual session or any special session held during that year; provided, however, that any measure making or supplementing an appropriation for a fiscal year submitted to or returned to the General Court by the Governor, under the provisions of Article LXIII of the Amendments to the Constitution, in the first annual session or in a special session held during that year shall cease to exist upon the termination of the first annual session.

[Adopted June 12, 1995.]

Papers to be Deposited with the Clerks.

13. Papers intended for presentation to the General Court by any member thereof shall be deposited with the Clerk of the branch to which the member belongs; and all such papers, unless they be subject to other provisions of these rules or of the rules of the Senate or House, shall be referred by the Clerk, with the approval of the President or Speaker, to appropriate committees, subject to such changes as the Senate or House may make. The reading of papers so referred may be dispensed with, but they shall, except as hereinafter provided, be entered in the Journal of the same or the next legislative day after such reference.

Papers so deposited previously to the convening of the General Court by any member-elect shall be referred in like manner and shall be printed in advance, conformably to the rules and usages of the Senate or House, and shall be entered in the Journal as soon as may be practicable.

A member or member-elect may include a brief written statement of intent with all papers intended for presentation to the General Court. Upon a favorable report by a joint standing committee, a committee may include a brief written statement of intent. Said written statement shall be dated and be limited in length to one double-spaced typewritten page and shall include the scope of the matter presented for consideration; provided, however, this rule shall not be construed to require the printing of such statement of intent presented pursuant to this rule.

[Adopted Feb. 7, 1890. Amended Feb. 2, 1891; Feb. 7, 1893; Jan. 25, 1894; Dec. 22, 1920; May 25, 1923; Feb. 15, 1933; Jan. 12, 1939; Jan. 9, 1941; Jan. 7, 1971; June 3, 1985.]

Dockets of Legislative Counsel and Agents.

14. The committees on Rules of the two branches, acting concurrently, shall have authority to prescribe the manner and form of keeping the dockets of legislative counsel and agents which are required by law.

[Adopted Feb. 2, 1891. Amended Feb. 19, 1920.]

Duties of the Clerks.

15. If any part of the report of a committee over the signature of the chairman or members of the committee is amended in either branch, the Clerk of that branch shall endorse upon the report such amendment.

16. All papers, while on their passage between the two branches, may be under the signature of the respective Clerks, except as to the adopting of emergency preambles and the final passage of bills and resolves. Messages may be sent by such persons as each branch may direct.

[Amended Feb. 21, 1919.]

17. After bills and resolves have passed both branches to be engrossed, they shall be in the charge of the Clerks of the two branches, who shall prepare the same for final passage in the manner prescribed by law; and when so prepared the same shall be delivered to the Clerk of the House of Representatives; and when the bills have been passed to be enacted or the resolves have been passed in the House, they shall, in like manner, be delivered to the Senate Clerk and Parliamentarian. If a bill or resolve contains an emergency preamble, it shall be delivered in like manner, to the Senate after the preamble has been adopted by the House of Representatives and before the bill or resolve is put upon its final passage in that branch. If the Senate concurs in adopting the preamble, the bill or resolve shall be returned to the House to be there first put upon its final passage, in accordance with the requirements of Joint Rule No. 22.

[Amended Feb. 24, 1914; Feb. 21, 1919; Jan. 7, 1971.]

18. [Omitted in 1971.]

19. The Clerk of the branch in which a bill or resolve originated shall make an endorsement on the envelope of the engrossed copy thereof, certifying in which branch the same originated, which endorsement shall be entered on the journals by the Clerks respectively.

[Amended Jan. 28, 1889; Feb. 24, 1914.]

20. Bills, resolves and other papers requiring the approval of the Governor shall be laid before him for his approbation by the Senate Clerk and Parliamentarian, who shall enter upon the journal of the Senate the day and date on which the same were so laid before the Governor.

[Amended Jan. 28, 1889; Jan. 7, 1971.]

Printing and Distribution of Documents.

21. The committees on Rules of the two branches, acting concurrently, may make regulations for the distribution of all documents printed or assigned for the use of the Legislature not otherwise disposed of, and such regulations shall be reported to and be subject to the order of the two branches.

Under the general order to print a bill or other document, the number printed shall be determined by the Clerks of the two branches as approved by the President of the Senate and the Speaker of the House of Representatives, except that such number, not exceeding two thousand, shall be printed as determined by the committee on Rules on the part of the branch in which the report is filed.

The Clerks of the Senate and House of Representatives, with the approval of the President and Speaker, may have printed, documents for use of committees.

Leave to report in print shall not be construed to authorize the printing of extended reports of evidence.

Bills, reports and other documents, printed under the general order of either branch, shall be distributed as follows, to wit: two copies to each member of the Senate and House of Representatives (to be placed on his file under the direction of the Sergeant-at-Arms, if desired by the member); three copies to each Clerk in either branch, and three copies to each reporter in regular attendance, to whom a seat has been assigned in either branch; twenty copies to the Executive; twenty copies to the Secretary's office; six copies to the State Library; one copy to each Public Library in the Commonwealth, which shall make due application therefor to the Sergeant-at-Arms, and shall make proper provision for the transmission and preservation thereof; and, when the document is the report of a committee, ten copies shall be assigned to the committee making the report. The Sergeant-at-Arms shall preserve as many as may be necessary for the permanent files to be placed in the lobbies, and distribute the remainder under such regulations as may be prescribed by said committees, acting concurrently.

The committees on Rules of the two branches, acting concurrently, may make such changes in distribution of documents as they deem necessary for expediting the work of the legislature.

[Amended Jan. 8, 1886; Jan. 28, 1889; Jan. 27, 1911; Feb. 19, 1920; Jan. 6, 1947; Apr. 5, 1967; Jan. 7, 1971.]

Emergency Measures.

22. The vote on the preamble of an emergency law, which under the requirements of Article XLVIII, as amended by Article LXVII of the Amendments of the

Constitution must, upon request of two members of the
Senate or of five members of the House of Representatives, be taken by call of the yeas and nays, shall be
had after the proposed law has been prepared for final
passage; and neither branch shall vote on the enactment
of a bill or on the passage of a resolve containing an
emergency preamble until it has been determined
whether the preamble shall remain or be eliminated.
If the two branches concur in adopting the preamble, the
bill or resolve shall first be put upon its final passage in
the House of Representatives. If either branch fails to
adopt the preamble, notice of its action shall be sent
to the other branch; and the bill or resolve, duly
endorsed, shall again be prepared for final passage without the said preamble and without any provision that the
bill or the resolve shall take effect earlier than ninety
days after it has become law. Procedure shall be otherwise in accordance with the joint rules and the rules of
the Senate and the House of Representatives.

[Adopted Feb. 21, 1919. Amended Jan. 30, 1923; Jan. 7, 1971.]

22A. Bills and resolves passed to be engrossed by
both branches and before being transmitted by the clerks
to the Legislative Engrossing Division shall be made
available to the committees on Bills in the Third
Reading of the two branches, acting jointly, who shall
examine them to insure accuracy in the text; that the legislation is correct as to form; that references to previous
amendments to any particular law are correct and to
insure proper consistency with the language of existing
statutes. These committees, with the approval of the
majority and minority leadership of both branches may
make corrections which are not substantive in nature. The
clerks of both branches shall be immediately notified, in

writing, of any such changes. Errors discovered by the committees of a substantive nature shall be reported to the General Court, which in turn shall take appropriate action under its rules. Upon completion of examination and possible correction of any such bills and resolves, the bills and resolves shall be returned to the clerks, who in turn, shall transmit them to the Legislative Engrossing Division to be prepared for final passage.

[Adopted Sept. 16, 1971.]

Legislative Amendments to the Constitution.

23. A joint committee to which is referred any proposal for a specific amendment to the Constitution shall make in each branch a separate report recommending either that the proposal ought to pass or ought not to pass no later than the last Wednesday of April. The committee shall file the said proposal, together with any official papers in its possession that relate thereto, with the Clerk of the Senate. When the time within which said committees are required to report has expired, all matters upon which no report has been made shall forthwith be placed in the Journal of the respective branches, with an adverse report under this rule; and shall then be placed on file in the office of the Clerk of the Senate. For further information of the members of the Senate and House of Representatives, the respective Clerks shall also place all such matters under a separate heading in the Calendar of each branch, as soon as is practicable. In each branch the report shall be read and forthwith placed on file; and no further legislative action shall be taken on the measure unless consideration in joint session is called for by vote of either branch, in accordance with the provisions of Section 2 of Part IV of Article XLVIII (as amended by

Article LXXXI) of the Amendments to the Constitution. A joint committee to which is referred any recommendation for an amendment to the Constitution made by the Governor or contained in a report authorized to be made to the General Court may report thereon a proposal for a legislative amendment, which shall be deemed to have been introduced by the member of the Senate who reports for the committee; and the procedure as regards reporting, filing and subsequent action shall be that provided for legislative amendments by this rule. Or it may report ought not to pass for the reason that no legislation is necessary or that the recommendation ought not to pass; and in such cases the usual procedure as regards similar reports by joint committees shall be followed. If such an adverse report is amended in the Senate by substituting a proposal for a legislative amendment, notice of the Senate's action shall be sent to the House and the said proposal, together with the official papers relating to the subject, shall be in the custody of the Clerk of the Senate; and if the said report is so amended in the House, the proposal, duly endorsed, together with the other papers, shall be sent to the Senate for its information and shall be kept in the custody of its Clerk. No further legislative action shall be taken in either branch on a proposal so substituted unless consideration in joint session is called for in accordance with the before mentioned provisions of the Constitution. If either branch calls for the consideration of any proposal in joint session, notice of its action shall be sent to the other branch; and it shall then be the duty of the Senate and the House of Representatives to arrange for the holding of the joint session not later than the second Wednesday in May. Subject to the requirements of the Constitution, joint sessions or continuances of joint sessions of the two branches to consider proposals for specific amendments to the Constitution, and all rules or provisions concerning procedure therein, shall be determined only by concurrent votes of the two branches. The rules relative to joint conventions shall apply to the joint sessions of the two houses.

[Adopted Feb. 21, 1919. Amended March 30, 1921; April 11, 1935; Jan. 12, 1939; Jan. 15, 1945; Nov. 9, 1951; Jan. 15, 1973; July 1, 1974.]

Executive Reorganization Plans.

23A. Any reorganization plan (accompanied by a bill) submitted by the Governor under the provisions of Article LXXXVII of the Amendments to the Constitution shall be referred by the Clerks of the Senate and the House, with the approval of the President and Speaker, to a joint standing committee within five days of the presentation thereof.

Said committee, to which is referred any such reorganization plan, shall, as required by said Article, not later than thirty days after the presentation of such plan by the Governor, hold a public hearing thereon; and shall not later than ten days after such hearing report that it either approves or disapproves such plan.

When recommending action, the committee shall make, in each branch, a separate report of its recommendations, and shall file said report together with the committee's recommendations and the reasons therefor in writing. Majority and minority reports shall be signed by the members of said committee. Any official papers in the possession of said committee that relate thereto shall be filed with the Clerk of the Senate.

If the committee recommends favorable action, the report shall be that the reorganization plan "ought to be approved". If the committee recommends adverse action, the report shall be that the reorganization plan "ought NOT to be approved". In each instance, the question shall be "Shall this reorganization plan be approved?".

In each branch, the report shall be read and forthwith recorded in the Journal. On the legislative day next following the Journal record, the report shall be placed in the Orders of the Day of the Senate and the House.

When the time within which a joint committee is required to report on a reorganization plan has expired, a matter upon which no report has been made shall forthwith be placed in the Orders of the Day by the Clerks of each branch and the question shall be "Shall this reorganization plan be approved?".

When such plan is before either branch, no motion relating to said plan shall be allowed except the motions to lay on the table (only in the Senate), to postpone to a time certain, or to commit or recommit (at the pleasure of either branch). The motions to take a recess, to adjourn, the previous question (if provided in the branch debating the issue), to close debate at a specific time, and the motion to reconsider shall also be in order.

A motion to discharge any committee to which is referred or to which is recommitted a reorganization plan shall not be in order prior to the expiration of forty days after the Governor's presentation of such plan. After the expiration of said forty days, a motion to discharge a committee shall be decided by a majority vote of the branch in which the motion is made.

Unless disapproved by a majority vote of the members of either of the two branches of the General Court present and voting, the General Court not having prorogued within sixty days from the date of presentation by the

Governor, the plan shall be approved and shall take effect as provided by Article LXXXVII of the Amendments to the Constitution.

Within seven days of the expiration of the sixty days from the date of presentation of said plan by the Governor, unless the question has already been decided, the Clerks of the Senate and House of Representatives shall place the plan in the Orders of the Day; and no motions except the motions to take a recess, to adjourn, and previous question, or to close debate at a specified time, shall be in order.

No such reorganization plan presented to the General Court shall be subject to change or amendment before expiration of such sixty days.

[Adopted June 13, 1967. Amended March 27, 1969; June 12, 1995.]

Joint Conventions.

24. The President of the Senate shall preside in Conventions of the two branches, and such Conventions shall be holden in the Representatives' Chamber; the Senate Clerk and Parliamentarian shall be the Clerk of the Convention, and a record of the proceedings of the Convention shall be entered at large on the journals of both branches.

25. When an agreement has been made by the two branches to go into Convention, such agreement shall not be altered or annulled, except by concurrent vote, excepting that it shall be in order to recess the convention from time to time upon a majority vote of said convention.

[Amended Jan. 7, 1971.]

26. No business shall be entered on, in Convention, other than that which may be agreed on before the Convention is formed.

Special Sessions.

26A. If written statements of twenty-one members of the Senate and eighty-one members of the House of Representatives, that in their opinion it is necessary that the General Court assemble in special session on a particular date and time specified therein during a recess of the General Court, are filed with their respective Clerks, such Clerks shall forthwith notify all the members of their respective branches to assemble at the State House in Boston on said date at the time so specified. When so assembled, the first business to be taken up shall be the question of the necessity of so assembling, in accordance with Article 1 of Section 1 of Chapter 1 of Part the Second of the Constitution of the Commonwealth. If twenty-one members of the Senate and eighty-one members of the House of Representatives judge by vote taken by call of the yeas and nays that such assembling of the General Court is necessary, specifying in such vote the facts constituting such necessity, the General Court shall then complete its organization as a special session and proceed to the consideration of matters properly before it. Nothing herein contained shall prevent the General Court from assembling in any other constitutional manner when it judges necessary.

[Adopted Aug. 7, 1939. Amended March 2, 1943; March 27, 1969; June 6, 1979.]

Joint Elections.

27. In all elections by joint ballot a time shall be assigned therefor at least one day previous to such election.

27A. In all cases of elections by ballot a majority of the votes cast shall be necessary for a choice, and where there shall be no such a majority on the first ballot the ballots shall be repeated until a majority is obtained; and in balloting, blanks shall be rejected and not taken into the count in the enumeration of votes, excepting that when the number of blanks shall be more than the number of votes received by the candidate having the highest number of votes, then the election shall be declared void and the balloting shall be repeated as provided herein.

[Adopted March 27, 1969.]

28. [Omitted March 28, 1972.]

References to the Committees on Rules.

29. All motions and orders authorizing joint committees to travel or to employ stenographers, or authorizing joint committees or special commissions composed as a whole or in part of members of the General Court to make investigations or to file special reports, all propositions reported by joint committees which authorize investigations or special reports by joint committees or by special commissions composed as a whole or in part of members of the General Court, all motions or orders proposed for joint adoption which provide that information be transmitted to the General Court, and all matters referred under the provisions of the second paragraph of Joint Rule 12, shall be referred without debate to the committees on Rules of the two branches, acting concurrently, who shall report thereon, in accordance with the provisions of Joint Rule 10. All matters which have been referred under this rule shall, in each instance, be reported back into the branch making such reference.

[Adopted Jan. 10, 1898. Amended Jan. 20, 1904; Jan. 28, 1913; Feb. 19 and Dec. 22, 1920; April 11, 1935; April 22, 1937; Jan. 27, 1955; Jan. 30, 1967; Oct. 18, 1971.]

30. All motions or orders extending the time within which joint committees and the committees on Rules of the two branches, acting concurrently, are required to report shall be referred without debate to the committees on Rules of the two branches, acting concurrently, who shall report recommending what action should be taken thereon. Such extension shall be granted by a concurrent majority vote if recommended by the committees on Rules of the two branches, acting concurrently; but no such extension shall be granted, against the recommendation of the said committees, except by a four-fifths vote of the members of each branch present and voting thereon. This rule shall not be rescinded, amended or suspended, except by a concurrent vote of four-fifths of the members of each branch present and voting thereon.

[Adopted Jan. 16, 1903. Amended Feb. 6, 1912; Feb. 19, 1920; Jan. 6, 1947; Jan. 27, 1955; June 7, 1965.]

Members.

31. A member of either branch who directly or indirectly solicits for himself or others any position or office within the gift or control of a railroad corporation, street railway company, gas or electric light company, telegraph or telephone company, aqueduct or water company, or other public service corporation, shall be subject to suspension therefor, or to such other penalty as the branch of which he is a member may see fit to impose. (See G. L. 271, sec. 40.)

[Adopted May 22, 1902.]

Accommodations for Reporters.

32. Subject to the approval and direction of the committees on Rules of the two branches, acting concurrently, during the session, and of the President of the

Senate and the Speaker of the House after prorogation, the use of the rooms and facilities assigned to reporters in the State House shall be under the control of the organizations of legislative reporters known as the Massachusetts State House Press Association and the State House Broadcasters Association. No person shall be permitted to use such rooms or facilities who is not entitled to the privileges of the reporters' galleries of the Senate or of the House. Within ten days after the General Court convenes the Massachusetts State House Press Association and the State House Broadcasters Association shall each transmit to the President of the Senate, the Speaker of the House of Representatives and the Sergeant-at-Arms a list of the legislative reporters with the principal publication or news service which each represents.

[Adopted Jan. 27, 1911. Amended Feb. 24, 1914; Feb. 19, 1920; April 17, 1925; May 23, 1979.]

Suspension of Rules.

33. Any joint rule except the tenth, twelfth and thirtieth may be altered, suspended or rescinded by a concurrent vote of two-thirds of the members of each branch present and voting thereon.

[Amended Feb. 7, 1893. Adopted in revised form Jan. 9, 1899. Amended Jan. 16, 1903.]

Audit of Accounts.

34. The committees on Rules of the two branches, acting concurrently, shall provide that an outside independent audit of joint financial accounts be conducted by a certified public accountant no less frequently than at the end of each second fiscal year. A copy of such audit shall be filed with the Clerks of the Senate and House of

Representatives and made available for public inspection
upon reasonable notice and during regular office hours.

[Adopted June 3, 1985.]

35. The committees on Rules of the two branches, acting concurrently, shall reexamine the Joint Rules of the
House and Senate as needed, but at least every four
years, and shall report to each branch any recommendations it may have to facilitate the work of the respective
branches and the joint standing committees.

[Adopted June 12, 1995.]

INDEX TO THE JOINT RULES OF THE TWO BRANCHES

[The figures refer to the numbers of the rules.]

715

CLERKS:

to certify bills and resolves to be rightly and truly prepared
for final passage, 17.
to submit certain petitions to State Secretary, 9.
to place unreported matters in Orders of the Day when time
for reporting expires, 10.
papers deposited late with, disposition, 12.
papers to be deposited with, and referred to committees, 13.
shall endorse amendments or reports of committees, 15.
papers on passage between the two branches to be under
signature of, except, etc., 16.
shall have charge of bills, etc., after passage to be
engrossed, etc., 17.
shall endorse where bill or resolve originated, 19.
Senate Clerk shall lay enacted bills, etc., before
Governor, 20.
Senate Clerk shall be Clerk of joint Convention, 24.
to notify members to assemble for special sessions, 26A.

COMMITTEES:

standing, appointment, number of members, etc., 1.
rules of procedure, 1.
oversight activities, 1, 12A.
open meetings, 1A, 1D.
public hearings, 1, 1B.
schedule of hearings, 1, 1C, 1D.
private sessions, 1D.
members of Legislature not to act as counsel before, 2.
travel of, 3.
report of, without being founded upon petition, 3A.
reports of, 4, 10.
reports of, may be made to either branch, except, etc., 4.
to report money bills to House, 4.
report of, subsequently referred to a joint committee,
to be reported to branch in which original report
was made, 4.

Memorials contemplating legislation deposited with Clerks
   late, disposition, 12.
Messages between the two branches, 16.
Motions, certain, to be referred to the committees on
   Rules, 29, 30.

New business, limit of time allowed for, 12.

NOTICE:

   of legislation specially affecting the rights of individuals
      or corporations to be given, 8.

Orders, certain, to be referred to the committees on
   Rules, 29, 30.
Orders of the Day, unreported matters to be placed in,
   by Clerks, 10.

PAPERS:

   to be deposited with Clerks, etc., 13.
   reading may be dispensed with, 13.
   certain, to be printed in advance, 13.
   written statements of intent, 13.
   on passage between the two branches to be under Clerks'
      signatures, except, etc., 16.
   requiring approval of Governor to be laid before him by
      Clerk of the Senate, 20.

PETITIONS:

   adverse reports on, to be made to branch in which
      introduced, 4.
   that a county be authorized to retire or pension or grant an
      annuity, or to pay any accrued salary or claim for
      damages, or to alter any county or municipal retirement
      law, or to reinstate former employees, to be reported
      adversely, unless, etc., 7A.
   for legislation affecting a particular city or town, 7B, 12.

NOTES OF RULINGS

OF THE

PRESIDING OFFICERS

FROM THE YEAR 1833.

PREPARED BY THE HONORABLE GEORGE G. CROCKER AND
CONTINUED BY HIM UNTIL 1913. SUBSEQUENT NOTES
HAVE BEEN ADDED BY THE CLERKS OF
THE TWO BRANCHES.

MEMORANDA. — S. or S.J. stands for Senate Journal, H or H.J. for House Journal. Citations from Journals which have never been printed refer to the duplicate manuscript copy in the State Library.

NOTES OF RULINGS

OF THE

PRESIDING OFFICERS
ON THE CONSTITUTION OF
MASSACHUSETTS

POWER OF PRESIDING OFFICERS TO DECIDE CONSTITUTIONAL QUESTIONS. — In a decision on a money bill, in which it was held that it was within the province of the Chair to decide the constitutional question involved, the following statement was made: "It is of course not intended to assume to the Chair any right of decision as to the constitutionality of matters of legislation in relation to their substance; but where the question relates to form and manner of proceeding in legislation, or, in other words, is one of order, it is the duty of the Chair to rule upon the same, although it may depend upon the provisions of the Constitution for its solution." Cases of a proposition to adjourn for more than two days, of proceedings without a quorum, of a faulty enacting form, and of neglecting to take the yeas and nays on a vetoed bill are cited. PITMAN, S. 1869, p. 341. SEE also STONE, H. 1866, p. 436; JEWELL, H. 1868, p. 386; BUTLER, S. 1894, p. 648; MEYER, H. 1894, pp. 509, 1399; DARLING (acting President), S. 1895, p. 578; TREADWAY, S. 1911, p. 506; YOUNG, H. 1922, p. 683; WILLIS, H. 1947, p. 528; FURBUSH, S. 1951, p. 1591.

A point of order having been raised that a proposed amendment was not in order for the reason that it was unconstitutional, it was held that it was not within the province of the Chair to decide as to the constitutionality of the amendment. BATES, H. 1897, p. 979. See also

728 *Notes of Rulings*

WALKER. H. 1910, p. 1480; BLANCHARD (acting President). S. 191 1. p. 1497; COTTON. S. 1939, p. 999; HOLMES. S. 1958, p. 1344.

That it was not within the province of the Chair to rule on the constitutional question that the House was in session on the Lord's Day contrary to the provisions of the Constitution; or whether the passage of a resolve would result in abridging the rights of a contract. HERTER. H. 1939, p. 2112; GIBBONS, H. 1953, p. 927.

That it was not within the province of the Chair to rule on questions as to legality or form of legislation involving decisions of the courts. HOLMES, S. 1958, p. 1429.

That an amendment to the General Appropriation Bill which, if adopted, would delegate the powers of the General Court to change general statutes to a commission and as such was clearly beyond the power of the House, raises a question of law, or of the Constitution, that was beyond the prerogative of the Chair to pass on. See GIBBONS. H. 1953, p. 1556.

That an amendment to the House Bill imposing limitations on property tax levies and expenditures of cities, towns and other local governmental units dependent on the property tax (House, No. 5757) would limit the appropriation power of the General Court as granted by the Constitution. McGEE, H. 1979, p. 562.

That an amendment to the General Appropriations Bill calling for a transfer of activities plan to be subject to the approval of house and senate committees on ways and means was unconstitutional because it was beyond the power of the Senate to delegate its powers to the committee on Ways and Means, it was ruled that it was not in the province of the Chair to rule on the constitutionality of the item. BULGER, S. 1981, p. 807.

For further rulings regarding the power of the presiding officer to decide constitutional questions, see MEYER, H. 1896, p. 254; MYERS, H. 1901, p. 1352; SALTONSTALL, H. 1934, p. 315; WRAGG, S. 1938, p. 836; COTTON (acting President). S. 1938. p. 1239; COTTON, S. 1939. p. 784; ARTHUR W. COOLIDGE, S. 1946, p. 1095. See also notes under Declaration of Rights, ART. XXX., CHAP. I., SECT. I., ART. II., CHAP. I., SECT. III, ART. VII., CHAP. VI., ART. II. and ARTICLES OF AMENDMENT XLVIII, LXII and LXIII.

DECLARATION OF RIGHTS, ART. XXX. — For a case in which it was ruled that it was not within the province of the Chair to decide as to the constitutionality of a bill that delegated legislative power to the Supreme Judicial Court, see WRAGG, S. 1938. p. 487. See also note to CHAP. II, SECT. I., Art. V.

In Joint Session it was ruled not to be within the province of the Chair to rule on the Constitutional question that it was an Executive intrusion upon the lawmaking power and authority of the General Court under Part the Second, Chapter I, Section I, Article 4 and Article XXX of the Declaration of Rights of the Constitution for the Governor to call a special session of the General Court with a restricted purpose of continuing the previous joint session. BULGER (*in joint session*). 1980 (Continuance of Joint Session), p. 4.

CHAP. I., SECT. I., ART. II. — *"No bill or resolve."* See LONG, H. 1878, p. 58; NOYES, H. 1880, p. 123.

"Laid before the Governor for his revisal." If either branch desires for any reason to revise an enacted bill, concurrent action of the two branches must be had, and the motion should be one providing that a message be sent by the two branches requesting the Governor to return the bill to the Senate. JEWELL, H. 1869, p. 645.

Notwithstanding this ruling, it is customary for the Senate, when it desires to revise an enacted bill, to request the return of the bill, without asking the concurrent action of the House. See SALTONSTALL, H. 1934, p. 710.

A motion to request the Governor to return a bill to the Senate having been made on the fifth day after the bill had been laid before the Governor and, during debate on this motion the five days within which executive action was required to be taken having expired at midnight, the motion was then ruled out of order. HOLMES (acting President), S. 1954, p. 1160.

"Who shall enter the objections . . . and proceed to reconsider the same." In a case in which a resolve and the objections thereto were laid on the table, it was held that it was then out of order to introduce a new resolve of a similar nature. GOODWIN, H. 1890, p. 613.

"But if, after such reconsideration, two-thirds of the said Senate or House of Representatives shall, notwithstanding the said objections, agree to pass the same, it shall, together with the objections, be sent to the other branch of the Legislature, where it shall also be reconsidered, and if approved by two-thirds of the members present, shall have the force of a law." Under this provision it has been held that in the branch first taking action a vote of two-thirds of the members present is sufficient to pass a bill. CLIFFORD, S. 1862, p. 625; BULLOCK, H. 1862, p. 586 (full discussion). See Kay Jewelry Company *v.* Board of Registration in Optometry, 305 Mass. 581. See also Walker *v.* State, 12 S. C. 200; Frillsen *v.* Mahan, 21 La. Ann. 79. *Contra,* see Co. of Cass *v.* Johnston, 95 U.S. 360; 2 Op. Att. Gen., 513 (1904, July 11).

In 1862, in a case in which, the President not voting, 33 votes were cast, of which 22 were in favor of the passage of the bill, it was held that the record of the yeas and nays was the only evidence of the number or the names of the members present, and that the necessary two-thirds had been obtained. CLIFFORD, S. 1862, p. 625. Later decisions do not support this position. SANFORD, H. 1874, p. 564; PILLSBURY, S. 1885, p. 584; HARTWELL, S. 1889, p. 589; BARRETT, H. 1889, p. 226. See also House Rule 67. See Brown *v.* Nash, 1 Wyoming Terr. 85.

It is permissible to reconsider a vote refusing to pass a bill over the Executive veto, notwithstanding the first vote is described in the Constitution as a reconsideration of the bill. SANFORD, H. 1874, p. 583; FROTHINGHAM, H. 1905, p. 1098. But see Sank *v.* Phila., 4 Brewster, 133. Wilson's Digest, 2058, 2151.

"Returned by the Governor within five days." It is not within the province of the Chair to rule on a point of order that a bill is not properly before the House for the reason that it was not returned by the Governor with his objections thereto in writing within the time fixed by the Constitution. MEYER, H. 1894, p. 1399.

"Both Sunday and a legal holiday. . . . are to be excluded in computing the five-day period." Opinion of Justices, S. 1935, p. 838. *Contra,* see Op. Att. Gen., Vol. III, p. 414.

Simply leaving the papers in the clerk's office after it is closed on the fifth day, with no official record whether left before or after midnight, is not such a return. CUSHING, H. 1912, p. 1879. [See notes to Articles of Amendment, LVI.] [Number of days Governor has to consider bills and resolves changed to *ten* (10), see Article LXXXX of the Amendments.]

CHAP. I. SECT. I. ART. IV.— *"All manner of wholesome and reasonable orders."* An order may not be used as the form for anything "on its way to become law." LONG. H. 1878, p. 60; SALTONSTALL, H. 1930, p. 229.

"To set forth the several duties, powers and limits of the several civil and military officers." For certain resolves defining the powers of the Legislature, especially the power to prescribe duties to the Governor and other executive officers, see PHELPS, H. 1857, p. 557.

CHAP. I., SECT. II. ART. VI. — See note to CHAP. I, SECT. III., ART. VIII.

CHAP. I., SECT. II., ART. VII. — For opinion of the Justices of the Supreme Judicial Court relative to the term for which officers of the Senate may be elected, see S. 1922, p. 3. See also Op. Att. Gen., H. 1921, p. 1027.

CHAP. I., SECT. II., ART. VIII. — For discussion of impeachment of public officers, see Senate document numbered 1535 of 1972, by Norman L. Pidgeon, Senate Clerk and Parliamentarian.

CHAP. I., SECT. III., ART. VI. — For a case of an arraignment of a State official at the bar of the House, see HALE, H. 1859, p. 149. [For discussion of impeachment of public officers, see Senate document numbered 1535 of 1972, by Norman L. Pidgeon, Senate Clerk and Parliamentarian.]

CHAP. I., SECT. III., ART. VII. — *"All money bills shall originate in the House of Representatives."* The exclusive constitutional privilege of the House of Representatives to originate money bills is limited to bills that transfer money or property from the people to the State, and does not include bills that appropriate money from the treasury of the Commonwealth to particular uses of the government or bestow it upon individuals or corporations. The Senate can originate a bill or resolve appropriating money from the treasury of the Commonwealth, or directly or indirectly involving expenditures of money from the treasury, or imposing a burden or charge thereon. OPINION OF JUSTICES, S. 1878, appendix; 126 Mass. 557; PITMAN, S. 1869, p. 340; COGSWELL, S. 1878, p. 279; GOODWIN, S. 1941, p. 1317; RICHARDSON, S. 1948, pp. 806, 815, 859. *Contra,* see JEWELL, H. 1868, p. 385; JEWELL, H. 1869, p. 630; LONG, H. 1878, pp. 197, 563.

See LORING, S. 1873, p. 409, for opinion that money bills should be allowed to originate in either branch.

It is the duty of the presiding officer of the Senate to observe with punctilious care the constitutional prerogatives of the House of Representatives. Without waiting for a point of order to be raised, he should cause a money bill which originates in the Senate to be laid aside or recommitted. In such case the action on the bill previously taken by the Senate is to be considered as not having been taken. BUTLER, S. 1894, p. 555; BUTLER, S. 1895, p. 378; SOULE, S. 1901, p. 753; McKNIGHT, S. 1920, p. 583; ALLEN, S. 1924, p. 450; WELLINGTON WELLS, S. 1925, pp. 376, 447 and S. 1926, p. 372; BACON, S. 1932, p. 670; FISH, S. 1933, p. 282 and S. 1934, p. 360.

An amendment to a bill relative to recycling of beverage containers that instituted a new fine was ruled as imposing a new penalty and not initiating a new tax. Therefore the amendment was properly before the Senate and did not need to originate in the House, BULGER, S. 1979, p. 1017.

It was formerly held that bills designating certain property as subject to or exempted from taxation, as well as bills imposing a tax in terms. were "money bills." BISHOP. S. 1881. p. 419: PINKERTON, S. 1893, p. 811. See also SANFORD, H. 1873, p. 283; STONE, H. 1866, p. 436. Later, an important bill exempting certain kinds of personal property from taxation was held not to be a "money bill." In rendering his decision, President BUTLER called attention to the fact that conditions which led to the adoption of this constitutional provision no longer exist. that the members of the Senate. like the members of the House, are now elected directly by the people, that the property qualifications of senators have been abolished, that representation in both branches alike is based on the number of legal voters, and that there remains no reason or excuse for construing into the Constitution a prohibition which does not clearly appear, that the bill was not in itself a proposition to impose a tax. and that in determining the point of order it was unnecessary to conjecture what results might accrue from its passage. BUTLER, S. 1895, p. 737.

It has been held that a bill exempting from taxation certain property in a particular town is not a "money bill." PILLSBURY (acting President), S. 1884, p. 259.

A bill abolishing certain existing exemptions from taxation and thereby subjecting to taxation property previously exempted, was held not to be a "money bill." TREADWAY, S. 1911, p. 506.

A bill, known as the bar and bottle bill, was held not to be a "money bill." WALKER, H. 1910, p. 941.

The words "money bill" do not cover bills merely creating a debt, but only bills relating to the taking of money or property from the people for the payment of a debt, or for some other public purpose. DANA. S. 1906. p. 1033.

A bill to provide for changes in the employment security law was held not to be a "money bill" for the reason that the money in the unemployment compensation fund is used only to pay benefits to certain employees and not for general purposes. FURBUSH. S. 1951. p. 991.

A bill granting a subsidy to the New York. New Haven and Hartford Railroad Company to aid in continuing service on a branch thereof was held not to be a "money bill." HOLMES. S. 1958. p. 1181. [See OPINION OF JUSTICES. S. 1958. p. 1139.]

A bill which amends an existing tax law is not a "money bill" if it does not increase the tax. FURBUSH. S. 1951. p. 1091.

A bill is considered as originating in that branch in which it is first acted upon. BRACKETT. H. 1885. p. 759.

For a case in which the Senate instructed a committee to report a bill to the House. see PILLSBURY. S. 1886. p. 702.

A bill providing for the payment of a filing fee for petitions for legislation was held to be a "regulatory measure" and not a "money bill" within the meaning of the Constitution. WELLINGTON WELLS, S. 1925, p. 609.

An amendment offered to the General Appropriation Act calling for a surtax of ten percent on corporations was laid aside. DONAHUE. S. 1964. p. 952. [See J. R. 4 "Money Bills."]

An amendment calling for a 20% tax on the commercial sale of blood by blood banks was ruled out of order in that the amendment proposed a new tax and should therefore originate in the House. BULGER. S. 1979. p. 1343.

An amendment to a deficiency budget calling for a two percent tax on gross receipts of petroleum companies, was ruled out of order because the pending amendment would convert the bill to a "money bill" which must originate in the House. BULGER, S. 1980, p. 1009.

[For discussion of "Budget — Powers of General Court and Executive Branch" see Senate document numbered 1525 of 1973, by Norman L. Pidgeon, Senate Clerk and Parliamentarian.] [For a discussion of what is a "Money Bill" and where should such bills originate, see Senate document numbered 2010 of 1973, by Norman L. Pidgeon, Senate Clerk and Parliamentarian.]

CHAP. I, SECT. III., ART. VIII. — *"Provided such adjournments shall not exceed two days at a time."* Sunday is not to be counted, but Fast Day must be counted. STONE, H. 1867, p. 270; JEWELL, H. 1868, p. 311. See also MEYER, H. 1895, p. 1313. [See also notes to CHAP. I., SECT. I., ART. II.]

CHAP. I., SECT. III., ART. X. — *"And settle the rules and orders of proceedings in their own House."* See LONG, H. 1878, p. 60.

CHAP. II., SECT. I., ART. V. — An amendment which would have made a certain bill provide that a special session of the General Court be called by the Governor was held not to be in order for the reason that such a provision would interfere with the prerogative of the latter. BLISS (acting Speaker), H. 1919, p. 1502.

CHAP. III., ART. I.— For discussions of "removal by address" — see Senate document numbered 1535 of 1972, by Norman L. Pidgeon, Senate Clerk and Parliamentarian.

CHAP. III., ART. II. — Opinions of the Justices of the Supreme Judicial Court may be required only when "such questions of law are necessary to be determined by the body making the inquiry, in the exercise of the legislative or executive power entrusted to it by the Constitution and laws of the Commonwealth" and "upon solemn occasions." OPINION OF JUSTICES, S. 1935, p. 448.

"Important questions of law" must be explicitly stated. OPINION OF JUSTICES, S. 1938, p. 382.

CHAP. VI., ART. II. — *"But their being chosen or appointed to, and accepting the same, shall operate as a resignation of their seat in the Senate or House of Representatives."* It is not within the province of the Chair to decide whether a member has forfeited his membership by accepting an office incompatible with his seat in the Legislature. HALE, H. 1859, p. 48.

ARTICLES OF AMENDMENT.

ART. I. — As to authority of Governor to approve within the five-day period after prorogation of the General Court of measures laid before him before prorogation. See Op. Att. Gen. 168, KNOWLTON, 1894; FINGOLD, 1956. [See also OPINION OF JUSTICES to Governor, Oct. 1956.] [See Article LXXXX of the Amendments.]

ART. VIII. See note to Constitution, Chap. VI., Art. II.

ART. IX. *(Annulled by Art. XLVIII.)* An amendment to the Constitution may be amended on the second year of its consideration, but such action will necessitate its reference to the next Legislature. BISHOP, S. 1880, p. 321; NOYES, H. 1880, p. 57; DEWEY (acting Speaker), H. 1890, p. 369.

It has also been held that an amendment to the Constitution cannot be amended on the second year of its consideration. PHELPS, H. 1857, p. 906; PHELPS, S. 1859, p. 323.

A vote agreeing to an article of amendment to the Constitution can be reconsidered. MARDEN, H. 1883, pp. 377, 422-427; MORAN (in joint session), S. 1935, p. 992, and H. 1935, p. 1289.

As to the method of procedure in acting on an amendment on the second year, and in providing for its submission to the people, see NOYES, H. 1881, p. 466. See also MEYER, H. 1896, pp. 255, 269.

That a named member may not be ejected for an extended period without a trial was not subject to a point of order because it was not within the province of the Chair to rule on constitutional matters. See BULGER (acting President), S. 1978, p. 1097.

That the report of the special committee on the naming of a member placed before the joint convention cannot be voted upon since it calls for the expulsion of the named member from the assembly unless he takes a course of action and also that the named member has not been afforded a trial prior to the meeting of the joint convention was not the subject of a point of order because there was ample precedence for the procedure being used. See BULGER (acting President), S. 1978, p. 1097.

ART. X.— *"But nothing herein contained shall prevent the General Court from assembling at such other times as they shall judge necessary."* As to methods of providing for such assembling, see OPINION OF JUSTICES, H. 1936, p. 1461. See note to CHAP. II., SECT. I., ART. V.

ART. XVII. In a joint convention for the purpose of filling a vacancy in a State office, the calling of the roll, and each member arising and announcing his choice, does not constitute a "ballot" within the meaning of this Amendment. WELLINGTON WELLS, S. 1928, p. 689, and H. 1928, p. 960.

A majority vote is necessary to elect a State officer to fill a vacancy, and a plurality vote is not sufficient. HOLMES (*in joint session*) S. 1958, p. 1356, H. 1958, p. 1860.

ARTS. XXI and XXII. See 157 Mass. 595.

ART. XXV. — The question being raised that the method of voting for a Councillor to fill a vacancy, by call of the roll, could not be considered a ballot, the Chair rules that this Article did not require the election to be by *ballot*, but by *concurrent vote*. GOODWIN, S. 1941, p. 389.

ART. XXXIII. — See note to House Rule 68.

It is immaterial that a quorum does not vote if a quorum is present. Pillsbury. S. 1885, p. 584; HARTWELL, S. 1889, p. 589; BARRETT. H. 1889, p. 226. See notes to House Rules 67 and 105, and note to Senate Rules under "Voting." *Contra*, see CLIFFORD, S. 1862, p. 625.

The words *"a majority of the members"* means a majority of the whole membership established by the Constitution. See Op. Att. Gen., Vol. I (1892), p. 36 (House Doc. No. 38). [See Senate document numbered 1496 of 1971.]

[For discussion of *majority* under certain circumstances, see Senate document numbered 1535 of 1972, by Norman L. Pidgeon, Senate Clerk and Parliamentarian.]

In ascertaining the presence of a quorum, senators who are in the chamber but do not answer to their names when the roll is called are to be counted. SOULE, S. 1901, p 1014.

ART. XLVIII. — See notes to Art. of Amend. IX. See also note to House Rule 80, *"And he shall receive no motion relating to the same, except, etc. "*; and note to Joint Rule 23. See Senate document numbered 1535 of 1972, by Norman L. Pidgeon, Senate Clerk and Parliamentarian for discussion of Initiative and Referendum. [See Mass. Reports 1956, Vol. 334, p. 757. See Statement, POWERS, S. J. 1960, p. 939.]

THE INITIATIVE. II. Sect. 2. (1) Attorney General has authority, under the Massachusetts Constitution, to refuse to certify a proposed initiative as not in proper "form" because it does not propose a "law," and (2) proposed initiative, relating to internal legislative procedures which are within the constitutional unicameral powers of the respective houses, did not relate to a "law" and, therefore, was not a proper subject for the popular initiative. [390 Mass. 593, 1983.]

THE INITIATIVE. II. Sect. 3. An initiative petition contains subjects that are not related; and also contains language which proposed to change a law which had been voted on ". . . in either of the last state-wide elections". [See OPINION OF THE JUSTICES, H. 1996, pp. 2013-2014; for printed document, see House, No. 5968 of 1996.]

THE INITIATIVE. III. Sect. 2.— It is not necessary to take action on a resolution providing for a legislative substitute before taking final action on an original initiative bill. WRAGG, S. 1938, p. 1029.

A proposed legislative substitute for an initiative bill, of the same general subject matter, although not confined to the particular wording or scope of the original petition, may be offered. RICHARDSON, S. 1950, p. 1097.

Various rulings on Legislative Substitutes to Initiative Measures. MCGEE, H. 1976. pp. 1668, 1669, 1670.

THE INITIATIVE. IV. Sect. 2.— Action must be taken on a proposed legislative amendment to the Constitution not later than the second Wednesday in June. See MCKNIGHT (*in joint session*), Journals of Extra Session of 1920, S. p. 61, and H. p. 87. [See also OPINION OF JUSTICES, S. 1921, p. 329.]

Such provisos or limitations as may seem fit may be added to proposed legislative amendments to the Constitution. FURBUSH (*in joint session*), S. 1954, p. 897, and H. 1954, p. 1504.

That members in joint convention had no right to vote on an amendment relative to reducing the size of the House of Representatives for the reason that said House was malapportioned, see DONAHUE (*in joint session*), S. 1970, p. 724; H. 1970, p. 878.

Amendments to a proposal for amendment to the Constitution which go beyond the petition forming the basis for the prayer, are not in order. See DONAHUE (*in joint session*), S. 1969, p. 1323; H. 1969, p. 1878.

Amendments to a proposal for amendment to the Constitution do not go beyond the scope of the petition because House Rule 90 had been suspended. See HARRINGTON (*in joint session*), S. 1978, p. 1031; H. 1978, p. 1459.

For discussion of degree of vote necessary on amendments to Constitution, See Senate document numbered 1496 of 1971.

THE INITIATIVE. V. Sect. 1. Neither house has power to take a vote upon the enactment of a law introduced by initiative petition later than the day preceding the first Wednesday in June. NICHOLSON (acting President). S. 1945, p. 981, and O'NEILL, H. 1950, pp. 1474 and 1475. [These rulings were based on an opinion of the Justices of the Supreme Judicial Court. See S. 1945, p. 925.]

Affirmative action having been taken on an Initiative Amendment to the Constitution providing for biennial sessions of the General Court and for a biennial budget, it was held (*in joint session*) that a motion to reconsider such action must be entertained. MORAN (*in joint session*), S. 1935, p. 992, and H. 1935, p. 1289. [This ruling was confirmed by the Justices of the Supreme Judicial Court. See S. 1935, p. 1084.]

THE REFERENDUM. II. — That nothing would be gained by the adoption of the preamble of a bill, in view of an opinion of the Justices of the Supreme Judicial Court that the bill is not subject to a referendum petition. HULL, H. 1926, p. 874.

An amendment proposing a state wide referendum on any bill is not in order, for the reason that this Article of Amendment (XLVIII) repealed Article XLII (authorizing reference to the people of acts and resolves) and substituted therefor a new method of referendum by petition. CAHILL (acting Speaker), H. 1935, pp. 1080, 1740; WRAGG, S. 1938, p. 836. [See also DOLAN, S. 1949, p. 717.]

As to the power of the Governor in declaring an emergency law, see 299 Mass. 191.

GENERAL PROVISIONS. II. *Limitations on Signatures.*

As to the validity of an initiative petition concerning an excessive number of certified signatures, See OPINION OF JUSTICES, S. 1950, p. 1054.

For a discussion as to the constitutionality of an initiative petition brought pursuant to Article 48 of the Amendments to the Constitution of the Commonwealth, entitled "An Act to ascertain and carry out the will of the people in 1970 relative to the calling and holding of a *constitutional convention* in 1971 to deal with subjects limited to the revision, alteration and amendment of the structure of government and to the arrangement, simplification and methods of amending the constitution; and to provide for a preparatory commission thereof, see *Opinions of the Honorable, the Justices of the Supreme Judicial Court,* 1970.

ART. LVI. — As to certain procedure in case of the return of a bill by the Governor with a recommendation of amendment, and for action taken in accordance therewith. See S. 1919. pp 749, 750; Op. Att. Gen., Vol. V. (1919), p. 349.

As to the practice of recalling bills from the Governor by the Senate. SALTONSTALL, H. 1934, p. 710.

A bill must be returned to the branch in which it originated. FISH, S. 1934. p. 562.

The Governor is restricted to amendments which are germane to the original proposition. YOUNG, H. 1924, pp. 630-632; SALTONSTALL, H. 1936. p. 1573; HARRINGTON, S. J. 1974. p. 2006. For a complete ruling on the matter of a Governor's right on proposed amendments, see B. LORING YOUNG, H. J. 1924, pp. 630-632.

That returning a bill with a recommendation that it be referred for further consideration and study to a special commission is an evasion of the responsibility of the Governor. CAHILL, H. 1938. p. 1622.

That the action of the General Court is limited to "amendment and re-enactment," and a motion to refer to the next annual session is not in order. ALLEN, S. 1923, p. 764. HULL, H. 1927, p. 639.

That after a bill has been returned by the Governor, and action thereon postponed, it is too late to raise the point of order that the message of His Excellency is null and void having lacked a signature when received and read. SLATER WASHBURN (acting Speaker), H. 1927, p. 683.

"Within five days." [See Article LXXXX of the Amendments.] Simply leaving the papers in the clerk's office after it is closed on the fifth day is not sufficient. SALTONSTALL, H. 1936, pp. 1191, 1250. [See notes of Rulings on CHAP. I., SECT. I., ART. II.]

As to the danger of substituting a new bill for one returned by the Governor, see SALTONSTALL, H. 1931, p. 910 and H. 1932, p. 458.

That, when a bill is returned by His Excellency the Governor with a recommendation of amendment specified by him, a motion to place the message on file is improperly before the House for the reason that the Constitution provides that "Such bill or resolve shall thereupon be before the General Court and subject to amendment and re-enactment." HERTER, H. 1939, p. 895. [Changed to *ten* (10) days for Governor to return with Amendment — see Article LXXXX of the Amendments.] [Entire bill open to amendment — General Court not limited to Governor's amendment.]

ART. LXII. — That it was not within the province of the Chair to rule as to the constitutionality of a bill providing for the loaning of money of the Commonwealth to individuals. ARTHUR W. COOLIDGE, S. 1945, p. 1229. See H. J. 1964 Const. of elections.

The requirement of a two-thirds vote on a bill providing for the borrowing of money by the Commonwealth is at the enactment stage. FURBUSH, S. 1951, p. 1601.

That it is not the prerogative of the Chair to rule on the constitutionality of a pending bill which, if enacted, might result in pledging the credit of the Commonwealth in contravention to the prohibition contained in the Constitution. ARTESANI (acting Speaker). H. 1952, p. 1433.

ART. LXIII. — Special appropriation bills may be enacted, on recommendation of the Governor, before final action on the general appropriation bill. COTTON, S. 1939, p. 852.

After final action on the general appropriation bill, or on recommendation of the Governor, special appropriation bills may be enacted, but such bills shall provide the specific means for defraying the appropriations therein contained. See YOUNG, H. 1922, pp. 683-685.

That an amendment, providing for the appropriation of a sum of money for further continuing the special commission (including members of the General Court) established to investigate the existence and extent of organized crime and gambling and other related matters, was improperly before the House for the reason that it made an appropriation prior to the passage of the General Appropriation Bill. The Speaker stated that the question raised was whether the proposed amendment came within the exceptions provided in Article LXIII of the Amendments to the Constitution. Because of the constitutional nature of the question, he was of the opinion that it was beyond the province of the Chair to rule thereon. SKERRY, H. 1955, p. 2020.

That a bill providing a loan through the issuance of state bonds was not an "appropriation bill." SKERRY, H. 1955, p. 2075.

That a bill which provided for carrying out the provisions of the proposed act only "after an appropriation had been made therefor" is not a special appropriation bill. HERTER, H. 1939, p. 1940.

That a bill providing a twenty per cent increase for certain officers and employees in the service of the Commonwealth is not an appropriation bill. WILLIS, H. 1948, p. 1643. [For ruling of Supreme Judicial Court on definition of an "appropriation bill," see H. 1948, p. 1556.]

That a bill providing for "a distribution of funds" is not an appropriation bill. CAHILL, H. 1938, p. 1217. That a bill authorizing a department to expend money for state functions "without appropriation" is contrary to facts, for the reason that a state department cannot operate without an appropriation. CAHILL, H. 1938, p. 1217.

That there is no law, provision of the Constitution, or legislative rule which would bar the General Court from considering the revenue "Bill to provide for state activities" prior to the passage of the General Appropriation Bill, see GIBBONS, H. 1953, p. 855.

On a point of order that appropriations must be made by bill and not by resolve, it was ruled that while it was not within the province of the Chair to rule on a question of interpretation of the Constitution, a precedent had been established for appropriating money by resolve. COTTON (acting President), S. 1938, p. 1239.

That an amendment proposing the insertion in the general [or supplementary] appropriation bill of an item not included *in the budget* is out of order, and defining the words "in the budget." HULL, H. 1926, p. 327; CAHILL (acting Speaker), H. 1935, p. 581; GIBBONS, H. 1953, p. 1536 and H. 1954, p. 1343; SKERRY, H. 1955, pp. 2377, 2380, 2381, 2383; DONAHUE, S. 1969, p. 1510.

That an amendment to a supplemental appropriation bill was not beyond the scope of the Governor's message for the reason that Section 3 of Article LXIII of the Amendments to the Constitution states, in part, that "the General Court may increase, decrease, add or omit items in the budget." MCGEE. H. 1977, p. 1856.

That the General Court cannot narrow the Governor's power to disapprove items or parts of items in a budget, or to veto any other legislation laid before him, but "on the same hand . . . the powers of the legislature cannot be narrowed, and one of said powers has always been the right to amend recommendations submitted by the Governor." HARRINGTON. S. 1978, p. 84.

As to competency of amendments which would introduce into appropriation bills subject-matter in the nature of new legislation "not required for reasonable financial control," see SALTONSTALL. H. 1935, pp. 879, 889; CAHILL. H. 1937, p. 775. See also SALTONSTALL. H. 1934, p. 1273; H. 1935, p. 1637; H. 1936, pp. 886, 926.

That it is not the intention of the Constitution to limit or deny the authority of the General Court in its ability to act in relation to the General Appropriation Bill. HARRINGTON. S. 1978, p. 821; Bulger. S. 1979, p. 960; S. 1983, p. 185; S. 1984, p. 463; S. 1987, pp. 1324 and 1330; S. 1993, p. 597; BRENNAN (acting President). S. 1985, p. 248.

An amendment to a Bill providing for a transportation development and improvement program for the Commonwealth relative to certain sections relating to the duties of the Massachusetts Convention Center Authority for which there was no petition filed was ruled in order due to the wide flexibility given amendments to appropriations bills and that members of the Senate should be allowed to insert or omit items or sections based on the merits of the subject matter. They should not be denied the opportunity to debate and vote on measures unless the amendment offered is clearly and without question beyond the scope of the legislation pending. BULGER, S. 1983, p. 1413.

As to competency of amendments of appropriation bills "reserving specific amounts for certain purposes and otherwise limiting the discretion of the Governor and Council," see SALTONSTALL, H. 1936, pp. 886, 926.

"The Governor may disapprove or reduce items or parts of items in any bill appropriating money." But the right to disapprove "does not extend to the removal of restrictions imposed upon the use of the items appropriated." "No power is conferred to change the terms of an appropriation except by reducing the amount thereof." SALTONSTALL, H. 1936, pp. 1323, 1424. [This ruling was based on an opinion of the Justices of the Supreme Judicial Court (from which the quotations are made),— see H. 1936, p. 1418.] BARTLEY, H. 1974, p. 2381.

As to advisability of the House amending its rule so "that budgetary items may not be moved a second time (except under suspension of the rules), on the ground that the Constitution recognizes and provides for separate action on individual items of an appropriation bill, thus giving them a separate entity," see SALTONSTALL, H. 1936, p. 1599; CAHILL, H. 1937, p. 846.

As to reference of budget recommendations to the House committee on Ways and Means only, see CAHILL, H. 1938, p. 246.

[For discussion of "Budget — Powers of General Court and Executive" see Senate document numbered 1525 of 1973, by Norman L. Pidgeon, Senate Clerk and Parliamentarian.]

ART. LXXI. — For opinion relative to the appointment of commissioners to divide the Commonwealth into representative districts, see 157 Mass. 595 (SJC 1893); S. 1939, p. 935.

ART. LXXIX. — See Article XVII.

ART. LXXX. — The intent of this provision seems to be to provide for the continued representation in the General Court of the people of a particular district pending action by the House itself in determining the question by seating one of the two individuals or by providing for determining the incumbent by means of a special election. QUINN (acting Speaker), H. 1965, p. 388.

ART. LXXXI. — If the two houses fail to agree upon a time for holding a joint session to consider proposals for specific amendments to the Constitution, which has been called for by either house, the governor shall call the same. For opinion on whether certain proposals were properly before a joint session so called, see FURBUSH (*in joint session*), S. 1955, pp. 861, 929; H. 1955, pp. 1354, 1435. [See FURBUSH (in joint session), S. 1956, pp. 902, 930; H. 1956, pp. 1404, 1432.] [Statement POWERS, S. 1960, p. 939.]

That members in joint convention had no right to vote on an amendment relative to reducing the size of the House of Representatives for the reason that said House was malapportioned, see DONAHUE (*in joint session*), S. 1970, p. 724; H. 1970, p. 878.

Amendments to a proposal for amendment to the Constitution which go beyond the petition forming the basis for prayer, are not in order, see DONAHUE (*in joint session*), S. 1969, p. 1323; H. 1969, p. 1878.

For a discussion as to the constitutionality of an initiative petition brought pursuant to Article 48 of the

Amendments to the Constitution of the Commonwealth entitled "An Act to ascertain and carry out the will of the people in 1970 relative to the calling and holding of a *constitutional convention* in 1971 to deal with subjects limited to the revision, alteration and amendment of the structure of government and to the arrangement, simplification and methods of amending the constitution; and to provide for a preparatory commission thereof, see *Opinions of the Honorable, the Justices of the Supreme Judicial Court, 1970.* See Mass. 585. S. J. 1893.

ART. LXXXIX. — That an amendment to a pending bill which had been filed with the approval of the mayor and city council of the city of Boston would be in violation of the Home Rule Amendment to the Constitution. MCGEE (acting Speaker). H. 1974, p. 1654. Home Rule.

That an amendment to provide for placing a binding question question on the ballot went beyond the scope of the petitions upon which was based the Bill reorganizing the school committee of the city of Boston. VOKE (acting Speaker). H. 1991, p. 814.

For various rulings by Attorney General, see:

1969 - (Boston - rent control) - see House, No. 5667 of 1969 (printed in full in House Journal for August 14, 1969, page 2545).

1969 - (city and town charters) - see House, No. 5655 of 1969 (printed in full in House Journal for August 13, 1969, page 2524).

1969 - (Stadiums) - see House, No. 5668 of 1969 (printed in full in House Journal for August 14, 1969, page 2549).

1970 - (West Springfield - taking of water from town of Southwick) - see House, No. 5517 of 1970.

[For opinion of Attorney General on appointments to special commissions by Governor, President of the Senate and Speaker of the House of Representatives, see H.J. June 29, 1973 - or House document numbered 7097 of 1973.]

That a petition relative to reforming the charter of the city of Boston was properly referred to the committee on Local Affairs and was not subject to the provisions of Joint Rule 12 for the reason that said petition was accompanied by an attested copy of an order showing approval of the city council and the mayor of the city. MCGEE, H. 1977, p. 16.

That an amendment to the Senate Bill establishing the Boston water and sewer commission and defining the powers thereof was improperly before the House for the reason that the pending bill was filed with the approval of the mayor and city council as required by section 8 of Article 89 of the Amendments of the Constitution, and to make a substantive change in the bill would require further approval of the mayor and city council of the city of Boston. MCGEE, H. 1977, p. 1566. [For similar ruling on a Somerville bill, see MCGEE, H. 1978, p. 1267.]

NOTES OF RULINGS.

ON THE

SENATE RULES

ORGANIZATION.

The election of the presiding officer being the first business necessary for the organization of the Senate, an order providing that the Senate proceed forthwith to the election of a President and determining the method of holding the election is in order even though no rules have been adopted to govern the Senate. HALEY (preliminary Chairman), S. 1949, pp. 4, 13, 14. See also pp. 27, 32.

An order for the appointment of a special committee to appoint committees was ruled out of order prior to the organization of the Senate, as business cannot be transacted by a legislative assembly until it is duly organized, the three essential parts of which are the qualification of the members, and the choice of the presiding and recording officers. MORAN (preliminary Chairman), S. 1935, p. 4.

THE PRESIDENT.

For opinion of the Justices of the Supreme Judicial Court relative to the term for which officers of the Senate may be elected, see S. 1922, p. 3. See also Op. Att. Gen. H. 1921, p. 1027.

The President has no power, either by general parliamentary law or by special authority vested in him by the Senate, to cause any document to be printed or distributed, or to prevent any document from being printed or distributed; and, upon the simple request of a member of the Senate, he has no authority to issue an order for the Sergeant-at-Arms to remove from the desks and files of the senators a report, portions of which are claimed to be unparliamentary. CROCKER, S. 1883, pp. 489, 575.

Under the rules of the Senate, and under the rules of general parliamentary procedure, the duties of the presiding officer are many. Several of these duties are: (a) to preserve order and decorum; (b) to restrain the members, when they are engaged in debate, within the rules of order; (c) to see that disorderly conduct of whatever nature is stopped; and (d) if the offending member persists in misconduct, the presiding officer is then *compelled* to invoke disciplinary action.

If a member violates the rules of the Senate by continually interrupting members in debate and thereby harassing the entire Senate, a member may arise to a point of order. BULGER, S. 1981, p. 1294.

While it is competent for a member of this branch to utilize the rules of procedure, once it becomes apparent to the presiding officer that said rules are being used in a dilatory manner and in such a way as to prevent the full body from taking action on the matter, it then becomes incumbent upon the presiding officer to rule the motion out of order so that the Senate may proceed to the business at hand and come to a conclusion of the question. BULGER, S. 1979, pp. 578, 1619; S. 1980, p. 418; S. 1981, p. 64; S. 1982, p. 903; S. 1983, pp. 507, 1312; S. 1985, pp. 903, 1708. FOLEY (acting President), S. 1982, p. 895; S. 1983, p. 465.

[For power of President to declare informal sessions or call off sessions, see Senate Rule 5A.]

CLERK.

[Senate Clerk shall be official Parliamentarian — see Senate Rule 7A.]

Rule 8. The suspension of this rule by itself does not take a bill out of the possession of the Clerk, nor does it preclude reconsideration moved in accordance with Senate Rule 53. JONES, S. 1904, p. 802; COTTON, S. 1939, p. 435; FURBUSH, S. 1951, p. 1349.

This rule does not apply to a bill which is referred to the committee on Ways and Means under the Senate rule relating to bills involving the expenditure of public money. SMITH, S. 1900, p. 885.

See notes to House Rule 70.

"*Except petitions, bills and resolves introduced on leave, orders,*" etc. As to the reason for these exceptions and their effect, see LORING, S. 1873, pp. 295, 299. It would seem that the right to reconsider the enactment of a bill, the reference of a petition or bill, or the adoption of an order, should expire when the bill, petition or order passes out of the hands of the Clerk.

[This rule was omitted in 1969, but the mere fact that the rule no longer exists in no way takes away or diminishes the right of a member to move reconsideration, as long as the papers can be made available.]

MEMBERS OF THE SENATE.

Rule 10. In the case of a bill relative to the common use of tracks by two or more street railway companies it was held that it was not a matter in which the private right of a senator who was president of a street railway company could be said to be immediately concerned as distinct from the public interest. CHAPPLE, S. 1907, p. 730.

A senator may vote on a measure affecting his private right if the vote is cast against his own pecuniary interest. FISH, S. 1934, p. 716.

In the case of a bill providing for the election by the General Court of the commissioners of the Department of Public Utilities, it was held that the private right of a member of the Senate who was a director of a division under the control of said commissioners was not distinct from the public interest. MORAN, S. 1935, p. 487.

The proper time tó raise a point of order questioning the right of a member to vote on account of interest is after the vote has been recórded and before the result is announced. WRAGG, S. 1938, p. 502.

For a case in which the private right of a member was declared to be immediate and distinct from the public interest, see WRAGG, S. 1938, p. 502.

See S. J. 1973, May 16.

See also notes to Senate Rule 56 and House Rule 63.

COMMITTEES.

Rule 12. For sundry rulings as to committees, see notes on Joint Rules "Committees" and "Sundry Rulings."

"*A committee on Ways and Means*" (*formerly "on the Treasury*"). See notes to House Rules 20, 25.

For ruling on inability to dictate type of report committee should make. KEVIN B. HARRINGTON, S. J. May 9, 1973.

Rule 13A. An order relating to procedure of the Senate is exempt from this rule. MORAN, S. 1935, p. 1181.

Rule 13B. The call for a minority caucus does not change or alter Senate Rule 42, which prohibits the interruption of a member while speaking. BOVERINI (acting President). S. 1991, p. 94.

Rule 15. A bill relating to the taxation of telegraph companies was held not to come within the provisions of this section, although it appeared that there might be but one such company in existence. HARTWELL, S. 1889, p. 732.

A bill to abolish an office in the State service was held not to come within the provisions of this rule. GOODWIN, S. 1941, p. 1415.

See also notes to House Rule 31 and Joint Rule 8.

Rule 16. A special act, as distinguished from a general law, is one which directly affects individuals as such differently from the class to which they belong or from the people at large. PILLSBURY, S. 1885, pp. 588, 589. It is not within the province of the Chair to rule that the object of an application can be secured under existing laws, or without detriment to the public interests by a general law. This question must be determined by the committee (PILLSBURY, S. 1885, p. 588; HARWOOD [acting President], S. 1899, p. 249). unless it appears on the face of the papers that the object can be secured under existing laws. PILLSBURY, S. 1886, p. 700. For a case in which it was held not to be allowable to substitute a general law for a special act, see PILLSBURY, S. 1885, p. 589.

Amendments which, if adopted, would change the character of a general bill to a special bill are not in order. PINKERTON, S. 1893, p. 505; LAWRENCE, S. 1897, p. 427; HENRY G. WELLS, S. 1915, p. 501; McKNIGHT, S. 1919, p. 1139; WRAGG, S. 1938, p. 489; COTTON, S. 1939, p. 1235; POWERS, S. 1963, p. 1663; KEVIN B. HARRINGTON (acting President). S. 1966, p. 394; DONAHUE, S. 1966, p. 1609; BULGER, S. 1979, p. 1242.

A bill applying to only one city or town is special in its application, and cannot be offered as an amendment to an adverse report of a committee on a petition for general legislation applying to the entire Commonwealth. SMITH, S. 1900, p. 873; JONES, S. 1903, p. 491; GOODWIN, S. 1941, p. 1300.

Upon the question whether a proposed amendment would change a bill from a general to a special law, see SOULE, S. 1901, p. 543.

A bill relating to the appointment of certain officers of the city of Boston was held not to be a special bill. JONES, S. 1904, p. 210.

An amendment affecting all permanent positions in a State commission was held to be special in its application. FURBUSH, S. 1951, p. 1489.

A bill which applied to any and all officials of a specified city was held to be a "special act" and not a "general law" and, therefore, not applicable to, because broader than the scope of, a petition which sought legislation relative to one particular official of that city. WELLINGTON WELLS, S. 1926, p. 494.

A new draft offered as a substitute for a bill based on petitions for special legislation was laid aside on a point of order as it was beyond the scope of the petitions and could not be considered a general bill as it did not accomplish the result desired by the petitioners. COTTON, S. 1939, p. 1164.

This rule applies to resolves as well as bills, so that a resolve which is special in its application should not be reported or moved as a substitute for one that is general in nature. A committee to which is referred a resolve, special in nature, should if feasible report a general resolve.

Amendments to a general bill which, if adopted, would eliminate certain counties, cities or towns from the provisions thereof, or which make the bill applicable to only certain cities and towns, are not in order as they would have the effect of converting said general bill into a special act. See COTTON, S. 1939, pp. 711, 1340; NICHOLSON, S. 1947, p. 675; DOLAN, S. 1949, pp. 437,

452; FURBUSH. S. 1951. p. 584; KEVIN B. HARRINGTON (acting President). S. 1966, p. 394.

However, an amendment to a general bill which would eliminate all cities of a specific classification from the provisions thereof, would be in order. DOLAN, S. 1949, p. 484.

That an amendment of the House Bill increasing the amount of contract assistance which may be provided by the Commonwealth to finance agreements with railroads to provide for passenger service to and from Boston for an extended period, was not in order for the reason that it would convert a general bill into a special bill. KEVIN B. HARRINGTON (acting President), S. 1967, p. 591.

That an amendment to substitute a "Bill abolishing the Walden Pond State Reservation Commission and transferring the care and maintenance of the Walden Pond State Reservation to the Department of Natural Resources", was laid aside for the reason that the bill was special and the petition upon which the matter was based, was general in nature. DONAHUE, S. 1967, p. 681. A resolution which is special in nature should not be reported upon one general in its application.

See also S. 1967, pp. 2200, 2228, 2230; S. 1970, p. 1375, with relation to special and general bills.

See notes to Senate Rule 50, House Rules 30 and 31, Joint Rule 7 and Sundry Rulings.

FORM OF BILLS AND RESOLVES.

Rule 17. Objection that this rule is violated cannot be sustained in the case of a House bill. PILLSBURY, S. 1885, p. 582.

INTRODUCTION OF BUSINESS.

[See Senate Rule 18 — Petitions introduced by members.]

Rule 19. Under this rule a bill based on a resolution was laid aside, for the reason that a resolution differs from a bill or resolve in that it is simply an expression of opinion by the General Court, has but one reading and is not laid before the Governor for his approval. CHAPPLE, S. 1907, p. 900.

Resolutions are not the proper vehicle for adopting rules of procedure for state offices and agencies. BULGER, S. 1982, p. 1024.

A bill reported on a joint order was laid aside. COGSWELL, S. 1878, p. 178.

A bill substituted by the House for an order was laid aside. NICHOLSON, S. 1947, p. 1245.

An order providing for the appointment of members of the General Court to make an investigation cannot be amended to include "persons to be appointed by the Governor". ARTHUR W. COOLIDGE, S. 1945, p. 720.

An order requesting opinions of the Honorable the Justices of the Supreme Judicial Court could not be substituted, in part, for local aid resolutions because the resolutions were simply declaring the intent of the Senate, were non-binding in nature and not a proper matter to be submitted to the court for opinions. BULGER, S. 1986, p. 55.

A bill which had been reported to the House and passed to be engrossed by that branch was laid aside by the Senate as the petition upon which it was purported to have been based had not been concurrently referred to the committee. WELLINGTON WELLS, S. 1927, p. 530.

A motion to substitute a resolve for an order is in order if the order is based on a petition properly introduced. WRAGG, S. 1938, p. 500.

Concurrent reference of the report of a State officer to committees for consideration is sufficient basis for legislation even though the report may not have been made in strict compliance with the General Laws. ARTHUR W. COOLIDGE, S. 1945. p. 810.

Rule 20. This rule requires that petitions for legislation be referred to "appropriate committees", but the fact that a petition has not been considered by the proper committee would not invalidate legislation which is reported on a petition regularly referred to any committee. FISH, S. 1933. p. 478.

The committee on Rules is required to report not later than the fourth legislative day succeeding the day of their deposit with the committee on any order or resolution referred to it under this rule. FURBUSH, S. 1951. p. 1788; BULGER, S. 1981. p. 366.

In order to come before the Senate (after the four day discharge period) the committee must make a report. BOVERINI, S. 1990. p. 401.

Resolutions relative to a prompt prorogation of the Senate were a proper matter to be referred to the committee on Rules, under the rule, even if they deal with procedure. BULGER, S. 1983. p. 1058.

See notes on "Committees" under "Sundry Rulings."

Rule 23. See notes to House Rule 47.

"Unless received from the House of Representatives." A bill coming from the House must be entertained even though it is not germane to the petition upon which it is based. PINKERTON, S. 1893. p. 470.

See notes on "Courtesy between the Branches" under "Sundry Rulings."

See statement of DONAHUE on "Introduced on Leave", S. 1967. p. 623.

Rule 24. For cases in which an order has been held to be unparliamentary in form, see SPRAGUE, S. 1890, p. 189; PILLSBURY, S. 1886. p. 140.

An order fixing the daily hour of meeting is not subject to this rule. FURBUSH, S. 1955, p. 1398.

A motion to lay on the table is a renewable motion and once debate or new information has come to the attention of the Chair, the motion to lay on the table is a proper motion at that time. FOLEY (acting President), S. 1981, p. 487.

COURSE OF PROCEEDINGS.

Rule 27. It is the duty of the committee to which bills or resolves have been referred under this rule, to report only "on their relation to the finances of the Commonwealth" and they may not recommend the addition of new subject-matter. NICHOLSON (acting President), S. 1945, p. 1002; NICHOLSON, S. 1947, p. 1176; FURBUSH, S. 1955, p. 521; HOLMES (acting President), S. 1956, p. 1282. [See FURBUSH, S. 1951, p. 1554.]

The question being on ordering to a third reading or passing to be engrossed a bill involving the *expenditure* of public money, and a point of order being raised that the bill had not been referred to the committee on Ways and Means, it was so referred. SMITH, S. 1898, p. 759; DANA, S. 1906, p. 517; GREENWOOD, S. 1912, p. 1373; MCKNIGHT, S. 1919, p. 356; S. 1920, p. 376; MORAN, S. 1935, p. 644; RICHARDSON, S. 1948, p. 652; DOLAN, S. 1949, p. 1302; FURBUSH, S. 1952, p. 334; BULGER, S. 1983, p. 1072; S. 1987, p. 1014; S. 1990, p. 404; S. 1991, p. 304; S. 1992. p. 577.

On a bill to increase the maximum speed limit in the Commonwealth, a motion to refer the bill to the committee on Ways and Means after it had been amended was in order because the bill had been amended and the motion to refer is a renewable motion. BULGER, S. 1990, p. 453.

After a bill has been passed to be engrossed, however, it is too late to raise a point of order that it should have been referred, under this rule. FURBUSH, S. 1956, p. 538.

A point of order having been raised that a bill *indirectly* involving the expenditure of public money, having had its third reading, had not been referred to the committee on Ways and Means, it was so referred. BACON, S. 1932, p. 425.

The question being on adopting an order which authorized the expenditure of public money for a special committee, and a point of order being raised that the order should have been referred to the committee on Ways and Means, it was so referred. EVANS (acting President), S. 1951, p. 1591; FURBUSH, S. 1951, p. 1724.

A bill having been referred to the committee on Ways and Means under this rule and having been reported by said committee, it is too late to raise the point of order that the bill does not come under the requirements of the rule. NICHOLSON (acting President), S. 1946, p. 939.

For an opinion relative to the limitations of this rule and to the authority of the committee to report thereunder, see MCKNIGHT, S. 1920, p. 797.

It was held that the rule did not apply to a bill which provided for the *payment of money to the Commonwealth.* See WELLINGTON WELLS, S. 1925, p. 609.

A bill to extend the time for filing returns of taxable property by foreign corporations was held not to come within the scope of this rule. HENRY G. WELLS, S. 1918, p. 487.

Exempting from taxation a certain sort of income does not involve the expenditure of public money or a grant of public property, under this rule. ALLEN, S. 1921, p. 298.

It was held that a provision in a bill requiring the State Secretary to furnish cards at cost to registrars did not come under this rule. WRAGG, S. 1937, p. 748.

A bill to establish two districts for the administration of criminal law in place of one was ruled to come within the provisions of this rule and was referred to the committee on Counties on the part of the Senate. COTTON, S. 1939, p. 1178.

General bills involving the expenditure of city or town money do not come under this rule, but only bills affecting a particular city or town. HOLMES, S. 1957, p. 519.

Under this rule, committees may report adversely or may recommend an investigation of the subject-matter referred to them. ARTHUR W. COOLIDGE, S. 1945, pp. 1116, 1144, 1199; NICHOLSON, S. 1947, p. 1201; RICHARDSON, S. 1948, p. 693; HOLMES, S. 1957, p. 1296.

A resolve substituted for a bill which already had been considered by the committee on Ways and Means, was held to be a "different measure from that acted upon by the committee on Ways and Means; that it was a measure 'involving the expenditure of public money'; and that, under this rule, it should be referred to the committee on Ways and Means." WELLINGTON WELLS (acting President), S. 1923, p. 785.

A bill may be referred to the committee on Ways and Means, on motion, even though it does not appear to definitely involve the expenditure of public money. RICHARDSON, S. 1948, p. 988; DOLAN, S. 1949, p. 741.

For a case in which the committee on Ways and Means exceeded its authority in recommending certain amendments, see POWERS, S. 1963, p. 1818; BULGER, S. 1980, p. 982; S. 1982, p. 214; S. 1983, p. 1054.

That a bill increasing the minimum salary of public school teachers, which was amended to provide that the Commonwealth assume the cost of the increased minimum, was held to come under the provisions of this rule and was referred to the committee on Ways and Means. DONAHUE, S. 1967, p. 1016.

"Senate Rule 27 requires bills to be accompanied by a fiscal note when, in the opinion of the committee on Ways and Means, the cost would exceed the sum of one hundred thousand dollars. In the absence of a fiscal note, it appears that it is the judgment of the committee on Ways and Means that one is not required." BULGER, S. 1979, p. 1576; S. 1986, p. 263; S. 1989, p. 1747; S. 1990, p. 321. *Contra,* FOLEY (acting President), S. 1983, p. 252; BRENNAN (acting President), S. 1986, p. 185; BULGER, S. 1987, pp. 1472, 1709.

See also notes on House Rule 44.

Rule 27A. Senate Rule 27A does not require that the bill appear on the Calendar, only that it "be in print and available to the members of the Senate at least five days prior to the date specified for action." BRENNAN (acting President), S. 1986, p. 438.

Rule 28. The subsequent rejection of a bill substituted for a report of a committee recommending "no legislation" does not revive the question upon the adoption of the recommendation of the report. The requirement that every bill shall be read three times does not render the substitution liable to be nullified by the rejection of the bill at a subsequent stage. BISHOP, S. 1881, p. 212.

Rule 31. For a case in which a bill was held to have been substantially changed, see SMITH, S. 1900, p. 487.

[See Senate document numbered 1053 of 1963 for discussion of this rule.]

Rule 33. Notwithstanding this rule, a motion to instruct the committee to report on a bill forthwith is in order. For sundry other rulings in a case in which, such instructions having been given and not having been complied with, some of the members of the committee were held to be in contempt, see JONES, S. 1903, pp. 769, 771, 778.

It is within the authority of the committee to recommend the adoption of a new emergency preamble in place of the one in the bill. HOLMES (acting President), S. 1955, p. 1629.

It is not necessary for an amendment to be approved by the committee on Bills in the Third Reading as being correctly drawn prior to its consideration by the body; but that a bill, if so amended, would subsequently be referred, under the rule, to the committee for examination. BOVERINI (acting President), S. 1986, p. 1033.

For a case in which the committee on Bills in the Third Reading exceeded its authority, see ARTHUR W. COOLIDGE, S. 1946, p. 1014; BULGER, S. 1979, p. 1165.

ORDERS OF THE DAY.

See note to House Rule 61.

RULES OF DEBATE.

See notes upon this division of the House Rules.

See paper on retaining floor after adjournment due to lack of quorum, by Norman L. Pidgeon, Advisor to Senate, S. 1976, p. 1941.

Rule 39. A member by yielding the floor to another member cannot thus transfer to the latter the right to the floor. Such right can only be secured through compliance with the rule. CHAPPLE, S. 1908, p. 696.

In a case in which pursuant to a standing order, the Senate adjourned while a member was speaking, it was

766 Notes of Rulings

held that such member was not in consequence thereof
entitled to the floor when the subject was again taken up.
CHAPPLE, S. 1908, p. 1139.

It is not necessary for a member to be in his seat in
order to raise objection to a request for unanimous
consent. HOLMES (acting President), S. 1956, p. 349;
BULGER, S. 1991, p. 1181.

Although this rule requires a member to address the
President, under Senate Rule 40, if more than one
member rises at the same time, the President has the
authority to designate the one who is entitled to the
floor, even though he has not verbally addressed the
Chair. HOLMES (acting President), S. 1956, p. 1656.

Resolutions condemning a member by name for certain actions not taken, were ruled in violation of this
rule. BULGER, S. 1981, p. 932.

It is *not* in order at *any* time during debate to impugn
the motives of any member of the Senate. BULGER,
S. 1981, p. 1224.

Rule 41. The principle of this rule, although exempli-
fying the principles of general parliamentary procedure,
was held not to apply in debate prior to the organization
of the Senate and the adoption of its rules for the current
year. MORAN (acting President), S. 1935, p. 6.

MOTIONS.

See notes upon this division of the House Rules.

A motion in its nature trivial and absurd will not be
entertained. SPRAGUE, S. 1890, p. 189; PILLSBURY,
S. 1886, p. 140. See also NICHOLSON, S. 1947, p. 1108.

The Senate having passed a general order that the
reading of the Journal should be dispensed with unless
otherwise ordered, it was held that a senator could not

require the reading of the Journal without a vote to that effect, and that a motion that the Journal be read was not a question of privilege. CROCKER, S. 1883, p. 290.

APPEALS. When Cushing was by rule the sole authority governing the Senate, it was held, in accordance with Cushing's Law, and Practice of Legislative Assemblies (Sect. 1467), that a question on an appeal could be laid on the table; and if such action was taken, the matter, whatever it was, which gave rise to the appeal, proceeded as if no appeal had been taken. CROCKER, S. 1883, pp. 288, 289. In the House it has been held that a motion to lay an appeal on the table is not in order. See MARDEN, H. 1883, p. 582. See also notes to House Rule 94.

It is to be noted that the Senate was required to follow Cushing's statement of Parliamentary Law, while the House, by its Rule 101, was simply required to conform to the rules of parliamentary practice.

In Crocker's Principles of Procedure it is held that an appeal cannot be laid upon the table separately from the proceedings out of which the point of order arose. Crocker's Principles of Procedure, Sect. 94.

Rule 44. A motion for a second legislative day does not have to be in writing. FURBUSH, S. 1956, p. 1227.

Rule 45. For an instance in which it was held that the adoption of an amendment inserting certain words precluded, except through reconsideration, striking out such words in part at the same stage of the bill, see SMITH, S. 1900, p. 530.

Rule 46. *"To adjourn."* A motion to adjourn is in order at any time. ARTHUR W. COOLIDGE, S. 1945, p. 1238.

It was held that when, upon a motion to adjourn, the yeas and nays had begun before the time fixed for

adjournment and had ended after that time, and the
Senate had voted in the negative upon the motion, the
refusal to adjourn had the effect of suspending the
operation of the order relative to adjournment, and was
equivalent to otherwise ordering. MORSE (acting
President), S. 1896, p. 912.

A motion to adjourn having been lost, a second
motion to adjourn was held not to be in order when the
only intervening business had been the rejection of a
motion to postpone further consideration of the pending
bill. DANA, S. 1906, p. 496.

For a case in which it was ruled that a motion to take
a recess was in order at any time. See WRAGG, S. 1938,
p. 928.

A motion to take a recess having been made and
action thereon having been delayed beyond the time
proposed, the motion was laid aside. FURBUSH, S. 1952
(Extra Session), p. 18.

A motion to adjourn to the first day of the following
legislative session was ruled out of order because when
the legislature is duly convened it cannot be adjourned
sine die or dissolved except in a manner prescribed by
the Constitution. FONSECA (acting President), S. 1983,
p. 1127.

See notes on House Rule 79.

"Or some other motion which has precedence."
Where the Senate assigned one matter for 2:30 P.M., and
one matter for 3:00 P.M., it was held to be the duty of
the presiding officer to call up the second assignment at
3:00 P.M., even though the consideration of the first
assignment was not finished. PITMAN, S. 1869, p. 316.

See notes to House Rule 80.

"To lay on the table." Pending the consideration of
one of the Orders of the Day, a motion to lay the Orders
of the Day on the table, is admissible. CROCKER, S. 1883,
p. 287.

A motion to postpone laying the Orders on the table is inadmissible. CROCKER, S. 1883, p. 287.

A motion to lay a bill on the table is in order pending a motion to refer the bill to the next General Court. COTTON, S. 1939, p. 586.

When Cushing was the sole authority governing the Senate, it was held that, if a motion to reconsider is laid upon the table, or is postponed to a specified time, the pending bill does not go with it. See PINKERTON, S. 1893, p. 627. *Contra,* see Crocker's Principles of Procedure, Sect. 62, and appendix note thereto. See also Senate Rule 62.

For an instance where a motion to *take from the table* was made by a person not making the motion to lay the matter on the table, see S. 1970, pp. 1961, 2118.

"*To close debate at a specified time.*" See notes to Senate Rule 47 and House Rule 80.

After the time for closing debate has arrived, the taking of the question cannot be postponed by a motion to adjourn or to commit, or that the Journal be read, and these motions cannot then be entertained. CROCKER, S. 1883, pp. 288, 289.

If a motion to close debate in one hour is reconsidered, the question does not recur upon the original motion, because that motion, owing to the lapse of time, is out of order. The debate will proceed without limitation unless a new motion to close it is made. PILLSBURY, S. 1885, p. 589.

"*To postpone to a day certain.*" A motion to postpone to a certain day having been negatived, the Chair may entertain a motion to postpone to a different day. NICHOLSON (acting President), S. 1945, p. 1018.

"*To commit (or recommit).*" A motion to recommit, with instructions to report a bill broader in its scope than the measures upon which the bill is based, is out of order. PINKERTON, S. 1892, p. 266.

"*To Amend.*" For discussion of "motion to amend" see Senate document numbered 1535 of 1972, by Norman L. Pidgeon, Senate Clerk and Parliamentarian.

A substitute which, by Rule 28, must have three several readings on three successive days, can be amended in the second degree. H. H. COOLIDGE, S. 1870, p. 416.

A proposed substitute bill can be amended, and should be perfected, before the question is taken on substitution. NICHOLSON, S. 1947, p. 232; RICHARDSON, S. 1948, p. 724; KEVIN B. HARRINGTON, S. 1970 (acting President), p. 1822; DONAHUE, S. 1970, p. 1846.

It is not out of order to substitute an entire bill for another entire bill. BRASTOW, S. 1868, p. 48. See also Senate Rule 28.

The substitution of a question on the rejection of an order for a question on the passage of the order is not a parliamentary substitution, because one is simply the negative of the other. CROCKER, S. 1883, pp. 575, 578.

If an amendment has been once rejected, the same or substantially the same amendment cannot again be moved at the same stage of the bill, but the rejection of the amendment may be reconsidered. HOWLAND (acting President), S. 1886, p. 611; BRADFORD (acting President), S. 1895, p. 715; GREENWOOD, S. 1912, p. 1553; CALVIN COOLIDGE, S. 1914, p. 930; GLOVSKY (acting President), S. 1956, p. 771; FURBUSH, S. 1956, p. 774.

If a new draft is substituted for a bill, it is not in order, at the same reading of the bill, to offer amendments which would convert the bill into a bill substantially the same as the bill for which the new draft was substituted. RICHARDSON, S. 1950, p. 1375; FURBUSH, S. 1951, p. 1353.

A motion is not in order to insert words previously stricken out by amendment or to strike out words previously inserted by amendment at the same stage of the bill. NICHOLSON, S. 1947, pp. 1159, 1197.

The substitution of a new draft for a bill is in effect striking out the entire text of the bill and inserting a new text. Inasmuch as words which are inserted by amendment cannot be stricken out in whole or in part, a substitute bill cannot be amended by striking out any of the words contained therein, unless the bill has been advanced to another reading. FURBUSH, S. 1951, pp. 1617, 1722.

An amendment adding a new section cannot be further amended at the same reading. HOLMES (acting President), S. 1955, pp. 944, 954.

See also an amendment embodying a rejected amendment cannot be entertained at the same stage. PINKERTON, S. 1893, p. 471; ROWE (acting President), S. 1947, p. 1179. As to whether an amendment is similar to one previously acted upon, see SOULE, S. 1901, p. 989; NICHOLSON, S. 1947, p. 1198.

An amendment which has been rejected at one stage of a bill can be offered again at a subsequent stage. JONES, S. 1903, p. 941; CHAPPLE, S. 1907, pp. 1004, 1095. So also action on an amendment at one stage of a bill can be reversed at a subsequent stage. ARTHUR W. COOLIDGE, S. 1946, p. 744; HOLMES (acting President), S. 1946, p. 867; RICHARDSON, S. 1948, p. 900.

It is not within the province of the Chair to rule as to the form or effect of an amendment. RICHARDSON, S. 1950, p. 1563.

That amendments which go beyond the scope of a message from the Governor are not in order. DONAHUE, S. 1969. pp. 1847. 1957.

That an amendment to Senate Resolutions urging the retention of the United States District Attorney calling for state Constitutional officers to stop their delay in appointing an Inspector General was ruled out of order because a matter which had been finally rejected cannot be admitted under the color of an amendment. BULGER, S. 1981. p. 63.

That an amendment is not in order for the reason that it is not proper to provide that acts of the General Court become effective contingent upon other states adopting the same provisions.

[For procedure relating to certain amendments in the Senate, see Senate document numbered 1535 of 1972, by Norman L. Pidgeon, Senate Clerk and Parliamentarian.]

"To refer to the next annual session." A motion to amend has precedence over this motion. NICHOLSON, S. 1947. p. 1198. [Motion to refer to next annual session repealed.]

This motion may be applied to an order for consideration in joint session of a proposal for an Amendment to the Constitution. FURBUSH, S. 1952. p. 761.

"To rescind." — For discussion of "motion to rescind" — see Senate document numbered 1535 of 1972, by Norman L. Pidgeon, Senate Clerk and Parliamentarian.

See notes to Senate Rule 45 and House Rule 90.

Rule 47. A motion to close debate in one hour is in order although a standing order requires adjournment before the expiration of the hour, and, if the Senate adjourns before the time allowed for debate has elapsed, the bill when again considered is open for debate for such portion of the hour as had not elapsed at the time of adjournment. CROCKER, S. 1883, p. 286; CHAPPLE. S. 1908, p. 735.

A motion having been adopted to close debate on the main question in one hour, and that time having expired, debate is not permissible on any subsidiary question. FURBUSH, S. 1956, p. 1209.

Rule 49. An amendment to an engrossed bill is not in order unless this rule has been suspended. COTTON, S. 1939, p. 433.

Rule 50. According to Cushing's Manual, Sect. 102, amendments proposing subjects different from those under consideration would be in order if they were not excluded by special rule. *Contra,* see Crocker's Principles of Procedure, Sect. 44. See also BRASTOW, S. 1868, p. 51; KEVIN B. HARRINGTON (acting President). S. 1966, p. 394.

For sundry cases in which a point of order has been raised that a proposed amendment is not germane to the subject under consideration, see the indices to the Senate Journals under "Order, Questions of." A list of cases which arose prior to 1902 may be found in the Manual of the General Court for that year.

If a committee reports only in part, amendments must be germane to that portion of the subject which is reported on. CROCKER, S. 1883, p. 86.

Amendments are admissible if they are germane to any portion of the subject-matter which is the basis of a committee's report. SPRAGUE, S. 1891, p. 715. [See also SOULE, S. 1901, p. 1049.]

An amendment may be inadmissible on the ground that it introduces a subject different from that under consideration, although it would operate as a limitation on the terms of the bill. BUTLER, S. 1894, pp. 644, 656-658.

A proposal to ascertain the will of the people with reference to the subject-matter, and provide for a report to the General Court, upon which legislation could be based, must be held to be germane, even though not requested by the petitioners. WRAGG, S. 1937, p. 928; H. J. 1938, p. 844.

Inasmuch as a bill coming from the House must be entertained, even though it is not germane to the petition upon which it is based, it seems that in such cases amendments which are germane to the bill are admissible, although they may not be germane to the petition. PINKERTON, S. 1893, p. 493. See also notes to Senate Rule 23. This does not, however, give the second branch the right to exceed the provisions contained in the bill coming from the first branch.

An amendment which, if adopted, would render the bill inoperative, may nevertheless be germane. PINKERTON, S. 1893, p. 556.

Amendments changing a special act into a general law are admissible because, under Senate Rule 16, the committee could have reported a general law. PINKERTON, S. 1892, p. 707.

Also, amendments to a general bill which are special in nature are not in order. KEVIN B. HARRINGTON (acting President), S. 1966, p. 394.

That a special act cannot be reported upon, or substituted for an adverse report of a committee upon, a petition for general legislation is a well established principle of legislative procedure, not that the special act is beyond the scope of the petition, which upon the principle that the greater is inclusive of the lesser cannot be said to be true, but that in specializing the legislation prayed for and restricting its operation to particular individuals or corporations a different question is presented from that which extends its operation to individuals or corporations as a class. JONES, S. 1903, p. 491.

After an amendment has been adopted, the objection that the bill in its amended form is broader than the scope of the petition on which it is based, cannot be entertained. BUTLER, S. 1895, p. 473.

It is too late to raise the objection that an amendment is not germane if the amendment has been considered and voted on at a previous stage of the bill. LAWRENCE, S. 1897, p. 848; ARTHUR W. COOLIDGE *(in joint session),* S. 1946, p. 995, and H. 1946, p. 1381.

That it is in order to eliminate exemptions from a tax bill just as it is in order to provide exemptions. KEVIN B. HARRINGTON (acting President), S. 1966, p. 396.

See S. J. 1973, January 8 and 9, for ruling on amendments to "Resolutions memorializing Congress."

See also notes to Senate Rule 16 and House Rule 90.

For cases where an amendment recommended by the Governor under Article LVI of the Amendments to the Constitution was ruled out of order as beyond the scope of the bill, see H. J. 1936, pp. 1573-1574; KEVIN B. HARRINGTON, S. J. 1974, p. 2006.

For a complete ruling on the matter of a Governor's right on proposed amendments, see B. LORING YOUNG, H. J. 1924, pp. 630-632.

Rule 51. Prior to the adoption of this rule it was held that the smallest sum and the longest time must be put first. COGSWELL, S. 1897, p. 376.

See notes to House Rule 91.

Rule 52. *"Not exceeding ten minutes shall be allowed for debate."* Time consumed in taking the question on a motion to adjourn is not to be deducted from the ten minutes allowed for the debate. CROCKER, S. 1883, p. 288.

See notes to Senate Rule 46 and House Rules 79, 80.

RECONSIDERATION.

Rule 53. The right to move a reconsideration is not limited to those who voted with the majority on the motion which is to be reconsidered. DANA, S. 1906, p. 500.

President LORING (S. 1873, p. 299) went so far as to say that there is no reconsideration of votes to commit petitions, etc.; but it would seem that a better position to take would be that there can be no reconsideration after such petition, etc., has actually been handed over by the Clerk to the committee. See SMITH, S. 1900, p. 885.

The same would be true, *mutatis mutandis* with reference to enacted bills. In the case of the latter, a method usually adopted is to request the Governor to return the bill, and then reconsider its enactment. See note to Constitution, Chap. I., Sect. I., Art. II.

The chair, having asked if there was objection to proceeding to the Orders of the Day, and hearing no objection, had read the first number in the Calendar, and a point of order having been raised that it was too late to move reconsideration of a matter, ruled that no action had been taken on the Orders of the Day and that the motion to reconsider could be entertained. RICHARDSON, S. 1950, p. 1548.

A motion to reconsider a vote recalling a bill from the Governor is not in order after the bill has been taken from the Governor's office. FISH, S. 1934, p. 578. See Senate Rule 8 and notes thereto.

As to the effect of a reconsideration of a vote to close debate at a specified time, see PILLSBURY, S. 1885, p. 589.

Previous to the change made in 1902, in a case where a bill had been amended and rejected, and when reconsideration of the rejection had been moved within the time allowed, and the motion to reconsider postponed until another day and then carried, it was held that a motion to reconsider the adoption of the amendment was not then in order. SOULE. S. 1901. p. 969.

Previous also to the change made in 1902, when the rule provided for reconsideration only on *"the same day or before the Orders of the Days are taken upon the succeeding day,"* it was held that if on the day following that on which the vote was passed a quorum was not present, such day should not be counted as "the succeeding day." SOULE. S. 1901. p. 955.

A motion to reconsider a *"subsidiary, incidental or dependent question"* may be moved at any time when the main question to which it relates is under consideration. MORAN. S. 1935. p. 1206: GOODWIN. S. 1941. p. 1264. A motion to amend by substituting an entirely new bill is covered by these words. CHAPPLE. S. 1908. p. 697.

"No reconsideration of the vote on the question of adjourning." Reconsideration of motions to adjourn, to lay on or take from the table and for the yeas and nays was held to be cut off by the rule as it stood in 1883. CROCKER. S. 1883. p. 287.

A motion to "Lay on the table" must be laid over until next session. See Senate Rule 24.

A vote to *lay a matter on the table* cannot be reconsidered. FURBUSH (acting President). S. 1950. p. 1272.

"When a motion for reconsideration has been decided, that decision shall not be reconsidered." The fact that the question has been decided once in the affirmative and once in the negative makes no difference. See DANA. S. 1906. p. 500: MORAN. S. 1936. p. 1131; WRAGG. S. 1937. p. 789.

Although a motion to reconsider the rejection of a bill may have been entertained and carried at one reading of a bill, a motion to reconsider may be entertained at a subsequent stage of the same bill. NICHOLSON (acting President), S. 1945. p. 624.

In a case where the rejection of a bill has been reconsidered and the bill has been substantially amended and passed to be engrossed, a motion to reconsider engrossment may be entertained, as the second motion to reconsider presents a different question from the first. WRAGG, S. 1938. p. 608.

An election vote cannot be reconsidered. GOODWIN, S. 1941. p. 1579: FURBUSH. S. 1953. p. 499.

See notes to House Rules 70 and 71 and note to Constitution. ARTICLES OF AMENDMENT XLVIII, THE REFERENDUM II.

REJECTED MEASURES.

Rule 54. See notes to Senate Rule 46 under the heading *"To amend,"* and to House Rule 49.

The rule is an expression of a principle of parliamentary law. For a discussion of its origin and effect, see BISHOP. S. 1880. p. 243.

General parliamentary practice not only forbids the introduction of a proposition which is substantially the same as a proposition previously rejected, but also forbids the introduction of a proposition substantially the same as one already pending, or substantially the same as one previously adopted or passed. In legislative procedure a bill is not passed within the meaning of the foregoing general parliamentary rule until it has been passed to be enacted. SPRAGUE, S. 1891, p. 713. [See also NICHOLSON, S. 1947. p. 1047.]

"Finally rejected." These words must be construed to refer either to a rejection by both Houses, or to such action of the Senate as amounts to a final rejection of the

measure independently of any action of the House.
PILLSBURY, S. 1885, p. 584. [See also BARRETT, H. 1889,
p. 864.]

"When an order is rejected, or a petition excluded, or
leave is refused to bring in a bill, or a bill or resolve is
refused any one of its stages of advancement, it is 'finally rejected.'" COGSWELL, S. 1877, pp. 301, 306.
Indefinite postponement is a final rejection. PINKERTON,
S. 1892, p. 808. See S. J. 1961, pp. 984-987.

"The phrase 'when any measure has been finally
rejected' must be construed to apply solely to such
measures as the Senate has power finally to reject, and
cannot of course apply to amendments which may be
offered at any stage of a bill, even if rejected at a
previous stage; nor has it ever been denied that an
amendment rejected by the Senate may be adopted by
the House and sent up for concurrence. A substitute is an
amendment differing only in this, that it is capable of
amendment in the second degree, and by rules of the
Senate, but not of the House, requires three several
readings. To propose a substitute is therefore only to
propose an amendment, and it does not become a
'measure' until it is adopted. The rule, being made by
the Senate, and applicable to the Senate alone, must
mean that no senator shall introduce a second time a
'measure', that it, a bill or resolve, and some kinds of
orders, which has been once and finally rejected by the
Senate. Any other interpretation would put it in the
power of a single senator to defeat any bill, which might
be pending in either branch or in the committee, and to
which he was opposed, by offering it as a substitute for
any other bill which he had reason to believe the Senate
was desirous of passing, and so compelling the Senate to
choose between two bills, both of which it might be
desirous of passing." H. H. COOLIDGE, S. 1870, p. 415.

This ruling was made before the adoption of Senate Rule 50. See also SMITH, S. 1898, p. 730; SOULE, S. 1902, p. 755. [See, *contra,* PITMAN, S. 1869, p. 517.]

In conformity with the foregoing it was held that a bill passed in the branch in which it began might be sent from that branch to the other, and so introduced, although a similar bill was there pending, or had been passed or rejected. COGSWELL, S. 1877, pp. 301, 306. See also BISHOP, S. 1882, p. 307; LAWRENCE, S. 1896, p. 1036; SMITH, S. 1898, p. 981.

A House bill, practically identical with a previous bill which had been received from the House and rejected by the Senate, was admitted, in recognition of the practice of the Senate that courtesy to the coordinate branch usually requires the consideration of a bill so received. SOULE, S. 1901, p. 931.

So, also in the case when a report "inexpedient to legislate" had been adopted by the Senate, it was held that the Senate was still bound to entertain a House bill on the same subject, if the report had not been concurred in by the House. PILLSBURY, S. 1885, p. 585.

When the above decisions of Presidents COOLIDGE and COGSWELL were given, the words "by any committee or member" were not embodied in the rule, and the rule ended as follows: "and this rule shall apply as well to measures originating in the House as to those originating in the Senate." These words were left out in 1877.

The fact that a bill has been finally rejected in one branch does not prevent its introduction in the other. HARTWELL, S. 1889, p. 822. Nor would the fact that a measure is pending in one branch preclude its introduction in the other branch. GOODWIN (acting President), S. 1939, p. 1364.

If, however, a bill or measure has been once rejected by both branches, general parliamentary law as well as this rule would prevent any measure substantially the same from being again introduced into either branch at the same session; and the fact that one branch had passed such measure and forwarded it to the other would not justify its introduction in the latter branch. Thus, where a report of "leave to withdraw" had been accepted by both branches, it was held that a bill (reported by a committee *after* such concurrent action) that embodied a measure substantially the same as that contemplated in the petition must be laid aside, even though the bill came from the other branch. CHAPPLE, S. 1907, p. 426; BISHOP, S. 1880, p. 243. [See also PILLSBURY, S. 1885, p. 583.] But, an adverse report on a measure having been accepted by the House and subsequently accepted by the Senate, a bill from the House was entertained and the alleged similarity of the two measures held to be immaterial because the bill had been introduced in the House previously to the Senate's action on the other measure. WELLS, S. 1916, p. 605; S. 1918, p. 318; FISH, S. 1933, p. 967.

It seems that, notwithstanding this rule, an amendment of the Constitution can be introduced, although it is substantially the same as an amendment which came from the previous Legislature and which has been rejected. PHELPS, S. 1859, p. 325.

"No measure substantially the same." A resolve providing only for biennial elections is not substantially the same as a resolve providing for biennial elections and biennial sessions of the Legislature. BRUCE, S. 1884, p. 581. [See also PILLSBURY, S. 1886, p. 635; SMITH, S. 1898, p. 893.]

For cases in which measures were ruled out under this provision, see HARTWELL, S. 1889, p. 804; BUTLER, S. 1894, p. 730; CHAPPLE, S. 1908, p. 945; CALVIN COOLIDGE, S. 1914, p. 710; S. 1915, p. 362; MORAN,

S. 1935, p. 510; NICHOLSON (acting President), S. 1935, p. 739; S. 1936, p. 1045; COTTON, S. 1939, p. 553; HOLMES (acting President), S. 1948, p. 795; RICHARDSON, S. 1950, p. 1437; DONAHUE, S. 1964, p. 1479.

For cases in which measures were held not to be substantially the same, see BUTLER, S. 1894, p. 804; JONES, S. 1903, p. 875; CHAPPLE, S. 1908, p. 883; TREADWAY, S. 1911, p. 1542; ALLEN, S. 1922, pp. 738, 750; S. 1924, p. 413; WELLINGTON WELLS, S. 1925, p. 616; BACON, S. 1929, p. 613; FISH, S. 1933, p. 477; S. 1934, pp. 398, 548; MORAN, S. 1935, pp. 463, 667, 1164; S. 1936, p. 1011; COTTON, S. 1939, p. 554; ARTHUR W. COOLIDGE, S. 1946, p. 477; NICHOLSON, S. 1947, p. 300; NUCIFORO (acting President), S. 1971, p. 1367.

"*Shall be introduced.*" The rejection of a measure does not prevent the consideration of a measure substantially the same, if it was introduced previously to such rejection. BOARDMAN S. 1888, p. 485; PINKERTON, S. 1893, p. 897. But the fact that an order was presented and laid upon the table prior to the indefinite postponement of another order practically identical was held not to be an introduction within the meaning of this section. PINKERTON, S. 1892, p. 808.

A point of order having been raised that a Senate bill was substantially the same as a bill previously rejected by the Senate, the President refused to lay the bill aside on the ground that the Senate, having first rejected the later bill and then having reconsidered its rejection, had indicated its willingness to act upon it. DANA, S. 1906, p. 882.

In the case of a bill which had been read a third time, it was held that it was too late to raise the point of order that it was improperly before the Senate because substantially the same subject-matter had previously been adversely disposed of. COTTON, S. 1939, p. 875.

Offering of amendment to bill held NOT to be reintroduction of a rejected measure. DONAHUE (acting President), S. 1962, p. 1207. [See change in Senate Rule 54, S.J. January 16, 1971, which provides that a measure which has been rejected cannot be offered as an amendment to another measure.]

A point of order having been raised that the Senate Bill requiring persons doing certain electrical work to be licensed, was improperly before the Senate for the reason that an adverse report on the same subject-matter had previously been accepted by the Senate, the point of order was well taken and the bill was laid aside. DONAHUE, S. 1967, p. 804.

VOTING.

Rule 55. A vote of less than a quorum is not conclusive proof that a quorum is not present, and is valid, provided a quorum is in fact present. SANFORD, H. 1874, p. 564; PILLSBURY, S. 1885, p. 584; HARTWELL, S. 1889, p. 589; SPRAGUE, S. 1890, p. 905; CHAPPLE, S. 1908, p. 470. See also Crocker's Principles of Procedure, Sect. 114, and appendix note thereto.

When the presiding officer by count ascertained that a quorum was not present at the time of the taking of a vote, the vote was declared void. LAWRENCE, S. 1896, pp. 633, 745.

As to what constitutes a quorum of the Senate, see rulings on Amendment XXXIII of the Constitution and Op. Att. Gen., Vol. I., p. 36, House Doc. No. 38 (1892).

A motion that the Orders of the Day be laid on the table having been entertained by the presiding officer but not stated by him, it was held that it was not then too late to verify a vote taken just previously, as the member that requested the verification had risen for the purpose of making the request in due season. GALLOUPE (acting President), S. 1896, p. 823.

Rule 56. For a case in which it was held that a request for the yeas and nays was made too late, see SMITH, S. 1900, p. 660; OLSON (acting President), S. 1951, p. 1949.

The Senate having refused to direct that a certain vote be taken by yeas and nays, it was held that verification by yeas and nays was not in order. PRESCOTT (acting President), S. 1919, p. 869.

Pending the taking of the yeas and nays, a point of order will not be entertained. WRAGG, S. 1937, p. 896; S. 1938, p. 394.

Contra, a member having arisen to ask for a call of the yeas and nays to verify a vote, a point of order was raised that he had not verbally addressed the Chair (see Rule 39), and after a ruling of the Chair and yeas and nays taken on an appeal therefrom, another point of order having been raised that it was too late then to ask for a call of the yeas and nays on the main question, it was ruled that the yeas and nays could be taken if the required number joined in the call. INNES (acting President), S. 1956, p. 1656.

A member may announce a pair with an absent member regardless of the vote required to carry the question. COTTON, S. 1939, p. 749. See S. J. 1963, p. 740.

The announcement of a pair with an absent member, being made before the call of the roll had been begun, may be withdrawn, after the completion of the call of the roll and before the result is announced, without unanimous consent. POWERS, S. 1963, p. 740.

See S.J. May 16 and 23, 1973.

Rule 57. "*Unless excused before the vote is taken.*" After a *viva voce* vote has been taken, a request to be excused from voting cannot be entertained. PILLSBURY. S. 1885, p. 583.

"*And no member shall be permitted to vote after the decision is announced from the chair.*" If other business has intervened, a vote cannot be cast even if this rule is suspended. HARTWELL. S. 1889, p. 650.

A vote for election to an office cannot be changed after a ballot has been cast or the name of the person voted for has been announced. FURBUSH, S. 1953, p. 499.

PARLIAMENTARY PRACTICE.

Rule 62. See notes to House Rule 101.

Rule 63. A report of the committee on Rules may make recommendations to change the suspension of certain rules from a two-thirds vote to a majority vote. BULGER. S. 1982. p. 1152.

The committee on Rules has the authority and may recommend certain special rules for procedure on a bill of a specific subject matter even though that bill has not yet come before the body after being reported out of the committee on Ways and Means. BULGER, S. 1982, pp. 1152, 1153.

NOTES OF RULINGS

ON THE

HOUSE RULES

[Rule number refers to the rule number beginning with the year 1979. Number in brackets refers to the rule number prior to 1979.]

SPEAKER.

Rule 7. [7A.] It is not necessary that the Speaker should be in the chair in order to make an appointment under this rule. Such appointment can be made by a communication in writing. LOMASNEY (Chairman), H. 1912, pp. 1158, 1284.

Custom makes it unnecessary for the Chaplain to officiate more than once during a calendar day. MYERS, H. 1903, p. 1065; WILLIS, H. 1947, p. 1558.

Rule 6. [8.] This rule applies only to a vacancy in the office of Speaker occurring after the permanent organization of the House. EAMES (Chairman), H. 1911, p. 4.

Rule 12. [13.] Custom makes it unnecessary for Clerk to have printed a Calendar of matters in the Orders of the Day when a second legislative day has been ordered. O'NEILL, H. 1949, p. 954.

It is not necessary for the Clerk to print on the Calendar a veto of part of the General Appropriation Bill. FLAHERTY, H. 1995, pp. 783, 1322.

MEMBERS.

For a discussion of methods of procedure in connection with the resignation of a member, see HULL, H. 1928, p. 601.

If objection is made, it is not the privilege of any individual member to have an amendment which is printed in the calendar read by the Clerk. MEYER, H. 1895, p.1211.

If the report of a committee that Mr. A., a sitting member, is not entitled to a seat, has been accepted, it is out of order for Mr. A. to take part in the proceedings, although a motion to reconsider the acceptance of the report is pending. PHELPS, H. 1856, p. 493.

Rule 15. [17.] *"No member shall absent himself from the House without leave."* The phrase "the House" refers to the Representatives' Chamber alone. SANFORD, H. 1874, p. 313.

The presence of a quorum is not necessary to excuse a member from attending. BARRETT. H. 1890, p. 774.

For a discussion of the power of the Speaker to order the doors closed when he believes a quorum is endangered or during a recess of the House, see WILLIS. H. 1946, p. 1508.

A point of order that the action of the Speaker in keeping doors closed during a previous recess cannot be entertained after the recess has come to an end for the reason that the question had not been seasonably raised. O'NEILL, H. 1949, p.1435.

COMMITTEES.

Rule 17. [20.] For sundry rulings as to reports of committees, see notes on the Joint Rules, under the head of "Committees."

"A committee on Ways and Means." Notwithstanding a previous investigation and report by the committee on Claims, or other committee, it seems that this committee has power to examine every matter before it as a new question, and decide for or against it, on its merits.

JEWELL, H. 1870, p. 454. But see notes to House Rules 30 and 33.

That a motion directing the committee on Rules to fill the vacancy in the office of Counsel was properly before the House for the reason that the adoption thereof would not amend the statute relating to such office. WILLIS, H. 1948, p. 977.

Rule 17A. A point of order that a bill was improperly before the House for the reason that the committee on Ways and Means did not maintain accurate records of proceedings was held not to be well taken. KEVERIAN, H. 1985, p. 487.

Rule 17B. A point of order that a bill was improperly before the House for the reason that report did not contain the signatures of members of committee on prevailing side was held not to be well taken. KEVERIAN, H. 1985, p. 130.

Rule 19. [24.] A point of order that a bill was improperly before the House for the reason that two of the members of the committee reporting it were ineligible under this rule was held not to be well taken. MYERS, H. 1900, p. 1431. A point of order of this nature should be raised before prolonged discussion. HULL, H. 1928, p. 587.

In the case of a creditor or stockholder of the Eastern Railroad, it was held that he could vote on the bill "for the relief of the Eastern Railroad Company and the securing of its debts and liabilities," inasmuch as such creditor's or stockholder's interest was not "distinct from the public interest, but was inseparably mixed with it." LONG, H. 1876, p. 181, and cases there cited. See also WINTHROP, H. 1838, pp. 202, 212.

A director of a bank which has petitioned for an increase of capital was held not to be excluded by interest from voting on a motion to instruct the committee on Banks and Banking to report leave to withdraw on all petitions by banks for an increase of capital. BLISS, H. 1853, p. 605. See also WINTHROP, H. 1838, pp. 77, 78, 79; WINTHROP, H. 1840, p. 207. (The latter ruling, which is in MS., may be found in print in the Addresses and Speeches of Robert C. Winthrop, Little, Brown & Co., 1852, p. 272.)

In the case of a bill "to equalize the bounties of our soldiers," which provided for paying certain sums of money to a particular class of persons described in the bill, it was held that a member who, under the provisions of the bill, would be entitled to $200, had such an interest as would deprive him of the right to vote. STONE, H. 1866, p. 364. See also cases there cited.

A member is not debarred from voting on account of private interest unless that interest is shown to be immediate, direct and unmistakably in conflict with the interest of the general public. YOUNG, H. 1921, p. 844; O'NEILL, H. 1950, p. 1578; MCGEE, H. 1977, p. 1204.

A member on the payroll of the city of Boston is not debarred from voting on the adoption of an order providing for the appointment of a joint special committee to investigate the finances of said city, because of a private interest in conflict with the interest of the general public. VALENTINE (acting Speaker), H. 1945, p. 1586.

That members of the House who are attorneys-at-law are not debarred from voting under the provisions of this rule on a bill providing for a reorganization of the district courts. GIBBONS, H. 1953, p. 1972; KEVERIAN (acting Speaker), H. 1977, p. 2398; MCGEE, H. 1977, p. 2398.

The proper time to raise a point of order questioning the right of a member to vote on account of interest is after the roll has been called and the member's vote recorded. BARRETT. H. 1892, p. 1125; HULL, H. 1928, p. 588; SALTONSTALL. H. 1934, p. 1357; WILLIS, H. 1948, p. 1437.

For other cases relating to this rule, see BANKS, H. 1852, p. 225; ASHMUN, H. 1841, p. 387.

[This rule was combined with House Rule 24 on March 15, 1977.]

Rule 20. [25.] See note to Rule 17.

It is in order for the committee on Ways and Means to include in a general appropriation bill an item of expenditure which, although not based upon any existing statute, is, however, based upon the budget recommendations of the Governor to the General Court, in accordance with the provisions of Article LXII of the Amendments to the Constitution. YOUNG, H. 1921, p. 425.

Said committee does not exceed its authority in "reserving specific amounts for certain purposes and otherwise limiting the discretion of the Governor and Council" (in appropriation bills), for the reason that "the House has a right in granting legislation to impose such provisos, conditions and limitations as to it may seem fit." SALTONSTALL, H. 1936, pp. 886, 926.

The committee does not have authority to insert in an appropriation bill a section providing for the discontinuance of a work which an existing statute (St. 1899, c. 477) orders to be continued, thus in effect repealing the statute. MYERS, H. 1903, p. 328. [For various rulings in respect to amendments of appropriation bills, see Notes of Rulings on the Constitution, Articles of Amendment, LXIII.]

An amendment of a supplementary appropriation bill must be entertained, even though the identical amendment was presented and rejected when the general appropriation bill was under consideration. SALTONSTALL, H. 1936, p. 1599.

The General Court must, when it passes a special appropriation bill, provide the means for defraying the new appropriation. YOUNG, H. 1922, p. 683.

See LONG, H. 1878, p. 347.

Said committee has not violated the provisions of this rule which requires it to report "the total amount appropriated" when reporting a supplementary appropriation bill for the reason that the section authorizing the transfer of monies from one state fund to another is not an appropriation within the meaning of the rule because such transfer does not in any way change the total funds belonging to the Commonwealth. GIBBONS, H. 1953, p. 1407.

Rule 22. [26.] It was held to be within the powers of the committee on Bills in the Third Reading to recommend an amendment containing provisions not found in a bill referred to said committee. KNEELAND (acting Speaker), H. 1919, p. 1002.

That the committee on Bills in the Third Reading had exceeded its powers in materially changing the provisions of a bill without reporting such changes to the House as an amendment. This point of order was sustained even though it was raised after the bill had several readings in the Senate in its changed form. SKERRY, H. 1957, p. 1938.

It is within the province of the committee on Bills in the Third Reading to report that a bill ought not to pass. BARRETT, H. 1890, pp. 862, 864.

That the committee on Bills in the Third Reading may recommend an amendment reinserting in a bill a provision which at a previous reading had been stricken out by the House. SKERRY, H. 1956, p. 2027.

When, the main question having been ordered, a bill is amended and referred, under Rule 50, to the committee on Bills in the Third Reading, debate may not be reopened when the bill again comes before the House. SALTONSTALL, H. 1934, p. 888.

A bill having been substituted for another bill, in the engrossment stage, and prolonged debate having ensued on the question on passing the substituted bill to be engrossed, it was held to be too late to raise the point of order that the substituted bill should have been referred to the committee on Bills in the Third Reading. CAHILL (acting Speaker). H. 1935, p. 1382.

On a motion to discharge all bills from the committee on Bills in the Third Reading, see BARTLEY, H. 1974, p. 2538.

A motion directing the committee on Bills in the Third Reading to report a bill could only be entertained by unanimous consent. MCGEE, H. 1976, p. 2172.

That the committee on Bills in the Third Reading had exceeded its authority in recommending amendments. KEVERIAN, 1985, p. 650.

[On March 15, 1977, the then House Rule 50 was consolidated with the then House Rule 26 and taken out of the unanimous consent category.]

Rule 24. [28.] On a motion to suspend paragraph two of this rule, it is beyond the province of the Speaker to rule on the question of the Mystic River Bridge Authority being a public agency or a private organization. MURPHY (acting Speaker), H. 1950, p. 656.

On a motion to suspend paragraph two of this rule in order to adopt an order directing the committee on Ways and Means to report a certain matter forthwith would require the unanimous consent of the members of the House for the reason that Rule 28 requires such orders to lay over for seven days before being considered. McGee, H. 1980, p. 1035.

Rule 26. [30.] A bill is special or general as it applies to one or all of the individuals of a given class. BATES, H. 1897, p. 182. See HULL, H. 1926, p. 668. See also notes to Senate Rule 16.

After a bill has been ordered to a third reading it is too late to raise the point of order that the bill is in violation of this rule. COX, H. 1915, p. 1158; CUSHING, H. 1914, p. 1466; BARRETT, H. 1892, p. 698; MURPHY (acting Speaker), H. 1949, p. 1387. See also MEYER, H. 1894, p. 350.

"Can be secured ... under existing laws." It is the province of the committee, not of the Speaker, to determine whether the object of an application can be secured under existing laws. MEYER, H. 1894, pp. 350, 485; BARRETT, H. 1892, p. 1160; MYERS, H. 1901, p. 1048.

Pending the point of order that the object desired by a bill could be secured by existing law, a motion to recommit was entertained. NOYES, H. 1887, p. 808.

Amendments extending the provisions of a private or special bill so as to make it general are admissible if the committee might have reported such a general bill on the order referred to it. YOUNG, H. 1923, p. 772; FROTHINGHAM, H. 1904, p. 628; MARDEN, H. 1883, p. 630; MELLEN (acting Speaker), H. 1893, p. 660; MEYER, H. 1894, p. 1146; MYERS, H. 1903, p. 1383; CUSHING, H. 1914, p. 1843; YOUNG, H. 1921, p. 488; SALTONSTALL, H. 1930, pp. 428, 889; H. 1931, p. 1057;

H. 1932, p. 855; Bartley, H. 1969, p. 1788; McGee (acting Speaker), H. 1974, p. 2180; McGee, H. 1976, p. 1977. See Senate Rule 16 and Joint Rule 7.

An amendment approving a certain contract by the town of Saugus was improperly before the House for it would change the character of a general bill to a special. Keverian (acting Speaker), H. 1983, p. 1514.

An amendment including town clerks in a bill relating to city clerks is permissible, on the ground "that many references in the General Laws to city clerks are applicable also to town clerks." Cahill, H. 1938, p. 958.

Resolutions general in their scope may be moved as a substitute for resolutions special in character. Barrett, H. 1890, p. 866; H. 1891, p. 60.

If the subject-matter referred to a committee is general in its character, it is not in order to propose amendments changing the bill reported thereon from a general law to a special act. Marden, H. 1884, p. 450; Noyes, H. 1887, pp. 700, 785; H. 1888, p. 600; Meyer, H. 1895, pp. 826, 1071, 1132; Bates, H. 1897, pp. 875, 968; H. 1898, p. 674; H. 1899, p. 332; Cox, H. 1915, p. 835; H. 1917, p. 738; O'Neill, H. 1950, p. 1324; Skerry, H. 1955, p. 813; Quinn, H. 1968, p. 2240; Bartley, H. 1969, p. 2102; H. 1970, p. 2017; H. 1971, p. 1893. See also notes to Senate Rule 50.

An amendment to a general bill which would eliminate the city of Boston from the provisions thereof was held germane. Willis (acting Speaker), H. 1943, p. 550 [See Hull, H. 1926, p. 668 and also ruling under notes to Senate Rule 16.] *Contra*, McGee, H. 1977, p. 2180.

An amendment excluding the city of Newton from the provisions of a general bill was not germane for the reason it would change a general bill to a special one. TYLER (acting Speaker). H. 1953. p. 1188.

That an amendment giving a veto power to certain cities and towns over the expenditure of funds for highway projects was not germane to a bill giving such power to all cities and towns for the reason it would change a general bill to a special one. THOMPSON, H. 1963. pp. 2288, 2289; BARTLEY. H. 1971. p. 1893.

That an amendment including towns to a Bill relating to providing minimum pay for police officers in certain cities was germane for the reason that it would, if adopted, make the proposed law state-wide in its application. TYLER (acting Speaker). H. 1953. p. 1188.

As to the rule of parliamentary procedure prohibiting special bills on petitions for general legislation, see ALLEN. S. 1924, p. 762; SALTONSTALL. H. 1931. p. 910.

"Or without detriment to the public interests by a general law." Prior to the adoption of this rule a committee could not change a special to a general bill. SANFORD. H. 1874. p. 502. Nor could the Legislature change a private or special bill by amendment into a general law. SANFORD. H. 1874, pp. 217, 513; LONG. H. 1878, pp. 117, 361. See also NOYES. H. 1888. p. 600.

On a petition for general legislation it is not permissible to report a special bill. FROTHINGHAM. H. 1905, p. 272.

Rule 28. That an order directing the committee on Ways and Means to report a certain matter forthwith would require the unanimous consent of the members present for the reason that this rule requires such orders to lay over for seven days before being considered. McGEE, H. 1980, p. 1035.

REGULAR COURSE OF PROCEEDINGS.
It is the custom of the House to have the Chaplain officiate but once during a calendar day. MYERS, H. 1903, p. 1065; WILLIS, H. 1947, p. 1558.

Rule 29. [37.] After a petition has been presented in accordance with the rules, and the question on its reference has been stated, it is then too late to call for a vote on its reception. HALE, H. 1859, p 64.

Rule 30. [40.] *"All motions contemplating legislation."* This rule does not prevent the introduction of orders of inquiry or investigation, but does take away the power of committees making investigations under such orders to report bills. The rule does not prevent suggestions of legislation. BATES, H. 1898, p. 456.

An order may not be the medium of effecting legislation. LONG, H. 1878, pp. 58-61; SALTONSTALL, H. 1930, p. 229; BARTLEY, H. 1969, p. 1217; H. 1971, p. 755 [See Mass. Const., Pt. the 2nd, Ch. I, the Legislative Power, Art. II.]

An order directing that a department of a city be transferred to and placed under the control of a state commission was laid aside on the ground that the result proposed could only be accomplished by legislation. WARNER, H. 1919, p. 1365.

"Founded upon Petition." A Senate order was improperly before the House for the reason that it directed a department head to participate in an investigation which would, if adopted, result in effecting legislation through the medium of an order. SKERRY, H. 1955, p. 1752. The loss of a petition, which the records show to have been duly presented, does not bar procedure thereunder. WALKER, H. 1909, p. 847.

A bill passed by the House was laid aside in the Senate on a point of order that it was not founded upon petition, as it purported to be, the Senate never having concurred in the reference of the petition to the committee which reported it. WELLS. S. 1927, p. 530 (see H. 1927, p. 734).

A bill will be laid aside if found to be broader in scope than the petition (or other subject matter) on which it was presented. SALTONSTALL, H. 1930, pp. 387, 691; H. 1931, p. 568; H. 1933, pp. 847, 1408; WILLIS, H. 1947, p. 1601; H. 1948, p. 917; BATAL (acting Speaker), H. 1950, p. 1866.

A bill authorizing the sale of soda water was held to be germane to a petition for legislation to authorize the sale of "soda" on the Lord's Day, on the ground that "soda" was the colloquial phrase for soda water, and was the term most often used. MYERS, H. 1902, pp. 917 and 920.

A bill providing for punishment of murder in the first degree by imprisonment for life was held not to be germane to petitions asking for "the abolition of capital punishment." CAHILL (acting Speaker), H. 1935, p. 1271.

For an instance when a bill was considered (in the interest of "justice, fair play and orderly procedure"), even though broader than the scope of the petition on which it was founded, see CAHILL (acting Speaker), H. 1935, p. 1384.

A petition which used the language "for the passage of the accompanying bill or resolve, and/or for legislation" contained in the printed blank incorporates, by reference, the provisions of the accompanying bill. KING, H. 1943, pp. 951 and 965.

"The committee on Ways and Means may originate and report appropriation bills. " See notes to Rule 20.

That an appropriation bill was within the scope of a message from the Governor and there have been no violations of the Constitution, or statutes by the committee reporting the bill. GIBBONS, H. 1953, p. 1406.

"Unless otherwise ordered. " In announcing that a message from the Governor would be placed on file, the Speaker is acting for and with the consent of the House, and his action becomes the action of the House if not disputed; and reference of the message to a committee is not required by this rule if the House thus otherwise orders. SALTONSTALL, H. 1936, p. 1473.

The Governor's budget recommendations cannot be "otherwise" disposed of, because of this rule, than by reference to the committee on Ways and Means under Rule 25, CAHILL, H. 1938, p. 246; DAVOREN, H. 1967, p. 806.

As to the right to require the submission of facts and information as aids to legislation (without requesting recommendations), see 14 Gray 239; Attorney-General *v.* Brissenden, April 15, 1930.

That reference of the Governor's budget message to the House committee on Ways and Means is a proper disposition of the subject matter thereof even though a portion of said message deals with the subject of taxation for the reason that there is no provision in the rules that makes mandatory the reference of taxation matters to the committee on Taxation. O'NEILL, H. 1951, p. 364.

That an "Order relative to requesting the police commissioner of the city of Boston to re-establish the so-called communist squad for the purpose of acquiring new evidence" was improperly before the House under Rule 30 as it was a motion contemplating legislation and as such should be "based upon a petition, a bill or a resolve." NATHANSON (acting Speaker), H. 1951, p. 2097.

Objection that a bill covers matter not referred to the committee cannot be raised after extended debate on the bill and amendments thereto have been acted upon and rejected. O'NEILL, H. 1952, p. 895. [Also see Sundry Rulings.]

An amendment originating new legislation was an improper amendment to an appropriation bill. BARTLEY, H. 1974, pp. 1218, 1219, 2032; McGee, H. 1976, pp. 1569, 1975.

Rule 31. [42.] *"No repealed law and no part of any repealed law, shall be re-enacted by reference merely."* HULL, H. 1926, p. 387.

Rule 32. [43.] When the question, "Shall this bill be rejected?" is pending, a motion to amend the bill is not in order (PHELPS, H. 1856, p. 323), but it is in order to move the previous question. PHELPS, H. 1856, p. 332.

Rule 33. [44.] As to the power of the committee on Ways and Means to examine a matter as a new question, see note to Rule 17.

A bill which would operate to deprive the Commonwealth of money to which it would otherwise be entitled, comes under the provisions of this rule. WALKER, H. 1909, p. 1020; COX (acting Speaker). H. 1912, p. 1467; COX, H. 1915, p. 1172; H. 1917, p. 533; HULL, H. 1928, p. 887.

For instances in which bills were held to come within the provisions of this rule, see YOUNG, H. 1922, pp. 508, 519; JEWETT (acting Speaker), H. 1921, p. 524; YOUNG, H. 1921, p. 919; HULL, H. 1927, p. 516; SALTONSTALL, H. 1934, p.777; CAHILL, H. 1938, pp. 845, 912, 1170.

For instances in which bills were held not to come within the provisions of this rule, see WALKER, H. 1910, p. 940; SALTONSTALL, H. 1934, p. 580.

A bill will be referred by the Speaker, under this rule, to the committee on Ways and Means, even though the fact that it involves expenditure of public money is not discovered, or brought to his attention by point of order or otherwise. until the question on its engrossment is pending. WARNER, H. 1919, pp. 644, 754; H. 1920, p. 1099; COX, H. 1916, pp. 454, 598; H. 1917, p. 684; CUSHING, H. 1913, pp. 1087, 1960; H. 1914, pp. 875, 893, 1067, 1318, 1373, 1467, 1516; COLE, H. 1907, p. 914; MYERS, H. 1900, pp. 640, 1303; BATES, H. 1899, p. 516; WHIPPLE (acting Speaker), H. 1899, p. 728; BRACKETT, H. 1885, pp. 709, 732; BARRETT, H. 1889, p. 795; H. 1892, pp. 330, 824, 1168; BATES, H. 1898, p. 742; HULL, H. 1926, pp. 417, 525; SALTONSTALL, H. 1930, pp. 397, 681; HERTER, H. 1939, p. 1149. See also BATES, H. 1899, pp. 619, 635; MEYER, H. 1894, pp. 756, 977.

For an instance in which this rule applies to county expenditures and to reference of a bill to the committee on Counties on the part of the House, see YOUNG, H. 1924, pp. 260 and 265.

A bill to provide for the widening and construction of Cambridge and Court streets, in the city of Boston, was held to come within the scope of this rule. YOUNG, H. 1923, pp. 750, 760.

A bill providing for an expenditure by the Board of Railroad Commissioners was referred under the rule, although provision is made by law for repayment to the State of all sums expended by or for said board. MYERS, H. 1902, pp. 936, 943. See YOUNG, H. 921, p. 729.

The committee on Ways and Means may recommend rejection of a bill which would bring money into the treasury of the Commonwealth. SALTONSTALL, H. 1933, pp. 967, 1409.

This rule applies to resolves providing for special investigations, notwithstanding "budget" recommendations. SALTONSTALL. H. 1930. p. 239.

That the language in this rule which relates to municipal expenditures requires that only bills which involve substantial expenditures of city or town money shall be referred to the committee on Municipal Finance on the part of the House. VALENTINE (acting Speaker). H. 1946, p. 1127.

A resolve providing for an extension of time within which suit should be brought under an act previously passed upon by the committee on Ways and Means was held not to come within the scope of this rule. MYERS. H. 1902, pp. 572, 971.

That resolves which affect state finances should be referred to the committee on Ways and Means. McGEE. H. 1980, p. 1034.

The operation of this rule cannot be reconsidered. SMITH. S. 1900. p. 885; P. MURPHY (acting Speaker). H. 1969, p. 2188. But the announcement of the reference to a committee of a substituted bill does not preclude verification of the vote. provided the bill is in the possession of the Clerk. SALTONSTALL. H. 1931, p. 869.

When the committee. making no recommendations. had been discharged from the further consideration of a bill. it was held that the rule did not require further committal for definite report. COX. H. 1915, p. 1216.

"New provisions shall not be added to such bills by the committee on Ways and Means unless," etc.

For an instance in which it was ruled that the committee on Ways and Means had exceeded its authority, see MCKNIGHT, S. 1920. p. 797; O'NEILL, H. 1950, p. 1607; SKERRY, H. 1955, p. 2397.

For an instance in which it was ruled that the committee on Ways and Means had NOT exceeded its authority, see BARTLEY, H. 1969, p. 715.

That the provisions of this rule which provides that "new provisions shall not be added to such bills by the committee on Ways and Means, unless directly connected with the financial features thereof" do not bar said committee from recommending amendments in the same manner that individuals may move amendments, so long as they are germane to the subject matter under consideration. YOUNG, H. 1921, pp. 889, 890; THOMPSON, H. 1963, p. 2694.

Also see COX, H. 1917, p. 810; CUSHING, H. 1913, pp. 1398, 1404; MYER, H. 1894, pp. 1197, 1219. See YOUNG, H. 1921, p. 425; HULL, H. 1926, p. 862.

After the House has ordered to a third reading a new draft of a bill recommended by the committee on Ways and Means, it is too late to raise the point of order that said committee had exceeded its powers in reporting to the House a new draft under this rule. WILLIS, H. 1946, p. 1199.

After the House has substituted a new draft of a bill recommended by the committee on Ways and Means, it is too late to raise the point of order that said committee had exceeded its powers in reporting to the House a new draft. DAVOREN, H. 1967, p. 2521.

That the committee on Ways and Means was not exceeding its authority in substituting a bill for a Senate order providing for a study of several unrelated matters for the reason that such action is not introducing "new provisions" not connected with the financial features thereof because the order was based, in part, on the pending bill. O'NEILL, H. 1951, p. 1827.

A bill should be referred to the committee on Ways and Means when there is any doubt that it affects the state finances for a determination by that committee as to whether or not state finances were involved. P. MURPHY (acting Speaker), H. 1969, p. 2188.

That the committee on Ways and Means had failed to attach a fiscal note. BARTLEY, H. 1971, p. 2303; McGEE (acting Speaker), H. 1974, p. 2222; BARTLEY, H. 1974, p. 2537; H. 1975, p. 2122; McGEE, H. 1977, p. 1977; KEVERIAN, H. 1985, p. 487; GIBSON (acting Speaker), H. 1986, p. 171; CORREIA (acting Speaker), H. 1986, p. 266; KEVERIAN, H. 1987, pp. 1652 and 1653.

That a Legislative Substitute for an Initiative Petition should have been referred, under this rule, to the committee on Ways and Means. McGEE, H. 1976, p. 1668.

Rule 33A. That a bill was improperly before the House for the reason that copies were not available for twenty-four hours. MURPHY (acting Speaker), H. 1983, pp. 1778, 1779.

That amendments were not being considered chronologically as submitted to the Clerk. BOSLEY (acting Speaker), H. 1996, p. 1805.

Rule 36. [47.] See notes to Rule 30.

As to whether it is proper under this rule to move to take from the files of last year a bill (which was then referred to the next General Court), and move its reference to a committee, without getting leave to introduce it, see LONG, H. 1877, p. 466 and OSGOOD, appellant, p. 469.

After a bill has been laid aside as broader than the scope of the petition, the petition may be recommitted but it is not in order to move to substitute another bill for the petition. SALTONSTALL, H. 1930, p. 691.

"Unless received from the Senate." See note to Senate Rule 23.

"Moved as an amendment to the report of a committee." After a bill has been substituted for the report of a committee, it is too late to raise the point of order that the bill is broader in its scope than the subject matter referred to the committee. NOYES, H. 1888, p. 463; HULL, H. 1927, p. 552.

Rule 37. [48.] Full reading may be requested of a bill not printed in amended form, if request is made at any time before the Clerk begins the calling of the roll. JEWETT (acting Speaker), H. 1933, p. 973. [Also see H. 1895, p. 1211.]

That a request for the full reading of a resolve must be made seasonably. ARTESANI (acting Speaker), H. 1958, p. 1408.

Rule 38. [49.] See notes to Senate Rule 54. See also "Courtesy between the Branches," under "Sundry Rulings," at the end of the notes on the Joint Rules.

"Finally rejected or disposed of by the House." The words "by the House" were added in 1890, following a ruling [that the House could send to the Senate two or more similar bills] by Speaker BARRETT, H. 1889, p. 864. [For a statement of the general parliamentary practice which differs from the position taken by Speaker BARRETT, see notes to Senate Rule 54.]

"A measure is rejected when the House refuses to allow it to take any of those steps necessary to its ultimate success." COGSWELL, S. 1877, pp. 305, 306. But "rejected" does not apply to a bill laid aside on a point of order. MEYER, H. 1894, p. 1219.

The words "or disposed of" were inserted in 1920.

An amendment in the form of a substitute bill is not to be debarred when an identical bill has been reported and is pending before the committee on Ways and Means, for pendency of a bill before a committee does not constitute final disposition. SALTONSTALL, H. 1936, p. 671. Also see KING (acting Speaker), H. 1941, p. 1915.

[Previous to the amendment of this rule adopted in 1920, it was held that a bill passed to be engrossed by the House but rejected by the Senate, is not by this rule barred from being again introduced in the House. MYERS, H. 1900, p. 1151. Also see CUSHING, H. 1913, p. 1908.]

The rejection of a bill providing for permanent clerical assistance does not exclude the subsequent introduction of a resolve providing for temporary clerical assistance. ADAMS (acting Speaker), H. 1900, p. 325. See also CUSHING, H. 1914, p. 1207.

It is not in order to move as an amendment a bill the same as one which has been passed by the House and then refused passage over to veto. MARDEN, H. 1883, p. 819. [Distinction should be made between a rejected *bill*, which had been reported by committee or substituted by the House, and a rejected *amendment* in the form of a proposed substitute bill. The latter, because of its rejection, never acquired standing as a bill, and would not come under this rule.]

After a bill "making appropriations for expenses of various charitable and reformatory institutions" was rejected, it was held that one of the sections of that bill could be introduced without violating this rule. MARDEN, H. 1883. p. 569. See also MEYER. H. 1894, p. 1226.

The final disposition of a bill accompanying an initiative petition does not prevent consideration by the House of a bill based upon a petition even though such measure is substantially the same. WINSLOW (acting Speaker), H. 1948. p. 1671.

Under this rule it was held that a bill from the Senate must be laid aside when the course of proceedings had been as follows: The petition with accompanying bill was originally presented in the Senate and there referred to a joint committee. in which reference the House concurred. The committee reported to the House, recommending reference to the next General Court; a motion to substitute the bill in question was rejected, and then the report was accepted by the House. In the Senate the bill was substituted for the report, and this bill, on its passage to a third reading in the House, was laid aside as coming within the scope of the rule. BARRETT, H. 1893, p. 856; MEYER. H. 1896, p. 1142. Also see BARRETT, H. 1891. p. 419. [These rulings are inconsistent with the present practice of permitting the same amendment to be moved at different readings or stages of a bill.] Subsequently, in the same session, in a case in which the House had previously adopted a report recommending that the petitioner have leave to withdraw, it was held that a bill substituted in the Senate for the report should be entertained. The distinction made was that in this case the bill itself had not been previously offered in and rejected by the House. BARRETT. H. 1893, pp. 961, 967.

Previous to the foregoing rulings it had been held that a bill may be received from the Senate and considered by the House. although a similar bill is there pending, or has been passed or rejected. Once in the House, and there referred to a committee of the House, a subsequent report of it back from that committee is a part of its career, and not such an introduction of it as to bring it within this rule as "introduced by a committee." LONG, H. 1877, p. 424; GOODWIN, H. 1860, p. 550. *Contra*, see SANFORD, H. 1875, p. 323; OSGOOD (acting Speaker), H. 1877, p. 416.

That this rule does not apply to amendments previously disposed of by the House, see HERTER, H. 1939, p. 1950; WILLIS, H. 1945, p. 1619. [Also see (under "Courtesy between the Branches") "Sundry Rulings."]

A bill changed in but a single essential provision is not substantially the same. SHERBURNE (acting Speaker), H. 1917, p. 1020; COX, H. 1916, p. 1146; CUSHING, H. 1914, p. 1590; NOYES, H. 1881, pp. 402, 446. See also MEYER, H. 1896, p. 1179; JEWELL, H. 1868, p. 204; SALTONSTALL, H. 1931, p. 1078; H. 1935, pp. 449, 1474; HAYS (acting Speaker), H. 1935, p. 1185; SALTONSTALL, H. 1936, p. 301; CAHILL, H. 1937, pp. 643, 716(2), 845, 994, 1198; H. 1938, pp. 354, 373, 1045, 1431; HERTER, H. 1939, pp. 821, 991; KEVERIAN, H. 1985, p. 1764; H. 1987, p. 1726; [Also see S. 1903, p. 875; S. 1922, p. 750; S. 1929, p. 613.]

Many proposed substitutes have been excluded, under this rule, when embracing measures or amendments substantially the same as those covered by previously accepted reports of leave to withdraw, inexpedient to legislate, no legislation necessary or ought not to pass. For examples see SANFORD, H. 1874, p. 349; BISHOP, S. 1880, p. 243; MARDEN, H. 1884, p. 555; FROTHINGHAM, H. 1904, p. 990; SALTONSTALL, H. 1933, p. 934; CORREIA (acting Speaker), H. 1986, pp. 878, 935.

When the House substitutes a bill for one of several adverse reports on the same subject, it may then accept the other adverse reports and the provisions of this rule cannot be raised as a bar to further consideration when the substituted bill again comes before the House. O'NEILL, H. 1950, p. 891.

An order cannot be excluded from consideration on the sole ground that its provisions contravene the provisions of an order previously adopted. HERTER (acting Speaker), H. 1937, p. 369.

For exclusion of an order limiting the number of cars to be run through the East Boston Tunnel, see WARNER, H. 1919, p. 1327.

When a report of leave to withdraw had been accepted by both branches, it was held that a bill, moved as an amendment to a subsequent report of the same committee to the same effect on a petition asking for substantially the same legislation as that on which the first report was based, must be laid aside. COLE, H. 1907, p. 540. See also Cox (acting Speaker), H. 1912, p. 1032; HERTER, H. 1939, pp. 1199, 1220.

After a bill reported on a petition has been rejected, the petition cannot be considered further. SANFORD, H. 1874, p. 511. See also SANFORD, H. 1873, p. 198; KIMBALL (acting Speaker), H. 1871, p. 400. But see notes under Joint Rule 5.

The acceptance of a report "no legislation necessary on the Governor's message" was held not to cut off action on a substitute for a bill previously reported by the same committee, although such bill and substitute covered matter embraced in the Governor's message. NOYES, H. 1888, p. 584.

In the case of a bill which had been read a third time, it was held that it was too late to raise the point of order that it was improperly before the House because it was substantially the same as a bill which had been previously finally rejected. BATES. H. 1897. p. 1197; SALTONSTALL. H. 1933. p. 1279; HERTER. H. 1939. pp. 1175. 1196; WILLIS. H. 1945. p. 1444.

It was held that this rule applied to an article of amendment of the Constitution based on a message from the Governor but substantially the same as one which the House. previously to the receipt of the message. had refused to agree to because the committee might have reported a constitutional amendment which would meet the Governor's recommendation and yet be materially different from the amendment the House had rejected. [In this case the Speaker refused to rule on the question whether. if the Governor had sent in a message recommending specific legislation which had already been rejected by the House it would. if reported by a committee. be such an introduction by a committee as would bring it within the provisions of this rule.] CUSHING. H. 1913. pp. 1864. 1874. [But see HERTER. H. 1941. p. 1849.]

"Introduced by any committee or member." As to the effect of these words. see LONG. H. 1877. p. 427. That the above words do not apply to reports of committees based upon Governor's messages. HERTER. H. 1941. p. 1849. [See *Contra* — SALTONSTALL. H. 1936. p. 1587.]

That an order providing for forwarding to the Massachusetts Bar Association the transcript of evidence presented before the committee on Rules in connection with the summonsing of Alfred B. Cenedella. Lawrence

R. Goldberg and other persons relative to corrupt acts by public officials and others is properly before the House, under Rule 38, for the reason that the prior subject matter was in the nature of a secondary amendment and as such presented a different parliamentary question. O'NEILL, H. 1951, p. 1925.

That an amendment to the "Bill providing for certain night parking of motor vehicles in the city of Boston" was properly before the House for the reason that its prior consideration had been at a different reading of the bill. BATAL (acting Speaker), H. 1951, p. 1960.

It is not in order to move as an amendment to the General Appropriations Act the contents of a bill previously disposed of by the House. McGEE, H. 1976, p. 1557; H. 1977, pp. 1282, 1286; PIRO (acting Speaker), H. 1984, pp. 550, 551.

It is not proper to offer as an amendment the text of a bill that has been approved by both branches and was presently awaiting the Governor's approbation. FINNERAN, 1996, p. 2317.

Rule 40. [53.] For effect, after reconsideration of enactment and the striking out of the enacting clause, of a motion to reconsider the latter action, see CAHILL, H. 1937, p. 1020.

Rule 41. [56.] It was held that the provision requiring a bill to be placed in the Orders of the Day for the next day did not apply in a case where a bill had been returned, without recommendations, by a committee, in response to an order to report forthwith, and the committee had been discharged. COX, H. 1915, p. 1192.

That a bill filed in the Clerk's office after adjournment and placed on the Calendar for the next sitting is properly before the House since the first reading of a bill is an undebatable stage and it has been the custom over a period of many years to dispense with such first reading without prejudicing members' rights. KIERNAN (acting Speaker), H. 1962, p. 1128.

Rule 42. [57.] See note to Rule 41.

That a request for the yeas and nays on the acceptance of an adverse report is not frivolous in its nature, but a main question. HULL, H. 1926, p. 292.

Rule 43. [58.] After a bill has been ordered to a third reading, it is too late to raise the point of order that it was not based on a definite recommendation of the majority of a special commission on whose report the bill was based. HULL, H. 1928, p. 738. Or that it is broader than the scope of the subject matter on which it was based. SALTONSTALL, H. 1934, p. 1058. [Also see rulings under House Rule 73.]

Rule 45. [59.] Matters in the Calendar must be acted upon separately. A single request that several matters be passed for debate is not in order. BARRETT, H. 1890, p. 604.

That an order for a second legislative day was properly before the House even though the House was considering the matters in the Orders of the Day since such an order was strictly a procedural matter similar to a motion to adjourn or to recess, which are always in order under House Rule 64. McGEE. H. 1979, p. 1899.

Rule 46. [60.] A point of order that the House is not complying with the disposal of matters in the Orders of the Day according to the provisions of this rule [and also Rule 47] is premature if raised before the House has met for the second legislative day. O'NEILL, H. 1949, p. 954. [Subsequently, after declaration of second legislative day, the point of order was well taken, p. 955.]

Rule 47. |61.| If a matter is discharged from the Orders of the Day, the vote cannot be reconsidered on the succeeding day, BLISS, H. 1853, p. 362.

VOTING.

It is the duty of every member to vote unless excused from so doing, or debarred "by private interests distinct from the public interest." BARRETT, H. 1892, p. 1207. See House Rules 19 and 48.

A member has no right to change his vote after the result is declared, even though the declaration is erroneous, and the right is claimed prior to a corrected statement. PHELPS, H. 1856, p. 496.

A vote may be declared null and void after it has been recorded. EDDY, H. 1855, p. 1570.

Pending a roll call it is not in order to move that the doors be closed, because such a motion, if adopted, might prevent members from coming in to vote. It is, however, in order to close the doors in case of a quorum call of the House, because it is the very object of the proceeding to ascertain who is present. HALE, H. 1859, p. 335.

Rule 48. [64.] Any member may require the observance by other members of the duty of voting while the vote is proceeding, and before it is declared; but it is too late to call for the enforcement of the rule after the voting has been completed and declared. SANFORD, H. 1874, p. 564.

The proper time to raise a point of order under this rule is before the vote has been completed and declared. O'NEILL, H. 1949, p. 1699.

A point of order that before the vote is declared the Speaker should secure applications from members desiring to be excused from voting was not well taken for the reason that the present rules of the House do not give the Chair the power to compel members to vote. O'NEILL, H. 1949, p. 1699.

"Members desiring to be excused from voting shall make application." etc. For a case which arose prior to the adoption of this provision, see BLISS, H. 1853, p. 367.

This rule applies only to main questions, and not to subsidiary, incidental or privileged questions. BRACKETT, H. 1885, p. 766.

"And shall not be subject to the provisions of rule forty-eight." This means that the yeas and nays cannot be taken on the question of excusing a member from voting. BARRETT, H. 1890, p. 607.

Rule 50. [66.] The privilege of a member to doubt a vote has been held not to be lost, although another member, desiring to offer an amendment, first secures recognition by the chair. UNDERHILL (acting Speaker), H. 1911, p. 1996.

For a case in which it was held that the verification of a vote was in order even though a motion to adjourn had followed and been rejected, see COX, H. 1918, p. 613.

Rule 51. [67.] *"And if a quorum is present the vote shall stand."* This is an expression of a general principle enunciated by Speaker SANFORD, H. 1874, p. 564; BARRETT, H. 1889, p. 226. See also notes of rulings on the Constitution, Articles of Amendment, XXXIII, and on the Senate Rules under "Voting."

Where the Journal showed that less than a quorum voted, and that the point of order was immediately raised that a quorum was not present and the House adjourned without determining whether a quorum was in fact present, it was held that the vote was void. MEYER, H. 1895, p. 370.

The absence of a quorum does not automatically adjourn the House and a motion to instruct the Sergeant-at-Arms to secure the presence of a quorum may be made. MURPHY (acting Speaker). H. 1949, p. 1442.

That general parliamentary practice supports the view that if the House is in the process of verifying a vote when a member doubts the presence of a quorum, that, upon the securing of a quorum, no further debate should be permitted. SKERRY. H. 1955, p. 1853.

On a rising vote being taken, after the announcement by the Speaker of the vote in any one division, it is too late to ask that the count of said division be retaken or verified after the announcement by the Speaker of the count in the next division. YOUNG. H. 1922, p. 645.

Rule 52. [68.] The call for the yeas and nays on the question of the disposition of a matter on the Calendar must be made before the consideration of the next matter on the calendar has been taken up. MYERS. H. 1902, p. 359.

When a question is before the House, and the yeas and nays have been ordered, a motion to reverse the roll call is not in order. BLISS. H. 1853, p. 299.

It seems that request for the yeas and nays cannot be laid on the table. See ASHMUN. H. 1841, p. 385.

Pending the taking of the yeas and nays a point of order will not be entertained. MYERS. H. 1902, p. 1232; WILLIS. H. 1945, p. 1562; H. 1948, p. 1455; O'NEILL. H. 1950, p. 1576.

After a request for the yeas and nays has been refused, a second request on the same question cannot be entertained. MYERS. H. 1900, p. 1314; WHITE (acting Speaker). H. 1910, p. 646.

"No member shall be allowed to vote who was not on the floor before the vote is declared." For a case arising when the rule provided that no member shall be allowed to vote who was not upon the floor when his name was called, or before the roll call was finished, see EDDY, H. 1855, pp. 1573, 1658.

A point of order was raised that the Speaker was in violation of the rules by interrupting a member who had the floor in debate for the purpose of allowing a member to vote. KEVERIAN, 1985, p. 576.

Rule 69. See notes on Rule 52.

RECONSIDERATION.

Rule 54. [70.] This rule was reconstructed and certain new provisions were added in 1902.

Agreement to an Article of Amendment of the Constitution can be reconsidered. MARDEN, H. 1883, p. 422; MORAN (in joint session), H. 1935, p. 1289.

Reconsideration can be had of a vote rejecting the report of a committee which declared that the seat of a member was vacant. HALE, H. 1859, p. 133.

As to reconsideration of votes to commit petitions, etc., and of the enactment of laws, see notes to Senate Rules 8 and 53.

When a vote has been passed to close debate at a specified time, and that time has arrived, it is too late to move a reconsideration in order to extend the debate. NOYES, H. 1880, p. 220.

A motion to reconsider a vote whereby a rule has been suspended cannot be entertained after business consequent upon the suspension has intervened. MEYER, H. 1894, p. 466.

As to whether the adoption of an order can be reconsidered after its execution has begun, see HALE, H. 1859, p. 270. ["The House alone has ample authority to make a committee, and may rescind its order for this purpose *before proceedings are had by the committee.*"]

[A motion was entertained to reconsider the adoption of an order providing for a joint committee to redivide the Commonwealth into congressional districts, although the members of the committee had been appointed in both branches. H. 1931, pp. 446, 453.]

[Speaker SALTONSTALL was prepared to rule that, upon reconsideration of a vote on which the main question had been ordered or debate had been closed, the bill was open for further debate. See bill creating a milk control board, H. 1934, pp. 880, 888, 895.]

A motion to rescind a standing or special order of the House may be entertained after the time for reconsideration of the order has expired. MEYER, H. 1894, p. 823; H. 1895, p. 982.

It has been held that a motion to reconsider a vote on an undebatable question cannot be debated. ROCKWELL, H. 1858, p. 331.

"On the next day thereafter on which a quorum is present." Before the requirement of the presence of a quorum (121 members) was inserted in this rule, it was held that a session held merely for the purpose of complying with the provisions of the Constitution, and not for the purpose of transacting business, was not to be considered as "the succeeding day." BARRETT, H. 1890, p. 1277.

When each of two or more daily sessions is declared to be a legislative day, each session is a day within the meaning of this rule. BARRETT, H. 1893, p. 1036.

During the last week of the session, the House having voted to remain in session until the completion of the matter under consideration and the vote thereon having been taken, it was held that a motion to reconsider was in order before adjournment. MYERS, H. 1900, p. 1444.

"Except during the last week of the session." These words may be construed as meaning the week prior to the date of final adjournment in case a date for prorogation has been voted by the House. BARRETT, H. 1889, p. 965. These words do not abrogate the right of a member to move reconsideration on the succeeding day. SALTONSTALL. H. 1932, p. 996.

"Before the Orders of the Day have been taken up." For a case in which a motion to reconsider was entertained after the Orders of the Day were taken up, see OLMSTEAD (acting Speaker), H. 1892, pp. 380, 381. But see also ST. JOHN (acting Speaker), H. 1892, p. 1202.

"First in the Orders of the Day for the succeeding day." Under a rule having a similar requirement, it was held to be necessary, notwithstanding the rule, to take up forthwith a motion to reconsider a vote that when the House adjourn it be to a day or hour different from that fixed by the rules. GOODWIN. H. 1860, p. 415.

"Shall be considered forthwith." This does not prevent a postponement of action on the motion to reconsider by vote to that effect. HALE (acting Speaker), H. 1874, p. 23.

A bill having been laid aside on the ground that it was beyond the scope of the petition on which it was based, a motion was made to recommit the bill under a suspension of the 5th Joint Rule. This motion having been rejected, and a motion to reconsider its rejection being before the House, it was held that the consideration of such motion could by vote be postponed to a time certain. WALKER, H. 1909, pp. 844, 851.

In the case of a motion to reconsider a vote whereby the House refused to discharge a matter from the Orders of the Day under a suspension of the rules, it was held that such motion should be considered at the time when made. TOBIN (acting Speaker), H. 1886, p. 524.

When a motion to reconsider is pending, it is too late to entertain a point of order that the matter under consideration is not properly before the House. SALTONSTALL, H. 1932, p. 428.

The acceptance of an adverse report having been reconsidered at the next sitting, and an amendment rejected at the preceding sitting also having been reconsidered, it cannot be held that the amendment is not in order on the ground that a similar amendment had been rejected at said next sitting. CAHILL, H. 1937, p. 1022.

That the House must proceed with a motion to reconsider the rejection of an amendment to the report of the joint special committee appointed to prepare rules for the government of the two branches, under the provisions of Rule 54, unless a motion to postpone prevails. O'NEILL, H. 1951, p. 519.

Rule 55. [71.] *"No question shall be twice reconsidered."* Where a bill had been rejected, and reconsideration was carried, and the bill was then amended in an essential feature, it was held that a reconsideration of a second rejection would be in order, because the question on the second rejection was not the same as that on the first. STONE, H. 1867, p. 218; HEYWOOD (acting President), S. 1865, p. 533.

The same question cannot twice be reconsidered. The fact that the question has been decided once in the affirmative and once in the negative makes no difference. BLISS, H. 1853, p. 721; CAHILL, H. 1937, p. 1020.

It has been held that this rule can be suspended so as to allow a second reconsideration. PHELPS, H. 1856, p. 481.

It is competent for the House to reconsider a vote refusing to pass a bill over the Executive veto, notwithstanding the first vote is described in the Constitution as a "reconsideration" of the bill. SANFORD, H. 1874, p. 583; FROTHINGHAM, H. 1905, p. 1098. See notes on the Constitution, Chap. I., Sect. I., Art. II.

RULES OF DEBATE.

[See Rules 57 to 61, inclusive.]

See paper on member retaining floor after adjournment due to lack of quorum, by Norman L. Pidgeon, Advisor to Senate, 1975, S.J., p. 1941.

Remarks should be addressed to the presiding officer, not to the House in general. BULLOCK, H. 1865, p. 155.

When a member yields the floor to another, he loses the right to it altogether. BRACKETT, H. 1885, p. 741.

When a member rises for the purpose of objecting to the granting of unanimous consent he is recognized for that purpose only and is not entitled to the floor in preference to another member. YOUNG, H. 1922, p. 178.

That a member by yielding the floor to another member cannot thus transfer to the latter the right to the floor. YOUNG, H. 1922, p. 474.

No person not a member of the legislative body has any right to take part in the debates. For a case in which application of this rule was made to the chaplain's prayer, see SANFORD, H. 1872, p. 291.

The uniform custom in the House has been to allude to a member by his residence. The pronouncing of the name of one member by another in debate is liable to lead to the excitement of personal feeling, and to a disturbance of that harmony and courtesy among the members which are essential to the highest style of order in a deliberative assembly. BULLOCK, H. 1865, p. 155.

A member is not debarred under the provisions of this rule from reading from the House Journal the names of members of the House. GIBBONS, H. 1953, p. 887.

That the uniform custom of the House has been to consider it improper to divulge what has taken place in executive sessions of committees. TYLER (acting Speaker), H. 1954, p. 1628.

That a member was not violating the uniform custom of the House which prohibits the divulging what has taken place in executive sessions of committees. SKERRY, H. 1957, p. 909.

Allusion should not be made to the opinions or wishes of the Executive for the purpose of influencing the decision of any question. This point is not one merely of formality or propriety, but one of principle, affecting the independence of the several branches of the government. The official acts and orders of the Executive, and his opinions officially communicated to the Legislature, are properly subjects of discussion and may well be referred to for the purpose of influencing the action of the legislative body; but it is irregular and unparliamentary in debate for member, with a view to securing the passage or defeat of a measure, to refer to the supposed opinion or wish of the Executive not officially promulgated. BULLOCK, H. 1865, p. 155; MORISON (acting Speaker), H. 1889, p. 800.

It is out of order for members to debate opinions of the Governor except in so far as said opinions are expressed in official messages and documents and that to impugn the motives of the Governor is clearly out of order. WILLIS, H. 1948, p. 1233; O'NEILL, H. 1951, pp. 1440, 1969; SKERRY, H. 1955, pp. 481, 846, 886, 1310, 1938, 2004.

That the remarks of a member related to official acts or orders of the Governor and even though they were not officially communicated to the Legislature, they were well within the ambit of previous rulings. O'DEA (acting Speaker), H. 1955, p. 1305. [Ruling of the Chair sustained on appeal.]

That considerable latitude is allowed in debating a question based on a message from the Governor which had been officially communicated to the House. SKERRY, H. 1956, p. 950.

A member, in presenting to the House his question of personal privilege, is not violating the general practice of legislative procedure which prohibits the introduction of the name of the Chief Executive in debate even though it directly relates to action of the Governor in relation thereto. VALENTINE (acting Speaker), H. 1946, pp. 1127, 1128.

When unanimous consent has been granted to make a statement a member must confine his remarks to a brief statement and not proceed to debate the passage of a bill. BURKE (acting Speaker), H. 1947, p. 1458; MACLEAN (acting Speaker), H. 1977, p. 2637.

After a point of order has been raised, the subject can be postponed to give the Chair time for consideration. NOYES, H. 1882, p. 446.

A point of order will not lie for the reason that a bill does not conform to the subject matter as stated in the title. BARRETT, H. 1892, p. 1160.

An order having been adopted that the Speaker should declare an adjournment on the completion of the business on which the House was engaged at 5 o'clock, it was held that a motion to take a recess until 7:30, made after 5 o'clock, was not in order, for the reason that the order had not been suspended. BRACKETT, H. 1885, pp. 771, 775.

Rule 58. [74.] A point of order that a member was not on his feet when he made a motion to adjourn whereas the objector addressed the Chair from his seat, was not well taken. SALTONSTALL, H. 1933, p. 1154. Also see BARRETT, H. 1893, p. 903.

Rule 61. [76.] The House has refused to sustain a ruling that the intent of this rule is to give the preference in speaking only to such members who have not spoken as rise at the same time with a member who may desire to speak a second time. HALE, H. 1859, p. 288. See also BARRETT, H. 1893, p. 908; O'NEILL, H. 1950, p. 1463.

That the Chair had not violated the provisions of this rule as the member who had the floor was speaking on the motion to suspend Rule 64 and that it was the first time he had spoken on that particular question. ARTESANI (acting Speaker), H. 1958, p. 1408.

Rule 62. [77.] That an amendment would be considered in legible form as it has been the custom of the Clerk to perfect, when possible, amendments that were not too clear as to the meaning. MOAKLEY (acting Speaker), H. 1959, p. 1465.

That an amendment was not in suitable amendment form as it could not, if adopted, be attached to the bill. QUINN, H. 1968, p. 2155.

In general terms, it is a principle of parliamentary law that no question can be moved a second time upon which the judgment of the House has already been expressed. See WADE, H. 1879, p. 540; HALE, H. 1859, p. 277; PHELPS, H. 1856, p. 530. Thus a report of leave to withdraw having been made and an amendment substituting a bill having been rejected and the report having then been laid upon the table, the same motion to amend is not in order when the report is again taken from the table. FROTHINGHAM, H. 1904, p. 767.

If a motion to lay on the table is lost, another motion to lay on the table is not in order until some substantial business has been transacted. The rejection of a motion to adjourn is not substantial business. BLISS, H. 1853, p. 281. See also CROCKER, S. 1883, p. 286.

A motion to suspend the rule limiting the time allowed to each speaker is in order pending a debate, although before the debate began a similar motion had been made and defeated. HALE, H. 1859, p. 603.

A motion that the further reading of a paper be dispensed with is not barred by the fact that at a previous point in the reading a similar motion has been rejected. HIGGINS (acting Speaker), H. 1894, p. 128.

No two resolutions nor any two bills contradictory to each other can be passed at the same session. See WADE, H. 1879, p. 540.

That an amendment substituting (in part) a bill for an order providing for an investigation of the disposition of "breaks" at horse and dog racing meetings cannot be entertained for the reason it would reverse what the House had already done and subsequently had refused to reconsider. WILLIS, H. 1948, p. 1440.

If, however, an amendment is made at one reading of a bill, inserting certain words, the same words, or any part of them, may be stricken out by amendment at a subsequent reading without reconsideration of the first amendment. SANFORD, H. 1874, p. 246. So also the rejection of an amendment at one reading of a bill does not bar the same amendment from being entertained at a subsequent reading. MEYER, H. 1894, p. 1187. For further modifications and explanations of this principle, see notes to Senate Rule 54 and House Rule 38.

A resolution disapproving of the course of a member is not admissible, unless such course has been a violation of the rules and privileges of the House. SANFORD, H. 1872, p. 292.

Rule 64. [79.] *"A motion to adjourn shall be always first in order."* A motion to adjourn is not in order "when a member in debate has the floor" or pending the verification of a vote. BLISS, H. 1853, pp. 275, 365.

If the main question has been ordered, a motion to adjourn is not in order until the main question is decided. BLISS, H. 1853, p. 275.

When a time has been fixed for taking a vote, and that time has arrived, a motion to adjourn is not in order, for the reason that adjournment would be a reversal of the decision to vote at a specified time. CROCKER, S. 1883, p. 289.

A motion to adjourn to a specified time is not entitled to precedence. BLISS, H. 1853, p. 302.

Although members' names are frequently used by presiding officers in presenting motions for adjournment this should never be done without the members' consent express or implied. THOMPSON, H. 1963, p. 2819.

If a motion to adjourn has been negatived, it cannot be renewed until substantial business has intervened. BLISS, H. 1853, p. 303; BACHELDER (acting Speaker), H. 1898, p. 780; DAVOREN (acting Speaker). H. 1963, p. 1650. See notes to Senate Rule 46.

If there is no other motion before the House, a motion to adjourn may be amended by specifying a particular day, and it has been held that it is not even then debatable. CROWNINSHIELD, H. 1849, p. 314.

The lack of a quorum does not automatically adjourn the House and a motion to instruct the Sergeant-at-Arms to secure the presence of a quorum is in order. MURPHY (acting Speaker). H. 1949, p. 1442.

See notes to House Rule 69.

Rule 65. [80.] See notes to Rules 52 and 64.

"Or some other motion that has precedence." If a special assignment is not called up on the day assigned for its consideration, it has been held that it falls through and loses its privilege, but this ruling was overruled by the House. BLISS, H. 1853, p. 347. See notes to Senate Rule 46.

"And he shall receive no motion relating to the same, except, etc." In the absence of specific authority under any rule, it was held that, pending the question on ordering to a third reading a certain bill introduced by initiative petition, it was not in order then to entertain a resolution proposing a legislative substitute, to be grouped with the said bill on the ballot as an alternative therefor. WARNER, H. 1920, p. 832.

"For the previous question." A motion for the previous question was held to be out of order where the only business intervening between it and a prior motion

for the previous question was the offering of two amendments and the rejection of a motion to postpone. MYERS, H. 1903, p. 349.

A motion for the previous question cannot be entertained by the Chair when another member has the floor. THOMPSON (acting Speaker), H. 1956, p. 973.

This motion may be renewed after "such length of time has been consumed in debate as to make it virtually a new question." JEWETT (acting Speaker), H. 1930, p. 923.

"To close the debate at a specified time." See notes to Rule 69.

"To commit (or recommit)." See CUSHING, H. 1913, p. 1317. See also note to Senate Rule 46.

"To amend." See notes to House Rule 73 and Senate Rules 46 and 50.

That a point of order that a recess declared by the Speaker was contrary to the facts since the question thereon had not been put to the House for its vote, is not well taken for the reason that it had not been seasonably raised. O'NEILL, H. 1951, p. 1971.

Rule 66. [81.] If the House adjourns pending a motion for the previous question, the consideration of said motion is not removed from before the House on the following day. BARRETT, H. 1890, p. 604.

After a motion has been made for the previous question, all debate upon the main question shall be suspended until the previous question is decided. WILLIS, H. 1947, p. 1622.

Rule 68. [84.] After the adoption of the motion for the previous question, and after it was shown, on putting the main question to vote, that a quorum was not present, the point of order that, upon securing the attendance of a quorum, further debate should be allowed, was held to be not well taken as not being seasonably raised. COLE, H. 1907. p. 794.

If a motion for the previous question is carried while a motion to reconsider the adoption of an amendment is pending, the motion to reconsider is not thereby made the main question. ELDRIDGE (acting Speaker), H. 1860, p. 288.

"And then upon the main question." The announcement of a vote for the preacher of the election sermon having shown that no person had a majority, a motion was made that the person having the highest number of votes be declared elected, and the previous question was then moved and carried, and it was held that the main question was the motion that a plurality should elect. BRADBURY, H. 1848, p. 273.

Rule 69. [85.] Unless the vote on a motion to close debate at a specified time can be taken at least thirty minutes before the time specified, the motion is improperly before the House. BATES, H. 1899, p. 505; WALKER, H. 1911, p. 1952.

When the hour mentioned in an order closing debate at a specified time has arrived, further debate is in order if the House, by unanimous consent, extends the time. WILLIS, H. 1945, p. 1533.

It has been held that a motion to close the debate must be put to the question before the time specified in the motion even if it is necessary to interrupt a speaker for the purpose of so doing. UPHAM, S. 1858, p. 448.

A motion to close debate at a specified time was held not to have been rendered inoperative by the fact that after the time had passed, but before the votes on various pending amendments and on the main question had been taken, the House considered and acted upon a special assignment and then adjourned. MYERS, H. 1903, p. 955.

The motion to close the debate at a specified time cannot be applied to a motion to refer a matter to the next General Court, for the reason that one subsidiary motion cannot be applied to another. BRACKETT, H. 1885, p. 599.

The adoption of a motion to take the vote at a specified time does not bar a motion for the previous question or a motion to extend the time. SANFORD, H. 1873, p. 262. When, however, the time fixed for taking the vote has arrived, it is too late to move a reconsideration in order to extend the time. NOYES, H. 1880, p. 220.

Rule 71. [88.] For rulings on recommittals see Joint Rule 5.

MOTIONS TO AMEND.

Rule 72. [89.] When an amendment has been adopted inserting or striking out certain words in a bill, the same words when taken in connection with other words, thus constituting a different proposition, may be struck out or inserted by subsequent amendment at the same stage. WARNER, H. 1919, p. 211; BATES, H. 1899, p. 909. See notes to Senate Rule 46, under "to amend."

A point of order against an amendment is premature when an amendment of the amendment is pending or when a motion to recommit is pending. HULL, H. 1927, p. 632.

Rule 73. [90.] The rejection of an amendment at one reading of a bill does not bar the same amendment from being entertained after a subsequent reading, or in connection with any other bill to which it would be germane. MEYER, H. 1894, p. 1187; SALTONSTALL, H. 1936, p. 1599.

That an amendment to provide for placing a binding question on the ballot went beyond the scope of the petitions upon which was based the Bill reorganizing the school committee of the city of Boston. VOKE (acting Speaker). H. 1991, p. 814.

An amendment proposing a state-wide referendum on any bill has not been in order since adoption of the "Initiative and Referendum" Article of Amendment (XLVIII) to the Constitution, which substituted a new method of referendum by petition. CAHILL (acting Speaker), H. 1935, pp. 1080 and 1740; O'NEILL, H. 1951, p. 2362; SKERRY, H. 1956, p. 958; DAVOREN (acting Speaker), H. 1964, p. 1388.

But an amendment adding a non-binding referendum question to the ballot would not be beyond the scope of the petition upon which the bill prohibiting the appropriation or expenditure of state or federal funds for abortion purposes, was based. McGEE, H. 1977, p. 1604.

An amendment providing for local acceptance of a bill providing for mass transportation facilities was held to be germane even though not requested by the petitioner. DAVOREN (acting Speaker), H. 1964, p. 2045.

An amendment eliminating certain taxes from a bill based on a message from the Governor was held to be germane even though the Governor had asked for legislation in the precise form of the bill submitted with such message. DAVOREN, H. 1965, p. 2588.

The words "or for such other legislation as may be deemed necessary" in a petition asking for legislation must be construed as limited to the principal subject of the petition. YOUNG, H. 1922, p. 518.

An amendment striking out a portion of a bill is not germane if it broadens the bill beyond the scope of the petition. MYERS, H. 1900, p. 918.

An amendment is not in order if it extends beyond
the scope of the subject matter on which the report of a
committee is based. MARDEN, H. 1883, p. 232;
BARRETT, H. 1893, pp. 1046, 1056; MYERS, H. 1900,
p. 1146; SALTONSTALL, H. 1930, pp. 290, 405, 642;
H. 1931, p. 938; H. 1933, p. 1194; H. 1936, pp. 533,
753; BIGELOW (acting Speaker), H. 1936, p. 609;
CAHILL, H. 1937, pp. 453, 572, 714; H. 1938, pp. 237,
526, 1495, 1560. The Governor, in returning bills with
recommendation of amendment, is not exempt from this
principle. SALTONSTALL, H. 1936, p. 1573; BARTLEY,
H. 1974, p. 2398; H. 1975, p. 2143; MACLEAN (acting
Speaker), H. 1976, pp. 1650, 1651; MAROTTA (acting
Speaker), H. 1984, p. 931; KEVERIAN, H. 1985, pp. 183,
487, 506; H. 1987, pp. 1653 and 1654. MENARD (acting
Speaker), H. 1991, p. 824; FLAHERTY, H. 1991, p. 1480;
M. P. WALSH (acting Speaker), H. 1991, pp. 1515, 1547;
VOKE (acting Speaker), H. 1992, p. 39; 1996, p. 1687;
SCACCIA (acting Speaker), 1996, pp. 2209, 2212, 2214.
[Also see ruling under House Rule 43.]

See notes to Senate Rule 50. See also ruling by
Speaker BARRETT (H. 1889, p. 842), cited in notes on
Joint Rules under "Committees."

For rulings as to amendments declared to be ger-
mane, see SALTONSTALL, H. 1935, p. 1064; H. 1936,
pp. 388, 463, 886, 926, 1038; CAHILL (acting Speaker),
H. 1936, p. 341; CAHILL, H. 1937, pp. 577, 1198;
H. 1938, pp. 661, 815, 1069; FLAHERTY, H. 1995, p. 165;
FINNERAN, H. 1996, p. 2417.

The scope of a bill sought to be amended is not
limited by the scope of an investigation which may have
been ordered, but includes the scope of the original petition and of any resulting bill or resolve which may have
been given legislative sanction. SALTONSTALL, H. 1930,
p. 765.

For amendments deemed not to be frivolous in their nature, see SALTONSTALL, H. 1935, p. 761; CAHILL (acting Speaker), H. 1935, p. 1280.

For an amendment deemed to be frivolous in nature, see C. F. FLAHERTY (acting Speaker), 1985, p. 12.

An amendment relative to the public *purchase* and operation of a public utility is broader in its scope than a recommendation for legislation relative to the public *control* and operation of such utility. HULL, H. 1928, p. 990; SALTONSTALL, H. 1931, p. 938.

An amendment increasing an appropriation to an amount larger than the specific sum recommended by the Governor in a special emergency message is not in order. YOUNG, H. 1922, p. 214. See notes to Amendment LXIII of the Constitution.

An amendment authorizing the playing of poker in connection with prizes to be won by chance, was held not to be germane to a bill authorizing the playing of "beano, or any similar game." CAHILL (acting Speaker), H. 1934, p. 1169.

A bill contemplating legislation is not admissible as an amendment to a report of a committee, leave to withdraw, on a petition which simply asks for a public hearing and not for legislation. TUCKER (acting Speaker), H. 1892, p. 460.

In a case where a bill permissive in its character was the subject matter referred, it was held that an amendment, which, if adopted, would make the bill mandatory, was not in order. MCDONOUGH (acting Speaker), H. 1888, p. 535. See also CUSHING, H. 1912, p. 1662; SALTONSTALL, H. 1933, p. 1193.

An amendment which provides for a *modification* of an existing law is not germane to a bill which provides for a repeal of the law. Cox, H. 1916, p. 288; MARDEN, H. 1883, p. 512; NOYES, H. 1887, pp. 523, 552; BARRETT, H. 1892, p. 786; DARLING (acting Speaker), H. 1894, p. 1085. [For an interpretation of "modification" see SALTONSTALL, H. 1935, p. 1740.]

On a petition for repeal of a law, it is competent to report or substitute a bill for repeal of a part of that law, on the ground that it is competent to grant a part of the request of the petitioner. SALTONSTALL, H. 1935, p. 1739.

On a petition asking for a study of the subject matter, it is not competent to substitute a bill. BARTLEY, H. 1970, p. 1669.

On recommendations for modification of the so-called compulsory motor vehicle liability insurance law, it was held not to be germane to move an amendment repealing that law. SALTONSTALL, H. 1935, p. 1414.

A bill regulating the giving of entertainments on the Lord's Day was held to be within the scope of and germane to a petition asking for the prohibition of such entertainments. MYERS, H. 1900, p. 738.

A substitute removing existing legal restrictions is not germane to a petition and bill imposing more rigid restriction. MYERS, H. 1900, p. 1007; WEEKS (acting Speaker), H. 1908, p. 749.

An amendment providing for the abolition of an official board was held not to be germane to a petition asking for the continuance of the board. MEYER, H. 1894, p. 825.

The House has a right in granting legislation to impose such provisos, conditions or limitations as to it may seem fit. BARRETT, H. 1892, pp. 536, 839. See also Cox, H. 1916, p. 837; CUSHING, H. 1912, p. 1645;

CAHILL, H. 1938, p. 527; O'NEILL, H. 1951, p. 1407; BARTLEY, H. 1969. pp. 1755, 1769; H. 1971, p. 1918; H. 1974, p. 1962.

An amendment proposing an investigation of *and report on* the subject matter of a resolve must be held to be germane, even though an investigation was not requested by the petitioners. HULL, H. 1926, p. 738; SALTONSTALL, H. 1932, p. 504; CAHILL, H. 1938, pp. 630, 844.

But an amendment is not in order if it seeks only to ascertain the will of the people with reference to the subject matter, for the reason that such a proposition would not result in a report to the Legislature on which legislation could be based. HULL, H. 1927, p. 501; SALTONSTALL, H. 1932, p. 430; HERTER, H. 1939, p. 923.

It is competent, in connection with a bill requiring the expenditure of a large sum of money, to provide by amendment a method of raising the money. SALTONSTALL, H. 1935. p. 1425; QUINN (acting Speaker), H. 1964, p. 1241. And to designate by amendment methods of financing a bill, "even from money already allocated for other purposes." CAHILL (acting Speaker), H. 1935, p. 1644. And to reduce by amendment an amount of money authorized (in the preceding year) to be expended. provided the money has not been spent. CAHILL (acting Speaker), H. 1936. p. 341.

An amendment relating to investments by savings banks is not germane to a bill based on a petition for legislation relative to the investment of savings bank deposits in the bonds of telephone companies. HULL, H. 1928, p. 241.

When the question is upon concurring with the other branch in the adoption of an amendment, such amendment only is the subject under consideration. COLE,

H. 1906, p. 982; QUINN, H. 1967, p. 2653. And it is not in order to move to concur with the Senate in an amendment of an item, with a further amendment striking out the entire item, for the reason that it is not competent for the House to eliminate by amendment an item which had been agreed to by both branches. SALTONSTALL, H. 1935, p. 889.

Where a report, no legislation necessary, had been amended by the Senate by the substitution, in part, of certain bills for so much of the report as related to the subject matter of the said bills, and the report (remainder) had been accepted by that branch and so endorsed, it was held that the subject matter covered by the said bills had been removed from the report, and only the remainder thereof was before the House for its consideration. YOUNG, H. 1921, p. 1005.

For sundry cases in which a point of order had been raised that a proposed amendment is not germane to the subject under consideration, see the appendixes to the House Journals under the title of "Questions of Order," or "Orders, Points of." A list of the cases which arose prior to 1902 may be found in the Manual for the General Court of that year.

An amendment in the form of a substitute bill may not be amended after adoption, until the next reading of the substituted bill. PHELPS, H. 1857, p. 984; DAVOREN, H. 1966, p. 1632; H. 1967, p. 2521; QUINN, H. 1968, p. 1716; BARTLEY, H. 1971, p. 2030; H. 1974, pp. 2470, 2586.

That an amendment to a proposed substitute bill is in order for the reason that it is always proper to perfect a proposed substitute bill before it is adopted. MCGEE, H. 1978, p. 1657.

A further amendment to a pending amendment declared to be beyond the scope. SERRA (acting Speaker), H. 1995, p. 331; NAGLE (acting Speaker), H. 1996, p. 2160.

That an amendment to strike out a sentence of a bill was improperly before the House for the reason that the sentence had been amended in the same reading of the bill. MENARD (acting Speaker), H. 1991, p. 1282.

It is too late to raise objection that a substitute bill is not germane to a petition after the substitute has been adopted. MEYER, H. 1895, p. 406; SALTONSTALL, H. 1935, p. 821.

So also it is too late to raise objection that an amendment is not germane to a bill after the amendment has been adopted (NOYES, H. 1888, p. 463; MYERS, H. 1902, p. 1276; H. 1903, p. 1032; SALTONSTALL, H. 1934, p. 774), or after the consideration of the amendment has occupied the attention of the House a portion of two sessions. SANFORD, H. 1874, p. 367. See also DEWEY (acting Speaker), H. 1877, p. 463; NOYES, H. 1881, p. 480.

Objection that a bill covers matters not referred to the committee cannot be raised after action on the bill, by amendment, or by passing it to a third reading, or even after continued deliberation in regard to it. [For citations on rulings based on the foregoing, see Sundry Rulings.]

See notes to Senate Rule 50 and to Joint Rules under the head of "Committees."

That an amendment, offered as a substitute (in part) for a special report of the committee on Rules relative to an investigation of certain acts and conduct of Alfred B. Cenedella, Lawrence R. Goldberg and other public officials, was improperly before the House for the reason that it was broader in its scope than the subject matter of the pending report. The amendment was in the nature of a resolve addressing the Governor to remove John S. Derham from the office of Justice of the Second District Court of Southern Worcester. As the removal contemplates concurrent action by the other branch and as the Senate had no part in authorizing the investigation, no amendment would be in order which would make that branch a party to the proposed action. O'NEILL, H. 1951, p. 1906.

That a point of order that the failure to adopt an amendment to a bill left it in a form where it was improperly before the House was held to be not well taken for the reason that the question raised was a matter of law. O'NEILL. H. 1952, p. 946.

That a point of order that a bill in its amended form is not properly before the House for the reason that the remaining provisions thereof were broader in their scope than the petition upon which the bill was based was held to be not well taken. because the amendments had already been adopted and the House had engaged in protracted debate on the question of referring the bill, as amended. to the next annual session. O'NEILL, H. 1952, p. 1576.

For ruling on amendment offered to a bill, where the Governor had recommended the enactment of the legislation in its *precise form* — —, see DAVOREN, H. 1965, p. 2588; BARTLEY, H. 1973. p. 3495.

That an item should not be in an appropriation bill but should be in a capital outlay bill. BARTLEY, H. 1973, p. 1090.

An amendment originating new legislation was an improper amendment to an appropriation bill. BARTLEY,

H. 1974, pp. 1218, 1219, 2032; McGEE, H. 1976. pp. 1569, 1975.

For rulings as to amendments declared to be beyond the scope of pending bills. McGEE, H. 1977, pp. 294, 309, 1118(2), 1203, 1427, 1804, 2037, 2038, 2585, 2606, 2673; McGEE, H. 1978, pp. 270, 505, 589, 618, 778, 1506, 1584, 1649; McGEE, H. 1979, pp. 90, 1570, 1571, 1883; McGEE, H. 1980, p. 454; McGEE, H. 1983, pp. 405A, 415A, 913; MURPHY (acting Speaker), H. 1983, pp. 1843, 1844; C. F. FLAHERTY (acting Speaker), H. 1987, p. 742; VOKE (acting Speaker), H. 1995, p. 534; DIMASI (acting Speaker), H. 1996, p. 2418; NAGLE (acting Speaker), H. 1996, p. 2553.

That amendments to the House Rules (in House Rule 19, Code of Ethics) were improperly before the House. McGEE, H. 1977, pp. 371, 372, 2222, 2263(2), 2264(2), 2266(2), 2290.

That an amendment to an order relative to the House rules declared beyond the scope. FLAHERTY, H. 1995, p. 10.

That amendments to the House Bill prohibiting the appropriation or expenditure of state or federal funds for abortion purposes were beyond the scope of the petition upon which the bill was based. McGEE, H. 1977, pp. 1605(2), 1606(2), 1614(2), 1615, 1616.

That amendments to the General Appropriations Act (House, No. 5560) were improperly before the House for the reason that they sought to amend various items in the budget and also to insert "outside sections." McGEE, H. 1978, p. 916.

That an amendment to the General Appropriations Act was improperly before the House for the reason that said amendment was not directly related to an item in section 20 of the bill. McGEE, H. 1980, p. 684.

That an amendment to the General Appropriations Act was improperly before the House for the reason that the House had previously engrossed and sent to the Senate a bill substantially the same as the amendment. McGee, H. 1978, p. 984; H. 1980, p. 652.

That an amendment to the General Appropriations Act (House, No. 6262) was improperly before the House for the reason that the amendment sought to amend an item which had already been amended at the same reading. McGee, H. 1980, p. 672.

That an amendment was improperly before the House for the reason that the subject-matter of said amendment had previously been considered during the same reading. Voke (acting Speaker), H. 1993, p. 990. See also Flaherty, H. 1993, pp. 1270-1271; H. 1994, p. 628; H. 1995, p. 8.

Rule 74. [91.] This rule does not save the right to amend when a simple motion to strike out *(i.e., a motion not embracing a proposition to insert)* has been made and rejected. Sanford, H. 1874, p. 499.

"A question containing two or more propositions capable of division." The question, "Shall this bill pass to be engrossed?" is not divisible. Thus, in passing to be engrossed a bill fixing certain salaries, the bill cannot be divided so as to allow the salary of each official to be voted on separately. Wardwell (acting Speaker), H. 1881, p. 490.

"Strike out and insert." See Noyes, H. 1880, p. 60.

Rule 75. [92.] See note to Senate Rule 51.

APPEAL.

Rule 77. [94.] An appeal from the ruling of the Chair must be taken at once. The right to appeal is cut off by the intervention of other business. PHELPS, H. 1857, p. 907. See also CROCKER, S. 1883, p. 289.

Upon the question raised by an appeal, a motion for the previous question is in order. MYERS, H. 1903, pp. 965, 1064.

For a case where the Chair refused to entertain an appeal because the question had previously been decided by a ruling of the Chair, which was confirmed by a vote of the House and thereby had become the judgment of the House, see BLISS, H. 1853, p. 365.

It has been held that, pending an appeal from the decision of the Chair on a point of order, a motion to suspend the provisions of a standing order requiring the Speaker to declare an adjournment at a specific time is in order. See Cox (acting Speaker), H. 1914, p. 652.

Rule 78. That resolves which affect state finances should be referred to the committee on Ways and Means, under Rule 33. McGEE, H. 1980, p. 1034.

REPRESENTATIVES CHAMBER AND ADJOINING ROOMS.

Rule 81. That the House was meeting in a formal session in violation of the requirement that all proceedings shall be televised. GIBSON (acting Speaker), H. 1985, p. 417; KEVERIAN, H. 1987, p. 1209.

QUORUM.

Rule 82. [105.] A vote of 82 to 21 does not necessarily indicate the lack of a quorum, but only that less than a quorum has voted. HULL, H. 1928, p. 964. [See Opinion of Attorney-General, 1892, Feb. 1, H. 1892, p. 118.]

Rule 85. [104.] That an order for a second legislative day was properly before the House since such an order was strictly a procedural matter similar to a motion to adjourn or to recess. McGee, H. 1979, p. 1899.

Rule 86. [101.] It is not competent for the House on motion to suspend the principles of general parliamentary law. The House could not suspend the rule that the rejection of a motion to strike out precludes amendment, any more than it could suspend the rule requiring a majority of votes to pass a motion. Sanford, H. 1874, p. 499.

NOTES OF RULINGS
ON THE
JOINT RULES.

***

COMMITTEES.

Rule 1. (See "Sundry Rulings.") For a discussion as to the creation of joint committees, and their relation to the two branches, see HALE. H. 1859. p. 269. [Opinion of the Counsel to the House of Representatives as to whether members of the General Court on existing recess commissions retain their membership on said commissions who fail of re-election to the General Court. See House Journal, 1939, p. 129.]

The committees on Rules of the two branches, acting concurrently, do not constitute a joint standing committee. SALTONSTALL. H. 1930. p. 228.

Under authority of the last paragraph of this rule, the committees on Rules of the two branches, acting concurrently, may report, recommending changes in the joint rules which tend to facilitate the business of the legislature and such changes may be adopted on a majority vote of the two branches, even though the joint rules have been finally adopted for the life of a General Court. For an instance where this occurred, see S. J. 1926. pp. 687-688.

Amendment to a report of the committees on Rules offered from the floor ruled beyond scope of report and would require a two-thirds vote to adopt. McGEE, H. 1976, p. 2209.

Rule 3. A delegation to represent the State, composed not only of members of the Legislature, but also of State officers, is not a joint committee within the meaning of this rule. BATES. H. 1898, p. 1068.

Rule 5. Under this rule a motion to recommit, made at a date later than that fixed in the rule, is out of order. BARRETT, H. 1891, pp. 866, 983.

This rule does not apply to a motion to recommit to a House committee. CUSHING (acting Speaker), H. 1911, p. 902. Nor does it apply to reports of the committees on Rules of the two branches, acting concurrently. SALTONSTALL, H. 1930, p. 228.

When a bill is declared to be broader in its scope than the subject-matter on which it was based, the subject-matter may be recommitted. BARRETT, H. 1892, p. 724; MYERS, H. 1900, p. 706; HULL, H. 1926, p. 862; SALTONSTALL, H. 1930, p. 397. See notes to Senate Rule 46. [See change in this rule adopted in 1953 which provides that a bill or resolve declared to be broader in its scope than the subject-matter upon which it is based shall be recommitted to the committee.]

Rule 7. *"Or other legislation."* Prior to 1891 this phrase was *"other special legislation,"* and special legislation was held to be that which directly affects individuals as such differently from the class to which they belong or from the people at large. PILLSBURY, S. 1885, pp. 588, 589.

It is the province of the committee, and not of the Speaker, to determine whether the purpose for which the legislation is sought can be secured without detriment to the public interest by a general law. MYERS, H. 1901, p. 1048; WARNER, H. 1919, p. 945. See also WALKER, H. 1910, p. 660.

See notes to Senate Rule 16 and to House Rule 30.

Rule 7B. A petition taken from the files of the preceding year is subject to the provisions of this rule, even though the rule had been complied with in respect to the preceding session. HULL, H. 1928, p. 219.

A bill relative to appropriations for school purposes in the city of Boston should have had the approval of the mayor and city council to comply with the last paragraph of Joint Rule 7B. WILLIS, H. 1948, p. 724. [In 1967 this rule was changed from one relating to requiring local approval on certain matters concerning cities, towns and counties, to one relating to home rule requirements under Article LXXXIX of the Amendments to the Constitution.]

NOTICE TO PARTIES INTERESTED.

Rule 8. See notes to Senate Rule 15 and House Rule 31. For a case in which it was unsuccessfully claimed that a bill, though general in its terms, was in fact special in its operation, and that therefore notice to parties interested should have been given, see WALKER, H. 1910, p. 1211.

A bill may be laid aside on the ground that it is in violation of this rule after it has passed through one branch. BISHOP, S. 1882, p. 307.

A bill which is offered as a substitute for a report of a committee must be germane to the subject referred to the committee. JEWELL, H. 1871, p. 342.

It is sufficient if the petition bears the certificate of the Secretary of the Commonwealth that the required publication has been made. It is not necessary to state in detail in the publication all the provisions of the legislation desired. BARRETT, H. 1892, p. 995.

It is not within the province of the Speaker, but within the province of the committee, to determine whether a petition has been properly advertised. BARRETT, H. 1892, p. 1160; WALKER, H. 1910, p. 1471. See also CUSHING, H. 1912, p. 1720.

"No legislation." Prior to 1890 the phraseology was *"no bill or resolve,"* and under that phraseology it was held that an order that a committee investigate the management and condition of a certain society and report what legislation is necessary was within the operation of the rule, because any bill or resolve embodying the conclusions of such investigation would be within the scope of the rule. BRUCE, S. 1884, p. 580. *Contra,* see PILLSBURY, S. 1885, p. 580.

A bill to incorporate the Boston Railroad Holding Company was held not to be such legislation as that described in this rule. TREADWAY, S. 1909, p. 1034. See also WALKER, H. 1911, p. 1800; WILLIS, H. 1948, p. 1215.

"Except by a petition." Prior to 1890 the words *"by amendment or otherwise"* were also used. For an instance in which under that form of the rule an amendment was held to be barred by the rule, see BISHOP, S. 1880, p. 333. For an instance in which an amendment proposing a new treatment of a subject already in the bill, and not the introduction of a new subject into the bill, was held not to be barred by the rule, see BISHOP, S. 1881, p. 384.

For an instance in which it was held that a communication from the Governor transmitting a subject-matter for legislation is, for the purposes of legislation, to be considered in the light of a message from him, and is entitled to the same consideration that such a message would have, and that a bill reported upon said communication is not in violation of this rule, see MYERS, H. 1901, p. 1048.

Also that recommendations for legislation contained in a special report submitted to the General Court by a board or commission duly constituted by law are not in violation of this rule. YOUNG, H. 1922, p. 201.

Prior to 1890 the following words were used: — *"Except by a report of a committee on petition duly presented and referred,"* and under this form of the rule various rulings were made. For cases in which a bill was ruled out, see LONG, H. 1878, pp. 116, 120; COGSWELL, S. 1878, p. 178; NOYES, H. 1888, p. 479. For a case in which it was held that the words "duly presented" did not require compliance with the provisions of chapter 2 of the Public Statutes in regard to notice; that those provisions were mandatory only to the petitioner, and that the Legislature might, if it saw fit, hear the petitioner, notwithstanding his failure to comply with the law, see MARDEN, H. 1883, p. 533. See also NOYES, H. 1882, p. 90.

"Objection to the violation of this rule may be taken at any stage prior to that of the third reading." For a case which arose prior to the insertion of these words, see DEWEY (acting Speaker), H. 1877, p. 463.

Rule 9. This rule does not apply to a message from the Governor or to recommendations contained in a report of a commission. COLE, H. 1907, p. 976; TREADWAY, S. 1909, p. 1034; WALKER, H. 1911, p. 1800.

For instances in which bills under this rule were referred to the next General Court, see COLE, H. 1907, p. 1064; CALVIN COOLIDGE, S. 1915, p. 894.

A motion to substitute a bill for a report "reference to the next annual session" (for the reason that the requirements of this rule had not been complied with) is not in order, unless the rule is first suspended. NICHOLSON, S. 1947, p. 1015. See also VALENTINE (acting Speaker), H. 1947, p. 1374; OLSON (acting President), S. 1951, p. 1270.

As to the form and evidence of publication, see notes to Joint Rule 8.

For a case in which a bill was held not to be special, but to be general and therefore not subject to the provisions of this rule, see WALKER, H. 1910, p. 1212. See also CUSHING, H. 1913, p. 1664.

The provisions of the Revised Laws, chapter 3, which are referred to in this rule, are mandatory only to the petitioner, and the General Court may hear the petitioner notwithstanding his failure to comply with the law. MYERS, H. 1902, p. 268; SKERRY, H. 1957, p. 2122.

A bill reported on a petition properly filed under the provisions of Section 5 of Chapter 3 of the General Laws is subject to amendment the same as any other bill. WRAGG, S. 1938, p. 436.

Under this rule it was held that a petition to establish the boundary line in tidewaters between two towns, involving the taking of land from one town and the annexing of it to the other, is, in effect, a petition to divide an existing town; and, since no publication of notice, as required by law, had been made and the rule had not been suspended, a bill reported upon such a petition was improperly before the House. MEYER, H. 1896, p. 947.

This rule having been concurrently suspended with reference to a petition before its reference to a committee, and the committee having reported "leave to withdraw," it was held that the rule was no longer operative on the subject-matter of the petition, and that a bill could be substituted for the report of the committee. DANA, S. 1906, p. 748.

Bills reported to the House in violation of this rule, and there passed to be engrossed and sent to the Senate for concurrence, referred to the next General Court in compliance with this rule. DANA, S. 1906, p. 712; CHAPPLE, S. 1907, pp. 898, 978; HOLMES, S. 1957, p. 1510.

A bill having been passed to be engrossed by the Senate and by the House, it was held that it was too late to raise the point of order that said bill came within the provisions of this rule. CUSHING, H. 1913, pp. 1941, 1959.

For the case of a bill which was held not to come within the provisions of this rule, see BATES, H. 1899, pp. 1036, 1061.

LIMIT OF TIME ALLOWED FOR REPORTS OF COMMITTEES.

Rule 10. If after the date fixed for final report a committee reports a bill, such bill must be laid aside. NOYES, H. 1888, p. 832; BARRETT, H. 1889, p. 897 and H. 1893, p. 706; COX, H. 1917, p. 641. So also a report of leave to withdraw will be laid aside. MEYER, H. 1895, p. 920. See also COX, H. 1915, p. 865.

After a bill has been substituted for an adverse report, it is too late to raise the point of order that the report was not made within the limit fixed by this rule. UNDERHILL (acting Speaker), H. 1911, p. 1791; HULL, H. 1926, p. 862.

General orders extending the time for reports of joint committees apply to these committees no less when sitting jointly than when sitting separately. MYERS, H. 1901, p. 1047.

That certain petitions pending before the committee on State Administration should be placed on the House Calendar with an adverse report (under Joint Rule 10). McGEE, H. 1980, p. 733 (2).

That all matters not reported by joint committees by the fourth Wednesday of April should be placed on the House Calendar with an adverse report (under Joint Rule 10) for the reason that any orders extending the time for committees to report should be adopted prior to that date. McGEE, H. 1980, p. 733. [Decision of the Chair sustained.]

COMMITTEES OF CONFERENCE.

Rule 11. It seems that any difference between the two branches can be submitted to a committee of conference. PILLSBURY, S. 1886, p. 702.

It seems that, although committees of conference must represent the vote of each branch, a fair interpretation of this rule, where the vote was not unanimous, would permit the appointment of two members from each branch representing the majority and the third the minority. COTTON, S. 1939, p. 1292.

That the Speaker had complied with the provisions of the rule requiring committees of conference to represent the vote of each branch, when the question before the committee was Senate amendments in which the House had non-concurred. SKERRY, H. 1955, p. 2215.

For a discussion of a situation in which, although the disagreement had been prolonged to the point where each branch had twice affirmed its position, neither branch asked for a committee of conference, see HALE, H. 1859, p. 116.

That which has been agreed to by both branches cannot be disturbed by a committee of conference. MYERS, H. 1900, p. 1403; O'NEILL, H. 1951, p. 2410; KEVERIAN (acting Speaker), H. 1977, p. 1573; FLAHERTY, H. 1996, p. 1771.

That a report of the committee of conference was improperly before the House for the reason that said committee has exceeded the total cost of the House and Senate versions of the capital outlay program. MCGEE, H. 1983, p. 1941.

It is competent for a committee of conference to report such change in the sections or portions not agreed to as is germane to those sections. BISHOP, S. 1882, p. 391.

The reception of a report of a committee of conference discharges the committee, even though the report is subsequently ruled out as beyond the scope of the reference, and the matters of difference may be referred to a new committee of conference. MYERS, H. 1900, p. 1463.

A question on concurring with the House in the appointment of a new committee of conference comes properly before the Senate even though the Senate has previously refused a motion for said committee. NICHOLSON, S. 1947, p. 1256.

A report of a committee of conference was laid aside on a point of order, for the reason that it recommended substitution of a new bill (special) for the bill (general) with respect to which the disagreement occurred. SALTONSTALL, H. 1931, p. 910.

That a report of a committee of conference on the General Appropriations Act was improperly before the House for the reason that said report contained language not referred to the conference committee. McGEE, H. 1979, p. 210; H. 1980, p. 1188; H. 1984, pp. 1126, 1127; FLAHERTY, H. 1992, p. 85.

That a point of order relative to a report of a committee of conference with reference to certain amendments to the General Appropriations Act was not seasonably raised. McGEE, H. 1980, p. 1189. [Decision of the Chair sustained.]

For warrant for departing, in connection with appropriation bills, from the usual procedure in respect to reports of committees of conference, and entertaining a motion for appointment of a further committee of conference on items on which the first committee had failed to agree, see CAHILL, H. 1937, p. 846.

For an instance where a new committee of conference had amended a part of the bill not in disagreement. BARTLEY, H. 1975, p. 2093.

For statement relative to representation on a committee of conference, see POWERS, S. 1962, p. 1569.

That a report of a committee of conference on a special appropriation bill was *"in part"* and that the committee could continue to deliberate upon the matters still in disagreement and report their recommendations at a future time. DICARLO (acting President), S. 1975, p. 1961.

For statement relative to NOT allowing motion to recommit conference committee report because committee is discharged after report, see DICARLO (acting President), S. 1976, p. 1537.

See paper on conference committee reports as to amendments, etc., by Norman L. Pidgeon, Advisor to Senate, S. 1976, p. 1940.

See "Sundry Rulings" (Courtesy between the Branches).

Rule 11A. That a report of the committee of conference on the General Appropriation Bill was improperly before the House for the reason that detailed information relative to the differences between the two branches was not made available. MCGEE, H. 1984, pp. 1125, 1126.

That an amendment to a motion for the appointment of a committee of conference on the General Appropriation Bill was improperly before the House for the reason that it would constitute an improper interference into the internal workings of a committee. FLAHERTY, H. 1994, p. 742.

LIMIT OF TIME ALLOWED FOR NEW BUSINESS.

Rule 12. This rule does not exclude matters of privilege. They may be considered whenever they arise. PILLSBURY, S. 1885, p. 583; BARRETT, H. 1890, p. 1259.

"All other subjects of legislation." See LONG, H. 1878, p. 572; BRACKETT, H. 1885, p. 354.

An order which is merely incidental to a subject of legislation before the House is not within the scope of this rule. MARDEN, H. 1883, p. 311.

"Deposited with the Clerk of either branch." In 1891 these words were substituted for the words *"Proposed or introduced,"* previously used. Under the rule as it stood prior to 1891, it was twice ruled that matter referred by one General Court to the next, when called up in the General Court to which it is so referred, must be considered as the introduction of a new business within the intent to this rule. In both cases the bill in question related to the compensation of members of the Legislature, and in both cases, on appeal, the decision of the Chair was reversed. LONG, H. 1877, pp. 466-473; CROCKER, S. 1883, pp. 521, 578.

"Shall, when presented, be referred to the next General Court." Under this rule, before the words "when presented" were inserted, in a case where a bill had passed to a third reading, it was held that it was then too late to secure its reference to the next General Court under the rule. DEWEY (acting Speaker), H. 1877, p. 463. See also WADE, H. 1879, p. 540.

For a case arising under a somewhat similar rule, see JEWELL, H. 1868, p. 591.

After the House had debated an order several times and had once adopted it, it was held too late to raise the point that the order came within the scope of this rule. BRACKETT, H. 1885, p. 354.

"This rule shall not be . . . suspended except by a concurrent vote." Pending the question on concurring in the suspension of this rule to admit a petition, it has been held not to be in order to move to lay the petition upon the table. NOYES, H. 1888, p. 260.

That a petition relative to reforming the charter of the city of Boston has properly been referred to the committee on Local Affairs and was not subject to the provisions of Joint Rule 12. McGEE, H. 1977, p. 16.

Introduced "On Leave" for statement, see DONAHUE, S. 1967, p. 623.

PRINTING AND DISTRIBUTION OF DOCUMENTS.

Rule 21. A resolve, not an order, should be the form used to provide for printing a document not for the use of the Legislature, and involving the expenditure of public money. LONG, H. 1878, p. 58; NOYES, H. 1880, p. 123.

The House can by its vote alone order documents printed for the use of the House. MEYER, H. 1894, p. 397.

LEGISLATIVE AMENDMENTS TO THE CONSTITUTION.

Rule 23. A proposal for a legislative amendment to the Constitution cannot be introduced by substitution for an adverse report of a committee on a petition calling for an amendment of the General Laws. ARTHUR W. COOLIDGE, S. 1946, p. 677.

That an amendment to an order calling for a joint session of the two houses could not be entertained for the reason that if it was adopted it would result in amending a proposal for a legislative amendment to the Constitution other than in a joint session. SKERRY, H. 1955, p. 1285.

Rule 25. An order having been adopted by the Senate for a joint convention to receive a communication from the Governor, the Chair refused to entertain a motion to reconsider the adoption thereof for the reason that the time stated in the order for the joint convention to be held had expired. HOLMES (acting President), S. 1955, p. 1576.

Rule 26. Can a committee reference made (rightly or wrongly) in a joint convention be modified subsequently by concurrent action of the two branches? SALTONSTALL, H. 1934, p. 500.

It is not competent for a convention, called for the purpose of receiving "such communication as His Excellency the Governor may be pleased to make," to refer any matter to a committee of either or both branches. MORAN (in *joint session*), S. 1936, p. 529, and H. 1936, p. 695.

A motion to commit may be made while a motion to reconsider is pending. SKERRY (*presiding in joint session*), S. 1956, p. 919; H. 1956, p. 1421.

SPECIAL SESSIONS.

Rule 26A. As to methods of providing for assembling in special session, see OPINION OF JUSTICES, H. 1936, p. 1461; H. 1939, p. 1853.

For ruling on calling special sessions during regular session of General Court, see KEVIN B. HARRINGTON, S. 1976, pp. 1859-1860.

JOINT ELECTIONS.

Rule 27. Pending the question on adopting an order that the joint convention proceed to the election of an

Attorney-General to fill a vacancy, and a nomination having been made and seconded for said office, it was ruled that nominations were in order pending the adoption of the order. HOLMES *(in joint session)*, S. 1958, p. 1355; H. 1958, p. 1860.

REFERENCES TO THE COMMITTEES ON RULES.

Rule 29. If the committees on Rules of the two branches, acting concurrently, are discharged from the consideration of a petition, and another committee reports on that petition a resolve subject to this rule, that resolve (even though it be the resolve originally accompanying the petition), should be referred to said committees, acting concurrently. SALTONSTALL, H. 1930, p. 622.

Rule 30. The committees on Rules of the two branches, acting concurrently, had recommended that extension of the time within which joint committees are required to report be granted. Under provisions of this rule, a majority vote is required for the adoption of the order. BULGER, S. 1988, p. 604.

SUNDRY RULINGS.

In a case in which a petition was accompanied by a statement of reasons in its support, it was held that such statement did not affect the scope of the petition. CUSHING, H. 1912, p. 1796.

When the rules require that legislation shall be based upon petition, the petition determines the scope of legislation. A bill filed with the petition does not enlarge the scope of the petition unless the petition contains phraseology which makes the bill a part of it. BUTLER, S. 1894, p. 940; JONES, S. 1903, p. 491. Neither does a bill curtail the scope of the petition which it accompanies. BATES, H. 1899, pp. 1036, 1061.

On a point of order that an amendment of a certain document could not be entertained because the petition, which had been considered and reported upon by the committee, was not in fact a prayer for legislation, but was merely a recital of alleged grievances, it was ruled that, inasmuch as the petition had been passed upon by both Houses and had been referred to a committee and had been considered and reported upon by that committee, it was essentially a prayer for legislation, and that the point of order was NOT well taken. WELLINGTON WELLS, S. 1926, p. 487.

COMMITTEES AND COMMISSIONS.

Committees must confine their report to the subject referred to them. For sundry cases in which the point of order has been raised that this principle has been violated, see indexes to the Senate Journals under "Order, Questions of" and appendices to House Journals under the titles "Questions of Order," and "Order, Points of." A list of the cases which arose prior to 1902 may be found in the Manual of the General Court for that year. See also H. 1908, p. 1359.

A report of a committee made without authority cannot be considered. BARRETT, H. 1892, p. 877.

A report adopted at a duly notified meeting of a committee, a quorum being present, was held to be a valid report of the committee, although an unsigned memorandum was written on the report to the effect that certain members, constituting a majority of the committee, dissented. BOARDMAN, S. 1888, p. 378.

It is not within the province of the chair upon a point of order to inquire into the internal workings of a committee with a view to determining whether the subject-matter in question has been properly considered by such committee. BARRETT, H. 1891, p. 1127; JONES, S. 1903, p. 457; GREENWOOD, S. 1913, p. 1154; WRAGG, S. 1938, p. 938; HOLMES (acting President), S. 1941, p. 1721; HUNT, S. 1943, p. 861; SKERRY, H. 1956, p. 408; KEVERIAN, H. 1987, p. 35.

When a report is received, the committee's duties as to the matter reported on are ended, and they can make no further report upon it unless the subject is recommitted to them by vote of the assembly. CROCKER, S. 1883, pp. 489, 576; MARDEN, H. 1883, pp. 529, 669; BARRETT, H. 1891, p. 789.

The reception of a report discharges the committee, even though the report is subsequently ruled out as beyond the scope of the reference. MYERS, H. 1900, p. 1463. For recommittal of subject-matter, see notes to Joint Rule 5.

Where a committee has referred to it several petitions on the same subject, or various papers involving either directly or remotely the same subject, whether simply or connected with other things, and the committee has once considered and reported upon any one subject involved in them, it has entirely exhausted its authority over that subject.

After such report has been once made, the subject passes beyond the control of the committee and becomes the property of the House.

Any papers left in the hands of the committee which may indirectly involve the same subject must be treated as if that question was not in them. It seems not to be within the power of a committee to withhold mention of any particular petition, report or other paper, and thus retain possession of a subject once reported upon as a basis for a new action and a new report.

General considerations support strongly this view. It is a maxim of jurisprudence that it is for the public advantage that strifes should come to an end. It is equally for the public interest that contentions in what our fathers called the Great and General Court should be settled once and for all. Many persons have a deep interest in the matters heard before committees. They appear in person or by counsel; and when the subject is. by report of the committee, brought before the Legislature, they appear to influence the action of members. as they have the right to do. When the matter is once disposed of, they depart. and suppose they may do so in safety. They have a right to believe their interests no longer require their presence. But if a committee may revive questions once reported upon and settled, there will never be rest. JEWELL, H. 1870, p. 480. See also NOYES. H. 1888, p. 584; SPRAGUE, S. 1891, p. 516; BARRETT, H. 1891, p. 790.

A joint committee having voted two weeks previously to report on a matter referred to it and the papers having been entrusted to a member of the committee to report, and that member having failed to make report and also having refused, upon repeated requests, to file the report or to surrender the papers, it would be competent under the circumstances for the chairman, on the request of the committee, to file the report without the original papers. YOUNG, H. 1922, p. 757.

Every report should conclude with some substantive proposition for the consideration of the assembly, such as, that a bill, resolve, order or resolution ought or ought not to pass, that the petitioners have leave to withdraw, etc., etc.

If a report recommends the passage of a bill or resolve, action is had upon the bill or resolve alone, and it takes its several readings, or is otherwise disposed of, as to the assembly seems fit. In such cases nothing is done about "accepting" the report. The statement of facts and arguments embodied in the report in support of the recommendation of the committee is not accepted or adopted. . . . and the assembly, by passing the bill or resolve, does not endorse that statement of fact or argument any more than, when it passes a vote, it endorses every speech made in support of the motion.

What is true of a report recommending the passage of a bill or resolve is equally true of a report recommending the passage of a resolution or order, reference to another committee or to the next annual session or any other action. The substantive proposition of the report is the motion, as it were, of the committee, and that proposition alone is before the assembly for its action. The preliminary statement of facts and of opinions contained in reports in the usual forms is not before the assembly for its action, and therefore cannot be amended. If, however, the proposition of a report is that its statement of facts and of opinions should be endorsed and adopted by the assembly itself, then and then only such statement would properly be before the assembly, and might be amended or otherwise acted upon. CROCKER, S. 1883, pp. 489, 576; BARRETT, H. 1890, p. 1254.

Whatever the proposition of the report is, the question should be so framed as to embody that proposition in distinct terms. The ordinary form of putting the question, namely, "Shall this report be accepted?" is inaccurate, ambiguous, misleading, and ought to be abolished. CROCKER, S. 1883, pp. 489, 576.

If a committee report in part only, its report should expressly state that it is "in part" and should clearly define what portion of the subject-matter committed to it is covered by the report. The use of the words "in part" is, however, not essential. If the committee intended to report in part only, and the phraseology of its report is consistent with such intent, its report will be treated as a report in part. CROCKER, S. 1883, p. 86; BARRETT, H. 1889, p. 843. See also SPRAGUE, S. 1891, p. 711.

When a committee reports only in part, a motion to substitute a bill which is germane to another part of the subject-matter referred to the committee is not in order. WALKER, H. 1909, p. 1245; BARTLEY, H. 1971, p. 1921 (2); MCGEE, H. 1975, p. 2463.

An order calling for the committee on Ways and Means to report revenue estimates for a fiscal year was ruled out of order because the committee reported out a bill only in part and thus amendments must be germane to that portion of the subject which is reported on. BULGER, S. 1984, p. 530.

A committee to which a report of a commission has been referred should make separate reports on the various subjects on which legislation is specially suggested, and a final report, — "no further legislation necessary." In a case, however, where a committee reported a bill on one only of several subjects, deeming that legislation on the other subjects was inexpedient, and plainly indicated that its report was intended to be a report in full, it was held that any amendment within the scope of the matter referred to the committee was admissible, though such amendment might not be germane to the subject-matter covered by the reported bill. Otherwise the committee would possess the power to bury by its own action, and without the power of revision, the issues referred to it. BARRETT, H. 1889, p. 842.

A committee to which the report of a commission has been referred may report a bill on the subject covered by the report of the commission, although such report omits to recommend legislation. NOYES, H. 1888, p. 670. But see HARTWELL, S. 1889, p. 733. See also SPRAGUE, S. 1891, p. 514.

There is no rule or statute that makes mandatory upon a committee the holding of a public hearing. It has always been a matter of discretion and the custom has been invariably to do so. WILLIS, H. 1948, p. 1215.

As to what legislation can be based on the reference to a committee of a report of a commission or board of trustees, see JEWELL, H. 1870, p. 478; NOYES, H. 1888, p. 670.

As to the scope of the report of a commission within which bills may be reported or amendments thereto moved, see SALTONSTALL, H. 1930, p. 765.

It is not necessary, however, that a bill should include all of the subject-matter considered by the committee. See WELLINGTON WELLS, S. 1928, p. 709; DOLAN, S. 1949, p. 497.

As to whether the same subject may be referred to two committees, see SANFORD, H. 1872, p. 419. It seems that such action would conflict with the principle of parliamentary law, that no bill or measure shall be twice passed upon in the same session. See BUTLER, S. 1894, p. 730. A recommendation of His Excellency the Governor having been referred to a joint committee, and a bill covering the same subject-matter having been referred to another joint committee, the Speaker, on a point of order raised when the latter committee reported, held that it was not within the province of the Chair to question the propriety of the consideration by a committee of a subject referred to it. FROTHINGHAM, H. 1904, p. 349.

If a bill reported by one committee is referred to another committee, the latter committee is not limited to the scope of the bill referred to it, but may report any measure within the scope of the propositions upon which the original bill was based. BUTLER, S. 1894, p. 920; LAWRENCE, S. 1897, p. 763.

If the report of a committee is ruled out as beyond the scope of the reference, the subject-matter of the reference is still before the House for its action. MYERS, H. 1900, p. 1463; WALKER, H. 1909, p. 844; UNDERHILL (acting Speaker), H. 1911, p. 1816.

A bill prohibiting the sale of intoxicating liquors was held not to be germane to a petition asking that the sale of malt and spirituous liquors be prohibited, for the reason that, as appears from 2 Gray 502, there are intoxicating liquors other than malt and spirituous liquors. BARRETT, H. 1892, p. 730.

In determining the scope of an application for legislation, it should be construed liberally; but the Chair is, at the same time, held to secure an observance of the rules made for obtaining well-considered legislation, and to the end that all citizens of the Commonwealth shall have full notice of matters brought before the Legislature affecting their interests. PILLSBURY, S. 1886, p. 703; BOARDMAN, S. 1888, p. 352; NOYES, H. 1888, p. 700; SPRAGUE, S. 1890, pp. 405, 886; TREADWAY, S. 1911, p. 1536.

For a case in which the scope of an order was construed liberally, see BARRETT, H. 1890, p. 1259.

A committee can report a larger sum than that named in the resolve referred to it. PILLSBURY, S. 1886, p. 700.

As the greater includes the less, it is a general rule that a bill will not be ruled out because it does not cover all the objects embraced in the order. PILLSBURY, S. 1886, p. 395; PINKERTON, S. 1892, p. 428. See also SOULE, S. 1901. p. 1049; COLE, H. 1908, p. 1005.

On a petition for general legislation it is not permissible to report a special bill. MARDEN, H. 1884, p. 450; FROTHINGHAM, H. 1904, p. 806 and H. 1905, p. 272; WALKER, H. 1909, p. 844 and H. 1910, p. 1255; CUSHING, H. 1914, p. 1322; WARNER, H. 1919, p. 546. See also COLE, H. 1908, p. 1005.

Also a report, leave to withdraw, on a petition which asks for general or special legislation, may be amended by the substitution of a general or a special bill. CUSHING, H. 1914, p. 1336.

When a bill for a rearrangement of the congressional districts was reported by a committee, under an order that directed that the districts as rearranged should conform to the districts as then established as closely as the lines of the existing wards and precincts of the city of Boston would conveniently admit, it was held that the Chair could not attempt to decide whether the lines of the proposed new districts conformed as closely to the lines of existing wards and precincts as convenience permitted, but that the committee was free to use its own judgment upon the question. LAWRENCE, S. 1896, p. 983; MEYER, H. 1896, p. 1211.

A message from the Governor transmitting a communication from a State commission calling the attention of the Legislature to a threatened abuse by a certain corporation, and suggesting that some appropriate action be taken, was held to be sufficiently broad in scope to permit a remedy of the threatened evil either by a general or by a special bill, or by both. MYERS, H. 1901, p. 1048.

If any part of a bill covers a matter not referred to the committee, or if a special bill is reported on a petition for general legislation, the whole bill must be withdrawn or excluded. It cannot be amended before it is received. SANFORD, H. 1872, pp. 422, 429 and H. 1875, p. 365; PILLSBURY, S. 1886, p. 702. *But such a bill may be recommitted.* See notes on Joint Rule 5.

Objection that a bill covers a matter not referred to the committee cannot be raised after action on the bill, by amendment, or by passing it to a third reading, or even after continued deliberation in regard to it. JEWELL, H. 1870, p. 477; SANFORD, H. 1874, p. 368; DEWEY (acting Speaker), H. 1877, p. 464; BRACKETT, H. 1886, p. 503; BARRETT, H. 1890, pp. 340, 1020 and H. 1891, p. 807; PINKERTON, S. 1892, p. 476 and S. 1893, pp. 387, 423; MEYER, H. 1894, p. 1248; BUTLER, S. 1895, p. 473; LAWRENCE, S. 1896, p. 941; ATTWILL (acting Speaker), H. 1898, p. 840; BATES, H. 1898, p. 940; SMITH, S. 1900, p. 660; NEWTON (acting Speaker), H. 1902, p. 479; DANA,

S. 1906, p. 480; COLE, H. 1907, p. 976; CUSHING, H. 1914, pp. 400, 1777; COX, H. 1916, p. 1053; WRAGG, S. 1937, p. 896. See also NOYES, H. 1881, p. 480; WADE, H. 1879, p. 540.

After a bill has been ordered to a third reading it is too late to raise the point of order that the recommendations upon which the bill was based were not filed on or before the time required by the statutes. YOUNG, H. 1922, p. 438.

For a case in which, the question being on passing a resolve to be engrossed, it was held to be too late to raise the point of order that under the provisions of a statute (St. 1907, c. 520, §3) the petition should have been referred to the next General Court, see CURTISS (acting Speaker), H. 1909, p. 1121.

As to cases in which orders would be suitable, see LONG, H. 1878, p. 58.

A motion that several bills comprised in one report should be placed separately in the Orders of the Day is not in order before the report has been received and the bills read the first time. SANFORD, H. 1872, p. 404.

A motion to require the committee on Rules to report forthwith on a petition was ruled out of order for the reason that there was nothing in the records of the Senate to indicate that such a petition was before the committee. RICHARDSON, S. 1950, p. 1489.

[*For opinion of Attorney General on appointments to special Commissions by Governor, President of the Senate and Speaker of the House of Representatives, see H. J. June 29, 1973 — or House Document numbered 7097 of 1973.*]

That an Order directing a joint committee to hold a public hearing prior to a certain date was improperly before the House for the reason that it would violate the long established precedent of authorizing committees of the General Court to schedule public hearings. McGEE, H. 1978, p. 123.

That an Order directing the House members of a joint committee to take certain action within the committee would be an improper interference into the internal workings of a joint committee by not allowing Senate members to partake in such action. McGEE, H. 1978, p. 124.

QUESTIONS OF PRIVILEGE.

A resolution declaring vacant certain contested seats is a resolution of high privilege, and need not be supported by a petition. MEYER, H. 1894, pp. 1192, 1198.

COURTESY BETWEEN THE BRANCHES.

Where one branch has passed upon a matter and forwarded it to the other, the latter is, as a rule, bound to receive and act upon it. This does not, however, give the second branch the right to exceed the provisions contained in the bill coming from the first branch. For instances in which this principle was followed, see PHELPS, S. 1859, p. 325; BULLOCK, H. 1865, p. 492; SANFORD, H. 1872, p. 125 and H. 1874, p. 392; COGSWELL, S. 1877, p. 306; LONG, H. 1877, p. 426; BISHOP, S. 1880, p. 243; S. 1881, p. 384 and S. 1882, p. 307; MARDEN, H. 1883, p. 523; PILLSBURY, S. 1885, p. 582; SPRAGUE, S. 1890, pp. 317, 794; PINKERTON, S. 1893, p. 470; LAWRENCE, S. 1896, p. 1036; MYERS, H. 1902, p. 1287; HENRY G. WELLS, S. 1916, p. 605; BACON, S. 1932, p. 802; NICHOLSON (acting President), S. 1936, p. 1126; NICHOLSON, S. 1947, p. 1233. *For exceptions* see COGSWELL, S. 1877, p. 300; BISHOP, S. 1882, p. 307; MARDEN, H. 1883, p. 478; BARRETT, H. 1891, pp. 790-

795; DANA, S. 1906, p. 712; CHAPPLE, S. 1907, pp. 898, 978; WELLINGTON WELLS, S. 1927, p. 530; BURGESS (acting Speaker), H. 1939, p. 1891.

One branch is not bound to entertain a matter from the other branch which has not been properly introduced in accordance with the rules. NICHOLSON, S. 1947, p. 1245.

It is not within the province of the Senate to question any action taken by a House committee in reporting a bill to that branch. ARTHUR W. COOLIDGE, S. 1945, p. 1061.

If a bill or an amendment, which is not germane to the subject-matter referred to a committee, comes to one branch from the other, such bill or amendment must be entertained out of courtesy to the branch from which it is received. MARDEN, H. 1884, p. 451; PINKERTON, S. 1893, p. 470; MEYER, H. 1894, pp. 466, 877; SMITH, S. 1899, p. 887; DANA, S. 1906, p. 982; O'NEILL, H. 1951, p. 1369; BARTLEY (acting Speaker), H. 1968, p. 2299; McGEE, H. 1983, pp. 1274, 1275. But see MARDEN, H. 1883, p. 478.

A point of order having been raised that a committee hearing on a matter was not called by the chairman in accordance with practice and that a report had been made in the other branch before the matter was referred to the committee, it was ruled that inasmuch as the House had received the report and passed the bill to be engrossed, the Senate must receive it and act upon it out of courtesy to the other branch. HOLMES, S. 1958, p. 665.

A point of order having been raised that a certain section of a report of a committee of conference on a supplemental budget contained subject-matter which was not a part of the matters of difference between the two branches, it was held that where one branch has passed upon the matter and forwarded it to the other, the latter is, as a rule, bound to receive it and act upon it out of courtesy between the branches. BULGER, S. 1981, p. 1817. See also, BOVERINI (acting President), S. 1982, p. 1303; BULGER, S. 1988, pp. 903-904.

See notes to Senate Rule 54 and House Rule 49.

CONCURRENCE IN AMENDMENTS.

Where a bill passed in the House was sent to the Senate and there passed with an amendment, and was then returned to the House for concurrence in the amendment, it was held that the House might agree or disagree with the amendment, or it might agree after amending the amendment, or it might refer the question of agreeing to the amendment to a committee, or might lay the subject on the table, or defer action to some day certain, because all such motions are supposed to be not unfriendly in their nature, at least not decisive or destructive. On the other hand, a motion to postpone indefinitely the whole subject, or any motion which carries with it an original purpose of destruction to the bill, is not in order, because the two branches have already agreed to the bill as a whole, and such a motion would be irregular in itself, and in its parliamentary effects uncourteous towards the other branch of the Legislature. BULLOCK, H. 1865, appendix, p. 493.

The question on concurring in the adoption of certain House amendments to an engrossed bill, being under consideration, it was held that a motion to refer the bill to the next annual session could not be entertained at that stage of the bill. ALLEN, S. 1923, p. 764.

Where a bill which has been agreed to by both branches and is sent from one branch to the other for concurrence in certain amendments, and the second branch, in addition to acting on the amendments, amends other parts of the bill *de novo*, it has been held that such amendments were not properly before the first branch. MEYER, H. 1895, p. 906; MYERS, H. 1900, p. 1403; DOLAN, S. 1949, p. 1265.

One branch, in considering an amendment to its bill made by the other branch, may amend such amendment, but its amendment must be germane to the amendment submitted for concurrence. SMITH, S. 1900, p. 978; FARLEY (acting Speaker), H. 1894, p. 1403; COLE, H. 1906, p. 982; QUINN, H. 1967, p. 2653; FONSECA (acting President), S. 1973, p. 2040; BARTLEY, H. 1969, pp. 2502, 2702; H. 1974, p. 2490; H. 1975, p. 1315.

For a discussion as to proceedings in case of a disagreement between the two branches in relation to amendments, see HALE, H. 1859, p. 116.

For ruling on amendment offered to a bill, where the Governor had recommended the enactment "of the attached bill in its precise form —", see H. J. 1958, p. 1507; POWERS, S. 1959, p. 298; H. J. 1961, p. 1533. *Contra*, see DAVOREN, H. 1965, p. 2588.

That a motion to concur with the Senate in its amendments to a House bill with a further amendment (inserting a new section) was improperly before the House for the reason that the only question before the House was concurring with the Senate in its amendments and that the proposed amendment was not an item in disagreement between the two branches. McGEE, H. 1977, p. 1435.

That a motion to concur with the Senate in its amendment to a House bill with a further amendment was improperly before the House for the reason that the further amendment sought to change wording in an item that had been previously agreed to by both branches. McGEE, H. 1977, p. 1500.

A point of order was raised on a House Bill further regulating the holding of public offices in certain small towns that the pending bill had previously received three readings in the Senate and subsequently received three readings in the House with a minor change and therefore should be before the Senate for concurrence in the House amendment, and it should not be on the Senate Calendar for three more readings.

It was ruled that the amendment adopted by the House was in the form of a new draft and, as such, the new draft required three more readings in the Senate. It was also stated that the Senate had no control over how the House chose to amend a bill, or as to what method the House used; but, as a rule, the Senate was bound to act upon it in the form in which it was received. BULGER. S. 1983, p. 1082.

MOTION TO RESCIND.

For discussion of "motion to rescind" see Senate document numbered 1535 of 1972, by Norman L. Pidgeon, Senate Clerk and Parliamentarian.

STATE OFFICERS.

A member holding a State office may retain his seat as a member of the Senate. HUNT. S. 1942 (Extra Session), p. 21.

For discussion of removal of public officers by "impeachment" or "address" — see Senate document numbered 1535 of 1972, by Norman L. Pidgeon, Senate Clerk and Parliamentarian.

RULES GOVERNING JOINT SESSIONS OF THE TWO HOUSES TO CONSIDER INITIATIVE AMEND-MENTS AND PROPOSALS FOR LEGISLATIVE AMENDMENTS TO THE CONSTITUTION.

[Adopted by the Senate and by the House of Representatives for the joint session held on May 14, 1997 and for any subsequent joint sessions which may be held.]

Rule A. After a Proposal for an Initiative Amendment has been read, the question shall then be on agreeing to the Amendment; whereupon it shall be open to debate and any motion provided for in special Rule F.

Rule A1. A proposal for a legislative amendment which has received the affirmative votes of a majority of all the members elected to the preceding General Court shall be read; whereupon it shall be open to debate, but may not be amended, and the question shall then be on agreeing to the amendment. A proposal for a legislative amendment which has not previously been agreed to in joint session of the two houses shall be read twice in immediate succession; and the question shall then be on ordering it to a third reading, whereupon it shall be open to debate and amendment.

Rule B. If it is ordered to a third reading, the proposal shall be read and considered at such subsequent joint session or joint sessions as may be agreed upon by the two houses or called by the Governor, in accordance with the provisions of the Constitution.

This rule may be suspended by a vote of four-fifths of the members of the joint session, present and voting thereon, in which case the proposal shall forthwith be read a third time; *provided, however,* that a motion to suspend the rule shall not be in order unless the committees on Bills in the Third Reading of the two houses, acting jointly, have examined the proposal and reported thereon in accordance with the provisions of Rule C.

Rule C. Before the proposal is read a third time, it shall be examined by the committees on Bills in the Third Reading of the two houses, acting jointly, and reported on by them in the manner provided in the standing rules of the Senate and of the House; provided, however, that a motion directing the committees on Bills in the Third Reading of the two houses, acting jointly, to report on a proposal which was ordered to a third reading at a prior joint session shall require a two-thirds vote of the members of the joint session present and voting thereon.

Rule D. After the third reading of the proposal, the question shall be on agreeing to the Amendment, whereupon it shall be open for debate or any motion provided for in special Rule F.

Rule E. If a Proposal for an Initiative Amendment is amended, before the question is taken on agreeing to the Proposal, it shall be examined by the committees on Bills in the Third Reading of the two houses, acting jointly, and reported on by them in the manner provided in the standing rules of the Senate and of the House.

Rule E1. Proposals which have not previously been agreed to in joint session and which are amended subsequently to their being ordered to a third reading, unless the amendment was reported by the committees on Bills in the Third Reading of the two houses, acting jointly, shall be referred forthwith to said committees and reported on by them in the manner provided in standing rules of the Senate and of the House.

Rule F. When the main question is under debate the President shall receive no motion that does not relate to the same, except the motion to adjourn or some other motion which has precedence by express rule or because it is privileged in its nature; and he shall receive no motion relating to the same except: —

For the previous question;

To close debate at a specified time;

To postpone until the two houses meet again in joint session;

To commit (or recommit), with or without instructions, to a special committee of the joint session composed of members of both houses;

To amend (excepting during consideration by the second successive General Court);

Which several motions shall have precedence in the order here arranged.

No motion to reconsider a vote on a main question shall be entertained unless made on the same day on which the vote was taken; and if moved, shall be considered at the time it is made.

Rule G. The sense of the joint session shall be taken by yeas and nays whenever required by thirty-five of the members present.

Whenever the yeas and nays have been ordered, the names of the Senators shall be called first, in alphabetical order; and the yea and nay vote of the House membership shall be determined in accordance with the House rules, excepting that those members of the House who have not been recorded in the usual manner as provided under the rules of the House may be recorded on a yea and nay list after the electric voting machine has been closed and before the final vote has been announced.

A pair with any member who is absent with a committee by authority of either or both houses may be announced, and shall be recorded, in the following manner:

If, before the question is taken, a member states that he has paired with another member who is absent with a committee by authority of the Senate or House, and how each would vote upon the pending question, the fact shall be entered in the Journals immediately after the record of the yeas and nays, and such member shall be excused from voting, but shall be included with the members voting for the purposes of a quorum; provided, however, nothing in this rule shall be construed as to permit pairing by a member on a question involving a required vote of two-thirds, three-fourths, four-fifths or a majority of a specified number of votes.

Rule H. It shall not be in order for the two houses to go into a Committee of the Whole when in joint session.

Rule I. If the two houses are in joint session ten minutes before the hour of meeting of either branch, the President shall declare an adjournment.

Rule J. The rules of the House of Representatives, including the last paragraph of House Rule 81, shall govern the proceedings in the joint sessions in all cases to which they are applicable, and in which they are not inconsistent with the provisions of Article XLVIII of the Amendments to the Constitution, or with these rules or amendments thereof, or with Joint Rules Nos. 23, 24, 25 or 26.

Rule K. It shall be in order to recess the convention from time to time upon a majority vote of said convention.

Rule L. Except as is otherwise provided in Rule B, Rules A to L, inclusive, may be altered, suspended or rescinded by concurrent votes of two-thirds of the members of each branch present and voting thereon in their respective branches.

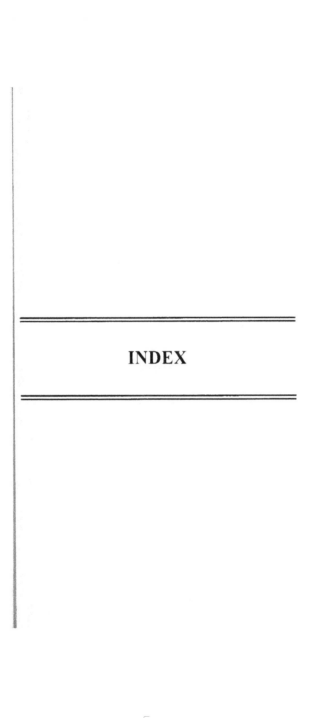

INDEX

INDEX.